"At the time it was happening I could only guess what my adversaries were thinking and planning to do to demolish us. Many of the accounts in the book I read for the first time. They may not have revealed everything and could have burnished their narrative for posterity. Nevertheless their recollections added spice to the narrative. I had pointed out some factual errors but told the writers to decide who is more reliable. The final version is their book and they had to exercise their editorial right."

~ *Minister Mentor Lee Kuan Yew*

"Without PAP, today's Singapore would not exist. The authors tell the story through the voices of the participants of this epic journey. They spoke to many people on both sides, the non-communists and pro-communists. They convey a vivid feel for what Singapore politics was like, how it has changed over the decades, and how the PAP itself has changed as Singapore was transformed under PAP leadership."

~ *Prime Minister Lee Hsien Loong*

"Fascinating, well-documented inside story of the PAP. It describes the intrigues between the Western-educated and Chinese-educated leaders for control of the party right from its inception."

~ *Othman Wok, old guard minister and former diplomat*

"In Singapore where PAP is the dominant party, it is rare to see the publication of a book with different political views. The writers interviewed former leftists such as Samad Ismail, Said Zahari, Dominic Puthucheary and S Woodhull to get their side of the PAP story. They even travelled to the Thai-Malaysian border to speak to former MCP leaders. Modern Singapore and PAP are inseparable. I strongly recommend this book."

~ *Fong Swee Suan, former left-wing trade union leader, and founding member and convenor of PAP who later joined Barisan Sosialis*

"This book is an apt reminder that there is always another dimension to the Singapore Story. It goes beyond the mundane stereotype in search of the true story. In some ways, it acknowledges the contributions of people who had shared a common cause and made sacrifices but were forced to depart from the scene for one reason or another. It is a timely read for all."

~ Lim Chin Joo, former left-wing student activist and trade unionist, and brother of Lim Chin Siong who led Barisan Sosialis in the battle against PAP in the 1960s

"*Men In White* gives a crystal-clear and complete picture of the PAP story since 1954. This is the first time I read a book featuring almost all key figures involved in the party since its early years, including those who broke away later. Such a book, which provides a more balanced account of our past, should have been written long ago. It is a must-read for every Singaporean and a perfect text on modern Singapore political history for our students."

~ Low Por Tuck, one of the 13 PAP legislative assemblymen who broke away from the party to form Barisan Sosialis in 1961

"The voices of the many individuals in this book reflect the battles in the PAP story. It will stimulate debate on Singapore's political history. Will the Men in White have the vision and the wisdom to lead Singapore for another 50 years? All Singaporeans should read this book."

~ Arthur Lim, eminent eye surgeon who served a brief stint in the Labour Front in 1958 as assistant to secretary-general Francis Thomas. Thomas was then-minister for communication and works in the Lim Yew Hock government.

"So many voices, so many people interviewed, even views of the communists are expressed ... Mrs Lee Kuan Yew's despairing comment that Harry should give up politics and stick to the law is touching; the story of the mysterious night soil carrier who became a PAP CEC member is fascinating; how chief minister Lim Yew Hock saved PAP by arresting its leftist officials showed what a close shave the party had! A wonderful read."

~ Maurice Baker, founding member of Malayan Forum, a political discussion group based in London which foreshadowed the formation of PAP

"In spare reporting language, the writers have brought to us the untold story of PAP. It tells of the subterranean struggle between the open English-educated leadership and the shadowy largely Chinese-educated leftist operators of the party branches and rural grassroots organisations."
~ Ngiam Tong Dow, former permanent secretary in several ministries and former chairman of Economic Development Board

"An authoritative, rich and compelling narrative of the men who founded PAP and their successors and how they shaped and continue to shape the destiny of modern Singapore ... The chapters on the transition of power reveal the PAP method of choosing leaders, the special mentoring of Lee Kuan Yew, the rough handling of Goh Chok Tong by Lee and a substantial account of the Goh Chok Tong years. No other book on Singapore politics and history covers as much ground."
~ Chan Heng Chee, Singapore's ambassador to the United States and author of The Dynamics of One Party Dominance: The PAP at the Grassroots

"*Men In White* is a perceptive work based on an incredible number of interviews that reveal, clarify, and breathe life into the emergence and success of PAP. This book introduces valuable new information and perspectives, and presents the most detailed and authentic analysis to date of the PAP's origins, rise to power, and governance of Singapore. For those who believe leadership decisions can provide useful insights and assist in making future decisions, this is the book to read."
~ Thomas J Bellows, professor of political science, University of Texas at San Antonio, who pioneered the academic study of PAP

"The goals of any political party in a democracy are to win elections, gain power and legitimacy, create a peaceful and prosperous nation-state and improve the well-being of the people from election to election. It is hard to find any political party that can match the record of PAP in all these dimensions. Hence, the story of *Men In White* is worth reading carefully. Political parties all over the world are struggling to deliver good governance. They too can learn valuable lessons from this volume."
~ Kishore Mahbubani, dean of the Lee Kuan Yew School of Public Policy, National University of Singapore. His latest book is The New Asian Hemisphere: the Irresistible Shift of Global Power to the East.

"A page-turner. Written in a fast-clipped journalistic style, the writers portray vividly the conflicts of the early years of the PAP's history, bringing to life a story rich in emotions—the hope of passions pursued, the anguish of betrayal and the grit behind politicking and policy-making. Part eyewitness account, part narrative history, and part political analysis, this book is wholly enjoyable in the richness of its material, the diversity of voices and the sheer zeal in its writing, while the meticulous research and interviews with new perspectives make it a must-read source book for any serious study of Singapore history. There is no other book quite like it on Singapore."

~ Chua Mui Hoong, senior writer, The Straits Times

"The authors wrote the PAP story in the grand tradition of journalistic scholarship. The accounts, from the horses' mouths and through the (un)reserved appraisals of supporters and critical narratives of regime bystanders, contributed significantly to our understanding of the inner psyche and ideological make-up of a group of leaders who pride themselves as men in white."

~ Ho Khai Leong, associate professor of political science,
Nanyang Technological University, and author of Shared Responsibilities.
Unshared Power. The Politics of Policy-making in Singapore

"Any future leaders from PAP or other political parties must satisfy a very demanding electorate for good governance. If they cannot, the people will vote them out of power. The track record of PAP therefore serves as a historical mirror for the new leadership driving ahead. This is a very good book to discuss Singapore's past and future so honestly and openly."

~ Yang Mu, coordinator, China cooperation programme,
East Asia Institute, National University of Singapore

"This is an impressive compilation of copious information and fascinating detail that ably and amply outlines the extraordinary rise and subsequent history of PAP and Singapore. It is to be hoped that non-Singaporeans who wish to know more of the country and its political development, will read the book around the world. Had it been available during my own research, I would certainly have reached for this book."

~ Meira Chand, Indian-Swiss author of seven novels residing
in Singapore since 1997

MEN IN WHITE

THE UNTOLD STORY OF
SINGAPORE'S
RULING POLITICAL PARTY

MEN IN WHITE

THE UNTOLD STORY OF
SINGAPORE'S
RULING POLITICAL PARTY

SONNY YAP, RICHARD LIM AND LEONG WENG KAM

MEN IN WHITE
The Untold Story of Singapore's Ruling Political Party

Published by Singapore Press Holdings Limited
1000 Toa Payoh North, News Centre,
Singapore 318994

Designed and produced by Marshall Cavendish International (Asia) Private Limited

Singapore Press Holdings Limited
1000 Toa Payoh North, News Centre,
Singapore 318994
Tel: (65) 6319 8346. Fax: (65) 6319 8258
E-mail: sphcorp@sph.com.sg
Website: www.sph.com.sg

National Library Board Singapore Cataloguing in Publication Data
Yap, Sonny, 1949-
    Men in white : the untold story of Singapore's ruling political party
    / Sonny Yap, Richard Lim and Leong Weng Kam. – Singapore :
    Singapore Press Holdings, c2009.
    p. cm.
    Includes index.
    ISBN-13: 978-981-4266-24-6

    1. People's Action Party (Singapore) – History. 2. Political parties – Singapore –
    History. 3. Singapore – Politics and government.
    I. Lim, Richard, 1949- II. Leong, Weng Kam, 1954- III. Title.

JQ1063.A98
324.25957 – dc22   OCN399087200

Printed in Singapore

DEDICATED TO

Singapore's greatest generation who grew up in untold
hardship and privations, suffered under British colonialism
and Japanese occupation, experienced social and political
upheaval, and yet picked up the pieces to rebuild their lives,
get married and raise families while laying the foundation
for the peace and prosperity of a new nation.

CONTENTS

FOREWORD

I READ Max Hastings' riveting account of the last year of the Second World War in Europe. The British journalist-cum-historian had access to UK, US, Russian and German archives and other documentary sources. His account covered all parties in the war based on military records and interviews of veterans.

I told then-prime minister Goh Chok Tong, who had told me that Singapore Press Holdings (SPH) was working on a book on the People's Action Party (PAP), that they should write it up as the Singapore story giving the views of all parties to the political conflicts. It will be compelling reading if it covers the views of all—those for or against the PAP. He suggested to Cheong Yip Seng, then-editor-in-chief of the English and Malay newspapers division, SPH, that they should get a team of writers and researchers to interview PAP's adversaries, read up the oral histories of PAP leaders and opposition players, and recount the events that brought Singapore to where it is today.

This book is the result of five years of research and interviews by an SPH team. Sonny Yap, Richard Lim and Leong Weng Kam wrote it up. SPH sent me their first proof copies for comments. I pointed out what I thought were errors of fact, but told them to accept or just give my different recollections. This is their book, not the PAP's.

The PAP secretariat had made available documents and records of the party. All sides in the contest were able to tell their side of the story. The SPH team interviewed many of the surviving players and read their oral histories, including of those who had passed away.

While writing this foreword, I asked the Internal Security Department (ISD) whether it was all right to disclose that Lim Chin Siong, a former PAP legislative assemblyman who was later detained for left-wing activities, had had clandestine meetings with a key underground communist leader called Fang Chuang Pi whom I dubbed "the Plen" or short for plenipotentiary. ISD agreed to the disclosure. Lim told ISD in his interviews in 1984 that he met the Plen three times between the late 1950s and early 1960s, and that one such meeting took place when the PAP split in 1961.

Lim was sketchy on specific dates and locations of the meetings. However ISD had information that Lim and the Plen met secretly in a secluded *attap* hut at 7½ milestone, Upper Thomson Road, on 16 July 1961, five days before the crucial motion of confidence in the 51-seat legislative assembly. Thirteen PAP dissident assemblymen abstained from the vote which resulted in PAP hanging on to power with 27 ayes against 8 nays and 16 abstentions.

In another corroborative statement in 1964, the Plen's former girlfriend, who is still alive, disclosed that one night she drove the Plen along Dunearn Road, picked up Lim, then went to Kallang Park where both men had a discussion. She did not provide the actual date of the meeting, but ISD assessed that it was sometime between late 1959 and early 1960.

These revelations showed that even though Lim denied he was a communist, he did make contact with the communist underground and that he collaborated with pro-communist and leftist PAP assemblymen in a bid to topple the PAP government in 1961. If he had succeeded, the future of Singapore would have turned out differently.

The writers have given a comprehensive picture of the events since the 1950s when a group of returning students from Britain conceived the idea of a new socialist-styled political party. My wife and I found the early chapters riveting. They re-created the tension and drama of those life-and-death situations the PAP was trapped in. It was a pity that it was left so late that some of the principal players had passed away, and the memories of those still with us were less crisp. It would have been a more gripping tale if the research was done 10 years earlier.

At the time it was happening I could only guess what my adversaries were thinking and planning to do to demolish us. Many of the accounts in the book I read for the first time. They may not have revealed everything and could have burnished their narrative for posterity. Nevertheless their recollections added spice to the narrative. I had pointed out some factual errors but told the writers to decide who is more reliable. The final version is their book and they had to exercise their editorial right.

I did not agree with the accounts of former cabinet ministers Toh Chin Chye and Ong Pang Boon that there was a vote at a central executive committee (CEC) meeting after the 1959 general election to decide who would be prime minister. They did not have to disbelieve what Toh and Ong said but simply stated my recall that there was no such vote, and that Toh had written me a letter in 1961 when his memory was fresher. I offered my resignation as PM to him as chairman of PAP. He replied that I had the unanimous support of the CEC to be PM in 1959.

Vividly stored in my memory were the early years from 1955 to 1975. There was a tense and drama-packed series of crises that left an indelible mark in my mind. They were struggles for survival. The first fight was against a formidable Communist United Front. And they had the support of a ruthless underground always lurking in the shadows, and directing them from time to time.

Next we found ourselves ambushed by UMNO Malay ultras who were determined to impose supreme Malay rule regardless of the constitution we had agreed upon, one that guaranteed our rights as full citizens of the Federation of Malaysia. We organised a pan-Malaysia movement for a Malaysian Malaysia in opposition to their Malay Malaysia. Tension became acute between Malays and non-Malays. Then-prime minister Tunku Abdul Rahman wanted Singapore to leave the federation or blood would flow, he told me. We separated and faced the formidable task of making a viable economy in an independent Singapore that had always depended on Malaya as its hinterland.

It is said the victors write up history. This is an SPH endeavour to muster all sources and cover the views of all who opposed the PAP. They had even interviewed those PAP legislative assemblymen who went underground, joined the Malayan Communist Party guerrilla forces and are now settled in the "Peace Villages" in southern Thailand.

Before we had solved the problems of making an independent Singapore viable, in 1967 the British government announced the withdrawal of all its forces East of Suez including Singapore. We weathered this loss of 20 per cent of our GDP from military spending and over 50,000 local jobs that supported or serviced its forces. The next shock was the oil crisis of 1973 when the Arab oil states embargoed the sale of oil to the US and Europe as Egyptian forces attacked Israel and crossed the Suez Canal. The price of oil quadrupled. We survived this with high inflation but no mass unemployment.

After that, it was the hard slog of building world-class infrastructure, attracting investments for jobs, and improving the education of our workers and their children. We had to make everyone learn English to have a common language. But all had also to learn their respective mother tongues to retain their sense of self-worth and not be de-culturalised.

My final task was to ensure that equally able and honest successors were in place to take over from the old guard. The governance of Singapore has become more complex. They have to maintain its security and stability, manage a more complex economy and continue to ensure social equity between our different races. Those painstaking efforts did not make news.

This account of the various forces that contended and resulted in the Singapore of today would interest present and future generations. It was a tortuous route Singapore had travelled to reach the First World. In the closing chapter, the writers have peered into the future to give their take on what lies in store. I do not necessarily agree with their crystal ball-gazing.

Lee Kuan Yew
Minister Mentor

PREFACE

IN May 2001, Mr Goh Chok Tong, then-prime minister and secretary-general of the People's Action Party (PAP), asked whether Singapore Press Holdings would be interested in publishing a book on the PAP, which would be 50 years old in three years' time in 2004. It should not be a commemorative one. It should be non-partisan, well-researched and not written for the PAP, but be the writers' version of history. I was enthusiastic because only such a book would justify the very substantial resources needed.

The PAP story has not been adequately told, certainly not one that spans half a century. The journalist in me knows it has all the ingredients of a gripping tale. How did the PAP engineer its transformation from a small coterie of largely English-educated intellectuals in a predominantly Chinese-educated population ruled by the British into a party that today is the overwhelmingly dominant political force in Singapore? How did it negotiate the turbulent, sometimes treacherous waters of colonial Singapore, and emerge triumphant from near self-destruction shortly after its formation? What is its formula for longevity? Will it survive its founding fathers? Indeed, it is a story of great courage, of betrayal, intrigue, and of deeply held opposing political convictions.

But what had the greatest appeal to me was the opportunity to reach out to a dwindling band of key players in the story. Not just the winners, but the losers, and interested bystanders as well. If their stories disappear with their passing, that would be an irretrievable national loss. The team that started work in 2002 knew there was little time to lose. In fact, by the time the final draft was reviewed in 2009, 25 of the more than 300 people the writers and researchers interviewed had died.

Not everyone we wanted to interview agreed to talk. For example, Ong

Eng Guan, who was in the PAP's first cabinet but who fell out with the leadership, would not even take our phone calls or receive us at his office. Fang Chuang Pi, leader of the communist underground in Singapore at that time, died in Hatyai, Thailand, in 2004 before we could reach him.

But many of those who cooperated had interesting tales to tell. Leong Weng Kam met Malayan Communist Party (MCP) members in southern Thailand. He writes: "I have seen pictures of those teenage Chinese schoolgirls in pigtails who were part of the leftist movement in Singapore in the 1950s and 1960s. Many landed themselves in the Peace Villages in southern Thailand, and are still living there. After more than 50 years, those I met in 2003 were frail (some could hardly walk), and were in their 60s and 70s. One of them told me she was the daughter of a rich businessman in Singapore living in a big mansion with servants at home and ate very good food every day. But she gave up all that to join the leftist movement, and went underground when security officers were after her.

"Eventually, together with many others, she escaped to Indonesia and later joined the MCP in the jungles along the Malaysian-Thai border. In the jungles as armed guerillas, they led very tough lives, ate everything from rats to elephants. One elephant, they said, could feed them for months. But they did not regret what they did."

In the end, we did not make the 2004 deadline despite deploying a full-time team of seven—three writers from *The Straits Times* newsroom, backed by four researchers. But I believe we have a better book as a result of the additional time we took. We made the effort to dive deep into declassified material in the archives in Singapore and London. The PAP gave us access to confidential party records. The Internal Security Department supplied records of key events we identified for research. Key players gave us permission to listen to their oral histories deposited with the National Archives. So did many others, including families of those who had died. In all, we listened to 200 oral histories. PAP leaders, from the founding generation to the current one, were generous with their time.

The most daunting part of the work was tracking down people not just in Singapore but scattered across the region—Malaysia, Thailand, Hong Kong and China. Among them were party leaders who had broken away from the Lee Kuan Yew faction of the PAP, whose version of history never made it to earlier books on the party. For this book to be worthwhile, their side of the story must be told. After finding them overseas, the writers had to cajole them to talk. Most of them were persuaded by the argument that if they stayed silent, their side of the story would never be told. It would be an injustice not just to themselves, but to past, present and future generations of Singaporeans. Their memories were not captured in the oral history archives. Getting their side of the Singapore story made a deep impression on our writers.

In Sonny Yap's words: "Although many of them spent years in detention and suffered tremendous privations, they betrayed no bitterness and rancour while recounting their experiences. Former firebrand trade unionist Fong Swee Suan was the very picture of gentlemanly geniality when he talked about how he started the 1955 Hock Lee bus strike, but not the riot. For the first time, former PAP leftists who were deported to China or exiled to Thailand broke their silence on their role in the PAP story."

Mining their memories has its limitations, however. Was what they remembered the full story? Memories might be selective and, as Sonny Yap put it, they could fall prey to retrospective rationalisation and dispense the wisdom of 20/20 hindsight. Painstaking work went into checking for accuracy. We cross-checked with archives of newspapers in three languages—English, Malay and Chinese—and, wherever possible, with the people involved. When there are contradictory accounts, we publish both versions of history, and let readers decide which to believe.

The book is in three parts. The first, written by Sonny Yap and Leong Weng Kam, covers the turbulent early years of the PAP when it was more often divided than united. In the second part, Richard Lim tracks its transformation into a formidable political force. In the third part, the team examines the PAP's survival strategy, and what could destroy it. For many generations of Singaporeans, especially those born after independence in 1965, the early years of the PAP are a very distant memory. If this book helps stimulate in them, as well as generations to come, an abiding interest in our past, the years of work that have gone into this book would not be in vain. We cannot be a strong nation if we cannot remember our past.

Cheong Yip Seng
Editor-in-chief
English and Malay Newspapers Division,
Singapore Press Holdings
1987–2006

ACKNOWLEDGEMENTS

Men In White would not have seen the light of day without the unstinting support and cooperation of the legions of people who contributed in one way or another, directly or indirectly, to the making of the book. We would like to record our deepest appreciation to:

• All the people who helped us to track down former politicians lost in the mists of time. In particular, we would like to thank Yio Chu Kang MP and NTUC assistant secretary-general Seng Han Thong for facilitating many of the interviews with past and present PAP ministers, MPs and party stalwarts. Our thanks also go to PAP executive director Lau Ping Sum for making it possible for us to attend key party events, and PAP HQ research executive Lua Bee Geok and her staff for helping us to contact former party activists and retrieve party records.

• Singapore Press Holdings Information Resource Centre for trawling through microfilms of newspapers from the 1940s to 1990s, opening up its photo archives and providing research support for the project. Thank you, Idris Rashid Khan Surattee and staff, for your patience and painstaking work.

• National Archives of Singapore for releasing more than 200 oral history interviews which represented a treasure trove of priceless memories.

• National University of Singapore Central and Chinese Library for identifying and locating books and material relating to the PAP story.

• Internal Security Department, Ministry of Home Affairs, for allowing us to read and cite Special Branch reports; Elections Department of Singapore, Prime Minister's Office; Housing and Development Board and Preservation of Monuments Board for helping our researchers and artist.

• National Archives of the United Kingdom for making available declassified documents relating to the politics of Singapore and Malaysia in the 1960s.

• Our long-suffering verbatim reporters Gavin Chua, Simon Tan and Serene Ng for rendering the hundreds of taped voices, accents and intonations into excellent, ready-to-use transcripts.

• Singapore Press Holdings Editorial Support Unit for providing us with administrative support and Information Technology Department Help Desk for bailing us out when we ran into technical difficulties.

• All the scholars here and abroad, community and religious leaders and former civil servants who shared their ideas and insights with us and added immeasurable value to our narrative.

• Most of all, to all the interviewees who opened their doors and hearts to us, and to family members of deceased oral history interviewees who consented to the release of their transcripts, we owe them an inestimable debt. To current and former political foes of PAP who cooperated with us despite their suspicions and cynicism over this project, we will never be able to thank them enough for giving us the benefit of the doubt. By granting us the privilege of tapping their memory bank, we were able to chronicle this epic journey into the forgotten and fractious past. It was indeed the ride of a lifetime.

• And finally, we must acknowledge the invaluable editorial guidance of former *Straits Times* editor-in-chief Cheong Yip Seng and editor Han Fook Kwang. If not for Cheong's leap of faith and sense of mission to "save" the fading and dying voices of a pioneering generation from oblivion, this book would have remained an impossible dream.

Sonny Yap, Richard Lim and Leong Weng Kam

PART ONE
BY

❧⸰❧

Sonny Yap and Leong Weng Kam

❧⸰❧

PROLOGUE
Lee's Blue-eyed Boy Unmasked

LIKE a lord surveying his manor, he could not help betraying his sense of pride as he showed off his prized possession squatting on a slope in the village of Bang Lang, a four-hour drive from Hatyai in southern Thailand.

As he took his visitor on a tour of the single-storey bungalow with the distinctive tiled roof and white concrete walls, he remarked wryly that a similar abode in Bukit Timah in Singapore would have cost at least a million dollars.

Just when you thought his estate ended with the well-tended garden, he pointed out that it extended over another two-and-a-half hectares of nearby land where 100 rubber trees were planted and their latex collected and processed by hired workers every day.

This was the rustic retreat where he and his wife returned to every three months or so from the garish lights and unremitting bustle of Hatyai to take a long weekend break and pick up the profits from their rubber smallholding—about RM300 ($150) a month.

What an idyllic life, you might say, for the childless retired couple who live in the city and still work to keep themselves mentally alive. When he was interviewed in 2003, he had just celebrated his 70th birthday and was working as a part-time private secretary to a Thai transport company boss while his spouse, nine years younger, taught in a private school.

But get to know Chan Sun Wing better and banter with him in his native Cantonese and he will tell you in a heart-wrenching manner that home was not Bang Lang or Hatyai but Singapore. That's where he was born, grew up, studied and worked as a Chinese newspaper reporter before becoming the close aide to a young lawyer who led a new political party to power in 1959.

Singapore was where his younger brother and three sisters still lived with their families. Sadly, whenever he wanted to see them, he had to go to Johor Bahru to meet them. Or they had to make the trek to Hatyai.

Chan is a refugee from Singapore who has been living in exile since 1963. He and his wife, Luo Yamei, were members of the Malayan Communist Party (MCP) who went into the jungle to fight for the founding of the Malayan Democratic People's Republic.

Formed in 1930, MCP gained tremendous popularity among the Chinese because of its armed resistance to the Japanese during the Second World War. But it was banned in 1948 when it initiated a revolutionary struggle to take over the Malayan peninsula. The insurrection only ended with a peace agreement signed between the MCP and the Thai and Malaysian governments in 1989.

Under the accord, some 1,188 guerillas laid down their arms and returned to civilian life in Thailand and Malaysia. Each MCP family, like Chan and Luo who remained in Thailand, was given some concessions by the authorities to secure its subsistence: one *rai* of land and a small sum of money to build a house and another 15 *rai* to plant rubber trees or grow a crop. A *rai* is a Thai term for land area measuring 0.16 hectare.

Four peace villages, as they were called, were designated for the occupation of former guerillas near the Thai-Malaysian border. Apart from Bang Lang where Chan and his former comrades built about a hundred bungalows, the other villages were Betong, Sukirin and Yaha.

When Chan reached the age of 60 in 1993, he received a monthly pension of RM50 from MCP to supplement his rubber proceeds and the pay from his half-day job.

His life story has all the ingredients of an action-packed novel. He fled Singapore in 1963 to escape a police manhunt and hid in Indonesia as a member of the communist underground for more than 10 years before donning guerilla fatigues in the Thai-Malaysian jungles in the early 1970s.

After undergoing military training, he worked as an English-Chinese translator and analyst for the MCP broadcasting station at its headquarters in southern Thailand, not far from Bang Lang. There he met his Johor-born wife, a surgeon who applied anaesthetic and extracted bullets from the wounded during the insurgency.

Luo said she joined MCP after two life-changing events: the death of her brother, an MCP member, in the Malayan jungle and her deportation to China after she was arrested by the Malayan government for possessing communist literature. From China, she was sent to Vietnam where she studied medicine and fought with the Vietcong against the Americans.

"Life as a communist guerilla was really tough," Chan bared his thoughts. "We ate everything we could find, including elephant meat. Do you know that one elephant could feed many people for many days?"

Age and the arduous life had taken a heavy toll on the rapidly balding, grey-haired man in a white short-sleeved shirt and loose trousers. But his facial features would remain recognisable to those who knew him well in Singapore. He still wore the over-sized thick-rimmed glasses of his younger days. His trademark buck tooth could still be discerned. And if there was anything that gave him away, it was his usual talkative and jovial self.

Sitting in a Hatyai hotel lobby, Chan was in a contemplative mood mixed with nostalgic wistfulness. "The Thai and Malaysian governments have been so magnanimous in allowing MCP members to return to their homes. I still don't understand why we are not allowed to go back even for a visit by the Singapore government."

⁕

FLASHBACK to June 1959, and you will find Chan ensconced amid the neo-classical columns of City Hall as parliamentary secretary to the prime minister after the People's Action Party (PAP) swept to power in the May 30 general election.

The 26-year-old had been elected PAP legislative assemblyman for Upper Serangoon in the polls which saw the fledgling left-wing party winning 43 of the 51 wards to overthrow the coalition government of chief minister Lim Yew Hock and take over the stewardship of self-governing Singapore.

Inaugurated in 1954, PAP comprised an odd mixture of British-educated scholars, self-styled socialists, Malay trade unionists and Chinese-speaking leftists who shared a common anti-colonial cause—to drive out the British rulers and set up an independent, democratic, socialist Malaya which included Singapore.

When its party secretary-general—a 36-year-old Cambridge-educated lawyer named Lee Kuan Yew—was installed as prime minister in City Hall in 1959, he took Chan along as his top aide. Chan's appointment signalled the ascent of an up-and-coming political star.

Educated in Chinese High School, Chan was a reporter with the now defunct Chinese newspaper *Sin Pao* when he came to know Lee, the ambitious Straits-born Chinese politician who was then struggling to learn

Mandarin to cultivate the Chinese ground. Chan became his friend and personal assistant.

At the party level, he was responsible for PAP's links with the politically restive trade unions and edited the Chinese-language edition of the party organ, *Petir*. As parliamentary secretary, he rendered Lee's English speeches into elegant idiomatic Chinese and acted as Lee's eyes and ears in the Chinese community.

No doubt Lee held him in high esteem and once remarked that he was the "most intelligent and politically educated of all the parliamentary secretaries". Other PAP leaders commended him for his political understanding and shrewdness.

By virtue of his position in the prime minister's office (PMO), Chan was regarded as the most powerful of the nine parliamentary secretaries who served the ministers of the first PAP cabinet. He headed the caucus of parliamentary secretaries who met the new prime minister regularly. Civil servants deferred to him because of his special relationship with Lee.

In the early days of the PAP government, the lack of water, electricity and roads was the all-consuming concern of the teeming population. Chan was entrusted with the chairmanship of the urban and rural services committee (URSC) which allocated these public amenities. People were overjoyed when they were given a standpipe with two taps or a bus shelter which was no more than a wooden shed with a zinc sheet roof.

Yet another unmistakable sign of Chan's growing clout was his appointment by Lee to take charge of the staffing for PAP branches and community centres. The latter came under the fold of the People's Association which was set up as a new grassroots organisation in 1960 to strengthen racial and social bonding.

Such was his influence in the corridors of power that he aroused much envy and resentment among his party colleagues. He was derided as Lee's blue-eyed boy, favourite and protégé. He was labelled a sycophant for dashing down the City Hall steps every morning to greet Lee when he arrived for work. His critics claimed that when he was on his own, he was amiable and sociable but when he stood next to Lee, he exhibited aloofness and arrogance.

Chan was born in 1933, the son of an engraving and signboard shop owner and hairdresser. He grew up in Kreta Ayer and worked briefly in his father's business before embarking on a journalistic career with pro-China newspapers.

Relating how he met Lee in the early 1950s, he said that it was his former Chinese High schoolmate and *Sin Pao* colleague, Jek Yeun Thong, who made the introduction. "We became friends discussing anything from characters in the Chinese classics to issues in the Chinese community." When he accompanied Lee on his trips to Malaya before he became prime minister, Lee would practise his Mandarin with him and "talk about anything under the sun".

In Lee's recollection, Chan was a "voluble fellow" who spoke Mandarin with a strong Cantonese accent. Yes, he practised speaking the language with Chan, but he made sure he did not adopt his pronunciation.

It was during a drive to Fraser's Hill with Lee and his family just days before nomination day for the 1959 elections that Chan was asked to stand as a PAP candidate. Lee told him that should the party form the government, his job would be to take care of the Chinese media.

If there was one more cherished memory of the trip, it was that of playing with the Lee children. Singapore's third prime minister would have probably forgotten about it but Chan said he taught a seven-year-old Hsien Loong how to put his hand behind his head to touch his nose.

⚬⟩•⟨⚬

THE lesson was plucked from an ancient Chinese classic titled "*xiao he yue xia zhui han xin*" (Xiao He pursues Han Xin under the moon). It told of two brilliant officials who served Liu Bang, the rebel leader who overthrew the Qin Dynasty and set up the Han Dynasty in 206 BC.

Xiao He was favoured by Liu while Han Xin was left out in the cold. When Han decided to leave, Xiao, knowing Han's potential and capabilities, pleaded with Liu to keep him but failed. One night Xiao learnt that Han had left the court. Immediately he gave chase and, under a full moon, succeeded in persuading Han to stay.

As Lee ploughed through the text in his City Hall office, he sounded somewhat surprised if not annoyed by the selection of a story of a would-be defecting aide. Sharply he asked his new tutor if he was trying to tell him something.

Foong Choon Hon, who recounted the anecdote, replied not at all but soon realised that Lee could be wondering if the story was meant to draw a parallel with the political upheaval at that time.

The lesson took place sometime in July 1961 when the PAP was breaking up over the issue of Singapore's merger with Malaya. Lee and company supported the idea of joining Malaysia but his leftist colleagues opposed the proposed union fearing that a conservative Malay-dominated central government would crack down on them.

As the PAP government struggled for political survival after losing two by-elections and faced relentless attacks from dissident party members, Lee moved a motion of confidence in the legislative assembly to flush out his adversaries from the party's remaining 41 representatives.

When the votes were tallied, he was not completely shocked that 13 PAP assemblymen had abstained from voting for their own government. But what distressed him deeply was that the aide who had worked closely with him in City Hall and the friend in whom he had reposed so much trust and confidence had turned against him. From Chan Sun Wing, it was the most unkindest cut of all.

As Lee recalled, Chan "was not acting like his usual self". "Once we decided on merger, he opposed it furiously. He became agitated and his boss must have told him to stop it. So he did his best to stop it," he said alluding to Chan's superior in the communist underground.

A greater trauma was to hit Lee and his anglicised associates when they discovered that the Chinese-speaking staff in the PAP branches and community centres were defecting en masse to the other side. Little did Lee realise then that when he placed Chan in charge of staff recruitment, his lieutenant was given carte blanche to pack both bodies with pro-communist members.

Chan had not denied that he was a communist operative planted by the MCP under the nose of the prime minister in the heart of the PAP government, or that he was at the centre of the conspiracy hatched by PAP single assemblymen in their Fort Canning quarters which culminated in The Big Split.

After crossing the floor in the chamber, the PAP rebels went on to form Barisan Sosialis with Chan taking on the mantle of propaganda chief and editor of its party organ. As the largest opposition party in the house, Barisan came close to bringing down the Lee government on several occasions.

But surely, you might ask, wouldn't Lee have known of Chan's communist background? Wouldn't Special Branch, the predecessor of Singapore's Internal Security Department, have alerted the prime minister that he was once a member of a communist cell controlled by none other than Jek himself?

After all, opposition leader Lim Yew Hock, who had access to intelligence reports when he was chief minister, had identified Chan as a communist in one sitting and asked home affairs minister Ong Pang Boon why he had yet to be arrested.

When interviewed in Hatyai, Chan said he believed that Lee was aware of his links with the communist underground from the outset. He recalled Jek telling him that when Special Branch warned Lee that Chan was a subversive element, Lee had replied: "I know, but he's of a different type."

Lee said he thought Chan was like Jek, a communist sympathiser who had changed. "Jek thought he had changed. I trusted Jek. On Jek's word, I thought I could trust Chan. What I did not know was that after Jek broke with the communists, Chan responded to a new controller. That was my mistake."

By his own admission, Chan was a member of the Anti-British League (ABL), a satellite organisation of MCP, when he was a student at Chinese High in the early 1950s. He was arrested twice for anti-colonial activities and was expelled from the school in 1952. When ABL was banned in 1954, he was notified that he had become a provisional member of MCP.

Lee viewed Chan's about-turn as treachery but Chan said he did not see himself as being disloyal to Lee but being loyal to his ideological cause. He parted company with Lee, he said, because he opposed merger.

To the besieged prime minister then, it was yet another misjudgement of character that exposed his naivete and taught him another painful lesson in politics. How personal relationships dissolved into ideological enmity would be a recurring motif throughout the PAP story of the 1950s and 1960s.

More than just a political saga of a party's struggle against colonialists, conservatives, communists and communalists, it tells the all-too-human story of friendships sealed and shattered by shifting political alliances and evokes the entire gamut of emotions from trust, hope and loyalty to betrayal, despair and anger.

Chan escaped the dragnet when a security operation code-named Operation Cold Store was launched in February 1963 to put communist activists behind bars. But later in the year, after he was elected Barisan Sosialis legislative assemblyman for Nee Soon in the general election, he went into hiding to avoid questioning by Special Branch in connection with a strike by pro-communist trade unions.

He revealed that he moved about in a van, confining himself to the rural areas. That he was able to do so without being detected, he said, testified to the mass support for the leftists at that time.

One dark night he boarded a smugglers' boat and landed on a neighbouring Riau island. From there he went to Jakarta where he met senior MCP leader Eu Chooi Yip. He never forgot Eu's greeting.

Eu: "What the hell are you doing here? Have you all forgotten about *bai pi hong xin*?"

The Mandarin maxim translates to "the skin is white but the heart is red", meaning that Chan should have continued operating within the PAP instead of coming out into the open.

Chan's reply: "But why didn't you guys tell me?"

1

To Be Young Was Very Heaven

IN a terrace house on Cromwell Road within strolling distance of Hyde Park and Harrods, three restless young men sat through the night huddled in animated discussion.

They had much to talk about as they had much in common—as fellow university students in London from British-ruled Malaya, as former fellow students of Raffles College in pre-war Singapore and as friends bonded by a traumatic wartime experience.

The trio were mature students resuming their education on colonial scholarships at the University of London after the disruption of the 1942-45 Japanese Occupation. Two were civil servants—Goh Keng Swee, then 31, was reading economics at the London School of Economics (LSE) while Abdul Razak Hussein, 27, was studying law. The third person, Maurice Baker, 29, was pursuing English literature.

The year was 1948. What kept them on edge was the series of heart-stopping events back home, particularly the latest British-sponsored scheme that separated Singapore from Malaya. They were seething with anti-colonial fervour as they regarded the indivisibility of both territories as sacrosanct.

But that evening, they were especially troubled by the lack of support from their peers in England for their latest anti-colonial initiative. Only days ago, Baker, Goh and a law student, Ali Hassan, had been to the Colonial Office to protest against the arrests of several leading members of the Malayan Democratic Union (MDU), the first indigenous political party to be set up in Singapore with a multi-racial and democratic platform.

Founded on 21 December 1945 by English-educated intellectuals to wrest independence for Malaya, MDU became intertwined with the Malayan Communist Party (MCP) which was operating legally after the war. When the communists resorted to armed violence, Britain imposed a state of Emergency on 16 June 1948. The MCP was banned and a crackdown on MDU followed.

What perturbed the three of them in the flat that night, wrote Baker in his unpublished memoirs, was the student apathy in London to the volatile situation in Malaya. Their contemporaries on government scholarships seemed fixated on their studies while those on "father's scholarships" preferred to live up to British author Samuel Johnson's dictum that "when a man is tired of London, he is tired of life".

Goh and Baker were also bothered by the memory of their experience in the second world festival of youth and students in Budapest, Hungary, in the past summer. They were there on a communist-subsidised junket but they could not help being struck by the political idealism of their counterparts from European, African and Asian countries.

Young Hungarians impressed them with their fierce determination to rebuild their war-torn country while young Indians left them in no doubt about their love for their motherland after it was freed from the British Raj a year earlier at the "stroke of the midnight hour".

In contrast, Malayan students appeared passive and complacent. Their shallowness of purpose and superficiality of thinking grated on Goh. One participant at the festival was Lee Kip Lin, then an architecture student at University College, London. Rattling off a roll call of recognisable names, the retired architect said scorchingly: "They went there just for the drinking and the womanising."

As the night wore on, the threesome kept coming back to the same vexing questions over and over again. India, Pakistan, Burma, Ceylon, Indonesia and the Philippines had found freedom so why was Malaya still lagging behind? Was it not time to instil political awareness among the young and prepare for inevitable independence? If the best and brightest from Malaya did not want to fight for freedom, who would? The communists?

Baker said he could not quite pinpoint whether the idea came from Razak or Goh. "We decided that something should be done to make the students more politically conscious so as to prepare for ultimate independence. We approached Razak and it was in Razak's flat on Cromwell Road that the idea of the Malayan Forum was born."

The aim: to attain independence for Malaya by constitutional means. The vision: an independent, socialist, non-communist Malaya.

Little did the three earnest young men who mooted the idea—Abdul Razak, Goh and Baker—have any inkling then that they were destined to be the future prime minister of Malaysia, the future deputy prime minister of Singapore and the future Singapore's high commissioner to Malaysia who would help to smoothen out troubled Singapore-Malaysia relations in later years.

WHY the name Malayan Forum?

There was no Malaysia yet. Whichever state they hailed from and whatever their race, the founding members of Malayan Forum could only conceive of themselves as Malayans. Goh, a Straits-born Chinese and son of an assistant rubber estate manager, was born in Malacca; Abdul Razak, son of a Malay chieftain, in Pekan, Pahang; and Baker, son of an English engineer and Indian housewife, in Alor Star, Kedah.

Whenever they mentioned Malaya, they meant Singapore as well. They were thus incensed by the British constitutional arrangements which hived off Singapore not once but twice from Malaya.

Before the war, Singapore, Penang and Malacca formed the Straits Settlements and came under the jurisdiction of the Colonial Office in London. To ward off the intrusion of other foreign powers, the British extended their influence to mainland Malaya by grouping Pahang, Perak, Selangor and Negri Sembilan under the Federated Malay States (FMS). Later they exerted control over the other states of Johor, Kedah, Kelantan, Perlis and Trengganu, which became known as the Unfederated Malay States (UFMS).

When the British re-occupied Malaya after the Japanese surrender, they dissolved the Straits Settlements. Penang and Malacca joined the other nine Malay states to form the Malayan Union on 1 April 1946. Singapore was excluded and kept as a crown colony under direct British rule.

But this scheme was opposed ferociously by Malay leaders as it meant conferring equal political status on the Chinese and Indian immigrant communities. Fearing that Malay interests would be undermined, they formed the United Malays National Organisation (UMNO) on 11 May 1946 to protest against the Malayan Union.

The British gave in. They scrapped the Malayan Union and replaced it with the Federation of Malaya in February 1948. Comprising the nine Malay states, Penang and Malacca, the new scheme restricted the citizenship of non-Malays. Once again Singapore was hived off as a crown colony because of its large Chinese majority and strategic importance.

To the London students, however, the notion of Singapore as a separate entity represented the height of geographical and socio-economic absurdity. The British-incubated schemes only strengthened their resolve to bring Singapore back to the fold.

Even in those halcyon days, the idealistic Goh preferred to stay in the background. His aversion to public speaking was already evident. Baker and Razak, who were then heading students' societies, had to prevail on their leadership-shy colleague to be the first chairman of the Malayan Forum.

Then the search began to rope in other kindred spirits. They inducted Mohamed Sopiee bin Sheikh Ibrahim, a social science student at LSE, as the secretary. He became so active that he had to be restrained from speaking too freely to the press. Making up the "original six" of the forum were law students Philip Hoalim Jnr and Fred Arulanandom.

Mohamed Sopiee, a founding member of UMNO, made his mark in later life as parliamentarian, diplomat and consumer advocate in Malaysia. Philip Hoalim Jnr became a well-known lawyer in Penang. His father, Philip Hoalim Snr, was the MDU chairman and a distinguished lawyer. Arulanandom later served as a High Court judge in Malaysia.

From the word go, they were acutely aware of the complex ethnic mix in Malaya and its chequered race history. That explained why they were very scrupulous about ensuring a multi-racial composition. As Hoalim Jnr remarked with a tinge of pride: "The Chinese were represented by Goh and myself, the Malays by Razak and Mohamed Sopiee. Baker represented the Eurasians and Arulanandom, the Indians."

As the grouping grew, the forum meetings moved to 44 Bryanston Square off Gloucester Place. Better known as Malaya Hall, it was leased from the Duke of Portland by the colonial government as a meeting place for Malayan students. Baker estimated that there were 340 out of 540 Malayan students then in the capital, mostly in London University and the Inns of Court. The other students were scattered in several provincial universities.

Malaya Hall was a happy hunting ground for the forum. One poor scholarship student from Taiping, Perak, known for his feistiness and punctiliousness, was dragged in by Baker and Goh. He was studying for his science degree in the University of London before going on to do his doctorate in physiology at Britain's National Institute for Medical Research. His name: Toh Chin Chye.

Before he joined the forum, Toh recalled, Goh and Razak had already discussed the future of Singapore and Malaya. Their starting point was the arbitrary detachment of Singapore from the peninsula under the Malayan Union and Federation of Malaya schemes. And their unswerving focus was on how to unite the two territories.

Malaya Hall, situated in a leafy square of central London near Marble Arch underground station and Madame Tussaud's, became the historic rendezvous where many future political leaders were to cross paths for the very first time. It was at the doorway of Toh's hostel room in Malaya Hall that *Utusan Melayu* journalist Othman Wok first met Toh when he attended a journalism programme in London.

While holding a social function on the premises one evening, Othman realised that he needed a "golden needle", a gold-coated stylus to play on the 78 rpm gramophone records. When told that the person holding it was Toh, he went up to his room and knocked. As the former social affairs minister recounted with a mock grimace: "I saw this short gentleman coming out looking unhappy that I had disturbed him while he was studying. He asked: 'What do you want?' I said: 'The boys downstairs told me that you keep these needles to play the radiogram.' He said: 'That's the trouble with you people. When you want to play the radiogram, you come and ask needles from me. I don't have the needle. You go and buy it out of your pocket. Leave me alone.' And he banged the door shut."

Another journalist who spent a year in London was Lee Khoon Choy, from the defunct Chinese newspaper *Sin Chew Jit Poh*. He attended meetings held by the Malayan Forum and China Society where Chinese students from China and Southeast Asia gathered. "At China Society, I saw the Kuomintang people and communists fighting one another and I felt that their fighting did not affect me; whereas at Malayan Forum, they were talking about my future," recollected the former senior minister of state and diplomat.

Often, the more spirited forum members would adjourn to the ubiquitous smoke-filled London pub where the growing intensity of their anti-colonial sentiments would match their progressive state of inebriation. Baker still cherished the memory of many an evening spent boozing away with Goh and Kip Lin while bantering about how to boot out the British.

One regular participant was Ghazali Shafie, then studying in the University College of Wales. Here's a flavour of a typical night out as recorded by the former Malaysian home affairs minister: "After listening to the classical records of Toh Chin Chye, going pub-crawling with Goh Keng Swee, or eating a free meal of Razak's most undelicious cooking at his apartment, we would eventually congregate somewhere with one topic in mind—the future of Malaya, which in those days included Singapore."

❧

LONDON 1949–50 could not have been more politically intoxicating for young impressionable minds. Never mind the dampness and shortages in a city recovering from the ravages of war; all around, the air crackled with the rhetoric of socialism. Students steeped in Wordsworthian poetry were wont to spout: *Bliss was it in that dawn to be alive, But to be young was very Heaven!*

Heaven was socialist and so was Britain under the British Labour Party which had ignominiously dumped the ruling Conservative Party of wartime hero Sir Winston Churchill just after the war in 1945. As encapsulated in the radical policies of Labour prime minister Clement Attlee, socialism proved to be intellectually exhilarating and liberating to Goh and friends.

The very notion of a system in which the means of production were owned and managed collectively for the public good appealed to their sense of idealism, fair play and equity. The Labour government's nationalisation of key industries won their unalloyed admiration. Even more enthralling was the enactment of the National Health Service which provided free medical services for all citizens.

What was more, the upsurge of nationalistic movements throughout the world which espoused socialism as their gospel electrified the Malayan Forum fraternity. Freedom was sweeping through Asia like a tsunami. Indonesia was liberated from the Dutch and Vietnam from the French in 1945, the Philippines from the Americans in 1946, India and Pakistan from the British in 1947, and Ceylon (now known as Sri Lanka) and Burma (renamed Myanmar) from the British in 1948.

Within the forum, members began to ask with growing moral indignation: why should the British who capitulated so easily during the war and exposed the Malayan people to the most horrendous atrocities of the Japanese be allowed to continue plundering the wealth of Malaya?

If the students gravitated to the British Labour Party, it was because they felt that it was sympathetic to their aspirations. It was Labour which granted independence to India, Burma and Ceylon. Styling themselves as socialists even though their theoretical understanding was nebulous, Baker admitted: "We were idealistic, hoping to eliminate the huge gap between the rich and poor through state control of the means of production."

But the forbidden fruit which they crunched into with great relish was Marxism, the revolutionary doctrine which postulated that exploited workers would eventually overthrow the capitalists and establish a new classless society. Baker still laughed at the memory of ploughing through the entire *Communist Manifesto* by Friedrich Engels and Karl Marx.

When warned that they should not read the *Daily Worker*, the British Communist Party publication, they lapped it up all the more, chortled Hoalim Jnr: "It's hard for me to convey to you the mood of the times. You had to live through it to understand what I mean. Those were the days when they said that if you are not a communist by 30, you are a fool, but if you are still a communist after 30, you are a bigger fool."

Goh and Razak were especially gripped by the iconoclastic views of Harold Laski, the guru of the Labour Party who taught them in LSE and who was to mould the thinking of a generation of students. They were so profoundly influenced by socialist ideals that they joined the Fabian Society which laid the ideological foundation for the British Labour Party.

The ideas jelled with their thinking. The Fabian Society did not favour the class struggle and instead preached social solidarity between workers and employers. The society's political philosophy was best reflected by its logo of a red tortoise signifying the superiority of gradual change over the hare of revolution.

Goh, who was raised in a strict Methodist household, found resonance in the Fabian beliefs of doing good and reforming society to help the poor. He reasoned that it was far better to improve the lot of the workers through the parliamentary system rather than through armed revolution as advocated by the communists.

In the parlance of the day, they all saw themselves as being on the left of the political spectrum, that is, they advocated change to the established order as opposed to those on the right who were against change and sought to retain the status quo. With the labels came varying hues and shades. If you were on the extreme left calling for the violent overthrow of the existing order, you were daubed "red"; if you held moderately radical views, you were "pink".

Perhaps the most dastardly label that you could pin on a person then was "reactionary" which ridiculed a person resistant to change and clinging on to an outmoded system.

In the Fabian Society, Goh and friends found their staunchest champion in Archibald Fenner Brockway, the chairman of the Movement for Colonial Freedom which was linked to the British Labour Party. It was no surprise that when the forum launched a series of talks to gauge the reaction of British politicians to freedom for Malaya, Brockway was their favourite speaker.

A typical talk, as Hoalim Jnr described it, would go like this: "What does the Conservative Party feel about independence for Malaya?" The same would be asked of the Labour, Communist even Fascist and Anarchist parties. Toh incurred the ire of colonial officials when he invited the British Communist Party to address the forum. One day, he said, Sir Gerald Templar, commander-in-chief of the British and Commonwealth forces, visited Malaya Hall, took him to the side and reprimanded him.

One prominent speaker was British high commissioner Sir Henry Gurney. His death a few months later brought home the terror of the Emergency to the students. He was ambushed and killed by communist guerillas on his way to Fraser's Hill in Pahang on 6 October 1951.

⁂

BUT one speaker who turned up at Malaya Hall on 28 January 1950 was not an eminent politician or intellectual—well, not just yet. The 27-year-old Straits-born Chinese had just graduated with a double first in law with a star for special distinction from Cambridge University.

Giving his parting shot as a returning student, he provided a personal assessment of the daunting political problems confronting Malaya on the road to independence, in particular, the race divide and the threat of communism. On a prescient note, he suggested the "development of a united political front that will be strong enough, without resorting to armed force, to demand a transfer of power".

In his view, society had to develop in a way which was not Malay or Chinese or Indian but Malayan, and be based on racial harmony and cooperation. If the various racial groups began organising themselves, he warned, the result could be another Palestine where one race was pitted against another.

Baker, who chaired the talk, remembered it as "a very important speech" which zoomed in on two critical issues—communalism and communism—which were to shape the speaker's lifelong political philosophy. He was Lee Kuan Yew or Harry Lee as he was known to his buddies.

Watching him from the sidelines was his wife Kwa Geok Choo whom he had married secretly in December 1947. A queen's scholar who also graduated in law with top honours from Cambridge, she was Lee's intellectual rival in Raffles College. Lee wanted to beat her in college but lost, quipped Baker, "... so if you can't beat her, you'd better marry her".

Lee, who was also attracted to Fabianism, was kept informed of the formation of Malayan Forum but could not take part in its activities as he was 80 km away in Cambridge. Hoalim Jnr likened Lee and the forum to "two streams". "We did not meet but he knew what we were doing and we knew what he was doing. He was doing a lot of things on his own because he too wanted independence for Malaya and Singapore," he said.

If Lee was able to clinch a place in Fitzwilliam College, it was because of the help of Cecil Wong who was residing there. Wong's parents were friends of the Lees. The college principal agreed to accept Lee on condition that Wong shared his lodgings with him.

As roommate for a term, was Wong ever privy to Lee's political thinking? "We talked generally about how to make the world a better place and about getting independence for Malaya. As a Christian, I was thinking in terms of promoting the Christian way of life. But Lee was not a Christian and his approach was more practical while my way was a bit up in the air," reminisced Wong, a retired accountant and company director.

When Lee rose to speak at Malaya Hall that evening, he was a nonentity to the powers-that-be. But he was no stranger to many in the audience who knew him from their days in Raffles College before their education was rudely interrupted by the war.

Opened in 1929, Raffles College was the premier institution in the arts and sciences for the English-educated in Southeast Asia. It ran parallel to the King Edward VII Medical School. Both were merged in 1949 to form the University of Malaya which later became the University of Singapore, the predecessor of the National University of Singapore.

Lee was in the same year as Razak and Wong pursuing English, mathematics and economics. They were two years behind Baker who was two years behind Goh who did so well in his studies that he was appointed economics tutor. Many of Lee's college mates went on to become movers and shakers on both sides of the causeway.

In those salad days, there was already a stark difference in attitudes between the English-educated and Chinese-stream students. Sheltered by the British military umbrella and assured of secure and stable jobs in the civil service and the professions, the English-educated hardly contemplated the prospect of independence. They read the British-owned *Straits Times* which was orientated towards colonial society and were only dimly conscious of the tumultuous upheavals in Asia.

Political interest was said to be virtually zero with their favourite pursuits revolving around girls, movies and sports. Edmund William Barker said he was apolitical, being more keen in games than in politics. Lim Kim San was "a bit of a dandy with lots of girl friends", according to his good friend, Goh. Describing himself as politically naive, Lim admitted that he did not know what communism was until he attended a briefing before graduation.

It was the Chinese-stream students in the college who were more politically attuned. Eu Chooi Yip, who studied in Shang Ban School in Kuantan and Yeung Cheng School in Singapore, was known for telling off the English-educated that it was morally wrong for Singapore to be run by the British.

The event that aroused their feelings to a feverish pitch was the full-scale invasion of China by Japan in 1937 which led to the fall of Shanghai and the "Rape of Nanking" in which hundreds of thousands of civilians were butchered by the rampaging conquerors.

While the English-educated took no more than a passing interest, Eu and company pitched in vigorously to raise money for the war-torn refugees of China. A "meatless day" was held on campus in which the money saved from not eating meat was donated to the China Relief Fund.

The Japanese invasion of the region showed up the courage of the Chinese-educated while exposing the timorousness of the English-educated. As the Japanese pedalled furiously down the peninsula towards Singapore at the end of 1941, many of the former but few of the latter enlisted immediately in a hastily organised force called Dalforce, named after Lt Col J D Dalley of the Malayan Police Special Branch.

After a 10-day crash course and armed with only grenades, shotguns and parangs, the volunteers fought the Japanese in suicidal hand-to-hand combat in northern Singapore. Cecil Wong remembered that they exacted such a heavy toll on the invaders that the Japanese went hunting for them after the surrender.

The vengeful conquerors targeted strong, young people whom they suspected could have been the Dalforce fighters. "That's how it happened. And you know, they took many away, they disappeared, they never came back, we didn't know what happened to them," said Wong in a poignant reference to the massacre which has yet to be accounted for to this day.

⁕

SO did the idea of forming a political party surface in the Malayan Forum?

In his first stint in London between 1948 and 1951, Goh said the members never mooted the formation of a political party. His recollection was that it was only after Lee returned home and started work with the trade unions to gather support that they decided to start a party.

Lee was not sure if they had decided to form a party then, "but we knew that when we returned, we had to join a party or form a party. You can't just go back and say, ok, let's start another discussion."

Toh was adamant that there was no talk whatsoever of forming a party during his forum days. "No, because we were not supposed to do so. There was the Emergency. We did not want to go back home, and be imprisoned for no rhyme or reason. And we knew that among those who attended our meetings, there were intelligence agents."

Indeed, agents from the Special Branch created by the colonial government to deal with subversion were not the only ones interested in the forum. Hovering around Malaya Hall was a group of radical activists led by Lim Hong Bee, a queen's scholar who gave up his law studies in Cambridge to devote his life to the communist cause.

Described as "one of the brightest in his generation" and a "kind gentleman but hard-core communist" by those who knew him, Lim acted as MCP representative in Europe. After Toh left London for home, Lim and his comrades seized control of the forum and put out a magazine supporting the communist insurgency in Malaya.

Goh was understandably upset that their "baby" had been hijacked. On his return to London in 1954 to read for his doctorate in economics, he and London University law student Chua Sian Chin plotted to oust them in the annual meeting.

For Goh, it was a sobering eye-opener into the communist tactics of filibustering and attrition but his group succeeded in mustering a vote of no-confidence against the leaders. Their strategy: getting the students to turn up and stay long enough to cast their votes. The carrot: providing free food and drinks.

And so the young starry-eyed idealists returned home one by one with dazzling academic honours and swirling socialist ideas. In August 1950, Lee sailed home and landed a job with the law firm of Laycock and Ong. The next year, Goh, with first class honours in economics, went back to the civil service and joined the social welfare department.

Toh was offered an opportunity to do further research in America but felt that it would be morally wrong to break his government scholarship bond. On his return in 1953, he assumed the post of lecturer in physiology at the University of Malaya.

As returning students who had stormed the bastions of British learning, they represented the new privileged class who would enjoy a status and pay and perks only second to the British expatriates.

In Toh's ringing words, they had a place in the sun.

Would they, as Lee asked in his Malayan Forum speech, become part of the vested interests of the colony or would they translate their political convictions into concrete action?

IT was in the shadow of the 31m-high clock tower at Chinese High that a 16-year-old Lim Chin Siong first met 18-year-old Fong Swee Suan in 1949. It was to mark the beginning of a bosom friendship and ideological comradeship that would last a lifetime.

Such was the intimacy of their relationship from their school ties to their involvement in the labour movement and politics to their detention and post-detention years that they were often depicted as *nan xiong nan di* (brothers who went through thick and thin together).

Reflecting on their lifelong friendship, former firebrand trade unionist Fong emphasised that it was cemented by "honesty, trust, dedication, political convictions and self-sacrifice". He said that he was very proud that whatever the ups and downs in their political career he "never betrayed Lim". Lim was 63 when he died of a heart attack in 1996.

Lim grew up in Telok Kerang near Pontian in Johor where his parents ran a provision shop. Fong was born to a laundry man and farmer in Senggarang near Batu Pahat, Johor. Both came from impoverished families and attended Chinese-language primary schools. Lim, a Hokkien, was the second in a family of 12 siblings while Fong, a Hakka, ranked third out of seven.

If they were older than their cohort in class, it was because their education was disrupted by the war. Like all Chinese-stream students throughout Malaya, they aspired to join Chinese High. Founded by philanthropist Tan Kah Kee in 1919 and funded by the Chinese community, it was the leading Chinese institution in Southeast Asia, attracting top teachers from China and the best and brightest students from the region.

Lim had spent a year at Catholic High, another Chinese-language school in Singapore, but found it too sedate. He made the switch to Chinese High because he wanted to meet the better read and progressive students there. Fong managed to persuade an elder brother, a tailor, to pay for his education at the imposing school on Bukit Timah Road.

Their school life coincided with the period of revolutionary ferment in Asia. No event seized their imagination and stirred their senses more than the day Mao Zedong stood at Tiananmen Square to proclaim the People's Republic of China (PRC) on 1 October 1949. In words that reverberated around the world, the chairman of the Chinese Communist Party (CCP) declared: "The Chinese people have stood up."

As Cheng An Lun, principal of Chinese High from 1948 to 1968, wrote in the school's 60th anniversary souvenir magazine in 1979: "The joy of the students was expected. The jubilant mood filled the entire school. The school auditorium and hostel rooms were decorated with portraits of Sun Yat Sen and Mao Zedong. The walls of the auditorium were pasted all over with newspaper articles on the new China."

Although Sun Yat Sen was the founder of Kuomintang (KMT) which lost to CCP in the protracted civil war, he was revered on both sides of the Taiwan Strait for leading the 1911 revolution that ended 267 years of Qing dynasty rule in China.

Like all their fellow students and teachers, Lim and Fong could not help being suffused by the euphoria of the communist victory with its utopian promise of social justice and egalitarianism. Just like their politically conscious fellow Malayans in London, they believed that the time had come for Singapore to cut off the British shackles.

They first met in *er jia* or class 2A, the top class in junior middle II which corresponded to secondary two in the present school system. Fong's first impression of Lim: "Polite, friendly and handsome." Then he found that they had much in common. "We were both ardent anti-colonialists and we were both fascinated by the surge of national movements in Asia and Africa."

No one who studied in Chinese High at that time could be immune to the revolutionary-like atmosphere in the school. "If you were a student, you could not escape it. The only question was … to what extent would you get involved," said former student Sze Lih Hwa referring to the political activism in the school.

Literature from communist China flowed freely into the school and Fong laid hands on a copy of Mao's famous poem, *The Long March*. Boys in khaki shorts and white shirts with silver buttons—the same uniform worn by today's students—lapped up the works of Chinese writers such as Lu Xun, Lao She, Guo Moruo, Ba Jin and Mao Dun who championed the cause of the working class. Just as popular were Chinese-language translations of Western literature, particularly books by Russian writers Maxim Gorky, Leo Tolstoy and Ivan Turgenev which highlighted similar themes.

Before Mao's victory in 1949, the school would raise the KMT flag as students sang the KMT song extolling the *san min zhu yi* (Three People's Principles) every morning. After Britain recognised the PRC in 1950, the school hoisted China's new five-star red flag and played the Chinese national anthem, *yi yong jun jin xing qu* (March of the Courageous), at its weekly assembly.

One eyewitness to this dramatic changeover was former student Chen Say Jame who remembered that the school could not find anyone to play on the piano on that day: "Then a teacher by the name of Qu Liang rose to go to the keyboard and started to play the new anthem and everyone sang … *qi lai! bu yuan yi zuo nu li de ren men* (Arise! People who are not willing to be slaves.)."

The British could not stomach the emotionally rousing songs and proliferation of red flags and soon put a stop to the morning ceremonies. Chen learnt later that the teacher had disappeared suddenly and believed that he was arrested as a suspected communist.

Still seared into his consciousness was the 31 May 1950 swoop when hundreds of policemen raided the school and detained 19 students and a teacher for pro-communist activities. Chen said the school was asked to show cause why it should not be closed and was only allowed to be re-opened in August after it sacked several blacklisted teachers and students and shut down its hostel.

The government action enraged the staff and students of the school whose anti-colonial sentiments were already fired up by British neglect of Chinese education and discrimination against Chinese-educated school leavers in the civil service and workplace.

According to Chen, the students organised themselves into groups to discuss current affairs and political issues. Meetings were held regularly outside the school, including weekend retreats in rented bungalows where students met their counterparts from other Chinese middle schools.

It was around this time, he believed, that elements of the MCP, which was banned in 1948, made their presence felt in the school. The MCP publication, *zi you bao* (Freedom News), was circulated freely in school. He recalled that copies were placed under students' desks in classrooms by five or six a.m. every morning.

Chen came to know Lim and Fong better in 1951 when they found themselves among 108 students attending the three junior middle III graduating classes. Seeing themselves as rebels against the British colonialists, they were struck by the number 108, which was the same as the number of heroes in the great Chinese classic, *shui hu zhuan* (*Water Margin*). The novel, set during the Song Dynasty (AD 960–1279) in China, depicts the valour of 108 righteous men and women who were compelled by a corrupt society to break the law and seek refuge in the mountain.

The students formed a special committee called *ji lian hui* (alliance of all the classes) to prepare for their graduation. With Chen as chairman, Lim as secretary and Fong as a committee member, they held discussions as well as picnics and other social events to foster comradeship.

A new flashpoint came in 1951 when the British authorities introduced a controversial requirement in the school. In addition to the school internal examination, students had to sit for a new common junior middle III examination which replaced the one conducted by the ousted KMT government in China.

Before 1949, to qualify for higher education in China, all graduating junior middle III students from Chinese-language schools in Singapore had to sit for an external examination administered yearly by the KMT government in China. But with KMT's defeat in 1949, admission to universities in communist China was banned.

The junior middle III students argued vehemently that the British authorities should discontinue the external examination as it no longer served any purpose. Fong noted that the students also saw no point in taking the examination as the certificate obtained would not qualify them for entry into government service or admission to a tertiary institution in Singapore.

In protest, *ji lian hui* transformed itself into a body called Students Opposing The Junior Middle III Examination. Members of the committee went round soliciting support for a boycott of the examination from students of other schools including Chung Cheng High, Nanyang Girls' High, Nan Chiao Girls' High, Chung Hwa High, Yock Eng High and Nan Hua Girls' High. Lim was a prime mover behind the boycott.

They also penned pamphlets and made speeches condemning British colonialism, calling for fair and equal treatment for Chinese-language schools and demanding social justice and freedom from British rule. "Lim Chin Siong was a good essay writer, so almost everyone respected him. Naturally he became the leader," said Fong.

Their activities caught the attention of Special Branch, and several student leaders including Chen and Lim were detained briefly for questioning before the examination took place over three days in October 1951. In all, 80 out of the 108 students in Chinese High boycotted the examination. They turned up for the examination but wrote only their names before handing in blank sheets.

All the students who took part, including Chen, Lim and Fong, were expelled. In one fell stroke, they lost their education and job prospects. Fong could no longer expect his brother to support him and so in 1952, he joined the privately-run Green Bus Company as a bus conductor. Two years later he was elected general secretary of the Singapore Bus Workers' Union (SBWU). He was only 23.

Lim enrolled in a private school to brush up on his English before joining Fong in the same union as the paid secretary of the Changi branch. He was barely 20. When he entered politics in 1955, Chen took over his post.

Under their radical leadership, SBWU became synonymous with union militancy and industrial strife. It became part of the Middle Road group of unions which was to form the most powerful labour movement in Singapore in the 1950s and whose support was crucial for any political party in search of a mass base.

Denied opportunities in education and employment, the sacked students of Chinese High, who did not even complete junior middle III (or secondary three today), would soon join forces with privileged English-educated scholars returning from London with top honours to coveted jobs in government service and the professions.

What happened when poor Mao-inspired socialists meet middle-class Fabian socialists? Watch out for the political combustion!

2

Lawyer: Lee Kuan Yew. Fee: $10

IT happened so frequently in the early 1950s that nobody thought anything was amiss. At the end of the day, Singapore General Hospital would dump its leftover food and poorly paid attendants would rummage through it and help themselves to the edible portions.

Then one day from out of the blue, they were accused by the hospital management of pilfering and threatened with disciplinary action.

They were perplexed. How could this be construed as stealing when they were "just picking up what the hospital was throwing away to feed their hungry children"? In exasperation, as Mofradi bin Haji Mohamed Noor, then hospital worker and chairman of the Singapore Medical Workers' Union recalled, they turned to their legal adviser for help.

The young earnest lawyer wrote a letter to the management to explain the situation and the matter was resolved satisfactorily. It was a small issue, acknowledged Mofradi, but the way Lee Kuan Yew handled it left a deep and abiding impression on the Malay hospital workers.

Mofradi was 40 days old in 1916 when his family fled to Singapore from Dutch-ruled Indonesia because of his father's involvement in an Islamic political party. After completing his religious education, he founded and taught in several *madrasahs* or Islamic religious schools before joining the hospital on Outram Road.

Wearing a white skullcap, the father of 10 and grandfather of 39 cut a gaunt but serene figure in his Teck Whye Lane public housing flat in 2002. What struck him about Lee in 1952 when he became the legal adviser to the union which represented some 12,000 hospital workers was his friendliness and modesty. "For example, when he attended meetings, he would not sit in front; he would sit among us," he said.

Mofradi's account had an unerring ring of familiarity which kept recurring in interviews with many former trade union leaders of the period—a union would have an industrial dispute, a work stoppage or a go-slow, or it would go on strike or enter into arbitration, and hey presto, its legal adviser would turn out to be Lee Kuan Yew.

Catch hold of Lin You Eng and he would regale you with the story of how as president of the Singapore Barber Shops and Hair-Dressing Salons Workers' Union (*li fa dian gong you lian he hui*), he once went to investigate a strike at a barber's shop which resulted in a smashing of mirrors and other fittings.

To his shock, the woman proprietor accused Lin of being one of the vandals and he was arrested together with the striking workers. Guess who came to the rescue? It was none other than Lee, the union's legal adviser who defended and cleared them of all the charges.

A barber himself who ventured into politics later, Lin remembered Lee as being very helpful and patient when dealing with them during the incident. "He spoke to us in halting Mandarin. He had no airs and showed he was willing to listen to the union members," said the six-footer with a thick shock of white hair who ran a garment contracting firm in 2003.

Walk down memory lane with Othman Wok and he would recall the year 1953 when he was secretary of the Singapore Printing Employees' Union (SPEU). The union had gone on strike against the British-owned *Straits Times* over the dismissal of a union official.

Othman was summoned to Central Police Station and told that the strike by 600 workers was illegal as it was called without giving due notice. No prizes for guessing who their legal adviser was. "Lee Kuan Yew came to my assistance and nothing happened to me," said the former journalist, minister and diplomat with a chuckle.

Lee had warned the union that it would lose the battle as it was facing a "very powerful employer" who represented British interests. He advised the strikers to return to work and offered to settle the dispute on its behalf. The union heeded his advice.

In his mind's eye, Othman could still visualise the scene in the union headquarters at 166-A Anson Road where they met after settling the strike. There were Lee, Goh Keng Swee, K M Byrne, G Kandasamy and S Rajaratnam. If the words still rang loud and clear in his head, it was because of what Lee said there and then: "Let's form a political party to protect all the workers in Singapore."

Dip into the Lee memorabilia kept by Mrs Lee, and you would come across all-and-sundry correspondence from trade unions naming Lee as, or inviting him to be, the legal adviser. One list reads like a directory of extinct trades: East Coast Mining and Industrial Workers' Union, Amalgamated Malayan Pineapple Workers' Union, Malayan Gold and Silver Workers' Union (Singapore branch) and Singapore Spinning Workers' Union.

Those who knew Lee in those days reckoned that he was the lawyer to no fewer than 50 unions and associations. No union was too small or humble for Lee to lend his name, be it for hawkers, taxi drivers, trishaw riders or bumboat operators. A letter by Wee Kok Kwang, president of the Singapore City Council Nightsoil Workers' Union to the City Council, copied to legal adviser Lee Kuan Yew, appealed for a $1 daily allowance.

According to Lee, many unions sought his service as legal adviser when he gained public prominence. "We decided we would not turn them down. So I became honorary adviser this, legal adviser that ... I used to go to some of their annual dinners or meetings to touch base with them."

Lee's friends from his youth lamented that the lawyer was so caught up in the hurly-burly of trade union work that they gave up on him. Ho Kok Hoe came to know Lee during the war when the Lee family was staying with prominent lawyer Richard Lim Chuan Hoe in China Building (now OCBC Centre) on Chulia Street. As he worked in Lim's law office in the building, he used to meet Lee.

After the war, Ho left for Australia to study architecture while Lee went to England to do law. One day, hoping to catch up with his old friend on his return, Ho visited Lee at his office in Laycock and Ong on Malacca Street. He saw Lee huddled with a group of workers talking all the time and figured that he was dealing with labour problems.

Lee greeted Ho and asked him to wait. Every now and then, he came by and said: "Kok Hoe, wait." And so he waited and waited and waited. When he reached the end of his patience, he blurted out: "Hey, Kuan Yew, I don't want to talk to you anymore, I don't care, I better *cabut* ("bolt" in Malay)." So off he went and they hardly ever met again, reminisced the retired architect who designed the National Museum in Kuala Lumpur and the old St Andrew's Junior School.

The "friendly and carefree" Kuan Yew he knew during the war who would come swinging into his office, put his legs on his table and chit-chat with him or teach him how to write English essays had taken a different turn. Clearly their interests had diverged.

How did a twenty-something who had returned from his law studies in England only recently end up with such a long string of legal positions? And why did he choose to work with poor and powerless workers rather than with rich and powerful clients?

⊱⋆⊰

IT was a day etched in the memory of Mrs Lee. She had just delivered her first child on 10 February 1952 and her husband was visiting her in the maternity ward of Kandang Kerbau Hospital, now known as KK Women's and Children's Hospital.

As she recalled, Lee sounded elated when he told her about his first union job while cradling baby Hsien Loong. "People would think he'd be cooing over the baby all the time instead of talking about union matters. But I think he was quite pleased at the prospect of acting for this union."

She was referring to the Singapore Post and Telegraph Uniformed Staff Union which was then locked in an acrimonious pay dispute with the colonial authorities. Several days earlier, union leaders Ismail Rahim and Perumal Govindasamy had visited Lee in his office and asked him to be their legal adviser.

Throughout the 13-day strike by the P and T union, as it was better known, which brought all mail services to a stop and unnerved British officialdom, Lee acted as legal adviser, official negotiator and eloquent spokesman—a high-profile role that was to catapult him into the headlines.

Basically, the dispute hinged on the difference between the government's offer of $90 and the postmen's demand of $100 on the maximum pay. It was a difference of only $10. But when the sheer reasonableness of the demand was met by the sheer intransigence of the response, it was transformed into a cause celebre.

Despite the massive service disruptions, people supported the postmen. The press cheered. Even some of the pro-British legislative councillors sympathised with the strikers. Eventually, the government gave in to the union's demands.

The triumphant resolution of the strike projected Lee as a champion of exploited workers in the public eye and turned him into a household name. Requests to Lee to act as their legal adviser came pouring in from trade unions and associations which nursed similar grievances against the colonial masters. To the establishment, Lee became anathema.

Obviously, the lawyer was not in it for the money as the unions comprised lowly paid workers who could barely afford to pay his legal expenses. If he really craved material rewards, he would have joined his contemporaries in servicing the big British trading houses and the Chinese banks or doing lucrative conveyancing work.

In his memoirs *The Singapore Story*, Lee said that he accepted the postmen's case without asking for legal fees. In a letter to Lee, his boss John Laycock complained that the firm had "suffered" from all his union cases and that it "must not take on any more of these wage disputes".

For an example of Lee's legal work, take this letter from Chan Tham Choon, general secretary of the Singapore City Council Services Union, to Lee dated 7 March 1956. It read: "My executive council has noted that there is no fee to be charged for the advice and help you have given to the union, and I am directed to convey the union's appreciation of your kind attention in this matter."

When *Utusan Melayu* journalist Samad Ismail was detained in 1951 for anti-British activities, his newspaper hired Lee as his lawyer. Living in retirement in Petaling Jaya, Kuala Lumpur in 2002, the grand old man of letters whose controversial career straddled both sides of the causeway was livid at the recollection of another leading lawyer who demanded $15,000 for his case. How much did Lee charge? "$10, a token sum," he crackled.

Former *Straits Times* news editor Felix Abisheganaden, who was acquainted with Lee in the 1950s and 1960s, noted that he hardly ever charged the unions for his work. "You can never say that he was ever in his life after any kind of financial gain—never, never, never."

If Lee was not in for the money, then what was he in for? To those who divined his thoughts and intentions, he was practising what he preached to his audience in his Malayan Forum speech in London: get involved in politics. And what better way to cut your political milk teeth than to take up the cudgels on behalf of underpaid workers?

Former student activist and unionist Chen Say Jame's observation was shared by many: "Lee was influenced by the Labour Party in Britain when he was a student there. So he was naturally inclined to be pro-labour and to build his network and power base through the trade unions. Hence his willingness and eagerness to help the unions as legal adviser."

Right from the start, noted former party chairman Toh Chin Chye, the trade union was recognised as an important source of support. "It was the unions that provided the mass base. Lee Kuan Yew was the legal adviser, so he had a mass base."

As Lee admitted, the free or almost-free legal service was extended to the unions when he was in Laycock and Ong. "I was working there for a salary at that time, service free. I mean even if I charged, it just went to the firm. Why should I charge them? John Laycock did not know. In the end I was working to get a following into the PAP! Had he known that, he would have stopped it."

The P and T union victory provided Lee with his entry point to a labour movement bristling with anti-colonial fervour. And it gave a big boost to his group from London who had resumed meeting in one another's home to keep their ideal of a united, independent socialist Malaya alive.

⚜

NO man is an island. Lee could not have pulled off one coup after another in the industrial arena without the surreptitious support of two friends in the colonial administrative service: Goh Keng Swee in the social welfare department and Kenneth Michael Byrne in the establishment branch.

Byrne, who graduated with arts and law degrees from Oxford University and attended Malayan Forum meetings occasionally, was also secretary of the Singapore Government Senior Officers Association which thus gave the group a ready-made platform for action.

Being familiar with the ins and outs of the public service, they provided Lee with backroom expertise on staff matters in the P and T union strike and other industrial disputes. Mrs Lee remembered that many of their meetings revolved around the technicalities of pay scales and vocational terms peculiar to each service.

Goh, a Straits-born Chinese, and Byrne, a Eurasian, were in the upper echelons of government. Yet despite their seniority, they found it hard to conceal their resentment of the imperious British and their discriminatory policies which favoured Caucasians over Asians in pay and promotions.

Goh had a poor opinion of his white bosses' competence and was incensed that he was paid only a third of their pay while doing all the work for which they claimed credit. Mrs Lee related how Goh once went on a one-man go-slow when he discovered that he was placed in a lower grade because he did not pass his Cantonese examination. "I don't know how long it lasted but in the end they passed him up to Grade 1."

In 1952, Goh and Byrne initiated the Council of Joint Action (CJA) to rally all local civil servants against their colonial superiors. They found the issue to ride into battle when the British authorities announced a plan to pay a new family allowance to expatriates but not to local civil servants. At a mass rally on 14 November 1952 in Victoria Memorial Hall, 2,000 officers representing 23 unions and associations slammed the government for discrimination.

When the recommendations of a pay review committee were rejected, some 10,000 government workers threatened to go on strike. To compound the issue, the outspoken and provocative Byrne was charged with insubordination and barred from being the chief spokesman in the negotiations.

The controversy finally simmered down when a new deal for a single allowance and salary scales for all 16,000 government employees was accepted. Byrne got off with a light reprimand. Once again, the rebels had won in a showdown in which Lee played a backseat role for a change while his two friends led the charge.

In their view, the issue transcended industrial relations. As Goh confessed, his motivation was political—to harass the British and build up a mass base. From the bruising encounters with the authorities, they drew some invaluable lessons: the importance of winning the mass support of lower income union members as well as the sympathy of the mass media.

For the neophytes, the CJA experience from 1952 to 1954 formed the crucible in which many of their political ideas were tested and political tactics honed in the heat of battle. Not surprisingly, the CJA had often been credited as the forerunner of the new political party that would be launched by the same ringleaders several months later. Where do you think the word "action" came from?

⚜

IF the postal strike transformed Lee into a champion of lowly paid, vernacular-speaking civil servants, a sedition trial made him a hero of high-minded English-educated intellectuals.

To cultivate as wide a spectrum of society as possible, he could not ignore the crème de la crème from his own language stream in the University of Malaya which was formed in 1949 from the merger of his alma mater Raffles College and King Edward VII College of Medicine.

Inspired by the rise of nationalism and socialism in Asia and inflamed by British imperialism, the most politicised of the cohort were concentrated in the University Socialist Club (USC) where they flirted with Marxism and engaged in vehement debates on the issues of the day.

Wang Gungwu was the first chairman of the club whose members included James Puthucheary, Sandrasegeram Woodhull, Ong Pang Boon, Chua Sian Chin, M K Rajakumar, Abdullah Majid, Poh Soo Kai and Lim Hock Siew. The eminent China scholar recalled that many USC members then were idealistic, adhering to political views which approximated those of Fabian Socialism.

Wang believed only his close friend and fellow hostelite Puthucheary had some idea of the complexity of what it meant to be a socialist. Influenced by the movement for Indian independence, he had served in the Indian National Army to fight the British in Burma during the Second World War and joined the Anti-British League, an underground group associated with the Malayan Communist Party (MCP).

According to Wang, the people who caught Lee's attention were obviously the people in the USC as they were interested in politics. This view was echoed by Woodhull who said: "When Lee returned from England, he made his way to the campus to meet us and became the legal adviser to the socialist club. The idea of forming a political party was already in his thoughts."

When the socialist club launched a journal called *Fajar* ("dawn" in Malay) to propagate socialist views, Lee headed the subscription list. Recalling a meeting held in Goh's home to discuss how Lee, Goh and Byrne could help *Fajar*, Woodhull commented that it marked "the beginning of a liaison" between the Lee group and the university socialists.

But what really congealed the connection between Lee and the students, he noted, was the sensational *Fajar* trial in which eight members of the USC editorial board were charged with sedition for publishing an article titled "Aggression in Asia" on 10 May 1954.

It labelled Malaya a police state and condemned the formation of the Southeast Asia Treaty Organisation (SEATO) by the Western powers to oppose communism in the region. One typically incendiary line read: "Malaya is one more pimple on the face of Asia where a colonial power rules with the help of quislings. As such our interests will always be sacrificed to imperial expediency."

Outraged, the British launched a dawn raid on the campus during the final examinations and arrested eight students: James Puthucheary, Poh Soo Kai, Kwa Boo Sun, M K Rajakumar, Lam Khuan Kit, P Arudsothy, Thomas Varkey and Edwin Thumboo.

Lim Hock Siew, who headed the *Fajar* defence fund, remembered Lee advising him how to phrase circulars to potential contributors to avoid being held in contempt of court as the matter was sub-judice. More significantly, Lee clinched the services of D N Pritt, a queen's counsel in England reputed for his espousal of socialist causes.

Amazingly, Pritt got the charges quashed in two and a half days in a packed courtroom before Justice F A Chua without the defence being called. The page one headline in *The Straits Times* on August 26 proclaimed: "Tremendous victory for freedom of speech." Pritt and Lee became the toast of the town.

Lim, a family doctor who later spent 20 years in detention under the Internal Security Act for alleged communist activities, reflected: "Politically, legally, it was a complete victory for the students." Looking back to the verdict, Wang could not resist conjuring up the campus elation then: "Lee had saved *Fajar*. All my friends in *Fajar*, they'd all been saved by Lee. He was a great hero."

⁂

WHILE nurturing his links with the Malay- and Indian-led public sector unions and the English-speaking intelligentsia, Lee was actually setting his sights on what he called "a world teeming with vitality".

This was the world that the English-educated reader of the day would be completely oblivious to if he read only *The Straits Times* where the governor's social calendar and the Raffles Hotel New Year's Eve ball enjoyed more coverage than the plight of the impoverished and the unemployed.

By family upbringing and education, Lee had no contact with the world brimming with revolutionary ferment. As the son of a Java-born father and Straits-born Chinese mother, he grew up speaking Malay at home and hardly knew Chinese. All his friends were English- and Malay-speaking. So how could he break into a world regarded as the exclusive preserve of the most powerful albeit illegal party on the peninsula, the MCP?

If Malay postmen handed Lee the admission ticket, it was Chinese boys in shorts and girls with pigtails who gave him a ringside view of the volatile labour movement. Their paths crossed as a result of a controversial government exercise to register people between the ages of 18 and 55 for national service in April 1954.

The Chinese middle school students opposed soldiering as it went against the grain of Chinese tradition embodied in the age-old saying "*hao tie bu da ding, hao nan bu dang bing*" (good iron should not be made into nails, good men should not become soldiers). Their fears were fanned by talk that a local garrison was being formed to coincide with the formation of SEATO.

A committee led by fiery student leaders from Chinese High and Chung Cheng High initiated the Movement for Exemption of Chinese Middle School Students from Conscription. It staged a series of protest actions which culminated in the May 13 incident at King George V Park on Clemenceau Avenue, now part of Fort Canning Park.

Police claimed that the students became violent and turned the demonstration into a riot. The students disputed the claim saying that they were marching peacefully to Government House (now known as the Istana) to petition the governor when the riot squad arrived and dispersed them with force.

One Chinese High School student, who was in the thick of it all, was Sze Lih Hwa, better known as Louis Hwa ("they couldn't figure out my surname"). Pointing to his right arm, the retired businessman who lived in Kuala Lumpur said he was hit twice with a baton by a policeman.

Limited by their youthfulness and lack of experience, and ignorant of the ways of a British-run colonial society, the students involved in the anti-conscription campaign soon realised they needed legal advice: how could they avoid being called up without ending on the wrong side of the law?

So imagine a group of Chinese High School boys roaming all over Raffles Place looking at 'advocates and solicitors' signboards and knocking on doors. Having learnt English in his early years in Trengganu, Sze was inducted as interpreter for the student leaders. Here is his account of how they sought to engage a lawyer:

The first lawyer they saw was C H Koh in his office on D'Almeida Street. The students told him they did not want to be soldiers and asked what he could do to help them legally. Koh agreed to be their legal adviser but after a few visits, the students gave up on him when he failed to give them any useful advice.

Then in an office around Kreta Ayer they met Philip Hoalim Snr, the famous lawyer who was chairman of the Malayan Democratic Union (MDU) before its dissolution in 1948. The students sought his legal opinion but instead received his personal opinion. "He actually advised us to be soldiers. So that was quite an anti-climax. So we left."

What Hoalim Snr said did not register with them then but now with the benefit of hindsight and in the light of history, Sze believed the lawyer was right and that he showed great foresight. He had told the students that when Singapore and Malaya attained independence, they would need Chinese soldiers to defend the country.

And so off they went in search of another lawyer. They met Richard Lim Chuan Hoe, the father of eminent eye surgeon Arthur Lim. He took the legalistic view that the law would be passed anyway and whether the students liked it or not, they would be conscripted. No solution again.

While wandering around the city, they bumped into *Utusan Melayu* journalist Samad Ismail who dropped the name of Lee Kuan Yew. And that was how they ended up visiting Lee in Laycock and Ong on Malacca Street and made their acquaintance with the up-and-rising politician in search of a Chinese base.

Lee vaguely remembered that it was either Sze Lih Hwa or Robert Soon Loh Boon who visited him at his home with an Indonesian Chinese girl. "They came in school uniforms. They wanted me to represent the students because they were being prosecuted for the May 13 incident." The girl left an impression on Lee. She came in a big car and spoke Malay, English and Chinese. Soon named her as Cheng Mei Nah of Nanyang Girls' School.

Lee was engaged as the lawyer for the seven students convicted of obstructing the police during the May 13 incident. Again he got Pritt of *Fajar* fame to take up their appeal on October 1954. But if they were hoping that the case would light up as much political fireworks as the *Fajar* trial, they were disappointed. Soon, then the foremost leader of the student movement, believed that the colonial government downplayed it to avoid "giving the students an opportunity to turn the court into a forum". The convictions were upheld and the boys jailed for several months.

When the students' anti-conscription committee was dissolved and reborn as the Singapore Chinese Middle School Students' Union (SCMSSU) in the same year, Lee was invited to be its legal adviser. He accepted it at once, said Soon noting that Lee and his associates were already preparing to form a political party and seeking to recruit members.

Sze recalled visiting Lee's home several times where the lawyer would ply him with questions about the Chinese and the student movement. "I was answering his questions all the time. For example, he would ask: 'Do you know many people? Do you have any Chinese friends?'

"In one conversation, he mentioned that he got so-and-so from this racial group and he said we got nobody from the Chinese side, so would you know anybody who could join us?"

To form a political party, convenors were needed. Sze disclosed that he introduced a few Chinese-speaking convenors to Lee, including his brother-in-law, Chan Chiaw Thor, secretary of the Farmers' Association and Fong Swee Suan, secretary-general of the Singapore Bus Workers' Union (SBWU).

Accounts might vary from person to person but there was no doubt that Lee came to know Lim Chin Siong and Fong Swee Suan through the students. Said Lee: "What I remember was that Lim and Fong were brought along either by Sze or Soon to my house. We wanted to get in touch with the Chinese-speaking unions, so they brought these two who were from the bus workers' union."

There was a cloak-and-dagger element in their newfound alliance. Chen Say Jame, Lim and Fong would meet Lee at Laycock and Ong to discuss union matters when John Laycock, Lee's boss and Progressive Party leader, was not in the office. "When Laycock was in, we had to hide," Chen mused.

Just as the P and T strike led to a clamour for Lee's legal services among the public sector unions led by English- and Malay-speaking leaders, the May 13 case paved the way for a string of legal appointments with the Chinese-speaking left-wing unions.

Clustered at No 149-151 Middle Road on the second floor of a bicycle shop, which had since been replaced by a four-storey building housing the Ma Guang Chinese Medicine and Research Centre, the strongest of the unions was the Singapore Factory and Shop Workers' Union (SFSWU). Led by Lim Chin Siong and open to all workers, it was called *kok giap* in Hokkien or *ke ye* in Mandarin, meaning "different trades".

Lee wanted to tap into the might of the Middle Road unionists even though he was aware that some were members of the Communist United Front (CUF). The term refers to an alliance of pro-communist organisations which operated "above ground" as opposed to the MCP which worked "underground".

Four months before he died in November 2003 at the age of 71, Woodhull said in an interview that Lee was consciously cultivating the left as he wanted to have as broad a front as possible even if it meant embracing the pro-communist camp.

The word he invoked to describe their relationship was "symbiosis", an arrangement in which two different parts came together and benefited from one another. He depicted Lee as "the rallying point" which brought the English-speaking students and Chinese-speaking leftists together.

James Puthucheary noted that "of all the open leaders, Harry was the most important. Everybody used to circle around Harry."

IN the dark of the night during the P and T strike of 1952, an associate editor of the *Singapore Standard* would come a-knocking on No 38 Oxley Road with the galley proofs of his editorial scheduled for publication the next day.

There was a conspiratorial air about the nightly rendezvous. It marked the first collaboration between Lee and Sinnathamby Rajaratnam, a leftist journalist of Jaffna Tamil origin who spent 11 years in London cavorting with Asian socialists. Introduced to Lee by Goh, Rajaratnam had no qualms about exploiting the tricks of his trade to advance the postmen's cause.

In his May 13 editorial on the colonial government's offer of a maximum pay of $90 versus the postmen's demand for $100, he wrote in his characteristic mix of sarcasm and irony: "Is it not the duty of a responsible government to give its prior attention to the lower paid workers than to the impoverished bureaucrats over the $1,000 mark? Why strain at a $10 increase when a $100 increase or more has been pushed through without the batting of official eyelid?

"Is the government so hard up that it cannot pay its lower ranks of workers decent wages? Or is there any spare cash to be used to alleviate the miseries of those higher up the ladder?"

Perhaps because of his exposure to Fleet Street in London and his frustrations in getting his messages through the British-run *Straits Times* and family-owned Chinese papers, Lee never underestimated the power of the press. Winning scribes over to his point of view was all part of his game plan.

Ironically, the newspaper most sympathetic to Lee then was *Utusan Melayu*, the predecessor of the Kuala Lumpur-based *Utusan Malaysia* known for its vitriolic attacks against Lee in later years. Founded in 1939 by Yusof Ishak whose face graced Singapore's dollar notes as the country's first president, the Malay newspaper was the voice of Malay intellectuals drawn to nationalism and socialism. Its leading writer was none other than Samad Ismail, a thin, scrawny man with dark glasses and a predilection for expletives.

While serving time from 1951 to 1953 for anti-British activities, Samad often received visits from Lee, his lawyer. They used to discuss politics including the formation of a new political party. "Lee wanted a party that would be very different from the others as he was very concerned about corruption in politics and the trade unions," he said.

When Othman Wok met Lee for the first time, it was with Samad in the *Utusan Melayu* office on Cecil Street. The lawyer asked the young Othman to play up the P and T strike because it involved Malay workers. In those days, politically conscious journalists had no compunction about aligning themselves with the interests of politicians, never mind the Fourth Estate principles of objectivity and impartiality. Former reporter Lee Khoon Choy said that newspapers allowed journalists to join political parties, noting that "Rajaratnam was then an openly PAP man".

Was it any coincidence that Lee planted himself in the heart of the newspaper industry when he became legal adviser to the Singapore Printing Employees' Union and the Singapore Union of Journalists, the predecessor of the Singapore National Union of Journalists?

Former *Straits Times* news editor Felix Abisheganaden was never in doubt that Lee was always wooing journalists and sizing them up. "Let's face it, he was after brains, not money and ostentation. He was just after thinking people."

Considering Lee's awesome aura today, it is hard to imagine how press-friendly Lee was in his early days, going by Abisheganaden's storehouse of anecdotes. Here is one of his favourites:

Below Lee's Malacca Street firm was a coffee shop where reporters would wait for the lawyer to return from court. On his way up to his office, Lee would join the reporters. "He would sit on a stool and talk with us for a few minutes and he would feed us with all kinds of stories—general, political and so on.

"He was flying ideas, a lot of ideas. He would tell you a story, he would intrigue you so much with the story, you'd say: 'Mr Lee, can I quote you?' He'd say: 'Yes, sure, go ahead.'

"So we all went back to the office all excited. Then we'd get a call from him. 'I say, Felix, remember I spoke to you just now, I don't think you can quote me.' We said: 'What's wrong, Mr Lee, it's a beautiful story. We can write it this way...' He said: 'Then don't quote me.'

"We said OK. The idea had sunk in. We were projecting his story without involving the master. You see how he worked." Abisheganaden let out a hearty laugh.

⚜

ON 3 December 2002, *The Straits Times* carried a full-page advertisement marking the 144th anniversary of the Singapore Char Yong (Dabu) Association and the opening of the Char Yong Building at No 29, Lorong 22, Geylang. It included a picture of Lee as the association's distinguished honourable adviser.

Char Yong town is in Dabu, a county in Guangdong province, China, where many Hakkas in Singapore came from. Lee's great-grandfather, Lee Bok Boon, hailed from Char Yong and the lawyer's connections with the clan go all the way back to his earliest political days.

As Mrs Lee narrated, every time Lee went upcountry on a case between 1951 and 1955—whether it was to Kluang, Muar, Batu Pahat, Ipoh, Penang or Sibu in Sarawak—the Char Yong Huay Kuan Hakka Association of each place would host a dinner in his honour.

When Lee made his political debut in the 1955 legislative assembly elections, one of his strongest supporters was Chong Mong Seng who lived opposite him on Oxley Road. Chong mobilised a fleet of cars to ferry voters to the polling stations.

More than that, Chong was the chairman of the Nanyang Khek Community Guild (*nan yang ke shu zong hui*), an umbrella body for all Chinese clan associations of Hakka origins in Singapore in the 1950s. Given the legendary clannishness of the Hakkas, who do you think they would root for at the hustings other than for one of their kind, and their legal adviser to boot?

But even as Lee spun his political web of contacts, he made sure he did not overlook the humble tradesmen and businessmen such as the Singapore Itinerant Hawkers and Stalls Association and the Singapore

Chinese Liquor Retailers' Association. As legal adviser, he had a firsthand feel of their problems.

For example, during the annual seventh and eighth moon festivals, hawkers would carry as many chickens as possible in their baskets on their bicycles to earn more money—and end up running foul of the law. With their summonses in hand, they would ask Lee to help them.

There was really no defence, Mrs Lee remembered her husband telling her, as the hawkers had committed an offence. He could only write to the authorities with the plea: "Look, these are just poor hawkers, having to make a living. Can you ask your policemen to just have a heart? Just let them make a living."

Once the liquor retailers found themselves in a legal quandary. Samsu and beer could be sold on their premises but beer was not allowed to be consumed there. The reason was that if you drank beer you needed a toilet and these shops did not have a toilet. So they saw Lee. Again there was no case and all Lee could do was to appeal on their behalf.

It seemed as if Lee was seeking to cover all political bases. He was not just networking with trade unionists, intellectuals and journalists but also with hawkers who overloaded their bicycles with squawking chickens and liquor retailers whose inebriated customers could not drink beer in their shops. And in between defending prominent clients in high-profile cases, he was writing petition letters for illiterate tradesmen.

The political payoff came when, apart from union members and students, all-and-sundry tradesmen turned up in droves to help Lee in the electioneering. When Lee's party needed an election office in the 1955 polls, the Singapore Chinese Liquor Retailers' Association offered its premises on Bernam Street in Tanjong Pagar.

When you had the support of the liquor retailers, Mrs Lee quipped, "it's like having every pub telling the drinkers that this is a good man, vote for him".

Meanwhile, with the whiff of elections in the air, friends and associates began straggling into No 38 Oxley Road. Mofradi noticed Lim Chin Siong had a habit of dozing off as the proceedings droned on in the late sultry afternoon. Toh Chin Chye sought to rein in Byrne's playfulness. Lee took notes furiously. The meeting was in order.

3

No Wives Please, Meeting in Progress

IF you happen to walk by the twin electric iron gates and sentry boxes, chances are that you would instinctively quicken your steps to avoid the expressionless gaze of two gun-toting Gurkha policemen in brown hats.

Camouflaged by foliage, ringed by a thick brick wall and flanked by low-rise apartment blocks with shuttered windows, the house exudes a forbidding presence.

Hard as it may be to believe now, there was a time when No 38 Oxley Road did not evoke such an aura of awe and mystique of power.

Indeed there was a time when people barged in unannounced, postmen rang the doorbell not to deliver letters but to lounge in the living room to plan a strike, and assorted characters streamed nonchalantly into the compound as if it was open house day.

If the walls of the home of the founding father of the Republic of Singapore could speak, they would narrate the unending procession of trade unionists, workers, tradesmen, students, journalists, civil servants, professionals and intellectuals passing through its gates in the 1950s asking for Harry, Kuan Yew or Mr Lee.

Here within a pre-war single-storey bungalow which stood on pillars, or *fu jiao lou* as the Mandarin speakers called it, was where the newly returned graduates from England took off from where they left off in their exhilarating Malayan Forum discussions in London.

Here in the basement room was where strained faces sat huddled around a long dining table littered with overflowing ash-trays.

Here beneath the whirring fan with three windows thrown wide open to dispel the heat and humidity was where ideas were tossed up, views argued, options weighed, issues thrashed and decisions made in hush-hush meetings which changed the history of Singapore.

Here towards the end of 1954 was where the People's Action Party (PAP) was born.

FROM whose lips came the words "people" and "action"? How did the name of the party come about? Who was the inspirational muse behind the red flash, blue circle and white background?

Notes were taken at these early meetings but to date no written records could be found with any of the founding members or with the PAP headquarters on New Upper Changi Road. They could have been shredded to avoid falling into the hands of the Special Branch. They could have been misplaced when PAP HQ moved from time to time. Or they could have been siphoned off by defectors during The Big Split of 1961.

What little is known has been gleaned from interviews with party founders between 2002 and 2005 and from oral history interviews lodged in the National Archives of Singapore.

The origins of the party's name and symbol are lost in the fog of memory as there was no unanimity in the accounts of six out of the 14 convenors who formed the party in 1954. The recollections of Lee Kuan Yew, Fong Swee Suan, Samad Ismail, Lee Gek Seng, Mofradi bin Haji Mohamed Noor and Toh Chin Chye were varied and nebulous and often contradicted those recorded in the archived interviews. Getting octogenarians and septuagenarians to reconstruct what happened more than half a century ago was a slippery enterprise in memory recall.

Philip Carlyle Marcus, Singapore's first local chartered accountant, was introduced to the party by his brother-in-law, K M Byrne. According to his recorded interview, he was told that the original name for the party was Singapore Democratic Front. On his return from England in 1954, he learnt that it had been changed to People's Action Party by Lee.

When he commented that the name had communist undertones, Lee replied that it would better satisfy the Chinese middle school student movement at the time as well as appeal to the Chinese-speaking community.

Well, in those revolutionary days, the word "people" or "*ren min*" in Chinese struck a chord among the Chinese masses inspired by the rise of the People's Republic of China (*zhong hua ren min gong he guo*) and the might of the People's Liberation Army (*zhong guo ren min jie fang jun*). Thus wouldn't "*ren min* (people) *xing dong* (action) *dang* (party)" have a deeper emotional resonance as it meant a party that acted for the people?

But Toh Chin Chye, the party's first chairman, dismissed Marcus' account insisting that they decided on the name rather quickly as the word "action" jumped right out from the Council of Joint Action which championed the cause of local civil servants only a few months ago. It was no coincidence, he pointed out, that the leaders of the council and the new party-to-be were one and the same.

"So we used the word 'action'. So 'Action Party'. But the Council of Joint Action was an exclusively civil service-orientated body. We wanted to involve the masses. So we added 'people'. So 'People's Action Party'."

Lending credence to Toh's version was the man at the vanguard of the council himself, Goh Keng Swee. He noted that several of those associated with the inception of the party were also involved in the council, namely, himself and Byrne; P Govindasamy, Ismail Rahim and Lee Gek Seng from the P and T unions; and A K Karuppiah from the Public Works Department Labour Union.

Lee also debunked any suggestion that the name was given by Chinese middle school girls. He did not think they would know the word "action" in English. "It's an English word. They didn't say '*xing dong*' and then we translated it into 'action'." Like Toh, he believed that the name was derived from the Council of Joint Action. "We wanted to differentiate ourselves from other parties by saying we're not just words, it's action."

An exposition by founding member Lee Gek Seng also sounded plausible: the members did not want to prefix the name of the new party with "Singapore" because they were "thinking in terms of a united Malaya". They gave "Malayan" a miss as it had been co-opted by mainland parties such as Malayan Chinese Association and Malayan Indian Congress. "So we decided on 'people'," he said.

Memories of the party's beginnings had eluded Fong Swee Suan. What he remembered distinctly was that the word "action" went down very well with him. "It distinguished the party from the inaction of the existing political parties and the legislative council where no action was taken to improve the living standards of the people."

Both Mofradi and Lee Gek Seng surmised that the word was picked because the group wanted a name to demonstrate to the people that the party was synonymous with action.

In fact, when translated into Malay—*Parti Tindakan Rakyat*—the meaning of the name became even more striking literally, explained Gek Seng, a Malay-speaking Straits-born Chinese. *Tindakan* means "action". Abbreviated, *Parti Tindakan Rakyat* becomes "Petir" meaning "a flash of lightning". In Tamil, People's Action Party is known as *Makkal Seyal Katchi*—*Makkal* for "people"; *Seyal*, "action"; and *Katchi*, "party".

Just as lost in the mists of time would be the origins of the familiar symbol displayed prominently on lamp-posts at every general election—the vertical red flash across the blue circle against the white background. Who conceived the design?

Such was the welter of claims and counter-claims that the question could best be resolved diplomatically by attributing the handiwork to what Toh called "a pooling of ideas". For what it is worth, here's a range of reminiscences:

Lee: "Well, the idea was to have something colourful and striking. So we used red for the lightning symbol—for action. When we say something, we do it; it's not just words, not just election promises."

Philip Hoalim Jnr: "At one meeting, we toyed with various symbols for the PAP. Everyone was asked to give a suggestion and I tried my hand at doing a design. But my idea was rejected because they said it looked like the symbol of a Dodge or Chevrolet."

Mofradi: "Ong Eng Guan suggested the design of a *rantai* ("chain" in Malay) but Byrne said that it was not symbolically strong and suggested a circle instead. Ismail Rahim, who was good in artwork, took up the idea and improved on it. Then Lee proposed putting a *petir* ("lightning" in Malay) across the circle."

Lee Gek Seng: "Ismail Rahim was called upon to work on the lightning and the circle. He submitted the design and we said okay, we would take it."

S Woodhull: "Well, the design came from Lee himself."

Samad Ismail: "Oh, I have forgotten all about it."

Toh Chin Chye: "It was Samad who came up with the idea of a lightning flash. Then I suggested we'd better add a circle because it looked very fascist."

Fascist? Toh could not pin down the reason for the unsavoury association but Fong recalled remarks by some people at that time that the flash bore an uncanny resemblance to a fascist sign. In fact, as press reports revealed later, it was identical to the symbol of British fascist leader Oswald Mosley—a flash and circle in black on a white background. Rajaratnam admitted that by the time they realised the similarity, it was too late as they had already designed the logo.

When PAP's political adversaries charged that even the slant of its flash was the same as Mosley's, Lee's tongue-in-cheek reply in *The Straits Times* on 7 February 1955 was "What else can a right-handed man produce?" before making the crack that "it is gratifying to know that even Sir Oswald

Mosley knew that a flash of lightning is an expression of action".

In the same report, Lee disclosed that the circle idea came from "the Olympic symbol of unity" and explained what the PAP symbol meant—lightning flash for "action" and red for "courage"; circle for "unity of the people of Malaya"; blue for "faith in unity"; and white background for "honesty" and "purity".

Today, the PAP symbolism endures except for the circle which now stands for the unity of all races in Singapore. Why "Malaya" was dropped is another story to be told in another chapter.

SO much for the name and symbol. What about the manifesto and constitution? Who weaved the thousands of words that formed the platform of the PAP and governed the running and organisation of the party?

Thumb through the very first manifesto and you would be bowled over by the armoury of facts and torrent of views which could have been lifted from a virulently anti-colonial tract.

Calling for an independent, socialist, non-communist Malaya, it pledged full support for labour and the ideal of multi-racialism. But its language was severe and uncompromising, accusing Britain of using Malaya's tin and rubber earnings to enrich the mother country and neglecting the plight of Malay farmers who depended on the rice industry.

Drawing on the rhetorical skills honed from an elite British education, the manifesto writers railed against the constitutional schemes which isolated Singapore from Malaya and favoured pro-colonial nominees in the legislature, and against the Emergency regulations which curbed the political rights of the people.

Commenting that most of Asia had already cast off the colonial yoke, they thundered: "Can we of Malaya afford to sit and watch the proud procession of free people of the world march past us? Must we crouch together trembling while so-called leaders warn us of the perils of being free? Our party is not afraid of freedom whether it be tomorrow or today. Far from fearing it, we thirst for national freedom—NOW."

Curiously, for such a well-researched and well-crafted document, it was not easy to authenticate the authorship of the manifesto. If you were a word sleuth, you might detect the characteristic hard-hitting style of the young Lee and young Rajaratnam.

Going by Lee's memory, he "put up the basic draft. Raja added the nationalistic flavour. Then it was tossed around, maybe many people gave ideas but finally Raja and I settled it." He noted that many of the ideas were adopted from the British Labour Party manifesto. Lee Gek Seng agreed that the draftsman must be Lee as he was "the best man to do it" given his legal and political skills.

Samad Ismail was certain that he had a hand in drafting the manifesto, noting that some of the ideas stemmed from the platform of the Malayan Democratic Union (MDU), the left-wing party which dissolved itself voluntarily in 1948 when the Emergency was imposed.

Scrutinise the manifestos of MDU and PAP and you will see an uncanny parallel. Both parties sought a reunited Malaya with Singapore and opposed any constitutional arrangement which hived Singapore off from Malaya; and both demanded full citizenship, full executive authority and a fully elected legislature based on universal adult suffrage.

The ever-sceptical Toh, however, shot down this claim. While conceding that the concept of a united Malaya formed the major plank in MDU's platform, he did not think that it necessarily originated with the MDU. "The idea of a union between Malaya and Singapore was the idea of all political parties," he argued.

In his recollection, the ideas for the PAP manifesto came from all members of the group. It was, as he paused to think of the right phrase, a "potpourri of ideas". Different people gave different ideas and so credit should be given where credit was due, he asserted in his clear, crisp voice.

Lee also pooh-poohed the idea of the PAP manifesto being adapted from the MDU's. "Maybe Samad Ismail made some suggestions based on the MDU manifesto. Maybe Raja knew about the MDU manifesto but I knew nothing about it. I did not look up the MDU manifesto."

The search is still on for the original party constitution. The earliest available copy with PAP HQ is the 1958 constitution, passed at the special party conference, which incorporated amendments setting out the cadre system.

By a stroke of luck, a copy in Chinese turned up among a pile of old political publications which a history buff handed over to a retired *Lianhe Zaobao* sub-editor. The document, printed by Sin Chew Kwang Hwa Printing Company, showed how loosely run the party was in those days: the central executive committee (CEC) was elected by ordinary members of the party, any member could move any resolution at the annual party conference and any 50 members could convene a special conference.

Fong could only remember being preoccupied with the structure of the CEC and the process for electing office-bearers. Toh said he was asked to put up a paper for discussion as the group thought that as an academic he would have time to work on it. "It was redrafted and redrafted and passed around. By the time it came out, it was no longer mine," he related with a rare smile.

If there were many amendments, he muttered, it was because of the pro-communist members who kept laughing at one part or another of the draft. One person he singled out as being particularly difficult because he fancied himself as "the party theoretician" was Chengara Veetil Devan Nair.

Although Mrs Lee was not privy to the goings-on in the basement, she believed she was involved in the drafting of the party constitution. She felt that she "must have had a hand" as drafting the rules of a society was her line when she worked in the law firm Laycock and Ong.

"I would not swear to it but who else would have drafted that constitution for them? I don't know who could have done it because my husband doesn't draft things. He was an advocate, he was a court lawyer. He looked into the law, he fought cases in court but he did not do paper work like drafting conveyances."

As she recalled, she had stopped work in 1954 to look after her first baby while waiting for the second one, Wei Ling, to come along. "I stayed quite happily at home playing with Hsien Loong and if my husband had any clients who went to him and wanted some drafting to do, he would fling it to me and say, how about doing this for me? And I helped him in his work and kept in touch that way."

Thus, she thought that Lee might have passed her the draft of the PAP constitution to work on. She did not think the others could have done the drafting as they were not lawyers but they could have told her what they wanted for inclusion.

It could not be verified, but Mrs Lee was also credited for registering the party with the Registry of Societies. Unfortunately, that piece of paper, which would have taken pride of place in a PAP museum, has been lost to posterity. Lee believed she submitted the application through Laycock and Ong.

What could be ascertained was that when the registry received the application, it sent a note to Special Branch inquiring if the party was "on adverse record". In response, Special Branch said that it "had no grounds not to approve the application".

❦

IF murkiness and mystery surrounded the early records of PAP, what could be said with greater certainty was that members of the Oxley Road group started gathering in the basement on Saturday afternoons from about 2.30 to 5.30 in late 1954.

"What I do remember is waiting for the meeting to finish so he could take me and my son out for a drive," said Mrs Lee who complained that when they dispersed, they would leave "a room stinking of cigarettes".

She attended the first meeting before she was kept out of the group. But while she could only sense the buzz below, she was very clear that the meetings were "for the express purpose of starting a political party ... it was specific: what'd be the manifesto, what's the programme, how's the party going to be organised..."

These meetings, she clarified, should not be confused with those held to discuss labour issues and salary scales for the public service workers whom Lee, Goh and Byrne represented. Neither should they be lumped with the beer-swilling bantering which the British-educated graduates indulged in from time to time.

Soon it was time to stop dithering and get serious because of the sudden rush of events in the year: if the *Fajar* sedition trial and the May 13 protest action had pushed politics into the forefront, the release of the Rendel Commission report spelling out a new partially elected legislative assembly meant that elections were in the air.

Headed by former British envoy Sir George Rendel, the commission reviewed Singapore's colonial constitution and proposed a new political structure aimed at enlarging public participation and paving the way for self-government. Under its plan, 25 out of the 32 representatives in the legislative assembly would be elected to form the basis for a ministerial form of government.

The local government would take charge of trade and industry, health, education and housing while internal security, foreign affairs, finance and external defence remained under the control of the British. The governor retained the right to veto any proposed law.

Should Lee and company form their own party or join an existing one to take part in the coming polls? Lee Gek Seng recounted talk of capturing the Labour Party, founded in 1948 by Indian trade unionists as Singapore's equivalent of the British Labour Party. But they ruled it out eventually as they felt that they could never get enough people into the party "so it's much better, easier for us to form a party". Goh said that they arrived at a consensus to form their own party by 1954.

Ask Toh, Samad and Fong how many people were huddled around the basement dining table, and their reply would be quite similar: "Just one long table full—about 20 people."

When Toh scanned the faces, he was struck by how motley the group was and noted that in the initial meetings, they were basically "sensing each other, feeling each other". They kept their rendezvous under wraps because of the preventive detention laws. Mrs Lee believed that the meetings might have started once a fortnight before becoming a weekly affair.

By most accounts, the meetings were formal and minuted. "No *main main* ("play, play" in Malay)," testified Samad. Toh took the chair while Lee was the secretary and note-taker. Lee remembered taking down "the conclusions". "I didn't keep the minutes because I was not a stenographer. For a three-hour discussion, it would have been too much effort and a lot of it would be waffle."

Lee Gek Seng said he was pulled in later as assistant secretary to "keep minutes and look after the administrative part of the party for the first few months" until Ong Pang Boon took over as organising secretary after the 1955 elections.

Sitting in the living room, Mrs Lee would have a close-up view of the people straggling down the stairs towards the basement. She would have greeted Goh, Byrne and Toh as friends as they were fellow Raffles College alumni and fellow students in British universities. Certainly, she would have more than a nodding acquaintance with Rajaratnam, the *Singapore Standard* journalist who collaborated editorially with Lee during the postal strike of 1952.

Samad Ismail would also be no stranger to her. The pencil-slim, chain-smoking journalist from *Utusan Melayu* whom Lee defended in 1951 often dropped by the house to talk politics. He still could not shake off his disarming arrogance when interviewed in 2002. When asked if it was true that Lee brought him into the party as mentioned in his memoirs, he snorted: "He didn't bring me in; I was already in. Ha!"

Samad was regarded by Lee's friends as a radical and sinister character with a mysterious background. He was a member of the underground Anti-British League (ABL) which identified and trained cadres for the Malayan Communist Party (MCP). During the Indonesian war for independence against the Dutch from 1945 to 1950, he smuggled weapons for the resistance fighters.

Goh had the impression that Samad cultivated Lee and took him under his wing. One tip that Samad was supposed to have given to Lee was: "The art of leadership will be to get someone to throw a stone at a target you choose. But the hand that throws the stone should never be yours."

It was Samad who introduced a fellow ABL member and former classmate from Victoria School to Lee—a Malayalee with over-sized spectacles who loved Shakespeare but hated the British. C V Devan Nair, a former secretary of the Singapore Teachers' Union and teacher with St Andrew's School, was destined to play a critical role in the history of PAP and Singapore.

Undoubtedly, their pro-communist dispositions were known to Special Branch and Lee. As Nair said: "I think Lee had decided that Samad and I could be the convenors although he knew we were on the wrong side. But at least he would talk to us. We had been to more or less the same kind of schools and we would talk the same language."

Hot on the heels of the English-speaking leftists came their Chinese-speaking counterparts whom Mrs Lee would have met when they paid an introductory visit with student leader-cum-interpreter Robert Soon Loh Boon. Lim Chin Siong and Fong Swee Suan came with the weight of the powerful Middle Road unions behind them.

Although they and Lee were poles apart educationally and socially, they were swayed by Lee's anti-colonial crusade and felt that his group would be "suitable partners to confront the colonialists and local collaborators", said Fong. "Lee told us that he intended to form a party to contest the elections with two aims—in the short term, to expose the inadequacy of the Rendel Constitution and in the long term, to create a socialist society."

More leftists or left-leaning persons followed their footsteps to the basement: Chan Chiaw Thor, a Chinese school teacher who later became secretary of the Farmers' Association, and the Tann brothers. Wee Tiong, married to an English parson's daughter who initiated him into Marxism, was a British-educated lawyer and legal adviser to a host of grassroots organisations and trade unions. Wee Keng was a violinist and English language teacher in Chung Hwa Girls' High School and president of the Chinese Schools English Teachers' Union.

Perhaps the friendliest faces who exchanged pleasantries with Mrs Lee were the people from the public sector unions who had worked closely with Lee in his celebrated cases and who also played an instrumental role in the success of the Council of Joint Action.

From the Singapore Post and Telegraph Uniformed Staff Union came secretary Perumal Govindasamy, an inspector of postmen, and assistant secretary Ismail Rahim, a postman. From its clerical counterpart, the Singapore Union of Postal and Telecommunications Workers, came its founder Govindasamy Kandasamy, a senior officer, and committee member Lee Gek Seng, a clerk.

It is interesting to note how fate lent a hand in deciding who would go into history as one of the 14 convenors of the PAP. Ismail Rahim was chosen to represent the lower or division four group of workers. For the upper or white-collar ranks, the choice was a toss-up between Kandasamy and Gek Seng.

According to Gek Seng, Kandasamy had just returned from England in 1954 and was going for an interview for a senior post. He was worried that his chances might be affected if he were selected as a convenor so he asked Gek Seng to meet Lee. Over lunch, Lee disclosed that a group of them was about to start a political party and invited Gek Seng to be one of the convenors.

The P and T people were soon joined by more representatives from the labour fraternity: A K Karuppiah and S Sockalingam from the Public Works Department Labour Union which represented government daily-rated employees. Both had little education but had the benefit of Lee's counsel in their fight for more humane working conditions. Sockalingam spoke poignantly of how public health workers used to work without boots which often resulted in their feet being pierced by pieces of glass.

Not to be forgotten was Mofradi bin Haji Mohamed Noor, president of the Singapore Medical Workers' Union. His experience typified labour's involvement in the party. "One day Mr Lee and Mr Byrne invited me to join PAP. I consulted members of my union and they supported my decision to join PAP. The reason why I joined was that PAP and its leaders had always defended the interests of the workers," he said.

Perhaps talking over the heads of the less literate members around the table were the University Socialist Club (USC) activists whom Gek Seng described as one distinctive group. Names that flashed across his mind included James Puthucheary, S Woodhull, Poh Soo Kai and Jamit Singh.

Dominic Puthucheary, a leading lawyer in Malaysia, was very sure that his brother James and his university mates were at Oxley Road to brainstorm the formation of PAP. Woodhull referred to one Christmas Eve meeting in which Lee urged Lim Hock Siew, Poh Soo Kai and M K Rajakumar to step "right out in the open" as a political group.

In Lim's recollection, the USC members were involved in discussions on the aims and directions of the party and on its draft constitution. But he thought that their bigger role was in influencing the various interest groups to support the founding of PAP.

Finally, as inauguration day drew near, came the roll call for the 14 convenors who would make history as the founding members of PAP: Lee Kuan Yew, Toh Chin Chye, S Rajaratnam, Devan Nair, P Govindasamy, Ismail Rahim, Lee Gek Seng, Fong Swee Suan, A K Karuppiah, Mofradi bin Haji Mohamed Noor, Tann Wee Keng, Tann Wee Tiong, Chan Chiaw Thor and Samad Ismail.

Break it down by race and you will count seven Chinese, three Malays and four Indians. How much more multi-racial could you get? By occupation—two lawyers, two journalists, two teachers, two postmen, a former detainee, an academic, a clerk, a hospital attendant, a *mandor* (Malay for "foreman") and a bus conductor. Could there be a better cross-section of society then? By labour affiliation—nine out of the 14 were trade unionists. PAP was pro-labour right from the starting line.

But why were Goh and Byrne, who stood shoulder to shoulder with Lee in many an industrial battle, missing from the list? As senior civil servants, they could not be identified publicly although their five junior counterparts in the public sector unions who became convenors were exempted from the rule barring them from taking part in politics.

Another glaring omission was Lim Chin Siong. Fong disclosed that Lim had asked him to be the convenor. Lim felt that Fong, as secretary-general of the Singapore Bus Workers' Union (SBWU), was better suited to be the "formal representative" whereas Lim was just a paid secretary of the Changi branch of SBWU. Lim also felt that the left was already well-represented by Devan Nair and Chan Chiaw Thor.

The public first woke up to the dawn of the new political party when they read a *Straits Times* report on 22 October 1954 announcing the inauguration of the PAP a month later. If some readers furrowed their brows, it might be because of the party's opening salvo from its first press statement: Why should six million Malayans remain political serfs when practically the whole of Asia has cast off the degradation of alien subjection?

⌘

THE day started bright and early for 22-year-old Chan Chee Seng when he turned up at the Victorial Memorial Hall to arrange the tables and chairs and put up the banners for the big occasion: the inauguration of the People's Action Party on 21 November 1954.

Ironically, for the launch of an anti-British party, the venue could not have been more colonial. Built in memory of Queen Victoria (1819–1901), the grande old dame projected a facade of Brittannia splendour with its classical columns and wrought iron gates.

When people started streaming in at about 10 am, the clerk with the Hong Kong and Shanghai Bank (now known as HSBC) stood by the side of the stage. "I was watching the crowd. If empty seats were not taken up, I would usher them to those places."

Chan might have been an eyewitness to unfolding history but in his typically self-effacing manner, he shrugged off his role as that of a "small fry". "I only helped to tie up banners, mail envelopes and arrange for volunteers to work."

Yet another person who confessed to playing a menial role was Mrs Lee. For the big event, she and Elaine, Byrne's wife, hand-stitched rosettes of the same colours as the new party's—red, white and blue. "We sort of knew you put a button in the middle and you needed safety pins. And we did it! They must have looked very primitive compared to the rosettes people wear today."

As PAP had no members yet, the convenors-cum-labour leaders were frantically rounding up as many of their union members and supporters as possible to fill up the cavernous hall. The postmen came, so did the hospital attendants, public works employees, teachers, busmen and workers from all-and-sundry trades and industries.

The Chinese middle school students known for their headline-making protests and sit-ins turned up in force too. "I mobilised them. I asked them all to put on trousers," Samad Ismail guffawed at the thought. Seated in the front row facing her convenor-husband on the stage, Mrs C V Devan Nair looked around and could not help being struck by the sight of the petite girls with pigtails.

When Lee surveyed the crowd estimated at between 800 and 1,500, he felt immense satisfaction that his painstaking efforts in cultivating a wide spectrum of society had come to fruition. By one count, some two-thirds of the wooden seats were occupied by blue- and white-collar workers of all races and language streams. Indeed the turnout had exceeded expectations as many had to sit on foldable chairs along the aisles and corridors outside the hall.

One press commentator referred to a "great mass of cars that all shone black and iridescent, like beetles in the sunshine before the stark white of the Victoria Memorial Hall". Then in the next line, he expressed surprise at the presence of a line of red lorries and an external loudspeaker relaying speeches in English when "not one in 10 persons in Singapore" understood the language.

As Singapore was still governed by emergency regulations because of the war in the Malayan jungle, the new party leaders were aware that they were under Special Branch surveillance. Taking a mischievous crack at the spooks, they placed a table on the platform and labelled it "Special Branch Office, CID". Before the meeting began, Lee invited Special Branch officers to take their place at the table. No one took up his offer.

When Mrs Lee read the article in the papers the next day, she felt that the reporters missed the sarcasm. The message to Special Branch, she said, was: "Well, you might as well pop up. If you want to listen, come and listen openly. Why sit down among there? And it must have raised a cheer from the crowd, not meant seriously."

To avoid any brush with the law, Mofradi recalled, people with suspected communist links were prevented from entering the hall by the organisers. For the same reason, Lim Chin Siong, who was already on the SB watch list, was kept off the rostrum. He was seated among the audience and did not speak.

It was perhaps to stave off official intervention and lend respectability to the occasion that two prominent persons were invited to grace the ceremony—Tunku Abdul Rahman, the president of the United Malays National Organisation (UMNO) and Tan Cheng Lock, the president of the Malayan Chinese Association (MCA).

UMNO was formed in 1946 by Malay chieftains and civil servants to oppose the Malayan Union plan which would deprive the Malay sultans of their status and grant citizenship to non-Malays liberally. MCA was founded in 1949 to prevent the British from repatriating the Chinese to China and to help resettle the Chinese in new villages. MCA later joined UMNO in the fight for Malayan independence.

While Toh agreed that the two VIPs "added leverage and lent prestige" to the PAP although they did not reflect the party's ideological thinking, the former leftists remembered that they were less disposed to their pro-establishment guests. As Fong said: "What common ground did the right-wing UMNO and MCA have with left-wing PAP?"

The inauguration provided the opportunity for the rank-and-file to see Lee in person for the first time. He was no longer just a name in the newspapers but a person on stage in flesh and blood, dripping with sweat when he introduced the convenors and unveiled the party platform for a united, democratic, non-communist Malaya that included Singapore.

The irony might have escaped him but under the severe gaze of previous governors in portraits adorning the wall, Lee attacked the British for delaying the transition to self-rule and independence and demanded an immediate end to colonialism. In a speech punctuated by shouts of *"merdeka"* ("independence" in Malay), the 31-year-old lawyer called for the creation of a democratic state based on universal adult suffrage and abolition of unjust inequalities of wealth.

Of the 14 convenors, nine were elected into the protem CEC with Toh as chairman, Lee as secretary and Ong Eng Guan as treasurer. Introduced by Rajaratnam, Ong, a 29-year-old accountant then, was embraced by the party with alacrity as it needed a treasurer desperately. Furthermore Ong was fluent in Chinese, English and Malay. He had graduated earlier in the year from Melbourne University with a bachelor of commerce degree and a diploma in public administration.

Lee did not find inauguration day particularly memorable, describing it in his memoirs as "a good but uninspiring meeting with no electricity or magic in the air". Mrs Lee thought that it did not make more of an impact as the group had been working for so long on the preparations to form the party that the day became just an official opening.

But for some of the listeners who sat through the four-hour event, fragments of memories of the day lingered on. One USC member who saw Lee on stage for the first time was retired doctor Sheng Nam Chin. "I was very impressed by him. Here was someone from an English-educated world, willing and able to lead what was then mainly Chinese-educated, politically-awakened Singaporeans."

Sze Lih Hwa, a Chinese High School student then, noticed "something unusual" about the ceremony that remained imprinted on his consciousness. In any big event in colonial Singapore, key officials would turn up in formal wear. It was no surprise that on that morning Tan Cheng Lock came in a lounge suit and Tunku in a wrap-around sarong outfit.

But Lee and his fellow convenors came without even a necktie, said Sze, and "they behaved like the common people". They were garbed no differently from those on the floor—in open-necked shirts, short sleeves or rolled up sleeves, and cotton trousers. Making their debut appearance in public, the Men in White were sending a sartorial signal as well as a political statement to the people of Singapore and the powers-that-be.

⚬⚬⚬

LOOK closely at the sepia photographs of inauguration day and you will see a young, bespectacled Lee in a white shirt with the rosette stitched by his wife standing in front of a table facing a microphone. Behind him, seated in a semi-circular row, were the 13 convenors.

All of them were men. For a party with the foresight and sensitivity to project itself as multi-racial, pro-labour and representative of society, why was there not a single woman on the platform?

The perception of PAP as a male-dominant, patriarchal party could be traced to the earliest days of the Oxley Road group. Although Mrs Lee was one of the first women to sign up as a PAP member, she was never admitted into the inner sanctum of the party.

Truth be told, she attended the first meeting with Rajaratnam, Byrne, Philip Hoalim Jnr and his wife Miki. She remembered her husband saying to her one or two days later: "'Look, the next meeting, we are dropping Miki and you'd better not come too.' So I said: 'That's a bit unkind and unfair.' He said: 'No, no, no, you can't. If we drop Miki and you come, there's going to be trouble. You'd better stay out and it'll just be a men-only thing.' So I was kept out."

From then on, she said, the meetings became strictly all-male. "The wives were dropped and I felt it was unfair that I should be dropped. I thought I could have made a contribution. But I did not take a strong stand about it."

Miki Goh-Hoalim Jnr, a well-known lawyer and women's welfare advocate in Penang, made her mark as a pioneering woman magistrate in Singapore before moving to the northern island with her husband in 1962. As she happily told this writer in April 2003, she and her husband retired the year before, after 50 years of legal work and 50 years of marriage.

The affection for her loquacious though frail husband beside her was unmistakable. Ever solicitous of his needs and taking pains not to disrupt his train of thoughts, she said that they had been inseparable since they married in London in 1952. "We were like two peas in a pod. That's why they always say 'Philip and Miki' or 'Miki and Philip'. Some say we were like *sam peh eng tai*," she said, referring to the Hokkien term for the Butterfly Lovers, the famous Chinese opera about the story of two scholars who were intimate friends.

Despite the passage of time, a sense of grievance still welled up in her when she recalled the Oxley Road incident. She was adamant that she was singled out and dropped from the meeting because she happened to be the wife of Philip whom the group suspected to be pro-communist. The first meeting, she said, revolved around personalities: Who should be in the group? Who should be out? Whom could they trust?

Subsequently, Alice (Goh's wife) and Elaine (Byrne's wife) phoned her for a meeting. "I can't remember where we met. It could have been the Cafe De Luxe on High Street when they told me: 'You know, this is a man's job. Our job is just to support them.'

"So I asked them: 'What? Sit down and knit socks while they drink beer?' I said: 'No, that's not for me, because Philip and I, we always work as a team.' So I told them: 'I'm going to see Kuan Yew.'

"I marched to his house to demand an explanation why I could not join the political party when it's just forming and we've all come back from England and there were no gender issues then. So why suddenly this gender issue now? His answer to me was: 'It's our prerogative. You are not invited.' That's what he said to me. I came back furious. So I told Philip, he was more furious."

That was the last time she visited No 38 Oxley Road. "After that I never spoke to him again," said Miki who radiated health and vigour as she swigged a glass of whisky at the Penang Club on that humid afternoon. Six months later, on 18 October 2003, she died suddenly from a stroke at the age of 81.

4

"I Bought Votes To Beat Devan Nair"

IT was billed as the battle of the Malayalees. In one corner was C V Devan Nair, 32, from the newly inaugurated People's Action Party (PAP). A former teacher and radical trade unionist recently released from prison, he had been barred from returning to government service.

In the other corner was A R Lazarous, 39, from the newly formed Labour Front (LF). A city councillor and community leader with the gift of the gab, he was a contractor who enjoyed British patronage.

Lending a hand to Nair were M K Rajakumar and James Puthucheary, the "*Fajar* boys" from the University of Malaya. Lazarous could count on the support of school teacher Michael Fernandez and kinsmen.

What did all these protagonists and antagonists have in common other than professing to be staunch socialists? Well, they all traced their roots to the small South Indian state of Kerala reputed for its high literacy level and highly developed political consciousness, and for electing the world's first communist government.

The Malayalees began arriving in Malaya in the nineteenth century to work mainly in the rubber plantations and British bases. Forward-looking and hardworking, they placed a premium on education which explains why despite being a minority within the Indian minority in Singapore, they have stamped their mark in politics, the professions, the unions and the media.

The Nair vs Lazarous battleground was Farrer Park, a sprawling area teeming with Tamil public works labourers, Malay villagers and Chinese shop workers. It was one of four wards in which the fledgling PAP was making its maiden appearance in the 1955 polls under the Rendel constitution. The other three were Tanjong Pagar, Bukit Timah and Punggol-Tampines.

The duo were among 79 candidates—69 on party tickets and 10 independents—who filed their papers to stand for 25 seats in the new 32-member legislative assembly drawn up by a commission appointed by the governor. It was supposed to mark the transition between colonial rule and self-government.

Michael Fernandez, who came from a fishing village in Kerala, was a teacher with St Patrick's School and an active member of the Singapore Teachers' Union when he joined the hustings. At 20 years, he was still a callow youth unable to crystallise the political differences between PAP and LF.

He did not know Nair and was unsure of PAP's platform. LF had a greater ring of attraction. Furthermore Lazarous impressed him as a role model in the Indian community, a successful self-made man who helped the poor and the jobless.

"He had a lot of money. He did not know what to do. He wanted power, I suppose." It was only later that Fernandez learnt that Lazarous grew rich as a contractor for the British war department by "helping himself to a lot of things and overcharging for contracts".

Money politics was rampant in the Rendel elections as it was called. As a political ignoramus, Fernandez found himself unwittingly helping Lazarous to buy votes. At that time, many sub-contractors or *kepala* ("headmen" in Malay) supplied gangs of workers to Lazarous for his contract jobs. The same arrangement was used to supply people who were eligible to vote.

"I was put in charge of paying these *kepala* who brought in the voters. I was entrusted with a lot of money to pay and record the payment," he said, noting that he also provided transport and food for the voters on polling day on April 2.

Nair campaigned vigorously for unity with Malaya, a fully elected legislature and a workers' charter. Yet despite his left-wing credentials, power of oratory and big turnout at his rallies, he lost to his fellow Malayalee by 366 votes. It marked PAP's first electoral defeat even as the other three wards recorded the party's first victories.

When Fernandez was interviewed in 2003, the former insurance executive-turned-education consultant still held the view that Nair lost because Lazarous bought the votes of those who depended on him and his *kepala* for work.

This would jell with the view of James Puthucheary who commented that PAP was severely disadvantaged by refusing to play the same game. There were "gangsters, little warlords walking around the place who said they had so many votes in their hands. They wanted money and we never offered them any money."

⚬⚬⚮⚬⚬

WELCOME to Singapore of the 1950s when vote-buying went hand-in-glove with the politics of intimidation and elections were equated with unsavoury practices. For PAP, the exposure to the seamy side of politics marked its baptism of fire. For the political babe in the woods, it was really a jungle out there.

Vote-buying was inextricably linked to gangsterism and secret societies in a still largely immigrant society whose welfare needs were ignored by the colonial government and whose impoverished masses had to fend for themselves. Often the lines between clans, guilds, self-help societies, trade unions and secret societies overlapped.

If you visited a Chinese settlement at that time, you would not fail to see the three figures from the period of the Three Kingdoms (AD 220–280) in ancient China. Idolised by secret societies, they were Liu Bei, founder of the state of Shu; his right-hand man and general, Guan Yu, deified as god of war; and Zhang Fei, a warrior. Hidden somewhere would be an armoury of parangs, bicycle chains and assorted weapons.

Secret societies or triads originated from the Heaven and Earth League or *tian di hui* (also called *hong men hui*) in eighteenth-century China which started as a mutual self-help society and became a resistance movement that swore to overthrow the Qing dynasty and restore the Ming.

When Chinese immigrants arrived in Singapore in the nineteenth century, they brought their triad culture along with them. Secret societies evolved into dialect-based gangs named after mystical numbers associated with *tian di hui* to distinguish themselves from one another. For example, the Hokkien gangs adopted "08", "24", "18", "108" and "36".

Many union chiefs also ran secret societies and coerced members to join them. Some were labour contractors who used gangsters as workers and vice versa. One former unionist admitted that he took part in "18" secret society activities and often roped in men from the "18" and "24" gangs during election time.

As the union boss and strongman for LF leader Lim Yew Hock, Lee Yew Seng said that a substantial number of union members were associated with secret societies. He noted that secret society members were among those who volunteered to help during elections.

A Special Branch report on the 1955 elections recorded that the Criminal Investigation Department was "embarrassed to find that several prospective candidates have consciously or unconsciously been employing secret society members as election agents".

The most damning revelations of the unholy pact between politicians and gangsters during the elections came tumbling out from a commission inquiring into allegations of corruption two years later.

Calling secret societies "the biggest menace to elections", M B Brash, who fought on a Democratic Party (DP) ticket in Queenstown and lost, testified that gangs controlled large blocks of flats and sold their votes to candidates. If a gang gave its allegiance to a candidate, he added, the politician was assured of the votes.

In his exposé of their modus operandi, he said that "it was the practice for gangsters to take voters to the polling booth and stand outside until the votes were cast". The gangsters could find out how the voting went and if the voters defied their instructions, there would be hell to pay.

Newspapers reported that bribes ranging from $10 to $25 were offered to electors to induce them to vote for certain candidates. Lazarous was said to have bribed Farrer Park constituents $5 each to vote for him.

Gangsterism was not confined to the Chinese. Some secret societies absorbed non-Chinese gangsters to swell their ranks. Samad Ismail was campaigning for his good friend Devan Nair when he learnt that Malay and Indian gangsters bought over by the opposition were bullying female Chinese students. So the man with the unfathomable past summoned the gangsters and threatened them "in a language they could understand".

As he related with relish, he warned one notorious gang called Bendera Merah ("red flag" in Malay) to lay off. They were the gangsters who were detained for being involved in the Maria Hertogh race riots in 1950.

Chen Say Jame was also stumping for Nair when he had a brush with gangsters in Farrer Park. "I remember clearly that when we went around to paste posters on the very first day after nomination, people would be right behind us, tearing the posters off. Those people were from the secret societies; they were instructed by our opposing party."

In sheer exasperation, he asked his union friends acquainted with secret societies for help. They tracked down the head of the gang who was giving them trouble—a mortuary worker in Tan Tock Seng Hospital named Ah Gu. They appealed to him and he gave the word to his men to back off.

Tanjong Pagar, the springboard for Lee's meteoric political rise, was not spared from roughhouse electioneering either. Wading into the squalor of Chinatown was a far cry from the genteel campaigning in church halls and rural schools which Lee did for Labour Party candidate David Widdicombe in Devon, England, in 1950.

At one rally, Lee was giving a speech when stones rained down on the crowd. A furious Chan Chee Seng, a black belt judoka in charge of rally security, went hunting for the culprits and eventually met their chief nicknamed Moh Peng ("pimples" in Hokkien) in a house on Craig Road.

Chan complained that his men were causing trouble in PAP rallies. Moh Peng told Chan not to worry, saying he would be at the rally the next day. Sure enough, he turned up. Not a single stone was thrown. There was no more incident. To cap it all, Chan chuckled, the gangsters threw in their support for PAP!

Those who lived in Tanjong Pagar in those days would remember how election politicking was enmeshed with triad activities. Ho Bee Swee, a paperbag dealer, was the head of the Ho clan and leader of the "108" gang.

When Lee came to campaign on Duxton Road and ask for his support, Ho agreed and rallied the other Ho clan members behind PAP. The Hos attended PAP rallies almost every day, said Ho, as they felt oppressed and wanted to free themselves from the harassment of other clans and secret societies in the area.

But a leader of the Teo clan based in the vicinity was a staunch supporter of diamond dealer Lam Thian, who was Lee's opponent from DP. A clan dispute broke out, resulting in the abduction of some Ho kinsmen by Gee Lian Kiat, a "24" triad group. The incident precipitated a series of fights with parangs and axes by triad members allied to both sides.

It culminated in a raid by about 100 members of the "24" gang on the Duxton Road premises of the Ho clan. Ho was filled with remorse as he felt that the problems that befell his clan were caused by his support for PAP. The feud between the Hos and Teos only abated when PAP won the city council elections in 1957.

There have been accounts that Lee helped to settle some of the secret society disputes but he dismissed them out of hand saying: "I'm a lawyer. How can I mediate?" He said he had no memory of the gang violence but remembered Ho Bee Swee as "a very thin, whitish opium addict" who was a very strong PAP supporter.

But wouldn't PAP have its fair share of gangsters? Yes, admitted Ong Pang Boon, the then-organising secretary, explaining that it had no means of knowing the background of the people who came to support the party at election time. But the big difference, he said, was that while the other side had to pay for secret society members, those who came to PAP volunteered their services.

⚜

"NOT even half a loaf." "Half a loaf." "Just a plain slice of bread without butter or jam." These were the bread and butter metaphors conjured up by politicians to explain to the less educated, if not undernourished, population why the new constitution was deficient.

As spelled out by the Rendel Commission, 25 out of 32 members of the legislative assembly would be elected to four-year terms with a council of nine ministers—three appointed by the British governor and six drawn from the political party with the largest representation in the chamber. The others would be nominated officials.

The governor would still have the right of veto and exercise control over external affairs, defence and internal security, and finance. In short, the constitution did not provide for a fully elected assembly with the supreme authority vested in the representatives of the people.

The lack of full autonomy reflected the position of pro-colonial members in the commission who felt that the transition to self-government should be gradual and stable because there were not enough local qualified people to take over the administration just yet.

Not surprisingly, the "don't rock the boat" Progressive Party (PP) welcomed it but the left-wing PAP and LF disparaged the reforms as inadequate and partial. PAP declared that the constitution was not workable. What was the point of seeking power under a limited government?

PAP decided to field only a token number of candidates with the aim of exposing the flaws of the constitution. It was short of manpower anyway. At a special party conference on 13 February 1955, it could only rustle up five names: Lee for Tanjong Pagar; lawyer Tann Wee Tiong for Changi; school teacher Chan Chiaw Thor for Paya Lebar; contractor Goh Chew Chua for Punggol-Tampines and unionist Lim Chin Siong for Bukit Timah.

But then the political virgin found that it had to wrestle not only with the availability but also the eligibility of candidates. Only British subjects born in the Straits Settlements could stand. Fong Swee Suan said he was barred by the rules from standing as he was born in Johor. For the same reason, the candidatures of Chan Chiaw Thor and Tann Wee Tiong were withdrawn.

So how were the candidates matched with their respective wards?

As Fong recalled, Tanjong Pagar was the natural choice for Lee as he was the legal adviser to the Singapore Harbour Board Staff Association (SHBSA) and the P and T unions based in the area. He could thus bank on the support of port and postal workers.

For similar reasons, Lim was picked for Bukit Timah, a humongous rural constituency which also covered Bukit Panjang, Pasir Panjang and Jurong. He was associated with the unions representing workers in the factories in the area such as Nanyang Shoes Manufacturing, Hume Industry, Green Spot, Lam Soon and Malayan Textiles.

Goh, a friend of K M Byrne, was nominated for Punggol-Tampines as he lived in the area and was well-known to the constituents. And of course Devan Nair went to Farrer Park because of the ethnic factor as many Indians resided in the ward.

Sembawang should have been a happy hunting ground for PAP but it could not unfurl its banner there. The ward was home to the 10,000-member Naval Base Labour Union (NBLU) whose legal adviser was Lee and whose vice-president Ahmad Ibrahim was a de facto party man.

So why did Ahmad, a watchman operator at Naval Base fire brigade, have to stand on an independent ticket? S Woodhull, whom Lee plucked from the University of Malaya to be general secretary of NBLU, said that its officials did not want the union to be involved directly with the PAP then. "They thought it might prejudice the status of our union."

Sembawang housed the biggest British naval base in the region which employed most of the residents there. The fear was that the union would be wrecked by dissension if its leader was seen as a representative of a left-wing political party calling for the withdrawal of British forces which would result in a massive loss of jobs.

<hr/>

TAKE a cursory glance at the headlines of the English-language press after PAP's inauguration and you will see how the party had to contend with a bombardment of smears. It was painted red, extremist, pro-communist and communist. It was accused of being a "communist-backed party". Lee was titled "commissar".

A hostile press was one of the first daunting challenges confronting the political newcomer. Typical of the reaction was *The Sunday Times* column published on 28 November 1954 which asked if a more intelligent dialogue could be heard at the party's inauguration or at a performance of an absurd film about a Persian princess and a shifty barber.

Dripping with sarcasm, it lamented that it was "sad to see a socialistic movement kicking off in such middle-class conditions, with people sitting on chairs in a room with fans keeping the temperature down". It ridiculed some of the PAP convenors as "charming and clever people, but hardly sinewy toilers".

If the British-run press was not friendlier, it was because it reflected the views of the British establishment. The colonial authorities were suspicious of PAP's cohabitation with leftist characters of dubious background. The Special Branch had even classified Lee as pro-communist.

The coverage by the family-owned Chinese newspapers ranged from mildly sympathetic to harshly critical. *Nanyang Siang Pau*, founded by tycoon Tan Kah Kee in 1923, and *Sin Chew Jit Poh*, started by Tiger Balm King Aw Boon Haw in 1929, were allied to big business interests and could hardly be euphoric about PAP's pro-labour orientation.

It seemed that only *Utusan Melayu* gave PAP its unflinching support as its leading journalist was also a party convenor. In fact, Samad Ismail was at the inauguration ceremony expounding on the PAP manifesto to the Malay audience. How much more politically partisan could a journalist be?

As PAP represented the left, its arch adversary was the right as embodied in the pro-establishment PP. The party of English-educated professionals was founded in 1947 by three lawyers—Tan Chye Ching, Nazir A Mallal and John Laycock, Lee's boss. It became the dominant party after winning six seats or two-thirds of the elected seats in the legislative council in the 1951 elections.

Like the Rendel Commission, PP favoured a slow and steady transition to self-rule. It fielded 22 candidates for the 2 April 1955 elections assuming that it would romp home as in previous municipal elections. The party was called Progressive because it believed in progressing by stages, according to former member Arumugam Ponnu Rajah.

The challenge from the right was not only posed by the local English-educated elite but also by the Chinese-speaking millionaires and merchants who played mahjong at their three-storey clubhouse on Bukit Pasoh Road. Founded in 1895, Ee Hoe Hean (or *yi he xuan* in hanyu pinyin) connotes a teahouse which radiates warmth and geniality.

Upset that their representation in the legislative assembly had been left out of the Rendel constitution, a coterie of Chinese businessmen including Tan Lark Sye, Ko Teck Kin, Lien Ying Chow, Tan Siak Kiew, Ng Aik Huan and Yap Pheng Geck got together to set up the Democratic Party.

Tan Eng Joo had just returned to Singapore after graduating in structural engineering from the Massachusetts Institute of Technology in the United States when he was asked by his uncle, rubber magnate Tan Lark Sye, to lead the party in the elections. DP put up 20 candidates in anticipation of forming the government.

The party championed citizenship rights for Chinese immigrants and supported Chinese education and culture, recalled Tan, best known as the man who broke a regional shipping cartel in the 1960s. "Under the British, you couldn't serve in the government unless you spoke English and knew English. The non-English educated had been here all their lives; why should they be second-class citizens?" he said.

Furthermore, DP wanted to counter PAP as Chinese businessmen grew increasingly apprehensive of the latter's radical policies. The party was perceived as anti-business and anti-employers. "We believed that the PAP was leftist and communist. We thought Lee was a leftist," said Tan.

The great irony was that when both PAP and DP went to the hustings to take up the cudgels on behalf of Chinese voters, they found themselves fighting over the same ground. Another delicious irony was that DP represented the wealthy merchants funding the schools which were churning out the most fervent supporters of PAP.

Just about the only party which did not pose more of a challenge to PAP was LF because of the semblance of ideological kinship. Both positioned themselves as left-wing, pro-labour, and shared the same platform— instant independence and abolition of the Emergency regulations.

LF was formed in 1954 by Lim Yew Hock, a stenographer-turned-trade unionist, and David Marshall, a leading criminal lawyer, from the remnants of the Labour Party and still-born New Socialist Party in 1954. In his memoirs, Francis Thomas, an English school teacher who joined LF, admitted: "We were not a real party but a haphazard collection of men brought together to contest the elections."

So if the dominant press, the English-educated middle class and the

Chinese business community were arrayed against PAP, who would be brave enough to throw in their lot with an untried and untested party?

⁕

BULAT Hamid and fellow postal workers sat in the verandah of No 38 Oxley Road scribbling away furiously. They were addressing "Vote for PAP" election bills for distribution to voters in Tanjong Pagar.

"Every day, after office hours, a group of us would be sitting there for one or two hours writing names and addresses," said the former P and T union member.

They had been taken to Lee's house during the run-up to polling day by their union leaders and founding members of PAP—postman Ismail Rahim, mail officer Perumal Govindasamy and senior officer Govindasamy Kandasamy. Bulat remembered Mrs Lee serving them orange juice and Lee making an impression on him as a "young, energetic and friendly man who spoke very well".

Mrs Lee did not forget them too, describing them as "invaluable" as they could write in English. She regarded them affectionately as "old faithfuls" who turned up regularly at party meetings. "I see their faces and recognise them as old friends. Although I don't know them that well, it's like meeting an old face that you know. They came and helped."

The postal workers were among the legions of volunteers and supporters who materialised during the elections to help Lee and his new party. They ranged from the unionists whom he represented and clan members to liquor retailers, shop assistants and hawkers—the ones whom Mrs Lee described as "honest-to-goodness straightforward workers".

"We didn't ask questions. Whoever was prepared to help, we would take the help. You can't be choosy. When you are in that position, you take help from where you can and they work for very little," she said.

At one meeting in Tanjong Pagar, she recollected, "a few hundred persons appeared. All his own personal contacts and friends of friends of Harry's. Some were people whom he met when he went canvassing. Some were people unknown to him who rang him up and offered their services and provided useful contacts".

Another source of support came from the students. Dominic Puthucheary, younger brother of James, spoke of how the University Socialist Club (USC) mobilised manpower for the campaign. "You would be surprised at the number of people who came to volunteer for Chin Siong because he was standing for Bukit Timah. The University of Malaya was in Bukit Timah. Some of his helpers later became prominent civil servants and judges in Malaysia."

Chinese middle school students linked arms and sang songs at rallies to drum up support for PAP candidates. Such was the unbridled enthusiasm of the girls with pigtails that even when constituents hid in the toilets, they would pound on doors and holler "Vote PAP" until they responded.

They would squat beside women washing clothes to exchange greetings and solicit their support. When they went door to door, as party worker Fong Sip Chee recounted, they would speak first to break the ice with the residents before letting the boys make their campaign pitches.

Many students did not attend school during the election period and went canvassing for votes in the streets in their uniforms. Why were they all rooting for PAP? According to former student leader Robert Soon Loh Boon, the Malayan Communist Party (MCP) had given the word that they should support PAP as it was regarded as the most progressive party in the elections.

⚜

WHATEVER you may say about the deficiencies of the Rendel constitution, at least one positive measure came out of it—the automatic registration of the Singapore-born which changed the voting profile overnight. The electorate for the 1955 polls ballooned to about 300,000 voters of which 60 per cent were Chinese-speaking. By contrast, the number of voters in the 1951 elections was a paltry 48,000.

In the days when voter registration was not compulsory, Indians outnumbered the Chinese on the rolls. The reason, as lawyer A P Rajah observed, was that Indians knew the importance of elections in India and were conscious of their vote while the Chinese did not understand elections and were thus not keen to register.

The extended voting franchise meant that if politicians wanted to engage the people on the issues of the day—be it the demand for independence, scrapping of preventive detention laws or better working conditions—they had to do so in the mother tongues. For the first time in an election, Chinese voters were in the majority. Suddenly the air at rallies all over the island crackled in a babel of dialect and Mandarin speeches.

Whenever Fong Swee Suan reflected on the 1955 elections, what flashed to his mind was the electrifying impact of the mass rally on the people and the rise of Chinese-educated politicians exemplified by his bosom buddy Lim Chin Siong. Although snubbed by the English press and English-speaking society, Lim was in his element every night, magnetising crowds by the thousands and rousing them to a heightened emotional state.

According to Fong, people who listened to Lim likened his performance to "watching a classic drama". "Some said he made them think, some said he made them dream." Toh Chin Chye, who used to sit beside Lim at mass meetings, said: "Huge crowds greeted him; it was amazing!" Fong Sip Chee: "A great speaker with charisma, he could move the people." Sze Lih Hwa: "He had the genius of speaking to the common people."

Then-medical student Arthur Lim recalled attending a rally in which Lim roared: "We are not getting independence and the British say we cannot get independence because we cannot stand on our own feet." Lim then paused before letting out a loud shout: "Stand on your feet and show the British!" "You know what," the prominent eye surgeon said, "people actually stood on their toes and chanted 'Down with the British!' "

But while Lim found Chinese speeches a breeze, his Tanjong Pagar colleague was having a tougher time because of his lack of Mandarin proficiency. Spotting Lee's Achilles heel, his DP opponent, Lam Thian, a Chinese High School-educated merchant, labelled him *er mao zi* or "pseudo-Westerner" and challenged him to a debate in Mandarin.

The derogatory phrase harked back to the late nineteenth century when peasants rebelled against Westerners in Qing China. The Europeans who were invading China were known as *chang mao* or "long hair" by the Chinese then. *Er mao* referred to a Chinese follower of Western culture. Soon it became shorthand for a Chinese who did not know Chinese.

A source of amusement during this election, said Mrs Lee, was the way her husband tried to avoid having to face Lam Thian. When the papers reported Lee as saying he preferred to have a multi-lingual debate, "the real reason was my husband could not possibly have debated in Mandarin then. He did not have the command of the language, he did not know enough Chinese..."

The debate never took place but Lee made his maiden speech in Mandarin for a few minutes at a mass rally on Banda Street, behind the former Oriental Theatre. Ong Pang Boon remembered that Lee rehearsed the speech. James Puthucheary remarked that the speech was written in about 100 Chinese characters by *Sin Pao* reporter Jek Yeun Thong. Mrs Lee said: "The writing was very big, the sort of writing you would write for a child learning to read for the first time."

⚜

A CAR buff strolling along Oxley Road on the morning of polling day would have enjoyed a visual treat. A procession of cars of all makes and models was streaming in and out of Lee's house. They ranged from the luxurious American Chevrolet, which the locals called *puay ki chia* ("aeroplane car" in Hokkien), to the ubiquitous Morris Minor.

They were on loan to Lee and his party colleagues and were deployed to ferry voters to the polling stations. The practice might seem absurd on hindsight but in those days voting was not compulsory and voters expected candidates to provide them with transport to the voting booths.

One dominant impression of the day for Mrs Lee was the whizzing of cars "like bedlam ... like Chinese New Year when a whole lot of cars are running around on the roads". Counting no fewer than 30 cars from a list in her husband's handwriting, she rattled off the names of those who had lent their vehicles to Lee:

Lee's younger brothers Dennis and Freddy, his sister Monica and her mother-in-law's sister Aunty Mary; friends Hon Sui Sen and his brother Louis and Fong Kim Heng; Byrne's friend Goh Khai Poh and brother-in-law P C Marcus; lecturers Tom Elliot and Charles Gamba; law clerk S Ramasamy; Hakka clan leader Chong Mong Seng and liquor retailer Ang Kok Seng. Also included were the cars from fellow party members— Goh, Toh, Byrne, Rajaratnam and Kandasamy.

There was a comical-farcical air as the cars cruised around picking up people. People jumped into the Austins and Hillmans for free rides to visit friends, related Fong Sip Chee. Then when they found themselves stranded without a return journey, they blamed those who had ferried them!

Mrs Lee remarked that some people treated it as a joke and took the opportunity to take a ride in those "great posh American cars". She mentioned how a laughing Dennis Lee, who was put in charge of car deployment, came back saying that he had just carried a carload of *sam sui por* (Cantonese term for the women construction labourers with red hats) to the polling stations.

But no matter how many cars were rounded up, there were never enough. So the PAP ploy, said Ong Pang Boon, was to ask people to hop into any car but, on reaching the polling station, to vote PAP. Mrs Lee cited her husband's election manifesto which read: "Never mind whose car you go in. Go in his car, but please vote for me."

Madcap as the to-ing and fro-ing might seem, it was serious business. Lee Gek Seng lamented that it was because of the lack of cars to ferry voters to the polling stations in time that resulted in Devan Nair's defeat in Farrer Park. He said he kept phoning for more cars but they came too late.

"I was at Farrer Park. It was true Devan received cars later. We would have won if we had gotten enough transport for the people. In fact when voting closed, there were queues of people outside the polling stations." He felt that many of the cars went to Bukit Timah instead to help Lim Chin Siong.

Mrs Lee recalled that when cars allotted to Farrer Park were late in turning up, Devan Nair's helper Kam Siew Wah "had the effrontery to throw a scene. Who the hell does he think he is?" She said that they had "a hell of a time" finding cars because most people lent cars to Lee personally and objected to cars going off elsewhere than to Tanjong Pagar.

⚜

INSULATED from society at large, the English-educated expected the Progressive Party (PP) to win the elections and work towards a gradual transition to self-government.

After all, the party had dominated the legislative landscape for years and its leaders were eminent professionals well-versed in the affairs of the colony. What's more, the Rendel Commission had crafted the rules to favour the party.

PP president C C Tan, the scholarly looking lawyer with iron-rim glasses, was introduced at rallies as the next chief minister. A shadow cabinet comprising John Laycock, N A Mallal and Lim Choon Mong was waiting in the wings.

But the verdict from the ballot box drew a collective gasp of disbelief— PP won only four out of the 22 seats contested. All its incumbents lost including C C Tan who was defeated by David Marshall in the upper middle class bastion of Cairnhill. Amazingly, a prominent politician had been trumped by a maverick lawyer.

Their Chinese-educated counterparts from DP, the Democrats, were just as devastated, snatching only two out of the 20 seats contested. Alas, the huge turnout at its rallies championing citizenship rights for Chinese immigrants had not translated into votes. Somehow its advocacy of Chinese language and culture had not paid off.

LF was also shocked by its victory in 10 out of 17 seats, thrusting it suddenly into the limelight as the majority party. As its Sephardic Jew leader Marshall exclaimed: "It was a miracle ... we did not expect to win ... we knew we were going to have two or three, suddenly we had this flood."

The party had not expected to win, let alone take over the running of the government. Its inexperience and unpreparedness in working a defective constitutional system explained much of the problems that were to trip up the LF-led government later.

Why did the PP fare so abysmally? The campaigning experience of its defeated candidate for Queenstown, Elizabeth Choy, was instructive. When the war heroine met her poverty-stricken constituents in the slums, they gave her a poor reception. "They said Progressive Party was for the rich and that they would lose their jobs if it got in. LF's election platform appealed to them because most of them were labourers," she said.

According to Syed Esa Almenoar of UMNO whose alliance with MCA won three seats in the 1955 polls, the Progressives were seen as being on the side of the capitalists and more interested in making money than in helping ordinary people.

The debacle of DP could also be attributed to its image problem. It was perceived as a rich man's party not helped by press reports of its candidates attending a sumptuous banquet with free flow of wine at the home of millionaire Ko Teck Kin.

An analysis revealed that vote-splitting by the Democrats accounted for several of the Progressives' losses. If the votes of the Progressives and Democrats were combined, they would have added up to 70,000 votes versus 42,000 for LF.

As Chan Kum Chee, then-PP secretary-general, said: "If the Democrats had not come in, those who voted for them would have voted for the Progressives. Then there wouldn't be any Labour Front." Marshall would not have won Cairnhill, the accountant said, if the Democrats had not put up Tan Khiang Khoo. Certainly Marshall, who won by only 775 votes, would have lost if Tan Khiang Khoo's 1,111 votes had gone to C C Tan.

Tan Eng Joo, who headed the Democrats then, agreed with this assessment. "I think Democratic Party took away most of the votes for the Progressive Party. And because of this, Progressive Party did not come into power." To the Democrats, it was some consolation that they blocked the Progressives as they feared that if C C Tan and company were to form the government, they would perpetuate the inequalities of society in favour of the English-speaking.

The surprising victory of LF was put down to its greater sympathy for the common people, its socialist platform and considerable union base. Its populist messages hit home with a populace aggrieved over British neglect and discrimination.

One of its leaders, Francis Thomas, was unequivocal about the reason for LF's triumph. "My own belief was that the deciding factor was a communist decision to back Labour Front against the Progressive Party and Democratic Party." He was not off the mark. Former Chinese middle school leader Robert Soon Loh Boon said that the communists supported PAP, LF and UMNO to widen the base for a united front. This referred to their strategy of working with a coalition of legitimate organisations to overthrow the British.

What about the PAP? Ecstatic over its electoral performance, it was only jolted by Nair's defeat in Farrer Park. In Tanjong Pagar, Lee secured a thumping win, beating PP's Peter Lim Seck Tiong, a teacher, by 5,121 votes and pushing DP's Lam Thian to a distant third with 760 votes.

His Bukit Timah comrade Lim Chin Siong romped home with a majority of 1,951 votes, trouncing DP's Tan Wah Meng, LF's A N Mitra and PP's S F Ho. In Punggol-Tampines, Goh Chew Chua vanquished DP's Anthony Goh and PP's H A de Silva by a majority of 1,209 votes. Ahmad Ibrahim, PAP's ally in Sembawang who stood as an independent, tasted sweet victory too by beating PP's Lim Kim Kee by 1,793 votes.

PAP was jubilant over LF's triumph as it meant that the left had edged out the right. In the counting centre at Victoria Memorial Hall, Lee shook hands with Marshall and promised to cooperate with him.

⚬⚬⚬

WHILE gangsters might be giving PAP cause for concern in Farrer Park, the sight of Chinese students campaigning aggressively for Devan Nair was raising more than eyebrows.

In her letters to Goh Keng Swee in London, Mrs Lee expressed her reservations about the "kids" and "brats". She complained about how they came to see Lee at all hours for advice, demanding for one statement or another to be issued to the press. When Lee refused to be pushed, they hinted that they could not help in the elections.

"I am not sorry Devan Nair lost in Farrer Park," she told Goh who was then involved in a tussle with pro-communist elements in the Malayan Forum. "With Nair in legislative assembly, you would have far more trouble than you are having in the forum, and the PAP would become just an apologist for the 'freedom forces'."

Referring to the Farrer Park defeat, she wrote: "They had masses of socialist club boys there and masses of kids and their whole organisation collapsed on polling day. Now I hear they are waiting for Harry to be unseated on petition and then they will put Devan in Tanjong Pagar. They've got a ruddy hope."

Two days after Lee won Tanjong Pagar in a landslide victory, his DP opponent Lam Thian challenged Lee's eligibility to sit in the assembly on the grounds that he had not lived in Singapore for the last 10 years, a Rendel requirement.

In London, Goh lobbied British MPs to sort out Lee's eligibility problem—Lee had spent three out of 10 years in Cambridge so technically he was not qualified. Eventually the government declared that Malayan students studying abroad should be treated as eligible to stand as candidates. The petition was dropped and Lee went on to represent Tanjong Pagar for the next five decades.

All the politicking, however, was beginning to grate on Mrs Lee. Evoking a tinge of despair, she said: "Sometimes I would much rather Harry got unseated and stayed out of politics and lived quietly on the law. What's the use of it all?"

5

The Night When Singapore Went Mad

"TAKE care of my gun, take care of my gun." The badly burnt man mumbled repeatedly as he staggered out of the overturned car. *Utusan Melayu* reporter Othman Wok thought he was delirious.

A posse of pressmen had rushed to help the terrified driver of the car set ablaze by a rampaging mob at a roundabout on Alexandra Road. "He was in a daze, and he showed us his gun," said Othman who only realised he was a plain-clothed detective when the police came to take him away.

The eyes of fright peeping out from the blackened face of Detective Corporal Yuen Yau Pheng as he kept his charred body upright became the most haunting image of the Hock Lee bus riot which shook Singapore on 12 May 1955. The 34-year-old Shanghainese later died in hospital leaving behind a widow and five children.

Another eyewitness was former *Straits Times* journalist Sit Yin Fong who wrote in his book *I Stomped The Hot Beat*: "His clothes were on fire, and he was literally burning. He was a ghostly figure as he strode ramrod straight away from the blazing inferno, which was his car and which might have been his funeral pyre."

The drama unfolded at about 9 pm at the traffic roundabout near where Thye Hong Biscuit Factory used to be. As Othman recounted, a crowd of strikers and supporters was demonstrating against the Hock Lee bus company down the road. People with masked faces were pelting the riot police with stones.

Two passengers in the car who were the detective's colleagues escaped unhurt. One of them, who turned out to be Othman's friend, related how Yuen was driving past the roundabout with them when he was stopped by the mob. When the detectives refused to divulge their identities, knowing that they would be killed if they did, the crowd became enraged. They overturned the car and set it alight.

The other tragedy of the riot seared into Othman's memory was the shooting of 16-year-old Chong Lon Chong by the police during a street battle. Instead of sending the Chin Kang School student immediately to hospital, the crowd paraded him for nearly four hours from Alexandra Road to Middle Road to demonstrate "police brutality". When the boy finally reached the hospital at around 1 am, he had died from a massive loss of blood.

Associate editor S Rajaratnam was putting the *Singapore Standard* to bed near midnight when he heard the commotion at the *Nanyang Siang Pau* premises not far from his office on Cecil Street. He learnt that the Hock Lee horde had dragged the wounded boy to the Nanyang office "so that chaps can take photographs, so that people can see".

At his funeral, Chong was hailed by Hock Lee strikers as a "working class martyr". Hung on poles near his grave were a giant wreath and two banners denouncing the police. A wreath sent by chief minister David Marshall, who contributed $200 for the coffin, was flung into a drain.

Yuen and Chong were not the only fatalities in "The Night When Singapore Went Mad" as Sit headlined in his article. Volunteer Special Constable Andrew Teoh Bok Lan was brutally hacked with a *changkul* and American journalist Gene Symonds was beaten to death by a mob.

To Rajaratnam, PAP founding member and ideologue, the Hock Lee riot signalled "the first demonstration of the ruthlessness of the communists and their capacity to unleash violence in Singapore since the start of the Emergency".

To Singaporeans who lived through it, the riot dramatised the industrial strife and social unrest which engulfed the island in the mid-1950s. It was a period of volatility and instability which gave Singapore a bad press and frightened the wits out of businessmen and investors. To the Confucianistic, it was divined as Singapore's equivalent of the disorder under heaven which portended an imminent change of government.

⚬⚬⚬

BROACH the subject of the Hock Lee riot with Fong Swee Suan and his response would be: "Of course, I was responsible for the strike. But it did not mean that I caused the riot."

Seeing the 70-year-old in a short-sleeved shirt and worn-out sandals in 2002, it was hard to imagine the genial grandfather as the fist-punching and table-thumping secretary-general of the Singapore Bus Workers'

Union (SBWU) whose strident cry once meant the instant downing of tools by hundreds of workers.

The incident had started as a muscle-flexing exercise between the Hock Lee Amalgamated Bus Company and the SBWU. The family-run company wanted to smash the closed shop system requiring all workers to join only SBWU. But the left-wing union was against management getting new workers to join a rival house union, the Hock Lee Employees' Union, and using them as strikebreakers.

When the company sacked 229 SBWU members on 24 April 1955 and recruited new workers with secret society connections, Fong's union launched a 24-hour hunger strike. Linking their arms, the strikers surrounded the buses to stop them from leaving the Alexandra Road depot until they were eventually dispersed by police.

A temporary deal which carved up the bus routes between members of the two unions and reinstated the dismissed workers was struck. But SBWU members still felt aggrieved as they were allotted old buses while new workers continued to be registered with the house union. Once again, they went back to the picket line.

On 12 May 1955, the riot squad arrived to drive them away from the depot. The page one picture in *The Straits Times* the day after showed picketing busmen in a crouching posture with their backs turned as Gurkha policemen aimed fire hoses at them. The jets of high-pressure water knocked some down while others were thrown in the air. Many were cut by granite chips churned up by the water.

Fong said he was outraged. Chen Say Jame saw workers collapsing as they were hit by the stones. Othman was shocked by the sight of pebbles flying through the water like "splinters from a bomb" piercing into human flesh.

Students of Chinese High and Chung Cheng High converged in 20 lorries on the Alexandra Road roundabout to join the strikers. A pitched battle between 2,000 rioters and the police raged round-the-clock from the bus depot to Tiong Bahru on May 12 and 13.

Stones and bottles were used by one side and teargas and desperate gunfire by the other. Calm was not restored until the dawn of May 13. The casualty count: four killed and 31 injured. *The Straits Times* declared that Singapore was in a state of crisis.

On the same day, 3,000 bus employees of the British-owned Singapore Traction Company (STC) joined 20,000 other workers in a series of sympathy strikes across the island. Public transport ground to a stop. The Chinese press and even the government-sector unions threw in their support.

A settlement was reached the next day in talks chaired by chief minister David Marshall—the house union was abolished and employees no longer fettered by management. The might of the Middle Road unions had prevailed.

Why did the Hock Lee strike escalate so rapidly into a riot? By most authoritative analyses, the riot was instigated by the communists to demonstrate the power of the underground and test the strength of the newly formed Labour Front-led government. Rajaratnam had no doubt about the unseen hand of the communists in "mobilising mass emotions to take on the government".

But while former leftists would not rule out the involvement of pro-communist elements, they believed the riots were compounded if not triggered off by secret society elements and agent provocateurs.

The constant refrain among interviewees was that the situation just spiralled out of control. For all his leadership clout, Fong said, he had no control over "outsiders", noting that there was nothing to stop students or any forces from joining the bus workers in their struggle.

Lee Kuan Yew, who was then SBWU legal adviser, agreed that Fong did not plan the riots. He doubted that Fong was acting on instructions to bring about a collision. The situation blew up, he said, because of "the overflow of revolutionary fervour among communist united front activists who believed that revolution was just the day after tomorrow". In such a hothouse atmosphere, these activists worked themselves to a feverish pitch in defiance of authority and in a strike, "there'd be a few inevitable toughies or semi-gangsters and off it went".

Painting an unflattering picture of the communist cadres as well, Samad Ismail said: "They couldn't control ... they lost control very quickly. They were scattered all over the place. There was no single leadership."

Likewise, S Woodhull believed that nobody would have been able to prevent the riot as it marked the beginning of an upsurge of the labour movement after years of suppression. "We were like little boys sticking our fingers in the dykes when they burst." Given the mood of the time, he said, "you couldn't tell people to halt in the middle of a battlefield, there was no effective command".

SUDDENLY they had blood on their hands. The scales from their eyes had fallen. Barely six weeks after securing three seats in the partially elected legislature, the political virgins had lost their wide-eyed innocence.

Socialist rhetoric had translated into real-life violence, intellectual abstractions transmogrified into real blood. The verbal cut-and-thrust in the august chamber had given way to mortal blows on the streets.

While the elected adhered to Erskine May, the bible of parliamentary procedures, the unelected swore by the dialectical texts of Mao and Lenin. While Lee and friends were engaged in a constitutional struggle, their leftist comrades had chosen to go down the extra-constitutional route.

The Hock Lee episode threw up in sharp relief the different outlook and approaches of the two camps within the PAP—one led by Lim Chin Siong who held sway over the powerful Middle Road group of unions; and the other led by Lee Kuan Yew and his coterie of like-minded English-educated intellectuals. As the popular Chinese idiom "*tong chuang yi meng*" goes, they share the same bed but have different dreams.

In the aftermath of the bloodshed, the member for Tanjong Pagar found himself in the invidious position of having to defend his rabble-rousing colleagues involved in the industrial turmoil and civil commotion. How could he distance himself from them without denouncing them openly lest he be accused of betrayal?

In the house, Lee was accused by chief secretary William Goode of deploring violence "after hell was let loose and men were killed ...What did he do to stop decent workers being turned into murderous rioters? Did he make any attempt to stop the extremists in the party staging this night of horror? Is his conscience clear? Or did he lose control to the member for Bukit Timah who sits behind him and drives the party?"

John Ede, the Progressive Party (PP) member for Tanglin, remembered that Goode "really went for Kuan Yew and got him on the defensive". The English cinema executive whose father-in-law was John Laycock observed that Lee often conferred with Lim who sat behind him as if he was "getting Chin Siong's okay to speak or to take a certain line".

If the budding party was hoping to project a positive image of itself from inauguration day, the riot put paid to it, recalled founding party chairman Toh Chin Chye. People became nervous and too frightened to join PAP. The leaders were derided as "young, immature and troublesome politicians," he said.

In the eyes of the public, the PAP leadership was perceived as an undifferentiated radical lump. In particular, the English-educated viewed it with much trepidation. MIT-educated Tan Eng Joo had the impression that Lim ruled the party while Lee was just an adviser.

Among party insiders, however, the cracks were beginning to show and the differences in the central executive committee (CEC) were becoming more apparent by the day. All the profuse public professions of "we", "our" and "us" could barely mask the divide between "them and us". Party comradeship was fast turning into an illusion.

From the outset, as Fong admitted, a line was already discernible between the two groups—Lee and company were disposed towards the Fabian-type of socialism while Lim, Devan Nair and he favoured a more radical approach.

While he admired Lee for his political convictions and leadership quality, Fong said, deep in their hearts his group lacked trust in him because of their different educational background and political outlook.

Devan Nair exhibited a similar wariness. When he joined PAP as convenor, he said, he was "still starry-eyed about the communists" and poured scorn on Lee and friends as intellectuals inspired by British Fabian socialism "for which I had developed a profound Marxist contempt".

S Woodhull also saw himself as part of the English-educated leftists in the party who had more ideological affinity for Lim than for Lee. His first impression of Lee was that he was "not left enough", "not ideologically deep enough", a "milk-in-water socialist", certainly "not one of us".

He, Lim, Fong, Nair and James Puthucheary comprised a group who met separately from Lee. Sometimes they caught up with Lee and moved closer on some issues, sometimes they distanced themselves from him. Their coexistence was based on the tacit understanding that the Lee group was free to control the party while the Lim group had full run of the trade unions and mass organisations.

Woodhull stressed that his group was more preoccupied with union than with party matters. Industrial action was more important than party organisation. "We were quite happy to let Lee go on. There was no attempt to clip his wings or oust him ... because we knew the organisation was not in his hands. The trade unions, street bodies, farmers ... you name it. He had not the men to control the ground but we had the capacity to organise that. So, never for one single moment did he trouble us too much."

So when did tension become more palpable between the two factions? Woodhull's ready response: when the left began acting independently in trade union activities and being involved in strikes and stoppages and making wage demands. Lee became upset because he was not consulted on industrial matters.

His view was borne out by Lee himself who said that although he was the party leader, he was not their superior. "They must have a superior in some cell and they could only take instructions from their superior." Referring to the Hock Lee riot, Lee said that he tried to dampen their demands but was ignored. "Where it does not suit them, they just don't listen."

Lee felt that the leftists were just using him "purely as a technician and buffer to manipulate the constitutional system to its limits for their exploitation. And they would do it only if it happened to be in their interest … They'd never do it because I told them to do it."

For example, the Chinese students would only accept legal advice from him when it suited them. "They wanted to know the technical position, where they could have been charged criminally in court, how to avoid that, they would take my advice. But where a course of action would lead to violence and the use of police force to quell violence, they wouldn't listen if it didn't fit in with their objectives or plans."

As Rajaratnam saw it, the communists wanted to see how far the Lee group could provide them with cover. The Chinese-educated always assumed that the non-communist PAP leadership was as fragile and vulnerable as David Marshall's and Lim Yew Hock's. They were rather condescending, he said, giving the signal that if "you want to prance at the front of the stage, that's okay by us but we are the masters".

So when Lee struggled with his Mandarin speeches at mass meetings, he noted, they would applaud him. Then they would get some Chinese speakers on stage and there would be greater applause. "They were making quite clear to us, yes, we applaud you but please remember that we can control the multitude."

❧

ARTHUR Lim Siew Ming was all eyes and ears as he circled No 3 Chancery Hill Road one night after the April 2 elections. All the lights in the compound were switched on. His job was to keep out intruders.

If the 21-year-old medical student who was to become a renowned eye surgeon had to patrol his own house, it was because of a hush-hush pow-wow going on inside the bungalow.

It was one of several marathon meetings that David Marshall was holding with politicians from several parties to cobble a coalition government after the 1955 elections. His Labour Front (LF) had captured 10 of the 25 seats but he needed the support of a few more representatives to achieve a working majority.

Ever paranoid about the British, the excitable lawyer refused to meet in any government building fearing that it would be bugged. So Arthur's father, lawyer Richard Lim Chuan Hoe, offered his home as the venue for the meeting which lasted eight hours and ended in the wee hours of the morning.

Arthur might have the privilege of witnessing the formation of Marshall's cabinet right in his home but he could not help musing how the chief minister was letting people go on and on and on. "Marshall could have just picked and announced his cabinet, but no, he believed in freedom of expression and the discussions became so protracted because some bums wanted to be ministers," he said in his Gleneagles Hospital practice.

Marshall roped in the three UMNO-MCA representatives as he felt that the Malays were a Cinderella community and should be in the ball. But he had not reckoned on UMNO president and member for Ulu Bedok Hamid Jumat clamouring for the portfolio with the biggest budget. Hamid grabbed it and became minister of local government, lands and housing. Mak Pak Shee, the LF member for Geylang, wanted housing and felt let down that he was only made assistant minister for labour and social welfare. Even more disappointed was the ambitious A R Lazarous who was left on the shelf or rather on the backbench.

The let-it-rip way in which Marshall put his line-up together illustrated his political naiveté and inexperience and gave a premonition of a style of leadership and governance that would soon drag him from one untenable situation to another.

From the day of his swearing-in as chief minister, he had been frustrated by the lack of full power and, given his short fuse, much of his nervous energy was consumed by frequent run-ins with colonial officials. He was incensed that governor John Nicholl placed the chief minister far down the protocol list. When he found he had no office, he threatened to put his table and office boy in the centre of the Padang.

Then barely had he found his footing in his new job when the Hock Lee riot erupted. It was not difficult to imagine the explosive impact this had on his tenuous hold on the administration as the hardline leftists kept pouncing on every opportunity to ambush the new government.

The prevailing view of the day was that his handling of the riot was weak and inept. The sympathetic view was that he should not be blamed entirely because of his limited power as chief minister and lack of administrative experience, compounded by a lack of support from the colonial authorities.

Weak—that was how Rajaratnam described Marshall's coping skills. He was astounded that Marshall never spoke out against the communists for allowing the 16-year-old schoolboy to die. "Marshall did not know how to handle this kind of situation. First, he did not have the organisation. Second, I think, temperamentally he did not have the subtlety or the knowhow to deal with communist tactics."

Inept was Lee's preferred word. He recalled sitting in his car on Jervois Road and looking towards the Hock Lee gates during the riot when he heard Marshall on the radio telling workers that he had telegrammed West Indian economist Professor Arthur Lewis for help to solve Singapore's problems.

"I nearly collapsed in an apoplectic fit. Here was a serious situation that had to be dealt with firmness. He's got a government. He had to show that he was prepared to govern. So I felt, this was unreal, this was surrealistic. There was a tense, physically volatile situation. Bus workers didn't know who Arthur Lewis was. In any case, how was Arthur Lewis going to solve this bus dispute? So I despaired."

Lim Yew Hock, who succeeded Marshall as chief minister, felt the latter lacked that degree of finesse to cope with the brand of politics rampant in those days and said "he allowed his heart to rule his head". Another LF colleague, Francis Thomas, said Marshall was not a practical politician, noting that there was in him "too much of the great tradition of the Jewish prophets".

Those who took a kinder view of Marshall's travails pointed out that he never expected to form, let alone run, the government. "Labour Front had been maligned. It was unprepared for its surprise win over Progressive Party. It had no cadres, no governing plan, no platform except vaguely to be pro-labour," reflected former civil servant Goh Sin Tub who served in his administration.

A P Rajah, who was with PP then, shared the same view saying that Marshall was surprised to find himself chief minister. "He had no training at all because he had never been in politics, he'd never been in the legislative council or city council. He had no political experience and was suddenly thrust into Singapore politics."

What about the thoughts of the man himself? Marshall confessed that he was lonely and lost during the Hock Lee bus riot, complaining that every legitimate grievance was manipulated for immediate political ends. He was infuriated with the British for leaving him in the dark about communist-fomented strikes but expecting him to approve the use of troops.

He disclosed that he was so deeply disturbed by his inability to obtain any information on internal security that he offered Lee his post as chief minister so that he could be assistant colonial secretary and learn the "mechanics of internal security". But Lee refused saying "history shows no one who takes office before independence ever retains office after".

Lee said he did not remember such an offer. "If the offer was made, I would have just laughed it off. We could not under any circumstances take office because then we would destroy ourselves. We knew that this half-baked constitution would not work and we would be in trouble. So we wanted to have nothing to do with it."

As Marshall summed up his philosophy: "We must learn to accept that we bark our shins and break our bones in the process of learning how to skate." When dealing with militant Chinese middle school students demanding the registration of their union, he said that his approach was to deal with the issue like a runaway horse. "You must run some distance with it and guide it to a halt, not confront it and get trampled to death by it or both of you will fall into the ravine."

This was why he allowed the Singapore Chinese Middle School Students' Union (SCMSSU) to be registered on condition that it promised not to get into politics. But the politically savvy knew he was kidding himself if he expected the hot-headed Mao-inspired youngsters to live up to their pledge.

Perhaps the best-known incident that reflected poorly on Marshall's leadership was the Merdeka Rally at Kallang Airport on 18 March 1956 when his rally platform collapsed like a pack of cards. The event was meant to showcase the people's desire for independence to visiting British MPs but it descended into mayhem and rioting.

Add another fault to Marshall—impatience fused with impetuosity. Singapore's history would have turned out differently if he had been more forbearing and accommodating when he led the negotiations in the first constitutional talks in London. He refused to accept anything less than a full loaf of independence. The talks failed and he had to keep his word—he resigned and passed the mantle of chief ministership to labour minister Lim Yew Hock on 6 June 1956.

Once again he fell into the ravine as the horse ran away from him.

ꙮ

TODAY Singaporeans track figures on economic growth, monitor stock market and property prices and watch the lips of the United States Federal Treasury chairman for any hint of interest rate movement. In the 1950s, their fathers and grandfathers were preoccupied with only one statistic— the number of strikes.

It was estimated that 275 strikes occurred in 1955, accounting for 946,354 man-days or working days lost. What made the figures even more chilling was that only one-third of the strikes were for better wages and working conditions—the remainder were launched as sympathy or protest strikes.

If there was one Hokkien phrase that sent tremors among businessmen and investors, it was *ba gang* or strike. Former Middle Road trade unionist Buang Omar Junid said that strikes were very common in those days. "I used to visit the strikers and ate with them. Sometimes the strikers clashed with the police and were arrested."

When Fong Swee Suan was arrested briefly in June 1955 for his involvement in the Hock Lee strike, Singapore Traction Company Employees' Union (STCEU) adviser Devan Nair called an immediate strike in the British-owned bus company. "I made sure they all walked out ... and it spread like wildfire."

Underpinning the radical labour movement was the Middle Road group of unions spearheaded by the omnibus Singapore Factory and Shop Workers' Union (SFSWU). Formed seven months before the November inauguration of the PAP in 1954 and led by party pioneer Lim Chin Siong, it became a power centre by itself.

SFSWU founding member Kwok Tai Ying recalled that the union was initiated in the wake of the May 13 riots in 1954. Aroused by emotional calls for a strong union, workers signed up in droves. By 1956 when the union celebrated its second anniversary, it had more than 32,000 members in about 200 factories and shops.

Certainly, the leftist trade unions had an agenda beyond simply exploiting legitimate grievances against appalling working conditions and high-handed management. Engineering industrial tension to create social chaos was all part of the united front strategy by the Malayan Communist Party (MCP) to overthrow the British.

When MCP found that it was losing its war in the Malayan jungles, it decided to embark on a united front struggle against the British in Singapore. As former MCP member Gerald de Cruz explained, the communists operated an underground movement which undertook revolutionary action and another which worked above ground through "all kinds of front organisations which have very democratic appearances".

These front organisations ranged from the trade unions and the student movement to old boys' bodies, guilds and musical troupes to associations of farmers and rural residents.

Much of Singapore then was rural, and pig, poultry and vegetable farming still figured as a key economic activity. In 1956, the Singapore Farmers' Association or *nong xie* in short was formed to fight for the rights of farmers and rural dwellers. It was modelled after a similar association in China under the Chinese Communist Party (CCP). One of its founders was PAP convenor Chan Chiaw Thor. Later *nong xie* gave way to the Singapore Rural Dwellers' Association or *zhu lian* and the Singapore Rural People's Association or *xiang lian*.

Ong Kim Seng was a 20-year-old *zhu lian* member when he was asked to meet a man along the railway tracks off Silat Road one evening. The man told him that people were fighting for the liberation of Malaya and Singapore and pleaded with him to go into the jungle. But Ong declined, saying he was his widowed mother's only son. "It was actually a call to join the Malayan Communist Party," said Singapore's famed watercolourist.

In the *zhu lian*, Ong was exposed to banned communist literature and songs. He attended makeshift theatre shows in secluded areas where performers staged revolutionary dramas such as the Red Lantern and sang songs in praise of the CCP and Chairman Mao.

It soon dawned on him that MCP was attempting to use the *zhu lian* to control the city eventually. It was a classic adaptation of the CCP's doctrine *yi xiang chun bao wei cheng shi* meaning "using the villages to surround the city".

When former MCP cadre Fang Mingwu was interviewed in southern Thailand, he related how he became a *zhu lian* general secretary and confirmed that the communist underground was using residents' associations to promote the communist cause.

The prime target for communist infiltration was the Chinese middle schools because of their vast pool of educated youths. Fang revealed that he worked as a foodstall vendor in Chung Cheng High to interact with the students. Another former MCP member Guo Ren Huey said he was posted to the same school to lead student activities. "At the end of 1949 or beginning of 1950, we were instructed to start launching an attack on the British to coordinate with the armed struggle in Malaya," he said.

The underground started the Anti-British League (ABL) to cultivate students for full party membership. One section was for the English-speaking and the other for the Chinese-educated. When ABL was dissolved in 1957, the most active members were absorbed into the MCP to carry out underground work while the rest were assigned to work "above ground" in the student movement, trade unions and political parties.

Communist penetration in the schools was manifested in the cell group or small student unit, *xue xi xiao zhu*. Hwang Soo Jin, a retired PAP member of parliament who was in Chung Cheng High between 1948 and 1953, said he was almost recruited into a cell group by a fellow student named Chen Fengchi. Once at Cathay cinema when a newsreel flashed images of Hong Kong policemen in the British crown colony, Chen stood up with his fist clenched shouting in Mandarin "*ying di zou gou!, ying di zou gou!*" or "British running dogs! British running dogs!"

On another occasion when they walked past an open-air Chinese opera on a makeshift stage, Chen condemned the performance as reactionary and superstitious and muttered that he would blow it up with a grenade if he could find one. Hwang said he declined to join the cell because he could not agree with the use of violence.

From the upper deck of any bus passing Chinese High, now known as Hwa Chong Institution, on Bukit Timah Road, you will enjoy a picturesque view of the majestic clock tower and lush expanse of green. Seeing the students in khaki shorts and white shirts with brass buttons streaming out of its gates, can you visualise them taking part in strikes, sit-ins, demonstrations and riots?

More than five decades ago, their predecessors wearing similar uniforms were often embroiled in such activities. In 1954 they protested vehemently against national service and the colonial education system. A year later, they joined the Hock Lee bus strikers at the picket line dancing and singing "Unity Is Strength" to the tune of John Brown's *Body*. "We became something like a gas stove providing heat and energy to the strikers," recollected former student leader Robert Soon Loh Boon.

Later the all-students Exemption from National Service Delegation was reincarnated as the Singapore Chinese Middle School Students' Union (SCMSSU). Such was its clout that it could instruct its legal adviser, Lee Kuan Yew, to work out a deal with Labour Front and UMNO—that the students would support them if they agreed to register the union should they form the government after the April 1955 elections. Marshall won and the union was registered in September.

One student at Chinese High from 1953 to 1955 did not join the union but knew the student leaders in his class well. Soon Loh Boon was seated on his right and Sze Lih Hwa was right behind him. They used to borrow his homework as they were too preoccupied with their student union activities. "They could make the teachers weep in the class ... they took over the school assembly, took the mike away from the principal. They interrupted our studies, boycotted classes and barricaded the gates. They also boycotted exams," said Ong Teng Cheong who was destined to be PAP chairman, labour movement leader, deputy prime minister and Singapore's fifth president.

Barely had Singapore recovered from the tears and trauma of the Hock Lee riot in May 1955 when another conflagration flared up a year later. Unlike Marshall, the new chief minister, Lim Yew Hock, had a low tolerance threshold for communist-inspired agitation. On 24 September 1956, he banned SCMSSU and ordered the arrest of its charismatic leader Soon Loh Boon and newly elected PAP CEC member and SFSWU official Chia Ek Tian.

In protest, Chinese school students staged a series of sit-ins backed by the Middle Road unions. Still embedded in the memory of older Singaporeans are the tear-jerking scenes of anguished parents outside Chinese High pleading with their children to leave the school.

On October 25, PAP held a rousing rally in the open field at Beauty World amusement park on Upper Bukit Timah Road. Lim Chin Siong worked up the crowds to a feverish pitch. Supporters piled into a fleet of lorries and headed for Chinese High in support of the students. The tinderbox was about to be lit.

Rioting raged for five days, spreading from downtown to Rochor Road and other parts of Singapore. Police barricades were smashed and tear gas used to flush out the students. Police cars were overturned and set ablaze. Curfew was imposed on October 26.

Once again Singapore made it to the headlines in the world press for rioting. The toll: 13 deaths and 123 injured.

THEY were all crammed into Lee's law office on Malacca Street on October 26 when the phone rang. Lee left the room to take the call. When he came back, he told the group that Malaya's chief minister Tunku Abdul Rahman had expressed concern about the situation and asked if he should despatch some troops.

Having backed the rebel students, Lim Chin Siong, Fong Swee Suan, S Woodhull, James Puthucheary and Devan Nair were huddled with their legal adviser and other PAP leaders to discuss their next course of action. They knew they were in the crosshairs of the authorities.

They agreed to meet in Lee's office again but realised that curfew was imminent. So with Nair behind the wheel, Rajaratnam was dropped off at his home on Chancery Lane and Lee on Oxley Road. Then the unionists returned to their Middle Road HQ to camp overnight.

Many people left stranded by the curfew were sleeping everywhere, on the floor and on the benches. "At four o'clock in the morning, the chains were cut and police walked in. There was this man called Richard Byrne Corridon and he said: 'Gentlemen, the game is up.' " This was Woodhull's vivid account of the big sweep which nabbed and bundled them off in black marias to Changi Prison.

Superintendent Corridon, who was in charge of the Indian and English-speaking section of Special Branch, led the operation authorised by the Lim Yew Hock government. It reflected the new "get-tough" policy of the fervently anti-communist pipe-smoking chief minister. Gone were the namby-pamby ways of David Marshall.

In all, the island-wide crackdown on the night of October 26 and the early hours of October 27 led to the detention of 259 people under the Preservation of Public Security Ordinance (PPSO). The PPSO, which allowed detention without trial, replaced the Emergency Regulations in 1955 and became the Internal Security Act (ISA) in 1963.

Leading the list were 14 PAP office-bearers and pro-communist PAP members, including virtually all the top officials of SFSWU. The most prominent were Lim, SFSWU secretary-general and PAP assemblyman for Bukit Timah; Fong, SBWU secretary-general; Puthucheary, SFSWU secretary; Nair, Singapore Traction Company Employees' Union (STCEU) adviser; and Woodhull, Naval Base Labour Union (NBLU) secretary.

In one fell swoop, all the trouble-making leftists who had been giving Lee one political migraine after another had been put behind bars. Lee's close PAP colleagues heaved a sigh of relief. Goh Keng Swee said that the timely detentions saved the party from communist takeover, and credited Lim Yew Hock for standing up to the communists in a way Marshall could not.

Rajaratnam was just as frank, admitting that the chief minister helped PAP because being a trade unionist, he understood power play and knew how to manipulate people and deal with the communists. "If Marshall was in charge," he said, "given his flamboyancy and his tendency not to think through every step, it would have resulted in the communists permeating into all fields."

As for Lee's reaction to the mass arrests, although he expected the purge, he was more concerned about its impact on PAP. As long as the arrests were confined to the communists or the pro-communists in the party, he said, he had no complaints even if it meant having to defend his leftist comrades in public.

"It's part of the prancing that has to be done. It's walking a tightrope. If I didn't, I would have been seen by the ground to have not lived up to what was expected of me. It's part of the anti-colonial front. So I had to go through the motions. Yes, of course, I was speaking purely for the record. I had no great passion to defend what the communists were doing."

IT is a story in PAP folklore that has been told and retold—how party chairman Toh Chin Chye faced the full frontal assault of belligerent pro-communist unionists for eight long hours and did not blink.

Date: 24 March 1957. Scene: PAP HQ on 140 Neil Road. From 8 pm until early morning, the PAP CEC was locked in a bitter battle of will and stamina with representatives of 19 Middle Road trade unions.

The gloves were off, civil courtesy flew out of the window and simmering dissension came to a boil in the left's first open challenge against the PAP leadership.

Lee was not present. The party secretary was in London as a member of the second all-party constitutional talks led by chief minister Lim Yew Hock. He had been given a mandate by the party CEC to obtain the best possible terms for Singapore's self-government.

But Lee was the very reason for the acrimonious party meeting. The leftists wanted to know if PAP was going to sell out to the colonialists in London and demanded that the mandate be withdrawn from Lee and that he walk out of the London negotiations.

They were up in arms over the PPSO, which enshrined detention without trial, and the Internal Security Council (ISC), a tripartite body comprising representatives from Singapore, Britain and Malaya which would act as the final arbiter on security matters. They were also angered by the clause banning detainees from taking part in the first elections under the new constitution.

No account of this debilitating, drawn-out meeting could have been better told than by Ong Pang Boon, the then–PAP organising secretary: "Dialogues were not conducted to elicit the simple truth. They were often long and inconclusive. Frank and honest personal views were rarely expressed. Simple questions requiring a 'yes' or 'no' were given long and tortuous dialectic replies.

"As arguments wore on, it became obvious that a new political line had been decided by the communist underground. The delegation from 19 trade unions had not come to seek clarification or listen to rational arguments but to force the new communist line on PAP.

"In this contest of patience, endurance, determination and will, the non-communist PAP leadership passed the test with flying colours. Sitting on hard wooden benches with no back or arm rests and without the luxury of coffee or tea, they held their ground for eight long hours without giving an inch. Despite the pressure of the unions, the majority of the CEC reaffirmed the party stand."

Ong commented that as spokesman for the CEC, party chairman Toh showed that he had the guts to face the challenge. Party stalwart Fong Sip Chee was filled with admiration saying "that man had got iron in him". Even though the unionists took a very truculent line, Goh weighed in, Toh slugged it out and gave them a severe scolding.

Memory was fast slipping for the increasingly infirm Toh. All he remembered was that "the left-wing members of the party pressed me to hold a special meeting to denounce the London talks. The meeting lasted until 3 am. The representatives of the left-wing unions were very tough-minded. I did not come from a union base but I had to show that I had as much stamina as them and that I could work just as hard."

The leftist adventurers, as they came to be labelled, failed to get Lee to walk out of the Merdeka talks. But five months later they got him to walk out in a way that they least expected—Lee walked out from the leadership of PAP.

6

The Kelong Plot That Backfired

STAND amid the cavernous emptiness, close your eyes, let your imagination roam and you might just hear reverberating echoes of the fiery smashes and fancy footwork that gripped the whole of Singapore on 5 June 1955.

Who knows, you might have been there as a child yourself to cheer Wong Peng Soon's breathtaking wristwork and Ong Poh Lim's dazzling "crocodile serve" which brought the world's greatest badminton prize—the Thomas Cup—to Malaya for the third time in this very hall.

Memories of the ear-splitting ovation for the world's unsurpassed players of the day when they thrashed Denmark 8-1 will forever be intertwined with the Singapore Badminton Hall on Guillemard Road.

Opened in 1952 and funded by public donations and a loan from "Tiger Balm King" Aw Boon Haw, the nondescript building trapped in an architectural time warp has been designated as a historical site.

Its walls did not just rock to the smashes of sporting history and the sounds of musical history—the legendary P Ramlee performed there in the 1950s and the Rolling Stones in 1965. They also bore silent witness to political history when the hall became the counting centre for Singapore's early elections and the venue where PAP members turned up by the thousands to elect their leaders.

One Sunday morning on 4 August 1957, lorry after lorry and bus after bus rumbled to its driveway pouring out a stream of humanity which soon swelled to about 3,000. The event: the PAP fourth annual party conference. The agenda: to elect a new 12-man central executive committee (CEC) to govern the party.

Mrs Lee Kuan Yew remembered the occasion because of the poor acoustics and the sight of garish banners and crude caricatures hanging on the stage. Toh Chin Chye sensed a "strange, tense atmosphere". Seated at the back, Goh Keng Swee found it hard to shut his ears off to the non-stop playing of communist-inspired music.

Party secretary Lee Kuan Yew was perturbed to see so many unfamiliar faces. Who were they? Were they really party members? Why were people whispering and casting quick sidelong glances?

The Lee group had put up a team of nine candidates including eight from the outgoing CEC and were prepared to concede three or four slots to the leftists. They also put forth six resolutions which included affirming the goal of an "independent, democratic, non-communist socialist Malaya" and endorsing the party line at the recent constitutional conference in London.

The party gathering came in the wake of two controversial events. The first was the marathon debate at party HQ on 24 March 1957 when the Middle Road trade unionists demanded a withdrawal of the mandate for Lee at the second constitutional talks in London. The second was the Tanjong Pagar by-elections on 29 June 1957 which saw Lee re-contesting and winning his seat following a challenge from David Marshall in the legislative assembly; the disgruntled leftists had worked covertly to support Marshall.

The party position was to accept the constitutional concessions and then work for independence through merger with Malaya. Self-government was seen as a step forward. Refusal to accept the terms would mean a deadlock and create a power vacuum which could be exploited by corrupt elements.

Applause greeted the candidates as they went up the stage one by one. Lee began to smell a rat when he realised that the more left the candidate was, the louder the applause.

One leftist candidate was Liang Chye Ming, who attended the same primary school in Johor as Lim Chin Siong. Recounting the varying intensity of the clapping, Liang said: "The applause given to the leftist members was very enthusiastic, more so than that given to Lee and his non-communist group. Mine was quite good." The applause was meant to signal to the audience which leftist candidates they should vote for, according to Liang, an English-language tutor in Hong Kong in 2003.

Although Lee and company had got wind of the challenge, the results from the secret ballot still came as a rude shock. They scored a thumping win with their resolutions which were carried by a vote of 1,150 to 112. But of the 12 highest vote-getters, only six of their candidates were elected. It was scant consolation to Lee that he clinched the highest number of votes (1,213). Toh took 1,121 votes followed by Ahmad Ibrahim (966), Goh

Chew Chua (794), Tann Wee Tiong (655) and Chan Choy Siong (621).

The other three candidates were booted out, the most ignominious being the downfall of party treasurer Ong Eng Guan, who with Lee and Toh made up the Big Three of the PAP then. The rejection of Haron Kassim and Ismail Rahim had the added effect of upsetting the party's Malay fraternity.

The leftists grabbed the other six seats. Three were from the outgoing CEC—Tan Chong Kin (with 811 votes), an English-educated bookkeeper from Farrer Park branch; T T Rajah (977), a Ceylonese lawyer and legal adviser to left-wing trade unions; and Goh Boon Toh (972), secretary of the Singapore Cycle and Motor Workers' Union.

The three new CEC officials were Tan Kong Guan (751), a welder and vice-chairman of Bukit Timah branch; Chen Say Jame (651) who took over as secretary-general of the Singapore Bus Workers' Union (SBWU) after the arrest of Fong Swee Suan; and Ong Chye Ann (762), a clerk in a car spare parts firm and vice-chairman of Farrer Park branch.

At six versus six, Lee's group and the leftists were deadlocked. Suddenly, the English-educated elite who had ruled the party from day one had lost its majority—and its grip on power.

⚜

IF the Lee people were flummoxed by the tie, it was because they thought there was a tacit understanding with the leftists that the latter should take only three or four seats in the ruling body. As the ratios in previous party elections showed, the leftists occupied four spots in the last CEC, virtually none in the second CEC and three in the first CEC.

Under this power-sharing arrangement, Lee and his lieutenants were supposed to control the party while the leftists had free run of the party branches, trade unions, students' bodies, farmers' associations and other grassroots organisations.

This agreement was crucial to Lee as he had no illusion that the leftists could have captured the CEC anytime if they wanted to as the party was open and loose with so many party members belonging to the Middle Road unions.

Goh was convinced that the communists had already taken over the party from the start and could have ejected Lee, Toh and him in its formative days. The reasons they balked, he believed, were that they knew they could not perform in the legislative assembly and that the party conferred respectability on them. Furthermore, as Toh noted, they still needed Lee as legal adviser to their unions.

Unquestionably, the left had exerted a strong influence on the party from the outset. The Malayan Communist Party (MCP) had instructed its open front operatives to join the party. Fang Mingwu, a former underground activist in Singapore who lived in exile in Thailand, explained that MCP supported Lee "because he was the best person at the time to partner us in the united front against the colonial power".

Among the 14 PAP convenors on inauguration day, 21 November 1954, four were leftists—Devan Nair, Samad Ismail, Fong Swee Suan and Chan Chiaw Thor. Nair, Fong and Chan went on to serve on the first CEC.

In the aftermath of the Hock Lee bus riot in May 1955, the leftists disappeared completely from the second CEC ostensibly to avoid tarnishing the name of PAP and giving an excuse to the Labour Front (LF) government to ban the budding party.

Fong, who led the Hock Lee bus strike, said they abstained from the CEC elections on 26 June 1955 to pre-empt any government action against the PAP leadership. James Puthucheary's account was that at Lee's request, Samad Ismail persuaded Lim Chin Siong and other leftists not to be in the power line-up. Nair said he advised the leading leftists to stay clear from the CEC to avoid a Special Branch crackdown.

Whatever the version, the upshot of it all was that the left withdrew from the second CEC elections. Nair, Chan and Fong did not offer themselves for re-election while Lim Chin Siong, S Woodhull and James Puthucheary stood down. According to press reports, Lim spoke to a thunderous reception at the conference saying that it was not necessary to be a CEC member to "get things done".

The Straits Times editorial commented that although "an air of beautiful unanimity and good party comradeship pervaded the PAP annual conference throughout the four and a half hours, it was possible to detect the echoes of muffled thunder behind the scenes on the PAP stage". Headlined "Forked Lightning", it warned that "the lightning may have forked but it is still the same streak of lightning".

Then the leftists staged a rousing comeback in the third party conference on 8 July 1956. They said that they were returning to the CEC at the request of Lee who felt isolated and needed the left to boost party support. Lee, however, took the view that the leftists wanted to use the

PAP CEC as cover as they anticipated further action against them.

Four leftists were elected then—Lim Chin Siong, Chia Ek Tian, Devan Nair and Goh Boon Toh. Lim chalked up the highest number of votes (1,537) followed by Lee (1,488). When Lim became assistant secretary, Toh said, it signalled that "if the Middle Road group had wanted to do so, they could have ousted Lee and his colleagues and captured the PAP central executive". Lee Khoon Choy interpreted the results as the first attempt by the left to capture the CEC.

Before the third CEC elections, Lee had made it clear that the leftists should be in the minority and was re-assured when they took only four out of 12 seats. So what happened at the fourth CEC elections? If the leftists were supposed to stop at four, why did they capture half the CEC depriving the Lee people of their majority? Was it a coup? Who orchestrated it?

⚜

TWO days after the August 4 party polls, T T Rajah and his five leftist colleagues turned up for the first CEC meeting at the Neil Road PAP HQ. When it broke up four hours later at 12.30 am, there was no sign of any office-bearers.

"Lee Kuan Yew shocked us by saying six of the 12 members would not hold office. We tried our best to persuade Lee but he was firm," said the Middle Temple-trained lawyer who acted as spokesman for the group.

Lee had dropped his bombshell—his team of six refused to hold office on the grounds that they had lost their moral right to enforce the resolution for an independent, democratic, non-communist, socialist Malaya. As he reflected later, they felt that they "should pass the ball to them" and let them be in charge when the party came to grief. If he and Toh had carried on, they would have become their prisoners and given them cover. "By turning the tables on them, we exposed them and we watched what they were going to do," he said.

The leftists were shocked to find themselves in such a quandary—yes, they wanted to dominate and dictate to the party but they wanted to do so with Lee and company providing the veneer of legitimacy. They were fearful that if they took over the party, their cover would be blown; the British were fighting a war against the communists in Malaya and would have no qualms about incarcerating them.

Furthermore, they did not want to split the party and weaken PAP's chances in the coming elections under the new constitution for self-government. They needed the party to win the polls so that they could secure the release of their beloved leaders in Changi Prison.

In increasing desperation, the leftists tried to persuade Lee to change his mind and assume office. Ong Chye Ann said he was the first to offer to give up his seat to any Lee nominee. Then Tan Kong Guan followed up with a similar offer. Lee's answer was no and no.

More peace offerings were made but Lee refused to budge. The party was thrown into disarray. The divided CEC met once more on 13 August 1957 to break the impasse. There was still no solution. Forced into a tight corner, Rajah said they had "no choice but to hold positions".

Rajah replaced Lee as secretary because he was English-educated and a legal adviser to the trade unions, said Tan Kong Guan who became the vice-chairman. Ong Chye Ann, who assumed the treasurer's post, remembered checking the party's kitty and finding that it contained only a few thousand dollars.

Tan Chong Kin took over Toh's chairmanship, Chen Say Jame became assistant secretary and Goh Boon Toh, assistant treasurer. What happened to the other six? Lee, Toh, Ahmad Ibrahim, Goh Chew Chua, Chan Choy Siong and Tann Wee Tiong remained as CEC members.

The new team drew up its plans to unite the party and open more new branches. But its reign was short-lived, lasting only 10 days. Just as Lee had predicted, grief came but earlier than expected when the Lim Yew Hock government rounded up five office-bearers as part of a massive anti-communist operation.

If there was a silver lining in the factional strife, it was that the educated public began to realise that the PAP was not a monolithic left but was split into two opposing camps—non-communist versus pro-communist. Even the hostile English language press became more discerning, dubbing the Lee people as "moderates" and stigmatising their opponents as "extremists".

❧❦❧

THE pretty young woman was about to climb up the wooden pier leading to the *kelong* when she was stopped by the owner. He believed that women might bring ill luck to the *kelong* and affect his catch at sea. *Kelong* is the

Malay word for a wooden structure built on stilts to trap fish.

A negotiation ensued. She took off her shoes and burnt some joss sticks and incense papers to appease the spirits. Only then were she and several other women allowed to join their menfolk.

Ye Ludi was the girlfriend of Chong Fun Liam, the secretary of the PAP central propaganda and education bureau which was hosting the overnight excursion-cum-meeting at the *kelong* off the Jurong coast on 6 July 1957. Set up earlier in the year, the bureau aimed to promote unity among party members from different branches. Its mission: *zu zhi qun zhong, jiao yu ren min*, or "mobilise the masses and educate the people".

PAP veterans swore that it was at this rendezvous under the moon and caressed by the breeze that a plot was hatched by a group of leftists to capture the 12-member CEC in the 4 August 1957 party elections. Among those in attendance were representatives of party branches and Middle Road trade unions.

The story had it that all night long, a merry party fished, sang and played games. Then, in the early morning the leftists turned solemn as they drew up a list of candidates—eight for themselves and four for the Lee camp namely Lee, Toh, Ahmad Ibrahim and Goh Chew Chua. They struck out party treasurer Ong Eng Guan whom they regarded as an anti-communist opportunist.

The meeting was said to be led by Tan Kong Guan and Goh Boon Toh, the respective chairman and vice-chairman of the bureau, and Ong Chye Ann, a radical trade unionist. The threesome were among the six leftists elected to the controversial CEC a month later.

For 45 years, Tan, who owned a food manufacturing business in Macau while Ong ran a food store in Hong Kong, kept the past to themselves. Then in separate interviews in 2003, they broke their silence denying that they held the *kelong* meeting to conspire against Lee.

Confirming that he hosted the get-together, Tan said: "It was supposed to be a retreat for party branch officials but unfortunately, it had been linked to the CEC elections. The meeting was just like any other party social event where members sang and had seafood for dinner. With so many people around, how could that be a secret meeting to plot against the PAP leadership?"

Taking the same tack, Ong said: "If I were part of a plan to take control of PAP, I would not have offered to give up my seat after the election when Lee refused to take office in the CEC."

Incredible as it might sound, both Tan and Ong maintained that they took part in the party elections to support and save Lee from a more extreme group which wanted to topple him from power. They claimed that they wanted to work closely with Lee in decision-making to make up for the loss of leftist representation in the CEC.

Tan made the startling revelation that two leftist groups were fighting for the allegiance of the Middle Road unions following the detention of Lim Chin Siong and other key leaders in October 1956 and the deregistration of the powerful Singapore Factory and Shop Workers' Union (SFSWU) four months later.

One group, led by Ong Chye Ann and his wife Kwok Tai Ying, was planning to revive the Singapore General Employees' Union (SGEU) or *fan xin* as a new umbrella body to replace the SFSWU. The other group, which Tan described as more radical, intended to use the Singapore National Workers' Union (SNWU) or *quan xin* as its front.

The latter was led by David Lim Yew Ku, a former Chinese High School activist; Chan Siong Koon, a radical unionist; and Zhang Hanqing, a taxi drivers' union activist. David Lim was the son of Nanyang Academy of Fine Arts founder Lim Hak Tai and younger brother of artist Lim Yew Kuan. Banished to China later, he was killed while fighting for the MCP in the Malayan jungle.

Tan said he belonged to the "moderate" group which felt that PAP should consolidate its strength and gain greater ground support first before seeking independence from the colonialists.

It appeared that the other group had given up on Lee completely, accusing him of collaborating with the colonialists. According to its members, he had sold out the left to the British and could no longer be trusted to lead the people to freedom. They wanted to abandon PAP and set up a new "revolutionary political party".

At the *kelong*, David Lim and company were heard shouting inflammatory slogans such as *xun su xing dong, cong xin xing qi ge ming de gao chao*, or "taking swift action to rekindle the revolutionary fervour". In other words, the leftists should go all out to win mass support within PAP and the trade unions.

Their disaffection stemmed from Lee's leadership and his acceptance of the new constitution for self-government which left security, defence and foreign affairs in the hands of the British. What really unnerved them was the provision for an Internal Security Council (ISC) which had the final say on security matters. They believed that it was directed at their comrades behind bars.

Tan related how the *kelong* discussion raged over the relevance of PAP. His group sought to persuade the more radical members not to split the party while the latter questioned the effectiveness of Tan and his colleagues outside the CEC. That was why they put their names down for the party elections, he said. "By getting elected to the CEC, we hoped we could be closer to Lee and influence him."

But former leftists and PAP stalwarts found it hard to buy Tan's story. If Tan really wanted to help Lee and keep PAP united, asked Liang Chye Ming, why didn't he speak to Lee about it earlier? Even if he was not able to do so because of the language barrier, said party veteran Choo Siu Heng, why couldn't he consult Ong Pang Boon, the bilingual organising secretary who was close to Lee?

Chan Chee Seng, who was at the *kelong* as a committee member of the Tanjong Pagar branch, was even more blunt and dismissed the meeting as "a brain-washing exercise and an attempt to enrol more lieutenants to support the leftists' cause".

Right from the start, he said, participants were organised into several groups as if they were taking up military formation before battle. Each group was given a name and a colourful flag to identify itself and assigned specific duties to perform.

Chong Fun Liam said he noticed a number of outsiders at the *kelong* whom he suspected to be MCP members. "I wouldn't know if other meetings were held by separate groups after we had gone to bed," said the prolific Chinese novelist known by his pen name, Tian Liu.

If PAP leaders blamed the leftists and the leftists blamed the extreme leftists, who then was actually behind the plot to capture the party? Or were there shadowy figures pulling the strings from behind?

Mention the August coup and one name that cropped up would be Lim Chin Joo, who, like his older brother Chin Siong, was also expelled from Chinese High for student agitation and was also involved in radical trade unionism.

Lee pointed a finger at him saying that he helped to organise the manipulation at the fourth party conference. "I'm not sure if Lim Chin Joo was the actual leader, but because he was the brother of Lim Chin Siong they may well have put him in the centre stage. So that aura or the mantle of Lim Chin Siong could be passed on to Lim Chin Joo because they had to re-gather the flock, get all the unions to coalesce around somebody."

Lim Chin Joo, the younger brother of Lim Chin Siong, appeared to implicate himself when he wrote a letter from prison, dated 22 December 1959, to Lee who read out this extract during a legislative assembly debate in 1960: "No one can deny that the August 1957 incident was virtually a battle for power sufficiently indicating the leftist adventurers involved were both childish and unscrupulous in their acts and I feel penitent about the wrongs I have committed while involved in the incident."

When interviewed in 2008, Chin Joo denied that he was involved in any conspiracy, insisting that he only attended the August conference as a paid secretary of the SGEU. He said that the letter was "not an admission that he was ever the mastermind behind or a player in any plot to capture PAP".

The part read out in the chamber, he said, came from a longer letter he wrote after visits by Lee and people close to him then. "The letter was thought necessary to help the Singapore government procure the agreement of the Internal Security Council to release me. It was not an admission of anything.

"Of course, it proved to be a futile exercise. What had never crossed my mind then was that a letter written in good faith under those circumstances could have been partially released and made use of while I remained under detention. A very painful lesson for me indeed!"

Could Lim Chin Siong be calling the shots from prison then? The leftist leader had said that he played no part and was not in favour of capturing the party. Or was Goh Boon Toh the man in the driving seat as suggested by Lee? Dominic Puthucheary recalled a meeting in which Goh kept saying that he wanted to oust Lee. What about Chen Say Jame? Goh Keng Swee thought that Chen might be the leader as the others were "not men of much ability".

When interviewed in 2003, Chen, a Chinese High School student leader-turned-trade unionist, still felt upset about being branded as one of the "left-wing adventurers" by Lee. He said that it was Lee who persuaded him to stand in the 1957 party elections to fill in the leftist vacancy after the 1956 arrests of PAP CEC members Lim Chin Siong, Devan Nair and Chia Ek Tian.

But because he won a lot of votes from leftist supporters, he was suspected to be one of the plotters. "My big mistake was that I did not ask Lee to nominate me for the election to the CEC when he persuaded me to do so. Instead, I asked somebody else who just happened to be around. That person was later found to be a member of the MCP," he said ruefully.

After the party elections, he said, Lee asked him to take over the post of assistant secretary to keep an eye on the secretary, T T Rajah, and to show him any statement issued by him. One day, when Rajah came to know about it, he asked Chen: "*Lu, hantu*?" ("You, a ghost?" in Malay).

Perhaps the most intriguing question mark hung over the role of imprisoned Devan Nair. At least three people said he was involved in the August plot—two were his fellow prison mates James Puthucheary and S Woodhull and the third was T T Rajah. But Nair denied it strenuously, saying that he was then questioning his commitment to communism and was already in contact with Lee.

Puthucheary said that Nair incited Rajah to take over the PAP against his wishes. "Devan wanted to run PAP from jail with T T Rajah as secretary, and it collapsed." In Woodhull's view, Nair "played a very, very important role in directing, in helping to encourage the remaining cadres to oust Lee ... preferably via T T Rajah".

Rajah noted that it was Nair who brought him into the CEC in July 1956. He said: "Sometime before the August 1957 elections, Devan told me that the left must have at least six or seven members in the coming CEC. We had three or four then. I told Devan there was a strong move from the left to throw out Ong Eng Guan and Ismail Rahim. I conveyed Devan's view."

When the six elected leftists were trying to persuade Lee to hold office after the deadlock in the party polls, Rajah said he was stunned when Lee asked him about his discussions with Nair. "He knew what Devan had told me. I was stunned. I could have straightaway implicated Devan. I did not do so. I felt it would be gross betrayal of trust to implicate Devan."

Former leftist Lim Hock Siew quoted Rajah as saying that Nair had indicated to him in prison that there should be "six-six in the incoming CEC". Rajah, the doctor said, must have transmitted what he thought was Nair's opinion to the other trade unionists who might have thought that it was also the opinion of the other top leaders in prison.

But Nair had rebutted all these allegations robustly. On the contrary, he said, when he heard of moves to capture PAP, he sent word through underground channels that Lee and company must retain leadership of the party. Otherwise, he warned, the British and Malayans would have second thoughts about the constitutional agreement which had just been secured for Singapore's self-government.

Lee said he found it hard to believe that an Indian could direct Chinese unionists to capture PAP. "It's utter rubbish. They would not have listened to him. He had no direct line to them. He had no influence over them. His influence was through his association with Lim Chin Siong and Fong Swee Suan."

The PAP leaders viewed the August conspiracy as a wild and reckless move by a gang of "left-wing adventurers" acting unilaterally or acting on a wrong reading of what their masters wanted.

Goh Keng Swee surmised that they were improvising on their own. Ong Pang Boon believed that there was a directive but because the instructions came from those who could not operate openly, the message became distorted as it went down the line.

Dismissing the plotters as a juvenile lot, Lee said it was incredible that the communist leadership would do something so stupid. "The feeling of the ground was against these young adventurers. First, they were nonentities. They had no capacity of leadership, they had no standing, no ability, no reputation."

He derided Tan Kong Guan and associates as followers rather than leaders. "They were used by others. Somebody had the idea that if they captured the CEC, then they could direct us, they could order us what to do in the assembly and direct the constitutional talks and so on. It's utter rubbish. It's a simple-minded solution to their problems."

Did MCP have a hand in the August affair? Fang Chuang Pi was a member of the MCP working committee which reviewed the episode at a meeting in Jakarta. When asked time and again in later years, he replied categorically that the move to oust the PAP leadership was "out of line" with MCP policy. The aim was to work with Lee and PAP to achieve self-rule and independence from the British.

It was because of the 1957 debacle that Fang had to surface from the shadows in Indonesia to meet Lee to "patch up the wounds" and forge a united front with the PAP in the coming elections. Lee came to know him through a series of clandestine meetings and gave him the monicker "the Plen", short for "plenipotentiary".

～❦～

WHEN Fong Sip Chee joined PAP in 1955, he was told that it was better for him to give his union rather than his home as the correspondence address as it would protect him from victimisation and Special Branch surveillance. He never received any notice of the 4 August 1957 party conference and therefore could not attend to cast his vote. He was mystified.

So was Lee Gek Seng when he turned up for the event—where were his P and T union friends who would have voted for Lee's line-up?

Looking around the Singapore Badminton Hall, Rajaratnam was puzzled too. He thought that most PAP members were from the civil service trade unions rather than from the pro-communist ones. So why was nearly half the crowd from the leftist side? He assumed that they were people who had just slipped in. But when the counting started, he realised they actually held admission cards which allowed them to vote.

The cat was soon out of the bag. The notices, which came with admission cards, were never received by many genuine members like Fong Sip Chee and Lee Gek Seng's friends because they were hijacked by leftist trade unionists and given to their own supporters with instructions to vote for their slate of candidates. The notices posted by PAP HQ literally dropped into their hands when they arrived at the unions.

By Lee's estimate, 1,500 to 2,000 admission cards went to SFSWU on Middle Road and SBWU on Queen Street.

On the day itself, he noticed people whom he had never seen before and was troubled that they were not interested in the speeches and the proceedings but only in laying hands on the ballot papers. Their body language betrayed their impatience and zealousness to vote.

But if the names were printed on the cards, why weren't they checked against the identities of the holders? Ong Pang Boon said that "identification was impossible in the absence of identity card numbers". There was no regulation requiring people to produce their identification cards for party registration. Besides, many people did not register with their real names for fear of being tracked by the authorities.

Ong shook his head when he recalled the blatant lobbying by the leftists on that fateful day. "Whenever a pro-communist candidate's name was called, there was prolonged applause from all sides—this was a clear signal to their supporters to vote for him. The applause was also calculated to influence and intimidate the waverers and the neutrals."

One candidate was leftist trade unionist Liang Chye Ming who noted that he was nearly elected. "I lost to the last elected candidate, Madam Chan Choy Siong, by a mere 18 votes but I was ahead of Ong Eng Guan," he said.

The defeat of party treasurer Ong Eng Guan shook Lee visibly. Tan Kong Guan said: "I remember Lee saying after the elections that losing Ong was like having one of his arms chopped off."

Thanks to a deceptively simple strategy by the other side, Lee and friends were left feeling incredibly naive and silly. By playing fair even though they were in charge of the party machine, Lee lamented, they had allowed the leftists to take advantage of them.

Calling themselves "fools", Lee said: "You must remember that the idea of going to a meeting with your votes already in your pockets so to speak, telling your supporters who to vote for was alien to the English-educated. The idea is members should choose and exercise their independent judgement. Well, we were being re-educated on the techniques of conspiracy and fixing of committees.

"It was part of our education and we learnt thereafter how to deal with them ... that there was no such thing as 'let's leave it to the good sense or good choice of the members'. They don't believe in a group of people to decide what's good and they get their members to follow suit and vote accordingly."

As Rajaratnam put it in his inimitable way: "You don't play according to Queensbury Rules with these chaps. First time we learnt how naive we were when playing even the constitutional game with the communists. They knew all the tricks. It was quite clear that they had fixed the whole damn thing."

The unnerving experience on that day gave the Lee camp first-hand exposure to the art of communist chicanery and tactics. It was a sobering eye-opener as they watched the way the leftists organised their people, campaigned for their candidates and engineered the voting.

Most of all, it taught the English-educated leaders the lessons of a lifetime, lessons which continue to be coded in their party philosophy to this day—that come what may, you must never lose control of your party, that you can't always play by the rules and you've got to fix them as you go along and that if you don't demolish your opponents, they will demolish you.

To understand why the PAP of today has become a closely knit and tightly controlled outfit which could never again fall prey to predators or be infiltrated by outsiders, go back to that humid day on 4 August 1957.

GUESS who was the knight in shining armour who came to save the distressed damsel from her folly?

On the night of 22 August 1957, chief minister Lim Yew Hock unleashed the Special Branch again, this time to sweep five of the six leftist PAP office-bearers out of Lee's way into prison. Only party secretary T T Rajah was spared.

For party chairman Tan Chong Kin, vice-chairman Tan Kong Guan, treasurer Ong Chye Ann, assistant treasurer Goh Boon Toh and assistant secretary Chen Say Jame, their reign lasted all of 10 days. The next year, Tan Kong Guan, Goh and Ong were banished to China. Under the banishment ordinance, trouble-making ethnic Chinese and Indians could be exiled to China and India.

In all, 18 PAP branch officials and members, 13 trade unionists and four journalists were nabbed. The mother of *Sin Pao* reporter Jek Yeun Thong was in tears when she called on No 38 Oxley Road to seek help for her son.

Defending his action in a white paper, the chief minister documented the communist penetration of PAP and stressed that the operation was aimed at preventing a repetition of the October 1956 riots.

Gerald de Cruz, his Labour Front (LF) colleague then, believed that Lim was compelled to act as the government could not afford to let PAP be captured by the communists. Its overwhelming fear was that if they captured the party and the entire trade union movement, then the whole of Singapore would be lost to the communists eventually.

But detractors saw a devious turn of mind in the chief minister. With elections to be called soon, Rajaratnam figured, the LF government thought that if the PAP was weakened, it would lose its following and take a long time to rebuild its strength. Lee's view was that "it's not so much saving the PAP as showing how ineffective the non-communist leaders were in the PAP".

What was most damaging to Lee were the widespread rumours that he colluded with the chief minister to put his leftist comrades out of circulation. Lee had foreseen that the new PAP leaders would get into trouble sooner or later but did not expect Lim Yew Hock to act so swiftly. "It compromised us. It made it appear as if we had deliberately exposed them."

From his prison cell, Nair was concerned that PAP would suffer severe political damage if the communist united front were to give credence to the charge that Lee was in cahoots with the chief minister. He said that he and Fong Swee Suan advised their colleagues outside "not to rock the PAP boat". The reason: "Because elections would then go against PAP and if PAP did not win, we would remain in the jug."

To dispel all the insidious innuendoes, Lee moved a motion in the legislative assembly to deplore the inaccuracies in the white paper. His main contention was that the chief minister launched the big purge not to save PAP but to save his power base in the 60,000-strong Singapore Trade Union Congress (STUC). Formed in 1951 by 28 non-communist white-collar unions, the STUC helped the LF to storm to victory in the 1955 polls.

Lee drew attention to a merger being negotiated between the STUC and the Singapore General Employees' Union (SGEU) which replaced the banned Singapore Factory and Shopworkers' Union (SFSWU) at the time of the arrests. When the police surrounded the Middle Road premises, he said, representatives of 32 unions were meeting to finalise arrangements to join and capture STUC.

Curiously, a key STUC official involved in the talks scoffed at any suggestion of a take-over by the Middle Road unions. "How were they able to take control of us when we did not even enter into any form of partnership with them?" asked Lee Yew Seng.

While he confirmed that merger talks were on, he noted that the left was not sincere and that STUC was "merely paying lip service". He said: "We never spoke truthfully from our hearts then. We did not really want to cooperate with them since we clearly knew that it was simply impossible for us to work with them."

But whatever the real motives of Lim Yew Hock might be, the indisputable outcome was that he saved the day for Lee by purging PAP of its communist elements. Rajaratnam admitted that the operation helped PAP. Goh agreed that Lim did PAP a favour and enabled the sidelined non-communist leaders to recover control of the party.

Gerald de Cruz eulogised that Singapore, PAP and Lee should be "eternally grateful to Lim Yew Hock and his advisers, whoever they were, for giving the PAP this chance of survival". What the chief minister did, he said, was "a very, very heroic thing" because it meant courting unpopularity among communist supporters and Chinese middle school students.

The big sweep gave Lee and friends the breathing space to take stock of the parlous state of the party and embark on a spring-cleaning exercise. After Rajah resigned on 25 August 1957 citing "poor health", they installed an emergency council with Toh as interim chairman to run the party.

On 20 October 1957, the fifth party conference was held. Dispensing with individual nomination and voting, Lee put up a new CEC line-up to be voted for and against en-bloc. Some 1,000 members signified their approval by a show of hands. There was no need for a secret ballot.

⸙

WHAT if, what if ... history is rife with such questions. In the story of PAP, none could be more tantalising than: What if the left had not captured the party in the tempestuous days of August 1957?

What if the leftists had not mounted their bid and alerted Lee and his politically inexperienced and naive colleagues to their clandestine manoeuvres and machinations?

What if, as Lee once speculated, they had "left us alone, played along with us and then captured it at a critical moment, say 1961, and expelled us from the party?"

The event altered the direction and nature of the party irrevocably and changed the course of many lives irreversibly. Looking back on the day which led to his 38-year exile in China, Tan Kong Guan said in 2003: "If I knew what was going to happen, I would rather not have been involved in the first place. I had nowhere to turn to, to express my innocence." Similarly, Ong Chye Ann reflected that if he had known things were going to turn out the way they did, he would not have taken part in that election.

In the history of PAP, party scribe Rajaratnam ranked it as one of its most critical moments while Fong Swee Suan and Liang Chye Ming called it a turning point.

Dominic Puthucheary was part of the new echelon of leftist leaders who stepped into the Middle Road power vacuum following the October 1956 crackdown. Leaning back in his black leather chair in his office in Bukit Tunku, a suburb of Kuala Lumpur, in 2003, the lanky lawyer looked pensively out of the window before describing it as the defining moment.

Why? Because Lee never trusted the left again and PAP was never the same again.

7

Mystery of the Night Soil Man

HE appeared from nowhere and disappeared into nowhere. With uncombed hair, in a crumpled short-sleeved shirt and shorts and tattered rubber shoes, he cut a forlorn figure of unabashed shabbiness, rather than spartan simplicity.

Passing his name off as Pang Teh Lin or Pan Tieren in hanyu pinyin, he introduced himself as a night soil carrier—that bare-bodied man of the 1950s and 1960s who went from house to house heaving a wooden pole with a bucket on either end to collect faeces.

Today you take the automatic flush system for granted. In those days, such workers collected human waste and stored it in vans which were divided into steel compartments. The waste was later tipped over at disposal stations and pumped into the sewerage works for treatment.

A queer character, remarked Fong Sip Chee. What a weird-looking person, thought Mrs Lee Kuan Yew when she first met him as an election helper at her Oxley Road home. She remembered Teh Lin as a "tall, skinny person who had a mole with hair sticking out". Chan Chee Seng's recollection: "A dark fellow who pretended to be poor and badgered you for treats and money."

Toh Chin Chye once confided to Fong about a secret encounter with him. At Teh Lin's request, he had turned up at what was supposedly his place of work. When the party chairman found himself at a sewerage facility, he felt the shivers thinking how easily Teh Lin "could have pushed him inside and got him killed and the whole world wouldn't know a thing".

For a humble worker, Teh Lin was a highly opinionated and effectively bilingual speaker. A speech he delivered at the second party conference on 26 June 1955 made the headlines in *The Straits Times* when he warned that the Singapore government had planted agents in PAP and called on the party to root them out.

He must have made enough of an impression on the party faithfuls to be elected to the second central executive committee (CEC) on the same day and to be re-elected to the third CEC on 8 July 1956 and appointed assistant treasurer to boot.

Then suddenly he dropped out of sight after that dramatic fourth party elections on 4 August 1957 which led to the leftists' takeover of the CEC and the big purge by the Lim Yew Hock government. As Fong put it, "he came out mysteriously and he just went off mysteriously".

How could a person appear from out of the blue to be a CEC member and then disappear without a trace? Lee Kuan Yew could not figure out how he was elected. "I don't understand it. It's one of those things that happened. We were not shrewd operators in the beginning. We were English-educated in a sense, so everything was open."

Racking his memory, Ong Pang Boon, who was the organising secretary then, admitted that he was still none the wiser about the circumstances surrounding Teh Lin's elevation to the supreme decision-making body in the party.

All he could recollect was that following the Hock Lee bus riot and a spate of accusations against PAP for being a communist stooge, the non-communist leaders in the party had insisted that the pro-communist faction should back out from the second CEC elections. "It was at this election that a mysterious person going by the name of P Teh Lin was elected," he said.

In a bid to unravel his identity, Ong visited his Beach Road address once and discovered that it was a dilapidated two-storey shophouse where no one there seemed to know him. Then an old man showed him the cubicle where Teh Lin supposedly lived—a wooden bunk with two or three empty wooden trunks. The old man said that Teh Lin was a seaman who was rarely seen.

If that was so, Ong wondered, how did he manage to receive party circulars and notices of meetings? Was the cubicle just a communicating address? Later he and other party officials made enquiries after his disappearance and found that he was not a night soil carrier at all. To their incredulity, they learnt that he had gone to Britain to study law!

So who was this now-you-see-him now-you-don't character? And what was he up to in the CEC? Ong's theory: "We suspected Teh Lin to be a Special Branch provocateur."

Toh said he was reliably told that Teh Lin was a Special Branch agent. "He was planted. We did not know it at that time. Our own screening was inadequate then."

Lee: "He seemed to have no faction, no group supporting him. So I suspected that he must be a Special Branch chap and that Special Branch used him to feed me with information. He was a useful source of information of who's who, what's what."

Former leftists believed that Teh Lin must have been a British agent as he spoke "so fiercely with impunity". Even Special Branch's Richard Corridon, who looked after the English-speaking section, could not pin him down when he was asked in his retirement years. He speculated that he could have been from the Chinese section.

❦

IF a "queer" and "weird" character of dubious background like Teh Lin could breeze into the PAP to sit alongside Lee and Toh, what did it say about the party? Well, it spoke volumes about the laxity and porousness of its organisational structure.

But seriously, how could an embryonic party in search of mass support afford to be fussy about membership criteria? At that time, anyone 21 years and above could sign up as a member. No photograph was required, no screening needed—just fill in a form and pay the subscription fee of $4.

No home address? Never mind, any address would do. Preferably, use a union address to avoid Special Branch surveillance. Anyway, what address could a person give if he lived in an illegally constructed squatter hut? Besides, what's the point of writing addresses in Chinese characters which could not be read by Malay postmen?

Peter Low Por Tuck was a former Chinese High School student twice detained for pro-China activities. Attracted by the radical aura of PAP, he resigned from Lee Wah Bank to join the party as a full-time worker. His monthly pay was $150. One key task was recruitment and one vivid memory was that of application forms piling up in a mess.

Filled-in information was often incomplete or unclear and subscriptions collected did not tally with the membership figure, he said. The reason was not hard to find: Middle Road unionists were recruiting members separately from the party officials and many did not hand in the forms and subscriptions to party HQ.

Perhaps the random and haphazard way in which the membership drive was conducted is best told in the anecdote of a Green Bus Company worker who recruited 2,000 members all by himself. What amazed Fong Sip Chee who related it was that the person was an illiterate who could not even sign his name. When he turned up for party meetings, Fong had to sign him in on his behalf.

When Goh Keng Swee inspected the membership records at party HQ one day, he found thousands of cards bearing names strewn all over. No one knew whether subscriptions for them had been paid. At party meetings, no one could tell whether a person was a member or not. Anyone could flash his party badge and walk in.

Many interviewees spoke of how they signed up for the party but had no idea whether they became members. Othman Wok remembered that when PAP convenor Samad Ismail returned to his *Utusan Melayu* office from the inauguration ceremony on 21 November 1954, he handed out membership forms to his staff. Othman filled in a form and submitted it to Samad. He never received any acknowledgement. "It was only in 1958 when Lee nominated me as chairman of Geylang Serai Changi branch that I knew I was a member of PAP," he said.

Sheng Nam Chin had a similar experience. The then-University of Malaya medical student said he applied to join PAP during its inauguration at Victoria Memorial Hall. "Yes, I did sign up but there's no trace of it in the party. I had to rejoin the party at the end of 1957 or beginning of 1958."

As a clerk with Hong Kong and Shanghai Bank, Chan Chee Seng dealt with two regular customers who turned out to be PAP convenors Tann Wee Tiong and S Rajaratnam. At their prompting, he applied to join the party but forgot all about it until Ong Pang Boon visited him at his girlfriend's home on South Bridge Road one day and asked him: "Are you Mr Chan?"

<hr />

IF Ong Pang Boon was earnestly rounding up people like Chan Chee Seng into the party, it was because of his new job as the first full-time official of PAP. As organising secretary, his brief was to strengthen the organisation and take charge of the day-to-day running of the party.

Born in Kuala Lumpur, the son of a treasury clerk in a rice trading firm came to Singapore to study at the University of Malaya on a Selangor state government scholarship. He joined the University Socialist Club and became acquainted with the *Fajar* boys S Woodhull and James

Puthucheary. In fact, Ong was summoned as a witness in the *Fajar* trial but refused to testify.

Weaned on a diet of left-wing Chinese papers and inspired by famous heroes in Chinese history, he developed an affinity for socialist causes. His campus stint served to heighten his political sensitivities to the tumultuous situation in Singapore.

It was James Puthucheary who initiated him into PAP. In early 1955, he took Ong to a Singapore Post and Telegraph Uniformed Staff Union gathering on Serangoon Road where he listened to party leaders expounding on the need to take part in the Rendel elections, and then to Oxley Road where he got roped into the April polls as election agent for Lee.

As election agent in Tanjong Pagar, he remembered he had "to do practically everything which had to do with elections"—from taking calls for the party, attending meetings with the police and applying for permits to organising and deploying election workers during the campaign.

In the meantime, having graduated in 1954, Ong had started work with the Federal and Colonial Building Society, the predecessor of the Malaya and Borneo Building Society. After the elections, he was transferred to Kuala Lumpur and was looking forward to the pursuit of a promising career and bringing home the bacon for his family when the phone call came from PAP.

It was a job offer which came with a 36 per cent pay cut. He was earning $700 then—a princely sum in those days of poverty and high unemployment—but PAP could only offer him $450 as organising secretary. In his memoirs, Lee mentioned that the money was taken out of his legislative assembly allowance of $500. Nevertheless Ong took the plunge into the political unknown.

As a paid official, he was not a member of the CEC but attended all CEC meetings to take down the minutes. CEC minutes were brief, recording only the decisions so that if they fell into the wrong hands, readers would not know who said what and the arguments leading to a decision. Ong explained that CEC worked on the assumption that the party was infiltrated by Special Branch and communist agents.

His administrative work was cut out for him—from registering members, issuing receipts, printing stationery and cutting stencils to responding to complaints and enquiries from party members and the public. He had a tough time balancing the budget as the party was run on very little. Funds came from members' subscriptions and well-wishers' donations. Bare furniture and fittings were provided by members and anonymous donors.

Getting premises for the party was one of his early challenges as landlords were generally unwilling to rent shop space for fear of being blacklisted by the authorities. By the first PAP anniversary in November 1955, the party could only form five branches namely Tanjong Pagar, Farrer Park, Punggol-Tampines, Bukit Timah and Bukit Panjang.

Fortunately the party was able to secure the front portion of a shophouse on No 140 Neil Road as its first HQ. It also doubled up as the Tanjong Pagar branch from 1955 to 1957 and became the gathering place for members and volunteers living in nearby Chinatown cubicles. They came not only to do party work but also to while away the evenings.

Chan Chee Seng could not wait to finish his bank work at 5 pm each day before rushing to party HQ where he would stay until very late running errands for the party or chit-chatting with the many people who wandered in and out of the premises. In a pre-TV age, it was a time of companionship and camaraderie which Chan cherished to this day.

In 2003, the historically significant address located amid a row of gentrified offices splashed in a palette of bright colours belonged to a film production company. Smartly turned out executives, men with ties and women in power suits, strode briskly along the *go kah ki* ("five-foot way" in Hokkien). Just about the only vestige of the impoverished 1950s was the sad sight of a bent-over old woman pushing a cart of old cardboards and newspapers.

Apart from his organisational and people-handling skills, Ong had another much-coveted quality among the politicians of the day. He was effectively bilingual, having been educated in Confucian Middle School and Methodist Boys' School in Kuala Lumpur and in the University of Malaya. Unlike the British-educated Straits-born Chinese PAP leaders, he could switch effortlessly from English to Chinese and vice-versa.

That quality made him eminently suited to play the bridging role between the leaders and members, and between party HQ and branches.

⚬⚬⚭⚬⚬

HO Puay Choo left Fujian province in China as a seven-year-old with her mother to seek a better life but they could not escape poverty in British Singapore. Unable to complete primary school, she had to sell porridge to keep herself alive before turning to sewing. Stricken by a sense of social injustice, she was naturally drawn to the anti-colonial speeches in PAP mass rallies.

As she listened to the leaders railing against social discrimination and income inequalities, she felt the pain and anguish of her sufferings. "I thought I ought to be a part of them since they would be focusing on rectifying the problems of the poor," she said.

Ong Chang Sam could not afford to continue school after secondary 2 and had to sweat it out as a sand quarry worker. Living in Punggol, he realised how "terribly underdeveloped" the place was—there was no electricity and the illiteracy rate was very high. He felt that if PAP were to assume power, the standard of living would improve. So he joined the Punggol-Tampines branch.

Ho and Ong were typical of the people who flocked to PAP in the early days—Mandarin- or dialect-speaking, Chinese-educated or lowly educated workers, petty traders, shopkeepers, hawkers and farmers eking out a hand-to-mouth existence. Living in city slums and *attap* colonies, they felt neglected by the colonial rulers.

A Special Branch report in February 1955 summed up PAP's membership as "poor" while describing the membership of the Progressive Party (PP) and Democratic Party (DP) as "wealthy" and that of Labour Front (LF) as "medium wealthy".

It did not require special intelligence to understand why the downtrodden, dispossessed and disenfranchised gravitated to PAP. All one had to do was to attend a rally and listen to the strident speeches against colonial iniquities and repressive laws, heart-rending advocacy for equality for Chinese education and impassioned calls for jobs and fairer working conditions.

Not surprisingly, the Chinese-speaking members of the party far outnumbered the English-speaking ones who were mainly from the government unions. Party veterans estimated that more than 80 per cent of the members were Chinese-educated then.

Unfortunately both groups did not mix well. Even in the branches such as Sembawang where there was a higher proportion of non-Chinese, Ong Pang Boon noted, Malay and Indian committee members were passive and uneasy not knowing what was being said or what was going on.

Consider Lee's bastion, Tanjong Pagar branch, which boasted more English-educated members. Yet they seldom dropped by No 140 Neil Road as they could not speak Mandarin, said Low Por Tuck who was bilingual, having studied in English primary schools and Chinese High.

The irony was that while the party chiefs took pains to ensure a multi-racial composition in the CEC, they simply had no control over the racial balance in the general membership. What could they do if Chinese-speaking workers were drawn to PAP like bees to honey while their English-speaking counterparts avoided the party like the plague?

Lee Gek Seng explained that the English-educated did not want to jeopardise their standing in society by being labelled left-wing and felt more comfortable with PP and LF. He confessed that he was initially afraid of being involved in PAP but was re-assured when the Singapore Union of P & T Workers negotiated for junior civil servants like him to be allowed to join a political party.

Ong attributed the party's failure to attract the English-educated to the "smear campaign" of *The Straits Times*, the antagonism of the colonial government against PAP and the fear of victimisation by employers.

The result was a growing dichotomy between the English-educated leadership and the largely Chinese-speaking membership, between a head comprising Fabian-styled intellectuals in party HQ and a body of Red China-inspired workers in the branches.

If the race and class divide was already hard to cross, the language barrier made it almost insurmountable. Many CEC members did not know what was going on in the branches. They depended on bilingual officials such as Ong and Low to do on-the-spot translation. With uncharacteristic bluntness, Ong said that as branch activists were Mandarin-speaking, "meaningful communication with Malays, Indians and the English-educated was well-nigh impossible".

It did not help that the kind of social and cultural activities—for example, Chinese folk dancing, harmonica bands, group singing—conducted in the branches only served to reinforce their "Chineseness" which in turn put off the non-Chinese. Instead they attracted even more like-minded Chinese to their fold. "Inevitably, the few non-Chinese and English-educated members in branch committees felt alienated and kept away from the branches," said Ong.

Mofradi bin Mohamed Noor, the hospital union chief and PAP convenor and founding member, was attached to Tanjong Pagar branch in 1955 but left before the year was out. One reason he cited was that he could not blend in with the Chinese-speaking branch committee members.

To top it all, there was little social interaction to bridge the divide. The anglicised bosses were perceived as intellectually forbidding people who had no time to engage in small talk with humble folks. "You know, you don't go for a drink with the top leaders," remarked Lee Gek Seng, "the only one you met in the *kopi tiam* was Devan Nair."

Fong Sip Chee described PAP as "a queer organisation" in which the top leaders were English-educated, the middle-level officials were bilingual and the lower-rung members were Chinese-educated. The divergence reached such a stage, he said, that the Chinese-educated sought to keep the branches as their exclusive preserve and barred the English-educated from entering the premises.

Although Fong studied in Chinese schools at primary and secondary level before switching to an English secondary school, he said he was branded as English-educated and was not welcomed in the Chinese-speaking branches. That was why, he said, as a campaigner during the 1959 elections, he was shunted to the English-speaking middle class wards of Cairnhill and River Valley.

The prejudice of the Chinese-speaking against the English-educated was all too disturbingly real and prevalent. He recounted an incident in a bus when he was conversing with a fellow Indian passenger in English. Two students from Chung Cheng High who sat nearby thought he did not know Mandarin and jibed that he *fang yang pi* ("emitted foreign fart"). He turned around and gave them the scolding of their lives.

⚬⚬⚬

VISUALISE big, burly K M Byrne doing a four-step harvest dance from China, his face turning redder as the pace quickened.

Called *yangko*, the farmers' dance originated from Yan'an in Shaanxi province, the bastion of communism in China. Adopted by the Chinese Communist Party as its signature item, it became a national dance which reached the height of its popularity during the Chinese Cultural Revolution in the mid-1960s.

When he heard the singing of *dong fang hong* ("The East is red" in Mandarin), *tai yang sheng* ("The sun rises") and *mei you gong chan dang jiu mei you xin zhong guo* ("There is no new China without the Chinese Communist Party"), Byrne might have suspected their communist origins but would have been none the wiser about what the lyrics meant. Throw in rousing games laden with political content and the jarring effect from the assault on all the senses of the Oxford-educated Eurasian was all but complete.

Ong Pang Boon and other PAP oldtimers could now relive these scenes with nostalgic relish but at that time they did not know what they were in for when they attended mass picnics or *ye can hui* organised by party branches at Changi, Pasir Ris and Punggol. If they thought they were going to have innocent fun by the sea, they were sadly mistaken.

It was certainly no picnic for no-nonsense party chairman Toh Chin Chye when he first stepped into one such party function. Listening to "pig-tailed Chinese schoolgirls singing songs from China", he felt ill at ease. Certainly, he did not feel welcome, he reminisced.

It was the same with Fong Sip Chee who said that he felt "like a pawn" mouthing revolutionary songs along the lines of *gu xiang* ("Your homeland") and *zhong hua er nu* ("Children of China") and keeping step in the *yangko*. But he marvelled at the boundless energy of the pig-tailed girls who could make them sing and dance tirelessly.

According to Chong Fun Liam, former Tanjong Pagar branch assistant secretary, these picnics were organised to circumvent the Emergency regulations which disallowed the gathering of more than five persons.

They became part of the plethora of activities hosted by the branches to recruit new members, propagate leftist ideas and instil collective discipline. Be they kindergarten and literacy classes or current affairs and cultural programmes, they were infused with an unmistakable pro-China if not pro-communist fervour.

The language and class divide between the English-educated leaders in party HQ and the Chinese-speaking members in the branches was also shading ominously into an ideological divide. While most CEC members were decidedly non-communist, much of the rank and file were wittingly or unwittingly falling along pro-communist lines.

The latter jelled with the Malayan Communist Party's (MCP) united front strategy of penetrating and using legitimate organisations as cover. As it considered PAP the most progressive left-wing party, the underground had instructed its "above ground" operatives to work with it to overthrow the colonial regime.

The branches were particularly vulnerable to infiltration as membership was approved freely and branch committees were elected directly by members. For some branches such as Bukit Timah and

Tanjong Pagar, membership could easily exceed a thousand. Goh Keng Swee observed that the branch committee officials were almost entirely Chinese-educated, unemployed, fierce and directed by the communist united front.

Most branches were controlled by the leftists from the Middle Road unions and residents' associations such as the *zhu lian* (Singapore Rural Dwellers' Association) and *xiang lian* (Singapore Rural People's Association). Insulated from party HQ, they could peddle their own agenda and flex their political muscles. Former Bukit Timah branch secretary Choo Siu Heng said that some branches did not take orders from the top and functioned as independent units. Fong Sip Chee noted that only the views of leftist union leaders filtered through to the branches; the views of Lee and Toh were blocked.

Party chiefs were often oblivious to the political slogans displayed at the branches. When Tunku Abdul Rahman and MCP leader Chin Peng failed to end the armed struggle during the Baling talks in 1955, Bukit Timah branch vice-chairman Tan Kong Guan put up a banner calling for the recognition of MCP, end of the Emergency, release of all political detainees and abolition of preventive detention laws. Tan recalled that the PAP CEC did not react to it until a Beijing newspaper reported it.

For the hard-pressed organising secretary, a recurring headache at party elections was when someone would slip in a resolution on the spur of the moment calling for the recognition of MCP. "We had to stop it as it was not in line with party policy and would endanger the very existence of the party itself," said Ong.

Even impish kids were not spared from communist indoctrination. When Othman Wok became chairman of the Geylang branch on Jalan Tiga Ratus, Upper Changi Road, he paid a visit to its kampung premises. He was shocked to find that "all the children wore red scarves and were singing communist songs, and the books were all communist books".

By Ong's frank admission, it was very difficult for the CEC to exert control over the branches. In current affairs classes run by the party, the most popular books used for raising the political consciousness of members turned out to be those which gave a Marxist analysis of class society. Teachers hired from outside disseminated ideas that were at variance with the party's position.

Indeed naive PAP leaders played into the hands of the leftists when they agreed to the setting up of the central propaganda and education bureau on 16 October 1956. It was supposed to coordinate branch activities but as events proved later, it became the vehicle for "leftist adventurers" to mount a takeover bid in the 4 August 1957 party elections.

The way the bureau spread its influence revealed its organising ingenuity and resourcefulness. With 13 branches at its disposal, it started a 100-man choir, a 100-man harmonica band and a 100-man folk dance troupe. It produced common material for news bulletins written on *da zi bao* (blackboards) and pinned on the walls of the branches.

On 1 May 1957, it published *dang xun* or Action Express for circulation among the branches to serve as discussion material. Initially the articles appeared innocuous and positive. Then views inimical to the party's interests began to creep into the newsletter. The CEC cottoned on to it after a few issues and suspended publication immediately. Lee and Ong were worried that PAP could be banned because of the publication.

When PAP started the publication of its magazine *Petir*, Ong had to keep vigil on the articles in the Chinese edition. "The editorial was supposed to be the same for both Chinese and English issues, which was usually written by Lee or Rajaratnam. Sometimes they got the translation right in the Chinese *Petir*. Sometimes they slanted it, conveniently leaving out certain points and making it more leftist."

At times the differences broke out into the open, all subtleties and niceties abandoned. When Ong and his staff went to help flood victims at Paya Lebar, he heard Paya Lebar branch activists telling farmers not to bring their problems to the PAP but to the pro-communist Farmers' Association and Rural Dwellers' Association. "Right under the nose of the organising secretary and his HQ party, these subversive elements were blatantly undermining the PAP," he said.

⚛

HO Puay Choo was dumbfounded when her bosom friend Chan Choy Siong asked her to stand for election to the CEC. She rejected the offer right away as she felt she lacked knowledge.

Then Ong Pang Boon came to persuade her but again she turned it down, saying, "I do not have any experience and I cannot shoulder such heavy responsibilities."

Not to be deterred, Ong and Chan took her to see the man himself. Ho recalled: "I told Lee Kuan Yew that I did not know or understand how things worked, thus I wasn't suitable for the position. Then he asked me: 'Are you willing to learn?' I answered: 'Yes, we ought to learn in life.' And he replied: 'That will be enough.' "

And that was how the 28-year-old samfoo-clad seamstress who did not complete primary school and could not speak English joined the 12-person high-powered line-up being put up for election to the fifth CEC at the special party conference on 20 October 1957.

The names were drawn up by the six-man emergency council set up to run the party after the arrest of the five leftist CEC members in August. As reported in the press, they were "to be voted for or against" under the new rules. The operative word was en-bloc—there would be no laundry list of individual nominations but a recommended slate.

En-bloc nomination and en-bloc voting were among the first slew of changes introduced to prevent the party from falling into the hands of the pro-communists. The game plan worked true to form at the party conference. The recommended team was approved overwhelmingly.

There were no fireworks as the pro-communist members stayed away to lick their wounds. There were no other candidates. "For the first time since the founding of PAP, there were no pro-communist or suspected Special Branch agents in the CEC," said Ong.

The six non-communist members in the last CEC were re-elected— Toh regained his chairmanship, Goh Chew Chua became vice-chairman, Lee was titled secretary-general instead of secretary; Ahmad Ibrahim was assistant secretary-general while Tann Wee Tiong and Chan Choy Siong remained as committee members.

The threesome voted out by the leftists returned to the CEC—Ong Eng Guan was back as treasurer along with Ismail Rahim and Haron Kassim as committee members. Interestingly, all three new additions to the fifth CEC hailed from Kampong Kapor branch known for its high level of activism—Wee Toon Boon, Suppiah Visva Lingam and Ho Puay Choo.

With the presence of Chan Choy Siong and Ho Puay Choo, women power had finally arrived in the PAP's highest echelon. Both sprang from the Women's League—the precursor of the Women's Wing today—which Chan helped to set up in early 1956. Its manifesto called on the women of Singapore to rally under PAP to fight for the emancipation of women.

Chan gained the distinction of being the first woman in the PAP CEC when she scraped through as the candidate with the 12th highest number of votes in the controversial 4 August 1957 party election. She made it six for the Lee camp versus six for the leftists.

"Choy Siong became the sixth person. If not for her, Lim Yew Hock might have banned PAP on the grounds that its CEC had been captured by the communists," said the man who put up her candidature and became her husband four years later.

Ong Pang Boon first met her during the 1955 elections when he was the election agent for Lee in Tanjong Pagar. The Nanyang Girls-educated party campaigner captivated him with her rousing public speaking skills and fluency in Mandarin and dialects.

Her political convictions were driven by her empathy for the poor and anger over the plight of abused women. She worked at her father's hawker stall before becoming a clerk in an oil milling company in Paya Lebar. When she was sacked by her employer for campaigning on behalf of PAP, she joined the party as a $150-a-month paid worker to take care of the accounts and subscriptions.

Chan went on to stamp her mark as PAP city councillor, legislative assemblywoman and member for parliament and pioneering woman activist who championed the cause of equal pay for equal work. Her husband noted that she played "a leading role in the party in agitating for the rights of women that finally took shape in the passing of the Women's Charter in 1961". The charter prohibited polygamy among the Chinese and made it obligatory for a husband to maintain his wife and children during marriage and after divorce. Tragically, her life was cut short by a car crash in 1981 at the age of 49.

Women's rights had been a key plank in the PAP platform right from the start. Like the communists, PAP leaders felt that women should be put on par with the men, given the same education and enabled to make their full contribution to society.

Perhaps this was best reflected in an English radio broadcast by Mrs Lee when she appealed to all women to vote for PAP during the 1959 elections. Lamenting that women did the same kind of work as men but did not get the same pay, she said: "Our society is still built on the assumption that women are the social, political and economic inferiors of men. This myth has been made the excuse for the exploitation of female labour." It was her one and only political speech.

With the election of the new line-up, the Lee team was back in harness. The two-and-a-half-month leadership crisis was over. Drawing lessons from the August debacle, the party bosses decided to put in place a foolproof system that would make it impossible for the pro-communists to launch a coup.

Their brainwave: a new system which would allow only specially selected members to be elected to the CEC and to elect the CEC. But first they had to weed out the pro-communists from the non-communists through a massive re-registration exercise. For the first time, all members were required to submit their particulars and photographs.

Predictably, the re-registration in May and June 1958 was opposed by the leftists who warned the rank and file that their photographs would end up in Special Branch. But in what must be seen as classic communist subterfuge, many shadowy figures signed up and remained with the party while waiting to be activated by the underground.

The exercise was not only held at party HQ but also entailed trekking into the countryside. S V Lingam related how he and party workers went to an area around Somapah Road in Changi one night but could only re-register a few people as the PAP Changi branch refused to co-operate with them. At about 11 pm, when they returned to their pick-up van, they were shocked to find that its tyres had been slashed.

According to Fong Sip Chee, of the 14,000 members, only a small segment of them had not re-registered. Lee Gek Seng was proud of his original membership No 2. But because he was late in re-registering, he found that his membership number had jumped to "3,900-something".

⌘

TRUST the meticulous Toh with his penchant for linguistic precision. When he first came across the word, he looked up the dictionary and checked with the books that he had borrowed from the erudite Rajaratnam.

The word was "cadre". In the mid-1800s, it referred to a military detachment but from the 1930s it was adopted by the communist party to refer to a small select group of members who could assume control of a revolutionary party or train others to do so.

The re-registration exercise was aimed at building up a cadre membership distinct from ordinary membership. All cadres had to be approved by the CEC. Only cadres could stand for election and hold office. Only cadres could cast their votes in party elections.

Cadre membership was kept hush-hush so no one outside the inner circle knew who was in and who was out. It led to much animosity and friction in the branches when some leaders found they were left out while their subordinates enjoyed that cachet.

What the new scheme meant was that the leftists could no longer be able to pack party conferences with their own people and engineer the voting. Only cadres could vote for cadres nominated as candidates by the outgoing CEC. In other words, what happened at the 4 August 1957 party conference could never be repeated.

Where did this ingenious and audacious scheme come from? Ask Toh and he would say crisply: "From the organisation of the communist party!" Lamenting how foolish they were in losing their own political party to the leftists, he said: "So we copied the communists. They had their own cadre system, that's why it's difficult to penetrate the communist party. It was not our idea, it was their system we copied."

Lee's account was that the idea came from the Vatican system. Just as the pope picked the cardinals who would in turn elect the pope, the party leaders would pick the cadres who would then elect the party leaders. So even if the pro-communists were able to dominate every party branch, he said, power would still rest with the executive.

As Lee elaborated: "They can capture branches, members, sections of the party but they will never capture the party. So that the symbol and what the PAP stands for—the reputation which we have built in the minds of the people—would be ours and not theirs."

Critics charged that these constitutional changes destroyed the democratic nature of the party as ordinary members lost their right to vote and be voted into the CEC. A system in which leaders appointed special members who then voted for the leaders was condemned as autocratic and designed to perpetuate Lee and his associates in power. Lim Hock Siew said that this marked the beginning of the leftists' disillusionment with Lee.

The cadre system, with some modifications, is still in place today. Cadres would be notified of the recommended candidates for party elections and they could vote for 12 or fewer names. The results would be announced by the party chairman but the vote tally would not be given unlike in the early days when it was routinely published in the press.

But the system did not preclude individual nominations at the party conference. The chairman would ask for any more nominations and wait for a few minutes before voting began.

Fong Sip Chee remembered that a cadre member named Tang Tuck Wah once stood for election by himself for the CEC and was duly defeated. When incumbent CEC member Tan Kia Gan was dropped from the recommended line-up, he asked someone to nominate him. He failed to muster enough votes.

⚬⚬⚬

ONCE again Singapore Badminton Hall played host to a special party conference on 23 November 1958. It was time to table the proposed amendments to the constitution providing for cadre membership and giving cadre members the right to vote and be voted into the CEC.

The usually publicity-hungry PAP turned publicity-shy. The press was barred. Strict precautionary measures were taken to ensure that only paid-up members attend the meeting.

The three-hour closed-door meeting was described in *The Straits Times* the next day as a move to prevent the infiltration of "political racketeers, opportunists and adventurers". Lee was quoted as saying that "unless a system is worked out, a man can just pay $4, walk into the party and have the right to decide the destiny of the party".

No longer would the British-educated leaders be laughed off for their naiveté and gullibility. Not only did they display their creative ingenuity in crafting the amendments, they also demonstrated that Machiavellian wiliness was not the exclusive preserve of the left.

Goh Keng Swee was still a senior civil servant forbidden from taking part in politics but he took his seat among the audience on that day to witness the proceedings. As usual, his ears were ringing from the ferocious speeches against the sins of British colonialism and the failings of the Labour Front government punctated by the rallying cries of "*merdeka*".

Amid the raucous din, he was not certain if party chairman Toh had explained in detail what the proposed constitutional changes meant. Even if he did, he said, he was doubtful if the audience understood.

What he remembered distinctly was that Toh moved the adoption of the new party constitution to the last item of the agenda. After completing his speech while moving the amendment, Toh said: "Those in favour, stand up and shout '*merdeka*' three times."

So they all did, and that was how the new constitution was adopted by the party. Whether the members realised it or not, Goh mused, they had passed an amendment depriving them of the right to vote for the CEC on that fateful day.

This was one of those rare moments in the early history of the PAP when the bookish English-educated scholars were one-up over the street-smart Chinese-speaking leftists.

8

Out with the Mace, In with the Broom

ABDUL Ghani Hamid felt a knot of anxiety as he stood to attention in the City Hall chamber. The 23-year-old city council clerk had been summoned there to act as the English-Malay interpreter for the event of the year: the swearing-in of the first mayor of Singapore on Christmas Eve 1957.

Imagine his rising nervous tension as the man of the hour strode into the room in open defiance of pomp and protocol—no mayor's cloak, no coat, not even a tie—in an open-necked white shirt and cotton trousers accompanied by his similarly garbed councillors from his political party.

A hush fell on the formally attired VIPs and dressed-to-the-nines audience as they realised they were in for a replay of the political histrionics which had delayed the ceremony by a day.

Just the day before, when Ong Eng Guan arrived at City Hall, he had been greeted by a barrage of fire crackers from boisterous supporters. When police demanded a "ceasefire", he declared that he had authorised the fireworks. A melee then broke out, resulting in the arrests of Ong and several city councillors.

On his release in the afternoon, he stormed into City Hall demanding that the swearing-in be reconvened. He shouted: "There is no power on earth which can stop this meeting today." Despite the lack of a quorum, he refused to leave his seat and only gave up at 4.30 pm with a show of clenched fists.

What would Ong be up to next, Abdul Ghani wondered. He did not have long to wait. After being sworn in as mayor, Ong defied tradition by refusing to trail solemnly behind the mayor's gold and silver mace. Instead he ordered its removal after taking a snap vote in which 26 councillors voted in favour and none against.

The mace symbolised the city status conferred on Singapore by royal charter in 1951. Measuring 1.28 m long and weighing 3.1 kg, it was embellished with heraldic symbols incorporating the coats of arms of

Queen Elizabeth II, Sir Stamford Raffles, the East India Company, the Straits Settlements and the Colony of Singapore. Within the central shaft of the mace was a cavity containing a lambskin scroll signed by the donor, cinema magnate Loke Wan Tho.

Ong delivered a speech lambasting the colonialists for neglecting the poor and needy. Then he strode to the balcony and spoke in Mandarin through a loudspeaker to the cheering crowd outside City Hall, punctuating his speech with cries of "*merdeka*". Liberal Socialist councillor Felice Leon-Soh exclaimed: "May God protect our city of Singapore."

For Abdul Ghani, it was an unforgettable encounter with the first PAP politician to assume the mantle of authority. As the first mayor of Singapore from 22 December 1957 to 18 April 1959, Ong gave the restless masses a sneak preview of what to expect from an imminent PAP government: power to the people, and shivers to the expatriates and civil servants.

On reflection, the retired Public Utilities Board finance clerk who later became a full-time writer and painter said: "Whatever you might say about Ong, he represented the PAP then and he showed how things could be done simply and fast. I believe he had done some good for the city council." Then he added: "By the way, the mayor did not need my services on that day. He spoke excellent Malay."

No councillor present at the ceremony could possibly shake off the memory of such headline-making political melodrama. From the PAP, Sze Lih Hwa recalled Ong condemning the mace as a "relic of colonialism" while Ho Puay Choo noted that the mayor also ordered the removal of the British flag and the photograph of Queen Elizabeth II.

From the Labour Front, architect and art-lover Ho Kok Hoe was mortified when Ong's xenophobic zeal extended to the Victoria Memorial Hall where oil portraits of previous governors were stripped and discarded. He remembered asking Ong to sell each portrait to him for $100 but he refused. "Where are they now? They must have been spoilt and mouldy by now. Do you know that the painting of Swettenham is a masterpiece?"

Thankfully, the larger-than-life portrait of former Singapore governor Sir Frank Swettenham by famous American artist John Singer Sargent had been retrieved. Measuring 2.59 m high and 1.44 m wide, it is now the property of the National Museum of Singapore. Its estimated value in 1998 was $4.3 million.

To mayor Ong, as he told foreign journalists later, the dumping of the ceremonial mace and all things British was analogous to the cutting of the pigtail by Chinese revolutionaries when they overthrew the Qing dynasty in 1911.

To the sinicised who drew a parallel between British colonialism and Manchu rule, it was most liberating. To the anglicised, it was nothing short of frightening.

⌘

AT last, PAP savoured its first taste of power. Ensconced in his mayor's chair, Ong was calling the shots in City Hall while his party colleagues— Lee Kuan Yew and Goh Chew Chua—continued to sit on the opposition bench in the legislative assembly. The third PAP assemblyman, Lim Chin Siong, sat in Changi Prison.

For the 32-year-old Malacca-born, Australia-trained accountant, it marked a remarkable political rebound as only four months ago he had been ejected from the party's central executive committee (CEC).

Thanks to the mass arrests of his leftist foes, he regained his treasurer's post in the party. The baby-faced, bespectacled man was picked as mayor by the PAP councillors and endorsed by the CEC following the party's resounding victory in the city council elections on 21 December 1957.

Winning 13 out of 14 seats and with the support of two UMNO-MCA representatives, the party was able to put together a minority local government. Seventeen other seats were held by three parties at loggerheads with one another.

The fully elected 32-seat city council was distinct from the 51-member legislative assembly which operated under the Rendel Constitution for limited self-rule. Taking over from the partially elected municipal council, the city council was responsible for public utilities and social services in downtown Singapore.

Although PAP was riven by factional fighting, its leaders decided to contest the city council polls as they saw it as a dry run for the forthcoming general election. "It was an election exercise to gauge voters' support," said Ong Pang Boon.

As they had little time and meagre resources, they put up only 14 candidates. Another reason, Lee explained, was not to scare the Lim Yew Hock government. "Had we beaten them, had we fielded all 32, my belief is that we would have won easily 25, if not more. And they would have then been resentful and would take action to cripple us."

After all, their main adversary was not one another but the Liberal Socialist Party which emerged from a merger of the Progressive Party and Democratic Party. Lib-Soc was regarded by PAP as a right-wing reactionary party backed by big money and the capitalist press. Under an electoral pact, PAP, Labour Front (LF) and UMNO agreed not to fight one another and split the left-wing votes.

Francis Thomas, who was LF's secretary-general, recounted meetings in which "the Labour Front leaders tried to bluff that they knew which seats they could win, while PAP leaders who were present quite obviously knew what they were talking about".

Then-LF organising secretary Gerald de Cruz disclosed that he gave away several constituencies to PAP because he felt LF was not nursing them and that PAP candidates were "men of far greater integrity".

The two Ongs in their thirties were the leading PAP candidates as they were university graduates and effectively bilingual. Eng Guan was described by Lee "as the ablest of the lot, not a profound thinker but quick-witted" while Pang Boon was considered "reticent but steady, reliable, sober and trustworthy".

The other 12 candidates were all in their twenties and less educated. They were picked from the party branches and trade unions or recommended by one another. Lee said that he wanted "young and active men and women who would be good examples of energetic, clean, honest and dedicated leaders that workers and hawkers and taxi-drivers could identify themselves with".

Sze Lih Hwa was asked to stand for Bras Basah as he was Hainanese and the ward comprised many Hainanese constituents. Chan Chee Seng felt inadequate and only agreed to be a candidate for Jalan Besar after Lee persuaded him that if he did not, "the bad fellows would take over the country". Ho Puay Choo said yes after she was assured that Kampong Glam was small and compact enough to be covered "with two legs".

To the flash and circle, the PAP added the broom to "sweep the city clean", literally and figuratively. Apart from seeking to eliminate corruption, the party pledged to ensure a courteous and efficient administration, and provide public services and social amenities to the people.

The 33-day campaign saw 70 candidates from five parties and 11 independents vying for votes in street rallies, mass rallies and door-to-door campaigns. PAP leaders were buoyed by a growing groundswell of support for the party in the wake of the unpopular government crackdown on its leftist leaders.

The Chinese middle school students and left-wing trade unionists threw in their support. Chan Chee Seng stood on a chair at street corners to catch the attention of people on the way to market in the morning. If he ran out of words, he would invite someone from the crowd to take over the chair.

Ho Puay Choo's sewing connections paid off as helpers came from tailoring firms to join her campaign. As she and her team went from house to house, they kept tabs on the reception by making a mark in their election booklets. This enabled them to estimate the level of voter support.

The results from the ballot box shocked the English-educated out of their wits. While PAP won 13 out of 14 seats, LF took only four out of 16 and Liberal Socialists, seven out of 32. PAP only lost in Sepoy Lines by 24 votes.

Of the votes cast, Ong Eng Guan clinched the second highest score with 82 per cent in Hong Lim, followed by Ong Pang Boon with 71 per cent in Tanjong Pagar. The top honour went to Chan Choy Siong with 86 per cent in Kreta Ayer. Undeniably, the masses had bought into PAP's thundering cry of sweeping City Hall clean with a new broom.

The turnout, however, was poor as only 165,526 of the 500,000 electorate, or a mere 33 per cent, cast their votes compared to the 1955 elections when 53 per cent voted. While rain could have been one factor, many letter writers to the press blamed it on the apathy of the middle class.

"While they waste their time at the cinema, games, parties and with their wives and girlfriends, you find the illiterate, the hawkers, the farmers and the labourers go in droves to the polls, conscious of their right to vote and to utilise that right as citizens," vented one reader to *The Straits Times*.

A one-line letter read: "The results of the Singapore City Council elections show that the day of the *towkay* has gone and that of the *towgay* has arrived." It was signed "*towkuah*". In Hokkien, *towkay* referred to the big boss or the rich, and *towgay* meant the humble beansprout, the poor. *Towkuah* denoted the beancurd, the simple fare of ordinary folks.

But one result dampened the PAP's euphoria somewhat—the debut performance of a new party formed a month earlier by David Marshall.

The Workers' Party, symbolised by the hammer, fielded five candidates and won four. The inescapable conclusion was that the leftists had backed the party as a possible alternative to the PAP. Fong Sip Chee's reading was spot-on: "The left did not want to put all the eggs in one basket."

⚜

THERE had been speculation that Lee would have preferred Ong Pang Boon to be mayor rather than deputy mayor.

But all accounts indicated that the natural and indisputable choice was Ong Eng Guan. As the party treasurer and only CEC member, he outranked all the PAP city councillors. By comparison, the other Ong, as organising secretary, was a paid employee of the party.

Call him a charismatic politician or a rabble-rousing demagogue, there was no question that he loomed larger than life in the council elections—to the great discomfort of his fellow party leaders as well as the leftists who were concerned that he was stealing their thunder.

No longer was he just a bookish bookkeeper in the background but a fiery leader in the forefront exhibiting a newfound revolutionary ardour and wildly populist style that set the masses alight.

Rajaratnam hailed Ong as the only non-communist orator who could match Lim Chin Siong at a time when Lee could not speak Hokkien. Those who heard Ong during the hustings swore that his Hokkien speeches were even more powerful than Lim's.

When the young Arthur Lim listened to Ong, he was reminded of a street corner storyteller whose tales drew hordes of housewives and youngsters. Former civil servant Goh Sin Tub remarked that his speeches had a hypnotic effect on him. Former leftist Ong Chang Sam admitted that he had a "special talent in winning the hearts and minds of the masses".

Giving the flavour of a typical anti-colonial speech, former PAP activist Chong Fun Liam said that Ong would highlight the difference between the generous salary of a British bus inspector and the trifling one of a local driver and asked why there should be such a whopping gap when the latter worked so much harder than the former.

Ong had this uncanny knack of making simple folks feel good and important, Chan Chee Seng said, noting that he would preface every speech by addressing everyone in the crowd as if he was addressing his family and relatives: "Ah Pek, Ah Mm, Ah Chek, Ah So, Ah Hia, Ah Tee..." These were Hokkien terms of respect which covered the whole gamut from venerable uncle to little brother.

To convey the mesmerising effect of his speeches, Chan invoked a Hokkien idiom which meant that "he spoke so well that even the birds would fly down from the tree to listen to him".

Ong's bilingual prowess could be traced to his growing-up years in Batu Pahat, Johor. His father, a hardware retail businessman, did not want his son to be Westernised and so placed him in a government school in the morning and a private Chinese school in the afternoon. After the war, he went to Australia and graduated from Melbourne University with a bachelor of commerce degree and a diploma in public administration.

When he began work as an accountant in Singapore in 1954, the political scene was stirring with the release of the Rendel report which called for a partially elected legislative assembly. PAP founder member S Rajaratnam said he met Ong and was so impressed by his linguistic ability that he invited him to join the party. Toh Chin Chye noted that the party was then scouting for a treasurer and Ong fitted the bill nicely.

Former trade unionist Philip Lau Liat Meng claimed he recommended Ong to Toh when the latter called him to say that they were forming a political party and needed a treasurer. "The name Ong Eng Guan sprang immediately to my mind," recalled the lawyer who lost in the 1957 city council elections as an independent candidate. He said he knew Ong well as they were colleagues in the Fred Waterhouse Workers' Union. He was general secretary while Ong was the auditor.

It was over dinner in Peking Restaurant on North Bridge Road, according to Mrs Lee, that the party leaders met Ong and decided to make him the treasurer. She thought that the decision was made with "precipitate haste" on the basis of just one meeting. "I did express some reservation but not very strongly," she said.

⚜

IF the British had expected Ong to play the titular mayor and bask in the trappings of office, they were in for a rude awakening.

Eschewing any ceremonial role and not satisfied with just presiding at meetings and shaking hands with visiting dignitaries, he plunged himself into the nitty-gritty of City Hall administration. He was hell-bent on being a hands-on, brook-no-nonsense, interventionist, reformist mayor.

Not only did he jettison all the mayoral regalia, he also turned down all mayoral perks and privileges. He announced that he would continue to live in his own home and drive his four-year-old Morris Oxford. Instead of using a government car, he walked to official functions from his City Hall office.

He made it clear that he did not smoke, drink, go to the races or attend cocktail parties. He instructed staff not to address any senior civil servant as *tuan* or sir, saying that these forms of address were used by colonial officials "to suppress the minds of the people". Call him Mr Ong, mayor, friend or brother, he told an audience of watchmen, peons, sweepers and lift attendants who broke into ringing applause.

The people's mayor sought to transform City Hall into a people's forum. The doors were flung wide open for common folks to pour into the august chamber. In slippers, sandals and even barefooted, they sauntered up the 23 steps that led to the public gallery to gawk at the horseshoe-shaped table where the 32 city councillors sat. Some were teenagers in singlets and shorts who did not comprehend what was going on but joined in the clapping, booing, catcalling and slogan shouting.

If the gallery was packed, they would "crowd and stand just behind us", said Ong Pang Boon. A *Straits Times* page one picture showed people literally breathing down the necks of the city councillors. Sze Lih Hwa remembered being taken aback by the sight of dozens of people squatting on the floor.

Fong Sip Chee likened the proceedings to a circus. Former City Hall accountant Chan Kum Chee compared it to a Chinese medicine show. Goh Sin Ee, who worked at the city council, said he could hear hawkers on clogs rushing to the council meetings every Friday and making a lot of noise. "The mayor gave too much face to the public," he moaned.

For a people who once felt intimidated by the forbidding chamber, City Hall became an extension of their public neighbourhood space. For the first time, they could follow the proceedings in their mother tongues—be it Malay, Mandarin or Tamil—thanks to simultaneous verbatim translations. The exclusivity of the English language was shattered.

Never mind if business moved at a tortuous pace because of the multi-lingual interpreting. Every word spoken was translated from English into Chinese, Malay and Tamil and vice versa. It took seven minutes to translate three minutes of speech.

When the mayor gave his stridently anti-colonial policy speech at the city council's first business meeting on 8 January 1958, his Mandarin speech was translated into Malay and Tamil but not into English. Lest the English-educated missed his message, he ordered all notices in all departments to be replaced by new ones in the vernacular languages.

Then he started cracking the whip to get development programmes going. When they were achieved, he would reel off the numbers to much fanfare. At a PAP cultural show on 28 June 1958, he recited the council's six-month achievements: more than 300 standpipes, 600 street lamps, 200 bus shelters, seven clinics, three creches and 20 playing fields.

Playing unashamedly to the gallery, he reduced the price of electricity from 20 cents to 12 cents per unit for domestic consumers and raised it substantially for big consumers such as hotels and cinemas. Licence fees were lowered for hawkers, trishaw riders and taxi drivers.

The origins of Singapore's reputation as campaign country could be traced to this period when month-long campaigns were held for "anti-spitting", "anti-litter" and "anti-pests". Chan Chee Seng spoke of how they would display two big brooms on the pickup to show to the people they were coming to clean up the place.

Under the mayor's stewardship, the meet-the-people session conceived by former chief minister David Marshall was instituted in his office every Saturday from 10 am to 1 pm. This gave Ong the opportunity to listen to any complaint of corruption, rudeness or administrative inefficiency. Soon all PAP councillors fell into line, thus beginning a weekly practice by the party which continues to this very day.

Another innovation was the Public Complaints Bureau which could be regarded as the predecessor of Feedback Unit, later renamed Reach. It struck Sze Lih Hwa as a novel idea at a time when people did not know where and how to make a complaint against a government official. All they had to do, he recalled, was walk up to the top of the steps of City Hall and they would see the desk manned by officials—in the open.

Complaints ranged from difficulties in getting electricity, water and gas supplies to harassment and corruption. Within a few weeks of the formation of the bureau, hundreds of people came to lodge complaints. *Nanyang Siang Pau* reported on 14 January 1958 that more than 400 cases of corruption were investigated and 20 cases brought to court for prosecution.

The first salvo was fired in the battle against the corruption which had plagued Singapore since the end of the war.

Look beyond the controversy of the Ong Eng Guan's mayorship, and you will realise that a number of municipal ideas and innovations which came to characterise the PAP government were seeded in the city council years.

⚜

WHEN the councillors trooped into a City Hall room for a meeting and found that there were not enough seats, Mayor Ong summoned R Middleton Smith, the acting chief administrative officer of the city council, and hollered: "Go and get chairs." The British expatriate left and came back carrying one chair after another.

Chan Chee Seng felt compelled to lend a hand. "I was a witness. I felt so bad I went to help him carry the chairs." The former city councillor, who related this anecdote, could not help admiring the stoic endurance and phlegmatic patience of British colonial officials who bore the brunt of Ong's berating and bullying. "They were really good and very cultivated. I could not understand why the mayor had to treat them in such a way."

Goh Sin Ee, who was a chief officer in the maintenance department in the city council, recalled attending a meeting convened by Ong for all the heads of departments. When the mayor commented that the Europeans were passing their work to Asian heads, an expatriate expressed disagreement. Goh was shocked when Ong "pointed his finger at the officer and asked him to get out".

Ong's crusade against the establishment has been described by some writers as the nearest to a Singapore equivalent of the fall of the Bastille in 1789 when peasants seized the symbol of royal tyranny and ignited the French Revolution.

Many heads rolled—metaphorically. It was a terrifying situation, Rajaratnam said, when Ong treated hawkers as top dogs and began sacking staff.

The mayor was particularly harsh on the expatriates as he wanted to expose their inefficiency and racial prejudice against Asians: a commercial secretary was sacked for allegedly embracing a young Chinese typist; a city engineer was reprimanded for insulting the dignity of the council by bringing his dog into City Hall; and a city analyst was fined $200 a month for a year for allegedly being rude to the mayor.

Ong abolished the monopoly of a European legal firm which enjoyed all of the city council legal work and rescinded the Malayanisation scheme which allowed for the gradual retirement of expatriates with handsome provident fund benefits.

Local civil servants who incurred his wrath were subjected to the humiliation of a dressing down in front of the people who complained against them. The mayor did not allow staff to read newspapers or drink tea or coffee at work. He would prowl around the office and eavesdrop on conversations. If anybody was found to be a bookie, he was sacked on the spot. If he was found to be rude to the public, he would have to give a lengthy and satisfactory explanation or face punitive action.

Ong could not tolerate long queues and tardy responses to letters and enquiries from the public. He expected bills to be settled within 15 minutes at the counter. A vehicle inspector with 22 years' service lost his job for allegedly keeping a taxi driver waiting for almost an hour before taking down a report from him. An efficiency officer was appointed to execute policies and investigate complaints.

Civil servants had to obey the mayor, recalled Goh Sin Ee, "if not, we had to get out of the job". If anyone failed to do his work properly, he would be downgraded and would have to settle for lesser pay, he said.

P C Marcus, who was the "efficiency expert" in the city council and later became the deputy chief administrative officer, summed it up by saying that Ong "put the fear of God in staff, both expats and local". Later even Marcus himself, who was close to PAP leaders, fell out with Ong.

The mayor had no compunction about ordering staff to get out of their offices to clean up the city. Retired civil servants still chafed at the memory saying it was akin to the hard labour imposed on professionals in communist countries. Forced to do menial labour, some felt as if Ong was behaving like a communist leader and that Singapore was going communist.

Fong Sip Chee recounted an operation dubbed Operation Pantai Chantek ("Beautiful Beach" in Malay) in which frightened civil servants were made to dig up stones and clean up Nicoll Highway.

City council officers were rostered to sweep different roads on different days. Goh Sin Ee found himself in a spot when he was assigned to sweep an area where he was known to most of the shopkeepers. He confessed that he had to buy a "big Chinese type of hat" to shield him from the sun—and embarrassment.

THE controversy surrounding mayor Ong's 16-month stewardship of the city council has cast a long shadow over his legacy, making it hazardous to weigh its pluses and minuses objectively.

In most PAP literature, he has been demonised as a tyrant, a megalomaniac and the Great Dictator, named after the Charlie Chaplin movie of the period which spoofed Adolf Hitler. Five decades later, he still evoked strong emotions among those who knew and worked with him.

Did Ong's enormous popularity, inflammatory anti-British rhetoric and much-ballyhooed municipal achievements contribute to PAP's victory in the 1959 elections? Historians leaned to the view propounded by American scholar Thomas J Bellows that the city council years were of inestimable benefit to the party and assured it of electoral success.

Whatever pejorative overtones it might have acquired through the prism of history, his administration gave the people—rightly or wrongly— an idea and flavour of what to expect from a national PAP government.

No less than the former deputy mayor himself, Ong Pang Boon, had acknowledged the achievements of the PAP city council in getting rid of corruption, providing vital services such as standpipes, street lighting, creches and public clinics and promoting the use of mother tongues in official communication for the first time. "All these were neglected by the previous council; the effect was to make people feel that the council was theirs," he said.

Toh Chin Chye also gravitated to the view that the council delivered the goods to the people. In particular, he noted that the liberal issue of hawkers' licences provided much-needed social relief by generating self-employment and jobs at a time when many people were out of work.

The PAP-run council demonstrated to the people that the party could get things done in a way different from other administrations, former councillor Sze Lih Hwa pointed out. "The idea began to form in people's minds that if the PAP could do so much in the city council when its power was limited, what more if the PAP were to form the government?"

Another former councillor, Ho Puay Choo, commended Ong's campaigns to instil courtesy and a sense of service among government officials as she related how ordinary folks were often oppressed by red tape and bureaucratic arrogance. She cited her visits to government departments where staff were reluctant to help her because she could not speak English.

After Ong became mayor, the situation at public counters was reversed. The member of the public was no longer expected to find an English-speaking person to translate for him. Instead the onus was on the department to look for an officer who could speak in the language of the person—be it in Mandarin, Malay or Tamil.

Fong Sip Chee took the view that Ong "did tremendous good by arousing the people in City Hall while Lee played elder statesman in the assembly". In the absence of Lim Chin Siong from the hustings, he believed that support for Ong helped to carry PAP through the 1959 elections.

It was because of the council's work, according to former assemblyman Ong Chang Sam, that people formed a good impression of PAP and regarded it as the ideal political party. Another former assemblyman S V Lingam had no doubt that the council's meet-the-people sessions were effective in swinging the votes to the PAP in 1959.

Even highly critical Lee Khoon Choy, known for his blunt comments, admitted that Ong made his biggest contribution as mayor of Singapore by working very hard and building up the image of "a very clean, very dynamic, efficient PAP which shook up the city council, fought the whites and backed the underdogs".

For a more authoritative assessment of Ong's legacy, consider Rajaratnam's contention that PAP's City Hall became far more of a forum in dealing with national affairs than Lim Yew Hock's legislative assembly. He argued that it helped to build up the reputation of PAP as the first political party with a mass character and ability to mobilise mass action.

Although former leftists disliked Ong intensely, they found it hard to dismiss his contributions altogether. Fong Swee Suan lauded his mass clean-up campaigns and his efforts in making government services accessible to the people. He agreed with the general view that Ong's popularity and the council's track record helped steer PAP to victory in the 1959 elections.

With the benefit of hindsight, former senior civil servants conceded grudgingly that Ong gave a timely wake-up call and reality check to the government. Sim Kee Boon, a retired permanent secretary, said it "shook the civil service out of its slumber". Ngiam Tong Dow, another former permanent secretary, wished, partly tongue-in-cheek, that there was a similar shake-up to jolt complacency in government service.

In an appraisal from the vanquished, Gerald de Cruz of Labour Front said that undoubtedly the mayor laid the foundation for greater PAP support and that much of the credit of the PAP victory in 1959 must go to

Ong. "He was a kind of a lesser David Marshall in a sense. He didn't have David Marshall's integrity, but he had the common touch. He knew what people wanted. He played on those needs and fears and aspirations."

The topmost PAP leaders, however, tended to downplay the electoral significance of Ong's mayorship. Goh Keng Swee slammed Ong for reducing the whole business of local government to absolute shambles. Even if there were no city council elections, he argued, PAP would have won because the masses could only distinguish between the good guys, the PAP, and the bad ones, the colonial stooges.

When Devan Nair commented on the way in which Ong ran the city council and demoralised the entire civil service, he could not help plunging into the scatological. By sacking engineers right and left, he said, he would have destroyed Singapore's flush system. "You pull the flush ... the *sai* ("faeces" in Hokkien), instead of going down, would come out."

Ong has disappeared from public view since his exit from politics in the 1960s. His voice is conspicuously missing in all the books on the PAP. The closest to getting his side of the story would be to read two articles that he penned for a PAP souvenir publication in 1958.

In the first, Ong wrote that he was "able to give a new interpretation to the role of mayor", one that was contrary to expectations that he would play the role of a mere figurehead. His aims, he stated, were to eliminate corruption and raise the efficiency of the council which had been synonymous with corruption for the past 10 years.

It was not possible for the party to make great changes as PAP lacked a majority, he said, so as mayor he conducted surprise visits in all the departments where he observed long waiting times to pay bills and rude treatment of the public.

"Instead of allowing key administrators in the city council to pass the buck, we told them what are our objectives and the target dates we expect to achieve those objectives. Almost every week I had to check progress reports, talk to men in charge and at times reprimand them for not being up to date," he said. For the first time, he added, the council could tell the public "how much they can give them and when they can give them".

In the other article, the mayor described the council which the PAP took over as "a cesspool of maladministration, corruption and inefficiency". For such a big public institution with nearly 13,000 workers and a budget of $125 million, he said, there was no proper accounting system and budgetary procedures.

He said that the way the council worked was not conducive to good government as no party could be held legally responsible for anything that went wrong. PAP councillors did not have the majority vote to push through their proposed schemes while councillors of other parties could obstruct them. For example, he noted that the meet-the-people sessions were stopped as the council refused to authorise a staff increase to cater for the extra workload.

Combine administrative cumbersomeness with Ong's penchant for theatrics and you would have the ingredients for some absurd situations. Once the mayor was 15 minutes late for a committee meeting and the non-PAP councillors elected a chairman and went ahead with the proceedings. When Ong arrived, he claimed they had exceeded their authority and rescinded all their decisions. The non-PAP councillors walked out. Ho Puay Choo spoke despairingly of meetings which started in the afternoon and ended around 3 or 4 am.

After 15 months of controversy in City Hall, the Lim Yew Hock government swung into action. On 27 March 1959, local government minister Hamid Jumat took over some powers of the council relating to staff and finance matters. Then he convened a commission of inquiry from 7 April to 26 May 1959.

With full press coverage, the shortcomings of a system in which the representatives of the local and central government came from different parties were exposed. The future of the city council hung by a slender thread as Singapore went to the polls a few days later.

✦

INITIALLY, the 33-year-old seamen's welfare officer welcomed the arrival of the "new broom" in City Hall.

But doubts began to gnaw at him when civil servants were rounded up on weekends to build a sea wall along Nicoll Highway. He felt that it smacked very much of communist methods.

Then with each sacking of an expatriate or a government servant, his apprehension grew. It did not help that rumours were rapidly making the rounds about civil servants who, if they were not booted out, would find themselves with a table but no chair in the office.

He admitted that this sense of persecution coloured his concerns about the PAP immediately before the 1959 elections.

What gave him cause for greater concern was that Ong and his minions seemed to be running the city council in a dictatorial way without being checked by the party leaders.

He found himself racked by soul-searching questions: Was the PAP like Ong? Was he doing all these things with the concurrence of the PAP? What was the stand of the PAP leadership? What could he expect if PAP formed the government?

Like most long-suffering civil servants, he braced himself for the unknown and the unpredictable as the general election went into full swing and threatened to bring Ong and his ilk to full power over a self-governing Singapore.

He was not sure if he had a future under a PAP government. But his name would one day be affixed to the highest office of independent Singapore: Sellapan Ramanathan Nathan.

9

Power to the Poor Man's Party

CALL him gruff, aloof and intimidating. But if there was anyone who had a finger on the pulse of Singapore in the 1950s, it was Goh Keng Swee who conducted a seminal social survey titled "Urban Incomes and Housing (1953–54)".

The language may be clinically dry but the 215-page text tells the story of degrading poverty, appalling overcrowding, abominable housing and jaw-dropping income disparities.

It painted a Third World Singapore mired in the sepia-toned poverty and squalor that Western writers and film-makers found so picturesque and exotic. But for elderly Singaporeans who remembered living through it all, the reality was one of long-suffering pain and unmitigated anguish.

It was a time when mothers took in the washing to earn a few dollars while fathers despaired of ever finding a job. Children shared everything from patched-up clothes to worn-out shoes and walked kilometres to school to save a few cents of bus fare. Meat was only seen during Chinese New Year reunion dinners.

People slept under an *attap* roof surrounded by chickens, ducks and pigs or lived with a dozen family members in a Chinatown cubicle where water came from a well and light flickered from a kerosene lamp. The toilet was just a hole in the ground.

As director of social welfare, Goh amassed a mind-boggling array of facts and figures which was later used as election ammunition when he joined PAP to fight in the 1959 polls. He could fathom the heart-wrenching issues of unemployment, housing and education in a way no huckstering politician could.

As an economist with a penetrating mind, he realised how tenuous Singapore's viability was—an island of 580 sq km (before land was reclaimed from the sea) with no natural resources. How could an economy based on entrepôt trade, farming and simple manufacturing support a population of 1.5 million and growing at 62,000 or 4.1 per cent a year?

With rare empathy for a privileged Straits-born Chinese, he understood the plight of the Chinese-educated who ended up as bus drivers and labourers. Their education was neglected and they were denied job opportunities in the public sector. Unlike their English-educated counterparts, they saw a dead end in British Singapore.

To the socialist in Goh, their sense of grievance and injustice was manifested in industrial strife and social unrest—the Marxist recipe for a revolution.

To rub more salt into their wounds, the Chinese-educated were given short shrift by the constitutional changes which led to a bizarre situation in which Indian voters outnumbered the Chinese. Treated as Singapore-born Chinese and citizens of China, they were not granted United Kingdom citizenship which would qualify them to vote.

In 1948 and 1951, many could not vote; in 1955, many did not bother to register and vote. It was only with the creation of Singapore citizenship, automatic registration and compulsory voting for the 1959 polls that they were empowered to put a cross on the ballot.

Suddenly the masses were in ferment—they wanted change but who would provide the change? Which party could drive the white man out of the country, remedy the social injustices and economic wrongs and give them hope and a better deal?

Should they vote for the upstart PAP or the newly formed Singapore People's Alliance (SPA), which led the ruling coalition government, or the Liberal Socialists (Lib-Soc), which resulted from an amalgamation of the Progressive and Democratic Parties, or UMNO/MCA which were affiliated to their parent parties in the newly independent Federation of Malaya?

⚬⚭⚬

ONCE again, PAP found itself at a political crossroads. Should it capture power under the new constitution which provided for a fully-elected 51-member legislative assembly or just sit on the opposition bench and let the ruling party make all the mistakes?

S Rajaratnam was against mounting an all-out bid as he believed that the government would run into difficulties given the lack of full independence, the dim prospects of immediate merger with Malaya and the enormity of Singapore's economic and social problems.

But the proponents of full power won the day. They argued that PAP could not afford to let the Lim Yew Hock government run down Singapore any further and they feared that it would not play by the rules in the next elections when the British were no longer around to act as referee.

Mrs Lee Kuan Yew recalled that her husband's concern was not whether PAP would win but what would happen if Lim Yew Hock continued for another term. "Would there be such a slide in standards in the administration that by the next election, say, 1963, the damage would have been beyond repair?" she asked.

Furthermore, it would be political folly to ignore the growing wave of support for the flash and lightning as evident in the December 1957 city council elections and the July 1958 Kallang by-election. Why should PAP give away its ground to another leftist party?

But it was tough scrambling around for 51 candidates at short notice after the legislative assembly was dissolved on 31 March 1959. PAP was all but snubbed by the professional class. The few tertiary-educated candidates included the leaders themselves—Lee Kuan Yew, Toh Chin Chye, Ong Pang Boon, Ong Eng Guan, Goh Keng Swee and K M Byrne.

They were so short of people that Lee roped in his brother-in-law and fellow Raffles College alumnus Yong Nyuk Lin. Married to Mrs Lee's older sister, Yong remembered that his father-in-law was hopping mad when he learnt that he was going into politics. After all, it was the banker Kwa Siew Tee who had encouraged him to make the career switch from teaching to insurance.

Rajaratnam was prevailed upon by Lee to resign from *The Straits Times* to join the field. The journalist said he had doubts about his capability and temperament to be a politician. "So I said, well, I'll think about it. Of course, he kept on arguing. And even my wife was not quite sure that active politics is what I'm cut out for."

There were no tea parties to invite potential candidates or formal interviews to screen them. Asked how they were picked, Toh replied: "Anybody who walked in. So long as from hearsay this chap was not a pro-communist or communist, he could stand for us."

Names were plucked from party branches and trade unions. Party workers who had barely left their adolescent years were shocked when they were asked to stand. Pitted against the prominent names of the day, they felt hopelessly inadequate in experience and expertise.

Ong Chang Sam said he was only 21, a shop assistant, poorly educated and financially broke when he was told to stand in Chua Chu Kang. "Ong Pang Boon said this was the decision of the CEC and I was not supposed to decline. I told him I did not even know where Chua Chu Kang was. I told him I could not stand but he said that was an order."

Lee's over-riding consideration was that the party should assemble a composite team reflecting the population in ethnic, racial and educational breakdown. "We wanted to present ourselves as a balanced party. Not of eggheads and intellectuals," he said.

The result of the party's first big talent quest was a motley collection of candidates ranging from doctorate-holders to school dropouts, from doctors, journalists, teachers and engineers to clerks, farmers, shopkeepers and dressmakers.

People knew Ong Pang Boon as a mild-mannered person who spoke in a soft monotone. But when queried why two barbers were chosen for the elections, he raised his voice by a few decibels: "So what! They had political convictions and had the courage to stand up and be counted with the PAP. They made their contributions, you don't always need people of ministerial calibre, you need the grassroots types to be in touch with the people."

One barber was Tee Kim Leng. He said that when he was picked to be the candidate for Punggol, the leaders of the Punggol branch protested saying they did not want a *ti tao kia* ("barber boy" in Hokkien) but a better educated person to be their legislative assemblyman. So vehement was their objection that they went to see Lee at his Oxley Road home to demand his removal as the candidate. Lee gave in and put a contractor Ng Teng Kian, who had at least a secondary school education, in his place.

Tee said that PAP then decided to field him in Pasir Panjang where it did not intend to contest originally. His independent opponent, H J C Kulasingha, a merchant, seemed assured of electoral victory as he was very popular with the residents. Tee felt vindicated when he became the first PAP candidate to win in the elections.

Nothing is more powerful than an idea whose time has come, said French novelist Victor Hugo (1802–1885). In 1959, the idea for the people of Singapore was PAP. Its platform pledging an honest, clean and responsive government struck an emotional resonance with the masses.

Propagated through mass rallies week after week, its manifesto called for an elimination of corruption, more jobs, more schools, support for Chinese education, a united labour movement, low-cost public housing and a women's charter.

Holding up a sheaf of yellowing speakers' notes in an interview, Sheng Nam Chin, who was then standing in Nee Soon, said that they were issued by PAP HQ to all candidates indicating what they could talk about. "We can emphasise whatever we like to emphasise. We can speak in whatever languages. But we can only speak on what is here, so every candidate's speech will be linked through a common thread."

For example, the speakers' notes on trade unions provided facts and figures and key points for the candidates to attack the Lim Yew Hock government for favouring big business and foreign interests at the expense of the workers. This was followed by an elaboration of what the PAP would do when it assumed power—provide more research facilities for workers, set up a permanent and independent court of labour, and involve trade unions in economic development.

Applying his prodigious analytical prowess to the way PAP organised the elections, Goh put it down to what he called "the principle of decentralised spontaneous organisation". Citing a mass meeting in Pasir Panjang as an example, he noted that the nearest branch to the ward would make all the physical arrangements such as hiring lorries, getting permits, renting loudspeakers, informing the speakers and climbing trees to put up banners and posters.

The support for PAP was so overwhelming that all one had to do was to set up a table anywhere, put up the party flag and helpers would turn up spontaneously. At a rally, he said, just shout "*merdeka*" and lambast the white men and there would be spontaneous applause.

To the English-educated middle class, the spectre of a pro-communist party in power evoked frightening images of being stripped of their property and thrown into communes. Their fears were fuelled by PAP's no-holds-barred assault against employers and big business for exploiting workers.

PAP did nothing to allay their suspicions during the campaign when Lee threatened to lock up editors and journalists if they soured up ties between Singapore and Malaya. Their sense of foreboding deepened when companies started making plans to leave Singapore.

To these people then, their last straw of hope lay with the anti-communist parties—the Singapore People's Alliance (SPA) under chief minister Lim Yew Hock which was formed from part of Labour Front (LF) and part of Liberal Socialists in November 1958, and Lib-Soc, as it was called, which emerged from a fusion of the pro-establishment Progressive Party and pro-business Democratic Party in January 1956.

For those banking on immediate merger with Malaya to foil the communist threat, their bet was on UMNO and the Malayan Chinese Association (MCA) which were affiliated to their parent parties in the newly independent Federation of Malaya.

Earlier attempts at forging an SPA-LibSoc-UMNO/MCA united front collapsed because of ego clashes, turf battles and internal bickering. Despite the formation of SPA, LF and Lib-Soc continued their independent existence.

The spectacular failure of the so-called united front was best seen in the results of the city council by-election for Kallang on 26 July 1958. Although LF and Lib-Soc put up a joint candidate, Chinese newspaper journalist Lim Ser Puan, they could not edge out PAP's Buang Omar Junid, a Middle Road trade unionist.

As the by-election was held before the general election that was to be called under the new constitution, Kallang was seen as a barometer of PAP support. Reeling on the ropes, Lim Yew Hock clung on to his coalition government until the very last day of its term before dissolving the legislative assembly on 31 March 1959.

Then-Workers' Party (WP) chief David Marshall recounted a rendezvous with the desperate chief minister in the vault of a bank during which Lim proposed to arrest Lee and several others and pleaded with the lawyer to keep his silence. "I said: 'Yew Hock, what are we fighting for? We are fighting for democracy. We are fighting for people to express their will. If they want PAP, that's the people's choice, although I think they are wrong. If you put them in prison, I'll shout from the housetop.' We parted very quickly."

⁂

ONE day Gerald de Cruz gave a lift to his neighbour, a broker named Norcutt Jansen. On their journey downtown, the LF organising secretary was baffled when his passenger asked for his help in contacting education minister Chew Swee Kee.

Jansen then made the shocking revelation that he was part of a syndicate which sold two tin mines in Ipoh to Chew for $600,000 and he wanted to collect his commission.

Where on earth did Chew, a former civil servant, get this kind of money? de Cruz alerted his party secretary-general, works and communication minister Francis Thomas, right away. Thomas checked with chief minister Lim Yew Hock and Chew himself but "found it very difficult to get a clear picture of where this money had come from".

As de Cruz related his role in the scandal that rocked Singapore, he noted that Thomas was a highly strung man of high principles. When the minister failed to obtain any clarification, he went to see the leader of the opposition who was none other than Lee Kuan Yew.

Arthur Lim, who was then the LF assistant secretary-general, remembered that de Cruz and he hung outside the chief minister's office while Thomas spoke to him for about an hour. "Lim Yew Hock laughed off this matter. Since he did not take it seriously, Thomas went to Lee," he said.

The information that Lee received was political dynamite. PAP chairman Toh laid the detonation charge at a mass rally in Hong Lim Green on 15 February 1959 when he revealed that an income tax investigation into a half-million-dollar account at the National City Bank of New York in the name of a minister was choked off quickly because the money, being a political gift, was not liable for income tax.

Two days later Lee tabled a motion for a commission of inquiry and fingered Chew, resulting in an uproar that led to Chew's resignation from the ministry and the legislative assembly.

During the inquiry, it was learnt that the money had been given to LF through Chew to finance the 1959 elections. It transpired that as LF president before he joined SPA, Chew had received a total of $701,593.47 on behalf of the party from a foreign source—$519,083.96 on 20 October 1957 and $182,509.51 on 24 April 1958.

Chew was quoted as saying that the source of the funds was "certain foreign well-wishers of Singapore Labour Front" and that they were meant to fight subversion and strengthen the party as an "effective bulwark against communism".

Recalling the bombshell revelation, Toh confirmed that the information came from Lee and was deliberately timed to maximise damage to the government. It was all orchestrated—he would fire the first salvo in a mass rally and Lee would unmask the minister in the chamber.

Mrs Lee recalled overhearing Lee, Goh, Byrne and Rajaratnam at a meeting in Lee and Lee. "I am quite sure they discussed Chew Swee

Kee, the money in that account, and whether Toh Chin Chye was going to announce it at that first meeting. I remember my husband saying, well, Chin Chye is letting off the bomb that's starting this election campaign."

There had been some debate on whether the Chew Swee Kee case fitted the definition of corruption. After all, he had declared the political donation to the authorities and income tax officers had not improperly exempted the gift from taxation.

But in PAP's book, you are corrupt if you "sell out" Singapore to outsiders by accepting gifts secretly from them.

What sunk Chew in deeper morass was that he embezzled the political donation for personal use. The inquiry heard that Chew dipped into the funds to buy houses and tin mines and give $50,000 worth of shares to Kartini binte Abdul Mulok, the wife of UMNO Singapore president and local government minister Hamid Jumat.

Whether it was Taiwanese or American or Central Intelligence Agency money, the damage to the ruling party was politically irreparable. de Cruz believed that the Chew Swee Kee scandal was "a great factor in destroying people's confidence in Lim Yew Hock."

His diagnosis was borne out in the ballot box. SPA lost 35 seats, hanging on to only the four middle class constituencies of Joo Chiat, Cairnhill, Tanglin and Mountbatten. Its ally, UMNO/MCA, was luckier, snapping up the three Malay-dominated constituencies of Geylang Serai, Southern Islands and Kampung Kembangan.

Not a single seat went to Lib-Soc. Out of its 32 candidates, 20 lost their deposits. The marriage between English-educated professionals and Chinese-speaking merchants had foundered on the rocks. The decimation of the right was complete.

The left-wing parties did not fare any better because of the decision by the underground to give unstinting support to PAP. Workers' Party ended up with nothing despite its amazing results in the 1957 city council elections. Partai Rakyat lost all four seats to the chagrin of Malay socialists.

PAP's victory was never in doubt. It won 43 out of 51 seats, exceeding Lee's expectation of 35. But he noted that although the party gained 84.3 per cent of the seats in the legislative assembly, it received only 281,891 of the 527,919 votes cast, or 53.4 per cent. Votes cast included 6,648 spoilt votes. If you go by the current Singapore Elections Department practice of calculating the result based on valid votes cast and excluding the spoilt votes, then PAP's win would be 54 per cent.

Putting it down to the vagaries of the first-past-the-post-system, Lee said that it was "a sobering reminder that the mass rallies, however impressive, didn't reflect the 47 per cent that didn't vote for us, that voted against us".

No one, however, could take away the magnitude and scale of its success. PAP won all seven straight fights. In 23 other constituencies, every PAP candidate polled more than the combined votes of all his or her opponents. Even less educated twenty-somethings could defeat seasoned politicians. Fung Yin Ching, a 25-year-old Chinese-educated woman welfare worker toppled 40-year-old commerce and industry minister J M Jumabhoy in Stamford.

Ong Eng Guan chalked up the biggest win with 8,834 votes in Hong Lim where he thrashed his three opponents with an absolute majority of 7,642 votes. At the other end in River Valley, Lim Cheng Lock with 3,430 votes beat SPA's Soh Ghee Soon by five votes on a recount. The first count was six. Third-placed Tan Ek Khoo of Lib-Soc received 2,529 votes.

The River Valley result reflected the impact of the split votes and the disarray of the anti-PAP parties. If they had an electoral pact, they could have denied PAP such a thumping victory. An editorial in *The Straits Times* on 1 June 1959 calculated that these parties could have won 18 instead of eight seats if they had combined their forces.

Indeed PAP's campaign strategy paid off handsomely. By holding the cards close to its chest until nomination day and unexpectedly fielding candidates in all 51 seats, the party threw the opposition off-guard. Had the latter read its intentions early, it could have redeployed its resources to meet the challenge.

PAP could afford to ignore the sensitivities of the English-educated minority as it capitalised on the mass sentiment for change buoyed up by its legions of leftist supporters from the trade unions and Chinese schools.

Even the constitutional reforms and electoral changes conspired to favour PAP. With the widening of the franchise and automatic registration, the Chinese-speaking masses could cast their votes and flex their political muscles. As former Progressive Party secretary-general Chan Kum Chee pointed out: "Lim Yew Hock gave citizenship to all but that killed him."

The morning after the elections, Mrs Lee went for a stroll with her husband and her second son Hsien Yang in the Botanic Gardens. A Malay gardener recognised Lee and greeted him "*Selamat Berjaya*". The congratulations were pouring in but there was little time to savour victory.

GOH Sin Tub was in charge of staff complaints in the education ministry when a St Andrew's School teacher named Francis Thomas came to see him one day.

For a moment, he wondered if the Welshman was about to gripe about his pay. He was right. Thomas wanted to talk about his expatriate allowance. But what he said floored the civil servant.

As he recollected, Thomas told him: "I've come to ask you to stop paying me the expatriate allowance. Now that I am a Singapore citizen, I cannot accept the allowance."

Despite Goh's clarification of his contractual entitlement, he refused to reconsider. "It was a matter of right and wrong with him, a matter of pride in his citizenship, not of wording of contract," he spoke endearingly of the man who went on to be communications and works minister in the LF government and a leading educationist and social worker.

Thomas was the very paragon of unimpeachable integrity. Reputed for his kindness and empathy for the less fortunate, he was held in high esteem by his former students, colleagues and all those who knew him. He was described by Lee as "the only honest man in the Labour Front".

Born in Wales in April 1912 and educated at Cambridge, the Anglican clergyman's son came to teach in St Andrew's School in 1934. During the Second World War, he was captured and sent to work on the Siam-Burma "Death Railway". After the war he became involved in politics, first with Labour Party, then with LF.

During the tumultuous days of 1959, he recorded his thoughts on the collapse of the LF-led government. The diary was supposed to form the basis of his memoirs titled *Politics of Defeat*. But he could only complete two chapters before he died of cancer in 1977 at the age of 65.

People knew how and why PAP won in 1959, he wrote in his account, but it took two hands to clap. "PAP had leadership and political skills to win elections but they needed the corruption and stupidities of the people then in power to get their landslide."

Giving his perspective from the losing side, he pinpointed several key factors which led to the defeat of the Lim Yew Hock government. The first was the organisational mess which saw LF losing control of its branches and reeling from one debacle to another—from the city council election fiasco to the string of by-election defeats.

The second was party president Lim Yew Hock's "habitual reliance on men of bad character" in the Singapore Trade Union Congress (STUC) who resorted to street corner coercion. The party was packed with gangsters "prepared to line up against the communists in return for licence to widen their field of intimidation and corruption".

Describing the July 1958 Kallang by-election as "very dirty", Thomas referred to a thug attack on PAP helpers. He said he was so concerned about the use of secret society men against PAP activists that he passed the word to the British Labour Party and political journalists and sought assurance that the government would not stand idle if gangsters gained the upper hand.

Next he cited an agreement to clean up the party to dispel widespread rumours of increasing corruption around Lim Yew Hock. As a start, at a party conference in early 1958, Thomas was elected secretary-general, Arthur Lim as assistant secretary-general and Stanley Chua as treasurer.

Thomas said that he then "waited for the other side of the bargain … getting rid of those who disgraced the party in the eyes of the voters … it was late but there might still be time to reconstruct the party and begin to win the local leadership to our side through which we could form a mass base, but nothing happened".

The crooked and strong-arm men remained, he penned despairingly. In the end, Thomas, Lim and Chua felt like "a dummy leadership". The three of them were "like the little figures of bride and bridegroom one sometimes see stuck on the top of a wedding cake. We were impotent, cut off from creative work, dummies intended to reassure the respectable public without being allowed to alter the character of the party".

Questioning Lim Yew Hock's leadership ability, he said that "there was no attempt to create genuine bonds of common understanding and purpose between the English-educated leadership and the Chinese-educated from whom most of the votes would have to come".

To make matters worse, they were often left in the dark about their leader's initiatives such as his collaboration with Lib-Soc and the proposed formation of the United Socialist Front. They had "to make the worst of the rumours and reports that reached them". That was the last straw for Thomas.

When Lee demanded a commission of inquiry into the allegations against Chew Swee Kee, Thomas crossed the floor and sat with the opposition. Towards the end, he said that he was quite clear that he wanted

Lee and his PAP to win the 1959 elections and that the future of LF was secondary.

During this time, he said he had "developed immense respect and affection for Lee. Partly he was clearly the man who might keep Singapore safe among so many dangers, but more important to me was his personal quality. He was a man capable of dedicating himself to the hardest kind of service to his fellow men, the almost intolerable burden of top-level leadership".

⁕

FROM the small town of Sadao in southern Thailand, the most hunted man in Malaya with a price tag of $250,000 was avidly tracking the run-up to the May 1959 elections.

MCP secretary-general Chin Peng had a vested interest in the result. *Ma lai ya gong chan dang*, as the party is known in Mandarin, had agreed with the town committee in Singapore—MCP's local branch—to support PAP.

In his memoirs *My Side of History*, he said that he could not place a figure on the voting population controlled by MCP in 1959. "But I can certainly say that most of the island's workers sympathised with the left-wing trade unions. Without the electoral support of MCP's supporters, sympathisers and fellow travellers, he contended, Lee "would never have achieved his stunning 43-seat victory in the 51 constituencies".

Former communist underground leader Fang Chuang Pi explained that they had to form a united front with PAP to fight the elections by proxy as they had been locked out of legal politics by the Emergency regulations.

But he complained that it was an unequal united front as the Mandarin-speaking did all the work while the English-speaking wielded all the power.

The communists supported Lee, another former MCP activist Fang Mingwu reiterated, but they did not trust him completely. He remembered that they had recommended many candidates to Lee for the 1959 polls who were rejected. Instead, he said, "We saw many names, including Dr Lee Siew Choh, whom we had never heard of. MCP was not happy but it was in a fix. Having given the support to Lee, it could not ask supporters to reverse it overnight."

Conventional wisdom had it that the PAP non-communist leaders rode to electoral victory on the mass support of the pro-communists. This was to give rise to the fabled metaphor that had come to embody the PAP story—riding the tiger.

No doubt the students and trade unionists directed by communist elements helped to campaign vigorously for the party. No less than Devan Nair, who had the inside track on the underground, stated categorically that the votes were delivered by the communist united front.

But the sceptics pointed out that PAP secured just over 50 per cent of the votes in the 1959 polls, meaning that the ground tended by the leftists could not have constituted an overwhelming majority of the population.

Goh Keng Swee maintained that PAP won because the masses did not distinguish between the Lim Chin Siong and Lee Kuan Yew factions in PAP. Lee argued that PAP triumphed because Labour Front was destroyed by its crackdown on Chinese High School and Chung Cheng High School students in the 1956 riots.

While Lee was dismissive of the lower echelon communist leaders, he placed a high premium on the leading leftists in jail. He wanted to get them on board so that they would not undermine the party at the hustings. But he was unsure of their allegiance.

Conversely, the detainees wanted PAP to win the elections to unlock the prison gates. Nair recalled that his prison mates were horrified one day when Lee said that PAP would not seek to form the government as he could not trust them. They pledged their support but Lee was not satisfied with verbal assurances.

Aided by Nair, the master wordsmith, Lee pinned them down in the drafting of a document called "The Ends and Means of Socialism" which would encapsulate their political stand and support for PAP.

The crafting of the document coincided with a period of intense soul-searching among the detainees. Affected by events in Eastern Europe which saw workers' uprisings being crushed by Soviet tanks, they were embroiled in heated debates on revolutionary communism versus democratic socialism.

One person in particular was beginning to come round to the view that it was wrong to apply communism to peninsular Malaya. Disillusioned by communist propaganda and Chinese chauvinism, Nair began maintaining a close liaison with Lee during his prison visits.

S Woodhull noticed their warming relationship and feared that Lee had gained a hold on him. "We could see that Devan Nair was changing his tune," he said.

As for the document, he said that it became the subject of much unpleasantness because of the wrangling over the release of the detainees. He and other leftists insisted on the release of all detainees and not just a few of them. "The position became extremely tense but Devan insisted that we sign it and that we must accept Lee's undertaking—at all costs."

Attributing it to the handiwork of Nair and Lee, Woodhull made clear that the document was "never volunteered by us and was produced under great reluctance by most of us". They all felt compelled to sign, he said, because not to sign would mean an open rift between them and Lee.

There were wild and frenzied scenes of joy for PAP supporters when the last results were announced at 2.40 in the morning. At the Gan Eng Seng School counting centre, Lee told reporters that "the people's verdict is clear and decisive. Nothing more can be added to it. It is a victory of right over wrong, clean over dirty, righteousness over evil."

A jubilant Lee Gek Seng and others hurried to No 38 Oxley Road to find out who's who in the new cabinet. "It was there that we heard CEC met and said that they would not take over the government unless eight persons that were named be released from prison."

AT 4 pm on Friday, 5 June 1959, in the City Hall chamber, Lee Kuan Yew raised his right hand and was sworn in as the first prime minister of the self-governing State of Singapore.

He was followed one by one by the other eight ministers who made up the first PAP cabinet. In keeping with their dress code, they wore open-necked white shirts and trousers. Taking the sartorial cue, Sir William Goode, the former governor who assumed the title of Yang Di Pertuan Negara (Head of State) under the new constitution, swopped his white ceremonial dress uniform and white plumed hat for a beige lounge suit.

The simple ceremony ushered in the PAP government which was to rule Singapore until today and transform a languid colonial outpost into a scintillating First World city.

Among those invited by the new government to the ceremony were Lee's brother, Dennis Lee Kim Yew, and friend, Edmund William Barker from Lee and Lee who acted as legal advisers to the PAP.

But conspicuously absent was another legal adviser from the same firm. "I was very disappointed I could not watch my husband being sworn in," lamented Mrs Lee Kuan Yew. Why? "I was told that because I was the wife, I could not go. He said: 'No, no. It will make too much trouble with all the other wives. You'd better stay away.' "

The event was somewhat subdued compared to the euphoria and excitement of the last few days following PAP's landslide victory in the general election on Saturday, May 30. It was the week that changed Singapore forever.

On Monday, June 1, Lee was summoned by the governor and asked to form the new government. He declined to do so unless his comrades in jail were released. On Tuesday, June 2, the governor announced the release after consulting Whitehall.

On Wednesday, June 3, at a minute past midnight, Sir William Goode proclaimed Singapore a self-governing state, ending nearly a century and a half of British colonial rule. That night, PAP staged a mass victory rally for 50,000 at the Padang before the flood-lit City Hall.

From the City Hall steps, Othman Wok made the rally announcement on radio in Malay. "I was the first to speak followed by the Chinese announcer. We made it Malay, Chinese, Tamil, English." This was to be the multi-lingual sequence for national announcements that remains to this day.

Standing by the Corinthian columns at the top of the City Hall stairs and listening to a radio was Mrs Lee. She expressed amazement at how young girls with pigtails could keep the massive crowd under control. She heard a sound she had never heard before, a murmur from the crowd like the sound of the sea. "It starts 'whooom' and then it comes up and it's 'whooom' it goes down—starting from one end of the Padang to the other."

Thursday, June 4, was the day of freedom for Lim Chin Siong, Fong Swee Suan, Devan Nair, James Puthucheary, Chen Say Jame, S Woodhull, Chan Chiaw Thor and Tan Chong Kin. They were greeted and garlanded by an ecstatic crowd outside Changi Prison. Pigeons were released and firecrackers lit.

They were taken to the party HQ at No 62-C South Bridge Road where they issued their signed statement "The Ends and Means of Socialism". As spokesman for the group, Nair re-affirmed their commitment towards achieving an independent, democratic, non-communist socialist Malaya by peaceful means.

"There was some cynical laughter from Goh Keng Swee which

somewhat annoyed me because at least as far as I was concerned, I was sincere. Lee Kuan Yew looked rather inscrutable. Rajaratnam and Toh Chin Chye were sombre. Lim Chin Siong was stroking his head and looking down," he said.

City Hall was picked as the venue for Friday's swearing-in and the administrative seat of the new government because of its intimate association with PAP during its city council years. Government House, or Istana as it is now called, was shunned as it was seen as a symbol of colonial suppression.

If you are curious about how the first PAP cabinet was formed, Toh said that as Lee was the prime minister, it was his constitutional prerogative to decide on the portfolios. According to Goh, Toh became deputy prime minister because he was party chairman. He became finance minister because he was the only economist.

Rajaratnam was culture minister because he was a journalist. Ong Pang Boon was appointed home affairs minister because he knew the linkage between party activists and the communist united front.

It seemed quite natural for Byrne, the legal brain behind many an industrial dispute, to be the minister for labour and law. The education ministry was thrust on former school teacher Yong Nyuk Lin.

Health went to Ahmad Ibrahim, a Naval Base Labour Union leader whom Goh described as "very honest and loyal". National development was handed to former mayor Ong Eng Guan as its importance corresponded with his status in the party hierarchy and because it absorbed many functions of the previous city council.

Reflecting on the toddling days of the PAP government, Toh said that they sorely lacked experience in administration—only the two Ongs had been involved in running the city council.

But he noted that they were fortunate to have two former senior civil servants in the cabinet. "Goh and Byrne gave us an idea what the government was all about, what the government departments did and therefore who should take charge of what," he said.

There were no assistant ministers as in the previous Labour Front-led government but nine parliamentary secretaries were appointed. Their brief was to support their respective ministers.

Low Por Tuck was flabbergasted but delighted when he was appointed parliamentary secretary for finance. "I had no experience in government work and was not sure whether I could manage my work. I learnt a lot from Goh," he said.

In the beginning, the bilingual Low pointed out, the Chinese-educated legislative assemblymen had difficulty following proceedings in the chamber. He said that he helped to explain, interpret and translate documents. As the party whip, he would inform members what stand they should take on issues.

The other parliamentary secretaries were Chan Sun Wing (prime minister's office), Goh Chew Chua (deputy prime minister's office), Yaacob bin Mohamed (national development), Sheng Nam Chin (health), Wee Toon Boon (labour and law), Lee Khoon Choy (culture), Tan Kia Gan (home affairs) and Leong Keng Seng (education).

After their release from prison, the leftists met regularly at Lee's home. Woodhull said that Lee wanted them to join the government immediately. "He said, we either sink or swim together. You can't be different."

He agreed to be political secretary to health minister Ahmad Ibrahim while James Puthucheary went to Industrial Promotion Board, the predecessor of Economic Development Board. Under pressure from Lee, Fong Swee Suan and Lim Chin Siong finally caved in to become political secretaries. Fong was posted to labour and law while Lim joined finance.

Chen Say Jame, however, chose not to get involved with PAP again on his release. He said that he was filled with a sense of foreboding. "I knew clearly in my heart that there was a time bomb within the party." He was proven right. It exploded two years later.

⁓⁂⁓

THE young Anglo-Chinese School teacher saw Lee for the first time during the 1959 elections. Lee was standing on a lorry at a Fullerton Square lunchtime rally denouncing foreigners and expatriates serving in British enterprises in Singapore.

Like many English-educated Singaporeans, he was struck by Lee's eloquence but startled by his stridency. "Lee was so persuasive I began to worry for Singapore's future. He seemed to be killing the goose that laid the golden egg," recalled Chan Chin Bock.

Was the new PAP government pro-communist? What socialist policies would it pursue? Would it confiscate private property and nationalise industries? These questions began making the rounds in the business community at that time, according to retired industrialist Tan Eng Joo.

The climate of confidence was further dampened by the local and international press which carried reports of capital, investments and entrepôt trade being diverted to Hong Kong, Bangkok and other cities.

Fear was increasingly palpable among the civil servants, the English-educated middle class and the Straits-born Chinese community. S R Nathan remembered reassuring a very worried Baba that the PAP government could not possibly nationalise an entrepôt economy.

Barely had the new government warmed its seat when it dropped a bombshell which confirmed their worst fears.

Postal clerk Lee Gek Seng was looking forward to his new government quarters on St Michael's Road. He had bought a refrigerator, radio and other appliances on hire purchase. Suddenly he found he could not meet his payments.

The PAP convenor and founder-member was so incensed that he put his name on a protest petition—against the PAP government.

10

Go Down on Your Bended Knees

IT was one of those sweltering days in May when the PAP candidate for Kreta Ayer and his canvassers went campaigning in the squatter slums and labyrinthine lanes of *gu chia chwee* ("bullock cart water" in Hokkien), the colloquial term for Chinatown.

Dripping in sweat and hoarse from making incessant pleas to residents to vote for the party, the group was relieved when Goh Keng Swee stopped by a sugar cane stall. As they huddled around the oasis expectantly, the former senior civil servant placed 10 cents, gulped down his drink and mumbled "I have paid for my drink. If you want to have a drink, go ahead", before walking away. They were stunned.

"We looked at him, the stallholder looked at us. We thought he would be giving all of us a drink." Chan Chee Seng, who accompanied Goh on his 1959 election rounds, was recounting yet another anecdote about the legendary thriftiness and frugality of Singapore's famed finance minister.

If that was not ample proof of Goh's parsimony, Chan found it when he rode in his car, a rattling Vauxhall which had seen better days. It was with a gasp of disbelief when he realised that part of the vehicle's floor panel had corroded to such an extent that "you could see right through to the road". "You see," he shook his head, "Goh did not even want to pay for a rubber mat to cover the gaping hole, let alone repair it!"

S R Nathan, who worked with Goh in the defence ministry in the 1970s, said that Goh was so averse to spending that whenever he travelled overseas he would carry soap flakes to wash his underwear in the hotel bathroom. Former diplomat Maurice Baker visited Goh in his hotel room during a trip one day and saw him drying his one and only underwear on the heater.

To today's Singaporeans, these penny-pinching habits would seem ridiculous and laughable but they formed the hallmark of PAP's founding fathers. Thrift was their name. Nothing was more repulsive than waste and extravagance. "I can count the number of treats they gave me on my fingers," Chan reminisced with a grimace. "If a minister offered us a cup of coffee, it meant a cup. He would not offer another cup and we wouldn't dare ask."

If you could not get a treat from them, it was even less likely you could get a loan. That Shakespearean maxim "Neither a borrower nor a lender be" would sum up their attitude towards money to a T. As an up-and-coming lawyer, Lee Kuan Yew would often receive an appeal for a loan and his Hamlet-like reply would be: "I am afraid I will not be able to make you a loan. It is against my principles to lend money to a friend because I have found from my personal experience that when I gain a debtor I lose a friend."

On that sultry day in Kreta Ayer, Chan and fellow party members felt much disconcerted by Goh's close-fistedness. Now with the benefit of hindsight, Chan realised that it embodied the qualities that made the man such a great steward of Singapore's hard-earned finances. "He wasn't squeezing us. He just didn't want to squander money. Every cent counted. We were lucky we had ministers like Dr Goh. That's why Singapore could save a lot of money and become one of the most affluent countries in the world," ruminated Chan.

Toh Chin Chye was lost in thought on a drive around the city in 2003. Many of the gleaming towering edifices were unrecognisable to him. What on earth was that, he asked pointing suddenly to the spiky durian-shaped structure on Marina Bay. As the car cruised around Rochor Road area where he used to be member of parliament, the sight of the teeming crowds at Bugis Village snapped him out of his reverie. "For what you have now, you've got to thank Dr Goh," he blurted out.

IN the political climate of the day when corruption, greed and self-serving opportunism was alienating the masses, PAP leaders were convinced that they had to hold themselves to a high standard of exemplary conduct. One that should equal if not exceed that of their leftist partners whose qualities of austerity and self-sacrifice resonated profoundly with the impoverished populace.

Lim Chin Siong and his comrades were reputed to toil ceaselessly night and day, living on very little. Money meant nothing to them, least of all material rewards. Their clothes were shabby and shoes well-worn. They often skipped meals and slept on wooden benches in their Middle Road union premises.

Giving an insight into the psyche of the communist, Gerald de Cruz who himself underwent rigorous training to be a full-fledged member of the Malayan Communist Party (MCP) said: "We had to lead exemplary lives. We had always to keep ourselves under control. They tried to make you into the perfect human being ... you had to be modest, self-disciplined, unassuming, self-controlled, totally honest, never telling a lie except to the enemy."

It was no secret that the hardcore Chinese leftists sniffed at colleagues who drank, smoked and womanised, labelling them as "happy-hour revolutionaries" who might betray them in a moment of weakness. One fellow leftist dubbed a "connoisseur of drinks and ladies" was Jamit Singh, secretary of the Singapore Harbour Board Staff Association. Fong Sip Chee commented that Chinese leftists "would never have tolerated Jamit had he been Chinese-educated".

An English-educated Straits-born Chinese who took a lot of flak was Lee Gek Seng. As a P and T union official, he would attend dinner and dance events at hotels and have a drink or two in cocktail lounges. Then to his dismay he would find himself being smeared by leftists who cried: "Look, he is wasting union money."

Lee Kuan Yew found it hard to conceal his admiration for the political convictions and simple way of life of the leftists. If his group wanted to win over the hearts and minds of the people from the left, he realised very early in his political career, it would have to "outleft the left".

But it was not easy to emulate their spartan lifestyle. Lee had to live down frequent charges that he was "a beer-drinking, golf-playing dictator who lived in a bungalow". To S Rajaratnam, the leftist view of life bordered on the puritanical. "I used to wear these colourful shirts, they used to give me long lectures. They felt that I should be soberly attired, just white shirt and white pants if possible," he said.

Former Middle Road trade unionist Dominic Puthucheary related a conversation with Lee on a boat trip to visit some detainees in St John's Island. "I was wearing a white shirt and white pants and I refused to smoke, I refused to drink and he was having a beer. He said: 'Dom, you're becoming like the Chinese-educated!'

"I was very impressed by the Chinese-educated, their capacity to organise, their dedication, their way of life. Well, I suppose I was very impressionable and so I tried to emulate them and Kuan Yew was worried about me."

If you ever wonder about the origins of the trademark garb that PAP adopted, all these white-on-white references would suggest that they go all the way back to the left and explain why to this day the party still strives to live by its oft-quoted maxim of being "whiter than white, purer than pure".

❧

WHEN the employees of Thorncroft company offered gifts to Lee in December 1956 for the legal assistance he rendered them, he replied that he could not accept anything for himself but would accept one item—a portable typewriter—for the party as a token of their appreciation.

Making clear that he had been directed by the CEC to accept the gift, he wrote: "We have started meet-the-people sessions in all our branches and the portable typewriter will be taken to the different branches and used at these sessions. I'm sure it will be most helpful to our party in its endeavours to help other workers and their families who are in trouble."

The values of the PAP pioneers were so instinctively internalised that they were inevitably embodied in the running of the party itself. Their "waste not, want not" ethos meant that a branch could only afford to occupy a portion of a dingy shophouse or a makeshift wood-and-zinc structure. Decor was threadbare with furniture and fittings contributed by supporters and sympathisers.

Indeed PAP started off as a poor man's party whose members were mainly hawkers, labourers, petty traders, clerks, shopkeepers and farmers. Its shoestring budget came from members' subscriptions, small donations, legislative assemblymen's allowances and funds raised from party activities and publications.

As organising secretary, Ong Pang Boon was all too familiar with the parlous state of party finances—the money collected each month was not sufficient to meet its expenses. For example, he noted that for August 1956, the party collected only $600 from subscriptions which could not even pay for the rent of the HQ and branches, much less staff salaries.

The party's first annual report from 1 December 1953 to 13 June 1955 showed that members' subscriptions totalled $8,143 and donations, $2,594.60. In a *Petir* article, Ong reported that the operations of its

10 branches cost $8,326.45 from June 1955 to June 1956. PAP was so financially strapped that it often delayed the opening of new branches and sub-branches.

At election time, unlike the more established parties, it could not count on big donors or resort to dubious sources of funds. When the party decided to take part in the 1955 elections, it appealed for funds and netted $2,700. Its first big donation came from Dr Chinnah Subrahmanyam, a party member and hospital pathologist who donated $1,001 after his racehorse won a top prize.

The 1959 polls required a much bigger war chest as PAP was fielding candidates in all 51 wards. As the election deposit stood at $500 each, it meant scrounging around for $25,500. As Toh admitted, the party had no campaign fund and expected candidates to cough up their own money or borrow money.

One account had it that Lim Kim San, a businessman running a sago-making factory and close friend of Goh Keng Swee, took out an overdraft of $10,000 to help pay the deposits for the candidates. Fong Sip Chee's version was that Lim originally put up $5,000 for 10 candidates but for some reason or other, withdrew the offer. Lim had no recollection of the offer.

According to Ong Pang Boon, it was businessman Goh Khai Poh who lent the party $25,000 to fund the deposits of the PAP candidates. He ran Swee Lian Finance on Prinsep Street and Khai Wah Battery Company on Rochor Road. This was corroborated by Fong Sip Chee who said that Toh signed an IOU on behalf of the party. The money was returned to Goh in full after the elections as no PAP candidate lost his or her deposit. Lee concurred with Ong's account.

Goh died in 1999. His son, Goh Ah King, confirmed that his father made the loan saying that he did it as a favour to K M Byrne who was his good friend. Noting that Lee was his father's lawyer, he recalled an occasion when Lee drove to the battery shop to get his tyres changed and he saw a young Hsien Loong sitting in the car.

Goh Khai Poh also provided transport during elections. His vans were used to distribute election posters and his lorries were joined to form election platforms. Sheng Nam Chin, who was standing in Nee Soon, said: "Whenever we needed a lorry or a loudspeaker, it was supplied by Khai Wah Battery Company."

Fortunately for the PAP, no huge capital outlay was needed for day-today campaigning as its hordes of helpers worked for free. Sheng said that his Nee Soon workers took their own meals. Tay Kum Sun, yet another friend of the gregarious Byrne who used to patronise his provision shop, noted that several hundred Chinese school students converged in Tanjong Pagar to canvass votes "without payment of money or promise of food or expectation of reward".

In contrast, the election workers for the other parties were said to be a mercenary lot. Fong Sip Chee estimated the average rate for each election worker at between $10 and $15 per day. It was a windfall for the jobless but for the unscrupulous, it turned into a scam—they would report for duty, collect the day's pay, dump the election pamphlets and adjourn to the coffee shop.

As a Labour Front (LF) candidate in the 1957 city council elections, Ho Kok Hoe was impressed by the discipline and zeal of the PAP workers who worked for free. What a far cry from his own workers, he bemoaned. On polling day, he was shocked when he discovered that almost all his workers had been "bought over" by his Lib-Soc opponent. He had to round up his friends at the eleventh hour to help him win the ward.

By keeping the party lean and self-reliant, PAP avoided the pitfalls and problems which tripped up the other parties. The Democrats were seen as being in cahoots with millionaire merchants, the Progressives as being protective of the interests of the English-educated professional class and the Labour Front as being locked in sinister embrace with rough gangsters and roughneck trade unionists.

Most of all, by not being beholden to any big donor, big business or big interest group, it kept money politics out of the party.

꧁ꕥ꧂

SO how did PAP fund itself in the absence of big donors? The simple answer: self-funding. The bulk of the party's funding still came from the pay of elected representatives. In 2005, the monthly deduction varied from $1,800 for a minister to $900 for an MP.

This time-honoured practice goes all the way back to 1955 when the first three PAP legislative assemblymen entered the chamber. Out of their $500 monthly allowance, a large chunk went to the party. In the case of Lee, $450 was used to pay the salary of PAP's first full-time employee—organising secretary Ong Pang Boon.

This funding formula obviated the need for contributions from businessmen and companies and ensured that no donor and interest group outside the party could exert political influence through patronage. In essence, the monetary sacrifice of ministers and MPs was parlayed into robust party finances.

Back then, PAP's pioneering politicians bore the brunt of the mandatory pay deduction much more than their latter-day counterparts who held high-paying full-time jobs. Many had to give up better paying jobs to work as full-time people's representatives. It was no surprise that Lee and his fellow leaders had to use all their persuasive if not coercive skills to get them on board.

Consider the PAP city councillor who received a monthly allowance of $200 of which $50 or 25 per cent went to the party. On top of that, he still had to fish into his pocket to pay for miscellaneous branch expenses. Could he and his family live on the balance?

Chan Chee Seng was earning $700 a month as a clerk in Hong Kong and Shanghai Bank when he was asked to stand for the 1957 city council elections. Naturally he declined as it would mean the loss of $500. He recalled that Lee kept pressing him saying: "You must stand, you cannot say you don't want to stand. You give up your job." I said: 'Give up my job? I got no money to give to my family.' He said: 'Never mind, you go and work that job.' " Chan finally gave in but fortunately, he said, he was a bachelor then and could live on less.

After the sensational PAP victory in the 1959 elections, the docking of allowances was extended to all its 43 legislative assemblymen. For ministers who earned $2,500 a month, the entire assemblyman's allowance of $500 went to the party. For the backbenchers, $150 out of the $500 was deducted.

As Ong summed it up: "That's how the party built up a regular source of funds. We didn't want to depend on donors." But he admitted that many assemblymen struggled to survive on their balance of $350. "Furthermore, they had to subsidise branch rentals and donate to funeral wakes and so on," he said.

Lee Khoon Choy was pocketing $1,200 a month as a journalist with *The Straits Times* when he was prevailed upon by Lee to resign and stand for the 1959 elections. He became a $500-a-month legislative assemblyman for Bukit Panjang. Then his mother, his first wife and father-in-law died within the same year and he was dead broke. "I did not have money to buy coffins," he said.

When Toh and Byrne attended his wife's wake, he requested a loan of $500 from the party. "Toh said that the party had no money. Toh and Byrne said they had no money. In the end, I asked Ong Eng Guan and he lent me $500."

Ho Puay Choo, the assemblywoman for Bras Basah, also felt worse off financially. Even after the deduction of her allowance for the party, much of the balance went to fund branch activities. She could not resume her work as a seamstress to supplement her income as all her time was taken up by meetings with her constituents and welfare work.

G Kandasamy finally rose to the rank of a division one officer in the civil service when he became assistant controller of posts in 1956. Then came the "invitation". As he recounted: "Lee Kuan Yew kept talking and talking and talking to me about standing for elections. Finally, I said okay, lah." Although the assemblyman for Kampung Kapor was appointed deputy speaker, a position which entitled him to another $500, he said that he suffered a big financial loss. "I could not make up the amount I was earning in the postal service. My mother was very upset."

One office-holder who felt utterly squeezed was Fong Sip Chee who was assemblyman for Stamford and parliamentary secretary (culture) in 1963. He calculated how despite having a pay of $2,150, he ended up with only $1,000. "My total pay was $2,150. $1,500 salary, $500 assemblyman's allowance, $150 transport allowance. Out of this amount, the party took away $1,150. I had only $1,000. It's more than 50 per cent. When I had my first child, I spoke to Dr Toh. He was kind enough—a man very tough in his words but very soft in the heart. He ordered the party treasurer to give me $100 more. Out of the $1,000 I received, I had only in cash $700. $300 was put in compulsory savings for me by the party." His child, Arthur Fong, followed in his father's footsteps by becoming West Coast GRC MP in 2001.

But did they not have any perks and privileges? All scoffed at the very suggestion. Ho Puay Choo put it in her typical homespun way when she said that life before and after being a PAP elected representative was exactly the same: "We cross the road, take the bus and eat at the street stalls."

A FEW days after PAP assumed power, newly minted finance minister Goh Keng Swee took a stroll from his office in Fullerton Building—now reincarnated as The Fullerton Hotel—to Empress Place. He wanted to inspect the currency vault but was stopped by Gurkha guards. He had to call the commander before he could gain admission.

It did not take long for the economic expert and former senior civil servant au fait with the inflow and outflow of government money to realise that he was scraping the bottom of the barrel. After discovering that the last government had dipped into the reserves and used up $200 million, he duly reported that there would be a deficit of $14 million for the year 1959.

For a party which preached the gospel of austerity, thrift and self-sacrifice and condemned the extravagant spending of the Lim Yew Hock government, it was time to put its socialist rhetoric into immediate action.

The values exemplified by the PAP leaders and their party were about to be extended to the governance of the country. The solution: a whopping pay cut. As Toh remembered: "Goh found that the government treasury was drying up with no money to carry on as a government. So his idea was just to cut expenditure. The easiest way was to cut manpower expenditure. So, salaries."

To set a personal example, the cabinet ministers agreed to Goh's proposal for a pay cut of $600 from their monthly gross salary of $2,650.

Then the bombshell was dropped: the variable allowances of all civil servants except the lowest rung workers would be slashed. Some 6,000 of the 14,000 government employees were hit. About 10 per cent suffered cuts of more than $250 a month while the highest paid lost a maximum of $400 a month.

The worst fears of the English-educated public servants were realised. With the memories of Ong Eng Guan's harsh mayoral rule still fresh in their minds, they agonised over whether yet another "reign of terror" would be unleashed. Was the pay cut the first swing of the axe?

In spine-tingling words that still reverberate in the minds of older Singaporeans, Lee told the legislative assembly on 21 July 1959: "I say to the civil service and their rather inept leaders at the moment ... if nothing else more catastrophic happens than the loss of allowances and the fact that government servants have to face fiercer competition from the non-English educated members of the service, then they should go down on their bended knees and thank the gods that their souls have been spared."

The reaction to the pay cut was visceral, running the whole gamut from anger, bitterness and disillusionment to humiliation, fear and sheer panic. There was a widespread perception conveyed by the English press and the opposition that this was vengeance wreaked on the English-educated for voting against PAP in the recent elections.

Goh Sin Tub, who was then principal staff officer in the education ministry, said that his colleagues felt "the pain and indignity" and were "completely demoralised". He could see anxiety writ large on the faces of the executive officers and the clerks.

S R Nathan, who was a seamen's welfare officer, recalled that he and his colleague in the labour ministry, Tay Seow Huah, were shocked as the pay cut took away a third of their monthly income. It was all the more traumatic because no one gave them any explanation. "We could not understand why a government which we were for should undertake such a serious step. It caused so much pain to many who were loyal and committed to helping a government led by people whom we admired."

It was fortunate, he said, that he and Tay had working wives which "lessened the pain" but he knew of colleagues who were devastated as their earnings were totally stretched by their financial commitments. "Some had to take drastic steps by either selling off their property or disrupting their children's education abroad."

Call it dramatic irony but the pay cut hit the PAP stalwarts all the harder as it came from their own government. To Lee Gek Seng, it was like a thunderbolt from the PAP lightning. The postal clerk was about to move into new quarters on St Michael's Road when his pay was slashed. How was he going to meet his hire purchase payments? "Luckily I got certain friends to advance certain money and this tied me over," he said woefully.

Even though he was a PAP founding member and convenor and close to the leaders, he was so aggrieved that he put his name in a petition against the pay cut and told off a minister. In similar vein, S V Lingam, then PAP assemblyman for Aljunied, lamented how public servants who helped the party rise to power had to suffer the ignominy of a pay cut.

Gloom and despondency gripped the civil servants as they pondered Singapore's future. Mohamad Ismail Haji, then registrar of births and deaths, worried that the communists had taken over. Nathan wondered if the Chinese-educated leftists were calling the shots in the government and whether the English-educated civil servants were being targeted.

"Our feeling was that our days in public service were numbered. Tay Seow Huah and I had many hours of quiet discussion about what awaited people like us. We even contemplated looking for work elsewhere in the private sector especially in areas of personnel management," said the president in his Istana office.

Just as affected was Sim Kee Boon, who worked first in the colonial secretariat and then in the administrative service. He wanted to leave and join the private sector but James Puthucheary, who was quite influential in government then, asked Goh to stop him from leaving.

Sim and Nathan stayed but many left. "I was devastated," said Chan Chin Bock, who was then a teacher at Anglo-Chinese School. "For reasons best known to itself at that time, PAP was not only highly critical of the English-educated but also thought poorly of all teachers in general. On a personal level, my teacher's pay was cut significantly by the PAP government's decision. This event led to my leaving the profession."

Fong Sip Chee cited an estimate of some 300 administrative and professional staff who moved across the causeway to flee PAP rule. Rajaratnam noted that quite a number of the English-educated went to Malaya because they thought PAP was pro-communist.

The effects of the brain drain began to be felt. In his annual budget statement at the end of 1960, Goh highlighted the seriousness of the dearth of professional staff, division one officers, engineers, architects and medical officers.

But there was a silver lining. If there was a talent vacuum, it had to be filled, and this led to the rise of high-calibre civil servants whom the PAP ministers were to rely on and work hand-in-glove to begin the Singapore Story. The roll call would include Sim Kee Boon, J Y Pillay, Howe Yoon Chong, G E Bogaars, Pang Tee Pow and K P R Chandra.

⌘

LIKE many young men of the 1950s, S R Nathan was hoping to clinch a coveted job with the city council. When he turned up at the interview, he found himself facing an Englishman and an Indian trade union leader who kept asking him in Tamil: "How many tables?"

As a Tamil, he understood the question but did not for the life of him knew what he was talking about. He did not get the job.

Later a senior civil servant asked why he failed to secure the job. Nathan replied: "Sir, I do not know. This man kept asking me how many tables."

But did you know what he meant? No, he said. Enlightenment only came when the officer explained: "What he meant was how many Chinese dinner tables were you prepared to provide if you got the job?"

As related by the former office boy who went on to become one of Singapore's most distinguished civil servants and diplomats before assuming the presidency in 1999, the anecdote was reflective of the rampant corruption in Singapore at that time.

Young people may barely stifle a yawn when they read about Singapore being ranked yet again by Transparency International as one of the least corrupt countries in the world. But do they know that corruption was once part of the way of life in Singapore? Just ask their elders.

There was a time when civil servants were routinely on the take. Hawkers and tradesmen had to bribe inspectors to get them off their back. Constables alternated between booking vehicles for road offences and accepting $10 from offending motorists on the spot. Parents offered gratification to school officials to secure places for their children.

Tee Kim Leng, the barber who became PAP assemblyman for Pasir Panjang in 1959, said that government departments were so corrupt that even office boys expected tips of between 10 and 20 cents for handing out an application form. "The police were corrupt and people had to pay officers to get them to investigate crimes. The rich and powerful could bribe the police to get people out of jail," he said.

Former PAP activist Chong Fun Liam used to work as a development officer at the former Singapore Improvement Trust. When he visited homes to verify the eligibility of applicants for new government flats, he discovered to his horror that many had already paid "coffee money" of $90 to government officials.

"Thousands of applicants must have paid the money which was a big amount considering our pay was only about $300 a month then," he said. He believed this explained why some civil servants could afford to live in big bungalows in those days.

In the 1950s and 1960s, corruption loomed as one of the biggest issues in the polls. At an Empress Place rally during the 1955 elections, then-Labour Front leader David Marshall was compelled to say: "There is much talk of corruption. If you have evidence against a Labour Front candidate, don't vote for him and report to the police."

Former *Straits Times* news editor Felix Abisheganaden had no hesitation declaring that the years preceding PAP rule "was the most corrupt period in the island's history". The culprits? "The bureaucracy, the police, the immigration and the politicians themselves under the Yew Hock administration," he said, noting for instance that citizenship could be bought for "a few dollars".

Chan Chee Seng was able to substantiate some of these allegations when he was posted to the immigration department on Anson Road after the 1959 elections. He described the department as the most corrupt in the government when he found that people were paying for immigration papers.

He remembered an old woman who appeared in his office one day offering him a paper bag. She wanted to thank him for helping her only son in China to enter and live in Singapore. Looking into it, he was shocked to see a bundle of $10, $5 and $1 notes. "I told her, if you give this to me, I become corrupt. You want me to be sacked? She took back the money."

The spectre of corruption haunted Lee right from the very beginning of his political career. Samad Ismail said that whenever Lee visited him in jail between 1951 and 1953, he would often talk about how he wanted to form a political party that would be very different from the others as he was "very concerned about corruption in politics and the trade unions".

It was Lee who called for a commission of inquiry into political corruption following the Tanjong Pagar and Cairnhill by-elections in June 1957. Reeling off a catalogue of corrupt election practices during a debate in the chamber, he expressed his greatest fear that if corrupt politicians were to take power after the 1959 general election, people would never believe in a democratic system.

In the 1948 elections, as he expounded on 18 July 1957, the stakes were low. Candidates could only aspire to become "the honourable Mr So and So" and get invited to Government House birthday parties. In the 1955 polls, under the Rendel constitution, the stakes were higher. A minister would be in charge of import, export and immigration permits and sell them at $50 or $500 each.

But with the stakes increasing after self-government in 1959, he warned, "it might be $5,000 for a bus licence or 50 bucks for a hawker's pitch. If one could be a minister for commerce and industry in self-governing Singapore, one could swipe a few million dollars very quickly."

Voicing his concern that there was no law to prevent a corrupt man from standing for elections, he said: "Nothing is more certain to destroy the democratic system of government than corrupt politicians. If your politician and minister is corrupt, your permanent secretary will become corrupt. Then your principal assistant secretary will take something for himself and the clerk will take something for himself. Finally the peons will not want to deliver anything unless you give him 50 cents for every letter."

His motion was passed unanimously and a commission of inquiry into corrupt, illegal or undesirable practices at elections was convened. It probed into how money was offered to buy votes, how candidates entertained voters with food and drinks and how gangsters were hired to intimidate voters.

If current elections are clean and orderly, some credit should go to the implementation of the commission's findings. They included the introduction of compulsory voting, a ban on cars to take voters to polling stations and the prohibition of canvassing on polling day. Other laws were introduced later to regulate the amount of money each candidate could spend in an election and mandate the submission of election expenses.

The PAP government's zero tolerance for corruption was dramatically demonstrated by its unrelenting action against its own ministers who deviated from the straight and narrow.

Tan Kia Gan, the former minister for national development, was stripped of all his public appointments in 1966 after being investigated for attempting to help his friend clinch the sale of Boeing aircraft to Malaysian Airways.

Wee Toon Boon, the minister of state (environment) was sentenced to four years and six months in jail in September 1975 after being convicted of several corruption charges involving $839,023. On appeal, his jail sentence was reduced to 18 months.

Teh Cheang Wan, the minister for national development, was investigated in November 1986 for accepting two bribes totalling $800,000 from private developers. He committed suicide before he could be formally charged in court.

Incorruptibility was the pivotal value which the PAP brought to governance and around which hung the other avowed principles of meritocracy, pragmatism and multi-racialism. As prime minister and senior minister, Goh Chok Tong had stated repeatedly that integrity was the single most important attribute of the PAP. His constant warning to party faithfuls: "If the PAP becomes corrupt, it must and should lose its ruling status."

❧

IT must have been a sight to behold when a milk vendor with three cows turned up at the ministry of national development on Upper Pickering Street. He complained that the animals had been shivering in the rain since his *attap* hut in Nee Soon had been pulled down. Parliamentary secretary Yaacob Mohamad promised to look into it.

A woman with marital problems sought the help of Ho Puay Choo at the labour ministry. The assemblywoman disliked the legalistic approach as it meant assigning a lawyer and posting a court order. She felt that this would only anger the husband and break up the family. Her solution: "I took her home and had a little talk with her husband, hoping that they would be fine after that."

When people appealed for their family members from China to join them in Singapore, immigration officers demanded proof of marriage and kinship. Chan Chee Seng, who was attached to the home affairs ministry, was bothered. How were they going to furnish any proof after being separated from their families for so long? Then he struck on a brainwave: ask them to submit a picture of the tomb of a deceased parent which carried the names of family members.

The early days of the new government saw a messianic zeal among the PAP leaders to live up to their election platform of keeping in touch with the man-in-the-street. Civil servants were pressured to serve common folks well. Parliamentary and political secretaries were appointed and legislative assemblymen assigned to all the ministries to help deal with people problems.

One high-profile manifestation of PAP's determination to stay connected to the masses was the setting up of a public complaints bureau in every ministry. In 1962, they were grouped under a central complaints bureau overseen by Lee Siew Choh, the member for Queenstown. It became the avenue for people to lodge complaints against bureaucratic arrogance, inefficiency and corruption.

For hapless civil servants, it was seen as yet another instrument of fear. Mohamad Ismail Haji said that he and his colleagues in the registry of births and deaths lived in trepidation knowing that if anyone filed a complaint against them, they would be subjected to investigation.

But the party's most potent problem-solving channel unfiltered by bureaucrats was the meet-the-people session conducted by every elected representative. There was nothing like meeting constituents face-to-face, listening to their woes and helping them to grapple with their problems that enabled PAP to keep its finger on the pulse of society. Where issues could not be resolved, said Ong Pang Boon, the least you could do was to express sympathy and explain.

Delivering good governance meant delivering the goods. Given the impoverished state of Singapore at that time, people were in desperate need for jobs, housing, education and health care. The pragmatists in Lee and Goh emerged, overriding any doctrinaire socialism that they had espoused in their campaign to gain votes and please the leftists.

Realising the limitations of an entrepôt economy and the dim prospects of an immediate common market with Malaya, Goh latched on to the idea of developing export-orientated industrialisation and attracting investments from multi-national companies. Singapore's masterplan was laid following the visit of a UN Development Programme industrial mission in 1960 headed by Dutch industrialist Albert Winsemius and his secretary I F Tang. The rest is history.

As head of the Industrial Promotion Board, James Puthucheary was involved in the plan to put up the Economic Development Board (EDB). The dyed-in-the-wool socialist believed fervently in the social ownership of key industries but lost the policy debate to the private enterprise camp represented by Goh and Winsemius.

Expressing his high regard for Goh in later years, he said: "I have not shared his great beliefs in private enterprise but I suppose he was right and I was wrong. Singapore has benefited from it." EDB was set up on 1 August 1961. The Singapore Story had begun.

But the PAP leaders did not abandon their ideological faith altogether. They applied it to public housing—with spectacular results. Taking over vast tracts of land under the draconian Land Acquisition Act, the government built low-cost flats for the poor and needy at record-breaking pace. It was PAP's greatest act of socialism.

As minister for national development, Ong Eng Guan was supposed to oversee this centrepiece of the PAP programme. He proposed a five-year programme without clearing it with the cabinet. His fellow ministers found it lacking in details and economic sense.

Finance minister Goh refused to give him the money and decided to outflank Ong by appointing a trusted friend and fellow alumnus of Anglo-Chinese School and Raffles College as chairman of the newly constituted Housing and Development Board (HDB) on 12 February 1960. Name: Lim Kim San. Salary: Nil.

Singapore's public housing miracle, unrivalled anywhere in the world, can be traced to the appointment of this self-made millionaire businessman whose gruff and straight-talking demeanour hid an uncannily analytical mind.

When Lim was finally summoned by minister Ong to see him in his Upper Pickering Street office, he found that he had not been given a parking lot despite his request. And when he was invited for lunch, he was served with "just rice and egg or something on top of it" although Ong knew that he was a gourmet.

But what Lim remembered most about the lunch encounter was what Ong, all of 35 years then, said to him: "You know, I'm the strongest of ministers. Among the new ministers I'm very strong." As if to demonstrate his vigour, he bent down to touch his toes with his fingertips. Replying that he was much older than Ong—he was 44—Lim also proceeded to bend down and touch the floor—with the palm of his hands.

11

Did Lee Become PM by One Vote?

THEY were still basking in the euphoria of their electrifying electoral victory on 30 May 1959 when they met in a small room in the law firm of Lee and Lee on Malacca Street sometime in the evening. The 12 CEC members of the winning party had to grapple with the all-important question: Who should be prime minister of the new PAP government?

Nothing in the party constitution had stipulated how a prime minister should be picked from the governing body. No convention had been set as no PAP government had ever been formed. Certainly, there was no assumption that the secretary-general should automatically be the prime minister.

Two names were proposed: secretary-general Lee Kuan Yew and treasurer Ong Eng Guan. Small slips of white paper were handed to the CEC members to write down their choice in a secret ballot.

When chairman Toh Chin Chye received the votes, he opened and counted them one by one. There was a hushed silence when he declared six for Lee and six for Ong. The deadlock could not have been more dramatic. Then exercising his prerogative as chairman, he used his casting vote to break the tie, and Lee went on to be prime minister and to preside over the miraculous transformation of Singapore for the next 31 years.

This cliff-hanger reconstruction is culled from the reminiscences of Toh and then-organising secretary Ong Pang Boon in a series of interviews for this book. It corroborated the account making the rounds in countless publications that there was a CEC vote to decide the premiership.

One oft-quoted source was Thomas J Bellows' *The People's Action Party of Singapore: Emergence of a Dominant Party System* in which the American scholar recorded that the CEC met to designate a prime minister after the elections and that party chairman Toh voted twice, first in the original vote and then as the result of a tie, a casting vote.

In 2006, the political science professor recalled that "the person I interviewed was an individual in whom I had especial confidence and was very courteous to a struggling graduate student". His dissertation for Yale University was based on extensive interviews with members and supporters of all major political parties in 1964 and 1965.

References to the vote were never refuted publicly. In fact, a column on 12 July 1960 by Gordon Hung in *The China Mail*, which preceded the *South China Morning Post*, noted Ong's tremendous popularity saying that "the only thing that seemed to stop him from becoming Singapore's first prime minister was the formality of a vote by the central executive committee".

Yak Keow Seng, a former PAP activist and close aide of Ong Eng Guan, remembered the former mayor and minister confiding in him and saying that there was indeed a CEC vote after the elections and that he lost to Lee by one vote.

In what must surely go down as the greatest mystery of the PAP story, Lee said he was completely puzzled by accounts of such a vote. "I don't remember any such thing. I cannot understand this, that Ong Pang Boon and Toh Chin Chye would say so. If one said so, I can dismiss it, but two said so ...

"I led the elections. I crafted the strategy. I made the major campaign speeches. I made the last major broadcast. It was assumed that I would be the leader. I was the man meeting governor William Goode before, during and after the elections, not Ong Eng Guan. I negotiated with him for the release of the detainees, not Ong Eng Guan."

He referred to an exchange of letters between him and Toh published in the press on 19 July 1961. Following the party defeat in the Anson by-election, Lee had written a letter to the then-chairman offering to resign as PM. In his reply, Toh recalled that the CEC was unanimous in choosing Lee as PM and that it had confidence in him to lead the government and party.

As a British-trained lawyer, Lee said that he was aware of the constitutional position—that to be prime minister, you have to be voted by the members of the assembly, not by the party's CEC. He noted that Ong Eng Guan could not have commanded the support of the majority of the elected representatives in the house.

On the prime minister's post, he added: "It's a job nobody wanted. Who wanted the job? Anybody who took the job knew that he was going to meet the communists and have a lot of trouble. So it was not a job that I sought. If I thought Ong Eng Guan could do the job, I would have happily given it to him."

S Rajaratnam was certain "there was no voting as there was no need to do so." Jek Yeun Thong thought likewise. "The choice of prime minister was obvious. There was no doubt. If there was ever a vote, it must have been held within the inner circle—Lee, Toh and Ong."

The date of the CEC meeting had eluded Ong Pang Boon but he was quite sure that it must have been held sometime before June 1 when governor William Goode summoned Lee and asked him to form a new government.

On 31 May, the day after the polls, a special cadre members' conference was held at the Hokkien Huay Kuan on Telok Ayer Street to elect the sixth CEC. But Ong believed that it was the fifth CEC elected on 20 October 1957 which met to "settle the premiership". This CEC, he pointed out, included three former city councillors close to the former mayor and one or two members sympathetic to him.

Of the 12 members of the fifth CEC, seven have died—Goh Chew Chua, S V Lingam, Chan Choy Siong, Tann Wee Tiong, Ismail Rahim, Haron Kassim and Ahmad Ibrahim. The remaining five were Lee, Toh, Ong Eng Guan, Ho Puay Choo and Wee Toon Boon. The latter two claimed they had no recollection.

Ong Pang Boon was not swayed by all the accounts to the contrary and insisted that there was a vote. "If there were no vote, how did Lee become prime minister?" he asked rhetorically. He was emphatic that he was present at the meeting although he could not vote as he was not a CEC member but a paid party official.

If the event was etched deeply in his mind, he said, it was because he thought it rather odd for two candidates vying for the top post to vote for themselves. "I always thought that you don't vote for yourself in meetings but I guess if you want to be a leader you have to cast your vote too."

What reinforced his memory further, he said, was that after the CEC meeting he was persuaded to be the minister for home affairs. Also playing on his mind then was his acute awareness of Lee's suspicions of the CEC members who might have voted for Ong Eng Guan. One was his wife-to-be Chan Choy Siong.

Toh was just as unequivocal about what he did at the fateful meeting. "I voted for Lee Kuan Yew because Ong Eng Guan was unstable and I counted the votes in front of everyone. I read up the rules about chairing meetings. So I used my casting vote and that's how Lee became prime minister. I used the chairman's vote."

Lending another intriguing note was an anecdote related by Low Por Tuck who joined Goh Keng Swee in the finance ministry after the elections. At one meeting with the parliamentary secretaries, Lee told them that Ong Eng Guan wanted to be prime minister after the election results were known and showed them a note written by Ong. Low said: "I don't remember reading the note, but according to Lee, it indicated Ong's desire to be prime minister."

Press coverage of the day made no reference to any CEC vote but suggested that the secretary-general was not the natural choice to be the prime minister. A *Straits Times* report a day after the May 30 polls quoted Toh as saying: "We cannot let you know at the moment who is going to be the prime minister or who will hold office, as the CEC has not made any firm decision."

A *Straits Times* report on June 1 noted that "24 hours after the PAP's landslide election victory, Singapore still does not know who will be its first prime minister". The next day the newspaper proclaimed Lee as Singapore's first prime minister with no mention of how he was selected. But talk of a vote persisted as typified in this remark by then-Progressive Party secretary-general Chan Kum Chee: "I understand when the prime minister was being chosen, Ong lost by only one vote."

⚬❖⚬

FROM today's perspective, it would seem inconceivable that anyone would dare to challenge Lee for the supreme job when his leadership of the party was virtually unquestioned from its Oxley Road days in the early 1950s.

After all, PAP was incubated in the bosom of his home. Lee saw through its gestation and was the principal convenor at its birth in 1954. He shot to prominence empowering the powerless and defending the defenceless. Painstakingly he cultivated a web of trade unions and grassroots organisations which provided critical political support for the fledgling party. Who else could top this sterling track record?

Some of his fellow founding members were older and more senior in work experience but they deferred to Lee's leadership from the start. Samad Ismail's comment was reflective: "Harry stood out from the rest. He had the personality, the energy and the intelligence." Others said that his legal mind gave him the commanding edge as issues of law and order were intertwined with the politics of the day.

Toh rued that he was just an academic with no mass base whereas Lee was a lawyer who brought in the support of the labour movement and was thus the natural choice to head the party. Having observed Lee in action in industrial disputes, Goh commended his legal ability to spot weaknesses in opposing arguments and latch onto issues that put the other side in an untenable position.

Rajaratnam noted that the "inner group" which included Toh, Goh and him had always accepted Lee as their leader and expected him to be prime minister when the party won the 1959 elections. Mrs Lee made a similar observation: "By some chemistry or something, they accepted his leadership without any question."

If you speak to former leftists, they were just as unqualified in their support for Lee then. PAP founding member and convenor Fong Swee Suan said that Lee was picked unanimously by the CEC as the secretary (before it was changed to secretary-general) because "he was sharp, outspoken and forceful with strong convictions and one who got things done very effectively". S Woodhull agreed that Lee was "the acknowledged leader of all" as he initiated the formation of the party.

It was true that a band of radical leftists launched a coup in the August 1957 party election to capture the CEC but their aim was to keep Lee at the helm to provide legitimate cover. Their plot backfired when Lee refused to hold office. They were dismissed as "maverick adventurers" who strayed from the Malayan Communist Party (MCP) line.

Former MCP secretary-general Chin Peng disclosed in his memoirs that the underground supported Lee. Fang Chuang Pi, who led MCP operations in Singapore, confirmed that he was instructed to back Lee as part of the anti-colonial united front.

Wildly speculative as it might be, the irresistible question that cropped up now and then was: Did it ever cross the mind of any PAP leader to dislodge Lee from the top? Was there no one with a shred of ambition to be primus inter pares?

As far as it could be ascertained, certainly not Goh who had confessed that he disliked politicking and public speaking, and said he lacked the charisma to be the leader. Not Toh either who had received Lee's letter of resignation on two occasions and could have accepted it and taken on the job himself. Instead he had ruled himself out, as he told our writers, because he believed in the principle of collective leadership and that "in politics, you need a legal mind".

What about the reserved and enigmatic Ong Pang Boon who was

once placed on the cover of an international magazine and touted as the next prime minister of Singapore? He had been described as immensely popular with the Chinese-educated cadres and there were frequent references to him receiving more support than Lee in party conferences. But former activists said Ong lacked the ambition and the fire and was completely loyal to Lee.

⚜

ONG Eng Guan was the third member of the nine-man cabinet to be sworn in as the minister for national development at City Hall on 5 June 1959. As treasurer, he ranked No 3 in the party after secretary-general Lee and chairman Toh. Together, they were dubbed the Big Three by pressmen and pundits.

At 34 years, two years younger than Lee, Ong was flying high. His stridently anti-colonial stewardship of the city council had captured the imagination of the neglected masses. He was lauded for his role in propelling PAP to a landslide victory. His ministerial portfolio commanded the biggest budget as it covered low-cost public housing, the centrepiece of the party's manifesto.

Yet one is hard pressed to find anyone in Singapore's history who had soared into the political firmament more rapidly and then plummeted into a black hole so abysmally. What really happened? Why did the most popular politician of the day risk it all by challenging Lee? Was he indeed the much maligned megalomaniac that he had been made out to be in PAP literature?

Ong had disappeared from public view since his exit from politics in 1965. He never spoke to the press again and never gave an oral history interview to the National Archives. All the much-documented allegations about his lust for power and his character defects have gone unrebutted by him.

Former politicians who used to know Ong well often expressed amazement that even in a small place like Singapore they had not crossed paths with him for decades. Ong Pang Boon, who was his deputy mayor, said he had yet to run into him since they parted company in the 1960s. Lee Khoon Choy's last sighting of Ong was sometime in the mid-1970s in Jakarta when he was Singapore's ambassador to Indonesia. He said that Ong had turned up at his embassy to seek some investment advice.

Chen Say Jame, a former leftist trade unionist, caught up with him in 1989 when they went on a two-week holiday in China. During their trip, Ong had asked Chen why the leftists in the PAP voted him out of the CEC in the August 1957 party elections. "I told him I was not involved in the ousting but I said I would have agreed to remove him anyway. I told him that I warned Lee about his ambition," said Chen.

Several attempts to interview Ong in his accountancy firm, Ong Eng Guan and Company, at Ubi Tech Park in Ubi Crescent, failed. On the last occasion in 2003, his accountant wife Claire Chan, whom he married in 1955, said that Ong visited his office only once in a while and that he would call back if he agreed to give an interview. He never did. When his wife died in November 2004, no obituary was placed in the press. His close friends said he had cut off contact with them.

Sadly, Ong's deafening silence will continue to be a glaring omission in the PAP story. To make up for his missing voice, let's listen to the people who knew him and worked with him in the 1950s and 1960s.

A woman friend of Ong and a former PAP member who requested anonymity defended Ong strenuously, saying that he was a much misunderstood man who only wanted to set things right for the party. "When he resigned his seat to contest in Hong Lim, he wanted to prove that the people—trishaw riders, hawkers, *samsui* women and so on—were behind him. Ong was very close to the ordinary folks and that made Lee very uneasy."

In her view, Ong was "neither anti-leftist nor an extreme rightist. He was simply an extreme anti-colonial fighter. In Ong's eyes, Lee was half-hearted in fighting the colonialists."

Like her, Yak Keow Seng believed that both leaders fell out because they could not see eye-to-eye on many issues. For example, he said, Ong was against the continuing employment of senior British civil servants such as George Thomson, A E Blades and P H Meadows. He felt that they were agents of the colonial government but Lee disagreed.

Many former PAP stalwarts and leftists believed Ong felt sorely disappointed at being passed over for a bigger post after the 1959 elections. Given the people's adulation, mayoral record and key role in the polls, he thought he was entitled to no less than the premiership or at the least the deputy premiership, they said.

They had no doubt about his ambition, noting that he was building a power base in the party and his ministry. Fong Sip Chee said that Ong sat on the panel which hand-picked cadres and was able to pack his own people at the party conference on 31 May 1959 to elect the new CEC. Rajaratnam observed that he was filling his ministry with his own political supporters. Ong Chang Sam said that Ong's followers were employed in government departments irrespective of their capabilities.

According to Chen Say Jame, Lee was warned repeatedly about Ong's quest for power. When he asked Lee to remove Ong from the CEC, the prime minister replied that he was his right-hand man. Chen recalled that he wanted to invoke an ancient Chinese fable to convey the danger posed by Ong. But because the prime minister was English-educated, he resorted to Shakespeare's Julius Caesar to make his point. "Caesar died at the hands of his good friend Brutus, didn't he? I told him that Ong would be Brutus in future, the Brutus within PAP."

Lee and company soon found that a style of governance that worked in an anti-colonial city council was very disruptive in an administration running a self-governing state on the road to independence. Ong's mayoral strengths turned into ministerial weaknesses. As mayor, Rajaratnam said, Ong could afford to be destructive by downing the British and civil servants but as minister, he had to be constructive by performing and producing results.

The way Ong ran his ministry began to grate on the nerves of his cabinet colleagues. Then-finance minister Goh recounted how Ong described his permanent secretary, Hon Sui Sen, as someone who could only write minutes and reports and could not get anything done. Ong told Goh that the way to administer was by pressing people from the top and from the bottom, "then they jump and get things done".

Lee remarked that Ong would not give any written instructions. "In fact, he told me once that a good administrator, a good leader, never writes minutes on file. He just brings the file, calls the officer up and tells the man, 'do this' or 'do that'."

When Ong announced a $415 million five-year plan to build 84,000 flats on September 1959, then-labour and law minister K M Byrne complained that was the first time the cabinet knew about it. Goh refused to give him any money saying that his submissions lacked financial logic. To outmanoeuvre Ong, Lee and Goh installed their trusted friend Lim Kim San as chairman of the newly constituted Housing and Development Board (HDB) on 12 February 1960.

Lim's appointment effectively cut Ong off from the most important job of his ministry. His wings had been clipped, his powers stripped. Could the ambitious populist take this lying down?

ONG was not enamoured of the left and the feeling was mutual. But being politically astute, he could sense the undercurrents of unease and tension between the left and Lee. He decided to exploit their differences.

Since the assumption of power by PAP, the leading leftists had felt shortchanged. On their release from detention, they were appointed political secretaries which Woodhull dismissed as sinecures with no say in government policy-making. Lim Chin Siong and Fong Swee Suan were denied cadre membership and isolated from party decision-making.

The opportunity for an open challenge came during a two-day party conference starting on 18 June 1960 at the Cultural Centre, a squat building with a slanted roof on Canning Rise. On behalf of his Hong Lim branch, Ong tabled 16 resolutions, many of which sounded as if they were plucked from the mouths of the leftists.

The resolutions took the party leadership to task for deviating from its anti-colonial party manifesto and failing to consult members when formulating government policy. They took issue with the deregistration of left-wing unions and preventive detention laws and also called for fresh constitutional talks with Britain.

The 16 resolutions were described by Fong Sip Chee as "a challenge to the fundamental precepts of the party". To Low Por Tuck, it was "just an excuse for Ong to fight the party". To Lee, it was a clearcut attempt to split the party and undermine his leadership.

But Ong had underestimated the mettle of the Lee camp. On the second day of the conference, Toh played executioner instead of chairman. Castigating Ong for challenging the collective leadership of the party and disrupting party unity, he swept the resolutions under the carpet and gave the members carte blanche to attack Ong.

A torrent of personal charges and counter-charges was unleashed at the meeting. In a typical exchange, Byrne said he was returning the silver cigarette case that Ong had given him as a Christmas gift lest he be smeared with corruption. Ong retorted that Byrne had given his son a piece of chocolate in return and that he was unable to force his son to vomit it out.

The coup de grace was delivered by Lee Khoon Choy, then parliamentary secretary (culture) who proposed that the CEC expel comrade Ong from the party. When Ong stormed out of the meeting with assemblymen S V Lingam and Ng Teng Kian, Toh asked for a show of hands and the proposal was carried unanimously.

Recalling the incident, K C, as he is better known, said: "I stood up and said that as a matter of principle, he should be sacked. He almost came to tears. In his defence, Ong said that the charges were cooked up by Lee and that it was unconstitutional to sack him." Toh's recollection: "We said, well, let us have a vote. It was voted on, he lost. After that, we told him: 'You're out.' "

On 20 June 1960, Ong was suspended as minister. On 27 July 1960, he and his two henchmen were formally expelled from the party.

For K C, it was a wrenching move as Ong was his good friend who had lent him $500 to buy the coffin for his late wife. "When I walked out of the Cultural Centre that night, Ong saw me. He stopped his car and gave me a lift home," he mused.

Ong had miscalculated. By championing issues close to the hearts of the leftists, he was banking on their support. But they were indifferent to what they perceived as opportunistic grandstanding from an anti-communist demagogue. Low Por Tuck noted that many members were also upset with him for creating a rupture so soon after PAP came into power.

But the sacking of Ong sparked off dissension in some branches which met to decide whether to support the 16 resolutions. Branches which supported Ong were re-organised. Several hundred members from the Hong Lim branch defected to join Ong and the party had to rebuild it from scratch.

At his Chua Chu Kang branch, Ong Chang Sam had to placate dissatisfied members who could not understand why Ong was expelled when he was regarded as a good mayor. He had to explain that Ong was not sincere and truthful and that he was using the 16 resolutions to build up his personal prestige to take over the party and change the government.

Then the sacked minister upped the ante dramatically when he alleged that M R Marcus, the secretary to the city health department, was appointed to the post because he was Byrne's brother-in-law. Two days later he charged that Kwa Soon Chuan was made the deputy commissioner of inland revenue (valuation) because he was Lee's brother-in-law.

On 19 December 1960, Toh, as leader of the house, moved a motion to condemn and suspend Ong for dishonourable conduct on the grounds that he used his privilege in the chamber to spread "malicious falsehoods".

In response, Ong said that the move was illegal and that it should be referred to London for a ruling. But to forestall suspension, he tendered his resignation on 29 December 1960 at 2.13 pm, 17 minutes before the assembly was due to sit.

This legislative controversy over whether a member could move a motion to condemn another was to result in time-consuming debates and research which led to the formation of the committee of privileges to deal with breaches of parliamentary privilege. As Toh reflected, it showed how much a new self-governing assembly had to learn not from precedent but from experience.

A commission of inquiry under Justice F A Chua was conducted between 20 January 1961 and 1 February 1961 to examine the allegations of nepotism. Its findings: Ong's allegations were "reckless and groundless".

Ong's past was raked up. The inquiry learnt that he had married a second wife before legally dissolving his first marriage. Facsimile reproductions of marriage documents appeared in the press to prove he was a bigamist. Ong accused Lee of smearing him. The dirt was flying as a writ was issued for the Hong Lim by-election on 29 April 1961.

⌖

GOH Keng Swee was so confident that PAP would snatch Hong Lim away from Ong that he placed a bet with British commissioner Lord Selkirk. The stake: 100 golf balls.

For the finance minister whose byword was frugality, it turned out to be a "very expensive foolish bet". Selkirk reminisced: "Goh gave me a gross of golf balls which I was very grateful for." Shaken by the results, Goh confessed that he spent so much time on government affairs that his political judgement was impaired.

The showdown of the year pitted the incumbent Ong standing as an independent against Jek Yeun Thong, his former private secretary in the city council. The Chinese newspaper reporter who replaced Ong as party treasurer and became political secretary to the prime minister came with revolutionary credentials—he was a former communist detained by the Labour Front government in 1957 and 1958.

Ong fought under the banner of the 16 resolutions and attacked Lee for being a dictator and his government for doing little for the poor. PAP went all out to expose Ong as an opportunist, liar and bigamist. The ruling party accused Ong of taking an oath that he was a bachelor and marrying another woman in Hong Kong when he was already married with three children.

Typical of the personal assault against Ong was that led by Oh Su Chen, a CEC member and PAP women's league chairman, who asked at a Hong Lim rally: "Would you trust a man like that?" Disclosing that Ong had offered her a "good future" if she remained neutral, she said that she would rather spit on the face of "such a man of no principles and brains".

It was an extremely bitter and intense campaign in which the PAP team covered every house, shop and hawker stall in the ward several times over. Lee led the full cabinet and all his assemblymen with hundreds of branch members in door-to-door canvassing. But it was all in vain. "If the ground is not yours, no amount of organisation can turn the tide," pronounced Fong Sip Chee.

In a resounding repeat of his 1959 victory, Ong polled 7,747 votes or 73.3 per cent of the total votes to trounce Jek by 4,927 votes. Ong's key had locked out Jek's lightning. To the common folks and ordinary party members, the result was a foregone conclusion but to the party leaders, it came as a crushing blow.

The former mayor was simply too entrenched in Hong Lim, a Chinatown ward teeming with hawkers, petty traders, bumboat men, riverside workers, taxi drivers and the jobless. Illiterate or semi-literate, they spoke Hokkien, the dialect of the impoverished Chinese majority.

The widely held perceptions of Ong as a man of the masses, advocate of the underdog and anti-colonial champion could not be dented by PAP propaganda. His mayoral record was still fresh in the minds of the people thankful for the rapid delivery of standpipes, street lamps and other public amenities. They were also grateful for his liberal issue of hawkers' licences and severe crackdown on rude and inefficient civil servants.

What happened on nomination day on 11 March 1961 gave a foretaste of the 49-day election campaign. A Special Branch report said that when Ong turned up to file his papers, he was cheered by members of the PAP Queenstown branch. One member was seen taking off his PAP badge and throwing it on the ground, saying that it was not worth anything. When PAP candidate Jek and fellow assemblymen appeared, they were greeted with boos, catcalls and obscene remarks.

In his rallies at Hong Lim Green, now known as Hong Lim Park, Ong mesmerised the massive crowd with his populist brand of Hokkien demagoguery. Jek, his Cantonese opponent, was simply no match when he spoke in his own dialect and gave Mandarin speeches. The coffee shop talk was that Ong was unbeatable and that even if Lim Chin Siong were to stand for PAP, the latter would have only a 50-50 chance. Betting syndicates gave Ong a 4,000-vote majority.

Ong had an uncanny rapport with people which is still talked about with wonder among former politicians today. K C said that he would squat with the labourers on the roadside and eat with them and ask his wife to help *samsui* women with their household chores. Wherever he went, Ho Puay Choo observed, he would greet people respectfully making them feel that he was close to them.

The sacking of Ong from the party conferred an aura of martyrdom on him and aroused strong anti-PAP feelings. What was so wrong with the 16 resolutions presented by Ong that warranted expulsion? they asked in indignation. Female support for him verged on the obsessive. Young girls fell on their knees, tore at their hair, burst into tears and begged people for the sake of their ancestors to vote for Ong.

Party campaigners realised that the ground which gave PAP the biggest constituency victory in the 1959 elections had turned cold. Very cold. The tell-tale signs were all too evident. While canvassing for Jek, Ho Puay Choo met residents who expressed sheer displeasure over Ong's sacking. "They neither seemed to care about our presence, nor bother to listen to us," she said.

Ong Chang Sam also sensed a drastic change of reception. In the last elections, he said, people would welcome PAP canvassers to their homes and offer them drinks. But in the by-election, "they refused to open the door and abused us when we said we were from PAP".

What went wrong? Reflecting on this low point in the party's fortunes, former PAP top guns concurred that it was well-nigh impossible to overcome Ong's tremendous popularity in Hong Lim. They also conceded that their campaign to expose Ong's personal life backfired miserably.

When PAP went public with Ong's bigamy, Rajaratnam said, it found that it did not have much impact on the people. Instead the attacks sparked off a wave of sympathy for Ong from people who felt that he had been treated unfairly.

"Why bring it out in the open? For the Chinese, having a second wife was not something to get indignant over. A second wife for a Chinese is nothing, it is part of his culture. Lots of Chinese in Singapore have mistresses, concubines. So in a way you are also indicting them," he said. Goh shared the same view noting that the "Chinese-educated thought it was unbecoming to reveal the private affairs of a person in a political fight".

In Devan Nair's mind, PAP went about exposing Ong in a rather legalistic fashion by taking him to a commission of inquiry and giving it wide publicity. "The Chinese electorate in Hong Lim must have decided that all this legal business was wrong."

⚜

THE Hong Lim debacle for the PAP begged one befuddling question: So what happened to its much vaunted support from the left? If the left could move the masses as it did in the 1959 elections, surely it could have swung the voters in favour of Jek who hailed from its ranks.

The answer: Ong had more than a little help from his "enemies". While the leftist leaders were pledging their support for PAP publicly, many of their rank-and-file supporters were helping Ong surreptitiously. A Special Branch report indicated that several leftist unions wanted to support Ong openly but dared not do so for fear of incurring Lee's wrath.

Depending on how you look at it, you could say that the leftists were playing a double game or performing a fine balancing act—letting some members go along with the anti-communist Ong to put pressure on Lee but not going all the way at the expense of losing their ground to him.

Rajaratnam noticed that their leftist comrades were less than forthcoming in their denunciation of Ong during the campaign. "In fact, the prime minister had to force Lim Chin Siong to come and speak on our platform. Which he did but in a very wishy-washy way. He was not walloping Ong. He said, yes, the 16 resolutions were anti-party but some of the resolutions were good and the PAP leaders should take note of them."

When he and his colleagues recognised the pro-communist types in Ong's mass rallies, they realised that the left was getting people from all over the island to turn up to support Ong. "So we knew at that time they were compelled to give verbal support to PAP but quietly they were mobilising support for Ong."

The party scribe concluded that the pro-communists did not mind an Ong victory. "They wanted him to win, to cut us down to size, to make us aware that without communist support, we could not get very far. They knew that if we won, then we'd be even more adamant about our relationship with them."

Ong Chang Sam recalled that he had similar doubts about the left: "The pro-communists knew what Ong's motive was but at the same time they did not want to say he was wrong. They were neutral and ambiguous. When we asked them to mobilise trade union workers to support us, they did it reservedly."

Devan Nair took the view that the left was neither working for nor against Ong. "He was seen as a populist hero at that time. They must have decided that it was not time to take on Ong. Let him destroy Lee first if necessary. But afterwards we would deal with him because his ground and our ground were the same."

The ambivalence of the left was reflected in the reminiscences of Woodhull. Viewing the Hong Lim tussle as a personality clash between Ong and Lee, he said the left would benefit by staying out of the fray. "Our attitude was really not to be over-committed publicly to Lee or Ong."

Although the 16 resolutions resonated with the leftists, they were suspicious of Ong. They felt that his election platform did not stem from his political convictions and that he was just courting their favour to spite Lee. They were especially concerned that he might hijack their issues— and their constituency.

There was no personal chemistry between both camps. Fong Swee Suan said that Lim Chin Siong and he hardly talked to Ong. They had fended off his overtures several times. One account had it that on the day the PAP cabinet was sworn in on 5 June 1959, Ong had asked Tan Gak Eng, a party assistant organising secretary, to arrange for a meeting with Lim Chin Siong to forge an alliance to check Lee but Lim declined.

Indeed the political manoeuvrings among Lee, Ong and the leftists at that time would make for a fascinating case study of Machiavellian machinations for any scholar. As Woodhull commented: "Everybody was watching the next move, circling around, hoping to make the maximum of a given political situation."

The PAP leaders were in a tight spot. How do you counter the most charismatic politician of the day without being held hostage to the left? For their radical comrades, it was a classic conundrum: How do you weaken

Lee to deepen his dependence on the left without empowering Ong at the expense of the left?

⚬⚬❧⚬⚬

REELING from the shock of the colossal fiasco, PAP went through an agonising soul-searching exercise. Why did the party fail so abjectly? Did Ong's overwhelming victory mean a repudiation of PAP and its policies?

Lee tendered his letter of resignation to Toh. Goh thought the resignation was constitutionally wrong as the prime minister should have tendered it to the Yang di Pertuan Negara rather than to the party chairman.

In his two-page letter, Lee acknowledged mistakes committed by the party and sought the reassurance of the CEC. His mandate was re-affirmed by the branches and the letter withdrawn.

His adversaries dismissed the letter as a ploy by Lee to gain public sympathy. Rajaratnam described it as part of the psychological warfare against the left. "I think it created some anxiety among the pro-communist elements because if the PAP leadership resigned, then either the British would take over or there would be a minority government, a caretaker government, which would probably swipe them again."

A review committee was set up on 18 May 1961 to conduct a post-mortem of the Hong Lim defeat, examine the errors of the government and party, and recommend measures for rectification. When the report was completed, Toh gave a summary which was most damning of his government.

Reforms were pushed through without adequate explanation or consultation with the people, the party chairman said as he read the indictment. "People could not follow the machine-gun rapidity of reforms and amendments to legislation and were confused. It was an indication of over-haste. Government should show a willingness to listen to constructive criticisms and if these were just, accept them without fear of losing face."

The bureaucracy was too rigid in the interpretation of rules especially those concerning citizenship and immigration. Civil servants were accused of dilatoriness and bullying the poor. Denied of the opportunity to be corrupt, some enforced regulations with a strictness calculated to arouse general animosity against the government. When people complained, they would say "that is the law as enacted by your own PAP government. If you are dissatisfied, go to your PAP assemblymen."

To remedy the failure in public relations between the governed and the governing, several recommendations were adopted. They included the launch of a courtesy campaign among civil servants and the setting up of a central complaints bureau.

Meanwhile, as party cadres drew bitter lessons from the Hong Lim defeat, they noticed that their leader had plunged into the learning of Hokkien with evangelical fervour. In their recollections, they believed that Lee took up the dialect seriously at this juncture to minimise his dependence on mass orators of dubious motives and mixed loyalties.

Devan Nair pointed out that originally Lee had preferred to operate behind the scenes and put others forward. For example, Lee had high expectations of Ong and wanted to let him "make all the fierce speeches in Hokkien while he would provide the intellectual leadership of the party".

But when Ong broke away from the party, he said, Lee "deliberately set himself out to develop his own style of speaking Hokkien, Mandarin, English, a uniquely conversational style which he didn't have before".

One effect of Hong Lim's defeat on Lee, according to his former parliamentary secretary Chan Sun Wing, was the realisation that if he spoke the language of the hustings like Ong, he could go it alone and need not rely on the pro-communists to rally the people behind him. "It changed Lee's relationship with the leftists. I think it was from then on that Lee believed he could win over the masses without the help of the leftists," he said.

Former PAP assemblyman Tee Kim Leng agreed, noting that it was only after the by-election loss that Lee felt he had to learn to speak Hokkien as well as Ong if he wanted to win over the Chinese ground.

Chan Chee Seng, who often drove Lee around in those days, remembered that when he first knew Lee, he could hardly speak Hokkien but through tenacious effort and constant practice, he was able to acquire fluency. "When we were in the car, he would ask: 'What is this, how do you say this in Hokkien?' Whatever little time he had, he would try to polish up his dialect-speaking skill."

The dust from the Hong Lim battle had barely settled when a new challenge against Lee began brewing in the most unlikely of places— the prime minister's office—and from the most unlikely of persons—the prime minister's parliamentary secretary.

12

"If We Win, We Will Shoot You"

AS provision shopkeeper Leong Keng Seng took a leisurely stroll along undulating Canning Rise, he found himself awash in a flood of sentimentality and nostalgia.

The scenic view of the hill evoked memories of his happy days as a bachelor politician when he shared the same quarters with six other single PAP legislative assemblymen.

Pausing in the public carpark at the foot of the imposing clubhouse of The Legends in Fort Canning Park, he indicated the exact spot where a government bungalow once stood. It was a place they used to call home not long after their radical left-wing party swept the 1959 elections.

The then-parliamentary secretary for education remembered that the double-storey colonial-styled house, with three bedrooms on the upper floor and the living and dining areas downstairs, stood on a slope facing the YWCA building across Fort Canning Road.

Dredging up his memories, Chan Chee Seng said that he occupied one room with Chan Sun Wing and Wong Soon Fong. Leong Keng Seng and Ong Chang Sam took the second room while the third was used by the two single assemblywomen, Chan Choy Siong and Ho Puay Choo.

When the PAP assumed power in June 1959, these Chinese-speaking representatives felt that their cramped Chinatown cubicles or rural *attap* huts were not conducive to legislative and constituency work, what with hordes of people calling on them day and night for help.

According to Chan Chee Seng, they raised their housing problem with finance minister Goh Keng Swee who promptly commandeered the Canning Rise bungalow for their use. Chan Sun Wing recalled that he was then living with his younger brother, an editor with a Chinese newspaper. "When I became the parliamentary secretary in the prime minister's office and was put in charge of the media, Dr Goh thought I should move to the quarters so that I would not be blamed for any news leaks to the press."

For a brief idyllic spell between late 1959 and mid-1961, the sprawling house overlooking a lush expanse of green echoed to the sounds of laughter, gaiety and animated conversations. It was a time of friendship and fellowship. Party colleagues dropped by to banter into the night. The then-political secretary to the prime minister, Jek Yeun Thong, often drove there. Two other political secretaries Lim Chin Siong and Fong Swee Suan treated it as a regular stopover. Home affairs minister Ong Pang Boon turned up discreetly to court Chan Choy Siong.

The single tenants took breakfast in the dining room every morning before going to work with unbridled fervour for their new, exciting, socialist government. After work each day, they left for dinner in Chinatown together. They shunned Orchard Road, dismissing it as a place for the anglicised.

Life did not revolve just around politics and there were lighter moments. Low Por Tuck, a frequent visitor to the hostel, said that the bachelor boys would sometimes cross the road to YWCA after dinner "just to look at the girls". Chan Chee Seng chuckled when he remembered how they trailed Leong Keng Seng and his girlfriend to the East Coast one night.

On Sundays they went on outings. "We were together almost all the time except when we went separately to our branches," reminisced Ong Chang Sam. To stretch their dollar, the $500-a-month assemblymen pooled their contributions to share meals and meet house expenses.

Then one morning Chan Chee Seng woke up to find that no one had knocked on his door reminding him to take breakfast. When he went down to the kitchen, he found that his housemates had left him without a scrap of food. No one invited him to join them for dinner either. At night, he had to walk alone to Koek Road for his meal.

Much to his consternation, he discovered that the group was not only barring him from eating with them but was also no longer talking to him. Something fishy was going on. He suspected that his fellow housemates were starting to organise among themselves.

Although he shared the same bedroom with Chan Sun Wing and Wong Soon Fong, they refused to talk to him. "They did their own business, I did mine. I was isolated, alone there. They became very cold towards me," he said.

It began to dawn on him that he was the odd man out among the group in the big debate on the issue of merger with Malaya. Before he was ostracised, they had been embroiled in acrimonious arguments over the pros and cons of the union broached by Malaya's Prime Minister Tunku Abdul Rahman on 27 May 1961.

The Chan Sun Wing camp had spoken vehemently against merger warning that it would lead to a severe crackdown by the Malayan and British authorities on PAP activists while Chan Chee Seng had defended it robustly, saying that they had nothing to fear if they were not communists.

Initially, the group tried to win him over but gave up when they realised he could not be moved. "They hammered me like hell. One even said, 'Chee Seng, how dare you challenge us? One day if we win, we will put you against the wall as a traitor and shoot you!' "Then they stopped talking to him.

◦◦◦◦

WHEN Goh offered the use of the bungalow to his unmarried colleagues in the chamber, he thought it would help to strengthen party bonding. Well, it did but in a way least expected by him—the closer they got together, the easier it was to conspire against their own government.

Differences between the leftists and the Lee people had existed from the outset of their partnership. Between them lay more than just disparities in world view, educational upbringing and social conditioning. Fong Swee Suan, who confessed that he was an ardent admirer of Lee's political dynamism, pinned it down to three simple words: lack of trust.

Mutual suspicions of each other's agenda dated back to Lee's participation in the London constitutional talks which resulted in several measures abhorred by the left: the retention of the preventive security regulations, the formation of the Internal Security Council (ISC) and the disqualification of detainees from standing for elections.

Some parliamentary secretaries resented their appointment believing they were more qualified than their ministers. The detainees who were released from Changi Prison and appointed political secretaries were aggrieved that they were kept out of government policy-making.

"Associated with but not involved in" was how S Woodhull described his job as political secretary for health. Leong Keng Seng said he was sidelined as parliamentary secretary for education: "They made all the decisions by themselves without consulting us."

Much disagreement centred on control of the party and direction of the government. With Lee and his inner group keeping a tight grip on power through the cadre system, the leftists felt cut off from the party. Lim Chin Siong and Fong Swee Suan were not even made cadre members, let alone co-opted as CEC members. It did not escape their notice that a party conference was held immediately after the 1959 elections but before their release from prison to pre-empt their nomination for the CEC.

As for the infant PAP government, Woodhull said: "We had no idea where it was heading to, what its policies would be, what its agenda was. For example, what was its commitment to trade union rights?" Lee was seen to be deviating from the PAP's socialist manifesto. The curbs on the labour movement did not go down well with the party's trade union rank-and-file. The free-market economic policies pursued by Goh were unpalatable to those who swore by state ownership.

Among the Chinese-educated leftists, the most emotional issue was Chinese education. Leong Keng Seng said that the PAP government promoted English-language schools at the expense of their vernacular counterparts and sought to put the people-funded Nanyang University under the control of the education ministry.

At the back of the minds of both factions was the premonition of an impending showdown. It was not a question of if but when. At a PAP election rally at Clifford Pier on 25 May 1959, Lee had declared that the ultimate contestants would be the PAP and the communists. "It is a battle that cannot be won by just bayonets and bullets. It is a battle of ideals and ideas," he said. Goh said they took it for granted that the big fight would come sooner or later.

When the communist underground reviewed the 1959 election results, Malayan Communist Party (MCP) secretary-general Chin Peng wrote in his memoirs, it predicted that the victorious Lee would move against the communists one day. James Puthucheary related a conversation with Goh in which the finance minister spoke ominously about "scrubbing out" Lim Chin Siong, Fong Swee Suan and even his brother Dominic from the party.

The fundamental issue acting as a lightning rod that brought all these simmering and subterranean differences to a boil was merger with Malaya. Tunku's proposal sent shivers down the collective spine of the left. But why should the leftists be against it when they subscribed to the PAP platform of striving for a socialist Malaya including Singapore? Didn't their leaders sign a statement endorsing this ideal on their release from prison in 1959?

Chan Sun Wing and company on Canning Rise were troubled by what they saw as Tunku's sudden eagerness to embrace merger. Why? Who put him to it? Didn't he oppose it from the start fearing that the entry of a predominantly Chinese Singapore would upset the racial arithmetic in such a union?

Fong Swee Suan admitted that he was baffled by Tunku's announcement and was concerned about the lack of details. Similarly, Low Por Tuck thought it was all suspect to him considering Tunku's fears about the Malays being swamped by the Chinese.

In Sheng Nam Chin's view, merger was part of a grand design put up by Whitehall to strengthen the anti-communist forces in the region. The idea, he contended, was to forestall anything that might happen in Indonesia under President Sukarno who was then aligned to the Communist Party of China (CCP).

Rightly or wrongly, the leftists all smelt a rat and believed it was a plot hatched by Kuala Lumpur and London, with the possible connivance of Singapore, to do them in. They figured that once the fervently anti-communist Malaya took over internal security, it would launch a massive operation to suppress them.

Their preferred stand was to press for full self-government with control over internal security as the first step on the road to independence.

Inevitably, suspicions fell on Lee. When the PAP leaders responded positively to merger, they believed that the prime minister must surely have had a hand in it. Merger was in Lee's interests, they argued, as it would help him to remain in power and keep the leftists at bay with help from the Malayan authorities.

Indeed, while the left saw merger as a conspiracy by Malaya, Britain and Singapore to demolish them, Lee saw merger as a lifeline out of his precarious political position. Expressing his apprehension over the communist threat, he said: "My own assessment of the future was a bleak one. I thought that without merger, their capacity to manipulate the ground on Chinese culture and Chinese language and Chinese civilisation on behalf of the communists would make Singapore ungovernable.

"I was fearful and I would have put our chances of surviving without merger as less than 50-50. And I believe merger was necessary to bring Singaporeans to their senses. Then they knew that first, that this was not a Chinese region, this was a Malay Muslim region..."

Then on 20 April 1961, in yet another twist of fate, a young, well-loved

PAP legislative assemblyman Baharuddin bin Mohamed Ariff died of a heart attack. His death triggered off a by-election in a constituency whose name had become synonymous with opposition challenge: Anson.

⚜

SITTING in the living room lined with Koranic scriptures and Arabic artefacts, the grey-haired man with the matching goatee looked like any doting grandfather in his 70s fussing over the little ones running around his feet.

Meeting him in his son's Housing and Development Board (HDB) flat in Serangoon North, it was hard to picture him as the militant trade union leader who once led busmen on strike while making fiery speeches laced with jokes and expletives, or as the humble bus conductor who rose to be the first president of the National Trades Union Congress (NTUC).

Mahmud Awang's mind flashed back to the tumultuous days of 1961 when he was president of the Trades Union Congress (TUC), an umbrella body for the labour movement, and head of the Singapore Traction Company Employees' Union (STCEU). He spoke of two surprises and three shocks.

Surprise No 1 came when he was asked by Ahmad Ibrahim to be the PAP candidate in the Anson by-election following the sudden death of Baharuddin. He declined but the health minister kept insisting that the prime minister wanted him to stand as he was well regarded as a trade unionist and Anson happened to be a working class ward teeming with Indian and Chinese harbour workers.

"I told Ahmad Ibrahim: 'I'm a layman, I cannot put any money for the election.' He said: 'Don't worry. We'll support you. You just put yourself up. You just talk.' " He said that he only relented when he was told that no less than merger with Malaya was at stake.

Surprise No 2: His opponent was none other than political heavyweight and prominent lawyer David Marshall of the Workers' Party (WP).

Then came Shock No 1 when he realised he had more than the flamboyant former chief minister to contend with. Throwing their weight behind him were his six comrades from the TUC and fellow PAP members—Lim Chin Siong, Fong Swee Suan, S Woodhull, Dominic Puthucheary, S T Bani and Jamit Singh. Dubbed the Big Six, they had turned against their own party and their own government over the issue of the day: independence through merger.

Even before nomination day on 10 June 1961, they had thrown down the gauntlet. If PAP wanted their support in the by-election, the party had to abolish the Internal Security Council (ISC) and the preventive detention laws. Instead of merger, they wanted a "genuinely full internal self-government". And they kept upping the ante with one demand after another: release all political detainees; unite the labour movement; liberalise citizenship criteria; allow freedom of press, speech, assembly and organisation.

Shock No 2 came when eight PAP legislative assemblymen came out in open support of the Big Six. They were Tee Kim Leng, Fung Yin Ching, Tan Cheng Tong, Lin You Eng, Teo Hock Guan, S T Bani and two of the conspiratorial occupants of the Canning Rise hostel—Ong Chang Sam and Wong Soon Fong. Their other house mates were still lying low.

A few days later, 42 trade unions issued a statement in support of their leaders' call for greater freedom for Singapore and the release of union leaders still under detention. It was clear that all these outright challenges signalled an unmistakable call to Anson workers to switch their support to Marshall who had cleverly co-opted leftist causes into his platform.

On the eve of polling day, Lee, with Goh in the front seat, drove past Marshall's rally and saw an enormous crowd. Goh recalled that when Lee dropped him on his way home, he said: "I dread tomorrow's result." Lee knew the chips were down and he was proven right when the ballots were counted. Mahmud was edged out by 546 votes. The lightning was extinguished by the hammer.

Looking back at the biggest shock of all, Mahmud said it was very clear why he lost—Lim Chin Siong's support for Marshall moved the ground against him. Low Por Tuck, who threw in his lot with Lim then, agreed that PAP lost because the trade unions had withdrawn their support for the party's candidate.

But Mahmud also believed that he lost several hundred votes because of a misunderstood eve-of-election speech by John Mammen, an Indian PAP assemblyman. It was construed by Indian voters as suggesting that if they were against merger and did not vote for PAP, they would be shipped back to India. Many Indians were offended and voted against the party, he said.

If the leftists were surreptitious in their support for Ong Eng Guan in the Hong Lim by-election, they had come right into the open with their backing for Marshall in Anson. In PAP lexicon, this break has come to be known as The Big Split.

Toh Chin Chye did not mince his words when he attributed the defeat to the treachery of PAP members who jumped ship midway through the campaign to aid the enemy. S Rajaratnam described the situation as irretrievable saying that the time had come for a showdown.

The sentiment was reciprocated by the left. "Both parties stood firm on their stand and the parting of ways was inevitable," reflected Fong Swee Suan. The united front had cracked.

No longer comrades-in-arms, Lim Chin Siong and Lee Kuan Yew were locked in a power tussle in which only one winner could emerge. As Fong put it in Mandarin, *yi shan bu neng cang er hu*, or "a mountain cannot have two tigers".

With two by-election defeats in two months, PAP had never sunk so low in its electoral fortunes. As its leader, Lee assumed full responsibility and submitted his letter of resignation as prime minister to the party chairman two days after the Anson defeat. The CEC spent the whole night deliberating on it before Toh penned its reply. Was Lee really throwing in the towel? Or was it just a tactical ploy?

❦

YOU might have read about the Mad Hatters' Tea Party in Lewis Carroll's *Alice in Wonderland*. But have you heard about the Eden Hall Tea Party which has passed into PAP literature as a classic tale of political duplicity? Today conspiracy theorists continue to garnish their stories while scholars ponder how it might have changed the course of Singapore history.

Depending on whom you listened to, you would get a varying interpretation of the meeting between the UK commissioner and four leading leftists at his white Edwardian-styled mansion called Eden Hall on 18 July 1961.

Given the various versions being tossed around, you could be reminded of yet another classic—the 1950 film "Rashomon" by famed Japanese director Akira Kurosawa, in which the rape of a woman and murder of a man were recalled from different and contradictory points of view to illustrate the gossamer elusiveness of truth.

The rendezvous took place one day after Lee withdrew his letter of resignation following the PAP CEC's pledge of full confidence in him and two days before he moved a motion of confidence in the legislative assembly to expose the rebels in his party.

On that sultry Saturday afternoon, UK commissioner Lord Selkirk together with his deputy Philip Moore met Lim Chin Siong, Fong Swee Suan, S Woodhull and James Puthucheary for tea in his Eden Hall residence on 28 Nassim Road. The get-together was initiated by Puthucheary at the request of Lim who wanted to ascertain the British position on a possible leftist takeover of the government.

As Fong recalled, they wanted to know if the British would back PAP in crushing them before they could put up a constitutional fight. In his recollection, Woodhull could not resist paraphrasing Selkirk's reply to them: "As Her Majesty's representative, I'm here to see the country move forward towards democracy. And we shall not use our powers unless there is a real threat to life and limb."

Were the British manipulating one group against another as alleged by PAP leaders? Woodhull stressed that he had no such impression and had no doubt whatsoever of Selkirk's openness and sincerity. "He played cricket," pronounced the retired lawyer who died in 2003 at the age of 71, four months after giving this interview in Kuala Lumpur.

Through Special Branch surveillance of Eden Hall, Lee came to know about the meeting and took umbrage. He accused the British lion of fraternising with the communist bear to overthrow his government. By giving the leftists confidence to capture the government, he thundered, PAP would be forced to fight back and suppress them—and that was what the British wanted all along.

In the reflections of former PAP leaders, the British were described as puppet masters who split the party and engineered a collision between both factions. They played a double game giving the impression to PAP that they wanted to lock up the pro-communists and giving the impression to the pro-communists that they could form an acceptable government.

It was all planned, declared Goh, noting that the British could have discouraged the leftists from making a bid for power. Ahh, the duplicity of man, he ruminated, how else could the British have run a vast empire with great success? Rajaratnam commented: "I don't believe for one moment the British would accept if the leftists won constitutionally."

But listen to the oral history interview with Selkirk and comb through all the British records of the period and you would glean a different impression. Selkirk made it clear that if there were no infringement of the constitution or recourse to violence, it would be quite improper for him to interfere in the political life of Singapore.

Here is one excerpt:

Question : If they were to win an election, Lord Selkirk, would you have been prepared to let them form the government?

Selkirk : Oh yes! I would.

Question : Lim Chin Siong and company?

Selkirk : Oh well, if they had had a majority in the assembly.

In one diplomatic despatch, he wrote: "I am certain that even if the next government is much further to the left or even communist-manipulated, we must allow the full democratic processes to work under the constitution provided that there is no threat to the internal security situation which requires our intervention."

What about Lee's accusations? Selkirk dismissed them as a "ridiculous fairy tale" concocted to put him in an anti-colonial light and to "throw a smokescreen over the grave dissensions within the party".

In his memoirs, Lee insisted that he could not accept Selkirk's explanation and was convinced the leftists had been tricked by an experienced politician. Well, who can unravel these varying shades of reality a la "Rashomon"? Where did unvarnished truth end and political spin begin?

⁕

LEE decided that it was time to draw a line in the sand. What better way to do it than to move a motion of confidence in the legislative assembly— every PAP member would be compelled to stand up and be counted. He knew that at least eight dissidents had turned against him during the Anson campaign.

It was a dangerous gamble to take in the 51-seat chamber. If 26 assemblymen voted against the motion, his government would fall leading to the possible formation of a leftist government or precipitating a general election in which the PAP was more than likely to lose in the wake of the double by-election fiascos.

As Low Por Tuck recalled, the prime minister convened a City Hall meeting and called on all PAP assemblymen to support merger and sign a form pledging full confidence in him. Low expressed reservations saying that "it was like signing a blank cheque to support merger" and requested a postponement for the signing. The next day, he received a notice for the motion of confidence sitting.

Ong Chang Sam said that some assemblymen appealed to Lee to change his policies in the light of the by-election failures and loss of popular support for the party. They expressed concerns that the merger could be used against the leftists but Lee turned them down and so they did not sign the forms.

Meanwhile the leftists were zealously soliciting support too. After being rebuffed by the CEC in their bid to stage a conference of all 51 party branches to challenge Lee, they held a flurry of meetings to cajole and coax their uncommitted colleagues to line up with them.

Buang Omar Junid, the then-member for Kallang, was roped into a City Hall meeting held by Lee Siew Choh and attended by a dozen assemblymen. He listened to Wong Soon Fong, Lin You Eng, Ong Chang Sam and Chan Sun Wing declaring that they no longer believed in Lee's leadership and urging the group to unite and leave the PAP.

"Everyone was asked in turn and each indicated his support ... When I was asked to speak, I said I wanted to find out if what was said was right or not," recounted Buang. Later he told Lee Siew Choh he would not join them as he had full confidence in the prime minister.

Lee Khoon Choy referred to another City Hall meeting held by Chan Sun Wing among the parliamentary secretaries. They talked about taking over the cabinet following Lee's threat to quit as prime minister. At one point, he said, Sheng Nam Chin turned to him and uttered: "You be the prime minister."

K C remembered that he almost burst into laughter when they discussed what portfolios they should take over—Chan Sun Wing as minister for education, Sheng Nam Chin as minister for health and Low Por Tuck as minister for finance. When he realised they were using him against Lee, he left the meeting. Chan Sun Wing and Sheng Nam Chin had since denied that there was ever such a meeting. Sheng retorted: "Who am I to offer him the post of prime minister?"

Yaacob Mohamed, one of the nine parliamentary secretaries then, cited a similar bid by leftists to topple Lee and seize power. His recollection was that Siew Choh would be prime minister with Lee Khoon Choy as deputy prime minister and Sheng Nam Chin as health minister. He said that he was offered a ministerial post if he were to join them.

In former British journalist Dennis Bloodworth's account, Lee had collected 24 signed pledges of support when he entered the house to move his motion of confidence. The whip was lifted to allow a free vote. The debate lasted a record-breaking 13 hours and 21 minutes, having started on 20 July at 2.34 pm and ending the next day at 3.55 am.

The jam-packed public gallery was treated to an unprecedented spectacle which saw PAP assemblymen lunging at one another's jugular with acidic barbs and stinging metaphors. Lim Yew Hock and his Singapore People's Alliance (SPA) colleagues gloated over the intra-party fighting. One UMNO representative derided PAP as a *gadoh-gadoh* ("quarrelling" in Malay) party.

They mocked Lee for bringing a party dispute into a public chamber at taxpayers' expense. The PAP leftists joined in the condemnation arguing that the motion should be thrashed out in the party rather than in the assembly. But Lee's key contention was that the ruling party must know where it stood as it prepared for merger with Malaya and settle the conditions before presenting it to the people.

As the time to call for a division or to take a vote neared, Lee made a headcount and found that he was short of one vote to secure a majority. All attention was focused on PAP member for Siglap Sahorah binte Ahmat, a plump Malay housewife who was then laid up in hospital with a big question mark over her party allegiance.

Chan Chee Seng volunteered to fetch her from hospital to vote for the motion. "At first PM dismissed my suggestion saying I would be wasting my time as the leftists had already won her over. But Toh told Lee to let me give it a try. And so off I went."

At Singapore General Hospital, Chan found Sahorah in tears. Complaining that no one in PAP cared about her, she said she had given her word to the leftists. Chan appealed to her not to switch sides saying that if she did not vote for her party, the PAP government would collapse.

She relented and Chan arranged for the hospital to send her to the assembly house in an ambulance. "Sahorah was carried up to the chamber. We walked in, the door closed and the bell rang. She voted just in time. I flashed a V sign to a smiling Lee," said Chan.

A July 22 report in *Nanyang Siang Pau* said that Sahorah was rushed by ambulance to the chamber to cast her decisive vote. It noted that she was helped to her seat by Chan Choy Siong and Ismail Rahim at 3.25 am when Lee was delivering his closing speech.

When the motion of confidence was finally put to a vote, the result revealed a fragmented house: 27 ayes, 8 nays and 16 abstentions. PAP clinched 26 votes from its own assemblymen plus one more vote from independent member C H Koh. WP's David Marshall and all SPA members voted against the motion. In all, 13 dissident PAP assemblymen abstained, joined by their former colleagues in the United People's Party (UPP)—Ong Eng Guan, Ng Teng Kian and S V Lingam.

Why did they abstain? Ong Chang Sam explained that they could not vote against the motion as they were still PAP members and were hoping that the government could be pressurised into changing its policy on merger. Low Por Tuck said that they had no intention of throwing out the PAP government.

❦

PLOUGHING through the speeches in the Hansard, or verbatim record of the marathon sitting, you could sense the poignancy of friendships lost and relationships severed.

For The Big Split was not just a political episode about the breakup of a ruling party, it was an all-too-human story about people caught up in a vortex of emotions as they turned against one another.

You could discern the note of sentimentality in Lee's voice when he said that it was with sadness that he watched the resolve of his friends and comrades melting in the heat of the battle. They were not crooks and rogues, he lamented, but they lacked the sternness of purpose in the face of strong persuasion and silent intimidation.

Referring to S T Bani as a friend twice, Lee recounted how they fought together to stop the Singapore Traction Company Employees' Union (STCEU) from falling under communist domination. Goh spoke movingly of his friendship with Lee Siew Choh, how it began over the chessboard and lasted through the years.

For Lee, perhaps "the most unkindest cut of all" came from his own parliamentary secretary, Chan Sun Wing, whom he had trusted as his aide and friend. He was shocked when he learnt from Special Branch that Chan was plotting against him in the Canning Rise quarters. Ditto for Goh when he found that his own parliamentary secretary, Low Por Tuck, whom he liked immensely, had also switched sides.

The PAP leaders also found that their faith in supposedly non-communist professionals was sadly misplaced. Medical practitioners Lee Siew Choh and Sheng Nam Chin had no qualms about crossing to the leftist camp and leading the charge against them.

To Lee, it was as clear as daylight that if you did not vote for his motion, you were against it. The 13 PAP assemblymen who abstained were sacked from the party. They comprised the five parliamentary secretaries—Lee Siew Choh, Sheng Nam Chin, Chan Sun Wing, Leong Keng Seng and Low Por Tuck, and backbenchers Wong Soon Fong, Ong Chang Sam, Tee Kim Leng, Lin You Eng, Tan Cheng Tong, Teo Hock Guan, S T Bani and Fung Yin Ching. The three non-elected political secretaries, Lim Chin Siong, Fong Swee Suan and S Woodhull, were also given the boot.

On the day of their expulsion, Low Por Tuck recalled, the assemblymen gathered at—where else?—the house on the hill to ponder their next move. They decided to form a new party called Barisan Sosialis ("Socialist Front" in Malay) to provide an alternative government for Singapore.

Formed on 13 August 1961 and registered on 17 September 1962, it became the biggest opposition party in the house. Lee Siew Choh was elected chairman, Woodhull vice-chairman, Lim Chin Siong secretary-general, Poh Soo Kai assistant secretary-general and Low Por Tuck treasurer. Its CEC members included Lim Hock Siew, Wong Soon Fong, Fong Swee Suan, Chan Sun Wing, Ong Chang Sam, S T Bani, T T Rajah and the Puthucheary brothers.

A five-pointed red star set in a blue circle against a white background was adopted as the Barisan logo. Its uncanny resemblance to the star on communist China's flag discomfited James Puthucheary who lobbied for a change to a four-pointed or three-pointed star without success.

But what really shook PAP to its very foundations was the mass defections of its branches and members. Some 35 out of 51 branches crossed over to Barisan together with 19 out of 23 branch secretaries. To Lee's dismay, he learnt that his Tanjong Pagar branch had been pulled like a rug from under his feet. His branch secretary, Chok Kor Thong, turned out to be the ringleader involved in mobilising all 51 PAP branches against the leadership.

When Toh went to his Rochor branch, he found that his branch secretary had vanished. K C said that his Bukit Panjang branch "just disapppeared" when more than half of his committee members, including his chairman and secretary, joined the exodus.

Many branches were literally stripped bare when their officials scooted. Desks, chairs, teacups, kettles, clocks, cupboards, fans and sewing machines were carted away only to re-appear at the Barisan branches. Barisan signboards were displayed brazenly at some PAP branches.

Giving their side of the story, Ong Chang Sam said that all the committee members of his Chua Chu Kang branch decided to join Barisan after he warned them that the government would use merger against the leftists. Sheng Nam Chin said that he would have been isolated if he had not allowed his Nee Soon branch to defect.

For PAP, the loss of 35 branches was just the first staggering blow. Two more, aimed at delivering the knockout punch, were to come.

To reach out to the people, the government had set up the People's Association (PA) in 1960 with its network of community centres. The Works Brigade (WB) was formed to train unemployed youths in bricklaying, farming, water pipe repairs and other vocational skills.

But unknown to the party leaders, communist agents had burrowed deeply into both organisations. A stark admission of communist infiltration came from a former MCP member who said that the underground gave him the signal to join PA.

Pro-Barisan PA employees mounted a 10-month strike from September 1961. Joining them were many community centre leaders as well as PA staff members. And when the strikers realised they could no longer return to PA, he said, they resorted to political agitation over merger against the government.

Over at the WB, some 2,000 unruly members staged a mutiny when they defied instructions and refused to work. The cabinet decided on an overwhelming display of force to overawe the strikers. It worked. When soldiers surrounded the camp with fixed bayonets, the youngsters capitulated.

Behind the uprising in the PAP branches and PA was none other than the prime minister's parliamentary secretary, Chan Sun Wing. Ong Pang Boon said that Chan was able to convince Lee to appoint many of the defecting PAP organising secretaries despite their security records. As Chan was also in charge of staff recruitment for PA, he enlisted many of the community centre leaders into his camp.

As for the instigator of the Works Brigade incident, all fingers pointed at Wong Soon Fong, who was attached to the labour ministry as "chief of staff" of the uniformed group. Goh believed that Chan and Wong were deliberately planted in the government by MCP cadre Fang Chuang Pi to outmanoeuvre Lee.

Chan Chee Seng and Wong were colleagues in the brigade when hostilities broke out. The tension spilled over into their Canning Rise quarters. When they went to bed in the same room, they turned away from each other without wishing one another good night.

⚜

TWO by-election defeats. Mass defections from the party. People's Association and Works Brigade under siege. Labour movement led by leftists. Rural, youth and student organisations captured by pro-communists. Public opinion swinging towards the opposing camp.

PAP faced its darkest hour in history as it teetered on the brink of collapse. From 43 seats in the 51-seat assembly in June 1959, its massive majority had dwindled to a wafer-thin 26-25 by July 1961 when the 13 PAP rebels crossed the floor.

Like a punch-drunk boxer, the party was reeling on the ropes. Lim Kim San recalled a despondent Goh saying that there were times when they thought of calling it quits and asking Lim Chin Siong to take over.

In a despatch to London dated 17 July 1961, Selkirk referred to a dinner with Lee and Goh and recorded: "I found them pretty broken men, extremely jumpy and uncertain of their political future."

Lee told him that he could rely on only 23 certain votes in the assembly and that he could hold on for another three months before the communists took over. "He now has considerable doubts whether Singapore can be governed on the basis of one man, one vote, and that the government of Singapore must now pass to the communists, the British or the Federation of Malaya," wrote the UK commissioner.

At a Special Branch briefing, its director Richard Corridon commented that what took place in the weeks after The Big Split was an "exact repetition of what happened under Lim Yew Hock with unions in full cry and rapid rebuilding of open front organisations". He warned that PAP was no match for Lim Chin Siong and the Middle Road unions.

As the merger debate gathered momentum, each sitting lent itself to high drama and cliffhanger suspense. The opposition smelled blood and called for a division at every opportunity. What grated Lee and company even more was that they had to depend on the support of their legislative enemies in SPA to fend off the advances of their former comrades.

One more turn of the screw came during a crucial debate on the Malaysia plan on 3 July 1962. Ho Puay Choo resigned from the party to be an independent saying that she did not agree with the terms for merger. When she joined Barisan on 11 August 1962, the pendulum swung to a perilous 25-26. The PAP had lost its majority.

As luck would have it, S V Lingam resigned from UPP and rejoined PAP, and it was back to 26-25. Phew!

Fate then intervened to give the power equation another hair-raising twist. On 21 August 1962, Ahmad Ibrahim, the minister for labour, died of liver disease at the age of 35 and the house was deadlocked at 25–25. As the prospect of another by-election loomed—with talk of Lim Chin Siong standing—the spectre of Hong Lim and Anson rose to haunt PAP all over again.

13

Devan Nair: "I Expected To Die"

THEY were comrades, friends and neighbours. But when they clashed during The Big Split, their personal ties became so strained they had to plan their day's movements to avoid crossing one another's path.

In 1960 and 1961, Devan Nair lived with his family on Youngberg Terrace off Upper Serangoon Road overlooking the sprawling Bidadari cemetery. Occupying the house next door was S Thendayatha Bani, a slender, handsome Indian, with a sharp nose and neat moustache.

More than just colleagues in the ruling party, they were fellow leaders in the Trades Union Congress (TUC) which sought to be the umbrella grouping for the labour movement. Both were also associated with the Singapore Teachers' Union (STU) and the Singapore Traction Company Employees' Union (STCEU).

When the battle lines were drawn over merger, Bani and five other TUC leaders dubbed the Big Six broke with Nair to oppose the Lee government. Bani was also one of the 13 dissident PAP legislative assemblymen who crossed the floor to form Barisan Sosialis.

As friendship gave way to enmity, the neighbours were no longer on speaking terms. Bani's political hostility, however, did not extend to Mrs Nair. Whenever he sniffed the aroma of her fabled cooking, the then-bachelor would make sure Nair was not around before popping next door to ask for a helping.

Ironically, Nair had moved to Youngberg Terrace to escape the politicking of another three of the Big Six—his fellow former inmates from Changi Prison. Following their release in June 1959, they were appointed political secretaries and housed in a bungalow on Nassim Hill.

But Nair, who was posted to the ministry of education, found his stay with the three political secretaries—Woodhull (health), Lim Chin Siong (finance) and Fong Swee Suan (labour)—and Industrial Promotion Board manager James Puthucheary a "distressing experience". It was like being embroiled in endless debates in Changi all over again.

He was upset that his colleagues were reneging on their pledges in the document "The Ends and Means of Socialism" which they had signed as a condition for their release. "After a hard day at the ministry, I would return home to be right in the middle of the plotters. They did not give up hope altogether in getting me back into the fold. I resisted, I told them they were on a collision course with PAP."

When he heard Tunku's proposed Malaysia plan on 27 May 1961, he was elated but knew that the pro-communists would oppose it fearing that they would be at the mercy of Kuala Lumpur. Returning to Nassim Hill that night, he saw gloomy faces all around. "I remember telling James: 'Why is everybody so glum? After all, we are committed to Malayan national unity.' And they said: 'No, no, this is bad for the revolution.' "

Nair knew that they were unhappy with him as he had given up on communism and thrown in his lot with Lee. Even before his imprisonment from 1956 to 1959, he had already been troubled by the brazen displays of Chinese chauvinism in pro-communist posters and the flogging of Chinese language and culture issues.

Behind bars, he grew so disillusioned with communism after pondering political developments in Eastern Europe that he wanted to go off and study law in London. As Mrs Nair recounted, a deal for his release was arranged by Special Branch's Richard Corridon with the help of Nair's good friend, Francis Thomas. "But there was a leak from the Lim Yew Hock government which resulted in *The Straits Times* reporting that Devan Nair had a "change of heart". So I told him not to go," she said.

Nair wrote to the British governor saying that if he were released he would denounce the colonial government. So the authorities extended his Changi stint. But he knew that sooner or later he had to signal his break with his comrades.

That moment came on the morning of 4 June 1959 as they were being released from Changi Prison and as jubilant supporters gathered outside the wall to greet them. "While we were waiting for the gates to open, I turned to Lim Chin Siong and said: 'Chin Siong, if you have any secrets to tell me, be careful. Don't tell them to me because whatever you tell me will go straight to PAP. And I am with PAP from now on.' "

NAIR sensed the inevitability of the split when he saw his Nassim Hill housemates being sucked into the Middle Road political hothouse. To his chagrin, his good friend Fong Swee Suan was swinging to the other side. He could not fathom the turnaround of James Puthucheary, the most strident anti-communist critic in Changi. They all seemed to have bought the myth of communist invincibility.

Having gone through thick and thin with his old comrades, he could not bring himself to confront them in public but was incensed that they were drawing government salaries as office-holders while preaching subversion. To free himself from their ideological clutches, he resigned from his government post in 1960 and returned to teach in St Andrew's School. He also moved to Youngberg Terrace.

But his classroom lessons were often disrupted by phone calls. "You are not supposed to be disturbed but when the call comes from PM, what do you do?" He said that Lee kept making him feel guilty by saying: "We are all fighting with our backs to the wall, you are correcting exercise books." After six months, he told Lee: "All right, I'll come back into the field full-time."

One early initiative of the new PAP government was to revitalise the Singapore Trades Union Congress (STUC) as a unifying body for the labour movement. Formed in 1951 by Lim Yew Hock and V K Nair, it drew mainly English-speaking members before falling into disrepute because of its links with gangsters and corrupt characters.

Perhaps to dissociate itself from its unsavoury past, it was re-labelled Trades Union Congress (TUC). Mahmud Awang, who headed STCEU, was appointed president. Taking over as secretary-general was G Kandasamy, then parliamentary secretary (culture). Joining him in the powerful secretariat were Nair, Bani, Lim Chin Siong, Fong Swee Suan, Woodhull, Jamit Singh, Dominic Puthucheary, Ow Kheng Tor and Buang Omar Junid.

Introduced to the public in the first May Day rally in 1960, they were dubbed Ten Tall Men—named after a Hollywood movie of the same name which starred Burt Lancaster and told the story of 10 French Foreign Legionnaires who foiled an attack by Muslim Berbers in Egypt.

The facade of unity, however, could not mask their differences for long as the wrangling between the pro-communist and non-communist unionists within TUC grew increasingly bitter. Nair spoke of how Lim Chin Siong and his associates were tightening their grip on the labour movement while Kandasamy and he had to fight a holding action. "We were hopelessly outflanked," he admitted.

The divergence of views became more discordant as they argued over labour laws and industrial relations practices. Dominic Puthucheary noted that the Chinese-educated leftists instinctively resisted the arbitration system and curbs on the right to strike. They feared that their role would be diminished "if it no longer depended on organisational power but on economics and arguments in court".

All these issues reached a flashpoint over the proposed merger with Malaya announced by Tunku and welcomed by the PAP leaders. The result: Six Tall Men withdrew their support for PAP in the Anson by-elections. By breaking ranks, they had turned against their own TUC president, Mahmud Awang, who was standing as the PAP candidate.

Lim Chin Siong, Fong Swee Suan, Bani, Woodhull, Dominic Puthucheary and Jamit Singh opposed the Malaysia plan stridently calling instead for full internal self-government with control over home security. The Big Six's big worry was that with merger, the anti-communist federal government would have no qualms about cracking down on them.

Their action in backing Workers' Party's David Marshall against PAP/TUC's Mahmud Awang was condemned as political treachery by the remaining non-communist Tall Men. Aghast, they pointed out that Bani was not only their TUC colleague but also adviser to STCEU of which Mahmud was president.

Nair said he made no secret of his fury when they declared their support for Marshall. "I remember warning them that that would be the beginning of the end. The beginning of the end of the kind of Singapore we wanted because my line was 'Look, you destroy PAP, you are going to allow Alliance-type politics to come over...' "

According to Kandasamy, the leftists did not consult the TUC leadership before jumping onto Marshall's platform. He remembered spending one whole night at the Queen Street headquarters tearing up documents to keep them from falling into their hands.

As an indication of the mutual suspicions in TUC, he said that during long meetings into the night, Lee would phone to find out what was happening. His assistant would enter the meeting room and say "your uncle on telephone" or "your mother" or "your sister wants you". After a while, Lim Chin Siong and company saw through it and said: "Yeah, Kanda, go lah, your uncle Lee Kuan Yew."

All the gloves came off at a forum on merger held by the University Socialist Club on 10 July 1961. To those who witnessed the verbal duel between Nair and Woodhull, it was a dramatic manifestation of the break. British journalist Dennis Bloodworth commented that it really brought the split out into the open.

Nair accused the leftists of veering away from their 1959 position on merger and using the PAP as their punching bag. Woodhull responded robustly throwing up one of his memorable quips that Nair was like a character in a George Bernard Shaw play who got closer to the right the more he progressed to the left.

The forum also featured a young law student who challenged PAP's contention that merger was necessary as Singapore lacked the prerequisites to go it alone. To cheers from the students, he presented the view that Singapore could survive as an independent economic entity. History has since proved him right. His name: Tommy Koh.

The forum fireworks gave a sneak preview of the impending showdown. Ten days later Lee moved a motion of confidence in the legislative assembly to separate the "sheep from the goats". The true colours of 13 PAP representatives were exposed when they abstained from voting for their own government.

The split in PAP was mirrored in the split in TUC as the leading protagonists and antagonists were the same in both the party and the labour movement. The Big Six were all PAP members. So were Nair, Kandasamy, Mahmud and Buang.

Just as PAP suffered a breakup leading to the formation of the breakaway party Barisan Sosialis, TUC experienced a similar meltdown with pro-PAP and pro-Barisan trade unions squaring up to confront one another.

When TUC was dissolved on 3 August 1961, the slate was wiped clean for the divided labour movement to regroup and re-register. Nair, Kandasamy and Mahmud set up a pro-tem body called National Trades Union Centre which was later renamed National Trades Union Congress (NTUC). Not to be eclipsed, Lim Chin Siong and company announced the formation of the Singapore Association of Trade Unions (SATU).

The starter's gun had sounded for the winner-take-all race to win the hearts and minds of Singapore workers.

LIKE Barisan Sosialis which had the upper edge over PAP at the outset, SATU enjoyed a similar headstart over NTUC. Just as one PAP branch after another was defecting to the other side, one trade union after another was following suit.

SATU had a flying start with the support of 82 unions. Seven out of every 10 Chinese industrial unions came within its fold. Its backbone was the Singapore General Employees' Union (SGEU) which replaced the defunct Singapore Factory and Shop Workers' Union (SFSWU). Called *fan xin* in Mandarin, it boasted 20,000 members and 32 affiliates.

Propped up by two other pillars—the powerful Singapore Business Houses Employees' Union (SBHEU) which represented private sector workers and the militant Singapore Bus Workers' Union (SBWU)—SATU epitomised the unshakeable might of the Middle Road labour movement under the helm of Lim Chin Siong.

James Puthucheary commented that SATU was riding high on the trust of the workers. Former left-wing unionist Chen Say Jame noted that SATU was already a strong and widespread union attracting large numbers of workers when NTUC had barely started its recruitment drive.

In their reminiscences, the pro-PAP unionists of the day agreed that SATU dominated the labour scene while NTUC was still struggling to find its feet. "By providing strong leadership, SATU was able to get a majority of workers especially the Chinese workers under its control," admitted Ho See Beng, the former general secretary of the Singapore Printing Employees' Union (SPEU) who later became NTUC president. His daughter, Ho Geok Choo, became West Coast GRC MP in 2001.

Such was the over-arching reach of the left-wing unions that their control extended to workers in many manufacturing firms and in strategically important areas such as the port, naval base and public transport.

SATU also had history on its side—radical trade unionism went back to the post-war years when it was heavily influenced by MCP and became integral to the anti-colonial struggle. Backed by student bodies and mass organisations and led by fiery ideologues, the left-wing labour movement proved to be a potent political force.

One key factor which gave SATU a sharp edge over NTUC in the early days was its leadership, according to former NTUC unionist and PAP MP Eric Cheong. Virtually all the leading unionists were on the other side, he pointed out. "SATU had the whole gamut of leaders. It had the Chinese-educated leaders like Lim Chin Siong and Fong Swee Suan; it had the English-educated ones like Woodhull and Bani. It had the Puthucheary brothers, Kam Siew Yee, Lim Shee Ping and so on. Whereas on our side there was only Devan."

SATU's English-educated unionists were articulate and conversant with labour laws. Bani was reputed for his intellectual approach to problems and negotiating prowess across the table. Dominic Puthucheary and Lim Shee Ping were commended for their skills in sewing up collective agreements.

Cheong, who worked with them when he was with SBHEU, said that they were very persuasive when arguing their cases for workers. He remembered that when Lim Shee Ping represented the Jardines branch, he negotiated an excellent union agreement for the workers. "For the first time, he got a very good increment across the board and that's why we got 100 per cent union membership. That was a tremendous achievement."

Of course, the threat of industrial action by the pro-communist unions compelled many employers to give in to their demands. Ho See Beng acknowledged that their militant brand of trade unionism attracted many Chinese workers influenced by the communist revolution in China.

In contrast, he said, the non-communist union leaders were seen as less motivated, less organised and less able to mobilise workers. "As they were mostly English-educated, they could not reach out to the Chinese-speaking workers," he said.

Left-wing unions appeared to enjoy a good press too. A newspaper article on 14 February 1960 described SGEU as one of the most active and successful unions on the island. It reported that in the last eight months, it had clinched more than $400,000 in arrears of overtime pay, leave pay, holiday pay and bonuses for workers through negotiations with employers. Its leaders were singled out for their earnestness and dedication.

As the beleaguered Nair looked at the overwhelming majority of trade unions lined up with SATU, he could not help thinking that the communist united front was unbeatable. How was his toddling NTUC going to survive? How could David slay Goliath?

Against the leading lights of the left, he could only rely on a handful of unionists namely Kandasamy, Mahmud, Ang Kim Thye, Ow Kheng Tor and Buang Omar Junid. He could only count about 12 unions or their remnants on his side. "We were a miserable minority. I personally thought we were going to lose," he said. Mahmud noted that it was because NTUC represented only the minority that it decided not to seek registration.

It was certainly an inauspicious start for the labour organisation whose acronym is synonymous with the success of Singapore today.

A top priority for Nair then was to ensure that the union he was most intimately associated with—STCEU—did not fall to the left. The union formed his personal power base which owed nothing to PAP or the pro-communists. It was his sterling leadership of the union during a five-month strike in the early 1950s which imprinted his name in the public consciousness.

When he was detained in 1956, his position as union adviser was taken over by Bani. On his release, he was welcomed as an "extra adviser". During The Big Split, Bani engineered a resolution that would recognise only himself as the adviser. Nair insisted on a secret ballot in the general council while Bani wanted a show of hands. "Most of them agreed with me. When the ballots were counted, out of 75 or so members, Bani had only six votes. All the rest were for me, so Bani had to leave," said Nair.

Fortune also smiled on him when many of the civil service unions allied themselves with NTUC. For that alignment, much of the credit should go to Kandasamy who had the vision to found an omnibus union for all government servants after PAP assumed power in 1959. The Amalgamated Union of Public Employees (AUPE) was all but impervious to communist blandishments. Although Nair and Kandasamy were not on the best of terms as they jostled for influence, their unions were to form the bedrock for NTUC.

S R Nathan was a seamen's welfare officer when he was asked by Kandasamy to help in the formation of AUPE and assume its presidency for a year. He agreed. Looking back, he believed that Kandasamy made an invaluable contribution to public service unionism by bringing all civil servants together. If AUPE had not drawn in all the government employees in the lower divisions, he contended, they could have been lost to the other side as they were so disenchanted.

With AUPE, instead of dealing with a multitude of feeble unions, he said, the government could negotiate with a single trade union on matters affecting the wages and terms and conditions of public service employees. More crucially, it prevented a further emasculation of public service unions which would have been favoured by the leftists in the PAP. "During the political crisis, any disarray in public service would have been fertile ground for the left-wing to exploit and even disrupt public services," said Nathan.

Another important union that switched to the NTUC camp was the Singapore Manual and Mercantile Workers' Union (SMMWU). That helped to halt the drift of white-collar workers to the SBHEU.

A small band of activists won Nair's everlasting gratitude for soldiering on in the face of the pro-communist juggernaut. Singling out SMMWU secretary-general Joseph Tan Meng Kwang as an example, he said: "He was one of those who really believed that we were all going to lose but decided that we would fight with our backs to the wall and we would die fighting on our feet and not on our knees."

⚜

AS a former comrade of SATU's top leaders, Nair knew how Lim Chin Siong and Fong Swee Suan lived and worked in their Middle Road HQ—sleeping on tabletops with newspaper piles as pillows and waking up to a simple fare of bread and coffee before plunging into the day's work. Poorly paid and adhering to a puritanical code of conduct, they were admired for their austere way of life and total dedication to their cause.

He recalled that Lim would ride on a bicycle in town while Lee was going around in his Studebaker and people would exclaim "see, workers' leader". To avoid suffering any invidious comparison with his leftist rivals, he said, he bought a "tumbled down old Fiat" to do his work.

Just as PAP leaders impressed on their rank and file to imbibe the virtues of simplicity, self-sacrifice and self-discipline—virtues found in the spartan left—their NTUC counterparts realised they could do no less.

They were acutely aware that their predecessors in Lim Yew Hock's STUC had sunk very low in public esteem because of their propensity to drink, gamble, womanise and dip their hands in the till.

The highest premium was placed on integrity, morality and probity. Nair remembered warning unionists that "now we have to set very high standards for ourselves. Any funny games and I will chop your heads and hands off." He left no one in any doubt that he would deal harshly with any NTUC leader found guilty of loose or corrupt behaviour.

May Day rallies became the focal points for both camps to show off the strength of their following. The pro-communist unions staged their rallies at Farrer Park with attendances by the thousands while their non-communist counterparts held theirs at Jalan Besar Stadium with a much smaller crowd. Nathan recollected: "Those present at the stadium were advised to spread out to give an impression of an even larger gathering."

It was at these rallies that he learnt how audience responses were orchestrated by union leaders. For some time, he had been puzzled over the uncanny way people were applauding at appropriate moments of a speech that was being given in a language they did not understand.

So on one occasion, he asked a worker if he knew what was being said. He said he did not. So how did he know when to clap? The worker replied that they had been briefed on how to respond. "The speaker would either raise his hand or point a finger towards them each time he made a point in his speech. When that happened, it was a signal to all to applaud even though we had no clue of the point that was being made."

To win hearts and minds, NTUC and SATU sought to outdo one another in championing the interests of the workers. The result was increased militancy which translated to more industrial action, work stoppages, pickets, sit-down protests, walkouts and strikes. In fact, 1961—the year of The Big Split—saw a sharp spike in strikes which cost Singapore nearly 400,000 man-days against 26,000 lost in 1959 when PAP came into power.

For an idea of a typical action launched by a left-wing union, take the strike at the Tanglin Club when staff walked out and members were forced to man the bar and the kitchen. Its European employers were depicted in crude caricatures crushing the bodies of Chinese employees and drinking their blood.

Mike Gorrie, who negotiated on behalf of the club, recalled that it conceded to almost every demand but to no avail. The issue was only resolved when the management threatened to close the club. On signing the agreement, Gorrie held out his hand but the union president—a tough-talking waiter—refused to shake it. Gorrie's view was that the employees "were being stirred up by people who had political grounds for doing so, to cause as many problems to Singapore as possible".

Businessman Tan Eng Joo's experience in dealing with Lim Chin Siong, Fong Swee Suan and James Puthucheary was just as disturbing. While negotiating an agreement covering 100 workers in his Pasir Panjang rubber processing factory, he had asked if he could sack anyone for stealing and if he could hire a technical person if needed. To both questions, they said: "No, you must seek the union's permission first." He closed down the factory.

It sounds incredible today but to clinch the support of the workers at that time, NTUC took a more confrontational stance, according to Ho See Beng. Between 1961 and 1963, NTUC led more strikes than SATU but Ho was quick to point out that while SATU strikes were politically motivated, NTUC strikes were driven more by industrial disputes and labour grievances.

Nathan's observation was that with the split in the labour scene, union militancy became more pronounced. As the seamen's welfare officer, he witnessed mounting labour agitation on the waterfront and had to intervene in a series of industrial disputes between shipowners/agents and seamen over real and imaginary grievances.

In one incident, he said, instead of seeking a settlement, a union activist was using a dispute to arouse discontent and create trouble on board ships. The purpose was to delay and disrupt the free movement of ships in the harbour. "It was obvious that this was to present to the world that Singapore was a place of growing industrial unrest."

❦

THE definitive saga of how NTUC finally prevailed over SATU has yet to be chronicled. Going by the reflections of people interviewed, NTUC's victory appeared to turn on its strategy of meeting the economic aspirations of workers and on drastic government action that decimated opposing unions.

The strategy: allow the leftist unions to rail against the iniquities of capitalism. Let them denounce employers as agents of neo-colonial oppression and let them indulge in anti-government posturing.

But among the NTUC unions, the word was: let's concentrate on mundane matters such as salary scales, timescales, increments and bonuses, never mind the tedious arguments before the Industrial Arbitration Court (IAC).

NTUC's view was that immediate cash benefits would be valued much more by workers than lofty political abstractions. After all, with the achievement of self-government and the prospect of independence through merger with Malaya, what mattered most were jobs, housing and schools, not more anti-colonial ferment.

As Ho See Beng recounted, NTUC focused on fighting for better wages and working conditions while SATU was mixing industrial action with political agitation. "SATU made the big mistake of using workers to peddle its political agenda," he said.

Nair agreed that SATU took the wrong turn by politicising its industrial battles and mentioned one Robinson's strike as an example. Its employees had genuine grievances against their employer, he said, but instead of giving its undivided attention to labour problems, the left-wing union turned it into an anti-Malaysia protest and added political demands on top of industrial issues.

If there was one high-profile case which boosted NTUC's stock considerably among the workers, it was the epic battle between Nair and *The Straits Times* (ST) in the IAC. Running over 42 sessions from 10 October 1961 to 26 June 1962, the wage dispute became the cause celebre of the time.

Nair represented the Singapore Printing Employees' Union (SPEU) and was aided by its president D Gopalakrishnan and secretary Ho See Beng. On the other side was a high-powered team led by industrial relations expert J J Rattray and ST general manager Graham Jenkins and advised by a battery of foreign accountants.

According to Nair, the British-run newspaper was so sure of victory that it decided that every word uttered in court would be published in full. "Rattray's submission on behalf of ST was brilliant. Everybody thought we had it. Woodhull thought I would be crushed."

But little did the management know that Nair had assembled a team to help him. "I got hold of some of the best minds in Singapore. They went through ST balance sheets, did all the costings. I would get them to argue with each other. As they argued, I would take down notes and then prepare my submission to IAC.

"Then I lumped all the evidence, presented it in court one by one and for weeks on end, ST had to keep its word. They had to publish every word, and that made a terrific public impact especially on the workers. We won the case."

If you wonder who his "backroom boys" were, one was Hsu Tse Kwang, a tax officer who later rose to be the commissioner of inland revenue; another was Roy Daniel, an economist from immigration department; and the third was none other than S R Nathan.

Seconded from the civil service, they formed the nucleus of the labour research unit (LRU) which acted as the brains trust for the labour movement. In 1965, it was renamed NTUC research unit. It is now known as the NTUC administration and research unit.

The idea for such a think-tank was pushed by Nair as he realised that unions should move away from the confrontational style of dealing with employers to intelligent negotiation based on accurate information-gathering.

As the unions lacked resources, Nair appealed to Lee and Goh for help. They agreed to fund it as well as deploy civil servants to get it going. Hsu was appointed director of LRU. Nathan received a posting order from Goh in 1962 with the "glorified title" of assistant director.

Nathan was told that many unions embroiled in disputes had broken away from SATU and that "unless they were properly serviced, they were in danger of returning to their former pro-communist fold".

From purely rendering advice and help in collective bargaining and arbitration cases, LRU soon found itself being sucked into the bruising battle to win the support of workers in new industrial enterprises.

Imagine Economic Development Board (EDB) struggling to attract investments to Jurong and assuring industrialists of industrial peace, and NTUC seeking to woo workers away from the leftist unions by flexing its muscles. It was a very difficult situation and Nathan remembered that many complaints were made to Goh to put pressure on the unions.

The rank-and-file unionists did not begrudge the help rendered by Hsu and company as they knew that they did not have the expertise to take on top management. As Eric Cheong noted, the best educated official in those days would have only a Senior Cambridge Certificate or the equivalent of 'O' level today. As for himself, he had only passed Standard Eight or Secondary Three before being expelled from school. Later, unionists were attached to LRU to learn the nuts and bolts of collective bargaining and industrial arbitration.

Former left-wing unionists, however, scoffed at the reasons cited by their NTUC counterparts for turning the tables on them. They argued that they were just as adept in negotiating with management and clinching tangible benefits for the workers.

What did them in was—in Dominic Puthucheary's words—executive action, referring to the full weight of government measures ranging from the freezing of union assets and deregistration to arrests and detention.

Operation Cold Store launched on 2 February 1963 was the devastating blow. Aimed at putting communist and pro-communist activists behind bars, it took Lim Chin Siong, Fong Swee Suan, Woodhull, Dominic

Puthucheary and other leading leftist unionists out of circulation.

Puthucheary said: "It wiped out the slate. It took us out and immobilised us." Woodhull: "All the leaders disappeared, gone. So there was nothing left." Even Nair and Ho See Beng agreed that the crackdown crippled SATU.

If Cold Store marked the beginning of the end for the leftist unions, their two-day strike on 8 and 9 October 1963 hastened their demise. When seven key unions were asked to show cause why they should not be deregistered for using union funds for political activities, a desperate SATU called for a general strike involving 100,000 workers from 105 firms.

The strike collapsed when the police declared it illegal and arrested 17 top SATU leaders including its president S T Bani, secretary-general Wee Toon Lip, organising secretary Teo Hock Guan, SGEU secretary Loh Miaw Gong and SBWU secretary Lee Tee Tong. Bani, Loh and Lee had just been elected Barisan Sosialis assemblymen in the general election a month earlier. Another two Barisan assemblymen, Chan Sun Wing and Wong Soon Fong, went into hiding.

The seven unions were deregistered on 30 October 1963. They were SGEU, SBHEU, SBWU and the unions for construction, brickmaking and machine workers and for seamen. Then the government dealt the coup de grace by rejecting SATU's long-pending application for registration on 13 November 1963.

It was during this period of confusion and anxiety spawned by the ill-conceived strike that many members of SATU-affiliated unions began their exodus to their NTUC counterparts. In one day, 50 branches from five SATU unions crossed over to SMMWU.

On 8 January 1964, 28 months after the breakup of TUC, NTUC was finally registered encompassing 48 affiliates and 85,000 members. It won government recognition because it had garnered the support of more than 60 per cent of the organised workers.

From being down in the dumps, NTUC had become the unchallenged trade union body in Singapore. The stranglehold exercised by the communists on the labour movement since the end of the war had been shattered. The might of the Middle Road unions had vanished.

Today, when you scan the glistening, towering edifice at No 1 Marina Boulevard, the new home of NTUC, it is hard to visualise the hole-in-the-wall office at the now-demolished Cultural Centre on Canning Rise where Nair plotted the defeat of his former comrades more than 40 years ago.

"In those days there seemed to be inexhaustible reserves of energy and a kind of cold determination that whatever may happen, the fight would continue," Nair said in an oral history interview in 1981. "I remember telling my children ... I was not merely ready to die, I expected to die, and there was a kind of recklessness because I knew that it was real danger. I did not have any bodyguard or personal escort in those days. About 10 years later, I was surprised to find myself still alive."

Up to the very end, he said that his leftist friends did not give up on him thinking that he could be swung over. "When the break came, they regretted the tolerance with which they had treated me. I think people like Woodhull and James Puthucheary took the view that history would have been different if only I had also joined them, that somehow or other the balance would have been tilted in their favour. James had said so among our people and they had reported to me: 'If only that b****** Devan had joined us.' "

14

Remembering PAP's Unsung Heroes

"THREE ways to say 'yes' and none to say 'no'." "Three choices which meant no choice." "No way to express a dissenting voice." "Terms of reference framed in such a way that only one possible answer could be given."

The 1962 Referendum on Merger which despatched Singapore into the political entity called Malaysia now seemed like an eternity ago but this sampling of reflections by former opposition politicians showed their lingering dissatisfaction with the way it was conceived and conducted.

"It was Hobson's choice, a battle we could never win," summed up Sheng Nam Chin, the former PAP parliamentary secretary (health) who defected to Barisan Sosialis.

The referendum, the first and only one held in Singapore so far, marked the culmination of the battle for merger between PAP and Barisan Sosialis, a year-long struggle which served as a full-blown rehearsal for the general election the following year.

Crippled by two by-election debacles and mass defections, and barely clinging to power in the legislative assembly, the ruling party campaigned vigorously for merger with Malaya to achieve independence. Merger was its political lifeline as a go-it-alone Singapore was politically unthinkable to Lee and company then.

Barisan opposed merger fervently fearing that an anti-communist central government would have no qualms about liquidating its leftist leaders. Instead, as a step towards independence, it called for a "genuine full self-government" in which Singapore would take full control of internal security and dispense with the need for the Internal Security Council (ISC).

A referendum, if you go by the dictionary, is a vote in which people are asked to show whether or not they agree with a particular policy or issue. But in the September 1 referendum, people were asked to vote "yes" to one of three options with no option to say "no" to any or all of them.

The opposition parties wanted only one question to be put to the people in the referendum: Do you accept PAP's merger proposal as outlined in the white paper? Yes or no? But the PAP government put down three alternatives on the ballot paper, all of which favoured merger but on varying terms. To recapitulate:

Alternative A: I support merger giving Singapore autonomy in labour and education, with Singapore citizens automatically becoming citizens of Malaysia.

Alternative B: I support complete and unconditional merger for Singapore as a state on an equal basis with the other 11 states in accordance with the constitution of the Federation of Malaya.

Alternative C: I support Singapore entering Malaysia on terms no less favourable than those given to the Borneo territories.

The wording and design on the ballot paper was skewed unapologetically in favour of Alternative A by juxtaposing it with the flag of Singapore. Alternative B was accompanied by the state flag of Penang, and Alternative C by the badges on the flags of North Borneo and Sarawak.

Given the familiarity of the Singapore flag symbol and the widespread use of government referendum posters showing a cross being marked next to A, critics charged that illiterate and undecided voters were being conditioned into voting for A.

To add insult to injury, when Barisan called on people to cast blank votes in protest, the government ruled that such votes were to be regarded as votes for the option that commanded majority support. The argument, surrealistic as it may sound, was that the person who cast such a vote could not make up his mind and therefore should abide by the majority decision.

Lee's rationale for not including a "no" was that all political parties had already subscribed to the principle of union with Malaya and so the question was not whether people wanted merger but what kind of merger they desired.

To his outraged opponents, it smacked of Machiavellian duplicity. But to those partial to PAP, it exemplified Machiavellian ingenuity. Even today, many older Singaporeans who voted in the referendum still marvel at the party's brazen audacity and verbal craftiness.

S Rajaratnam remembered that the three choices were plotted by Lee and Goh Keng Swee and approved by the cabinet. Ong Pang Boon attributed their uncanny verbal tinkering to their familiarity with the ins and outs of the British political system. "Trust Lee and Goh to have that kind of mind," he muttered.

British officials were astounded by the way the referendum was planned to ensure that whichever way the vote went, the PAP government would not face defeat. Even if people voted for B, it was still a vote for merger, remarked Philip Moore. The former deputy UK commissioner noted that Lee had been troubled by the referendum vote in Jamaica on 19 September 1961 which favoured secession and led to the breakup of the Federation of West Indies.

If people had been able to vote "yes" or "no" to merger, the result might have turned out differently, Sheng contended. Then as an afterthought, he said: "It was very cleverly done, and looking back, better for Singapore. I am prepared to concede that whatever PAP did, it was for the better of Singapore."

⚬⚬⚬

THE period from late 1961 to end-1962 must surely rank as one of the most politicised in Singapore's history. It coincided with the battle for merger in which politics was literally thrust into the face of every Singaporean. Like it or not, he had to make a stand on merger.

With PAP and the opposition parties evenly matched in the chamber, the ruling party knew that it might lose if it called for a general election. Its organisation was in disarray. Its socio-economic achievements had yet to be visible. It was plagued by a host of issues ranging from unemployment and industrial strife to city squalor and discontent over Chinese education.

At this critical fork in the road, political salvation seemed to lie with Singapore's absorption into the proposed Malaysia and letting Tunku deal with the communists on the island. As Philip Moore wrote to London on 12 July 1962: "It was clear that the government could not face a general election and that their only course was to seize the initiative offered by Tunku."

By August 1961, Lee had hammered out an agreement with the Malayan premier. As spelled out in the white paper on merger released in November, the federation would take over defence, external affairs and internal security while Singapore would retain control of labour and education. In exchange for autonomy in these two areas, Singapore was allotted only 15 seats instead of the 25 which it should be entitled to based on the size of its population.

In addition, the 624,000 Singapore citizens would not become federation citizens on merger although they would be given Malaysian nationality and passports. Singapore citizenship was not equated with federal citizenship as Tunku did not want Singapore Chinese to vote across the causeway and upset the political dominance of the Malays in the federal parliament.

Barisan pounced on these issues with predatory glee. Although the leftists subscribed to eventual reunion with Malaya—their dream was a socialist Malaya or a communist republic of Malaya—they had not bargained on merger happening so soon and on the terms thrashed out between the two prime ministers which ceded control over internal security to Kuala Lumpur.

When they realised that merger was unstoppable, they resorted to a tactical ploy—they declared that they were in favour of full and complete merger, with proportionate representation for Singapore in the federal parliament and automatic federation citizenship for all its citizens. Knowing full well that these conditions were unacceptable to Tunku, they were hoping to throw a giant spanner in the works.

They accused PAP of selling Singapore short by getting only 15 seats for a population of 1.7 million vis-a-vis 16 seats for Sabah, with one-quarter of Singapore's population, and 24 seats for Sarawak, with half of Singapore's population. By being granted separate citizenship, they alleged, Singapore Chinese would end up as second class citizens in Malaysia.

Ong Chang Sam recalled that when he was acting parliamentary secretary in the prime minister's office, he read the cabinet documents on merger and took part in heated arguments over citizenship rights. "I felt it was not a good plan. I argued: 'Why should we become second class citizens after merger and not be treated as equals?' That was why I opposed the party CEC and went over to the other side."

Similarly Ho Puay Choo said she felt aggrieved over the terms of the merger. Citing her exasperation over the lack of explanation by her party leaders, she said: "Although I was a member of the CEC, there were a lot of things I did not understand as I did not know English. In fact, we did pose a number of questions during CEC meetings but not all of the answers were satisfactory."

At the sitting held to pass the motion on merger, she said that after she listed her queries on merger, another PAP assemblyman, Lee Teck Him, rose to speak on the same subject. "However the session was dismissed even before he had a chance to finish his speech. That was the reason why I was unhappy about the party. I mean, they should not have passed this merger motion without any detailed discussion within the assembly." That was why she resigned from PAP, she said.

⚬⚬⚬

THE story of how Goh Keng Swee outwitted Lee Siew Choh in a radio forum on merger on 21 September 1961 has become part of PAP annals. It tells how the finance minister ambushed his adversary when the latter demanded that Singapore opted for full and unconditional merger with Malaya.

He exposed the Barisan chairman's ignorance by pointing out that if Singapore were to go for a Penang-type merger, only half of the 624,000 adult Singapore citizens born on the island would automatically become federal citizens. Those not born in Singapore would have to apply for registration as citizens under stringent qualifications which included knowing the national language, Malay. The likelihood was that hundreds of thousands of Singaporeans would be disenfranchised.

Goh had been waiting to spring such a trap on his opponents after meeting James Puthucheary in his Fullerton Building office one day. Puthucheary had told him that Barisan would outsmart PAP by asking for complete merger on the same terms as any other state of Malaya. Then he scribbled some figures on a piece of paper which indicated that the Chinese would outnumber the Malays in a combined Malaya and Singapore—a demographic situation that would favour the pro-Chinese Barisan.

But Goh was privy to a crucial fact that Puthucheary did not know— that if Singapore were to go in on equal terms, a proposition that would be utterly unacceptable to Tunku anyway—not all Singapore citizens would automatically enjoy federal citizenship.

Expecting Puthucheary's view to be adopted by the leftists, he said that Lee, Rajaratnam, Toh and he met and all thought that this was "good grounds to take them on because this meant if we had complete merger, Singapore would be treated on the same basis as other states, then nearly half of Singapore citizens would lose their political rights. James did not know or overlooked this, and so issue was joined on merger."

Devan Nair described Goh's intervention in the radio forum as masterly. "It went down in a very great way because nobody in his senses would want to lose his citizenship." Fong Sip Chee said: "Lee Siew Choh plunged into the most grievous blunder. He must have cursed James Puthucheary bitterly for misleading him. Really James was equally ignorant of the matter and it was a case of the blind leading the blind."

Casting his mind back, Sheng agreed that Goh had outfoxed Lee Siew Choh by equating his stand for complete and unconditional merger with entry into Malaysia on the same basis as Penang and Malacca as presented in Alternative B.

Thus if Singapore joined Malaysia under the Penang system, out of the 624,000 Singapore citizens, 230,000 might be disenfranchised. "And as that was put down as Alternative B," said Sheng, "we could not ask people to vote for it."

Realising it was trapped, Barisan reverted to its anti-merger stance. Deriding the referendum as dishonest and a travesty of democracy and dismissing all three alternatives as unacceptable, the opposition party unsheathed its next weapon: cast blank votes to reject merger.

As Ong Chang Sam reasoned, as there was no "yes" or "no" vote but a "yes" for three different forms of merger, Barisan called on the people to cast blank votes in protest. By doing so, Ho Puay Choo argued, it meant that people did not support any of the conditions attached to Alternatives A, B or C.

But once again they had not reckoned with the devious creativity of the PAP in foiling the challenge. The law was duly changed so that blank ballots would be counted together with whichever of the options commanded majority support. Call it disingenuous or ingenious, the PAP view was that any person who cast a blank vote could not make up his mind and was therefore leaving it to the legislative assembly to decide for him.

If this was not perplexing enough for the poor voter, Lee later warned that if Alternative B won more votes than PAP's Alternative A, then the blank ballots would be counted for the Penang-type merger. British journalist Dennis Bloodworth wrote: "This artful move threw half of the electorate not born in Singapore into a state of confused panic which Goh cultivated by sending out some 40 trucks fitted with loudspeakers to warn flummoxed masses that if they cast blank votes, they stood to lose their citizenship."

Hanging on to power by the skin of its teeth, PAP was fighting back with everything it could muster, never mind the niceties of Westminster-styled democracy. It mounted an all-out offensive to win the hearts and minds of the people through what was famously termed the "open argument".

There was open debate not only over the air but also on campus and other public forums where PAP and Barisan and other opposition parties were enjoined in a running war of words. Nair said that PAP took the argument on Malaysia right into the open. "These debates helped a great deal because the English-educated and others who had voted against the PAP in 1959 were won over because they realised Lee and company were not communists."

A memorable highlight in the battle for merger was the series of 12 radio talks delivered by Lee between 13 September 1961 and 9 October 1961. Through the airwaves, Lee sought to explain the political upheaval to Singaporeans and sell his message that merger was "as inevitable as the rising and setting of the sun".

More sensationally, the talks were a no-holds-barred exposé of the communist united front and its tactics and techniques. Drawing from his experience of working with the communists since PAP's inception in 1954, Lee gave a graphic account of their modus operandi.

He reprinted documents in Lim Chin Siong's handwriting to prove that he was a communist open front leader and used the pseudonym Laniaz to refer to an important communist cadre who was none other than his good old friend who used to visit him at Oxley Road and introduced him to Nair—Samad Ismail. Lee also revealed his series of clandestine encounters with senior communist leader Fang Chuang Pi whom he dubbed "the Plen", short for "plenipotentiary".

To many listeners, it was a riveting eye-opener to the threat of communism. There was a cloak and dagger air about it and elements of skulduggery which kept them on tenterhooks as Lee ended each talk with a preview of what to expect in the next.

But to the leftists, there was outrage and shock over what they perceived as a monumental breach of confidence by Lee in his tell-all exposé. They asked why Lee was spilling the beans on the so-called communists when he chose to associate with them right from the beginning. They claimed that Lee was under siege and could not find a way out except by ratting on his former comrades.

Low Por Tuck believed that the radio talks were aimed at frightening the people by linking Barisan with the communists and putting the party in a sorry light in the eyes of Tunku. Lee wanted to convince the Malayans and British that although he worked with the communists, he was not a communist or a pro-communist, he said.

The leftists were also incensed by the PAP's use of government machinery in the battle for merger which was after all synonymous with the battle against Barisan. Low complained that it was tough to counter PAP propaganda when "all the facilities were under the control of government". Former Alliance leader A P Rajah observed that Lee was very adept at using all sources of information dissemination.

To the PAP, however, merger was seen as a national rather than a party issue and it saw no reason why it should be coy about exploiting its advantages as an incumbent government. In fact, the radio talks were printed in four languages at the Government Printing Office, packaged in a 138-page booklet titled *The Battle for Merger* and distributed widely.

Indeed no stone was left unturned to promote merger—whether it was by relying on Special Branch for information or by making use of radio and publications under the Ministry of Culture and facilities in para-government outfits such as the People's Association and Works Brigade.

The year-long publicity exercise, ranging from radio forums, pamphlets and posters to neon signs and jingles, was the longest ever launched by the government. Left unsaid but not gone unnoticed was that the widespread use of government facilities at its disposal helped the ruling party to make up for an organisation in shambles, the mass defections and loss of many branches. As some might say, all's fair in love and war—and politics.

⚜

THE referendum could easily be mistaken for a general election with its accompanying sound and fury from mass rallies, street meetings, house-to-house visits and the daily propaganda barrage. The only difference: no candidates but only a ballot paper with three choices.

Where the line between the Lee camp and the leftists was hazy in the 1959 elections, it came into sharp focus during the referendum campaign. On one side of the battle for merger were the non-communists and on the other side, the pro-communists and communists.

What was at stake at the mark of a cross was no less than the future of Singapore—and the fate of PAP. The governing party advocated merger to achieve political stability and economic security in a greater and stronger entity. Barisan condemned Malaysia as a neo-colonial plot which did not offer real independence to the people.

It was a bitterly fought campaign. Goh remembered how PAP was chased from pillar to post by the emotive arguments that Singaporeans would become second-class citizens after merger and that the island would suffer from inadequate representation in Kuala Lumpur.

Given the political murkiness of the time, forecasting the results proved to be a hazardous exercise. Buang Omar Junid thought that PAP should be able to garner only 50 per cent support from the people. The most positive response, he said, came from the Malay community which was looking forward to life in an enlarged Negeri Melayu (Land of the Malays). He found it harder to read the enigmatic reactions of the Chinese, many of whom chose to keep silent.

According to a former Special Branch chief, when his men monitored the betting in the early days, the odds were very much in favour of blank votes. He said that a very senior officer predicted that PAP did not have much of a chance and was immediately challenged to a wager by Lee.

In the Barisan camp, the battle cry was "oppose Malaysia, reject all three options, cast a blank vote". Low Por Tuck said that his campaigning was aimed at countering Lee's charges that Barisan was linked to the communists and reassuring people frightened by a threatened loss of citizenship if they did not vote for Alternative A.

As the Barisan official in charge of applications for permits then, Ong Chang Sam noted that his party's rallies were very well-attended compared to PAP's. He recalled that the last Barisan rally of the campaign was staged in the vacant land on Shenton Way. "It was packed to the fullest capacity. I remember seven lorries were arranged to make a platform for the speakers. That was why I thought we were going to win."

Barisan was so confident of victory that thousands of party members and supporters, in white shirts and blue trousers or skirts waving flags and slogans, surrounded the Singapore Badminton Hall when vote-counting began on referendum night. Counting went on into the following morning. At dawn, the crowds were given a secret signal to disperse. The preliminary results were read out. Barisan chairman Lee Siew Choh insisted that the counting of votes was wrong and demanded a recount. But as the recount was underway, he and his followers left. It was just an excuse to make their exit, said Chor Yeok Eng.

The final results were announced at 11.25 am by a bleary-eyed official. Out of an electorate of 624,000, 561,559 (or 90 per cent) had voted. Alternative A: 397,626 (71 per cent); B: 9,442 (1.7 per cent); C: 7,911 (1.4 per cent); and blank votes: 144,077 (25 per cent).

Finally, after two by-election fiascos, mass defections which split his party asunder and near collapse of his government, Lee had scored an overwhelming victory. Breaking into tears, he declared: "The verdict of the people is a terrifying thing for the politically dishonest."

Unbelievably, with the blank votes counted in favour of Alternative A, PAP's percentage of victory soared to 96 per cent! Lee Siew Choh rejected the results claiming that people had been intimidated into voting for PAP's option. "Some of the crosses were shaky indicating that the voters were shivering," he said in his typically mocking, deprecatory tone.

So what really accounted for PAP's triumph? Rajaratnam was surprised as he had expected 50 per cent of the votes for his party and 40 per cent for the opposition. After all, he said, PAP performance in previous polls had always hovered around the 51 to 53 per cent mark.

He surmised that most people, like his branch supporters, voted for merger as they felt that it was "the only way out" even though they were not happy or were unsure about it. In his view, the 25 per cent who cast blank votes were the pro-communists and the disaffected.

Lee's diagnosis was that PAP won because it stayed consistent to its cause—independence through merger—while the opposition kept changing its tune. Originally, Barisan was committed to union with Malaya, then it demanded full self-government with no ISC, then merger along the lines of Penang and Malacca, and later merger on equal terms. Then they said: reject all alternatives. "So they deserted the cause and we joined issue. It was not possible for them in one or two years to convince people that they had never supported merger," he said.

To leftists' charges that Singaporeans would end up as second-class citizens, Lee managed to take away the sting at the eleventh hour. He was able to get Tunku to agree that with merger, Singapore citizens would become Malaysian citizens instead of nationals although their voting rights would continue to be confined to the island.

Undoubtedly, the big swing came about because the English-educated and Malays lined up solidly behind PAP unlike in the 1959 elections when they harboured suspicions about its leftist leanings. While the middle class bought into PAP's arguments about Singapore's lack of economic viability as an island entity, the Malays were euphoric over the prospect of unification with Malaya and the elevation of Malay as the national language.

Certainly, the impact of PAP propaganda on the mass media could not be underestimated. On referendum day, then-commissioner of police John Le Cain told a Special Branch officer that PAP would win hands down. The reason? When he visited one polling booth, he saw an old woman shouting in dialect at the top of her voice: "I want Singapore flag, I want Singapore flag."

When Gerald de Cruz asked his amah where she was going early in the morning, she said she was going to vote in the referendum. "I said to her: 'And how are you going to vote?' And she said: 'I'm going to vote A of course.' I said: 'Oh. Why are you going to vote A?' She said: 'You silly man! The radio has been telling me to do so for months. Aren't you going to vote A too?' "

As for the leftists, they were thrown into deep despondency wondering why the number of blank votes fell so short of the number of their supporters. It was a great blow, admitted Ong Chang Sam who agreed that they lost because they did not have the support of the English-educated.

In opposing Malaysia, he felt that his party should not have adopted the same propagandistic approach used by the communists as it scared off the English-speaking. "In our review, our CEC stated that the government had relied on threats to win the referendum. We said that the government had control over the propaganda machine and had manipulated it to win the referendum, used unfair methods and that we were not given a choice. But the fact was we lost because we had not gained the support of the English-educated."

Other former leftists blamed PAP for warning the people repeatedly that if most of the votes went to Alternative B, then the blanks would also go to it. This had the effect of stopping many from casting blanks to ensure that Alternative B did not win by default, they said. The thought of losing their citizenship was just too frightening for people to contemplate.

Another factor was cited—the open support for merger by the Singapore Chinese Chamber of Commerce. Its president, Ko Teck Kin, had warned the public that as Singapore was only a trading port with no resources, it would only have a future if it merged with Malaya. "Rumours of Singapore not being able to survive spread widely, so once the voters were taken in by these rumours, we lost more of our votes," said one former leftist.

The referendum saga ended on a comical, if not farcical footnote. On 5 September 1962, a motion was moved by the government to let the opposition decide to which Alternative—A, B or C—the 144,077 blank votes should go. All 13 Barisan assemblymen and David Marshall of Workers' Party walked out in protest. PAP, SPA and UMNO abstained. Ong Eng Guan and Ng Teng Kian of United People's Party (UPP) voted against it and the motion was defeated 2–0!

The September 1 victory marked a turning point in PAP's fortunes. Toh Chin Chye commented that it shattered the myth that the masses were solidly behind Barisan and the left-wing trade unions. For the first time, reflected Rajaratnam, "we suddenly discovered, that given time and the right approach, PAP could build itself up as a considerable force in Singapore politics".

To Fong Sip Chee, it signified the coming-of-age of PAP. "From that day, we were endorsed by the people of Singapore as a political force in our own right without the myth and stigma that we survived on the support of the communists and their united front. We had proved to the people that the communists were not unbeatable. The party had dismounted from the communist tiger."

⚬⚬⚬

COLOURFUL buntings fluttered from street lamps. A ceremonial arch framed the entrance to each kampung. A banner in English, Malay, Chinese and Tamil read: "Welcome Prime Minister."

The makeshift stage, where a Chinese opera was staged nightly to draw crowds from the wood-and-zinc squatter colonies, had been transformed into a platform to give a rousing welcome to the guest-of-honour.

An air of festivity suffused the largely rural ward which still lived up to its Malay name in the 1960s—*ulu*, meaning an upriver remote place, and *pandan*, the fragrant screw pine leaf used in food flavouring and basket weaving.

Grassroots leaders accompanied the prime minister as he wended his way through the labyrinthine lateritic lanes. At each of the 13 kampungs, villagers turned up in force as he stopped to shake hands and give a speech. Along the way, petitions requesting water, electricity, bridges, roads and other amenities were submitted to him.

When the prime minister visited a Malay kampung, the Malays presented him with a songkok. When he met Indian dwellers, they painted a dot on his forehead. And when he arrived at a Chinese temple, he lighted up an incense stick. These scenes, which were replayed over and over, were to leave a deep impression on Low Tiow Lye.

They showed how important it was for a politician in Singapore to be open and neutral about religious issues, said the Fujian-born businessman and community leader as he gave a vivid account of how the village leaders of Ulu Pandan hosted the prime minister's visit. Low was then chairman of the Ulu Pandan welcoming prime minister working committee.

The event was part of the the prime minister's islandwide constituency tours beginning from May 1962 to just before the September 1963 general election. It all started when Lee returned from an Afro-Asian mission to a rousing reception. From the airport, he proceeded to Kreta Ayer for a tour which lasted until the early hours of the following day.

Drenched in sweat and in a voice which sounded hoarser by the day, he visited one ward after another speaking in Malay, Mandarin, Hokkien and English. If he agreed to act on any problem raised by a community leader, he would direct the civil servants accompanying him to attend to it immediately. In the words of Gerald de Cruz, it was an "extraordinary virtuoso performance".

Constituents looked forward to the prime minister's arrival knowing that it would spell improvements in the area, said Low. When his committee members found that the roads leading to the kampungs were in bad condition, they wrote to the Public Works Department. The roads were repaired on the day before the prime minister's visit. Ditto with street lights and other public amenities.

Veteran PAP activist Choo Wye Foo remembered that Lee sometimes ended his tours at 2 am and had to overcome resistance and hostility in places influenced by the leftists. In one incident, the retired businessman said, eggs were thrown at Lee who merely wiped off the mess from his clothes before resuming his itinerary.

Lee's marathon walkabouts were to evolve into the ministerial visits to the HDB heartlands that Singaporeans are so familiar with today. The raison d'etre remains the same: to feel the pulse of the local community and address its needs and aspirations.

In retrospect, it could be said that taken together with the battle for merger in the referendum, the constituency tours which stretched Lee's political acumen, linguistic skills and physical endurance to the utmost helped to turn the tide in favour of his beleaguered party.

⚜

NERVOUS Singaporeans braced themselves for the fall of the Lee government as they watched the balance of power see-sawing in the 51-seat chamber—from PAP 25–Opposition 26 with Ho Puay Choo's resignation from the party to 26–25 when S V Lingam rejoined PAP from UPP to 25–25 when Ahmad Ibrahim died on 21 August 1962.

The spectre of Hong Lim and Anson rose to haunt PAP again. What if a by-election were held in Sembawang and Lim Chin Siong stood for Barisan? He would surely win, wouldn't he? Under public security laws, Lim could stand as long as he was not in detention at the time of nomination.

PAP prudently left the seat vacant. But the leaders knew that Barisan was courting their Chinese-educated assemblymen and working on the waverers. Any more defections, and the government would fall with weeks to go before referendum day on 1 September 1962.

Tongues were a-wagging at that time that if Ho Puay Choo crossed the floor, could Chan Choy Siong be far behind? Both assemblywomen were the best of friends who came from an impoverished background, studied in Chinese schools and shared similar views on women's rights. For a spell, both had lived together in that hotbed of leftist activities—the Fort Canning singles' quarters.

Chan's husband, Ong Pang Boon, scotched all such speculation stressing that she had always stood by the party. "If she had wanted to leave PAP, she would have joined Ong Eng Guan, who was very good to her, at the time he tabled the 16 resolutions against the party leadership."

To illustrate her unflinching loyalty to the party, he related how she was hurt while protecting the PAP emblem at the Neil Road PAP HQ during a police raid in October 1956. When a British officer ordered his men to remove the PAP symbol on the wall, she resisted and was hit on the hip by a police officer with his metal-tipped swagger stick.

"She saved the party emblem but she was so painfully hurt that she was unable to go home for two days. Today one may laugh at her for saving what might be regarded as a replaceable emblem made of cloth but for those steeped in the history of China and fired by the deeds of heroism in modern revolutionary literature, the party emblem symbolised the cause for which one would lay down one's life if the occasion demanded it."

Looking at the total domination of PAP in parliament today, it seemed incredible that there was a moment in its history when every vote for the ruling party counted—literally. Sahorah's vote mattered. So did the votes of Chor Yeok Eng, Lee Teck Him, Ismail Rahim and John Mammen. Lee mentioned that Jamit Singh promised John Mammen, his colleague in the Singapore Harbour Board Staff Association (SHBSA), a great future in Barisan if he defected. He did not.

Of all the PAP's men, Chor was singled out by Barisan as the best bet given his humble background. He was the son of a pawnshop clerk and a construction worker and had only a secondary-level Chinese school education. Furthermore he helped to campaign for Lim Chin Siong during the 1955 elections.

As Chor narrated, when Barisan activists failed to recruit him, Lim visited him at his Bukit Timah home with a prepared statement of support and coaxed him to sign it. He refused. Lim asked Chor if he wanted a CEC seat or any position in return for his help in toppling the PAP government.

"I asked him to answer what the long-term objectives of the leftist organisations were since they did not want merger. The secretary-general did not answer, instead he rebutted and asked me if I deliberately wanted to oppose them. He said his people had the backing of a strong force and that they would fight to the last man instead of folding their hands and awaiting arrest."

When Lim found he could not make any headway, he suggested to Chor that he give up politics and take up business instead. He said that all Chor had to do was to resign from the legislative assembly and Barisan would compensate him with a sum of about $200,000. Chor said he rejected the offer, knowing that if he accepted the money, the PAP government might fall in the vote of confidence in the house. "To me, $200,000 was a big sum of money in those days but I just couldn't take it because I was in politics for the party and the people, not for personal gain," he said.

After he rebuffed them, he said, the leftists began to harass him calling him names such as Lee's *zou gou* ("running dog" in Mandarin) and Lee's *kuei kia* ("adopted son" in Hokkien). One day he found a dagger stuck in the door of his party branch in Jurong. Then he received a knife wrapped in a parcel from the post office.

Former Barisan leader Fong Swee Suan, however, denied that the party had ever made such an offer to Chor. He said that Barisan was a poor party and did not believe in using money in politics. Former leftists quoted Lim as saying that they could not possibly offer such a bribe as they never had so much money.

Chor has since been held up by PAP as a shining example of party loyalty. Lesser known and obscured by history, however, were the ordinary members and grassroots activists who stuck with the party during The Big Split. At a tumultuous time when most of their comrades were fleeing to Barisan, they struggled to salvage what remained of their party branches and keep the party going.

Choo Wye Foo spoke of how jittery he felt when most of his colleagues deserted the Kreta Ayer branch and warned him that PAP's days were numbered. "It was tough staying on the side of PAP. You must be strong in your faith in the party. It was much easier to go over to the other side. Even your friends would start calling you names, such as 'running dog' and 'traitor', and they would spit and talk bad things about you behind your back."

The retired unionist said he stayed with the party because he was put off by the leftist threats of violence and was moved by the sincerity and dedication of Lee and Goh in seeking to create a fair and equal society.

Chua Boon Siong confessed that he was an ardent admirer of Lim Chin Siong and would have joined the leftists if not for their unruly behaviour when they resigned en masse from PAP. "They took everything away from the Delta branch including the sewing machines for the dress-making classes, and they threatened to beat me and my assistant secretary Ho Cheng Choon," said the former student activist who later became a time-keeper with Singapore Bus Services.

Ng Boon Chong found himself isolated in the Bukit Panjang branch when many of his colleagues defected. The travel agency manager recalled that some leftists visited his home and asked him to leave the party. "They told me if I did not support Barisan, I would be committing *li shi de zui* or 'a crime in history'."

Perhaps no one is better placed to pay a tribute to the legions of party loyalists who kept PAP from going under in the 1950s and 1960s than its former organising secretary Ong Pang Boon. He said: "These were the people who worked day and night in the branches, writing out banners and posters, drawing up sketches and putting them on lamp posts, walls and party platforms, selling *Petir*, distributing leaflets, canvassing from house to house, getting people to attend mass rallies, serving as stewards, assembling platforms on lorries for mass meetings and doing the thousand and one chores that had to be done to win mass support of the people for the PAP cause.

"They had nothing to gain materially but everything to lose. In fact, some were victimised and some lost their jobs. Others were beaten up by gangsters while some got picked up by the colonial police and roughed up in police stations. Yet others had taunts and abuses heaped upon them by erstwhile comrades.

"These were the unknown and unsung heroes, without whom PAP would not have been able to rebuild itself after each purge and to soldier on from strength to strength."

15

What if Barisan Had Won in 1963?

THE knock on the door of a terrace house on Carlisle Road off Farrer Park came in the early hours of the morning.

As Fong Swee Suan rubbed the sleep off his eyes, he was astonished to see Chew Tong Li, his former neighbour and friend from his hometown in Johor, in a policeman's uniform toting a long gun. Memories of their basketball-playing days in Senggarang flashed through his mind.

But this was no courtesy visit. Chew was part of a team who had come to arrest the Barisan leader and radical trade unionist in an islandwide sweep dubbed Operation Cold Store on 2 February 1963. Fong recalled: "He stood there for a few minutes looking stunned. I told him: 'It's okay, you do your duty.' Then he said: 'Wah, it's you. How could it be you?' "

Fong was driven in a car with several detainees from his home in Singapore to Kuala Lumpur. It was only when they stopped for lunch did he learn about the scale of the operation. After spending a night in the capital, he was taken to a forested area and kept in solitary confinement for six months.

Then he was packed off to another camp where he found himself in the same cell with fellow PAP founder-convenor and rural association head Chan Chiaw Thor. Fong and Chan were among the eight detainees released on 4 June 1959 as a condition for PAP's assumption of power after winning the elections.

As Fong recollected: "It was a cement cell. Even the bed was made of cement. Except for a few books, nothing was supplied to us as they wanted to make sure we would not use a blanket or whatever to commit suicide.

"I was interrogated day and night for six months. I was asked about all my activities. They tried to find out if I had a communist connection. At night, they put an alarm clock outside my cell which rang every 15 minutes. I couldn't sleep."

Other than Fong, the big names caught in the dragnet were Barisan CEC members Lim Chin Siong, Lim Hock Siew and Poh Soo Kai, and unionists S Woodhull, James Puthucheary, Jamit Singh and Lim Shee Ping. In all, 113 people were rounded up including 24 Barisan members, 21 trade union leaders, 17 Nanyang University (Nantah) students and graduates, seven members of rural associations and five journalists. However, all 13 Barisan legislative assemblymen and party chairman Lee Siew Choh were spared.

Planned by the Internal Security Council (ISC), the round-up was named Cold Store because it was meant to put communists and suspected communists "away for a little while", explained a former Special Branch officer involved in the operation.

The PAP government told the public that ISC acted against the detainees for seeking to sabotage Malaysia and supporting the armed insurrection which broke out in Brunei on 8 December 1962. Led by Brunei Partai Rakyat leader A M Azahari, the revolt was aimed at foiling the entry of the Borneo territories into Malaysia but it was crushed by British troops flown in from Singapore.

Barisan secretary-general Lim Chin Siong was accused of meeting Azahari in Singapore on the eve of the rebellion and conspiring to stage a simultaneous uprising in Singapore. Fong Swee Suan, however, strongly denied all these charges saying that what Azahari and Barisan had in common was just the aim of getting rid of colonialism.

The big sweep took place against the backdrop of Confrontation or Konfrontasi launched by President Sukarno of Indonesia on 20 January 1963 to abort the proposed Malaysia union. The unofficial war, which combined military action, political subversion and infiltration of agents, was instigated by Partai Komunis Indonesia (PKI) or the Indonesian Communist Party which was allied to the Chinese Communist Party (CCP) and the Malayan Communist Party (MCP).

Toh Chin Chye maintained that Operation Cold Store was meant to pre-empt the communist united front from mounting any violence or creating any disorder in the closing stages of the establishment of Malaysia. "Malaya could not allow Singapore to become the Cuba of Malaysia, a safe base from which MCP could launch a political offensive against Malaysia."

The "clean-up" was necessary, argued S Rajaratnam, because of Indonesia's hostility and plans by communist parties in Malaya and the Borneo territories to disrupt Malaysia.

Nair remembered discussing with Lee the need for such an operation in view of growing public opinion against Confrontation and public disillusionment with Barisan for backing Sukarno. "As PM once said, you can't afford to be sentimental when you are fighting for the life of a community. The outcome was crucial not only for ourselves but also for the ideals we were working for ... we had to grow what is known as calluses."

According to declassified British diplomatic correspondence, ISC gave the greenlight for the operation on 16 December 1962 but it was canned after the Malayan and Singapore governments disagreed over the list of detainees. It was revived as Operation Cold Store on 2 February 1963. Fong Swee Suan was in the list of 169 names. So were many of Lee's former comrades. Lim Chin Siong was offered safe passage out of Singapore but preferred to go into captivity.

The crackdown was greeted by cries of foul play by the opposition. Its leaders charged that it was all part of a conspiracy by the British, Malayan and Singapore authorities to demolish the left and destroy organised opposition in the proposed Malaysia. "The Brunei armed revolt provided a good excuse to put us in," contended Fong.

OTHMAN Wok was typing a report in *Utusan Melayu's* Kuala Lumpur office when he received a call in early August from Rahim Ishak in Singapore. The PAP CEC member told him: "Don't mention this to anyone ... PM would like you to stand for elections soon, please get half a dozen photographs of yourself."

Then about a month later came the urgent request for him to be in Singapore in two days. Given such short notice, the journalist had no choice but to pull a fast one over his editor. He pleaded for a few days' compassionate leave saying his mother was ill. That very night, he left for the railway station.

His train was delayed by a Malayan Railways strike. When he reached Tanjong Pagar station late in the evening, he went straight to PAP HQ on South Bridge Road where he met PAP CEC member Wee Toon Boon. Wee took him to Government House for an election briefing by Prime Minister Lee.

Othman remembered seeing all the candidates in one room. "It was there that I learnt I was going to be in Pasir Panjang. Lee told me 'Don't worry. It's going to be a safe seat.'" Othman had lost narrowly to an UMNO candidate in Kampong Kembangan in the 1959 elections. Pasir Panjang was held by Tee Kim Leng, one of the 13 PAP assemblymen who defected to Barisan.

Come nomination day on 12 September 1963, he discovered that the opposing candidate from UMNO was Ahmad Rahmat, a school teacher and close friend. When they were in school before the war, they used to cycle together around Telok Blangah. Othman never extended his leave from the office and never returned to *Utusan Melayu*.

Polling day was scheduled on 21 September 1963, five days after the proclamation of Malaysia. The nine-day election campaign was the shortest possible allowed by law—a controversial practice which continues to this day. As it coincided with the Malaysia Day celebrations, campaigning time became even more truncated.

Barisan called it "snap election—blitzkrieg style" and "the most unfair and undemocratic elections in the history of Singapore".

According to British colonial officials, Lee wanted to hold elections while the machinery of the state was still in his hands. The idea was not to give the central government enough time to take over the police and exercise any significant influence on the conduct of the elections.

PAP fielded candidates in all 51 seats, followed by Barisan in 46, Ong Eng Guan's United People's Party (UPP) also in 46, and Singapore Alliance (comprising SPA, UMNO, MCA and MIC or Malayan Indian Congress) in 42. The Workers' Party put up three candidates, Partai Rakyat three, Pan Malayan Islamic Party two and United Democratic Party one. Sixteen independents also joined in the fray.

But the electorate knew that the real battle was between PAP and Barisan. It was to be the mother of all Singapore elections, a colossal clash which would determine the course of Singapore's history. If the results had gone the other way, the Singapore of today would have turned out differently.

For the rapidly diminishing band of old warriors on both sides, the memories of an intensely fought campaign are hard to shake off. Ong Pang Boon talked about opponents who brazenly played the chauvinistic card by accusing PAP of being anti-Chinese and about secret society elements and thuggish unionists who intimidated voters.

When Goh Keng Swee visited the rural areas in Changi and Chua Chu Kang, he encountered hostile reception and could not help noticing earnest youths holding evening classes for children of farmers—they were evidently seeking to win hearts and minds for the pro-communist cause.

While canvassing as the PAP candidate in Punggol, Ng Kah Ting said he and his supporters had to put up with threats of physical injury and acts of vandalism. Street lamps were smashed and public telephones ripped off. Some of his opponents warned the former school teacher: "When we come in, we will settle the score with you—*wo men hui gen ni men suan zhang.*"

Tay Boon Too, who was helping K M Byrne in Crawford, said he was labelled a "barking dog for the master". In one incident, the then-Yock Eng School teacher faced a volley of stones and had to run and hide in a drain to avoid being hurt.

Tang See Chim was an election agent for Yip Sai Weng, who was challenging PAP incumbent-turned-Barisan strongman Wong Soon Fong in Toa Payoh. On one of their rounds, said the former minister of state and lawyer, they were chased by parang-wielding gangsters.

Another PAP activist lending a hand to Yip was Quah Wee Ho who remembered watching helplessly as Wong Soon Fong's wife and a group of people went around ripping off PAP posters. "I couldn't do anything. We put up a poster, they tore it down."

The poster war reflected the heat of the hustings. Othman said they would start bright and early in the morning to put up PAP posters. "By noon, Barisan posters would be placed over ours. Then we got our chaps to put ours over theirs. By 3 pm, the Barisan posters would be placed over ours again."

To be fair to the leftists, thuggery was not a one-way street. Barisan campaigners were also at the receiving end of rough-house tactics. They cited instances when Works Brigade members broke up their meetings and smeared their posters. A *Straits Times* article on 18 September 1963 reported that four Barisan supporters in a van with loudspeakers were attacked by a group of 50 youths from the Works Brigade at Sembawang. Chio Cheng Thun, the Barisan candidate for Chua Chu Kang then, referred to an incident in which his supporters were beaten up and landed in hospital.

Apart from Malaysia, the other issues dominating the campaign were the detention of leaders and Chinese education. The latter became a hot political potato when 10 Nantah graduates joined the Barisan line-up to make up for the absence of the party's top guns who had been detained under Operation Cold Store.

They were financed by none other than the founder of the university himself Tan Lark Sye, a rubber tycoon and community leader who was at loggerheads with the government over the treatment of the Chinese-educated. In public speeches, he made no bones about his support for the Chinese-educated and expressed the hope that in the event of a Barisan victory, a Nantah graduate should become education minister.

The Nantah graduates were Lam Chit Lee, Lim Huan Boon, Ong Hock Siang, Lim Chien Sen, Leong Kwan Fai, Thio Kheng Lock, Chia Thye Poh, Poh Ber Liak, Ng Hui Sim and Shie Shing Min. Some were fielded against PAP ministers on the understanding that they would hold ministerial posts if they won.

Ong Hock Siang, who was then a fresh Nantah graduate, found himself confronting Lee in Tanjong Pagar. "I didn't choose to fight him but I was sent there by the party. I remember at our party meeting the leaders just read out who was to stand against whom and in which constituency. That's it," he said.

The Nantah influx did not escape the attention of Lee who noted that a new breed of communist intellectuals—the university graduates—was coming. They were going to where the blank votes were cast in the referendum while the less educated assemblymen were being "sacrificed" in the middle-class English-speaking wards, he said.

The schism between the tertiary-educated and lowly educated members in Barisan became apparent when incumbent assemblymen in humble occupations were asked to step down. Tee Kim Leng said: "Lin You Eng and I had to give way to the better educated as both of us were barbers."

Barisan candidates were supported by left-wing unionists, members of rural residents' associations and students from Nantah and Chinese middle schools. Their expectations of victory were boosted when they saw their rallies pulling in crowds of 30,000 compared to PAP's 3,000.

Even PAP candidates were worried about the outcome. Othman Wok described the elections as "touch and go". Lee said: "Many people feared we would lose to Barisan. They made detention of their open front leaders and our alleged 'sell-out to Malaysia' burning issues of the elections."

Goh said he was not optimistic. This was, after all, the general election they had avoided since The Big Split of 1961. "If there were no merger issue, and we had to fight on Chinese education, language, culture, trade unions, we would lose," he said.

On the eve of the polls, no pundit and no newspaper predicted a PAP victory.

❧⚜☙

VOTING ended at 8 pm and the ballot boxes for the four rural wards of Bukit Timah, Bukit Panjang, Choa Chu Kang and Jurong were carted to the counting centre at Jalan Teck Whye Secondary School. All four PAP candidates knew they had lost even before the counting was over. The constituencies happened to be the areas where large numbers of blank votes were cast in the referendum.

Chor Yeok Eng, who was standing for Bukit Timah, was filled with foreboding when he saw thousands of people wearing red armbands descending on the school. Some burly characters carried bottles, water pipes, rods and motorcycle chains. Were they preparing to attack PAP supporters if Barisan swept to victory?

His fears were allayed when he learnt that although he was defeated, PAP had scored a resounding overall victory. "That ended their plans for violence. When the results were announced, the reckless ruffians were frightened away and bloodshed was avoided," he said.

Lee Khoon Choy, the then-candidate for Bukit Panjang, recalled that he was inside the counting centre when he overhead a Barisan official giving the order "*bu yao rang ta men chu qu*" ("don't let them out" in Mandarin) on learning that his party had won all four seats. Taking a nervous look outside the building, K C spotted several parang-wielding mobsters.

He listened to the radio which—to his great relief—broadcast one victory after another for PAP, giving it a total of 37 against Barisan's 13. When the belligerent hordes heard the final score, they slipped away. He could not imagine what would happen to him and his aides if Barisan had won the elections.

At Monk's Hill School where counting for Cairnhill was underway, Lim Kim San was on tenterhooks. The self-made millionaire and unpaid chairman of the Housing and Development Board (HDB) was not sure how the votes would go as he had faced hostile reception from the old Orchard Road market stallholders who felt victimised by the *tua kow* ("big dog" in Hokkien), a reference to the police.

Milling around the school were many young Barisan suppporters carrying bottles. He had better luck than his rural counterparts beating his Barisan opponent, Lim Ang Chuan, by a handsome majority of 5,306 votes. "If they had won, the police would be on their side and they would have resorted to violence ... I couldn't sleep after the excitement. For the first time, I took a sleeping pill," said Lim.

It was the longest and darkest night in the history of PAP—two ministers were toppled and another four ministers nearly toppled. Barisan's game plan to wipe out half of the cabinet almost succeeded.

Health and law minister K M Byrne fell to S T Bani by 193 votes in Crawford while national development minister Tan Kia Gan lost to Kow Kee Seng by 750 votes in Paya Lebar.

Deputy prime minister Toh Chin Chye scraped through by 89 votes over Lee Siew Choh in Rochor. Culture minister Rajaratnam pipped Tan Jing Quee by only 220 votes in Kampong Glam. Home affairs minister Ong Pang Boon edged out Lam Chit Lee by 403 votes in Telok Ayer. Education minister Yong Nyuk Lin had a close shave, beating Un Hon Kun by 618 votes in Geylang West.

Barely clinging to power in the last assembly, PAP had finally secured a solid majority. But a sober analysis revealed how close its victory was. It had to thank Ong Eng Guan's UPP for splitting the votes which would have otherwise gone to Barisan. A British diplomatic note recorded that four ministers would almost have been defeated had the UPP candidate in each case not polled between 1,000 and 1,500 votes.

An angry Lee Siew Choh ranted after the elections: "Four PAP ministers will have to thank UPP for saving their skins by doing the dirty work of splitting left-wing votes." The Barisan chairman blamed his 89-vote defeat in Rochor on vote-splitting by UPP candidate Pan Teck Tai who received 1,067 votes. Toh agreed that the vote-splitting saved him.

Lam Chit Lee lost to Ong Pang Boon by 403 votes but UPP candidate Goh Hong Keng obtained 1,484 votes which could be identified as anti-PAP votes. If there were no UPP challenge, the seat would have certainly gone to Lam.

There were other close calls for the ruling party. Ong Pang Boon's wife, Chan Choy Siong, beat Middle Road union strongman Wee Toon Lip by a hair's breath—63 votes. If only Wee could have just a fraction of UPP candidate Chen Chia Kuang's 2,233 votes. Teong Eng Siong snatched victory from Chen Poh Cheng, Fong Swee Suan's wife, by 154 votes in Sembawang.

In all, 584,433 people or 95 per cent of an electorate of 617,650 voted. PAP clinched 272,924 votes or 79,623 more votes than Barisan's. Although it secured 47 per cent of the votes, it garnered 73 per cent of the number of seats—thanks to the first-past-the-post system.

This meant that although PAP collected less than half the total votes cast, it could form the government. By comparison, Barisan obtained 32.1 per cent of the votes but took only 13 seats. UPP retained only Hong Lim through Ong Eng Guan, with 8.3 per cent of the total votes. The Singapore Alliance comprising SPA, UMNO, MCA and MIC also took 8.3 per cent of the votes but did not earn a single seat.

To this day, PAP's 47 per cent score in 1963 remained its lowest electoral mark in history. Its highest was 86.7 per cent in 1968 as a result of the Barisan boycott. It garnered 54 per cent in 1959 and 66.6 per cent in 2006. Its average score over 12 general elections between 1959 and 2006 would be 67 per cent. Calculations are based on valid votes cast. Figures cited in other publications would be different if they are based on total votes cast which included spoilt votes.

Among the 92 candidates who lost their deposits was David Marshall who won Anson as Workers' Party chief two years ago with leftist support. As an independent, the former chief minister could muster only 416 votes. The ward was recaptured by PAP's P Govindasamy.

Press analyses of the day concurred that PAP romped to victory not just because of its strengths but because the votes were hopelessly split. The general finding was that PAP had actually won only 20 seats by outright majority and had taken the other 17 seats because the combined anti-PAP votes were fragmented in three-, four- and five-cornered fights.

A calculation showed that PAP won seven working-class constituencies because of vote-splitting by UPP. This explained Lee Siew Choh's wrath when he attacked UPP for causing the defeat of Barisan in Rochor, Telok Ayer, Kampong Glam, Kampong Kapor, Delta, Geylang West and Sembawang.

Barisan was particularly strong in the countryside because of the support from the farmers, and rural residents and country people's associations. Of the 13 seats captured, nine were in rural areas, two in the city (Havelock and Crawford) and the other two in wards where squatter colonies proliferated (Toa Payoh and Bukit Merah).

One analysis showed that the combined Barisan-UPP votes exceeded PAP's in 21 constituencies. This meant that if there were no vote-splitting and if Barisan had fielded the right candidates to influence the floating voters, it could have won another eight seats in addition to its 13 thus leaving PAP with 29 seats.

Looking back to the elections which paved the way to the Singapore of today, Ong Pang Boon agreed that Barisan could have won more seats if it knew how to fight the elections better. Lee Khoon Choy said that if Barisan's top leaders were not detained and could stand in the elections, it would certainly have done even better.

Was it divine providence or cruel fate that Barisan missed the golden opportunity to be a formidable political force in Singapore? Would Barisan have been able to form the government if there were no Operation Cold Store?

⚜

"I LOST because I forgot one very important factor—to meet and shake hands with the people. Even though the government had spent $2 million and built 12 community centres for my ward, these things did not matter." More than four decades later, Lee Khoon Choy still stuck to this view to explain his defeat as the incumbent in Bukit Panjang.

As parliamentary secretary (culture), he said, he was too preoccupied with organising cultural festivals and as a PAP official, he was too bogged down in party work. As a result, he did not spend much time with his constituents and paid the price.

Tay Boon Too put it simply and bluntly when asked why Byrne lost in Crawford. "He was too straightforward. Many residents faced resettlement. Yet when they pleaded with the minister to postpone it for one or two years, he refused to do so."

The defeats in Paya Lebar and Toa Payoh were blamed on land clearance schemes for the construction of an airport and public housing flats respectively. Resettlement schemes which displaced farmers cost PAP many votes in rural wards such as Jurong and Chua Chu Kang. Where such local issues festered, Barisan candidates were able to exploit the people's dissatisfaction at the expense of their PAP counterparts.

For all the defeats and near-defeats, however, there was no running away from the fact that PAP had scored a surprising landslide victory.

Lee attributed it to the support of right-wing votes which had previously gone to Lim Yew Hock's party and other members of Singapore Alliance (SA). In his view, the 1963 results gave a more accurate reading of ground sentiment than that of 1959 when PAP was perceived as a pro-communist party. "So Malays, Indians and the English-educated voted for PAP because they wanted merger and believed that the other side was pro-communist," he said.

The English-educated voters were seen as especially crucial. In 1959, they were averse to PAP's leftist orientation. But by 1963, as a result of The Big Split, they could differentiate the non-communists from the pro-communists. Unlike the Chinese-educated who were influenced by the rise of revolutionary China, they had no truck with communism believing that the ideology would only lead Singapore to social chaos and economic ruin.

The key factor in PAP's triumph was merger. That was the verdict of many former politicians. Othman said: "PAP won because most people especially the Malays supported merger and feared that if Barisan won, the communists would take over and abort merger."

Some former leftists agreed. They noted that Barisan failed to get the support of the elderly and womenfolk who listened to government messages on Radio Singapore and Rediffusion. Ong Chang Sam said: "People supported merger. They did not accept our policies. They did not sympathise with us just because a few of our leaders had been arrested."

The timing of polling day five days after the promulgation of Malaysia on the steps of City Hall also put PAP in an unshakeable position while pushing Barisan into a corner. How could Barisan possibly reconcile its anti-Malaysia stand with a Malaysia that was a fait accompli during the election campaign? Indeed Lee Siew Choh had cited Malaysia as one factor for his party's defeat.

Related to the merger issue was the communist scare and the Indonesian threat that could have strengthened the resolve of many people to go all the way with the PAP despite their misgivings. There was a palpable fear that if PAP votes were split, Barisan might sneak in to form the government. Rajaratnam said that many of his party workers and constituents were not in favour of merger but kept faith with PAP.

To secure more votes, PAP had no qualms about playing up the communist menace in its propaganda. A British diplomatic despatch noted that PAP threw up an eve-of-poll scare by alleging a central government plot to take away votes from PAP through the SA and UPP.

This would enable Barisan to win the elections, it said, and allow Kuala Lumpur to suspend the constitution and instal Lim Yew Hock as governor of Singapore.

Low Por Tuck recalled that at a PAP mass rally on the eve of polling day, Goh made the threat that if Barisan won and formed the government, Malaysian troops would march across the causeway into Singapore. "That warning was the fatal blow that turned the tide against Barisan. It was Goh's eleventh-hour strategy. The warning came at about 10 pm that evening, leaving us with no time to respond."

He only realised how potent the speech was after the elections when he asked relatives and friends why they voted for PAP. "They said they were afraid of the consequences described by Goh," said Goh's former parliamentary secretary.

Barisan made many strategic and tactical errors during the campaign but none was more devastating than its support for Indonesia and the Partai Komunis Indonesia (PKI) in opposing the formation of Malaysia. PKI, led by Aidit, was then the third biggest communist party in the world. When Jakarta declared Konfrontasi, Barisan found itself on the wrong side.

Voters were unnerved by the outbreak of anti-Malaysia demonstrations in Jakarta after Malaysia Day in which mobs stormed the British and Malayan embassies screaming "*ganjang* Malaysia" ("crush Malaysia" in Malay) and set cars ablaze.

As news broke of guerilla activities in Borneo and Indonesian troop manoeuvres in the last few days of the electoral campaign, Singapore was gripped by a sense of national crisis.

Whatever advantage Barisan might have had on the issues of Chinese education and culture was lost in such a heightened state of anxiety and uncertainty. Ong Pang Boon commented that Barisan was completely out of touch with the ground when it embarked on an anti-Malaysia campaign. Devan Nair reflected: "The greatest mistake they ever made was to support Indonesia Confrontation. That was fatal."

Viewed against the backdrop of Konfrontasi, the battle between a pro-Malaysia PAP and a pro-Indonesia breakaway left took on the dimensions of a Cold War tussle between two neighbours. The America-led Western alliance saw Malaysia as part of the plan to stop the dominos from falling into the Red camp while the pro-Soviet and China Eastern bloc saw Malaysia as part of a neo-colonial plot to serve the interests of the white powers.

Three days after the elections, the first bomb exploded at Katong

Park opposite Ambassador Hotel on Meyer Road injuring a driver. On December 10, another bomb went off on Vaughan Road claiming two lives. Up to May 1965, 41 blasts occurred in all maiming or killing 60 people and damaging homes, buildings, schools, bridges and water mains. Konfrontasi had struck home. Terrorism had come to Singapore.

⊶⊱⊶

MERGER and confrontation, however, did not fully account for PAP's sensational turnaround in fortune. The party had one more trump card which was fast gaining visibility by 1963.

All around, people were beginning to see the towering blocks which epitomised the Singapore Dream of the 1960s. The joy of moving from a squalid squatter hut to a clean, spacious flat with its own toilet and kitchen is still remembered by many older Singaporeans with a deep sense of gratitude.

Determined to eliminate Third World squalor, PAP made public housing top priority in its 1959 manifesto. By March 1963, about 350,000 people or 20 per cent of the population were living in subsidised housing with rents ranging from $20 to $60 per month. The rentals were within the means of 75 per cent of the working population whose monthly incomes ranged from $100 to $500.

Some 26,000 flats were built in a little over three years by HDB under the chairmanship of Lim Kim San. In contrast, only 23,019 units were constructed by its predecessor, the Singapore Improvement Trust, in its 32 years of existence.

Undoubtedly, public housing exerted a powerful hold on the imagination of a largely impoverished population. It spelt hope and a new beginning. Lee had stated unequivocally on several occasions that it was the building of Everton flats in Tanjong Pagar that helped him win the ward.

If the homeless were moving to new flats, the unemployed were finding new jobs created by the government's nascent industrialisation programme—jobs that lifted them out of poverty, gave them dignity and enabled them to take care of their families and, most importantly, send their "baby-boom" children to school.

Jobs were certainly one factor that influenced many voters, said Chan Chee Seng who wondered how many young Singaporeans today realised how poor their parents and grandparents were in those days. "When I went to school, I walked bare-footed with my shoes slung around my neck. I only put them on when I entered the school. This was to make sure that the shoes would not be damaged or worn out as they were my one and only pair."

Between June 1959 and April 1963, factories with a total paid up capital of $131 million were set up to manufacture products such as plastic tooth brushes, cotton wool, zip fasteners, mirrors, condensed milk and—believe it or not—chewing gum. A picture in a PAP publication showed rows of women treading on sewing machines with a caption proclaiming the rise of a new industry—garments.

No municipal achievement was too big or too small for the PAP government to pitch to the voters—from the $40-million Ulu Pandan sewerage scheme to the 15,604 street lamps and 2,426 water standpipes built by April 1963. Impressive statistics were rolled out for the same month showing the number of homes which enjoyed electricity (128,520), piped water (128,500), gas (34,973) and telephones (69,000).

Roads, bridges, bus shelters and drains were built. The Paya Lebar Airport runway was extended. Some 112 community centres went up. For islanders, jetties were erected, water supplied and goats distributed to improve their livelihood. For farmers, banana planting was introduced and free inoculation provided for pigs.

If one new flat was built every 45 minutes, as the PAP mantra went, one new school was built every three weeks. From 1959 to 1963, primary school enrolment rose from 267,000 to 333,000 and secondary school enrolment nearly doubled to more than 80,000. Free health services were extended to the people. Women's rights and welfare was promoted vigorously.

As Lee summed it up in his election victory speech: "The 26,000 homes, the Jurong industrial site, water, community centres, clinics together with the open argument clinched the issue." Thanking civil servants for helping him to accomplish these social objectives and confront the communists, he said: "Without their cooperation, the other half of the open argument would not have been carried through."

The 1963 elections witnessed the arrival of the pragmatic Singaporean voter. He was not pro-any ideology, just pro-jobs, pro-housing, pro-education, pro-higher standard of living. Shedding their socialist straitjacket, Lee and his fellow leaders felt vindicated—it was far better to fulfil meaningful material aspirations than satisfy abstract ideological yearnings.

WHILE most eyes were glued to the outcome of the gigantic clash between PAP and Barisan, the ruling coalition in Kuala Lumpur was keeping vigil on the fate of its offspring south of the causeway—the Singapore Alliance.

With the proclamation of Malaysia and Tunku lending prestige at election platforms to rally the crowd, the SPA-UMNO-MCA-MIC coalition was expecting the electorate to swing to its side for the sake of solidarity.

Although SPA head Lim Yew Hock did not contest the elections, he was the chief spokesman making the case that Singaporeans would be better off with the Alliance as it was part of the federal government. He accused PAP of covering up for the communists when it came to power and took issue with Lee for meeting the Plen secretly.

Why did the former chief minister pull out of the race? In press reports, he said that his move was related to his decision to take court action against PAP for indulging in a smear campaign against him. But in his book *Reflections* published in 1986, he said that he was asked to retire by Tunku at the request of his partner, Singapore UMNO.

If the left was punished in the 1963 polls, the right was pulverised. Singapore Alliance did not win a single seat although it held seven seats in the previous assembly and fielded 42 candidates. To add to the indignity, all its seats fell to PAP with increased majorities and no fewer than 31 candidates lost their deposits.

Its new leader, Yap Pheng Geck, was pushed into third place in River Valley. So was its best bet, incumbent A P Rajah in Farrer Park. The Alliance secured just under 49,000 votes or only 8.3 per cent of the votes cast in 1963—a big drop from 27.1 per cent in 1959.

But what shook UMNO to the core was the loss of its three Malay bastions—Geylang Serai, Southern Islands and Kampong Kembangan— to PAP's Malay candidates. Tunku was shocked as he had visited the three wards before election day to address the crowds and had thought that Singapore Malays were staunchly behind him and UMNO.

The seeds of conflict between PAP and UMNO were sown. No one foresaw it at that time but a big brutal battle between the two ruling parties on both sides of the Johor Straits was about to begin soon—with disastrous consequences.

16

PAP's Biggest Electoral Fiasco

WHOOSH—an egg flew in an arc hitting the speaker on the stage and splattering the white and yolk all over his face before trickling down to his sweat-soaked shirt.

It is 1964. The PAP rally had come to Kuala Lumpur, to a rip-roaring reception but someone among the estimated 20,000-crowd had a different notion of hospitality.

Chan Chee Seng was mingling with the masses when he spied the flying missile. "Ong Pang Boon didn't seem to know what hit him and he didn't seem to care. He just wiped it with his hand and carried on talking," recalled the former PAP stalwart.

Ong, known for his stoicism under adversity, preferred not to make much of the incident merely saying that he knew something had landed on him but kept on talking as he did not want to show any sign of fear.

In yet another incident in Kuala Lumpur after a PAP rally one night, Chan and fellow campaign workers were returning to their pickup van when they were confronted by parang-wielding gangsters. They ran and piled into their vehicle. "I accelerated to the utmost but the bloody thing wouldn't move," he said, "it was very frightening as they came near us. Fortunately after several attempts, the van started."

Former PAP activist Quah Wee Ho, who took charge of the sound system and lighting for PAP rallies then, still remembered how Ong and Chan tried to rent space for a PAP HQ in Kuala Lumpur. "They would pay rent, then the next day the owner would ask them to take back the rent. Somebody must have told the owner to return the rent."

When they realised they were being tailed on their office-hunting expedition, they would travel in several cars dropping people at various stops to obscure their trail. Eventually PAP managed to secure its HQ on the sixth floor of Central Electricity Board Building on Batu Road, now known as Jalan Tuanku Abdul Rahman.

Start a conversation with any party oldtimer involved in PAP's participation in the 1964 federal elections and such anecdotes would come tumbling out in a torrent. They captured in all its manifold manifestations the culture shock encountered by the party in its first and only electoral foray outside the island.

Accustomed to the ins and outs of the island's political arena, PAP found the mainland milieu a strange new world. In Singapore, the party took voluntary help for granted. In Kuala Lumpur, Ong experienced his first rude shock when his efforts to recruit campaign workers were met by the blunt question: "How much?"

Lee Kuan Yew said that in Singapore, people worked for PAP out of sheer enthusiasm. "You gave them a soft drink or coffee and that's that. But there in Malaya they demanded $5 or $3 a day. And if you don't pay, no posters went up."

It was ironical, he noted, that people expected to be paid for working for a party of the working people. "The workers wanted cash. Because that's the norm—no cash, no work. So it was a costly business. I don't know how we managed. I think we ended up $20,000 or $30,000 in debt, in the red, at the end of the campaign."

The bruising experience on the Malaysian hustings exposed the party's first-generation leaders to the pitfalls of money politics and left a permanent imprint on their psyche. The lessons learnt were reflected later in new election rules designed to prevent a similar situation from occurring in Singapore.

In retrospect, you could say that the egg on Ong's face was an apt metaphor for PAP's performance in the elections, a fateful event that triggered off a chain of consequences—intended and unintended—that was to put Singapore on the road to separation.

⚜

CALL it hypothetical hogwash or just a semantic game but one what-if scenario which continued to haunt many older Singaporeans would be: What if PAP had not taken part in the 1964 federal elections? Could the communal riots of July and September 1964 have been averted? Would Singapore have remained part of Malaysia?

What's hard to disprove was that PAP's decision to throw its hat into the ring sent shockwaves across the causeway and set in motion a sequence of events that was to lead to much grief and sorrow. What began as intense

PAP-MCA competition for the urban votes ended as an incendiary PAP-UMNO clash over diametrically opposing ideologies which culminated in the riots and separation.

Scholars now look at the 1 March 1964 announcement by PAP chairman Toh Chin Chye to field a token team in the first Malaysian general election in apocalyptic terms. They sprinkled their text with phrases such as "crossing the Rubicon" and "breaching the Maginot line".

Although Toh made it clear that PAP's aim was not to fight UMNO but the anti-Malaysia parties, his words were construed as a frontal and unwarranted challenge against the UMNO-led coalition. This was not helped by Lee's repeated assertion that MCA was replaceable and that PAP wanted to ensure that the protest votes against MCA did not go to the Socialist Front (SF), the Malaysian equivalent of Barisan Socialis.

Broach this seminal episode with former politicians on both sides of the Straits of Johor and talk would swing inevitably to this pivotal question: Did Lee breach an agreement with Tunku not to take part in the 1964 elections? What exactly was the agreement about?

The Malaysians had no doubt whatsoever that there was an agreement and that Lee violated it. Mohamed Khir Johari, former UMNO strongman and a confidante of Tunku, was absolutely certain that PAP was not supposed to take part in the 1964 polls and that when it did, Tunku was very upset with Lee.

Tan Siew Sin, then MCA chief, said he was horrified by Toh's announcement as he had been told by Tunku that PAP had given an undertaking not to take part in at least the first Malaysian elections. Former MCA MP Michael Chen recalled that both sides were not supposed to compete with one another as there was "a sort of understanding that Singapore was Singapore, peninsula Malaysia was peninsula Malaysia". In other words, the twain were not supposed to meet.

Lim Kean Siew, former SF leader, gave a similar account. "Tunku never thought Lee would come into Malaysia and set up the PAP. He thought that as PAP was a Singapore party, it would remain in Singapore. Thus when Lee came in and started attacking Tan Siew Sin and MCA, Tunku got very angry."

The reminiscences in the PAP camp were less clearcut. S Rajaratnam said: "As far as I know, there was no agreement signed or even explicitly stated by the PM that we should keep away from involving ourselves in Malaysian politics." The Malaysian leaders just assumed that PAP would not participate, he noted, given Tunku's view that Singapore should just make money and be the New York of Malaysia and leave politics to its Washington, Kuala Lumpur.

Goh Keng Swee's understanding was that Tunku did not want PAP to conduct any political activities in the peninsula. He quoted the Malaysian prime minister as saying words to the effect: "Let's go our separate ways. We look after your communists, you don't bother us."

Lee's own recollection? Yes, there was a gentleman's agreement made on the golf course in which Tunku said that UMNO would not take part in Singapore's politics and Lee said that PAP would not do so in the first elections after the formation of Malaysia.

So whose decision was it to take part in the 1964 polls? Devan Nair recounted a 1979 visit to Tunku in his retirement home in Penang. The father of Malaysia complained that Lee broke faith with him when he contested the elections. "I told Tunku, you are wrong. The decision was taken by PAP when Lee and I were touring the African countries. The decision was taken by Toh, Rajaratnam and company. When Lee returned, he was saddled with a fait accompli. Tunku found it difficult to believe that when I told him. But that was the truth."

Lee was then leading a Malaysian delegation on a 35-day mission to 17 African countries. He said that he was not aware of Toh's announcement until his return from his trip. "There was no communication. I didn't have an Air Force One to communicate with Singapore. Out of contact, completely out of contact."

But there had been suggestions that Lee could not possibly be unaware of such a major party decision. As one former party activist muttered: "How could the secretary-general of the party not be consulted about a decision as critical as taking part in the federal elections?"

By all accounts, it appeared that the Malaya-born PAP ministers agreed to field a team in the elections during a cabinet meeting in Lee's absence. Taiping-born Toh Chin Chye, Kuala Lumpur-born Ong Pang Boon and Rajaratnam who grew up in Seremban had a strong emotional attachment to their hometowns. They felt that they had the right to engage in Malaysian politics and that it was in line with PAP's fundamental objective of achieving reunification between Singapore and Malaya.

Ong confirmed that he was one of those who favoured participation. "On the face of it, what's wrong with taking part? We had gone into merger, surely we should take part in the Malaysian general election if we wanted to. We were exercising our right as Malaysian citizens to take part."

An increasingly infirm Toh could not remember much of his role in the fateful proceedings. What he could say was that as PAP believed in a united Malaya including Singapore, he felt that the elections would be a good time for PAP to win some ground and fight for a common identity.

Rajaratnam's account was that with merger, Singapore-born citizens were not allowed to take part in Malaysian politics but Malaya-born citizens could do so. Taking issue with the dual identity, they decided to form a PAP in Malaysia to put up Malaysians for the elections. "So I and Dr Toh decided we would field a few PAP candidates just to make it quite clear that we had not given up our ultimate aim of a Malaysian political entity."

According to Lee, Rajaratnam and Toh were most enthusiastic about PAP going into Malaysia and that he was roped into it because he had to abide by the party decision. But he admitted that he did not really set out to resist it. "I could have demanded another meeting and put my point of view. I decided not to because I persuaded them to make it only a token participation and to re-open the issue would be high-handed on my part, unless I felt very strongly about it. Because there was only one reason why I could have objected, namely that I had agreed with the Tunku not to participate.

"But the Tunku had come down during our general election. He sent his UMNO bigwigs down and he himself came down to a dinner. Well, so the agreement had been breached by him. I was really not in the position to say that we have to honour our side of the bargain. He did not honour his own compact with me."

Indeed what swayed the doubters in the cabinet was that the Malaysian leaders had meddled in the 1963 general election in Singapore. MCA senators Khaw Kai Boh and Tan Tong Hye came down to revamp Singapore MCA and canvass for the support of Singapore Chinese. Likewise Tunku and Khir Johari came to lobby for the UMNO candidates in the three Malay strongholds of Geylang Serai, Kampong Kembangan and Southern Islands. Tunku made no secret of his support for Singapore Alliance when he made an eve-of-election appeal: "It is my prayer that the people of Singapore will give favourable consideration to the party of which I am the leader."

Describing himself as a technocrat with no interest in the political process, Malacca-born Goh Keng Swee said he decided to go along with

Rajaratnam and Toh when Tunku broke his word. "I had reservations, having understood Tunku and Malay leaders better than others but I could not counter their arguments. They intervened in our elections, why should we not take part in a token way in theirs?"

⌘

WEARING a beige cap and blue jacket, the small-sized, bespectacled man would pass off unnoticed on the streets as a nondescript senior citizen.

But this was the Sungei Ujong Club where heads turned to greet him "Good evening, Dr Chen" when he breezed in. And this was Seremban, Negri Sembilan, where people knew him all too well as the state's leading opposition MP in the Malaysian parliament until his retirement in 1999.

With a faraway gleam in his eyes, private practitioner Chen Man Hin talked about the day PAP came to town. A fellow doctor in Seremban, S Seeveratnam, the brother of Rajaratnam, had asked Chen if he could meet the PAP people and help them in the coming elections. "I agreed and we got together to start the PAP branch in Seremban. I became secretary and Seeveratnam, chairman."

The meeting marked the launch of Chen's political career that was to see him taking the helm of the Democratic Action Party (DAP) for more than three decades. DAP succeeded PAP Malaysia in 1966 following its deregistration after separation.

But Chen did not stand in the 25 April 1964 elections. Another medical friend of Seeveratnam was picked to be the PAP candidate for Seremban Timor. Lau Kit Sun, a graduate of Hong Kong University, joined the PAP line-up of 11 parliamentary and 15 state candidates in the first Malaysian elections to elect 104 parliamentarians and 278 state assemblymen.

With no party machinery in the peninsula, PAP had to rely on its Malaya-born ministers with relatives and friends in their hometowns to start the ball rolling. Rajaratnam took overall charge of the election campaign. He was aided by Toh, Ong and Lee Khoon Choy.

They had to scramble for Malaya-born candidates as Singapore-born citizens were not eligible. Except for those residing in Singapore, Rajaratnam admitted that the leaders had no personal knowledge of many of the recommended candidates. This was unlike the situation in Singapore, he said, where the party could observe a person for a couple of years before it decided to put him up as a candidate.

Despite his reservations about PAP's participation, Lee Khoon Choy went up north to scout for potential candidates. He remembered inducting three candidates in Kuala Lumpur—Too Chee Cheong, a former MCA member and general practitioner; Goh Hock Guan, an architect and town planner; and Lam Khuan Kit, a lawyer and former member of the University Socialist Club, University of Malaya. Another Selangor candidate was K V Thaver, an educationist and unionist.

In Penang, PAP managed to woo Tan Chong Bee and Kang Eng Wah away from the Socialist Front (SF) to stand for elections. Tan was a former SF state assemblyman and president of the National Union of Teachers. Kang was also a trade unionist. Another Penang candidate was Lee's friend from his Cambridge days—Lim Ewe Hock, a lawyer and queen's scholar. Other candidates were accountant Ng Cheah Chim, law clerk Charlie Leong Tuck Wah and teacher Yao Ke Yuan.

The PAP chiefs were more familiar with the Malaya-born candidates despatched from Singapore—Lai Tha Chai, a Nanyang graduate working in PAP HQ; Liang Teck Sum from the Singapore Manual and Mercantile Workers' Union (SMMWU); Chua Sian Chin, a lawyer with Lee and Lee; and Wong Lin Ken, a history lecturer in the University of Malaya. Coincidentally, Chua and Wong were brothers-in-law who married two sisters and later became home affairs ministers in Singapore.

Of course, the best known of the bunch was NTUC secretary-general Devan Nair who stood for Bungsar, which included Petaling Jaya. Lee said that originally the party had no intention of fielding Malacca-born Nair as it wanted to keep his wife's seat Moulmein for him when he became a Singapore citizen. Mrs Nair was elected in the 1963 polls. "But when the time came, we were scampering and looking for suitable candidates and there was Devan who was a Malaysian citizen."

Nair recalled that he refused the prime minister twice when he was asked to contest. "I was having my hands full keeping the communist united front at bay in the trade unions. I didn't want to be away from my family, my children were growing up, so I said 'no' twice.

"But PM had a way of putting on a long face and saying 'well, that means we lose one good voice', subtly suggesting you were the selfish chap, self-centred. So I got fed up and finally said: 'All right, put me up. I don't care where you put me up.' "

As Rajaratnam related, PAP "went in blind" with a campaign run on a shoestring budget. Lee admitted that they were banking on the party's reputation. "We had no organisational links with the people there and we had no members who had influence in the streets, clubs, clans or guilds."

Almost everything needed for the campaign—equipment, posters, cars and manpower—was supplied from Singapore. Lee Khoon Choy noted that its entire fleet of cars came from Singapore. Chan Chee Seng recalled driving an old Austin pickup filled with audio equipment and loudspeakers for 10 hours from Singapore to Kuala Lumpur. Quah Wee Ho said he recruited manpower from the Works Brigade to set up electrical and sound equipment and build rally platforms.

On the hustings, PAP campaigned for a unified, prosperous and more equal Malaysia. It criticised MCA for not doing enough for the Chinese and it turned its guns on SF for backing Indonesia's Crush Malaysia policy. Casting his mind back over more than four decades, Chen Man Hin said that the thrust of the PAP campaign was to eliminate corruption and fight for a more just and equal society.

PAP's overall strategy was not to fight UMNO while competing with MCA and SF for the urban votes. Thus when the party found that its candidates Liang Teck Sum and Mohamed Noor bin Jetty were facing UMNO in Johor Bahru Timor and Johor Bahru Barat, it ceased campaigning immediately thus reducing its parliamentary slate from 11 to nine.

Did PAP aim to replace MCA as the UMNO partner as popularly believed? Chen did not think so as he said that PAP did not field enough candidates to replace MCA and that its objective was limited to just having a voice in parliament.

But MCA's Michael Chen, who stood against Lam Khuan Kit in Damansara, firmly believed that PAP wanted to replace his party in the Alliance. The rivalry between the two parties became so intense, he said, that Tunku had to intervene to declare that "even if there were only five members left in MCA, UMNO would still support and cooperate with MCA". Khir Johari made it clear that UMNO had to defend MCA as an attack on MCA was considered as an attack on UMNO.

Just as agitated with PAP was SF which PAP treated as its bitterest enemy while fighting against MCA, recalled then-party leader Lim Kean Siew. The retired Penang lawyer, who was with Lee in Cambridge, said: "I can tell you why. Kuan Yew was very ambitious. He wanted to remove anybody in the socialist camp who could oppose him so that he could be the only socialist leader." Well-respected Tan Chee Khoon was infuriated with PAP for stigmatising his party as "crypto communist".

A breathtaking highlight of the PAP campaign was the staggering crowds that gathered at its mass rallies whenever Lee made his appearance. Michael Chen remembered Lee turning up in Damansara to speak for Lam Khuan Kit. "Oh, what a crowd. He was the big draw, a very eloquent speaker. PAP didn't have much organisation but when it held a rally, it attracted thousands and thousands of people. The crowd could number as many as 10,000, 20,000."

Similarly, Lim Chong Eu of the United Democratic Party said that when Lee surfaced in Tanjong, Penang—the constituency he was standing in—thousands converged on the PAP rally. SF's Tan Chee Khoon, who was standing for Batu, said that when the PAP held its rally there, it drew the biggest crowds that Kuala Lumpur had ever seen.

What accounted for the crowd phenomenon? Ong Pang Boon put it down to curiosity: people wanted to find out more about the Singapore party which dared to champion meritocracy and multi-racialism, a policy at variance with the Alliance's concept of Malay political supremacy.

Chen Man Hin agreed, saying it was curiosity about PAP which drew the crowds. "PAP had a good name in Singapore. It formed a very popular and effective government. They wanted to come and listen to what it had to say. And also what it said touched a chord in the hearts of the people. It was representative of what they wanted—justice, equality, fairness."

But while the rallies were attracting never-before-seen crowds that flattened the long coarse grass called *lallang* and caused traffic snarls, PAP campaigners were sensing different vibes on the ground. The reception to their door-to-door canvassing was decidedly cool.

Lee Khoon Choy cited instances when Chinese supporters pulled back suddenly for fear of antagonising the authorities. Their sentiment was: "What will I gain if I support you? Even if you win all nine seats, you will still be in opposition. And then the government will fix us for supporting you."

Relating his experience in Malacca, Bulat Hamid said that as PAP campaigners neared a Malay kampung, they could see villagers talking or playing games. But when they reached the doorway of one house after another, they were surprised to see them lying on the floor. "They were pretending to sleep to avoid making contact with us. So what could we do but walk away?"

Othman Wok noted that many Malay constituents would treat them politely even inviting the PAP canvassers into the house for a drink. "They listened to us but at the end they would say smilingly 'You sounded very good but we still want to vote for the sailing boat,' " he said referring to the symbol for the Alliance.

In Chan Chee Seng's words, the rally was hot but the ground was cold.

◦◦◦◦◦◦

LEE was so confident that PAP would win at least seven parliamentary seats that he placed a $10,000 bet. He was shocked when he heard the results in Rumah Temasek on Jalan Tun Razak where Singapore officials used to stay in Kuala Lumpur. The party lost all nine but one and crashed in all 15 state seats.

In their reflections years later, former key PAP players still could not get over their biggest electoral fiasco in history. Rajaratnam called it a "total massacre". Devan Nair dubbed it a "disaster". Goh said he thought PAP could shock MCA but it got shocked instead.

The tremendous crowds at their mass rallies had boosted their expectations that they were in for a very big win. They were to learn a very bitter lesson which would be stamped indelibly on the party's institutional memory—that a massive turnout did not necessarily translate into votes.

The ruling Alliance scored a landslide victory winning 89 seats in the federal parliament with nine going to Pan-Malayan Islamic Party (PMIP), the predecessor of Partai Islam Semalaysia (PAS); two to People's Progressive Party (PPP); two to Socialist Front (SF); one to United Democratic Party (UDP); and one to PAP. Devan Nair salvaged the party's pride by scoring a narrow 808-vote victory over SF's V David in Bungsar.

If PAP had sought to dent MCA's standing, it had failed abysmally with several of its candidates suffering the further ignominy of losing their deposits altogether. What's more, MCA improved its performance by clinching 27 out of 34 seats contested compared to 18 out of 31 in the 1959 elections.

What went wrong with the PAP's election strategy? Did it lack understanding of peninsular politics? How could its reading of the Malaysian Chinese mind and Malay psyche be so off-the-mark? Historians and scholars have advanced their grand hypotheses, now let's hear it from former protagonists and antagonists who were in the thick of action.

One commonly-held view among them was that PAP plunged into mainland politics too soon and too hastily without establishing a strong party machinery and grassroots network. Not enough groundwork was done to study the constituencies and voters' profiles. Its resources were stretched thin from Penang to Johor.

Many of its candidates were political babes-in-the-woods unknown to the constituents. They were bursting with zeal and good intentions but lacked political experience and acumen. They were simply banking on PAP's name, reputation and track record in Singapore and its eloquent leaders to carry the day.

Toh put it bluntly when he muttered: "We never did our homework well. We were just selling the PAP as a trade brand. Our personal touch was not there." He added that the PAP's style of politics was regarded as distinctly Singaporean and alien to the Malayan electorate.

PAP lost, he said, because Singapore had been separated from Malaya for too long. "Since the party's inception, it had made no effort to develop a pan-Malayan character and had little understanding of the attitude and mores of the Malayan population. So there was no affinity. Our roots were not there. People were more familiar with UMNO and MCA."

Rajaratnam's indictment was just as severe: "We just jumped into the pool and hoped for the best." PAP had no idea that a constituency could be bigger than Singapore and was ignorant of the physical difficulties of campaigning, he said, recounting how he got lost while trying to find his way to a rally in Port Dickson.

It was only when they examined the electoral register that they realised that a town such as Seremban and Malacca would include a rural area where UMNO was well-entrenched among the kampungs. Thus PAP found it difficult to canvass for votes without knowing the *kampung ketua* ("village chiefs" in Malay).

The biggest stumbling block was that most Malays were hostile to PAP because of UMNO propaganda and the widespread perception that PAP was a Chinese party from Singapore seeking to intrude into the Malay heartlands. As former UMNO leader Khir Johari put it, the Malays were against PAP for trying to "enter their *rumah* (house)".

Nair's personal view: "We frightened the lives out of the Malays, the terrifying efficiency of the PAP, the record of our success against Barisan, our public image with the non-Malays." Felix Abisheganaden's journalistic view: "The PAP came here and made a great impression but at the end of the day, it's whom you mingled with in the *kampungs* and the outlying areas that mattered."

Lee's reading of his party's crushing defeat was that the people did not buy into the idea of token representation. They might have thought differently if PAP fielded a large enough contingent to be a force if elected, he said, "then we could bargain from strength and affect their lives". His view was shared by Ong who said: "People asked: Was it worth voting for PAP when it was not fighting to win and form the government?"

Being Malaya-born was no help to the candidates from Singapore either as having spent all their working lives on the island, they had lost touch with their hometowns. Chan Chee Seng, who campaigned for PAP candidates in Kuala Lumpur, commented: "Singapore representatives were strangers to the voters. They didn't know anything about you. They only knew Lee Kuan Yew. You had no relationship with them. Why should they elect you?"

Chen Man Hin's diagnosis was that the Malaysian electorate had always been very conservative and PAP was viewed as a party that would shake the status quo. Michael Chen, who beat his PAP counterpart in Damansara, agreed: "Malaysian Chinese might be fascinated by PAP slogans but after balancing the pros and cons, they would prefer to have a more conservative but safer sort of party like the MCA."

Then there were those who believed that PAP fell victim to its own all-too-subtle propaganda which all but befuddled the less sophisticated voters. How could the party claim to support UMNO in one breath and then attack its coalition partner MCA in the next? How could it seriously expect Tunku to abandon his finance minister and MCA chief Tan Siew Sin?

The moment Tunku declared full support for MCA, they said, PAP's position was unravelled. UMNO would never agree to accept PAP in place of MCA, said Khir Johari who often cited the cautionary tale of the Arab and the camel to warn of the danger posed by PAP: "Out of kindness, the Arab invited the camel into his tent. It ended up with the camel taking over the whole tent and driving out the Arab altogether."

Nair acknowledged that their campaign was too subtle and that they over-estimated the sophistication of the electorate. "Basically it went like this. Confrontation was going on, you must support the Tunku. Vote for the PAP candidates wherever they were, but otherwise vote for Tunku and Alliance. And the people took Lee seriously and they did vote for Tunku."

Undoubtedly, Indonesian Confrontation loomed large as one key factor that influenced the outcome of the federal elections. Malaysia was threatened by President Sukarno. People rallied behind Tunku in the spirit of national solidarity. In particular, the Chinese did not want to line up with the wrong side. True, PAP was against Confrontation but unfortunately, its stand was not readily discernible to the people because of its opposition language, said Chen Man Hin.

To some pundits, what was surprising was not that PAP lost so badly but that Nair won at all. What were the reasons for Nair's victory in Bungsar? His former party colleagues said that he was the best known of all the PAP candidates, having carved a name for himself as a leading trade unionist and anti-colonial fighter on both sides of the causeway, a charismatic speaker and indefatigable campaigner.

According to Rajaratnam and Ong, Nair's election pitch had a greater impact in Bungsar as it had a large English-educated middle class with a significant number of Indians and fewer rural Malay voters. It was urbanised, compact and relatively easier to canvass.

One controversial issue that emerged from the hustings has since been the subject of endless debate: Was the election fiasco due to Lee's lack of sensitivity to the Malay psyche when he campaigned vigorously for equal citizen rights for all races—a political philosophy opposed to UMNO's concept of Malay political supremacy and special rights?

You can argue one way or the other until the cows come home but for what it is worth, here is a range of reflections:

Devan Nair: "Historically I think the judgement will be that however brilliant PAP was in its analysis of the situation in Singapore, in Malaysia we underestimated the Malay reaction. And we misread the situation completely."

Lee Khoon Choy: "PAP made the assumption that because it won the three Malay strongholds of Geylang Serai, Kampung Kembangan and Southern Islands, it could also do so in Malaya. But Malays considered Malaya as *tanah melayu* or "land of the Malays" and non-Malays as outsiders."

Tan Chee Khoon: "PAP didn't know the psychology of the Malays. In most of the constituencies, Malays formed a strong and sizeable proportion of the electorate ... The PAP, being very brash then, went headlong alienating them."

Tan Siew Sin: "PAP misunderstood Malay psychology. If you go through the records, in the 1964 elections, every Singapore minister except Goh Keng Swee campaigned. Keng Swee knew Malay psychology. I'm told he flatly refused to campaign. He never made an election speech. He never crossed the border. Keng Swee knew this would not work and the result proved it."

Lim Kean Siew: "Lee didn't understand the Malays. He didn't understand Malay psychology. He thought Malays could easily be pushed around."

Chen Man Hin: "I do not agree that Lee lacked understanding of the Malays. He was trying to put across the point that this country required a different type of politics—one which stressed justice and equality. When you pushed that, then of course you upset the Malays. Kuan Yew being Kuan Yew, he's very forceful when he put across a point of view. There's no intention to antagonise the Malays but to say what he thought were the facts."

Lim Chong Eu: "I wouldn't say that Lee had no understanding. He had deep understanding but maybe his understanding was different from that of others."

⚜

TUNKU would often invite Goh to lunch or a round of golf whenever he was in Kuala Lumpur. He grew fond of Goh because he thought he was the odd man out in the PAP, having stayed out of the 1964 federal elections.

The former finance minister recollected an enigmatic exchange with Tunku after a game one day.

Tunku : Tell Lee he must change, I cannot change, I am too old to change.

Goh : Tunku, I don't understand.

Tunku : Tell him lah, he'll understand.

Goh : All right, Tunku. I'll say so.

Tunku kept repeating that he was too old to change. On his return to Singapore, Goh passed the message to Lee and asked: "Do you understand?" Lee's reply: "I haven't the foggiest idea. I don't know what he is talking about."

It was with the benefit of hindsight that Goh understood years later. "Tunku was a feudal leader with certain standards, values and ways of behaving," he said, "but we were totally different. We were motivated to modernise at the fastest pace. He was conservative and expected us to change to his style of leadership. So he became disillusioned with us. He felt that the communists were less troublesome; he could lock them up but he could not do the same with us."

This anecdote captured the divergent thinking of Tunku and Lee, UMNO and PAP, Kuala Lumpur and Singapore—a polarity in political philosophies that would put them on a collision course and lead ultimately to separation.

Both parties saw the world from two completely different and irreconcilable positions. PAP stood for a multi-racial Malaysia which would grant equal citizenship rights to all races. UMNO swore by a Malay-dominant Malaysia that accorded special rights and privileges to the Malays.

PAP's clarion call was to translate later to the emotionally electrifying slogan "Malaysian Malaysia"—a challenge viewed by UMNO as an all-out attack on its fundamental tenet that Malaysia was the land of the Malays and should be ruled by the Malays.

The inter-party strife was compounded by acrimonious debates in the federal parliament and vexatious wrangling between the two governments over a host of issues ranging from the proposed common market to the sharing of government revenue. Hitting a brick wall again and again, Goh concluded that his Malaysian counterpart and second cousin Tan Siew Sin had little intention of giving Singapore any leeway in trade and investments.

In the aftermath of the federal elections, the PAP-Alliance antagonism spilled south of the causeway. UMNO HQ took over the Singapore branch and sent its representatives to rebuild the Malay ground. Their most potent weapon was *Utusan Melayu* which could only be read by those who knew the Jawi script. The newspaper, which used to support PAP in its formative days, had fallen into UMNO's hands. Raising the banner of "religion, race and homeland", it championed the cause of the Malays and accused the PAP government of oppressing the Malay community.

Led by the fiery Syed Jaafar Albar, the UMNO leaders highlighted the plight of poor and jobless Malays and exploited the dissatisfaction of Malay kampung dwellers who had to make way for urban renewal. They stoked up their emotions over the absence of special rights which their mainland counterparts enjoyed.

The Malaysia Agreement had stipulated that special privileges granted to the Malays of Malaya would not be extended to Singapore Malays. PAP's stand was that Malays had a "special position" but not "special privileges". But this did not stop the ultras, as Lee labelled them, from demanding that privileges such as job quotas and land reservations be extended to Singapore Malays.

To address the grievances of the Muslim community, Lee and social affairs minister Othman Wok proposed to meet their representatives at Victoria Theatre on 19 July 1964. But they were pre-empted by an UMNO-sponsored convention at New Star Cinema in Pasir Panjang a week earlier on July 12.

Attended by several thousand people and representatives of 150 Malay organisations, the convention condemned the government over its treatment of the Malays and empowered a 23-member action committee to speak for the Malay community. Inflammatory speeches were interspersed with chants of "Kill Lee" and "Kill Othman". The political mercury was shooting up. Racial tension was palpable.

Nine days later, a procession marking the birthday of Prophet Mohammed assembled in the Padang and began its march to Geylang. It was a day that would go down in infamy, a day that saw the outbreak of a communal bloodbath. The final casualty count: 23 killed and 454 injured.

Come every July 21 when Singaporean students parade in their ethnic costumes to celebrate Racial Harmony Day in schools, do they know that they are actually marking the anniversary of the worst racial riots in Singapore's history?

17

Malay Heroes Who Changed History

THE unthinkable and the unimaginable had happened. For an island where the races had lived cheek-by-jowl for generations and which sought to be a shining beacon of multi-racial harmony, the most nightmarish scenario had materialised: Chinese-Malay racial riots.

The eerily surreal scenes of death and devastation which unfolded on 21 July 1964 could have been lifted from any media coverage of a Third World country in ethnic strife today: shophouses razed, cars burnt, buses smashed, properties vandalised, innocent people killed and maimed.

Buried in the subconsciousness of older Singaporeans are the memories of being stranded on the streets and frozen in fear as violence broke out and the economy ground to a halt. Hawkers scurried away. Cinemas cancelled screenings. Airlines bypassed Paya Lebar Airport. Causeway traffic ceased. Stock and property prices collapsed.

Frightened Chinese villagers fled from Malay-dominant estates while Malay villagers bolted their doors in Chinese-majority areas. Gangsters sharpened their knives. Desperate constituents pleaded with their assemblymen for help. PAP ministers met in cabinet in a state of shock.

In the absence of an official inquiry, the carnage had lent itself to varying interpretations. What's indisputable was that on the day itself, some 25,000 Malay Muslims had assembled on the Padang to commemorate Prophet Mohammed's birthday before marching towards Lorong 12 in Geylang.

As the procession turned from Victoria Street into Kallang Road, an incident occurred near the Kallang gasworks sometime after 5 pm. Within hours it escalated into a riot that spread quickly from the *lorongs* ("lanes" in Malay) of Geylang to the streets of the city. At 9.30 pm, a curfew was imposed. It was lifted at 6 am the next morning but was reimposed at 11.30 am when racial violence erupted again. By the time the curfew ended on August 2, 23 people had died and 454 were injured.

What's disputable was who triggered off the riots. Then-Malaysian deputy prime minister Tun Abdul Razak put the blame on a Chinese man who flung a bottle out of mischief at the procession as it passed through the Kallang area. "It sparked off a fight which turned into a riot," he said.

As former chief minister Lim Yew Hock elaborated, the empty bottle hit a Malay who exclaimed: "Oh my God! A Chinese hit me!" When the Malays, who were in a heightened state of religious fervour, heard the accusation, they lost their heads and started beating up Chinese bystanders.

"The news spread like wildfire. The Chinese shouted that they were being assaulted by the Malays and so the Chinese retaliated. The Malays shouted that they were being assaulted by the Chinese and the Malays retaliated."

According to this account which Special Branch originally believed to be the reason that led to the riots, the incident happened at about 5.30 pm. A man named Syed Alwi bin Syed Mohd was on his way home when he saw a young Chinese man throwing some joss papers through the window of the first floor of a coffee shop named Yew Seng Restaurant on 277 Kallang Road.

It was believed he scolded the youth for throwing the papers and in return the youth threw a bottle at him. It hit him on the head and wounded the left side of his face. While he was being taken away, he told members of the procession that he was hit by a bottle thrown by some Chinese. This resulted in some Malays rushing into the coffee shop and assaulting the Chinese there.

The versions cited by the PAP camp differed. According to Lee Kuan Yew's radio broadcast that night, a federal reserve unit policeman had asked a group of people who were straggling away from the procession to rejoin the main group. But instead of being obeyed, he was set upon by the group. Thereafter a series of disturbances occurred as more groups became unruly and attacked passers-by and bystanders.

Othman Wok, who was heading the PAP contingent then, recalled that the procession stopped suddenly as it passed Kallang: "I saw people running around and shouting that there was a riot. I saw several Malays punching a policeman." Anticipating trouble, he led the PAP marchers to the old Kallang airport building which housed People's Association.

Later, Special Branch noted that there was no conclusive evidence to corroborate the bottle-throwing incident. On the other hand, another

Special Branch report that the riot began with the assault on the police constable was supported by numerous witnesses residing along Kallang Road.

Whatever the version, it begged the all-important question: Was the riot spontaneous or pre-planned?

In his radio message, Lee said he believed that "all the indications show that there has been organisation and planning behind this outbreak to turn it into an ugly communal clash". His view was that the violence was started by a minority group of extremists but thugs took advantage and created more trouble.

Othman said: "I believe the riot was planned; it did not erupt spontaneously. They were very smart to choose a religious procession so that if we had stopped it, we would be called anti-Muslim. The inflammatory communal and racial speeches made by Malaysian UMNO leaders worked up Malay sentiments in Singapore."

He cited a conversation he had one week after the riots with an *Utusan Melayu* reporter in Kuala Lumpur who told him that at 2 pm on July 21, he already knew that the riots were going to happen. "I asked: 'How did you know beforehand that the riots would take place?' He replied: 'Oh yes, we knew beforehand. We have our sources, you know.' "

Yaacob Mohamed, the then-assemblyman for Southern Islands who was also marching with his PAP colleagues, said he was told that people from Malaysia had come down to start the riots and that stones were thrown from homes to create unrest.

Toh Chin Chye was sure that the riots were sparked off by the communal agitation of *Utusan Melayu* and UMNO secretary-general Syed Jaafar Albar. Goh Keng Swee said he had no doubts that the riots were started by Albar. S Rajaratnam believed that "somebody" must have triggered off the race riots as a warning to PAP that it should pipe down. He noted that the Chinese policeman who was beaten up had vanished without a trace, "reinforcing my suspicion that this was a political offensive".

PAP's views were reflected in the declassified despatches of the British, Australian, New Zealand and American diplomats based in the region. They all pointed their fingers at UMNO extremists for running and condoning a communal campaign against the PAP government which precipitated the riots. Britain's high commissioner in Kuala Lumpur, Anthony Head, told London he had "no doubt that this extreme element of UMNO played a considerable part in stirring up the first communal riots".

But UMNO people denied all these allegations placing the blame instead on communist instigators and Indonesian agents. Tunku said he had evidence that Indonesia was stirring up the grievances of Singapore Malays. Syed Esa Almenoar, who was leading the UMNO contingent on that day, attributed the riots to "several Malays and several Chinese fighting at the junction of Lavender Street and Kallang". He was insistent that none of the UMNO marchers took part in the riots and suggested that pro-communist elements could be behind the violence.

A second wave of riots broke out from September 2 to September 11 ignited by the alleged killing of a Malay trishaw rider by a group of Chinese men on Changi Road. Unlike the July riots, the violence was contained speedily and the perpetrators arrested before it could spread. Thirteen persons were killed and 106 injured in the September violence.

There was less contention among UMNO and PAP leaders about the cause of the riots which coincided with the landing of Indonesian troops at Labis in Johor. Federal government officials believed that Indonesians were behind the disturbance. Then-acting prime minister Toh Chin Chye said that the September riots should be considered in the context of a fresh attempt by Indonesia to weaken Malaysia.

Will the truth of the July riots ever emerge? Who can trace the smoking gun? A commission of inquiry set up by the Malaysian government never got off the ground. Professor Wang Gungwu, who was appointed one of the panellists, said that the commission never got to the bottom of it because of separation. "Once Singapore was kicked out, it became a foreign country. So what rights would a Malaysian commission have?"

Syed Esa Almenoar lamented that he did not have the opportunity to appear before the commission. "I was supposed to give evidence, final evidence together with, I remember Albar, but unfortunately, Singapore separated. So, the commission of inquiry died a natural death."

Rajaratnam noted that the PAP government's memorandum outlining the evidence leading to the riots was submitted to the commission but it was never published because Singapore was suddenly thrust out of Malaysia. Why was the inquiry not held? He believed that if the evidence comprising statements by Malaysian leaders and *Utusan Melayu* editorials were produced, non-Malays in Malaya would know that what happened in Singapore could happen to them too.

IT was a frantic time for the PAP leaders as they sought to keep their wits about them and figured out how to calm a terrified population. They felt powerless as they had no control over internal security.

Although Lee and his cabinet colleagues agreed to a curfew right away, it took some to-ing and fro-ing between the police and the federal authorities before it was finally imposed at 9.30 pm on the night of the riots.

Rajaratnam recalled a frustrated Lee failing to contact Razak on the phone and suspecting the Malaysian deputy prime minister of being "deliberately absent". He said that Lee had to warn Police HQ at Pearl's Hill that if the anti-riot squad was not sent out immediately, "I'll go on TV and denounce that you are deliberately not doing anything".

The traumatic experience taught PAP a very bitter lesson: the folly of not being in charge of the police and army. As Goh reflected later, they were so engrossed in the financial and economic terms of merger that they did not pay sufficient attention to what he called "power in the naked form". Invoking Mao Zedong's dictum that "power grows out of the barrel of a gun", or *qiang gan zi li mian chu zheng quan*, he said they realised too late that "the gun was not in our hands".

What worried Rajaratnam most was the danger of an increasingly agitated Chinese population taking the law into their hands. He recounted the expressions of relief among the Malays living in the Istana Kampong Glam, the former palace for Malay royalty, and the Sultan Mosque area when he visited his constituency. They told him that they were living "in a sea of Chinese and were afraid of Chinese retaliation".

To bridge the racial divide, the ruling party set up goodwill committees in all 51 electoral wards. Called *jawatankuasa muhibah* in Malay or *qin shan wei yuan hui* in Mandarin, they comprised community leaders and village elders who worked with the authorities to check unruly action or behaviour and squash rumours that would fuel racial tension. The aim was to protect lives and property.

The committees also set up special funds to buy food for needy Malay constituents and arranged for Chinese residents to accompany their Malay neighbours to market. These goodwill committees became the forerunner of today's ubiquitous Citizens Consultative Committees (CCCs).

There was a bright side, though, to this nightmarish chapter in Singapore history as stories of Chinese risking their lives to help the Malays and vice-versa emerged and remained etched in the memories of a fast diminishing ageing generation.

In one incident recorded by Low Tiow Lye, then chairman of the Ulu Pandan goodwill committee, legislative assemblyman Chow Chiok Hock and several committee members visited a Malay village behind what is now Coronation Plaza in Bukit Timah. They found themselves surrounded by a group of Malay youths who wanted an assurance that the Malays would not be beaten up and a guarantee that the police would not step into their mosques to make spot checks.

As night fell and the crowd grew increasingly hostile, Low realised that their lives were in danger. As luck would have it, a Malay village leader had the presence of mind to invite them to his house for tea as other elders persuaded the youths to disperse. "They were saved by Malays who trusted them," Low said.

Yaacob Mohamed told the story of Kampong Sireh off Upper Serangoon Road where 70 Malays in eight families lived among 3,000 Chinese. Twice a gang of Chinese youths gathered in front of the Malay houses and challenged the occupants to a fight. Twice Chinese elders came and told them that if they touched a strand of hair of any Malay in the area, all their Chinese friends would defend them. The hooligans left in a huff.

If there was yet another silver lining, it was that the riots brought a temporary respite to the acrimony between PAP and Alliance. Top Malaysian leaders from Kuala Lumpur joined their PAP counterparts in touring affected areas to render aid and restore confidence.

Khir Johari remembered a wild rumour about the murder of an imam in Geylang. At the request of then-culture minister Rajaratnam, he went on television with the Malay religious leader to prove that the latter was alive and kicking. "It was my first appearance on the screen as TV had yet to be introduced to Malaya. In one move, we managed to calm the Malays."

For two weeks after the July 21 riots, he said that he was the "uncrowned king of Singapore" as Tunku had appointed him director of operations with full power to work with the security forces to restore law and order.

Initially, there was wariness on both sides in view of their mutual hostility. Khir Johari admitted that his PAP counterparts were not cooperative and kept their distance in the beginning. "They were afraid that we might nab a few PAP leaders. But that was not our aim. I never received any instruction to arrest any PAP leader," he said.

He recalled phoning Lee to suggest going out to meet the people. "One of the first places we visited was in Upper Serangoon Road, not very far from where Hotel New World collapsed. So we went there and met the people to calm them down." Goh conceded that once the Malaysian leaders got into the picture, they acted expeditiously.

❧

WHEN Rahmat Kenap accompanied Lee on his round in Geylang Serai to calm the jitters of the constituents, the PAP assemblyman for the worst affected ward during the race riots was taunted by fellow Malays as a *babi* ("pig" in Malay) who had joined the Chinese.

Othman Wok was branded a *kafir* and *pembelot* ("infidel" and "traitor" respectively) to the Malay race—possibly the worst curses to inflict on a Malay. Mahmud Awang and Ariff Suradi were accused of selling their soul to the Chinese and to Lee.

During the 1963 general election, Malay PAP candidates were condemned as running dogs of the Chinese. Othman was stunned to see his posters in Pasir Panjang smeared with human faeces while his campaigner Bulat Hamid was told in his face that when he died, he would not be allowed to be buried in a Malay cemetery.

It was the worst of times for the Malay PAP stalwarts who had to endure insults and threats of physical injury and death from UMNO extremists. But it was also the best of times for them as their heroism, courage and fortitude shone through those dark days of Singapore.

To the ruling party, it was an incredible stroke of good fortune that they turned out to be men of sterner stuff who remained unswervingly loyal to their party and completely immune to the menacing words or sweet blandishments of UMNO. Not a single Malay PAP assemblyman jumped ship at this critical juncture.

They adhered to the PAP ideals of meritocracy and multi-racialism and refused to go along with UMNO's notion of Malay political supremacy and Malay special rights even though they would benefit the most from such a political ideology. In fact, some harboured reservations about the non-extension of special rights to Singapore Malays but did not allow UMNO's emotive appeal to override their belief in PAP's cause of a more just and equal society.

Through the ups and downs of the 1950s and 1960s, they remained loyal to PAP. They joined the party even though it was labelled Party Anak Peking ("child of Beijing") by segments of the Malay community. They saw the party through The Big Split of 1961. They fought valiantly in the elections, losing the three Malay bastions of Geylang Serai, Kampong Kembangan and Southern Islands to UMNO in 1959 and then snatching them back in 1963.

They braved a torrent of verbal abuse from UMNO and mainland Malays when they went up north to help campaign for PAP candidates in the 1964 federal elections. Most critically, as Singapore sunk into communal carnage later in the year, they did not wilt under pressure but pitched in passionately to help Lee restore confidence in the Malay community.

If they had abandoned PAP the way the 13 PAP assemblymen (12 Chinese and an Indian) did in 1961 when they crossed the floor to form Barisan Sosialis, the Singapore of today would not have materialised. If they had been won or bought over by UMNO, Singapore would have in all probability remained in Malaysia as a backwater state.

They changed Singapore's history, and no one knew it more poignantly and profoundly than Lee himself. In a thank-you letter to an ailing Rahmat Kenap in 1998, he wrote about how the former assemblyman stood by him while walking the streets of riot-torn Geylang Serai in 1964: "I cannot forget that for as long as I live ... You never wavered. I was fortunate to have in you a staunch, stout-hearted and loyal comrade."

In his 75th birthday dinner speech in 1998, Lee shed tears when he paid tribute to Othman. Relating how the former minister supported him wholeheartedly during the turbulent years in Malaysia and the race riots, he said: "Because of the courage and leadership you showed, not a single PAP Malay leader wavered. That made a difference to Singapore."

Lee's roll call of heroic Malay assemblymen included Rahim Ishak, Yaacob Mohamed, Buang Omar Junid, Mahmud Awang and Mohamed Ariff Suradi. Not many people were aware that several of PAP's leading Malay cadres originally hailed from UMNO.

The exodus from UMNO to PAP was led by Yaacob Mohamed, a barber-turned-teacher who made his mark as a charismatic speaker. As a Singapore UMNO CEC member, he became disillusioned with his party for not championing PAP's cause of fighting for independence through merger. He crossed over to PAP HQ to register as a member and 30 UMNO members followed suit.

The entry of a devout Muslim like Yaacob helped to change the perception of the Malay community towards PAP and opened the gates for more Malay members. Tunku's response to the mass resignations: "Good riddance."

Rahmat Kenap and Buang Omar Junid also left UMNO because they believed in PAP's multi-racial line and its ability to meet the promises of its voters. Mahmud Awang, who was elections secretary of UMNO Alexandra branch, said that as a trade unionist, he felt that he should not support any race but support all workers instead. PAP was thus the logical choice.

Why was there no reverse flow from PAP to UMNO? That was because the Malay party never bothered to woo them, they said. According to PAP founder and convenor Mofradi Haji Mohamed Noor, when he was struggling to resolve workers' problems in the Singapore General Hospital, UMNO never tried to reach him while it was Lee and Byrne who offered their help.

Similarly, Ariff Suradi recalled that when telephone board employees went on strike, they sought the assistance of then-UMNO chief and Labour Front minister Hamid Jumat. "We went to his house but he did not bother to meet us. That's why we turned to Lee for help," said the former president of the Singapore Telephone Board Employees' Union.

PAP's sensitivity to Malay interests was amply demonstrated right from the days when Lee and company sat around the dining table in the basement of No 38 Oxley Road to brainstorm the formation of the party. A radical Malay journalist, Samad Ismail, was Lee's confidante. Samad, Mofradi and Ismail Rahim were the convenors on inauguration day. Mofradi of the medical workers' union and Ismail Rahim of the postal workers' union sat on the first CEC.

As Mofradi recollected: "The reason why both Ismail Rahim and I were appointed was to help PAP know what was happening in the Malay community." As a senior *Utusan Melayu* journalist, Samad lent editorial support to the new party and conveyed PAP's messages to the Malay community. It was Samad who rounded up journalists like Othman Wok and Baharuddin bin Mohamed Ariff to join PAP.

Samad noted that Lee's rapport with the Malays was enhanced by his ability to converse in Baba Malay and by his popular standing as a legal adviser to many trade unions with a high proportion of Malay workers. Whether they were postal, telephone or harbour workers, they saw Lee as their advocate and champion.

No listing of Malay luminaries on the PAP record book would be complete without naming Ahmad Ibrahim, the leader of the Naval Base Labour Union who became the first Malay minister in the PAP government. He was reputed for standing up to Malay extremists and for drawing many Malays to the PAP fold. Ariff Suradi remembered Ahmad telling him: "If you don't join PAP, there'll be no Malays to represent the Malay community."

If UMNO won the three Malay strongholds in the 1959 elections, it was because of its communal appeal as a Malay party and the intervention of Tunku whose word as Malaya's new prime minister carried much weight. But in the next polls in 1963, all three wards slipped from its grasp—much to UMNO's shock and disbelief.

Ariff Suradi and Yaacob Mohamed toppled the two UMNO incumbents Mohamed Ali Alwi and Ahmad Jabri Akib in Kampong Kembangan and Southern Islands respectively while Rahmat Kenap vanquished UMNO strongman Ahmad Haji Taff in Geylang Serai. How did PAP effect such a dramatic turnaround?

The victories were attributed to the ceaseless efforts of the Malay PAP leaders in working the ground even though they were UMNO-controlled wards. Undeterred by threats and taunts, they sought and obtained much-needed amenities such as water tanks, jetties, standpipes, street lamps and schools for the residents.

Ariff Suradi said he made regular house-to-house visits and attended almost every wedding ceremony in the ward and even made donations to UMNO-sponsored events. Rahmat said he pledged to tackle the municipal problems in Geylang Serai neglected by UMNO during its two terms—from clogged drains, mosquito breeding and floods to untarred roads and lack of street lighting.

According to Othman, the main factor that favoured PAP in the Malay heartlands was merger. Among all the races, the Malays were keenest about merger with the mainland and they wanted to make sure that PAP, which negotiated merger with Kuala Lumpur, would be voted in to make a success of Malaysia. As Rajaratnam put it: "They knew that if UMNO won, they could only sit in opposition whereas if PAP won, PAP Malays would be in positions of power."

When Tunku heard the 1963 election results, he could not sleep blaming the defeat on those who betrayed UMNO. *Utusan Melayu* pinned the debacle on the split in the Singapore UMNO leadership which confused the Malay voters. Syed Esa Almenoar, then-Singapore UMNO secretary-general, linked the loss of confidence to its chairman Hamid Jumat because of his association with the Chew Swee Kee scandal. Chew was the education minister in the Lim Yew Hock government who received

$700,000 from an American source to finance his party's battle against the leftists in the 1959 elections.

Khir Johari, who oversaw Singapore UMNO then, was brutally frank. He said that the UMNO assemblymen did not fulfil the promises they made to voters after being elected. "They had neglected to visit the kampungs, talk to the people and find out what their needs were."

⊱✢⊰

AT 15 minutes past midnight on 9 May 1965, Lee Khoon Choy, political secretary to the prime minister, emerged from the stately Sri Temasek in the Istana grounds and walked across Orchard Road to hand a piece of paper to PAP HQ, then housed in an elevated red-brick building on the spot facing Concorde Hotel formerly known as Le Meridien Hotel.

At 7 am when the participants re-assembled in the designated but never-used residence of the prime minister, they were pleasantly surprised to see copies of the agreement on their tables—all ready for the final vetting and signing. One of them remarked to K C: "Is this how the PAP works?" At 9.30 am the press statement was ready to roll.

If you trust the memory of Fong Sip Chee who was part of the HQ staff then, this was how the declaration of the newly formed Malaysian Solidarity Convention (MSC) saw the light of day, a seminal statement that was to reverberate throughout the peninsula. Taking issue with the way Malaysia was being governed by a Malay-dominated alliance of communal parties, it called on Kuala Lumpur to recognise the democratic principles enacted at the formation of Malaysia and invited all Malaysians to unite to "fight for the ideal of a Malaysian Malaysia".

Among those who talked deeply into the night were Toh Chin Chye, Ong Pang Boon, Lee Khoon Choy, Othman Wok and E W Barker from PAP; D R Seenivasagam from the Ipoh-based People's Progressive Party (PPP); Lim Chong Eu, Lim Meng See and Abdul Wahab Mohamed Yassin from Penang-based United Democratic Party (UDP); Stephen Yong and Marican Salleh from Sarawak United People's Party (SUPP) and Leong Ho Yuen and Michael Buma from Machinda, another party from Sarawak.

Coalescing under the rubric of MSC, the five political parties staged their inaugural rally on 6 June 1965 to an overflowing crowd beneath the sweeping cantilevered roof of the National Theatre at Fort Canning

Park. Chen Man Hin remembered he felt uplifted by the "very inspiring" keynote speeches. Lee recounted a speech by Buma which was so devastating that the English papers were afraid to publish his punchlines. The Machinda leader had said that every time he listened to the radio, the announcer gave the time as *waktu tanah melayu* ("the time of the land of the Malays"). Why was it not *waktu tanah Malaysia*?

The idea of a Malaysian Malaysia electrified the imagination of the masses. As propounded in MSC rallies: "A Malaysian Malaysia means that the nation and the state is not identified with the supremacy, well-being and interests of any one particular community or race. A Malaysian Malaysia is the antithesis of a Malay Malaysia, a Chinese Malaysia, a Dayak Malaysia, an Indian Malaysia or a Kadazan Malaysia."

But to the Malaysian leaders and UMNO, the idea was anathema. It was seen as a direct challenge to Malay political supremacy and special rights, and an attack on their system of governance under which the ruling political parties were organised along racial lines—UMNO for Malays, MCA for Chinese and MIC for Indians.

So who incubated the idea of MSC? Toh and Rajaratnam said that they were the prime movers. Rajaratnam included Lee as well noting that the then-prime minister was convinced that "things had moved to such a pitch that Malaysia was not going to work, so we had to make the next move". The move was MSC.

Rajaratnam admitted, however, that he was more strident than Lee about the notion of Malaysian Malaysia. He said that Toh and he felt strongly for it for "emotional and personal reasons" as they were from Malaya where they had relatives and friends. Lee, he said, had only contacts with individual Malays and had no deep attachment to Malaya.

Toh was singled out by Goh as the leading figure in the MSC who did not pull his punches. The MSC strategy, Goh said, was to bring in disaffected politicians from the other territories. It was like "borrowing the communist united front strategy of enlisting the support of others to fight a bigger man".

Did the concept of Malaysian Malaysia breach the special position of the Malays in Malaysia as enshrined in the Federal Constitution? Rajaratnam did not think so saying that the special position of the Malays also existed in the Singapore Constitution, that is, Malays were regarded as indigenous people and accorded special treatment from other non-Malays but no privileges were granted.

He argued that the special position of the Malays had never been defined in legal terms and that it was a political concept to assure the Malays who lost out in education, economic power and other fields that they would be helped to catch up. It was only when UMNO came into power in Malaya, he noted, that laws were passed to provide land reservations, job quotas in the civil service and other privileges for the Malays.

"Singapore therefore never subscribed to these things. We only accepted what was in the Federal Constitution—the special position of the Malays. We don't believe in special rights, privileges. But we define the special position of the Malays, in terms of giving opportunities to better themselves," he said.

From UMNO's point of view, the Malaysian Malaysia campaign was a calculated move to strip away the rights and privileges of the *bumiputras* or "the sons of the soil". Khir Johari argued that the Malays were in the weakest position economically and educationally and that unless these imbalances were corrected, a Malaysian Malaysia would not work. "We had to do something to help them attain the standard to compete with the rest; there was nothing wrong with it," he said.

As MCA's Michael Chen saw it, Tunku's "let the Malays govern the country and the Chinese do business" philosophy was not quite understood by people like Lee who did not grow up in a Malayan environment. "These simple approaches made the Malays and Chinese comfortable with one another. MCA knew that no Chinese could be PM and that the Malays could have run Malaysia without the Chinese."

Perhaps what alarmed the Kuala Lumpur leaders most was the spectre of Singapore, Sarawak and Sabah, and possibly Penang and Malacca, coming together in a new grouping or an alternative arrangement if MSC were to succeed in its objectives. Such an idea had been alluded to by Lee and sensationalised in press reports with the screaming headline: Partition.

There was a "very, very strong rumour" that the three Ss—Singapore, Sarawak and Sabah—would come together and UMNO was very concerned, recalled Syed Esa Almenoar. He said he did not buy it but certain people in UMNO believed that it would come into being.

The MSC had been depicted as the final blow, the point of no return and the death knell for UMNO-PAP relations which hastened the eviction of Singapore from Malaysia. Lim Chong Eu agreed that it was the breaking point. Referring to PAP in Singapore, UDP in Penang and SUPP in Sarawak, he said: "The fact that these parties came together, that they could be stronger than the Alliance was quite clear and that I think was the basic reason why Tunku and his people began to think that it was better to let Singapore go off."

Rajaratnam believed that MSC was the proverbial straw that broke the camel's back. Here is an elucidating extract from an oral history interview with the former foreign minister on why PAP embarked on such a politically dangerous venture.

Question   : At the time when PAP undertook the MSC, were there already suspicions that this would lead to Singapore's expulsion?

Rajaratnam : Well, vaguely we thought that we'd get into trouble. I don't know to what extent. Whether there'll be mass arrests, banning of the party. In fact, we didn't think that separation would have been the alternative. We thought it'll be some kind of crippling of PAP.

Question   : Why was PAP willing to risk something like that?

Rajaratnam : No, it is not a risk. Because we knew, once we got in there, as I said, after merger, we suddenly became conscious of the fact that Malay ambition was a Malay-dominated Malaysia. So this awareness began to dawn on us. So either you sit back and do nothing. And eventually it's too late, then you've got to accept the inevitable. Or we'd better see whether we can, while we're still strong, retard it or reverse the whole political concept in Malaysia.

Question   : In other words, PAP was willing to martyr itself for the cause.

Rajaratnam : It's not a question of martyr. Everybody goes into politics for specific reasons, specific beliefs. The Malays have gone into politics for the belief that Malays must rule. We have gone into politics because we believe in a multi-racial Malaya or Malaysia. Because without these beliefs, politics becomes meaningless.

❧❧❧

FROM out of the blue, Ong Eng Guan shot back into the headlines when he resigned on 16 June 1965 as assemblyman for Hong Lim, the seat he won four times since 1957. On the first two occasions, he stood for PAP and in the last two, he stood against it.

His sudden decision to quit politics paved the way for a by-election on 10 July 1965. The stage was set for a battle royale between PAP's Lee Khoon Choy, the political secretary to the prime minister, and Barisan's Ong Chang Sam, its organising secretary. Both were defeated candidates in the 1963 elections.

The duel occurred amid Indonesian Confrontation and continuing tension between PAP and UMNO over their opposing ideologies on the governance of Malaysia. Rumours circulated of moves to suspend the Singapore Constitution and detain Lee. Toh mentioned a possible assassination attempt against Lee and PAP leaders mulled over the idea of a government-in-exile in Cambodia.

Until Ong emerged from seclusion to give his side of the story, why he quit would continue to be one of the big question marks in the PAP story. Ong's ostensible reason: it was futile to serve in the assembly when the PAP government had suppressed the mass media.

But PAP leaders were convinced that an unseen hand in Kuala Lumpur had engineered Ong's resignation to put PAP's standing to the test. That the populist United Progressive Party (UPP) chief resigned on the second day of an UMNO convention in Singapore fuelled speculation that the Malay party might be behind it.

Their suspicions were reinforced when UMNO leaders called on people to vote for Barisan. To Fong Sip Chee, it was curious and unbelievable that *Utusan Melayu* should support Barisan openly knowing that it was a pro-communist outfit which had pledged to crush Malaysia.

Lee's view was that the federal government had influenced Ong to resign through Gary Wang, an MCA member who used to be Ong's former political secretary when he was mayor from 1957 to 1959.

Goh believed that Ong's decision to resign for no apparent reason must have been at the insistence of the Malaysians and the Kuala Lumpur Special Branch. He fingered S V Lingam, Ong's former chief lieutenant and Aljunied assemblyman, whom he said was later discovered to be an agent of KL Special Branch. Lingam was a double defector—first to UPP and then back to PAP.

Rajaratnam said that they could only go by Lingam's word that the Malaysians had induced Ong to quit but conceded that this was just a theory as there was no concrete evidence.

Some of Lingam's friends, however, found the theory incredible saying that they knew him as a poor, simple man lacking in curiosity and the requisite qualities of an agent. Chan Chee Seng dismissed it completely arguing that if he were an agent, he would have been taken care of by the Malaysians and not died a pauper. Ong Pang Boon also thought that Lingam's behavior was very uncharacteristic of an agent.

Lee conceded he had no proof but asked why Lingam, whom he viewed as a political survivor, should leave PAP to join Ong Eng Guan. "There was no future. It did not make sense. I am thinking—this is ex post facto—why did the man make that move? Because he was told to make that move, keep in touch with them. Goh Keng Swee said he was a member of the Special Branch. I think they must have told Goh but it was not told to me and I believe that to be true."

The by-election has since been described as a defining moment in the history of PAP and Singapore. No less than the future of the island was said to be at stake as the intense straight fight between PAP and Barisan was also viewed as a do-or-die proxy battle between PAP and UMNO.

As Lee put it, in a clear reference to the Malaysian leaders: "They wanted a by-election to test how much support the PAP had. If Barisan could defeat us, they could neutralise PAP leaders using the Internal Security Act without much agitation against our detention."

Lee Khoon Choy: "Ong resigned to enable Barisan—and UMNO—to test our strength. If we had lost, Malaysian troops would have come in and we would all be arrested."

Fong Sip Chee: "Defeat would have been a disaster for PAP and Singapore and would almost certainly change the course of the island's history. It was either a party's victory in Hong Lim or the people's defeat in the whole of Singapore."

But seriously, would Malaysia have sent its forces across the causeway if PAP lost? When the question was put to UMNO's Khir Johari in 2003, he laughed it off saying: "I knew Tunku through and through. He was a fair man. He would never do such a thing."

MCA's Michael Chen said he did not think Tunku, being a Western-educated prince, would resort to such action. "I don't think he would be pressured into detaining Lee. He must be thinking that you could not solve the problem by detaining Lee."

The 10-day campaign revolved around the issue of Malaysia. PAP fought for public endorsement of its concept of Malaysian Malaysia as opposed to the Alliance's communal Malaysia. Barisan found itself in a quandary because of its Crush Malaysia platform. It could not respond adequately to charges that it supported Confrontation and by implication, of condoning the Indonesian bombings that killed innocent lives.

At last Ong's bastion was breached. Hong Lim returned to the PAP fold when Lee Khoon Choy beat Ong Chang Sam by 2,052 votes on 10 July 1965. The tide that had been turning in PAP's favour against the leftists had reached a new high-water mark. Lee hailed the victory as a clear endorsement of Malaysian Malaysia. Less than a month later, Singapore was out of Malaysia.

In his reflections, Goh commented that it was PAP's defeat in Hong Lim in 1961 that compelled Tunku to come up with his Malaysia plan to prevent Singapore from going red. But with PAP's victory in the same ward in 1965, Tunku no longer had such fears and was free to contemplate what to do with troublesome Singapore.

In other words, the rationale for merger—to keep Singapore from falling into the hands of communists—had disappeared. This was one of the A to Z factors that went through Tunku's mind as he recuperated from shingles in a London hospital and agonised over the most momentous decision of his life: to expel Singapore from Malaysia. Was separation the unintended consequence of the Hong Lim by-election?

⸎

ON his journey back to Kuala Lumpur, Tunku stopped over in Singapore on August 5 at 3.50 am. Whatever troubling thoughts he might have had on his mind was masked by his usual genial and expansive self.

Later in the day, Syed Esa Almenoar sent him off at Paya Lebar Airport. As Tunku prepared to board the plane, he bid the Singapore UMNO secretary-general "Goodbye, my Esa."

Four days later came that fateful phone call. Top UMNO official Ghafar Baba was coming to meet Singapore UMNO urgently. Syed Esa rounded up all his party colleagues for the gathering at UMNO House, now renamed PKMS Building, on Changi Road. The future Malaysian deputy prime minister broke the news and many officials broke down immediately.

It was there and then that Syed Esa realised the poignancy of Tunku's parting words at the airport. "It never occurred to me until afterwards, because he never used to say, 'Goodbye, my Esa.' He would say, 'I will be seeing you.' " Goodbye Esa meant Goodbye Singapore.

18

Separate or Face a Bloodbath

EDMUND William Barker had barely settled down in his new job as minister for law when he was summoned to Lee's City Hall office for the most important assignment of his life.

As a lawyer with Lee and Lee before being cajoled into standing in the 1963 elections, the queen's scholar who graduated from St Catherine's College, Cambridge University, was familiar with the drafting of all kinds of agreements.

But nothing in his experience and expertise could quite prepare the 45-year-old Eurasian for what the prime minister was about to thrust upon him: drafting the agreement to separate Singapore from Malaysia, the amendment to the Malaysian Constitution allowing Singapore to separate and the proclamation of Singapore's independence.

As Barker related, he hit the law library of the University of Singapore and found a precedent in the break-up of the Federation of West Indies. Using it as a model, he drafted the three historic documents that were to effect secession and give birth to the Singapore of today.

It was typical of Lee's foresight that he thought of and insisted that the water agreement between Johor and Singapore be enshrined. It should have been placed in the separation agreement, Barker recalled, but it ended up in the amendment bill instead.

He spotted the legal discrepancy over dinner with Malaysian deputy prime minister Tun Abdul Razak but "because Siew Sin wanted this clause and Dr Goh wanted another, I forgot about it". Finally just before they signed the papers, he realised that it was in the wrong place but decided to proceed anyway.

Later he told Singapore chief justice Wee Chong Jin that the water clause should not have been inserted in the amendment to the constitution. Wee's judicial response: "Never mind. If it's in the constitution, it's even stronger."

And that's the story of how Section 14, which continues to be a source of controversy between both governments over their interpretations, found its way into the very document—the Constitution and Malaysia (Singapore Amendment) Act 1965—which established the independent and sovereign state of Singapore.

Just to recap, it read: "The Government of Singapore shall guarantee that the Public Utilities Board of Singapore shall on and after Singapore Day abide by the terms and conditions of the Water Agreements dated Sept 1 1961 and Sept 29 1962, entered into between the City Council of Singapore and the Government of the State of Johore.

"The Government of Malaysia shall guarantee that the Government of the State of Johore will on and after Singapore Day also abide by the terms and conditions of the said two Water Agreements." Singapore Day referred to Separation Day—9 August 1965.

When Barker, who represented Tanglin from 1963 to 1988, died in 2001, Lee highlighted his "unique role" in settling the final documents for the separation of Singapore from Malaysia. If Lee was the founding father of independent Singapore, you could say that Barker was its legal midwife.

⁓⁂⁓

HISTORY records that Tunku made his heart-wrenching decision while recuperating from shingles, a nerve disease of racking, unbearable pain, in a London hospital on 29 June 1965. He fell ill while attending the Commonwealth Prime Ministers' Conference.

As he reflected in his column in a Malaysian newspaper, *The Star*, on 7 April 1975: "I never knew before what it felt like to be stretched out on a bed without being able to move one's legs or to turn to one side or the other for days on end. Every movement caused grinding pain, but my mind was alive and active; so I lay there, I was thinking of Lee. And what I thought did not drive the pain away but made it worse.

"The more pain I suffered, the more I directed my growing anger at him pitying Singapore for all its self-imposed problems. Whichever way my restless mind turned, I could not help but come to one conclusion—and that was to cut Singapore adrift from the rest of Malaysia."

In his mind, the alternative was a bloodbath if the political and racial tension between Kuala Lumpur and Singapore kept on rising. Despite pressure from UMNO extremists, he could not contemplate arresting

Lee, suspending the constitution and taking over Singapore by decree.

Bapa Malaysia, or "Father of Malaysia" in Malay, was at the end of his tether. There was simply no end to the issues bedevilling relations between both parties: UMNO's defeat in the 1963 Singapore elections, PAP's debacle in the 1964 federal elections, UMNO's move to revitalise its Singapore branch, PAP's plan to open more branches on the mainland, the launch of Malaysian Solidarity Convention (MSC), the controversy over the common market, the collapse of a two-year political truce and the raging war of words in parliament, press and public.

The straw that broke the camel's back, according to the Kedah prince, was a speech by Lee in the federal parliament on 27 May 1965 when he moved an amendment to the motion of thanks to the Yang di-Pertuan Agong's address. Lee expressed regret that the king had not assured the people that the country would move towards a Malaysian Malaysia.

In his speech, Lee argued that PAP could do as much if not more for the Malays and the indigenous people. Taking issue with Alliance's policies for benefiting only Chinese millionaires and a few Malay millionaires, he questioned how the imposition of Malay rights could raise the living standards of the Malay *raakyat* ("people" in Malay).

"He brought up many issues which disturbed the equilibrium of even the most tolerant members of the house ... nothing said or done after that speech of his could improve relationships between Lee and some of our party members who grew very bitter about him," Tunku wrote.

Devan Nair, who attended the sitting as PAP member for Bungsar, noted that Lee held the whole chamber spellbound when he switched his speech to Malay. "But unfortunately it had quite negative results. It increased the feeling of insecurity of the UMNO, MCA and MIC leaders."

From his London hospital bed, Tunku relayed his let-Singapore-go proposition to Razak in Kuala Lumpur and asked him to discuss it with senior Malaysian ministers and PAP leaders. The Malaysian deputy prime minister replied that he had already met Lee for nearly two hours to resolve issues but "our minds did not meet on most points". Then he mentioned that when Goh saw him after returning from medical treatment in Germany, the Singapore finance minister had expressed the view "that the only way to stop a headlong collision is to separate Singapore from central government".

If you comb through the newly declassified documents on Australian foreign policy relating to Malaysia between 1961 and 1966, you would be irresistibly drawn to the conclusion that Goh played an instrumental role in Singapore's separation.

Thomas Kingston Critchley, the then-Australian high commissioner to Malaysia, referred to Lee's heavy dependence on Goh and quoted Malaysia's home affairs minister Ismail bin Dato Abdul Rahman as saying that Lee was not prepared for a showdown with Goh. "I am satisfied that Goh played a big part in the settlement and this is confirmed by Razak," he said.

This view was reinforced by William Beal Pritchett, the then-deputy high commissioner in Malaysia (Singapore), who said that Goh told him that if Kuala Lumpur was not going to cooperate with Singapore economically, then "Singapore might just as well be out of Malaysia".

The all-abiding impression gleaned from the Australian despatches to Canberra was that unlike Goh, Lee was not prepared for a complete break, preferring instead a looser association with economic and financial autonomy for Singapore but with defence and external affairs remaining with Kuala Lumpur.

Did Goh exceed or ignore the mandate given by Lee when he opted for separation right away? Did the former finance minister attempt to explore other constitutional alternatives to keep Singapore within Malaysia?

Stonewalled by his Malaysian counterpart and second cousin Tan Siew Sin at every turn during negotiations over the common market and other economic arrangements, Goh was more than convinced that merger was not working out.

When Goh was interviewed by writer Melanie Chew for the book *Leaders of Singapore* published in 1996, he revealed that he met Razak and Ismail on July 20 and told them that the only way out was for Singapore to secede completely.

Leafing through what he called the Albatross file, he read: "It should be done quickly, and before we got more involved in the solidarity convention. As you know, Rajaratnam and Toh were involved in the solidarity convention. You want to get Singapore out and it must be done very quickly, and very quietly, and presented as a fait accompli." Refusing to divulge any more details, he said that Razak and Ismail agreed that Singapore must get out. The question was: How to get Singapore out?

According to Critchley, the Malaysian ministers told him that by July 20 there was an understanding on how separation should be achieved and that Barker was asked to go ahead with the legal drafting.

When interviewed, both Toh Chin Chye and Ong Pang Boon said they were not aware of the Albatross file. Lee said that he knew about the file although he had not read it. "Goh told me: 'I've got an Albatross file where I put all the things that went wrong.' "

Lee noted that the file contained more than just Goh's notes on his negotiations with Razak for separation. It also dealt with his frustrations with the then-Malaysian finance minister over the common market. "Tan Siew Sin was doing everything possible to fix us. So Goh saw this going to a dead end. He was in favour of breaking up. I was not in favour."

Would these accounts debunk the notion that Singapore was booted out ignominiously? Did they suggest that Tunku decided on separation and Goh seized the idea with alacrity ruling out any other constitutional option? In other words, secession was not foisted on Singapore unilaterally but was worked out jointly and deliberately by Goh and Razak.

⚬⚬⚬❦⚬⚬⚬

IF you view the separation agreement displayed in the National Museum of Singapore, you should be able to make out the 15 signatures of the five Alliance ministers and the 10 PAP cabinet ministers that made it a legally binding document. Officially, it is called the Independence of Singapore Agreement 1965.

According to Australian diplomatic correspondence, Goh pressed Lee to accept separation rather than fight on and both Goh and Barker gave categorical assurances to the Malaysians that Lee would accept the agreement.

A hesitant Lee was still hoping for a constitutional re-arrangement that would keep Singapore in Malaysia but with full autonomy. In fact, he made a last ditch effort on August 7 to persuade Tunku to pursue other alternatives. But Tunku had cast the die.

How did the PAP cabinet react to the separation agreement? Barker, who drafted the document, said that he signed happily because he never understood why his colleagues wanted to merge in the first place. He commented that "separation was the best thing to happen to Singapore".

Othman Wok recalled driving from Singapore on August 7 to Temasek House, now known as Rumah Temasek, on Jalan Tun Razak in Kuala Lumpur where he met his grim-faced colleagues. "PM called me into a room and asked me if I were prepared to sign the separation declaration.

I said: 'PM, I will sign it without hesitation but what about the communists in Singapore?' He replied: 'Don't worry, I will handle them.' "

For Rajaratnam and Toh, the driving force behind PAP's foray in the 1964 federal elections and the MSC, it was a gut-wrenching moment. They had strong emotional affinity for the mainland and were prepared to run the risk of resisting separation.

Othman saw a visibly upset Rajaratnam complaining that they had all worked so hard for Malaysia so why should they quit and Lee giving the curt rejoinder, "don't make my position difficult". Barker said that Lee "had a devil of a time convincing them" noting that "if they didn't sign, they would have to leave the cabinet".

This snapshot of cabinet tension was also captured in a diplomatic message by Critchley who quoted Lee as telling Tunku that "it was Goh that mattered and that if he had to choose, he would be prepared to do without Toh and Rajaratnam".

At Lee's request, Tunku scribbled that oft-cited August 7 letter to Toh making it clear that "there is absolutely no other way out". On reading the note and realising the inevitability of separation, Toh fell in line followed by Rajaratnam.

What if they had refused to sign the agreement? Lee said he told Toh that if he did not sign, he would have to take over the fight. "I am not going to carry on anymore. I will just hand over to you, you will carry on the fight. You will be responsible for the bloodshed because Tunku said bloodshed. I said: 'You carry on.' Then he signed."

For Ong Pang Boon who grew up in Kuala Lumpur, signing was Hobson's choice. "We were at Temasek House when Toh showed us a copy of the agreement. We asked: 'We fought so hard for Malaysia, was this the only way out?' They said the other way was going to jail, facing a racial massacre…"

On their return to Singapore, Lee summoned the ministers who were not in Kuala Lumpur to Sri Temasek to sign the agreement. Barker observed that Lim Kim San and Yong Nyuk Lin signed willingly. Lim said that Lee had always known that he favoured an independent Singapore. Jek Yeun Thong's signature completed the document. Signed and sealed, it was delivered by a Royal Malaysian Air Force aircraft to the federal capital at midnight—10 hours before the proclamation that would shock the region.

TRUST the lawyer in Barker to spot yet another legal incongruity on the day itself—Singapore's independence was announced before the amendment bill providing for its separation was passed in the Malaysian parliament and senate. "It should have been the other way round," he said.

At 10 am on Monday, August 9, a radio announcer read out Lee's proclamation that "Singapore shall be forever a sovereign democratic and independent nation, founded upon the principles of liberty and justice and ever seeking the welfare and happiness of her people in a more just and equal society."

A few minutes after 10 am in Kuala Lumpur, Tunku broke what he described as "the most painful and heartbreaking news" to the *dewan raakyat* or parliament. He said: "In all the 10 years of my leadership of this house, I have never had a duty so unpleasant as this to perform."

He moved the Constitution and Malaysia (Singapore Amendment) Bill 1965 on a certificate of urgency to sanction the legality of Singapore's separation and independence. It was passed by 126 to nil with one abstention. Likewise the senate or the upper house gave a unanimous aye. This explained why to this day, whenever a bilateral row erupted, Malaysian commentators would gloat over the fact that Singapore owed its independence to an act of parliament in Malaysia.

If the bill was passed speedily, it was because the government MPs had been briefed minutes earlier and instructed to vote for it. A number of Alliance ministers and MPs opposed Tunku's decision but had to toe the party line. UMNO secretary-general Syed Jaafar Albar refused to enter the chamber to vote. When home affairs minister Ismail warned him that Tunku would be angry, he muttered: "I don't care."

The opposition MPs were caught off-guard completely. Former Socialist Front chief Lim Kean Siew still chafed at the thought that he did not have a chance to debate it. His party colleague Tan Chee Khoon was abroad when he read about Singapore's separation in the papers. In his recollections years later, he accused UMNO and PAP of *pakat-pakat* ("collusion" in Malay).

Just as the news was about to go on air at 10 am, Lee was giving a last-minute briefing to senior civil servants and diplomats. All were thunderstruck as they had no inkling of what was to happen. A top official remembered a sad and subdued Lee talking about how their efforts in getting into Malaysia and fighting for it had all been undone. He was struck by the prime minister's remark about "how ironical that we have to go into Malaysia to come out independent".

At noon, Lee gave his press conference at Radio and Television Singapore (RTS)'s studio on Caldecott Hill. Televised at 4.30 pm, it showed a visibly distraught Lee breaking down at one point—a scene that was to be seared into the memory of a generation.

In a choked voice, he said: "What has happened has happened. But be firm and calm. We are going to have a multi-racial nation in Singapore. This is not a Malay nation, not a Chinese nation, nor an Indian nation. Everybody will have a place in Singapore...

"Every time we look back to the moment we signed this document, it is for us a moment of anguish. For me it is a moment of anguish. All my life, my whole adult life, I have believed in merger and unity of the two territories. We are connected by geography, the economy and ties of kinship ... It broke everything we stood for ... would you mind if we stop for a while?"

The recording stopped. Tears rolled down his cheeks. He buried his face in his hands. He started to speak then broke down again. Foong Choon Hon and Mohamed Ghazali Ismail were seated next to Lee as his translators. "When he broke down, both Ghazali and I were totally at a loss as to what to do next. I could only look down at my notebook," said Foong, who was then RTS executive producer.

Chan Chee Seng was among those in the studio who saw Lee overcome with emotion before continuing with the press conference. He said: "I believe Lee felt responsible for the happiness and future of the millions of people who looked up to him as their leader. He brought about merger which gave them hope. To see it broken, he must have felt very sad. All of us there felt very sad."

When Ghazali Shafie heard the news on August 9, he was shocked. He was well-acquainted with PAP leaders from their Raffles College and Malayan Forum days. And as then-Malaysia's permanent secretary for foreign affairs, he often shuttled between Kuala Lumpur and Singapore acting as what he called an "honest broker" between both sides during thorny negotiations. "That afternoon I rushed down to Singapore and called on Lee at his office in the City Hall building overlooking the Padang. He looked terrible, with his eyes red and swelling. He had been at a press conference earlier to announce the separation.

"When he saw me, he broke down; so did I. We were both distraught at the prospect of having to live in two different countries, a prospect for which neither he nor I was prepared. Lee was at once angry and sad, and we spent about an hour consoling each other."

For the PAP leaders involved in expanding the party across the causeway and launching the MSC, breaking the bad news to the Malaysian branches was a heart-rending exercise. Recalling his meeting with party colleagues in Kuala Lumpur, Ong Pang Boon said: "I don't know if they felt abandoned but I felt like I was abandoning them."

To the prime movers behind MSC, the anguish was particularly acute as they had coaxed the leaders of the other political parties in the various states to join PAP in fighting for the ideal of a Malaysian Malaysia. Lee Khoon Choy noted that they were actually organising an MSC rally in Penang when separation occurred.

It was terrible. Toh did not mince his words when he said he had instigated Lim Chong Eu and other party leaders to join MSC and attend its inaugural meeting in Singapore. When the break came, he said, "they looked at it as a betrayal. They thought we had betrayed them and that we made use of them."

Reflecting on that fateful day more than four decades later, Lim Chong Eu, the then-chief of United Democratic Party who later became chief minister of Penang, said that his predominant reaction was one of shock. "We didn't feel abandoned but we felt upset, unsettled, uncertain..."

Chen Man Hin, who became chairman of Democratic Action Party after the change in name from PAP, remembered he felt sad but not abandoned. After all, this was politics, he said, and those who were left behind knew they would have to fight their own battles from then on without counting on PAP in Singapore.

Suddenly families were split asunder as members ended up as citizens of two different countries. To their distress, the Nairs found themselves not only separated by distance but also by citizenship. While Bungsar MP Nair remained a Malaysian, Moulmein legislative assemblywoman Mrs Nair became a Singaporean along with her children.

Lee felt responsible for Nair's predicament and wanted him to return to Singapore. But Nair refused saying that "it was a matter of honour. I had been elected there and I must go through my full term.

"Lee feared that my life was in danger and I would end up with a kris behind my back. He was distraught, did not sleep for quite a few nights, so much so that his doctors and his wife were very deeply concerned..."

"I remember Mrs Lee telling me about his condition, and I said I would see him and tell him he need not have me on his conscience. So I went to Oxley Road and over a meal I told him quite categorically that neither he nor anybody else in Singapore including my wife would be able to persuade me to leave the Malaysian parliament and return to Singapore."

Foong recounted several occasions when he saw Lee breaking down in a Changi chalet and using a white towel to wipe away his tears. "Once, when he was making a call to Kuala Lumpur, I overheard him instructing the person on the other line to ensure the safety of Devan Nair. After putting down the phone, he just broke down. From this incident, you could see how concerned he was about the safety of the comrades who fought with him."

⁂

LOOKING back, Toh said that in one fell stroke, PAP's vision of a united Malaya and Singapore vanished. To Rajaratnam, separation meant the crushing of his dreams. As PAP stood against the notion of an independent Singapore, he said: "We got to eat our own words, disprove our own thesis..."

To Nair, it meant the collapse of an ideal. "Because we had never seen, even in our wildest dreams, Singapore as an independent place. We were Malaya-centred."

Initially he refused to accept separation. "I personally carried on in Malaysia for the same ideal. But it took me, I think, three, four years at least just before the 1969 general election which I did not contest, to realise that this ideal was in shreds. Like Humpty Dumpty, the pieces could never be put back together."

The intoxicating dream of a united, democratic, socialist Malaya with Singapore conceived in the beer-swilling days of the Malayan Forum had ended in the weeping and gnashing of teeth.

The nightmarish challenge of getting an improbable strike-infested tiny island-state going with no natural resources, common market and hinterland had begun.

The curtain had fallen abruptly on the Malaysian Dream. The next act—the Singapore Story—was about to unfold.

19

Come On, Was There Really a Tiger?

IT was close to midnight. As Lee Siew Choh lay stricken with lung cancer in his Dunearn Close bungalow, he was still dictating from his handwritten manuscript.

Sitting by his bedside, his only daughter was typing furiously away on her personal computer. Elaine, a lawyer, was struggling against sleepiness to help her father complete his memoirs which he started writing soon after he was diagnosed with the disease in early 2000.

The founding chairman of Barisan Sosialis knew he was in a race against time to tell the story of his 32-year career in politics which changed the course of Singapore's history.

The medical practitioner wanted to rebut what he saw as flagrant untruths perpetuated by PAP. "If I don't write, the truth will never be told," he said in his last interview in 2001 when he gave our writer a peek into his memoirs which ran into 50 chapters.

Sadly, before he could find an editor and publisher, he died the following year at age 84. Elaine explained that publication was delayed not because it was politically contentious but because the draft required considerable editing. "The memoirs lack a head and a tail. Many chapters are short and need to be expanded with more backgrounding."

Recalling her dictation work, she said that she and her father would sometimes argue over how a description could be better written, or whether a sentence should be re-phrased to avoid sounding rude. "I told him it was not very nice to say things in a certain way but he insisted on it. When he found that I had corrected or deleted it later, he would change it back."

According to Elaine, the memoirs range from his boyhood days in Kuala Lumpur where he was born to his final exit from politics in 1991 after serving as a non-constituency MP for three years. It also covers her father's relationships with the political leaders of the day.

Siew Choh's is a story that many older Singaporeans have been waiting to read with bated breath. When Lee Kuan Yew learnt about his ailment, he sent his former foe a note saying that he admired his gutsiness in the face of cancer and that he was looking forward to reading his memoirs.

His revelations could shed light on the most befuddling questions in Singapore's political annals: Why did he order the withdrawal of Barisan MPs from parliament after separation, a move which resulted in the disappearance of a robust backbench opposition? Why did he stage the boycott of subsequent by-elections and the 1968 general election which led to parliament being handed over to PAP on a silver platter?

When parliament was convened on 9 December 1965 to table the Singapore Independence Bill and the Constitution Amendment Bill, the rows of red benches reserved for the 13 Barisan MPs were conspicuously empty. Two Barisan MPs were then under detention—Loh Miaw Gong (Havelock) and S T Bani (Thomson); and another two were on the run—Chan Sun Wing (Nee Soon) and Wong Soon Fong (Toa Payoh). The remaining nine stayed away.

Siew Choh had ordered a boycott declaring that parliamentary democracy was dead and accusing PAP of using the house to "rubber stamp" one fait accompli after another.

Some Barisan MPs, however, objected to his stand arguing that a boycott would mean breaking faith with the constituents who elected them. On 31 December 1965, Lim Huan Boon resigned from his Bukit Merah seat in protest followed by Chio Cheng Thun (Chua Chu Kang), Kow Kee Seng (Paya Lebar) and Bani.

Siew Choh was undeterred and announced on 7 October 1966 that the remaining seven Barisan MPs would resign from the august chamber to take "the struggle against imperialist oppression into the streets". Chia Thye Poh (Jurong) and Lee Tee Tong (Bukit Timah) quit on October 18; Koo Young (Thomson), Ong Lian Teng (Bukit Panjang), Poh Ber Liak (Tampines) and Tan Cheng Tong (Jalan Kayu) on October 28; and Loh Miaw Gong (Havelock) on November 1. The pull-out from parliament was complete.

A series of by-elections was held for the vacated seats. Thanks to the Barisan boycott, PAP was awarded walkovers or returned with landslide victories in seats contested by independent candidates. By 7 March 1967 when the last by-election was completed, PAP had bagged 49 out of 51 seats with the two seats held by the missing Barisan MPs hanging in limbo.

Then came the 1968 general election which PAP called to seek a new mandate from the people to tackle the unemployment problems arising from the proposed withdrawal of British troops from the island. On nomination day, 51 out of 58 PAP candidates were returned unopposed. On polling day, PAP prevailed in the remaining seven seats contested by two Workers' Party (WP) candidates and five independents to score an incredible 58 out of 58. Singapore had entered the era of total one-party rule.

By the time Barisan realised the futility of its extra-parliamentary struggle and re-entered the electoral arena, the tide had turned inexorably against it. It could not win a single seat in the 1972, 1976, 1980 and 1984 general elections and finally sank into oblivion when it merged with WP in 1988. Siew Choh, however, made a re-appearance in the house as the first non-constituency MP when his WP team in Eunos became the best loser in the 1988 polls.

Barisan's boycott of parliament and the polls had been described by Rajaratnam as the biggest turning point in Singapore's political history as it led to the establishment of a one-party parliament. Calling it "a stroke of destiny", Lee said that the absence of opposition allowed the ruling party to focus on economic and social development unhindered and undistracted by politicking. "Had they stayed on, they would have adjusted to the constitutional situation and become a real left-wing party which would then make us right-wing," he noted.

In press interviews in later years, Siew Choh expressed regret about boycotting the 1968 elections. With the benefit of hindsight, he agreed that if not for the boycott, PAP might not have been so dominant in parliament today and Barisan might still be the main opposition party. Elaine said that her father admitted that he did not think about the long-term effects of the boycott.

Born in Kuala Lumpur in 1917, the son of a Chinese school teacher and housewife graduated from King Edward VII College of Medicine and worked at Kandang Kerbau Hospital—now known as KK Women's and Children's Hospital—before setting up his own medical practice, International Dispensary. At the hospital he met his wife-to-be Kathleen Fam Yin Oi, a volunteer nurse and school teacher. Besides Elaine, they had three sons.

It was on campus that he met Goh Keng Swee during a chess tournament and became firm friends. He came to know Lee through the Chinese printing workers' union where they acted as medical and legal adviser respectively. Both Goh and Lee persuaded him to join PAP. In the

1959 general election, Siew Choh won the Queenstown seat and a year later was appointed parliamentary secretary for home affairs.

The doctor's government stint was, however, short-lived when he clashed with his party bosses in 1961 over the question of merger and led 12 other dissident PAP assemblymen to form Barisan Sosialis. He spearheaded the Barisan charge in the 1963 elections winning 13 of the 51 seats but lost by a mere 89 votes to then-PAP party chairman Toh Chin Chye in Rochor.

In character and temperament, he could not have been more different from the man who would otherwise have led the party if he had not been put into cold storage. While Lim Chin Siong was soft-spoken and patient, Siew Choh was garrulous and impetuous. Witness his record-breaking speech in the chamber when he spoke for nearly seven-and-a-half hours during the merger debate on November 20 and 21 in 1961.

Goh noted that Siew Choh was a decent and honest man and felt sorry for getting him involved in politics. Describing his former chess partner as a very aggressive player who took big risks, he said that the way to beat him was to play a safe game, build up a strong position, let him make his adventurous moves and then just break up his attacks.

In Ong Pang Boon's view, Siew Choh was an individualist, not a schemer, and one who would express his unhappiness readily and say anything that came to mind, including ideas passed to him, without realising they were communist-inspired. Perhaps British journalist Dennis Bloodworth summed it up best when he said Siew Choh was a good man but a bad politician.

Given the parlous and bizarre state of the opposition under Siew Choh and the fact that he was never arrested, many a wagging tongue had suggested that he was a PAP plant. Rumours circulated about him being on PAP's payroll. It did not help that S Rajaratnam called him "God's gift to PAP". Fong Swee Suan commented that PAP should be happy with Siew Choh as his policies cut Barisan off from the electorate.

In the interview with our writer before his death, the doctor confessed that he was troubled by these allegations for decades. Whenever he attended a university seminar, he said, someone would inevitably ask him: "Doctor, all your colleagues were arrested. Why were you spared?"

His response would be that he was not a communist and that with the arrest of his able colleagues, he would therefore not pose a threat anymore. "PAP wanted to use me as a facade for democracy. It could always turn round and say, look, the leader of the opposition is free and can do what he wants."

Former Barisan colleague and fellow doctor, Sheng Nam Chin, dismissed all the insinuations and innuendoes about Siew Choh saying that he had been unfairly treated. "They said he was working for the PAP. That's a joke to me. Siew Choh would not stoop that low."

. What did the communist underground say about him? With undisguised affection, former Malayan Communist Party (MCP) cadre Chan Sun Wing described Siew Choh as a frank and straightforward person saying, "I don't think he had any ulterior motive. He was politically very naive."

⁕

BENEATH all his ranting and raving about the "death of democracy", "phoney independence" and "Lee's fascist dictatorship", what really drove Siew Choh to initiate the boycott of parliament that changed Singapore's political equation irrevocably? Was he acting unilaterally? Or was he acting on someone's order?

Although he regretted the boycott of the 1968 elections, he maintained until his dying breath that the 1965 parliamentary walkout of Barisan MPs was the right move as it drew people's attention to the "undemocratic practices" of the PAP government.

As he told our writer, after the September 1962 referendum, Barisan kept on pressing the government for an open meeting on merger. "We wanted to know exactly what had happened. But we were always ignored. For quite a number of months, there was hardly any meeting in parliament. And while we were waiting, Singapore's independence was declared!"

Instead of holding any sitting, he charged, "there were only arrests, arrests and arrests of our people. So we wanted to expose PAP's non-democratic practices by walking out". He was referring to Operation Cold Store in February 1963 which put 113 leftist politicians and trade unionists behind bars.

The PAP government's rationale was that the massive security operation was necessary to prevent anti-Malaysia elements from establishing a "Communist Cuba" in Singapore.

Several former Barisan activists came to Siew Choh's defence maintaining that he should not be held wholly responsible for the pull-out as the decision was not just his but the party's.

Leong Keng Seng said that the MPs had no choice but to walk out because there was no parliamentary democracy. "By doing so, the party hoped that it could force the PAP government to hold a fresh general election. But that was not to be. Barisan miscalculated."

Ong Chang Sam pointed out that most Barisan central executive committee (CEC) members and Barisan branches supported the move to quit parliament. He agreed with Siew Choh then that Singapore's independence was questionable because of the way the island was separated from Malaysia.

Sheng Nam Chin advanced the view that Siew Choh adopted the extreme line "out of sheer frustration" as he figured that all was lost in the parliamentary arena. "There was no more fight. You could not win. Why fight when the odds were against you? Therefore, if there was any other chance, any chance of fighting, it was extra-parliamentary."

If you take the word of former communist cadres, Siew Choh was definitely not taking instructions from MCP. This was because the underground was in disarray, they said, after its guerilla war in Malaya went badly and successive waves of mass arrests decimated its ranks and sent its leading cadres on the run.

According to former MCP member Chan Sun Wing, the Barisan chairman took the battle from parliament to the street because he was influenced by John Eber after attending the Afro-Asian Latin America conference in Havana, Cuba on January 3, 1966.

Hailed as the most powerful gathering of pro-communist, anti-American forces in the history of the Western hemisphere, it proclaimed the right of people to oppose imperialist violence with revolutionary violence. This included coordinating subversion and guerilla activity on a worldwide basis.

Eber, a member of the Anti-British League (ABL), a subsidiary of MCP, was the Cambridge-educated Singapore Eurasian lawyer based in London who led a pro-communist faction to take over the Malayan Forum in the early 1950s and was later ousted by Goh and friends.

Chan remembered that Siew Choh professed great admiration for John Eber and Cuban leader Fidel Castro. "I observed that after his return, he became more aggressive and his opposition to the authorities grew even stronger."

Another former Barisan assemblyman and MCP cadre noticed that Siew Choh became a changed man after his trip and related a heated argument between them. The party chairman had ordered him to revamp Barisan branches on the instructions of an international communist party. He refused insisting that they should only take orders from MCP. Siew Choh then replied: "Have you heard of John Eber?"

When Lee Khoon Choy met Fang Chuang Pi, better known as "the Plen", in Hatyai in 1996, he raised the issue of the Barisan boycott. The communist chief's response, he recalled, was that Barisan walked out of parliament without consulting MCP and that "Siew Choh didn't listen to us. He was listening to John Eber after the meeting in Cuba."

Rajaratnam also took the view that Siew Choh was inspired by the Havana conference which called for a world revolutionary struggle. It might have worked in Africa and Latin America, he said, but Siew Choh applied this principle in Singapore without modifying it and came up with "struggle in the streets". The trouble with Siew Choh, he said, was that he took ideas literally.

But if Siew Choh was taking his line from Eber, could Eber be taking his line from Beijing? In August 1966, the Cultural Revolution was launched by Chinese Communist Party chairman Mao Zedong to arouse the masses against their leaders. Militant youths called Red Guards took to the streets attacking government institutions and officials.

Ong Hock Siang, who lost to Lee in Tanjong Pagar in the 1963 polls, was convinced that Siew Choh's boycott decision was influenced by the revolutionary upheaval in China. "The wave was coming too strongly and he was just being swept along," he said. Fong Swee Suan noted that Siew Choh's extreme line coincided with Mao-inspired attacks in China against government leaders regarded as revisionist social democrats.

Former Partai Rakyat chairman and Operation Cold Store detainee Said Zahari saw it in the same light—that Siew Choh sought to launch a similar cultural revolution in Singapore by instigating Barisan members to go into the streets to fight.

The extra-parliamentary struggle was manifested in illegal strikes, sit-down protests and street demonstrations, vandalism of public property, clashes with police and recitation of Mao's quotations.

Said recalled that when many arrested cadres joined him in prison, they even tried to launch an ideological struggle among the inmates. "I could see how extreme they were, their politics was very infantile, very naive. That was the kind of politics that Siew Choh tried to inculcate among the cadres of the Barisan in line with the Cultural Revolution."

KOW Kee Seng was sorely missed by PAP backbenchers when he absented himself from parliament. The Barisan MP for Paya Lebar brought guffaws to the sombre proceedings with his entertaining speeches. Fong Sip Chee said that Kow reminded him of a Hollywood silent film comedian.

Born in 1932, educated in Nan Zhong Primary and Chung Cheng High, Kow joined the ABL and became a member of MCP. At one time or another, he was president of Singapore Rural Dwellers' Association and secretary of Singapore Bus Workers' Union.

Together with fellow MPs Lim Huan Boon and Chio Cheng Thun, they crossed swords with their mercurial party chairman over the boycott and resigned from parliament in protest at the end of 1965. They felt that having been elected by the people and being paid an allowance by them, they should serve the people even though they were "suppressed" by the PAP government.

According to those who took issue with Siew Choh, the doctor had cited three reasons for the boycott—there were too few parliamentary sessions, Barisan's loss in the 1963 elections was because of vote tampering, and it was meaningless to have a parliament where PAP MPs were voted in by people out of fear.

Their counter-argument was that if the people had the guts to fight it out in the streets and clash with the police and had no fear of being detained, why should they be afraid of casting their votes for Barisan?

One former Barisan assemblyman said that their relationship turned sour when Siew Choh accused him of siding with PAP. At almost every Barisan meeting, he noted, disagreement would break out. "It seemed like a short circuit, where wires were not connected properly ... As the number of disputes escalated, the stability of the party was at risk." Several Barisan branches attempted to oust Siew Choh from the leadership, he disclosed, but the bid failed as the CEC had full confidence in him.

"In the end, the CEC gave way to him simply because he was a doctor and was English-educated. At that point, I was totally upset. I felt that it would be pointless for me to carry on receiving my allowance if we continued to boycott parliament," he said.

Putting it all down to bad leadership, another former dissident Lim Huan Boon said that he quit because he could never see eye-to-eye with Siew Choh who often derided him as a capitalist because his father happened to be a wealthy building contractor.

Yet another party stalwart who disagreed with Siew Choh's notion of fighting in the streets was Low Por Tuck. He felt that it did not fit in with the Singapore situation and that it endangered democratic principles. "Since I cannot convince them or persuade them to fight in parliament, then it's no point for me to remain in the party. Since it was against my will, I just called it a day."

While former leftists blamed the PAP government for causing most of their problems, they did not exonerate Barisan from making its share of blunders. They pointed the finger at Siew Choh for not playing his cards better and adopting the appropriate strategies and tactics to counter the PAP challenge. Without the guidance of the leaders in detention, they said, he was ill-advised and prone to erratic, unilateral acts.

For example, his bravado in despatching his best candidates to meet the PAP bigwigs in their seats backfired on him and the party in the 1963 polls. He abandoned his Queenstown ward for Rochor under the delusion that he could topple Toh Chin Chye. Fong Swee Suan thought that Barisan might have won the elections narrowly if Siew Choh had pursued more pragmatic policies which appealed to the middle class and the workers.

The sudden independence of Singapore also compelled many leftists to rethink their position. Although they felt vindicated by their opposition to merger, they were confounded by Siew Choh's continuing attack against independence. Ong Chang Sam said that even when Singapore became a member of United Nations on 21 September 1965, Siew Choh was still claiming that its independence was phoney.

Lim Huan Boon made it clear that he stood for elections in 1963 because he opposed merger. So when Singapore broke away from Malaysia and became independent on 9 August 1965, he saw no necessity to remain as an opposition MP.

Indeed Barisan's contradictory if not convoluted positions on merger perplexed many of its members. They felt that if the party opposed merger, then it should fight for independence but instead it sought "total internal self-government" which ironically meant continued reliance on the British in security and financial matters.

The bickering in Barisan also spilled over into the left-wing labour movement and came to a head during one May Day celebration. Siew Choh had quarrelled bitterly with Tan Sin, the militant president of the Singapore Commercial Houses and Factory Employees' Union (SCHFEU) which succeeded the banned Singapore General Employees' Union (SGEU) as the latest Middle Road incarnation. Siew Choh held a rally with six trade unions while Tan Sin and some 23 trade unions broke away to stage another.

Stories about the widening split were leaked to the press. In the *Sunday Mail* of 16 April 1967, political journalist Jackie Sam wrote about how Tan Sin, described as one of the last of the brilliant minds in the unions, was ousted and the job entrusted to Ong Chang Sam.

The same report recorded the fate of those who challenged Siew Choh and fell into limbo—Poh Ber Liak, Kow Kee Seng and Chio Cheng Thun. It said that even Chia Thye Poh, a Nanyang graduate, had become a mere ordinary member because he had the temerity to speak out against Siew Choh. Chia held the record for serving the longest political detention in Singapore, from 1966 until 1998 when all restrictions were lifted.

If the strength of Barisan was sapped by the detention of its leading lights, it was not helped by the release of its detainees who gave public statements—whether voluntary or coerced—detrimental to the cause of the party. A number of leftists held Siew Choh responsible for bad leadership and decided to renounce politics and make public confessions.

Former MCP member Tan Chong Kin was PAP chairman for 10 days in August 1957 before he was arrested. The ranking official of the Singapore Association of Trade Unions (SATU) was arrested again on 8 October 1963. On his release in December 1965, he castigated his Barisan comrades for refusing to admit that Singapore was an independent and sovereign state.

In January 1966, the public was presented with the novel spectacle of S T Bani appearing on television to denounce his party. He had just resigned from Barisan and criticised it for not wanting Malaysia and not wanting an independent Singapore either. He argued that political, economic and social problems could be resolved without a communist-led revolution.

In 1969, Barisan was dealt a shattering blow when its foremost and most charismatic leader Lim Chin Siong recanted. He condemned the party's extra-parliamentary struggle and declared the independence of Singapore genuine. The resignation of the man whom Lee once introduced as the future prime minister of Singapore spelled the beginning of the end for the party.

IN seven years, PAP had swung from the brink of collapse to an absolute monopoly of seats in parliament. Barisan's "street parliament" had turned into a theatre of the absurd and the Middle Road labour movement was reduced to a pale shadow of what it used to be. MCP influence was on the wane as its key cadres disappeared into the Riau islands.

Intertwined with the PAP saga is the story of the rise and fall of the left. Led by impassioned ideologues, the movement partnered the party on its ascent to power riding on the wave of mass support from the predominantly Chinese-speaking population. Yet it could not save itself from political extinction.

In their moments of introspection, many former leftists lamented that they put their lives on the line to help PAP drive out the colonialists but failed to receive their due recognition, let alone enjoy the fruits of their contributions and sacrifices.

As MCP leader Fang Chuang Pi bemoaned in a press report: "It was an 'open united front' in which the leftists were in prison and the rightists were made government officials. It was an 'open united front' in which the Mandarin-speaking did all the work while the English-speaking wielded the power."

Why did the leftists fail so ignominiously? One oft-cited factor was that they broke up with PAP too prematurely. They said that they should have avoided The Big Split of 1961 and instead waited for a more opportune time to challenge the party leaders.

A former MCP cadre disclosed that the underground was not in favour of the leftists leaving PAP so soon. Interestingly, he said that MCP was not happy with Barisan's action during the 1962 referendum. MCP favoured Alternative "B" which represented full and unconditional merger with Malaya while Barisan rejected all three options and called on people to cast blank votes in protest.

As he explained, MCP was planning on a long-term basis and believed that if Singapore joined Malaysia on equal terms, it would be able to spread its influence through political parties, trade unions and other mass organisations in the peninsula. But Lim Chin Siong and other leaders in the frontline opposed the Malaysia plan stridently because they knew that once Singapore merged with Malaya, the central government would crack down on them.

Fang Mingwu, a former MCP activist living in exile in southern Thailand, also felt that Chan Sun Wing and Wong Soon Fong should have stayed put in PAP. As parliamentary secretary in the prime minister's office, Chan was close to the bosom of power while Wong exercised much influence in the Works Brigade.

As he dwelt on those turbulent days, he pinpointed another weakness of the left—it relied too much on its own kind, the Chinese-educated. He said: "MCP should have co-opted more diverse groups. Lee was smarter. He got the postal workers, the Malays and English-educated."

In later years, Fang Chuang Pi admitted that he had overlooked the fact that the Chinese in Singapore consisted of two groups—the Mandarin-speaking and the English-speaking. He was only aware of the Mandarin-speaking group and knew nothing about the latter. This divide was the reason why the left-wing movement could not go far in Singapore, he said.

Furthermore, the left was no monolithic entity. Just as the early PAP was wracked by personality clashes and factionalism, so too was Barisan. And just as PAP grassroots cadres resented the parachuting of the tertiary-educated types into top party posts, their Barisan counterparts felt the same way when they found themselves sidelined by Nantah graduates.

The two barber assemblymen, Tee Kim Leng and Lin You Eng, were dropped from the Barisan 1963 election slate. Tee said that he and Lin, among others, were asked not to stand following "a lot of bargaining" between Siew Choh and the underground which threatened to withdraw its support if its recommended candidates were not fielded.

There was also simmering tension between the Chinese leftists and non-Chinese leftists. The latter felt that they were not wholly trusted by the former and grew increasingly disillusioned with those who took the chauvinistic line and sought to impose an austere way of life on them.

The English-educated middle class types were considered the weakest in the link, said former Barisan and SATU leader Dominic Puthucheary, a Malayalee who worked as a teacher and civil servant before going into politics. "They saw us as weak, opportunistic, bourgeoisie, and they called us names. We were all drinkers, softies. If you smoke, it's wrong. If you drink, it's wrong. If you go to a woman, it's wrong. You can't do anything right. I mean there's nothing human. The only thing that's human, that's normal is considered weak."

A stark illustration of this schism was captured in Said Zahari's narration of the travails of Partai Rakyat in his memoirs *Dark Clouds at Dawn*. The writer, who was the party chief before he was detained under Operation Cold Store, depicted it as a betrayal of the Malay left by the Chinese left.

Set up in 1955, the small Malay-dominated left-wing party fielded four candidates in the 1959 elections on the understanding that it would be supported by MCP which was then throwing its whole weight behind PAP's bid for power. But at the eleventh hour, support was withdrawn and all four lost dismally. Said suspected that Lee and Fang Chuang Pi made a secret deal to abandon Partai Rakyat.

According to Fang Mingwu, MCP withdrew its support for the four Partai Rakyat candidates because it feared that PAP might not win the elections. It wanted to pour all its resources into supporting PAP to ensure its victory. "If PAP could not form the government, our plans would fail and our comrades in prison would not be released," he said.

Pinning the blame for the fiasco on Fang Chuang Pi, Said said that the communist leader "seemed to have lost his bearings, a result of his failure to read Lee's politics, personality and character". He charged that every political step taken by the Plen was crushed by the combined strength of Lee, Tunku and the British.

In his reply to Said published in a Chinese Malaysian newspaper on 19 March 2001, Fang explained that the decision was made to "stabilise the situation then so as to strengthen the position of PAP in negotiating with the British". But he admitted that "it was a mistake as a result of our wrong decision to give full support to PAP".

Yet another factor handicapping the leftists, as they acknowledged readily, was their youth and lack of education, knowledge and awareness of the larger forces at work in the region—be it the Soviet-China split, the Cold War or the incompatibility between communism and Islam.

In contrast with the British-educated PAP leaders who included two doctorate-holders, they had barely finished their school education when they plunged into politics. Many dropped out or were expelled. Lim Chin Siong and Fong Swee Suan were in their 20s when they assumed leadership positions. Chin Peng was only 23 when he became secretary-general of MCP.

Fang Mingwu noted that many leftists did not even have a good grounding in Marxism-Leninism. "We were so young then. We did not read enough. Few knew what communism was all about. We had only a simplistic view of communism," he said.

Even if they wanted to, there was not enough literature for them to read, pointed out Dominic Puthucheary who said that as a twenty-something trade unionist, he was too young to grasp the complexities of communism.

The leftists' analyses stemmed simply from a "romanticisation of China". "We saw everything in this light, even the tinned food from China was better than the tinned food from the West. Tsingtao beer was better than the beer from anywhere else."

In Lee Khoon Choy's analysis, the fall of the left in Singapore could be attributed to the collapse of communism in Indonesia. Barisan wanted to capture power with outside help from Jakarta where the Malayan National Liberation League, an MCP-linked underground organisation which opposed the formation of Malaysia, was based.

But when the Partai Komunis Indonesia (PKI) or the Indonesian Communist Party was liquidated following an abortive coup in 1965 which led to the rise of President Suharto, the Barisan leaders lost all hopes of victory.

In his reflections, Lee said "he was struck by the impetuosity and impatience of young communist activists who acted as if a successful revolution was going to happen in Malaya and Singapore the day after tomorrow". He noted that their slogans and actions were totally imitative of what the Chinese Communist Party was doing in China.

"They couldn't understand that this was Malaya, this was Singapore, and this was not China," he said, "so they were muddled in their thoughts. Their backdrop was wrong. Their data on which they based their decision was irrelevant."

If anybody could recognise the geo-political significance of Singapore, James Puthucheary told Dennis Bloodworth, that person was Harry. Nobody in the left understood the importance of Singapore's standing at the crossroads of world traffic, he said.

To be sure, the left was mortally wounded by the sweep of drastic government action: wave after wave of detentions, de-registration of left-wing unions and freezing of funds, ban of pro-Barisan organisations and left-wing publications and other restrictive measures.

Grossly unfair? The PAP rejoinder, in the words of S Rajaratnam, had always been that politics in Singapore could not be played by Queensbury rules. It was winner-take-all. The other side would have done exactly the same thing if it formed the government, and if the communists won, it would be a permanent win with no more elections.

ON the cover of a comic book titled *To Tame A Tiger: The Singapore Story* by Joe Yeoh, Lee is depicted riding the wild beast with David Marshall caught in the clasp of its claws as Lim Yew Hock gives a petrified look.

Some people have compared the then-PM to Wu Song, a legendary figure from the great Chinese classic, *Water Margin: The Outlaws of the Marsh* (*shui hu zhuan*), who throttled a tiger with his bare hands.

Wu song da hu ("Wu Song kills the tiger") is lifted from a treasure trove of stories about the 108 heroes who helped the poor fight against evil officials at the end of the Northern Song period in the 12th century.

This riding-the-tiger imagery has now passed into Singapore's political literature. It encapsulates the PAP story of how a group of courageous if not foolhardy leaders rode the communist tiger without being swallowed up by it.

Conjured up by past and present PAP leaders, journalists and academics over the decades, the metaphor has become conventional wisdom, an unchallenged thesis. In Mandarin, Ong Pang Boon called it *qi lao hu* or "riding the tiger".

As Lee Khoon Choy summed it up, Lee rose to power by riding on the back of the communists—the tiger—and defeating it. Any other weaker leader would have been eaten up by the communists, he said.

Former MCP cadre Gerald de Cruz drew a parallel with the experience in other countries where non-communists worked with the communists in a united front. Eventually the communists would come out on top because they were much more organised, disciplined and ruthless.

He recalled warning Lee that if he played around with the communists, he would be distrusted by people. "He said: 'Oh, it will be all right, Gerry. One day I'll put all my cards on the table and then they will understand the game I've been playing.'

"And I said: 'But if they distrust you by then, it doesn't matter what cards you put on the table, they still won't believe you. So don't carry this on too long.' I couldn't really judge how this policy would emerge. But of course I was wrong. Because Lee Kuan Yew was one of the very, very few in history who have turned the tables on the communists."

Well, try invoking the same metaphor in a conversation with former leftists and you would be slapped by sharp, mocking responses such as: What tiger? Come off it, did the PAP really ride on the tiger? Well, if there was a tiger, what kind of animal was it?

With typical philosophical equanimity, Dominic Puthucheary asked rhetorically: "Was there really a tiger? Did the tiger want to swallow anybody? Or was there a movement with a wide range of political views from extreme left to social democratic right which attempted to create an alternative to a colonially-designed society, an embryo for creating a new Malaya?"

S Woodhull dismissed the tiger metaphor as nonsense, saying that it was just an overworked cliche which simplified a much more involved situation. "Where was the tiger? Who was there to give the ferocity?" he sniffed.

Said Zahari also gave short shrift to the catchphrase contending that Lee chose to fight the left very early on. "Lee knew how to fight against the left by gaining the support of the stronger force. He had already been assured by the British and Tunku that they were with him but he must make sure that these people were finished. So there was no question of riding the tiger."

If there was a tiger, Samad Ismail chortled, it was a tame one with no claws. Sheng Nam Chin remarked wryly: "Maybe the tiger was a little domesticated, not really a communist tiger. If the tiger was made up of truly dedicated communists like Zhou Enlai and Lin Piao, few would have survived riding it."

Assuming there was a tiger, some former communists said, it would have been very much weakened by MCP's defeat in the guerilla war, its organisational shambles and the detentions of its top cadres. As one put it, how fierce could the tiger be when so many guns were pointed at its head?

Fong Swee Suan turned the metaphor on its head: "PAP riding the tiger? I would say that it was just the other way round. We were riding on the real tiger—the Internal Security Council, the army, police, Tunku, Lee, the Malayans and the British. They were the real tiger who colluded against the leftists."

⁂

SOONER or later the question had to be put to Fong Swee Suan: "Mr Fong, were you ever a communist?" His reply: "I had answered this question many times in prison in response to the Special Branch. Would I answer you differently now?"

Detained thrice for suspected communist activities, the PAP founder-convenor and former leading trade unionist said that he had always insisted on irrefutable proof from the authorities that he was a communist but had yet to see any.

Put the same question to Samad Ismail and he replied with that evasive, elfish look: "I don't think so. I was just ABL." ABL refers to the Anti-British League, an auxiliary organisation of MCP. But his old friend, Devan Nair, had declared that Samad was already a full MCP member by 1949.

Many former PAP members-turned-leftists interviewed in Singapore, Malaysia, Hong Kong and Southern China denied they were ever communists but admitted readily they were inspired by the Chinese Revolution and were sympathetic to the communist cause at that time.

Just about the only people who confessed openly to being communists were those living in the Peace Villages in southern Thailand such as Chan Sun Wing and Fang Mingwu.

So what made a communist? How would you define a communist? According to the Collins Cobuild dictionary, a communist is someone who believes in communism which is the political belief that all people are equal and that workers should control the means of producing things.

Ong Hock Siang, the Barisan candidate who lost to Lee in the 1963 general election and was once arrested for pro-communist activities asked: "If you supported the Chinese Communist Party's victory in China in 1949, did it make you a communist? And if you didn't, did it make you an anti-communist?"

Ong Pang Boon, who dealt with many leftists as minister for home affairs and PAP organising secretary, defined a communist as one who swore allegiance to MCP and was a card-carrying member of the party or its communist organisations.

Woodhull described a communist as a person who was either a member of a communist party or was acting under the instructions of the party. Sheng Nam Chin said that a communist was one who would give up his life for his belief in a revolution to establish the dictatorship of the proletariat.

The difficulty in pinning down a definition, according to eminent China scholar Wang Gungwu, was that communism developed from Marxism and that the degree of support for Marxist principles varied from person to person. Even capitalists subscribed to some Marxist ideals. In his view, Marxist ideas were modified by Lenin, Stalin and others into a set of doctrines for a communist party and if you joined it, you became a communist. "At least that's the definition that I feel confident with. Any other use of the word 'communist', I say, 'how would you know?' As long as they are not members of a communist party, they are quite justified in disclaiming being communists."

Devan Nair, who admitted that he was a communist, once gave a rundown of his former leftist associates: James Puthucheary was not a communist. Neither was Woodhull even though he was regarded as a Marxist intellectual. Dominic Puthucheary and S T Bani were pro-communist sympathisers, not communists. Chia Ek Tian was almost certainly an MCP member. Soon Loh Boon and Chan Chiaw Thor might have been communists.

Puthucheary recalled a conversation he once had with Lee who said: "Dom, you and James could never be communist because both of you are romantics." As the former radical unionist elaborated: "That's true. We could never be. We would have been shot long ago. At the very most you can say that we were romantics who had read something about communism and its ability to wipe out poverty and racial discrimination in one revolution. We were quite naive. Yes, you can say all that. But you can't say that we're communist in the sense that we were members of MCP or that we worked with MCP."

Back to the decades-old question in Singapore history that refuses to go away: Was Lim Chin Siong a communist?

He had denied being a communist until his death. His close associates were adamant that he was not a communist. Even some of his critics agreed, noting that a communist would not have abandoned politics the way Lim did.

Lim Chin Joo said he believed his brother: "Different people would like him to be remembered as a communist. By doing so, his detractors could justify his removal from the political scene and MCP could claim credit for his contributions to the cause of national independence and freedom."

Chan Sun Wing said that Lim was close to being an MCP member but lost contact with his "superior" in his cell who "disappeared" suddenly. To be a communist, according to Chan, one was required to take part in a special initiation ceremony. He recalled that he had to take a pledge before the portraits of Mao, Lenin, Karl Marx and Engels in a solemn ceremony in the late 1960s before he became a member.

Likewise, Lee noted that Lim was a communist cell member who was on the way to becoming an MCP member. "Technically, he was not a communist, but he was taking orders from the party. He was not acting independently."

Going by a strict legal definition, Lee said, a communist would be a member of a communist party. But he adopted the popular usage of the term "communist" to include anybody who took orders from either the communist party or its affiliates.

According to information from the Internal Security Department (ISD), Lim admitted in 1984 that he met the communist leader, Fang Chuang Pi, also known as Fong Chong Pik, three times between the late 1950s and 1961. Fang was dubbed "the Plen", short for plenipotentiary, by Lee.

Lim was vague on specific dates and locations of the meetings. He told ISD officers that one of the meetings took place when PAP split in 1961. In a corroborative report, ISD noted that Lim held a secret meeting with Fang in a secluded *attap* hut at 7½ milestone, Upper Thomson Road, on 16 July 1961, five days before the make-or-break vote of confidence in the legislative assembly.

ISD had information that Lim exerted all his efforts to win over the pro-communist and wavering elements in PAP in a bid to topple the government. The vote, which could have changed the course of Singapore forever if it had gone the other way, saw the PAP government clinging on to power by 27 ayes against 8 nays and 16 abstentions including 13 by dissenting PAP assemblymen.

Another Lim-Fang rendezvous was revealed by Fang's girlfriend in a statement to ISD in 1964. She said that one night, she drove Fang along Dunearn Road, picked up Lim before going to Kallang Park where both men had a discussion. She did not provide the date of the meeting but ISD assessed that it was sometime between late 1959 and early 1960.

Ong Pang Boon conceded that Lim might not be a card-carrying member of MCP "but by his actions and speeches in the 1950s, he sounded like a communist and he supported communist objectives".

EPILOGUE
Coming Full Circle

IF you visited the bustling southern Thai city of Hatyai in the 1990s and early 2000s, you might have rubbed shoulders with two elderly men who were once the target of an intense police manhunt in Singapore.

Chan Sun Wing and Wong Soon Fong made the headlines in October 1963 as the two Barisan Sosialis assemblymen who went missing after staging an illegal workers' strike. Elected in the polls just a month earlier, the former journalist and electrician never took their oath of office in the chamber.

Instead they vanished into the shadows of the Indonesian Riau islands, hid in Indonesia as members of the communist underground before surfacing as Red guerillas along the Thai-Malaysian border in the 1970s to fight for the founding of a people's republic on the peninsula.

But it was a lost cause. In 1989, together with more than a thousand guerillas, they gave up their bloody insurrection when the Hatyai Peace Agreement was signed between the Malayan Communist Party (MCP) and the Thai and Malaysian governments.

Chan and Wong, who began their political career as PAP legislative assemblymen in 1959, were among the 30-odd guerillas from Singapore who laid down their arms and returned to civilian life. Given a piece of land by the Thai government and a small monthly pension by MCP, they settled down in Bang Lang, one of four designated Peace Villages. The other villages were Betong, Sukirin and Yaha.

Each village comprised about 100 households living in single-storey concrete houses equipped with satellite dishes to receive television programmes from around the world. Amenities included a community hall, provision store, coffee shop and kindergarten.

When we met Chan in Hatyai in 2003, the 70-year-old former parliamentary secretary in the prime minister's office was a part-time personal assistant to the boss of a shipping company. His job: to read and translate e-mail and correspondence from English to Thai and Chinese.

Wong, then 69, was the assistant managing director of a tourist company called GBL, a cooperative formed by residents of Bang Lang. If the former Works Brigade supremo was not held up by administrative work, he would be ferrying visitors in a mini-bus on the two-hour drive between Hatyai and the peace village.

Singapore tourists shopping and dining in Hatyai and Yala, another nearby southern city, might have patronised retail outlets and restaurants without realising they were run by former comrades-in-arms of Chan and Wong.

An example of a guerilla-turned-entrepreneur was Tee Ai Hua who ran a small travel agency, a shop selling leather handbags and fashionable wear and a traditional Thai massage service centre on Sanehanusorn Road, a popular shopping street in downtown Hatyai.

Remember the pig-tailed girls of the 1960s who fled Singapore? Among them was Guo Renluan, a Nan Chiau Girls' School student who joined the communist underground then. In 2003, she was living in Yala with her husband and daughter and working as a Chinese-language tutor.

After they escaped to Indonesia, their five-year-old daughter was sent to school in China with other children of MCP members. Guo only saw her seven years later, when she was 12, in Hainan island. "When we met again, my daughter couldn't recognise me as her mother and called me 'auntie' instead," she said.

Then there was Shi Mei Chiao, a factory worker in rural Singapore who became involved in trade union and political activities. She spoke about how she became a fervent supporter of Lim Chin Siong and Lee Kuan Yew in the early days of the PAP.

Married to former MCP cadre Wei Kang Chun, they had to go on the run when their underground cover was blown in 1962. Together with about 100 other young students and workers, they left in the still of the night by boat and in batches, first to the Riau islands and then to other parts of Indonesia.

They spent more than 16 years in Indonesia, moving from one city to another disguised as hawkers, shopkeepers and tradesmen while carrying out communist activities. They had a daughter and three sons who were also sent to China by MCP to relieve the parents of the burden of raising their children while on active duty.

With the liquidation of Partai Komunis Indonesia (PKI) in 1965, Indonesia was no longer a safe haven for MCP members and they started leaving for Hong Kong, Macau and China. In 1980 the couple moved to the Thai-Malaysian border where Wei joined the propaganda unit responsible for publication and broadcasting while his wife dealt with the logistics of transporting food and other material to the insurgents.

As they looked back over the decades from their rustic Bang Lang home, did they ever harbour any regrets about how their lives had turned out? A pensive Wei admitted that when they were young, they did not realise the enormity of the sacrifices they had to make for their beliefs.

"We were just being swept along by the wave," he said, "but we were prepared to give up our lives for our cause as there was no turning back." Recounting how he escaped death several times, he said: "Once in the jungle, I faced an enemy who pointed a rifle at me but he ran out of bullets."

In stoic resignation, his wife acknowledged that life had been very tough on them but said that "what we experienced over the years had enriched our lives".

Indeed the poignant yearning for home was most palpable in the peace village community. Chan and company confessed that they missed their families and friends in Singapore. Although they had heard and read so much about the island's phenomenal growth, they had yet to see it for themselves.

They said they could not understand why they were still banned from returning home when they were already in their twilight years and posed no political threat to the PAP government. Former left-wing unionist Liu Bo asked why he could not even visit his homeland as a tourist.

It was scant consolation that they could only view the skyline and shoreline of Singapore from across the causeway in Johor Bahru. That's where they put up whenever they wanted to meet their relatives and friends. Chan often shuttled south to JB to keep in touch with his siblings and their families. When Wong's daughter married in 1998, she hosted her dinner in the southern state capital so that her father could attend the occasion.

One reason cited for the continuing ban was that the 1989 Peace Agreement did not cover Singapore. The stand of the Singapore government had always been that they would only be allowed to return if they denounced communism publicly, cut their ties with MCP and satisfied the Internal Security Department (ISD) that they had done so.

Although MCP had ceased operations, it had not been formally dissolved, according to former party secretary-general Chin Peng who was given a permit to attend a seminar in Singapore in October 2004. He said that it might happen sooner or later.

In an interview in 2005, minister mentor Lee Kuan Yew reiterated that they could return to Singapore provided they sought clearance from ISD. "We said, you make a clean statement on what you did and so on after you left and that you are now broken off, finished, closed, then you come back."

"In other words, we are politically neutering them," he said, warning that if they were allowed to come back unrepentant, they might "restart the links and cause trouble". The government had made an offer to them, he noted, but they turned it down because they wanted their return to be unconditional.

In fact, Fang Chuang Pi, the former communist underground leader whom Lee dubbed "the Plen", had made several requests to return to Singapore. The government once offered a one-week social visit pass to Fang and his wife on condition that it should not be treated as a precedent for his fellow communists in southern Thailand. But Fang declined the offer. He died in 2004.

Ironical as it might seem, while Chan and his comrades could not visit Singapore, Singaporeans could visit the Peace Villages and even take up board and lodging in their homes. They could tour the village museum showcasing the history of MCP through exhibits such as photographs, propaganda materials and military equipment and go on excursions to its former jungle camps.

Such is the strange world of history and politics that when the guns fell silent and armed men and women swopped their fatigues for civvies, the sites which once witnessed life-or-death battles are transformed into tourist attractions.

⚜

HEONG *Kei* ("fragrant sign" in Cantonese) is the name of a household brand of food products familiar to consumers in Macau, Hong Kong and the southern Chinese cities of Zhuhai, Shenzhen and Guangzhou.

Made in a factory in Zhuhai and distributed through a wide network of retail outlets, its items range from the popular Singapore-styled barbecue pork (*bak kwa* in Hokkien) and pork floss to almond biscuits, candies and other sweets.

Few people know that the man behind Heong Kei was a former pro-communist PAP chieftain from Singapore named Tan Kong Guan. Even fewer would know that he was one of the six radical leftists who took control of the party following its stormy conference on 4 August 1957.

Derided as "maverick adventurers" by the Lee camp and chided by the communist underground for "going out of line", Tan, who was then PAP propaganda bureau chief, and his associates were accused of holding a midnight *kelong* meeting to plot the capture of the party. It was said that they wanted to run the party while using Lee as cover. But their plan backfired when Lee and his five non-leftist central executive committee (CEC) members refused to hold office.

Compelled to take over the CEC, Tan assumed the post of vice-chairman while Tan Chong Kin replaced Toh Chin Chye as chairman and T T Rajah succeeded Lee Kuan Yew as secretary. Chen Say Jame became assistant secretary; Goh Boon Toh, treasurer; and Ong Chye Ann, assistant treasurer.

For 10 days, they ruled the roost until the Lim Yew Hock government launched a massive crackdown on suspected communists. Tan Kong Guan, Ong and Goh were banished to China a year later in 1958, together with about 30 other party, union and student activists.

When interviewed in 2003, Tan, Ong and other former leftists said they were still perplexed over why they were deported to China when they were not born there. Tan was born in Thailand in 1932 and grew up in Singapore. Ong was born in Penang in 1929 and worked in Singapore.

Ong's wife, Kwok Tai Ying, known as Quek Check Hwa then, who was born in Johor in 1932, was also banished to China together with Ong in 1958. She was a paid secretary of the Singapore Factory and Shop Workers' Union (SFSWU) before she was arrested. Both tied the knot in Guangdong in 1963.

She recalled protesting to the prison officer when told that she would be sent to China. She argued that as she was born in Malaya, she should be deported to Malaya, not China. "But the officer said that the Malayan government did not want me and that because I am Chinese, I must go to China. I had no choice."

Together with the 30-odd detainees, Kwok left on a train to Kuala Lumpur and joined more than 200 other deportees on board a ship bound for Guangdong. She noted that the group, which included communist party and secret society members, formed the 36th batch of deportees to be sent to China since the Emergency in 1948.

When their ship reached port, they refused to disembark. Kwok said that Chinese officials came on board to persuade them to leave but they hung on and argued until late at night. It was only when the officials assured them that they would be allowed to keep their nationalities and leave China later that they agreed to disembark.

After working in farms and factories in Guangdong for two years, Tan, Ong and Goh were sent to Beijing where they spent the next eight years at the People's University studying at the information department and attending courses in politics and the social sciences.

Tan and Ong said they were not sure why the Chinese government despatched them to Beijing. "They treated us as leaders of PAP and thought we might help strengthen ties between Singapore and China in future," surmised Tan in Macau.

Liang Chye Ming, a former leftist who was also deported to China in 1958, thought so too. "They were probably picked because of their past record as former PAP office-bearers and CEC members," he said in Hong Kong. Some observers saw this as irrefutable proof that Tan and Ong were communists.

The Chinese government kept its word. At the height of the Chinese Cultural Revolution between 1966 and 1976, then-Chinese premier Zhou Enlai issued a statement allowing overseas Chinese born outside China to return to their countries of birth. Many former trade union and student activists from Singapore, including Ong and Kwok, wanted to return home but could not do so because of the banishment order.

Tan went to Macau where he started his Heong Kei food business in 1970. Ong moved to Hong Kong with his wife and started a shop selling Heong Kei food products in 1974. China-born Goh moved from Fujian to Hong Kong a year later in 1975 and worked as a trader in Chinese tea.

When the former self-styled revolutionaries were interviewed in 2003, they were all well-entrenched in the capitalistic way of life. Tan had just scaled down his business after selling his factory in Zhuhai and passing his remaining retail outlets to his eldest son, Yang Sheng. His younger son, Yang Kong, was operating a VIP gambling club in Macau.

Ong and his wife retired in 2005 after closing their shop in Shatin. They lived on the rent they collected as owners of a factory floor in an industrial building. They bought a small apartment in Kwun Tong, Kowloon, where they lived with their accountant daughter.

As they reflected on PAP's ascent to power in 1959, they said they had high hopes that as deported PAP members they could return to Singapore. In the same year, Tan remembered, two PAP friends, Jek Yeun Thong and Chan Choy Siong, visited him in Guangdong.

During their meeting in Jek's hotel room, the former culture minister told him that "if he and the others would denounce communism and support PAP's non-communist, socialist, democratic principles, they could return to Singapore anytime". But Tan and Ong declined the offer on the grounds that "we were forced to leave Singapore against our will and it's our right to return without any conditions".

According to Ong's wife, the Singapore government did allow them to visit the island on special request. "Once my husband's elder brother was very ill and he managed to return to Singapore to see him with a special permit," she said.

Others made short trips to Singapore without permission by using travel documents which spelt their names in English differently. One former unionist related with some hilarity how he visited Singapore as a member of a Hong Kong tour group!

The first deportee to return to Singapore for good was Choo Siu Heng, a familiar face in PAP grassroots circles. After his banishment, the former PAP Bukit Timah branch secretary appealed to then-home affairs minister Ong Pang Boon giving the assurance that he was not a communist and pledging his loyalty to the party.

The minister brought up his appeal to the Internal Security Council which comprised British, Malaya and Singapore representatives. The Malaya representative was convinced and voted with Singapore in favour of Choo's return.

On his return with his wife and baby daughter in 1962, Choo resumed his work with PAP in the Ulu Pandan branch and became intimately involved with grassroots organisations. When he was awarded a commendation medal from the party in 2005, the 75-year-old had served the party for 49 years.

Then one day in August 1996, Ong, Kwok and other former leftists received a letter from the Singapore government informing them that the banishment orders issued to them in 1958 had been revoked. The notification read: "I am pleased to inform you that the Minister for Home Affairs has agreed to revoke the Banishment Order issued against you. You are now allowed to enter Singapore as a normal visitor."

Since then, they have returned to Singapore on several occasions. Goh Boon Toh became a permanent resident so that he could live with his wife and two sons in Singapore.

The revocation, which took effect six months after the death of Lim Chin Siong, did not make the news in Singapore and many past and present PAP members were not aware of it. Lee Khoon Choy was visibly surprised when he was told in 2003 that Goh was living in Singapore. He asked: "Why is he in Singapore? Is he allowed to return?"

In an interview in 2005, Lee was asked why the banishment order was lifted. He replied that they were no longer a threat and that conditions had changed. "Their usefulness to the MCP is gone and we knew that they were disappointed with China. So no harm letting them come back and they will disabuse our people of the folly in believing that China's a paradise."

⊰⊱

IT sounded like any lunchtime banter among old friends punctuated by peals of laughter, the occasional ribald jokes and good-natured ribbing. To any casual observer, the camaraderie was unmistakable and infectious.

If you were present at the Mitzi's Cantonese Restaurant on Murray Terrace that Saturday afternoon in 2004, you could have easily eavesdropped on the dozen diners talking about an absent member of the group who was then on holiday in China.

Chan Chee Seng was in his element regaling the company with an anecdote about how 79-year-old Lin You Eng visited Geylang almost every day to look for a young China girl.

As he related mirthfully, Lin had met the twenty-something girl on the plane from China to Singapore and discovered that she was heading for one of the lorongs in the notorious redlight area to work as a call girl for a short stint. Horrified, he tried to persuade her to change her mind but she turned a deaf ear saying she needed the money desperately.

When they parted company at Changi Airport, Lin was still feeling unsettled. In a last ditch attempt to rescue her from the brothel, he combed the lorongs of Geylang for the next few days—to no avail. "You Eng is a kind-hearted and silly old man," a diner cracked as another round of laughter resounded around the table.

Lin was no dirty old man but a chivalrous old knight who wanted to save a young damsel from vice. He was the barber-turned-PAP city councillor for Rochor (1957–1959) and PAP and then Barisan legislative assemblyman for Moulmein (1959–1963). He was one of the 13 PAP rebels who crossed the floor to join the opposition over the issue of merger.

After he left politics, he set up a hair-styling salon in Hilton Hotel with a few friends before he went into garment manufacturing. "I once cut the hair of former US President Richard Nixon when he was staying at the Hilton here," he said with pride. Don't believe it? He whipped out a photocopy of Nixon's signature on his visitors' book.

Older Singaporeans dining near the table on that Saturday could not have mistaken it for just an ordinary senior citizens' gathering. Some of the faces were quite recognisable—former cabinet ministers Ong Pang Boon and Jek Yeun Thong, and former senior parliamentary secretary Chan Chee Seng. Other faces might be harder to place especially those of former leftists Tee Kim Leng and Lim Huan Boon.

The Saturday lunch for former political warriors had been a regular fixture since the early 1970s. Once they plotted against one another, now they took turns to host the get-together rotating it among their favourite restaurants—Red Star on Chin Swee Road, Beng Tin on Chulia Street, Beng Hiang on Amoy Street and Mitzi's on Tanjong Pagar Road.

Less recognisable would be Liao Wen Ming, a former left-wing PAP activist who later became a timber merchant. He was entrusted with the task of informing the group of the date and venue of each lunch.

Liao revealed that it was Chan who initiated the idea of a lunch powwow for PAP office-holders and MPs when Chan and the other two founding members, Ong Pang Boon and Toh Chin Chye, were still holding government positions.

As Chan explained, when they were in government, they had little opportunity to talk to MPs and so the lunch was conceived as an informal forum for them to meet one another and exchange views. Later when they left politics, they continued meeting for lunch as a group of retired politicians.

By the 1980s, Liao said, the lunch was thrown open to former PAP members who broke away to form Barisan Sosialis. Lim Chin Siong came along. So did Lin You Eng, Tee Kim Leng and Ho Puay Choo. Even Ng Teng Kian who deserted PAP to join Ong Eng Guan's United People's Party (UPP) joined in. After all, as they pointed out, both Barisan and

UPP were spun off from PAP.

But with each passing year, the attendance began to drop as old age and illness exacted their toll. Some could no longer turn up because of failing health.

Toh Chin Chye, known for his short fuse, stopped attending the gathering after he lost his patience with Chor Yeok Eng for being frequently late for lunch. Toh reprimanded Chor severely, Liao remembered, adding that other members soon gave up on Chor as they found it hard to track him down and ensure his attendance.

Of course, there were some former PAP politicians who frowned on the fraternisation with former foes. "Don't forget," remarked one agitated former MP, "if the other side had won, we would have been liquidated and they would certainly not be socialising with us today."

Chan Chee Seng, however, believed in letting bygones be bygones. His view was that they all started as colleagues in the same party but took different political paths later. "We were friends once, then some went to Barisan and some remained with PAP. After we retired, there's no more politics and we are back to normal. So it's back to friendship again and there are no hard feelings. Our past political differences do not matter."

Another former PAP leader commented: "When we meet, we don't talk about our past differences. But as former politicians, we still discuss the issues of the day and express our views on government policies freely and sometimes quite critically."

Indeed, seeing former PAP and Barisan politicians seated around a table indulging in two of life's greatest pleasures—good companionship and good food—you could not help concluding that they had come full circle. They used to be friends before they became foes, and now with their do-or-die battles a distant memory, they had become friends all over again.

Heard of the M K Club? Well, that represented yet another merry band of former PAP stalwarts and political adversaries. It was set up in 1981 by former members of PAP's very first branch, Tanjong Pagar, which used to share premises with PAP HQ on 140 Neil Road between 1955 and 1957.

The founding members were former PAP organising secretary Ong Pang Boon and his late wife, Chan Choy Siong, and Low Por Tuck; they were PAP's first three paid officials. Other founding members were Chan Chee Seng, Ho Puay Choo, Robin Sim, Chong Fun Liam and 40 other former Tanjong Pagar branch activists.

Chong, a reputed writer of Chinese novels and plays, said that the group had wanted to register itself as Merdeka Club but the name, which meant "independence" in Malay, was rejected as it had political connotations. So they simply used M K and called it Makan Club whenever people asked what the initials stood for. After all, *makan* or "eating" in Malay was one of its activities.

Each year the club holds functions to coincide with its annual general meeting and to celebrate Chinese New Year or the Mooncake Festival. In the past, members used to go on excursions and overseas tours together.

At its peak in the 1990s, the group grew to more than 110 members but dwindled to 78 by 2005. "Many are getting on in age. At least one would pass away in a year. There was one year when we lost four of our members," lamented Chong.

Chairing the club then was Ho Puay Choo, a former PAP legislative assemblywoman who defected to the Barisan Sosialis and later became a businesswoman dealing in building materials. She said: "We were all members of the party's Tanjong Pagar branch and I am happy that after all these years, we still meet at least once every year just to keep in touch."

As for the former leftists, the social highlight of the year is the annual Chinese New Year lunch, usually held on the third day of the Chinese New Year, where they exchange greetings and Mandarin oranges. No speeches are made to keep the occasion strictly non-political.

The event on 2 February 2006, at Tai Seng Restaurant in People's Park, saw the biggest ever attendance of some 150 people as it also marked the 10th death anniversary of Lim Chin Siong. Before lunch, guests observed a minute of silence in memory of the Barisan Sosialis leader who died on 5 February 1996.

Present at the lunch were Lim's widow Wong Chui Wan, his brother Lim Chin Joo and bosom friends Fong Swee Suan and his wife. Kathleen Fam Yin Oi, widow of Barisan chairman Lee Siew Choh, also turned up with daughter Elaine.

Also present among former Barisan members were Leong Keng Seng, Sheng Nam Chin, Ong Chang Sam, Low Por Tuck, Tan Cheng Tong, Ho Puay Choo, Lin You Eng, Teo Hock Guan and Fung Yin Ching, the sister of Fang Chuang Pi. The others were former activists from the trade unions, student groups and rural residents' associations, and former political detainees.

Former trade unionist Chen Say Jame said he always looked forward to the event as he found it a meaningful and joyful occasion to catch up with one another. Otherwise, the only time when they saw one another would be under sad circumstances—at the funeral wake of yet another former leftist.

⚜

WHEN Lim Chin Siong died of a heart attack at the age of 62 in 1996, Toh attended his wake and told reporters that Lim and MCP played a very important part in Singapore's political history. "If they had won, Singapore would be very different today," he said.

In his message of condolence to his family, Lee wrote that Lim and his comrades fought tenaciously for their beliefs and forced the English-educated leaders to set high standards of personal integrity and lead simple lives to withstand their political attacks.

On the death of Lee Siew Choh in 2002, Lee commented that "the part he played in Singapore politics helped change the course of history". In his tribute, then-prime minister Goh Chok Tong said that the former opposition leader was very much a part of the history of Singapore and PAP and that in his own way, he contributed to the island's political development.

So what then constituted the contributions of the leftists to Singapore? As history favours the victors, much has been written from their vantage point. But how did the vanquished figure in the PAP story? In what way did the political losers make a difference?

"Insofar as they carried Lee through the 1959 elections"—that's how Sheng Nam Chin put it in a nutshell. To former leftists, their greatest legacy was obvious—helping Lee and PAP to capture power in 1959 as part of their combined anti-colonial struggle for independence.

Samad Ismail noted that the left was the only group who really took on the British seriously and provided the sinews for Lee and company. Fang Mingwu confirmed that the communists were instrumental in rallying popular support for the fledgling PAP.

In Said Zahari's view, Lee would not have become prime minister if Lim Chin Siong and fellow comrades had not mobilised mass support for the young English-educated lawyer. "Had it not been for the left-wing movement, the British would not have allowed Lee to take over the country so easily," he said drawing an analogy with the situation in Malaya where "had it not been for MCP guerillas taking up arms, the British would not have given independence to Tunku so easily".

Dominic Puthucheary agreed: "Even though the left failed to capture power, we had succeeded in helping Malaya and Singapore to achieve freedom with greater speed." If the British had resisted, Woodhull said, the militant left would have become even stronger and more popular.

According to Fang Chuang Pi, such was the impact of the anti-colonial struggle on the population that the British government had no choice but to make special constitutional arrangements to reduce the pressure from the people who were clamouring for liberation.

Lest you think the former leftists were making a self-seeking appraisal of their role in history, their views were shared to a large extent by those in PAP. Ong Pang Boon agreed that the leftists had contributed to Singapore's history by raising the political consciousness of the people, building up mass support and helping to get rid of the colonialists.

"Not all things done by the communists were bad," said Chan Chee Seng noting that PAP took a leaf from its book. "They were pro-people, pro-jobless and pro-underdogs. They sought to alleviate poverty, they went to the people, they listened to the poor."

Yet another contribution cited by the left was its intense competition with the PAP in striving to work for the welfare of the people. The result, as even Lee had acknowledged, was that PAP sought to emulate if not "outleft" the left.

Listing many of the progressive policies in public housing, education and health care conceived by the Lee government, Dominic Puthucheary said: "PAP had to undercut or take the ground from under the feet of the left by providing solutions which were as good if not better than what the left could do."

PAP had to make capitalism succeed to prove to the left that it was better than socialism, the lawyer said. "So this competition between the left and PAP produced a positive effect in that PAP had to prove that capitalism was more democratic, more socially orientated, that it had a heart and a human face."

According to some former leftists, the PAP government did so well in improving the livelihood and living standards of the people that they had to admit in their soul-searching moments that they could not have done better if they had taken over the running of the island.

No doubt the legacy of the left had left an indelible imprint on the psyche of the PAP pioneers. Indeed the lessons which the party absorbed from the climacteric clash with its arch adversary have been internalised in its institutional memory and transmitted to succeeding cohorts of new members. That perhaps explains the unyielding reflexes and instincts which characterise its no-holds-barred approach towards the opposition to this day.

To Lee, what stands out most in his mind was the dedication and selflessness of the leftist leaders. As he often expounded: "They put the hurdle very high for us ... to compete with them, we needed to show the people that we were just as determined and as dedicated as they were.

"They forced us to establish very high standards for ourselves in order to survive and even after we defeated them, we decided that without those standards, we would go down. We maintained those standards. I think that was their contribution. It was very important."

Chan Chee Seng exemplified the PAP rank-and-file who stood by their beleaguered leaders during The Big Split of 1961. He remained unmoved even when he was threatened by his fellow assemblymen in their Canning Rise quarters for refusing to defect. Lee lauded him as a man of great courage and loyalty who was impervious to intimidation.

Sitting in the conference room of the ISS International School on Preston Road off Depot Road, which he headed after retiring from politics, Chan could not help waxing philosophical. With a rhetorical twist, he acknowledged that Barisan made its contribution to Singapore—by playing a negative role. "Without the negative, how would you know the positive? If Barisan did not go against you, how would you know PAP was doing the right thing?"

Tracing the influences which shaped his political outlook, he said that as a student in the English-medium St Anthony's Boys and St Joseph's Institution, he had no access to political texts except books glorifying the British Empire but in the Chinese-medium Yeung Ching Primary and Catholic High, he was initiated into the great Chinese classics.

The man with a penchant for spouting Mandarin maxims and dialect dictums said that he joined PAP because he imagined that its leaders were like the 108 legendary heroes in *Water Margin* (*shui hu zhuan*) who fought against a corrupt and unjust government—the Chinese equivalent of Robin Hood.

Then drawing from yet another Chinese classic, he said that just as the rights and wrongs depicted in *Romance of the Three Kingdoms* (*san guo yan yi*) enlightened him on the political and civil strife in third-century China, the rights and wrongs in the historic struggle between PAP and the communists in the 1960s taught him lessons on the politics of Singapore.

"Actually it's the errors that educate us, that help us to understand what is right and what is wrong. Actually the battle between PAP and Barisan gave us a lot of knowledge and experiences and taught us that life was worth living … and fighting for."

The day that changed Singapore forever: No photograph existed of the swearing-in of Lee Kuan Yew as prime minister in City Hall on 5 June 1959 as it was closed to the press. This scene was re-created by artist Lai Kui Fang, based on interviews and research. The oil painting was unveiled in 1992.

Handover of power: Goh Chok Tong being sworn in as Singapore's second prime minister in City Hall on 18 November 1990. The ceremony, witnessed by President Wee Kim Wee (*right*) and 600 guests in the chamber and an adjoining room, was televised live.

Changing of the guard: Lee Hsien Loong reciting his oath as Singapore's third prime minister at the Istana on 12 August 2004. He is standing next to President S R Nathan and Chief Justice Yong Pung How. The event was witnessed by 1,400 guests on the Istana lawn and watched live on TV.

All photographs courtesy of Singapore Press Holdings, unless otherwise stated.

No 38 Oxley Road:
The pre-war bungalow
of Lee Kuan Yew as
it looked in the 1950s
before it was fortified
by security grilles and
its frontage walled off.
This was where PAP
founding members met
on Saturday afternoons
and where an unending
procession of people
came to meet Lee to
initiate political action.
(Illustration by Miel)

Where the PAP was conceived: Some of the party's founding members meeting in the basement dining room of Lee Kuan Yew's home to discuss the design for the party's symbol. *(clockwise from top right)* Ismail Rahim, Lee *(standing)*, K M Byrne, S Rajaratnam, Devan Nair, Toh Chin Chye, Goh Keng Swee and Samad Ismail. *(Illustration by Miel)*

Lee quits: Lee *(third from right)* and company outside PAP HQ on Neil Road after announcing they would not take up party posts on 6 August 1957. Goh Chew Chua is at the doorway; Toh Chin Chye is third from left; and Lee Khoon Choy is on the extreme right.

Banished to China in 1958, free to return in 1996: *(from left)* Former PAP vice-chairman Tan Kong Guan, former member Liang Chye Ming, former treasurer Ong Chye Ann and wife Kwok Tai Ying. They were deported by the Lim Yew Hock government after the leftist takeover of PAP in 1957.

From incarceration to liberation: Released detainees from Changi Prison meeting the press at PAP HQ on 62-C South Bridge Road on 4 June 1959. *(from left, sitting)* Fong Swee Suan, S Woodhull, Lim Chin Siong, Devan Nair, James Puthucheary and Chan Chiaw Thor; *(from left, standing)* Lee Khoon Choy and Lee Kuan Yew.

When every vote counts: PAP assemblywoman Sahorah binte Ahmat being carried on a stretcher by ambulance from Singapore General Hospital to the chamber to cast her decisive vote in the motion of confidence debate on 21 July 1961.

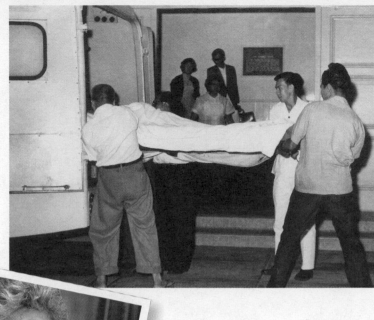

No wives please: Mrs Miki Goh-Hoalim Jnr *(left)* was dropped from early PAP meetings, and so was Mrs Lee Kuan Yew, and the party became a "men-only thing".

Women power: The 1959 polls saw the election of five PAP legislative assemblywomen *(clockwise from above left)* Chan Choy Siong, Ho Puay Choo, Oh Su Chen, Sahorah binte Ahmat and Fung Yin Ching. Chan, Ho and Oh were also CEC members.

From swords to ploughshares: Former MCP member Liu Bo showing the display of destroyed rifles at a makeshift museum in Betong, southern Thailand.

Jungle parade: MCP leader Chin Peng inspecting communist guerillas in southern Thailand in the early 1980s. In the forefront is Fang Bai Lian who provided this picture.

Homesick exiles:
(clockwise from left)
Former PAP parliamentary secretary Chan Sun Wing provided this early 1980s photo of himself in guerilla fatigues; Chan and wife Luo Yamei in Hatyai in 2003; Fang Mingwu; Fang's wife, Fang Bai Lian, with a picture of herself as a pig-tailed Chinese middle school student in Singapore.

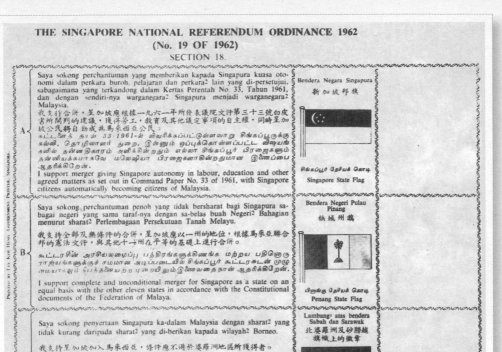

THE SINGAPORE NATIONAL REFERENDUM ORDINANCE 1962
(No. 19 OF 1962)
SECTION 18.

A

Saya sokong perchantuman yang memberikan kapada Singapura kuasa oto-nomi dalam perkara buroh, pelajaran dan perkara² lain yang di-persetujui, sabagaimana yang terkandong dalam Kertas Perentah No. 33, Tahun 1961, dan dengan sendiri-nya warganegara² Singapura menjadi warganegara² Malaysia.

我支持合併，星加坡應根據一九六一年所發表議院文件第三十三號白皮書所開列的建議，獲得勞工，教育及其他議定事項的自主權。同時星加坡公民將自動成為馬來西亞公民。

கட்டளைக் தாள் 33, 1961-ல் விவரிக்கப்பட்டுள்ளவாறு சிங்கப்பூருக்கு கல்வி, தொழிலாளர் துறை, இன்னும் ஒப்புக்கொள்ளப்பட்ட விஷயங்களில் தன்னிகாரம் அளிக்கின்றதும் எல்லா சிங்கப்பூர் பிரஜைகளும் தன்னியக்கமாகவே மலேஷியா பிரஜைகளாகின்றதுமான இணைப்பை ஆதரிக்கிறேன்.

I support merger giving Singapore autonomy in labour, education and other agreed matters as set out in Command Paper No. 33 of 1961, with Singapore citizens automatically becoming citizens of Malaysia.

Bendera Negara Singapura
新加坡邦旗

Singapore State Flag
சிங்கப்பூர் தேசிய கொடி

B

Saya sokong perchantuman penoh yang tidak bersharat bagi Singapura sa-bagai negeri yang sama taraf-nya dengan sa-belas buah Negeri² Bahagian menurut sharat² Perlembagaan Persekutuan Tanah Melayu.

我支持全部及無條件的合併，星加坡以一州的地位，根據馬來亞聯合邦的憲法文件，與其他十一州在平等的基礎上進行合併。

கூட்டாரின் அரசியலமைப்பு பத்திரங்களுக்கிணங்க மற்றய பதினொரு ராஜியங்களுக்குச் சமமான அடிப்படையில் சிங்கப்பூர் கூட்டரசுடன் முழு மையாகவும் நிபந்தனையற்ற முறையில் இணைவதை நான் ஆதரிக்கிறேன்.

I support complete and unconditional merger for Singapore as a state on an equal basis with the other eleven states in accordance with the Constitutional documents of the Federation of Malaya.

Bendera Negeri Pulau Pinang
槟城州旗

Penang State Flag
பினாங்கு தேசிய கொடி

C

Saya sokong penyertaan Singapura ka-dalam Malaysia dengan sharat² yang tidak kurang daripada sharat² yang di-berikan kapada wilayah² Borneo.

我支持星加坡加入馬來西亞，條件應不遜於婆羅洲地區所獲得者。

போர்னியோ பிரதேசங்களுக்கு அளிக்கப்படும் சலுகைகளுக்கு எவ்வகை வீழ்ப் குறைவற்ற முறையில் சிங்கப்பூர் மலேயாவின் சேர்வதை நான் ஆதரிக்கிறேன்.

I support Singapore entering Malaysia on terms no less favourable than those given to the Borneo territories.

Lambang² atas bendera Sabah dan Sarawak
北婆羅洲及砂勝越旗幟上的徽章

Badges on the Flags of North Borneo and Sarawak
வடபோர்னியோ சரவாக் கொடிகளிலுள்ள சின்னம்

Three ways to say yes, none to say no: Facsimile of ballot paper for the 1962 referendum on merger showing Alternative A, B and C.

Vote for A please: Goh Keng Swee *(second from right)* canvassing for votes among the porridge-eating elders of Chinatown in August 1962.

345

Signed, sealed and delivered: The 15 signatures of the five Alliance ministers and 10 PAP ministers that sanctioned Singapore's separation from Malaysia on 9 August 1965. Officially, the document is called the Independence of Singapore Agreement 1965.

Cultivating the Malay ground: *(clockwise from top left)* Samad Ismail, Mahmud Awang, Ariff Suradi and Mofradi bin Haji Mohamed Noor were among the pioneering Malay leaders in PAP.

Day of infamy: Two overturned cars at Paya Lebar Road on 23 July 1964. Some 23 people died and 454 were injured in the worst race riots in Singapore's history.

Goh in the 1976 slate: Some other candidates include *(from left)* Yeoh Ghim Seng, Shaari Tadin, Fong Sip Chee, Mansor Sukaimi, Phua Bah Lee, Teo Chong Tee and Rahim Ishak. Goh Chok Tong is on the extreme right.

Deng comes to Singapore: Lee Kuan Yew welcomes then-Chinese vice-premier Deng Xiaoping at the Paya Lebar airport (1978).

Setting up links in Batam: Second-generation contenders *(from left)* Goh Chok Tong, Bernard Chen, S Dhanabalan and Lim Chee Onn quench their thirst with coconut juice on neighbouring Indonesian island, Batam, during their one-day visit (1979).

Lesson in the rain: Lee Kuan Yew shows he can hold the attention of a crowd even in pouring rain at the Fullerton Square rally (1980).

Rally on Prophet Mohammed's birthday: Ahmad Mattar addresses a 20,000-strong crowd at the National Stadium at a mass rally organised by MUIS (Islamic Religious Council of Singapore) together with other Muslim bodies (1981).

A break-through win: Opposition candidate Chiam See Tong at a rally in Potong Pasir, the ward which he eventually wins (1984).

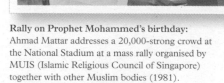

Church cover: Lee Kuan Yew meets Archbishop Gregory Yong at the Istana to discuss the Marxist conspirators who used the Catholic Church as their cover (1987).

Goh becomes prime minister: Goh Chok Tong waves to his well-wishers at the Padang after his swearing-in ceremony in the City Hall as Singapore's second prime minister (1990).

"You won't enjoy this": Lee Hsien Loong at the Singapore General Hospital shows reporters the portable pump which feeds chemotherapy and anti-nausea drugs into his body, as he battles cancer (1992).

Singapore's first elected president: Supporters congratulate Ong Teng Cheong on his victory in the first presidential election (1993).

Traditional Indian welcome: Goh Chok Tong at the Indian community's grand dinner held at the Shangri-La Hotel (1997).

Community centres keeping up with the times: The Marine Parade Community Club, which cost nearly $30 million and took three years to build, opens its doors to the public (2000).

A third-generation leader: Teo Chee Hean *(second from left)* on a walkabout to canvass votes in Nee Soon Central with veteran Ong Ah Heng (2001).

Party's main man: Wong Kan Seng handing out a thermometer to a stallholder during the SARS crisis (2003). Wong is very much in charge of party affairs as first assistant secretary-general in the CEC.

Hari Raya celebrations: Tony Tan and Yaacob Ibrahim *(behind him)* being welcomed by mosque officials at the Petempatan Melayu Mosque (2004).

Key players in Goh's team: NTUC chief Lim Boon Heng *(left)* and George Yeo, who opened up the cultural scene as the minister for information and the arts, at a May Day dinner (2004).

And the confetti rains down: PAP leaders at the 50th anniversary rally at the Singapore Indoor Stadium (2004).

Old Guard at anniversary: Present at the PAP's 50th anniversary dinner are *(from left)* Chan Chee Seng, Ch'ng Jit Koon, Ong Pang Boon and Ho Kah Leong (2004).

One candle stays lit: Lee Kuan Yew blows out the last candle on the cake as Goh Chok Tong, Tony Tan and Lee Hsien Loong look on, at the party's 50th anniversary dinner at Suntec City Convention Centre (2004).

Swearing-in at the Istana: Unlike the case of the two previous prime ministers, Lee Hsien Loong's swearing-in ceremony is held at the Istana, watched by 1,400 guests from all walks of life (2004).

The third and the first: Newly sworn-in prime minister Lee Hsien Loong shakes hands with Singapore's first prime minister Lee Kuan Yew. President S R Nathan watches on (2004).

Veteran PAP grassroots leader: Choo Siu Heng has served the party for more than 40 years.

More women officials in the new century:
Eight women PAP MPs flag off a walk at Marina
Promenade to mark International Women's Day.
(from right) Lily Neo, Amy Khor, Halimah Yacob,
Cynthia Phua, Lim Hwee Hua, Ho Geok Choo,
Irene Ng and Penny Low (2005).

A victorious day:
PM Lee being carried
by jubilant supporters
at Woodlands Station
after the 2006 general
election results were
announced.

**His third National
Day rally:** Lee Hsien
Loong impresses
with his eloquence
at his National Day
rally, at the same time
showing a different
side of him (2008).

PART TWO
BY

Richard Lim

20

The Turning Point—1984

Sleepless in Singapore

IT was past two in the morning but Singapore was still wide awake. In many homes across the island, people huddled in front of their television sets to watch a press conference that was being telecast live from the Singapore Conference Hall. On the screen was a grim-faced Lee Kuan Yew, secretary-general of PAP and prime minister of Singapore since 1959, fielding questions from a roomful of reporters.

This was the 1984 post-election press conference and Lee was understandably grim.

The ruling party had suffered its biggest drop in majority votes since the 1968 general election and for the first time, two opposition candidates were returned, confirming that the 1981 Anson by-election win by J B Jeyaretnam of the Workers' Party (WP) was not a fluke.

The results—64.83 per cent of the votes, a steep plunge of 12.8 per cent from the 1980 general election—surprised everyone, including PAP. With Jeyaretnam and Chiam See Tong of the Singapore Democratic Party (SDP) winning the two seats, PAP finally lost the political dominance it had enjoyed since 1968.

And it looked as though the party might never have total dominance again. Singapore had changed and so had the people.

In the years since autonomous rule in 1959 and independence in 1965, PAP had shaped the people. Now these same people had used their votes to signal to the party that it was time it reshaped itself to adapt to them.

As Lee said at the press conference: "The results of the election show a highly sophisticated electorate. They wanted a PAP government, they were sure they had one, they wanted to put pressure on PAP. They wanted some people in parliament to get us to either go slower or to be more generous in our policies, less austere and so on ... We've lost two seats ... The signal has been sent."

In the 1950s and during the 1960s, the people in Singapore were witness to Lee and his team's successful fight against the British and then the communists and communalists. Those were tumultuous years, marked by labour strikes, riots, communal strife, curfews and the panicked hoarding of food by the population. But by the late 1960s, the people had begun to know order and stability.

So when the PAP government took harsh and often painful measures to ensure Singapore's survival after it was turfed out of Malaysia in 1965 and after the British withdrew their troops in 1971, the people were willing to grit their teeth and go with their leaders.

Lee and his team set about laying the infrastructure for their ambitious industrialisation programme at the same time that they undertook a wholesale resettlement of the population. People were moved out of their slums and squatter colonies, and re-housed in new high-rise public housing flats that were built at a dizzying speed. Farmers had to give up their little plots of land and find alternative ways to make a living.

The different races, brought together by empire and encouraged to live in their own enclaves, were integrated in the new public housing estates. There was, in effect, a shuffling of the population. Although the government had decreed that there would be four official languages—English, Chinese, Malay and Tamil—Lee decided from the beginning that English would be the language of government and commerce and the neutral medium for the socialisation of the different races.

These were massive changes, and they touched and shaped the lives of just about every man, woman and child. If there were painful adjustments to be made, the people coped as best as they could. They trusted that their leaders would deliver them a better tomorrow.

Their trust was not misplaced. In the short span of two decades, they saw their lives transformed. They had become a property-owning people with a stake in the land and access to a middle-class way of life. The scruffy place they had known was now a modern metropolis, unmatched by any capital city in Southeast Asia. The slums, squatters and squalor of yesteryear were but a memory.

It was an outstanding achievement by any measure. No other post-colonial society had seen such a leap in so short a time.

But, as Lee pointed out at the press conference, the generation that provided "a very firm, solid base for high endeavour, that generation has grown old, diminished in numbers. A younger generation has got to find its own goals, decide what it wants out of life in Singapore and what there is to put in."

That new generation was better educated and more demanding of their leaders. The struggles and hardships of the early years of independence the younger generation could never know, except as a history lesson from their textbooks. "Even for the older voters," a PAP post-mortem report on the 1984 election noted, "the memories of hard times are fading."

The ruling party had succeeded in its nation-building job perhaps too well. Now that the people were no longer hungry and anxious about the morrow, they were less willing to accept the kind of tough policies that PAP still pushed out—this time not just for Singapore's survival but for what it believed would be the country's longer-term good.

When a man is well fed and has a comfortable life, he is more concerned with current irritations than visions of the future. "I think that's always the case," Lee said.

And so, by the early 1980s, Singaporeans had begun to see the PAP government's long-term policies as excessive interference in their private lives. The party that had given them the good life was now overbearing and authoritarian.

Through the ballot box, they sent PAP that "sophisticated" signal.

LEE faced the press, flanked by four of his core second-generation leaders—Goh Chok Tong, who had led in the organisation of the election campaign, Tony Tan, Ong Teng Cheong and S Dhanabalan.

Ong was an architect and urban planner when he was inducted into PAP in 1972. The other three had come on board in the mid- and late-1970s. Goh was formerly the managing director of the national shipping line. Tony Tan and S Dhanabalan were fast-rising stars in the banking sector. All four had impressive academic credentials and were early achievers. In 1984, they were in their mid- to late-40s, the prime of their lives.

Lee himself was only 61 years old. But he had begun his search for a successor generation of leaders more than 10 years earlier. At the time, his Old Guard peers were entering their 60s and, as he was younger than them, he could see that they were slowing down and losing their reflexes.

He had also seen in other countries how "by hanging on for too long, a creator generation lost the chance to facilitate and to ease the way for its successors, and thus to have more influence in determining the nature of its successors", as he told a party conference in 1980.

In that speech, he recounted the last time he saw Jawaharlal Nehru in 1964, a few months before he died: "He was tired, exhausted by his age and the endeavours of a lifetime."

Nehru, the first prime minister of independent India, was 75 when he died. His daughter Indira Gandhi was likewise "weighed down by gigantic problems, with few young and able men with the zest and drive to help her solve them". She was the country's third prime minister, after Nehru's successor Lal Bahadur Shastri died of a heart attack just 19 months into the job.

In his search for talent, Lee did not restrict himself to the party. He recognised that those grassroots leaders who were thrown up from the party's rank and file had come largely from a generation that did not have access to universal education. And if they had some education, it was in their vernacular languages. Their political experiences were formed mainly in the trade unions. They might be fearless fighters and effective mobilisers but they were not equipped to manage the complex apparatus of government.

So Lee looked beyond the party to cherry-pick the best and brightest in the land. After a few false starts—brightness alone was not enough, there had to be other qualities like strength of character and integrity—he found his men and fielded them in the 1976 general election and the by-elections of the late 1970s. Except for Ong, the men with him now in the room with the press were from those cohorts.

By 1980, he was able to test their leadership potential in the general election. He got them to pick the new candidates, organise the campaign and fight the polls. In their second outing in 1984, he had them blooded.

"Have you got a team equal to them and that can run this place? You haven't, you know," Lee said, looking at the television viewer in the eye towards the end of the press conference.

It was a sober poser for the viewer to sleep on when the session finally ended just before dawn.

The New Got "Choppered" In

WHEN Lee got his new team into the field in 1980, he kept the old on the bench.

His two closest teammates, Goh Keng Swee and Lim Kim San, supported his plan to run-in the second-generation team early. They understood their captain's sense of urgency and volunteered leaving the field together to force the pace of renewal.

Lim, the man who kick-started Singapore's hugely successful public housing programme, did so in 1980. He went on to head the Port of Singapore Authority and then the public-listed Singapore Press Holdings. He resigned as the media group's executive chairman in 2002 but stayed on as its senior adviser until the end of 2005.

In 2003, in his office in Singapore Press Holdings' News Centre in Toa Payoh, the still spritely 87-year-old said: "We've got to make room for new blood and fresh ideas to succeed us if Singapore is to succeed. I supported the idea of renewal and was more than ready to go."

Goh, Lee's deputy and the economic architect of Singapore, followed suit in 1984. He was the deputy chairman of the Monetary Authority of Singapore from 1985 to 1992 and from 1992 to 1996, the executive chairman of the Institute of East Asian Political Economy, later renamed East Asian Institute. In 1985, he was also appointed the economic adviser to China on coastal development and the tourism industry. He crossed over to the private sector in 1994, joining Hong Leong Asia as deputy chairman. His health started to decline in the late 1990s.

In an interview in 1982, he said: "It's time to call it quits. I'll be 65 next year. But I'll be available. Maybe to advise the second echelon leaders … and I'd rather have that sort of relationship than an official one…" That it would be difficult to make the adjustment to being a private citizen, he acknowledged as much. "But it has to come and you might as well reconcile yourself to it," he said.

The other Old Guard leaders still around in the early 1980s were E W Barker, S Rajaratnam, Toh Chin Chye, Ong Pang Boon and Jek Yeun Thong. But by 1984, none of them was in the party's central executive committee (CEC). All the CEC posts were filled by the second-generation leaders, except for Lee Kuan Yew and two veteran grassroots leaders, Ch'ng Jit Koon and Ho Kah Leong, who were popular with the party's rank and file as well as on the ground.

There was naturally some unhappiness among the sidelined Old Guard and those lower down in the ranks who had to make way for new blood. Economist Augustine Tan, a non-party member who was "helicoptered" in for the 1970 by-election, recalled that "there was a lot of strain". "You could feel it ... tension, resentment," he said.

He pointed out that the self-renewal process was a very daring move because some of the older MPs and ministers who were displaced had been very popular on the ground. "So I think Lee Kuan Yew was really risking political capital in the process. It was something which I felt that, at that time, even many of his colleagues would not have supported if they could have voted on the situation."

When Toh was moved to the backbench in 1980, he became a vocal critic of government policies in parliament. "How can I remain a dumb cow?" said the man who was once the chairman of the party and the deputy prime minister of the country.

Twenty years on, in 2004, few people recognised him on the street. In his modest house in Bukit Timah, where he tended an orchid garden, the 83-year-old said of the party's renewal process: "Well, it was a renewal of substance. You had to do it. It was getting rid of some bodies and finding some new bodies. For old party members who had been loyal, it was a painful process. You don't repay their loyalty by throwing them out. We had the responsibility to help them find jobs."

Even Ong Pang Boon, a party stalwart known for his measured responses in public, could not maintain his silence on the Old Guard's disappointment over being eased out. At a constituency dinner to celebrate the 25th anniversary of the party in 1979, where both Goh Chok Tong and Tony Tan were seated at the main table, he made the pointed comment that Singapore was a parvenu society where if a person was not successful, he would be forgotten and neglected. "Thus, the Old Guard members, once they retired, were often regarded as 'losers'. Their contributions would be buried and forgotten," he lamented.

But despite the unhappiness, there was no breaking of ranks. These men had fought shoulder-to-shoulder for a common cause and they shared a bond that had been forged in the white heat of life-and-death battles.

Ong, who had held a senior management job in the diversified Hong Leong Group since he quit politics in December 1984, said in an interview 20 years later: "There was no jostling for power. Our aim was the same and, if there were any differences, they were not so great."

In Toh's case, there was speculation for a while that he would form a splinter party to fight the election in 1984. But in the end, he stood as a candidate on a PAP ticket. It was his last term in politics. He joined the management of a small hotel group and in 1990 was made an adviser to one of the subsidiaries of Keppel Corporation. He retired in 1996.

Augustine Tan believed that the continued success of PAP was what had prevented the resentment and bitterness of the Old Guard from becoming a political factor. "I mean, if PAP had faltered in any way, those resentments which had boiled over could have divided the party," he said.

❧

LEE'S way of "helicoptering" in new leaders would become a standard feature of PAP, even after he stepped aside as secretary-general of the party in 1992. It is a feature probably unique to PAP and Singapore.

In other countries, political leaders rise from the party ranks. Aspirants fight their way up, often paying for patronage to pave the way. Upon arrival in office, those who are beholden to patrons would want to entrench themselves since they have too many interests at stake. It would cost them dearly to lose their positions and often, they would want their pound of flesh from the party in return.

In Malaysia, for example, Abdullah Badawi of the dominant party UMNO found that out when he became prime minister in October 2003. He had dropped several old divisional leaders when he drew up the new UMNO state positions. One of them, Ibrahim Ali, the divisional chief in Kelantan, kicked up such a fuss in public that it would be funny if it were not a serious matter. "I still love UMNO, but it appears UMNO does not love me anymore. If I challenge the decision, it is because my dignity has been hurt," he moaned like a jilted lover.

He threatened to join an opposition party. He went away for a trip and when he arrived home, some 10,000 supporters showed up at the airport to welcome him back. And they gave the UMNO leadership a 30-day ultimatum—reinstate him or else. When he was not reinstated, Ibrahim contested in the 2004 general election as an independent candidate. He was expelled from UMNO.

There were other unhappy axed divisional heads who could have plotted to do damage to UMNO behind the scenes, by sabotaging the party election machinery, for instance. "This is what many UMNO leaders do after they are dropped," said a senior Kelantan politician. "The only difference is that some do the damage quietly while others make threats in public."

Among other things, it was the fear of this kind of costly backlash that had kept the ruling party from renewing itself. A number of divisional chiefs had been around for more than 25 years and had begun to just coast along and enjoy the perks of their titles.

Former prime minister Mahathir bin Mohamad was not able to scratch out the non-performers from his list of candidates for the 1999 elections because his support in UMNO was considerably weakened after he sacked his deputy Anwar Ibrahim in the previous year. As a result, many of the old and discredited faces in UMNO either lost or had their majority votes slashed.

But Abdullah, with no baggage, had signalled by the third month he was in office that he would play hardball with the likes of Ibrahim Ali. In fielding more than 240 new faces in his coalition Barisan Nasional slate for the March 2004 general election, he faced noisy protests, withdrawal of support and even sabotage from candidates who were dropped. He was, therefore, careful not to chop all the dead wood at one go, even after he had a landslide victory.

PAP must have been relieved that its change of guard was smooth, even uneventful. But that was because Lee, ever the planner who took the long view, had laid the groundwork for it for more than 10 years.

A question on every pundit's lips after the 1984 election was—would the setback affect the handover of power to the new team?

They had their answer in the new year. The new team was still firmly in place, with additions from the 1984 cohort, as more members of the Old Guard were shed.

A new generation of voters had emerged, as Lee had said. It required a new team of younger leaders. But much more than that, because for Lee, renewal could not wait; mortality loomed large. When one of his most trusted lieutenants, Hon Sui Sen, was hospitalised in the Singapore General Hospital in late 1983, Goh Keng Swee was in the next room. Hon died of a massive heart attack in October that year. He was 67. At about the same time, Rajaratnam, then 68, had a heart attack when he was in America and underwent a bypass operation in London. Back in Singapore, he had a part of his lungs taken out.

No doubt the 1984 general election had been a brutal rite of passage for the new line-up of PAP leaders but it was better that they were put through it sooner than later, for the Old Guard leaders might not be around for too long.

The No-mercy Post-mortem

PAP did not expect its share of votes in 1984 to be as high as 1980's 77.66 per cent. After all, it had already suffered a loss—its first since 1968—in the 1981 Anson by-election. Many of the issues that contributed to that loss might be specific to the ward but the result was also an indication of a growing trend among the people to vote for the opposition.

PAP was surprised and disturbed, however, by the scale of the swing— 12.8 per cent—and the plunge in majority votes in almost all the wards across the island.

In material terms, there was no reason for the people to be unhappy. The four years from 1980 to 1984 had been exceptionally good years. Salaries had gone up by 8.7 per cent in every one of those years. By August 1984, the PAP government had also succeeded in housing 80 per cent of the population and three-quarters of them owned their HDB flats (public housing flats built by the Housing and Development Board).

So what were the reasons for the swing?

"We tempted fate," was the blunt answer the party gave in its own post-mortem report that was released for the first time for this book. "Had it not been for the tremendous depth of support which PAP enjoyed, we would have been voted out of office."

The report was a merciless piece of self-examination. It identified, with no punches pulled, the reasons for the swing against the party and made recommendations on what the party should do to rebuild the kind of extensive support which the PAP government had enjoyed.

But it was more than just a post-mortem exercise. If the 1984 general election marked a major turning point for PAP, then the 33-page document was a significant signpost that pointed to that turn. From it, one could trace the transition of the Old Guard leadership to the new and the shift in the party's style.

What had remained unchanged, though, was the substance of its policies. The PAP government would always work for the long-term good of Singapore.

The shift in style had been gradual, so gradual in fact that one could take in its full measure only by stepping back at the end of the 1980s and looking at how much the society had changed.

It was just as well that the PAP government started making the change in the mid-1980s. It helped prepare both the party and people to adjust to the new demands of globalisation and the exponential growth of new information technologies that came full throttle in the 1990s. Because the new technologies shortened business cycles and forced a faster pace of change, society had to become more nimble and rely less on its old command-and-control approach to doing things.

The post-mortem report was put together by a task force set up by Goh Chok Tong, who joined the party in 1976 and had, by 1984, become the party's assistant secretary-general. Chaired by Ong Teng Cheong, it was made up entirely of the key members of the 1980 and 1984 cohorts.

Lee Hsien Loong, a member of the task force, wrote up the report. The eldest of Lee Kuan Yew's three children, he was 32 years old in 1984. He left the army, where he was brigadier-general, to go into politics. In the general election, he fought against a lightweight—Giam Lai Cheng—from an inconsequential party in the new, largely working-class ward of Teck Ghee in Ang Mo Kio. As he recounted more than 20 years later, his team was sure he would take away her deposit (which all election candidates were required to put down and which would be forfeited if they failed to collect at least 12.5 per cent of the votes) but he did not.

Lee Didn't Stop at Two

PAP had tempted fate by rolling out one controversial policy after another in what was an election year, the post-mortem report noted. It was never done in past election years.

In the first six months of 1984, Lee Kuan Yew, worried about potential problems 30 to 50 years down the road, pushed through two policy ideas that roused a population which had become apathetic with growing affluence.

From the 1980 census, he discerned a trend of "lop-sided procreation". The better educated women were not marrying and if they did, were producing at the most two children. Less educated women, however, were producing more children when, in most instances, they did not have the resources to raise them, much less give them a good education.

So a graduate mothers policy was launched. Lee gave graduate mothers their pick of pre-school or primary school for their third child. It sparked off a public outcry. The papers were inundated with angry calls and letters, even from tertiary educated women who, at the time, made up only 1.3 per cent (14,515) of the female population.

The Straits Times published the more considered responses but allowed room also for the more emotional ones, such as that sent in by an incensed 40-year-old single professional: "I am deeply insulted by the suggestion that some miserable financial incentive will make me jump into bed with the first attractive man I meet and proceed to produce a highly talented child for the sake of Singapore's future ... The only fanatics who have done such things were the storm troopers of Nazi Germany."

Eugenics, or the science of selective breeding to improve the hereditary qualities of a breed or a race, was an idea as old as Plato but it was discredited when the Nazi regime used it to justify its racial superiority and sent thousands of "inferior" Jews to the gas chambers.

No post-war leader in the developed world would go near that idea. It would be political suicide. But Lee was not one to flinch from his conviction. He believed that human intelligence was innate and carried in the genes, and that nature did not distribute its gifts evenly among all people.

Tony Tan artfully dismantled the controversial policy soon after the election but Lee must have felt vindicated by findings that advances in genetics and evolutionary biology turned up afterwards. A human being does not come into the world a blank slate and there are inherent biological limits to what he can be and do which are specific to him because of his genetic make-up. The right environment will allow him to achieve his fullest potential but it cannot extend by very much the limits set by his genetic make-up.

The other potential problem Lee tried to anticipate was the prospects of Singapore becoming a greying society. According to an official estimate, about 20 per cent of the population would be aged 65 and above by 2030. The elderly could be a heavy burden on future generations if they did not have the means to support themselves and take care of their medical needs.

Lee got Howe Yoon Chong, a former senior civil servant who crossed over into politics and was made the health minister, to form a committee and study the problem. Howe and his team took great pains to put together a comprehensive report with a list of recommendations. They did not expect it though to become a bomb that blew in their faces after

Lee released it to the public.

There were many useful recommendations in what came to be known as the Howe Yoon Chong Report but what drew the public's exclusive attention was the one which suggested the raising of the retirement age from 55 to 60, then 65 eventually, and pushing back accordingly the age when people could withdraw their savings from the Central Provident Fund (CPF), a government-managed pension scheme.

The public outcry was even louder this time. Alarmed, the government put it on the backburner, pending more studies to be done in the area.

The post-mortem report said the people felt insulted and were deeply resentful of the two policies: "The CPF proposal suggested that people could not be trusted to look after their own money even in old age. The graduate mothers policy ... implied that not every citizen's child would be equally talented or valued, and worse, that parents too were not equal."

Lee, seemingly unfazed by all the fuss, did not stop at two.

In the second half of the year, he proposed that parliament be allowed to have three non-constituency MPs if no opposition candidate won in a general election. These MP seats would be offered to contestants who had failed to win the election but garnered the highest votes in the opposition camp. They could debate freely in parliament but not vote on critical matters. Critics saw it as a salve to the younger electorate's wish for some opposition presence in the House to check PAP.

He also mooted the idea of an elected president whose principal task would be to safeguard the nation's reserves from future governments that might be tempted to dip into them for all the wrong reasons. Under the constitution, the government appointed the president whose role was largely a ceremonial one.

"It was a long list of new ideas for the electorate to digest," the post-mortem report said.

The report was also candid in its admission that the PAP's election strategy was wrong. The party had planned to take the high ground, focus on long-term issues and ignore the controversies that had been stirred up by the slew of policy changes during the year.

In an article published in *The Straits Times* after the general election, political commentator Chan Heng Chee of the National University of Singapore said: "Harsh and unpopular policies introduced in the context of immediate threats to economic survival such as measures deemed necessary after separation from Malaysia and the withdrawal of British troops were better understood and borne with. The population as a whole has been much less swayed by the necessity of controversial measures to ensure the continued development, prosperity and stability of Singapore in the twenty-first century."

The opposition appeared to have understood this well and to have gauged correctly that the people's anger and resentment had not been defused by the time the election was held. It tapped into that latent disaffection and exploited it to good effect in the nine days of campaigning.

Pushed against the ropes and put on the defensive, PAP was forced to beat back the opposition on those very issues that it had originally ignored. But it was a case of too little, too late.

The party had also misread the ground although the second-generation leaders had spent three years tilling it after the loss of the Anson seat in 1981. Their constituency walkabouts had been too well stage-managed by local grassroots leaders who were eager to bear only the good news, the report said.

Its nerve network of party branches, citizens' consultative committees, community centre management committees and residents' committees was no longer the effective feedback loop that the leadership thought it was. The branches, dormant outfits that came to life only during elections, had to be reinvigorated and new members had to be encouraged to staff them. They had to also consciously campaign for the party even during the non-election years.

The post-mortem team also found that the mass media, though supportive of the government, did it no favours. Instead, in overplaying PAP, the print media created doubts and disbelief among the voters. Their emphasis on the defects and deficiencies of the opposition helped stir up more sympathy for the opposition rather than hurt them. And voters were indifferent to the party broadcast and the daily press conferences at the party headquarters.

Ang Peng Hwa, dean of the School of Communication and Information at the Nanyang Technological University, agreed that the approach that the newspapers took during the run up to the election was "too obviously 'pro' the ruling party". "It hurt the papers' credibility as well as the PAP's," he said.

At the time, Ang was a young reporter at the newly launched afternoon daily, *The Singapore Monitor* (now defunct), and was part of the team covering the election. He remembered: "The circulation of *The Singapore Monitor* was climbing steadily before the GE. But after the event, it plunged. Readers were perceptive."

⚜

To Win Anew the Right to Rule

A pertinent point made in the post-mortem report was that the right to rule had not been transferred automatically from the Old Guard to the New. It was probably not transferable.

"The most important priority of the new leadership must be to establish a close rapport with the people, to win the right to rule," it said.

First, the party had to revamp its image. People had come to see it as arrogant and unfeeling. It did not understand the problems of the less fortunate and showed no compassion for them.

PAP also had to change its purely rational approach towards selling its policies. People needed to be engaged emotionally. Logic alone was not enough to win them over. The party had to stop harping on the quality of its candidates as it only reinforced the perception that its super-achievers were too removed from the ground and had no feel for the common man.

"The PAP must find some visible way to demonstrate that it has ordinary people in its inner circle and for people to identify themselves with the candidates even though the candidates are not poor or ill-educated," the report said.

Feedback and later on, EQ (or emotional quotient) would become buzz words as the party, led by Goh Chok Tong, developed a more consultative style of governance.

Although the party had always maintained a low profile, the wide range of essential services that the PAP government provided such as the day-to-day maintenance of HDB estates had made it omnipresent in people's lives. "The government must do less, rather than more, for the people" was the report's recommendation. Most significantly, the report accepted that "the opposition is here to stay". The conjunction of events that made possible the high degree of consensus in the first generation was unlikely to repeat itself, it pointed out.

In and out of parliament, PAP had to engage its opponents in ways different from those of the past. The party's objective was to maintain a large and stable majority for PAP rather than to eliminate the opposition altogether.

⁕

IT had been the practice of PAP to begin introducing its new candidates for a general election a month or two before the event. Parliament would be dissolved and two weeks or 10 days before nomination day, the respective dates for nomination and election would be announced.

For the 1984 general election, however, Lee Kuan Yew gave a full year's notice.

There were several reasons for the long notice, he told his audience at a rally. Chief among them was that the year-long process "would be political initiation for the post-Malaysia generation, the under-30s, the generation that has not personally experienced strife and deprivation". It would be "the education of a whole generation of young voters", he said.

Lee achieved his goal at some cost to the party. But more than that, he succeeded in jolting a population out of its comfort zone. It was an apathetic population that believed that the PAP government would take care of its every need even as it chafed at the restraints.

Looking back some 20 years later, Lee said that there was method in the way he shook up the electorate. He was certainly not playing brinkmanship, as was suggested by Chan Heng Chee in her 1985 article in *The Straits Times*.

Lee said: "The percentage could go down but we could not lose. And even if we were to lose, how many seats could we lose? Not many. The position is not one of just happiness as we go along, up and up and up. Every now and then, it's a bumpy ride. Put your seat belts on. Turbulence. That's life."

It was a lesson that the younger generation had to learn.

More importantly, Lee thought it was necessary to have a proper shake-up before the handover "so all the weaknesses, all the potential anti-votes, could be identified".

The anti-communist phase was ending. The communists and their supporters had been resettled and although for some years they still voted against PAP, the antipathy had largely dissolved. Their children had grown up and were doing well.

But new problems were cropping up. As Lee elaborated: "One phase had ended where we met an economic and social problem of inequality because of lack of opportunities. But we have created a new problem of equal opportunities but not equal results. So this had got to be defined so that people would understand it."

The meritocratic system had led to a new divide in society, not by wealth but by ability. There were winners and losers. The less able could be resentful and vote against PAP. The new leaders had to be made to see this. They had to attend to the less able without resorting to the kind of welfare policies that had debilitated the workforce in once-successful economies like Germany and France.

So 1984 was indeed a turning point. The post-mortem report, besides being a signpost, would also serve as a roadmap for PAP in the 1990s.

21

The Foundation Years

When Deng Came to Town

A joke that made the rounds of the *kopitiam*, or coffee-shops, during Deng Xiaoping's three-day visit to Singapore in November 1978 was that he was taken to view the Chinese Gardens in Jurong, which was modelled after the Summer Palace in Beijing.

It was not true, of course. But Deng did visit Jurong, which was a showcase of Singapore's industrial programme. At the Jurong Town Corporation (JTC) offices, its chairman Teh Cheang Wan briefed him on the programme—its difficult initial years, its eventual take-off in the late 1960s and its move from labour-intensive to higher-technology industries in the mid-1970s.

When it came to recreation amenities in the Jurong industrial estate, Teh highlighted the Chinese Gardens. It was popular among Singaporeans who could not afford to go to Beijing to enjoy the real thing, he said, which drew laughter from Deng's delegation.

The centrepiece of the Summer Palace in Beijing is a marble boat built by the Manchu Empress Dowager Cixi. At the Chinese Gardens in Jurong, the replica was cast in concrete. "Stone would have been too expensive," Teh had said.

It was a small detail but the obvious attention paid to costs and the thoughtful provision of recreation amenities in an industrial estate, such as gardens, a zoo and a bird park—which his wife Cho Lin visited—would not have escaped Deng, then the senior vice premier of China.

In Singapore, Deng also saw for himself the success of the public housing programme. From the window of his car, as he was being ferried from one appointment to another, he would have noticed the Housing and Development (HDB) blocks which dominated the skyline. Almost 70 per cent of the population lived in HDB flats. Less than 20 years earlier, most of the people were living in crowded slums in the city centre and scruffy squatter clusters on the fringes of the city.

At the HDB headquarters in Maxwell Road, after a briefing by the board's chairman Michael Fam, the Chinese leader could not stop asking questions: What were the utility charges for a three-room HDB flat? Did residents have to pay for the maintenance of lifts?

The small country's great leap forward in so short a time would have impressed him. After its independence in 1965, Singapore's gross domestic product recorded double-digit growth from 1966 to 1973. Growth rates dipped in 1974 and 1975 following the global oil shock and subsequently recovered to 8.5 per cent in 1978. Per capita gross domestic product rose from $1,567 in 1965 to $7,581 in 1978. Foreign direct investment rose from $1,398.3 million in 1970 to $4,649.5 million in 1975 and to more than $11,200 million in 1980.

Prime Minister Lee Kuan Yew had welcomed Deng at the Paya Lebar airport. A picture taken at the airport shows the 74-year-old leader looking stout in his Mao jacket as he shakes Lee's hand. He was short, coming up to only Lee's shoulders. They had talks over two sessions at the Istana where Deng and his wife stayed.

The visit might have been brief but the Chinese leader left Singapore with deeply etched impressions. A year later in China, when Deng told his officials that China needed to have foreign investment to play catch-up with the developed world, he related what he had seen in the small city-state: "Singapore benefited from factories set up by foreigners in Singapore. First, foreign enterprise paid 35 per cent of their net profits in taxes which went to the state; second, labour income went to the workers; and third, foreign investment generated the service sectors. All these were income for the state."

Fourteen years later, in his historic *nanxun*, or southern tour, to Wuhan, Shenzhen, Zuhai and Shanghai, Deng would cite the city-state's "good social order" in his speeches. "They govern the place with discipline. We should draw from their experience and do even better than them," he said.

A stream of Chinese officials would afterwards pour into Singapore every year to study its various government programmes.

Deng's endorsement of Singapore was the best kind of accolade that the first-generation PAP leaders could have. After all, China was behind the communists against whom PAP was fighting in the 1950s and 1960s.

DENG Xiaoping's visit to Singapore, the last stop in a three-nation swing which included Thailand and Malaysia, came less than two years after he wrested control of the Chinese Communist Party (CCP) and the state from an extremist group led by Mao Zedong's fourth wife Jiang Qing. Mao had died in September 1976.

By the time he came to Singapore, Deng had, in effect, begun playing the leadership role, although nominally. Mao's designated successor Hua Guofeng was still chairman of the party and the country's premier. The former head of security was eventually eased out in 1981.

In the 10 years before Deng seized control at the helm, while Singapore and the other "East Asian Tigers" (South Korea, Taiwan and Hong Kong) enjoyed explosive growth, China was mired in nationwide chaos and convulsions. To hold on to his power, Mao, a lion in winter, had launched what he called a cultural revolution and set loose the country's young on a costly, destructive rampage.

Deng himself had been purged twice during the revolution. In Singapore, as he took in the city-state's achievements, he must have felt even more keenly the urgency to repair the damage wrought by the follies of Mao and put China on the path of growth.

Lee had posed him a challenge before his departure. There was nothing that Singapore had done that China could not do or do better, he said. After all, the majority of Singaporeans were ethnic Chinese, the descendants of largely illiterate peasants from southern China who had sailed down to the Nanyang more than 100 years ago.

The Cultural Revolution had its repercussions beyond the Great Wall. It frightened a number of multinational firms that had just begun their Asian operations in South Korea, Taiwan and Hong Kong. At the time, silicon chips and semi-conductors had just been developed and because their assembly was labour-intensive, electronics companies had looked to Asia where labour was cheap to set up their assembly plants. But now they found that their operations were too close to China. What if the chaos were to spill over the Great Wall? As they cast around for another spot that was farther away to relocate their factories, Singapore went to them to make its pitch as a choice location complete with generous tax incentives.

As Lee's ablest lieutenant Goh Keng Swee recounted in an interview in 1982 that was never released: "During that period (between 1968 and 1970) ... we had large numbers of genuine interest as against the casual application. When a company sent its number one man, like Rollei or Bell

& Howell did, then you knew they were very disturbed."

Goh, in his second stint as finance minister, felt confident enough at last that Singapore would succeed in its economic take-off. In his first stint, between 1959 and 1965, there was no economic growth to speak of, he said, although some infrastructure was laid down.

So confident was he that in a speech in 1970, the year before the British ran down their bases in Singapore and withdrew their troops, he predicted that Singapore's per capita GNP would overtake Britain's before the end of the decade. There would also be a desperate shortage of workers and many would have to be imported from neighbouring Malaysia, he said.

⚬⚬⚬⚬

Right Bets and Tough Calls

THE turbulence in China presented an opportunity to Singapore and the PAP leaders were quick to seize it. MNCs came to set up their plants on the island. In less than four years, they had filled up Jurong and the other industrial estates and helped solve Singapore's unemployment problem. A labour shortage became the new problem. Malaysian workers made a beeline across the Singapore-Malaysia causeway to work in factories in Singapore.

Goh's confidence was not misplaced after all. He had taken a bet and it proved to be a winner. It was one among many winning bets which the PAP leaders took in the early years of nationhood and for at least the two decades when the party had dominant rule, the people were willing to throw in their chips with them.

Independent Singapore succeeded where many others had failed. Many former colonies in Asia and Africa found themselves floundering after they had gained independence. Although their failures could be attributed to a number of causes, the absence of strong leadership was always the principal reason.

In most instances, the early decisions taken by leaders on how they would govern their newly sovereign states were crucial to their subsequent success or failure. Equally important was the execution of the leaders' visions and here too, many states tripped up. The grandest vision remains a vision if it is not carried through. Execution requires effort, political will and the participation of the people even when it can mean some pain to them in the short term.

In Singapore's case, the PAP leaders were practical men who made their bets grounded in reality. They did not allow themselves to be held hostage by the fancy economic theories of well-intentioned development experts and were not afraid to go against the current of the times.

In the early post-empire days, for example, it was not politically correct, especially when one claimed to be a democratic socialist, to woo MNCs to set up factories in one's country. To do so was to exchange one set of colonial exploiters for another, as most former colonies saw it, and the people would be oppressed again.

Influential development economists at the time pronounced that the era of export-led growth was over and that trade could not be an engine for growth for developing countries. Countries should instead produce the goods that they had been importing from the West to end their dependence on the developed countries. The jargon for it was "import substitution".

Goh, himself a trained economist from the London School of Economics, had a healthy scepticism of academic experts who presumed to direct the growth of developing countries from the commanding heights of their ivory towers when they had little or no practical ground experience to speak of. He said in a 1966 speech: "If I may be so presumptuous as to give advice to others ... I would ask them to throw away all the books published on economic growth since World War II."

By the 1970s, import substitution as an economic strategy for developing countries had proven to be a failure.

Lee and Goh trusted the judgement though of one trained expert—the Dutch economist Albert Winsemius who was first sent to Singapore in 1960 as the leader of a United Nations Development Programme mission. He would play a pivotal role as Singapore's economic adviser for more than two decades, until 1984.

Goh had always been seen as the architect of Singapore's economic success. But in the 1982 interview, he said Lee's contribution to Singapore's economic growth had not been generally understood. When it was clear that the island's entrepôt trade would not be enough to support a nation of two million people and that it had to industrialise, it was Lee who thought up the strategy of drawing the MNCs.

Singapore would never have that broad industrial base which larger territories like Taiwan, South Korea or even Hong Kong, with China as the hinterland, had. The MNCs, however, would bring with them their international markets. Singapore could also benefit from the transfer of technological know-how from the foreign engineers and managers to the local people.

When Goh made his prediction that Singapore would be desperately short of workers, it was Lee who saw immediately how the situation would lead to a rise in workers' wages. It would be relatively painless, then, for the workers to put more money into the CPF, the government-managed pension scheme, as their wages rose.

"So between us," Goh said, "we worked out a scheme whereby CPF contributions increased as wages increased."

A large sum of real savings was thus built up. Loans from these savings at low interest rates were used to build the necessary infrastructure to support an industrialised economy. Without it, MNCs could not operate in Singapore. The Chinese have a saying, *zao chao yin feng*. To attract the phoenix, one has to build a nest. And that requires capital investment.

Lee had a hand too in restructuring industry in the mid-1970s towards the direction of higher skills. The switch from lower to higher technology industries pushed up wages and phased out the less efficient industries which could not afford the new wages. The MNCs moved their labour-intensive operations to Malaysia and Thailand where labour was cheaper but kept their regional head offices and high-end plants in Singapore.

Goh said of Lee: "He sees problems with long-range implications and has a deeper grasp of what has to be done, both to forestall problems as well as to get things going."

Yet, Goh's own contribution to the building of independent Singapore was much more than that of a deputy prime minister. It was encompassing. One finds his fingerprints in almost every area: defence, finance, industry, science and technology, education. They are also in the 'soft' areas: the Singapore Symphony Orchestra, a world-class zoo and bird park. For a while, he also had an all-girl bagpipe band, which livened up the annual national day parade.

And there was a dream team—Toh Chin Chye, E W Barker, Lim Kim San, S Rajaratnam, Ong Pang Boon, Devan Nair and Othman Wok. Hon Sui Sen crossed over from the civil service to join them. These men were fighters but most of them were also able administrators, each gifted in his own way. They were their own men but they kept a united front.

"We learnt that from the communists," said Toh. "You challenged PAP, and there was always 'a formidable core' you had to take on."

THE PAP leaders made another winning bet when they chose to retain the language of their former colonial masters. To this day, English remains the medium of communication in science and technology and international commerce. It is also a neutral medium that holds the different ethnic groups together.

Several former British colonies had thrown out English in a grand gesture of nationalist pride. But when they did so, they locked out their future generations of citizens from the larger world where English was the main language. It was sad, more so if the crucial decision was taken by leaders who had had themselves the benefit of a modern education in the developed west but who, upon their return to their homeland, chose to go native to pander to populist sentiment.

Typically, revolutionary leaders who fought against empire came from the elite class in their societies and more likely than not, had the advantage of being educated in the west.

There were also those who did not go native but who made the other common mistake of mimicry. They tried to transplant into their own less developed countries, the modern ideas and social attitudes that they had absorbed abroad without recognising that they had come from a small privileged class and that the larger population outside of their class, in rural countries especially, was still held down by age-old traditions and superstitions. The new social attitudes of a modern industrial society, you cannot impose on a custom-bound people overnight, and when you dismantle their traditions at the same time, you inevitably create a new class of dispossessed people.

Goh Keng Swee had observed: "Modern ideas of liberalism, egalitarian ideals, welfare state concepts ... all these are appropriate in an affluent society, but are largely irrelevant to a nation struggling to escape age-old poverty ... These concepts encourage a propensity to laziness and inaction, inculcate a belief that society owes every man a comfortable living and proliferate trade unions whose main purpose is to get more pay for less work."

The revolutionary Indian leader Jawaharlal Nehru was one who subscribed to the noble ideals of democracy and socialism. He believed a modern India could be built on moral principles and he clung stubbornly to the idea that the country should be self-sufficient and not rely on imported goods.

As it turned out, the system which he had set up in the name of the poor in the end did very little for them, even after many years following his death. In the year 2000, half of the people in India were poor by the international standard of US$1 a day and a third of the world's poor were in India. Four out of 10 Indians were illiterate. In 1960, India's per capita income was higher than China's. In 2000, at US$450, it was half its neighbour's.

The Indian writer Gurcharan Das records in his much-lauded book, *India Unbound* (2000): "Democratic institutions were set up before we had the chance to create an industrial revolution ... We set up intricate regulatory networks before the private economy had transformed a rural society into an industrial one. We began to think in terms of welfare before there were welfare-generating jobs ... In a sense, we tried to redistribute the pie before it was baked. The result, as we have seen, was a throttling of enterprise, slow growth, missed opportunities."

Nehru occupied the imagination of a whole generation of Indians— which Indian of a certain age could forget his historic 1947 independence speech?—and it was not until 1991 that P V Narasimha Rao could overturn his policies and begin sweeping liberalisation. At the time, India was in a financial hole and faced pressures to reform from the International Monetary Fund and the World Bank in exchange for a bailout package.

Rao, seen widely as a "stop-gap leader" following the assassination of Rajiv Gandhi, seized the opportunity to unleash what was the biggest revolution since 1947—turning his Congress Party's 40-year socialist legacy on its head.

Sadly, while he had the administrative ability, the elderly premier—he was 70 when he took over the hot seat—lacked the stamina and political will to sustain the reforms. By 1994, when the crisis receded and pressures to reform eased, all the entrenched politicians and bureaucrats who had vested interests in the old ways were quick to pull the brakes on liberalisation.

Rao lost the election in 1996 because of a corruption scandal. The Bharatiya Janata Party (BJP), which succeeded Congress, continued with the reforms and the country enjoyed considerable growth. The fruits, however, went largely to the educated in the cities and not enough attention was paid to the rural poor, who still formed the majority of the population.

Political pundits who had been impressed by the growth in cities like New Delhi, Mumbai and Bangalore were shocked when the BJP was voted out in the May 2004 election. Sonia Gandhi's Congress Party, which had worked hard to cultivate the rural communities outside of the key cities, formed the new coalition government. Sonia, the Italian-born widow of Rajiv, knew only too well that she would never be wholly accepted by the people of India and had the smarts to make Manmohan Singh, the economist who had been the driving force behind Rao's reform, the prime minister.

Four years into the new millennium, India looked set to become a world power, like its neighbour, China. But so many years and so many opportunities had been lost.

Certainly, one cannot measure Singapore's achievements against the more apparent failure of a huge and complex country like India. Yet, there were things that the PAP leaders had done right which India had lately seen fit to learn, just as China had by sending its officials to study Singapore.

Nehru was an inspiration to Lee. Like him, Lee too came from the elite class in Singapore and had his university education in England. But perhaps he was of a more practical bent; he was not burdened with high idealism, unlike Nehru. Also, as the country came into independence almost two decades later, Lee was able to learn from the mistakes that the Indian leader and others had made.

Sociologist Kwok Kian Woon of the Nanyang Technological University observed: "I don't see a great deal of idealism in Lee Kuan Yew and the party—idealism in the sense of very, very deep and profound human values. They were professionals out there who wanted to get the job done, they were very realistic about things and they knew that whatever one said about equality and democracy, some things had to be put in place."

Veteran opposition leader Chiam See Tong acknowledged that PAP had achieved much for Singapore. One of its weaknesses, though, he said, was that while it catered to the broad base of people, it generally did not do enough for the small minority at the bottom of society.

Said Chiam, a devout Christian whose grandfather and father were both pastors: "PAP is too business-like in its policies, rather than human. As Jesus Christ said, even if it is only one lamb that has been lost somewhere, as a good and caring shepherd, you will go and look for that single lost lamb and bring it back to the fold."

Chiam was talking about the realm of the soul, where saints rule. In the concrete here and now, political rulers in democratic systems work to serve the larger good. There will always be a small minority who, for whatever reasons, feel that their needs are not served. They are the ones who consistently cast their votes against PAP, no matter who the opposition is.

The PAP government, more pragmatic than pious, would say that it had always had various schemes that served as safety nets for those who had fallen between the cracks. It did not, and could not, neglect the bottom segment because it knew that a small society like Singapore could ill afford a disgruntled underclass.

Noble ideals of deep and profound human values are all very well and good. But when these ideals are not translated into positive results for the population at large, as in the case of Nehru's India, they breed cynicism, which eats away the soul rather than nourishes it.

If the first-generation PAP leaders were not driven by the kind of idealism Kwok spoke about, they were, however, not unlike an order of priesthood, given their austere ways and full commitment to the country.

When Lee Kuan Yew took office in 1959, he made it clear that the PAP government would not tolerate corruption, a practice common in Asian countries. No one was above being investigated for corruption and when found guilty, he would be duly punished no matter how loyal he had been to the party or government. Lee placed the Corrupt Practices Investigation Bureau directly under the charge of the Prime Minister's Office (PMO).

Teh Cheang Wan, the JTC chairman who briefed Deng in Jurong, was probed for corruption in 1986 when he was minister for national development, a post he had held since 1979 after winning a by-election on a PAP ticket. He was accused of taking bribes from a property developer. When the investigations led to his suicide in December 1986, it became one of the most high-profile corruption cases in Singapore. It was also one of the most intensely scrutinised. A commission of inquiry into the case was formed after Chiam See Tong had asked for one in parliament.

Wee Toon Boon, an old party faithful and a minister of state, and Phey Yew Kok, an MP and a leader of the National Trades Union Congress, were two other casualties. Wee was jailed. Phey fled the country.

It was a testimony to the system Lee had set up that he himself, together with his son Lee Hsien Loong, then deputy prime minister, were the subjects of a corruption probe ordered by his successor Goh Chok Tong in 1995. They had enjoyed discounts for the purchase of two properties each. The investigations showed there was nothing improper in the 5 to 7 per cent discounts that developers generally gave to selected "early bird" buyers to test the market.

Lee asked for the case to be given an airing in parliament and to also be covered live on television. There were older viewers who found the proceedings painful to watch. For them, this was a man who had led in the building of a wealthy Singapore and here he was being held to account for a few hundred thousand dollars that he had gained from a legitimate discount. Nowhere in Asia could one see a spectacle quite like it. But then, Lee would not have it any other way.

⤜❧⤛

Singapore Reloaded

LEADERS can make all the right bets and tough calls, and yet, a country can still fail to perform. This can happen when there is a lack of attention to details and ideas get lost as they are delegated down the chain of command. The ball is passed—then someone sits on it.

In an essay titled "What Slows Us Down?", Gurcharan Das argues: "It is the unhappy inability to translate thought into action that afflicts our public life with devastating consequences. Nehruvian socialism need not have deteriorated into licence raj had our civil servants possessed better management skills ... East Asia grew twice as rapidly as India between 1965 and 1985, not only because of better strategy, but because of better execution..."

When it came to execution, the first-generation PAP government was ably supported by a small corps of top civil servants who had been trained under the previous British administration. This group of men was fired up by the vision of their new leaders and saw in their work a mission. "We wanted to be the masters of our own destiny," as one of them, Sim Kee Boon, said.

They worked closely with their political masters but were content to remain largely faceless, even as they took on one daunting task after another. Yet, they were not your "yes, minister" types. They were not afraid to stand up to their bosses or make tough calls themselves.

Sim was a good example. When he retired as head of the civil service in 1984, Lee Kuan Yew sent him over to Keppel Shipyard to save it from sinking. Then a government-linked outfit, the shipyard had used up an enormous amount of funds the previous year to buy up another company in a move to diversify its business. But the timing could not have been more wrong. It coincided with a severe downturn in the ship-repair industry and a full-blown recession.

McKinsey, the consulting firm to which the government paid $1 million to study the ship-repair industry in Singapore, recommended in its report that Keppel be merged with another shipyard, Jurong. The ship-repair business was pronounced a "sunset industry".

But Sim took a tough call and went against McKinsey's merger recommendation. He trimmed Keppel's sails and cut down on its crew. The western financial media practically buried him for his action but in less than two years, he had turned Keppel around. With Sim at the helm, Keppel would go on to become a Singapore company with a global reach.

A lot was at stake but in having the confidence to act based on his own judgment and not on advice dished out by expensive experts who could be a convenient scapegoat should things go wrong, Sim showed he had what John Maynard Keynes called "animal spirits".

J Y Pillay, best known as the man behind Singapore Airlines, was another illustrious example. He was the deputy secretary of the Economic Planning Unit in the mid-1960s when he sent a promising young officer Goh Chok Tong for a master's degree course at Williams College in Massachusetts in the United States. Upon Goh's return, prime minister Lee tried to poach him to work as his principal private secretary.

But Pillay did not invest a costly year in Goh just so he could end up in the PMO. He went to see his boss Lim Kim San, then-minister for finance, who persuaded Lee to let Goh serve in the Economic Planning Unit.

Both J Y Pillay and Sim Kee Boon were blooded in the early to mid-1960s, especially during the years when Singapore was part of Malaysia. "Every day was a crisis day" was how Sim remembered that time.

So in 1968, when Pillay was tasked to help Hon Sui Sen manage the pullout of the British troops, the 34-year-old took it in his stride.

Singapore was the main logistics base of the British Far East Command whose operations stretched from the east coast of Africa to the farther reaches of the Pacific Ocean. Four main bases that amounted to 10 per cent of the land were set up on the island. Spending by British troops was as high as $500 million a year, or about 20 per cent of Singapore's GDP. These bases remained even after Singapore ceased to be a colony.

But by the mid-1960s, it was clear that Britain could no longer afford to keep even the last vestiges of its imperial power out in the Far East. The British economy was faltering and its sterling was under attack. Its taxpayers who had endured the post-war privations of the 1950s now wanted public money to be spent on their own welfare, the people of former colonies be damned.

In 1967, the British Labour government released a Defence White Paper announcing the rundown of its bases in Malaysia and Singapore. No exact dates were set but the British indicated that they would withdraw half of the 26,000 troops based in Singapore by March 1971 and the rest by 1975.

Singapore thus faced the prospect of losing about 20 per cent of its GDP. Lee Kuan Yew made several frantic trips to London to try to fight to keep the bases but to no avail. He was not too worried about the economic fallout; after all, he had nine years to work to cushion it. What worried him more was how Singapore was going to defend itself.

The presence of British troops was vital to the country's industrialisation plan. It would serve to reassure foreign investors, especially when there was a war going on in Vietnam and neighbouring Indonesia had just recently ceased its hostile confrontation.

But as Lee and his ministers made preparations for the base rundown by 1975, they were delivered a rude shock in January 1968—the date for the complete pullout of the British forces had been pushed forward to 1971.

The economic fallout would now be immediate. Besides the loss of income, the spectre of massive unemployment, which PAP had tackled since it took over in 1959, loomed large again. About 70,000 people who worked directly or indirectly for the British would lose their jobs. On top of this number, there was the annual stream of 25,000 school-leavers who would require jobs.

It was, as Lee described it then, "a matter of life and death". He called for an early election in February to have a new mandate from the people to push through a number of defence and economic policies that would ensure industrial stability and bring in the MNCs more quickly.

After he had the mandate—PAP won all 58 seats—Lee moved the Employment Bill and had the Industrial Relations Ordinance amended to make the interests of the unions subordinate to national ones. Disruptive strikes were outlawed although workers' rights would be protected and there would be no sweatshops. What Lee wanted was a harmonious industrial climate and a workforce that was disciplined, efficient and productive.

At the same time, he created a Bases Economic Conversion Department (BECD), headed by Hon Sui Sen, to negotiate the terms of handover with the British. Hon picked two deputies—JY Pillay, to handle economic matters and K P R Chandra, who was in the land office of the Ministry of Law, to work out the allocation of the British-owned land.

Three decades later, in his office in the Singapore Exchange Limited where he was the chairman, Pillay spoke about the period: "It was just three years after separation and that was already a blow to our hopes of establishing a common market, a free trade area with Malaysia. Then, we had to build up our military forces which meant greater expenditure.

"At the same time, the economy was still sputtering. Our effort to bring the multinationals into Singapore was accelerating but hadn't produced too many results at that stage. The international financial sector had not made the mark until 1969, 1970 ... So it's not surprising that the mood was grim."

Together with Hon, the young civil servant sat down at the negotiating table with the British and got them to agree to a £50 million payout— 25 per cent in grants and the remaining 75 per cent in interest-free loans. "Fifty million pounds by today's exchange rates is $150 million. In those days, £50 million would have been about $300 million to $400 million. That's a lot of money in the context of our budget," Pillay said.

The retrenched civilian workers in the bases received more than adequate compensation. About 8,000 non-citizens, mainly Indians and Malaysians, were able to return home. There were also those who could afford to retire. The rest of the workers were reabsorbed by the new commercial entities created by the BECD in the former bases, such as Sembawang Shipyard.

"So things turned out reasonably well. Our aspirations, our ambitions were not so great," Pillay said. "Looking back, it didn't seem like they were very major initiatives. But at that time, they were relevant, they were pertinent, they were large in relation to what else was going on [here]."

He added: "The economy started to pick up towards the end of the 60s. So the great concerns that the government had in 1967 and 1968 about the devastating impact of the withdrawal on our economy and the loss of British military protection did not eventuate. We were fortunate and I suppose we carried out more or less the right policies."

The Financial Times in London was not as understated in its assessment of the city-state's performance. It said in a commentary: "Singapore's response to the withdrawal can be seen in retrospect as one of the most striking achievements by any developing country in recent history."

For someone like E M Sundaram, who had worked for 20 years as a motor mechanic charge hand in the British naval dockyards, the whole bases rundown episode seemed almost a non-event. When the dockyards were converted into Sembawang Shipyard, he was made a foreman, a job he retained till he retired 10 years later.

What had been more eventful for Sundaram was his fight against fellow leaders in the Naval Base Labour Union in 1963. The union, which was controlled by the Barisan Sosialis, led a strike that year. Sundaram had refused to take part in it and had actually formed a committee to fight against it. He lost many friends as a result but as an active PAP grassroots leader in Sembawang since 1960, he had seen how the people's needs were better served by constructive work carried out by the ruling party than by the destructive actions of the communists.

Sundaram would serve PAP as a cadre member for almost four decades until his retirement in 1997. The father of eight was a veteran of seven elections where he volunteered as party organiser, election agent and counting agent.

In 2003, in his four-room HDB flat in Yishun Ring Road which he had lived in since 1982, the 74-year-old proudly displayed his Long Service Gold Award that PAP had bestowed on him. He also had the PBM (*pingat bakti masyarakat*) and the BBM (*bintang bakti masyarakat*) medals—public service medals and stars respectively—to show. These were given by the government, usually on National Day, to those who had contributed to the people of Singapore or the grassroots.

⁓⊙⁓

THE accelerated British pullout was not without its blessings. It forced Goh Keng Swee who was then building up the armed forces to speed up the pace. It also drove him to build an air force in double quick time. He told *The Straits Times* a few years later: "It really scared me. When we started MINDEF (Ministry of Defence) in 1965, the British were still there. We thought we had plenty of time ... But in 1967, they were going to withdraw and that gave urgency to the build-up of the SAF (Singapore

Armed Forces). In 1968, they said they were going to withdraw in three years and it really scared us. What was necessary then was to build up an air force as fast as we could..."

On the economic front, Goh launched a $900 million stimulus package to prevent a recession which could come with the pullout. The money was used to build defence, public housing and infrastructure in the three years from 1968 to 1971.

To create demand for public housing, Lee and Goh moved, in 1968, a Bill to allow the people to use their CPF savings to buy HDB flats. It put the flats within the reach of most people and there was practically a stampede for them. The Housing and Development Board, which was formed in 1960 and which had built some 90,000 flats by 1968, stepped up its construction programme. It built more than 150,000 flats between 1968 and 1975.

By 1978, when Deng Xiaoping came to Singapore, the HDB had built almost half a million flats, housing about 70 per cent of the population.

The round-the-clock building of public housing, factories, roads, drains and parks transformed the island. The slums and *attap* hut kampungs of the colonial days had largely disappeared. Up in the sky, there were hauling cranes everywhere one looked which the *kopitiam* wags hailed as the national bird. When silhouetted against a rising or setting sun, they made a poetic sight, an emblem of the modernisation of Singapore.

It was a case of Singapore reloaded. Lee had delivered on the promise he had made before the 1968 general election: "There will be nobody, whether in 1969, 1970, 1971 or 1972, sleeping on pavements, doing their ablutions by the drain and raising their families on the five-foot-ways of Singapore. We are going to keep this the cleanest, brightest, greenest city on the equatorial belt."

Although it meant a better quality of life for the people, still the initial change was wrenching and dislocating for some, especially the older and rural folks.

Under the British, the different racial communities—and even the different dialect groups among the Chinese—lived in separate enclaves. Moving into the high-rise HDB blocks, they lost the security and familiarity of their old neighbours and had to get along with new neighbours of other races and dialect groups. They had to learn to cultivate a new social attitude to cope with the demands of a modern industrial city.

But old habits die hard. There were those, for instance, who persisted in urinating in the public lifts for many years even after laws had been passed to penalise such behaviour. In the end, security cameras had to be installed to catch culprits in their act.

Also, when people were allowed to sell their flats and buy new ones, the different races, which had been shuffled, began to regroup again. The HDB had to set a racial quota system for every block of flats to encourage multiracial living.

In the earlier days of the HDB, MPs on the ground had to do much persuading and cajoling to get kampung folks and those in the rural areas to resettle. The tightly knit Malay community especially found it hard to move into the new HDB high-rises. It did not help that during the years when Singapore was part of Malaysia, political leaders from across the Singapore-Malaysia Causeway had come down and told the Malays that it was against their culture to live in what they called pigeonholes. Guard your kampung homes with your lives, they had exhorted.

Othman Wok, a Malay himself and then-minister for social affairs, played a critical role in resettling the community. He first got the Division 3 and Division 4 Malay public servants, who were living in free government quarters, to move into the HDB flats. Word of mouth soon got around that HDB living was not so bad after all. You had your own water supply, electricity and privacy.

HDB living became so popular that the Malay political party UMNO formed a cooperative and got the HDB to build three blocks of flats for it in Geylang Serai, the heart of the Malay settlement.

Another sensitive problem cropped up when old, dilapidated mosques and *suraus*, or small mosques, had to be demolished for urban development. Unlike the case of other races, the identity of the Malays was very much tied up with Islam, their religion. The mosque was the centre of their daily lives.

After sitting down with Othman to discuss it, Lee decided that a piece of land would be reserved for the building of a mosque in every new HDB estate. It would be sold to mosque leaders at market price. A Mosque Building Fund was set up and all Muslims were encouraged to donate a small sum to it from their monthly CPF contributions.

It was not necessary to make such a provision for the building of churches and Chinese and Indian temples. Those who wished to build them had to tender for the land.

SINGAPORE'S public housing programme is clearly one of PAP's supreme achievements. It is not surprising that Deng Xiaoping had shown so much interest in it back in 1978. He had also obviously seen in Singapore a model for his dream of a revitalised, twenty-first-century China.

22

Party Shake-up: Guerilla Outfits Dismantled

Lee's Task Force

AFTER PAP had won the fight to govern Singapore, the party took a back seat, as it were, as its top leaders engaged themselves fully in the building of the new nation.

As far as the people were concerned, there was no division between party and government. The ruling party was the government, or *cheng hu* in Hokkien.

The people went to the *cheng hu* only when they needed help with their housing or a job or arbitration in a neighbourhood dispute. They would go to the PAP branch office in their constituency, usually situated on the ground floor of an HDB block, and petition the member of parliament when he held his meet-the-people session.

These sessions were—and still are—clinics conducted by MPs once a week in the evening, usually from 7 pm to about midnight. On hand to help the MPs run the sessions were the local grassroots leaders—unpaid volunteers who might or might not be party members.

Except for these weekly sessions, the branches were more or less dormant. The rank and file PAP members in the branches had little say and practically no role at all in party affairs or national politics, except during election time when they would be called upon to mobilise supporters and help in the campaigns.

Old party faithfuls who participated in PAP's early struggles and who still sought fulfilment in grassroots politics had to adapt themselves to the changed environment. Their new duties, such as helping out at their MP's meet-the-people sessions and organising events at the community centres, were more mundane than exciting but no less rewarding if their motivation was to serve the community. They would still get their adrenalin rush, though less frequently, when elections were held.

The shift of power away from the branches was also partly by design. In The Big Split of 1961, when 13 PAP assemblymen defected and formed the Barisan Sosialis, about 20 out of 25 branch organising secretaries and their committees crossed over as well. Before they left, they trashed the offices and destroyed equipment and records. Lee Kuan Yew and his lieutenants would not forget that experience.

In an article in the party's 15th anniversary souvenir magazine in 1969, PAP's ideologue S Rajaratnam put the new party position in perspective: "When a party becomes a ruling party, you should not think of government and party as two separate entities. A party in power is still the same political party. The difference is that its functions have become different.

"Its preoccupation, once in power, is to govern a country ... So if today some of you feel that the party is taking a back seat, it is only so in the sense that our party is no longer performing the functions of a party which is striving to achieve power."

He pointed out that the 1970s would see major changes. A new generation of better educated Singaporeans would take for granted the previous achievements of PAP. The party's new role must be to "attract, recruit and train leaders" from among the young to replace the old who would be "out of touch with the new world they helped to forge".

"The party must become a workshop for forging bold new ideas to meet the requirements of a rapidly changing society and a rapidly changing world…"

He articulated the top leadership's position on the need for self-renewal in the party when he said: "One of the most difficult tasks of politics is not how to acquire power but how to transfer it to a new generation of leaders. More difficult still is for leaders to deliberately create new and able leaders to systematically take over from the older when the time comes."

He urged party members not to "put barriers in the way of able and energetic newcomers who must displace us".

That article was one of the first clear signals to the Old Guard that they had to make way for the new. A year before it was written, PAP had already begun its first major recruitment of talent outside of the party when it fielded a number of PhD holders, academics, professionals and senior administrators in the 1968 general election, which it won by a landslide, thanks to the walkout by the Barisan Sosialis.

In 1970, it pushed out five Old Guard leaders including the only woman MP, Chan Choy Siong, and brought in new men in a by-election. More candidates with better academic qualifications were again introduced in the 1972 general election.

But as it turned out, many of the high flyers who had come in amid much hype and high expectations during this period had their wings singed very quickly. Men with impressive academic credentials like Tan Eng Liang, Singapore's first Rhodes scholar, and Ong Leong Boon, a surgeon and former student leader in the university, took a sharp nose-dive and disappeared before they could even take off. They had barely made their presence felt on the political stage.

There were others whom the party leadership assessed would still be useful on the backbench even though they had failed to make the cut for a cabinet position. Stanford-trained economist Augustine Tan, who was for a while Lee Kuan Yew's political secretary, was one of them. He did not take his lesser duties any less seriously. For two decades, he played a valuable role as an outspoken backbencher and was a widely respected MP in his Whampoa ward.

Lee admitted that PAP did make some mistakes in the early self-renewal process. When he first made the admission to the book's writing team in a meeting in 2003, Mrs Lee, who was by his side, turned to him and said, "You thought the PhDs would do it."

It was one of the few interjections she made at that preliminary meeting. She did so only when her husband's memory of past events needed some jolting. And they could be pithy remarks like the one above. Mrs Lee was, after all, her husband's memory bank. In those early years when he was fighting one crisis after another, Lee certainly did not have the luxury to keep a diary, much less a detailed record. But the woman behind the hard-driving man had a prodigious memory. A lawyer as bright as her husband, she had also helped draft many an important document for both party and government in those years.

When he was writing his two-volume memoirs, Lee tapped on his wife's memory, besides research provided by a small team.

In a later interview, in his office on the second floor of the Istana Annex, Lee explained why he thought initially that PhD holders could fill top leadership positions. He had looked at Toh Chin Chye and Goh Keng Swee, both PhDs, as examples.

"But I had not realised these were unusual PhDs," he said. They had lived through the Japanese Occupation, a traumatic experience that had tested them and brought out other attributes in them. The new generation of PhD recruits had not gone through a similar life-transforming experience.

"And as a general rule, when a man goes to the university to teach and his whole career has been academic, that means he's less interested in the world. He's interested with ideas, words, concepts and the presentation of concepts," he said.

Lee picked his candidates for the 1976 general election more carefully and tested them more rigorously. He settled on 11, among whom were the potential second echelon leaders. These included Goh Chok Tong from Neptune Orient Lines and S Dhanabalan from DBS Bank. They were in their 30s when they were inducted into the party.

He added more high-calibre recruits in the two by-elections in 1977—Bernard Chen and Lim Chee Onn—and a by-election in 1979 that had a slate of seven candidates including Tony Tan from OCBC Bank.

Many of these candidates had proven track records as technocrats. But a criticism made of them by opposition party leaders and critics, even from among the PAP Old Guard, was that they were removed from the ground since they were mainly in the scholar-elite class.

But Lee believed they could learn to connect with the common folks. They just had to be exposed to grassroots politics, with the help of seasoned MPs. So after the 1976 general election, he set up a task force that comprised seven older MPs to help break them in on the ground.

Lee remembered he set up the task force because, with the number of new MPs, "it was getting to be too much work to do myself".

"So I said, 'Okay, get it filtered first.' I asked Hwang Soo Jin and a few others to monitor them, see how they fit in..."

Hwang, the MP for Jalan Kayu, was picked to head the task force mainly because he was effectively bilingual. In those days, most of the grassroots activists were Chinese-educated, while the new cohort of MPs were mainly English-educated.

Hwang had a Chinese school education at Chung Cheng High, then went over to London where he obtained a degree at the Chartered Insurance Institute and stayed on to work in the city for five years before returning. He was the general manager of an insurance firm when he was approached by PAP to stand for election in 1968.

He was a dapperly dressed and urbane 68-year-old when we met him in 2003. He was chairman of the Singapore Reinsurance Corporation Ltd, whose office in Amoy Street was a small museum of his collection of Asian art and his own paintings. He said his performance as MP in Jalan Kayu, a big ward and a former Barisan Sosialis stronghold, could also have been a deciding factor in his being made the task force coordinator.

Lee confirmed this. "He held his ground ... and he's quite shrewd."

Jalan Kayu was one of the four wards affected by the 1971 British pullout when the Seletar air base was shut down. One of Hwang's first tasks as its MP was to help residents and small businessmen who depended on the air base for their livelihoods find their feet again.

In the early 1970s, pig farms from all over the island were relocated to two designated areas, Jalan Kayu and Punggol, so that the disposal of the pig waste could be better controlled. Hwang had to help those coming into his constituency to settle in. At the same time, he also had to defuse the unhappiness of the landed property owners in Seletar Hills who, newly arrived at wealth, sniffed at having to put up with foul-smelling pig farms in their neighbourhood.

⚬⚬⚭⚬⚬

THE task force, which was formed in January 1977, was kept small. The other MPs in the task force were Lee Khoon Choy, MP for Braddell Heights; Sia Kah Hui (Upper Serangoon); Ho Cheng Choon (Geylang East); Ong Soo Chuan (Nee Soon); Yeo Toon Chia (Ang Mo Kio); and Lai Tha Chai (Henderson).

Its job was not simply to guide and break in the new MPs. Its members were also charged with spot-checking on the younger men and monitoring their attributes like character, temperament and motivation. Eventually, they were instructed to rank the better ones among them.

Lim Chee Onn and Bernard Chen were also put under its charge after they had come on board in the 1977 by-elections.

Lee said of the monitoring: "It was a useful exercise because it saved me time. I could cross-check with my own interactions with them whether it was a good assessment. It also gave me an idea of their (the older MPs') own prejudices and biases.

"It helped in the sense that you got a feel of the man, not just his ability, but his character, temperament, personality. But the final test was in the performance. We sent them to various jobs to see how they performed. Because there was intense interaction with the minister in charge and they attended cabinet sometimes, you got a lot of feedback. So finally, it was on-the-job performance."

The new MPs did not know, however, that they were being so closely monitored by the task force. Ow Chin Hock, who was in the 1976 cohort, said: "On looking back, I believe the task force had another agenda which we did not know at that time. It was to identify those with office-bearer potential."

Goh Chok Tong did not know that Lee had, at the end of the exercise, instructed the task force to rank him and four others who had emerged top of the class, so to speak. When asked about it by the authors many years later, he said it was the first time he had heard of it. But he laughed and said: "I am not surprised that he did. Are you?"

Singaporeans know well Lee's penchant for ranking talents and institutions. It was he who suggested the annual ranking of schools, which Goh Chok Tong as prime minister introduced in 1992. In 2004, in a major revamp of the education system, it was modified to an exercise in which schools were ranked in bands instead.

⚜

Lee's Letter: "I Want Your Assessment"

AS head of the task force, Hwang Soo Jin had to submit regular reports to Lee. He also got to work with him personally. What he remembered vividly from that period was Lee's sense of urgency. "So, whatever you did, you did it with despatch," he said.

Hwang, who quit politics in 1984, two years after the task force was disbanded, also spoke of Lee's attention to detail. Leaders are often supposed to attend to the big picture and leave the details to their subordinates. But not Lee. When he asked for feedback on the new MPs, for instance, he did not do so with one source only but with many. He checked and double-checked the feedback he got, the former MP said.

Hwang believed that even as he was monitoring the work of the new MPs, Lee could have also put someone, perhaps Lee Khoon Choy, another member of the task force and an older party faithful, to watch over him.

But Lee maintained that since Hwang had to see him regularly, he had a "pretty good assessment of him personally".

He said: "I think when you appoint a chap, a person, to an important position, you've got to make sure that he's up to the job. If he's up to the job, then you can leave him to do the job. If he's not up to it, you'll be coming back, supervising him and eventually replacing him, which means trouble, unnecessary work."

The secretary-general asked for reports not only from Hwang but from the other members of the task force as well. The way he gathered feedback from them cannot be better described than in his own words in this confidential letter he sent to Hwang and some other members of the task force in April 1981, long after the group was disbanded in April 1979:

"Can I have a frank assessment of the 18 new MPs? What impressions do they leave you after three months? Who are likely to make a contribution in (1) the government, (2) in parliament, and (3) in the party? Are they, as a group, a credit to us? Do any look like becoming liabilities?

"You have watched their interaction with the older MPs, parliamentary secretaries and ministers of state. What is the mood and attitudes of the older MPs, parl-secs and ministers of state? Do they feel sad that they are going to be bypassed by the younger, higher educated new MPs? Or do they accept that this is necessary and good for the party, the government and the country?

"Do any of the new MPs behave in a superior or arrogant way? Who are the easy mixers, who are approachable and able to get along with people?

"Which new MPs have potential for leadership? Of the five younger cabinet ministers—Ong Teng Cheong, Goh Chok Tong, Dhanabalan, Tony Tan and Lim Chee Onn—whom have you the most confidence in? Can you give me in strict confidence your merit rating of the five for: (1) Ability, (2) Reliability, (3) Ability to speak and influence people, and (4) Strong character?

"When I am present, I assume they are on their best behaviour. When they are with MPs, they are likely to be their natural selves. An old MP, like you, can see them for what they are. Give me short thumbnail sketches of what you make of each of the five younger ministers. How do you rate them in potential as a leader?

"Have you any fears that when I have stepped down, there will be dangers of factionalism in the party? Or is there growing rapport between the old and new MPs, and the older and younger ministers?"

❧

SINCE 1980, Lee introduced psychological tests to assess potential candidates. He also adopted the system devised by the Anglo-Dutch oil company, Shell, to assess a candidate's potential based on four qualities: the ability to see the big picture and simultaneously zoom in on the critical details, power of analysis, imagination and a sense of reality. "Straight

IQ, logic, reasoning is very easy to determine. But the character, the temperament, the values, the motivation—these we had to find out the hard way," he said. The tests are now applied not just on potential PAP candidates but also among government scholarship applicants.

Yet, as Lee pointed out, they are not foolproof. He gave the example of a potential PAP candidate who achieved a perfect score in the tests but failed the interview with him. As it happened, the person got into trouble later. Psychologists have a term for people who can ace such tests—they "fake good".

A Shell study had shown that the ability to assess a person was a natural-born gift. One either had that gift or not. Lee agreed with it. He cited Tan Teck Chwee, a former chairman of the Public Service Commission, as one of those natural assessors who could read a person fairly accurately, even when he was "faking good".

Lim Kim San was another one who could make sharp, intuitive assessments of a person quickly and for many years, he was the head of the party's final selection panel for potential candidates.

Branches were "Guerilla Outfits"

AT the end of December 1977, Lee Kuan Yew decided it was time the party branches had a shake-up. The PAP power pyramid, especially its base, was due for a much-needed overhaul. Lee would use the task force for the purpose and injected Goh Chok Tong, Lim Chee Onn, Bernard Chen and Ahmad Mattar (from the 1972 batch), and Sidek bin Saniff (from the 1976 cohort) into the team.

Lee said of his decision: "By then, we had decided that ministers, MPs, grassroots leaders … they had got accustomed to one another and they didn't want to change. In a way it was natural and probably good because you knew who were the people you could depend on. But at the same time, you got people entrenched in the jobs and active new people were kept out. So it needed to be shaken out. There had to be a turnover."

According to Hwang, the party headquarters was dominated by a group of Chinese-educated cadres. There were factions and cliques at the party branches, and the way some branches had raised their funds and used them was questionable. For instance, he said one MP put out a publication that reportedly collected about $1 million worth of advertising.

The CPIB had to move in to freeze his account.

Some branches were running cooperatives and businesses on the premises. There was even one which set up a barber shop. Many party branches ran kindergartens, which generally contributed the most money to their coffers. But there was hardly any system to keep track of all this money.

Lee cited the case of an MP who "organised things and built up a little war chest of his own". He said: "It was inevitable in the early days because you needed people who were self-reliant, who could muster their own resources … not just money but manpower. So they often had either friends or union contacts or old schools, old boys associations and so on.

"In those days, we had many more Chinese-educated because the Chinese-educated at that time were a larger percentage of the population."

The shake-up was necessary because "we were making sure that they (MPs and grassroots leaders) abided by certain rules, that they could not be as freewheeling. Most important was the honesty and integrity of the people. We didn't mind them collecting money, showing resourcefulness. But it must not lead to petty benefits that would lead eventually to corruption. Because the greatest asset of the party is that it is not corrupt, and once the party becomes corrupt, then the government will become corrupt."

The shake-up saw an influx of younger volunteers who were English-educated. The entrenched Chinese-educated grassroots leaders who had to accommodate them were not exactly excited by the entry of these young Turks whom they saw as having little community experience and who could appear aloof, arrogant and perhaps self-serving. The English-educated were more task-oriented and more detached emotionally. But in community work, that approach could make them seem more impersonal and less caring of the constituents.

A veteran grassroots leader Chen Chi Yuen who had served at the Bukit Timah branch for more than four decades, first for the MP Chor Yeok Eng and since 1984, for Wang Kai Yuen, put it bluntly: "Lee Kuan Yew depended on us Chinese-educated. Then he moved us aside."

Perhaps he could not forget his disappointment in 1976 when he was shortlisted as a possible PAP candidate for the general election but was subsequently dropped. Also, back in 1962, in the wake of The Big Split, Chen, who was teaching at Chung Cheng High School, was among the more than 90 Chinese-educated teachers who were sacked from their jobs for their links with the breakaway party, Barisan Sosialis.

He got back his job a month later, only after Chor had written to the Ministry of Education and the PAP leadership to make clear that Chen was not a turncoat even if he had friends and colleagues who had crossed over to the Barisan.

He would remain a teacher at Chung Cheng until his retirement at 60. Then he spent another seven years as a teacher in Li Chin Secondary School. For a while afterwards, he worked in a food court on weekends collecting plates and cleaning tables before he got a job as a cashier in Bukit Timah Plaza, a suburban mall.

Throughout the years, he had remained loyal to PAP. In 2003, at 72 years old, he was still the vice-chairman of the Bukit Timah branch and continued to help out at the meet-the-people session every Wednesday.

Back in 1984, together with Chor Yeok Eng, he had helped the Stanford-educated Wang Kai Yuen fight his crucial first election. Chor, then 54 years old, was making way for a new man after having dedicated his life to PAP. He, too, came from a Chinese-educated background. At a farewell dinner organised by his branch supporters, he betrayed his hurt when he introduced Wang to those present. He remarked, seemingly in jest, that the new man was a *phor shi*, or professor, while he was just a *phor-tu*, a man of the earth.

Chor and Chen belonged to that group of dedicated Chinese-educated community leaders whose lives were touched and shaped by the revolutionary fervour of the Kuomintang and the CCP that spilled out of China in the first half of the twentieth century.

"It was a phase in history," Lee said.

He did not neglect to put on record in his memoirs Chor's bravery as a PAP assemblyman at a time when the communists were fighting to topple the party. The stoutly built man had lived in communist-infested Bukit Timah and faced real physical risks when he rejected the Barisan Sosialis' overtures to get him to become one of them.

Chor confessed that he was a member of the communist party when he was in his teens. But after he had seen how the party members burned down the factories in Bukit Timah and destroyed buses and taxis during the 1948 Emergency, he threw all his communist books into a bonfire. "They were supposed to be fighting the British, but the factories, the buses and taxis, all belonged to the locals. The violence did not make sense to me," he said. When PAP came by in the mid-1950s, he knew it was the party to join.

Chen Chi Yuen's service did not go unrecognised by PAP. In 1992, he received a commendation award from the party and a public service medal from the government.

At the turn of the new century, there were still a number of old hands like Chen working the ground. They provided continuity in the party and could be tapped for their institutional memory. PAP recognised this and accorded them the due respect even as it pushed for regular renewal to ensure a constant injection of new blood and new ideas.

THE largely disorganised state of the branches was a surprise to the new leaders like Goh Chok Tong, Lim Chee Onn and S Dhanabalan. They were "a group of guerilla outfits", said an incredulous Dhanabalan. They had assumed PAP to be a well-oiled machinery. But that well-oiled machinery was in the government where the top PAP leadership had focused all its energies.

When Dhanabalan was elected treasurer of the party's central executive committee (CEC) in 1984, one of his first tasks was to look into the party finances. He remembered: "I was worried when I looked at the funds the branches were handling and the lack of control. In many cases, the MPs left it to the grassroots leaders and they did not have the time to follow up on how the funds were used.

"There was a potential for abuse. It was very tempting for somebody with the wrong motives to get into the branches and start using the money. Here was a big fat fish with a lot of cats around and you just trusted the cats not to eat the fish? We didn't."

Some branches had accumulated large reserves. But because they were not legal entities, they had no legal basis to hold the funds. Dhanabalan introduced a corporate structure to the party, with the headquarters in full command of party finances and proper accounting in the branches.

Later, in 1986, he helped formed the PAP Community Foundation (PCF). One of its functions was to collect funds from all branch kindergartens which would be channelled back to the community instead of to the individual branches. Goh Chok Tong directed Tay Eng Soon, who was then senior minister of state for education, and MP Arthur Beng to organise the kindergartens into a proper island-wide preschool network.

The need for self-renewal in the party became clear when Goh and his team proved they were up to the task of carrying out the long overdue overhaul of the party.

Still, because PAP was a political party, there were times when corporate practices could not apply. One instance was when Goh suggested that a tall building be built on Napier Road to house the PAP HQ. Its prime location opposite the Botanic Gardens could draw major firms to set up offices in the building and so ensure a stream of revenue for the party.

But Lee advised against it. His explanation: "Most governments lose their capital cities in elections because the government leaders became too familiar figures to the people. We fight and win in a city so we will have to be a different kind of party. Not being ostentatious is a crucial part of the party that we are." So PAP made a modest black-and-white colonial bungalow in Napier Road its headquarters. It was kept spartan, had a skeletal staff and on weekends, grassroots leaders from the different branches took turns to sweep the premises.

In that way, the party has not changed. Fifty years after its founding, its headquarters is a nondescript building tucked away in a HDB estate in New Upper Changi Road. You could easily miss it if you do not look out for it. Foreign delegations that have been taken there are often surprised to find it so small and manned by a staff of around 11. The UMNO headquarters in Kuala Lumpur, for example, is palatial by comparison.

⌘⌘⌘

Chok Tong Drew up New Party Objectives

IT was Hwang Soo Jin's contention that if Lee Kuan Yew had not pushed for renewal and a shake-up in the late 1970s, perhaps no other top PAP leader would have done so, since they were fully stretched in their government roles. The consequences then could have been dire for the party. Feelings among some of the Old Guard were hurt when they had to be moved aside but it was the necessary thing to do to keep the party vital and relevant to the times.

The danger was very real for the party to become fixed in its ways and its sinews hardened "into inflexible postures", to borrow the words of Tony Tan from his speech at the PAP conference in 1982 when, as first assistant secretary-general, he sought the cadres' endorsement of the draft of a revised constitution.

The draft was based on one that was drawn up by Goh Chok Tong in 1978. It was one of Lee's key assignments for the task force as the original constitution adopted at PAP's inaugural meeting on 21 November 1954 had become obsolete. Its objectives of ending colonialism and establishing "an independent national state of Malaya" had lost their relevance since Singapore gained independence in 1965.

Goh led a committee to work on revising the original party objectives. To prepare the new draft, he canvassed views from the different cohorts of MPs—those who joined the party in the years 1959, 1963, 1968, 1972 and 1976.

In a letter to these MPs, he said: "Party objects are the cardinal precepts upon which we determine the party's programmes and raison d'etre. Hence, in the current revision exercise, it has been decided to involve as many MPs as possible."

Goh drew up the final draft only after another series of brainstorming exercises had been carried out by the MPs. Based on that draft, a new party constitution was crafted and four years later, it was adopted after Tony Tan had won the cadres' support for it.

The party objectives in the new constitution are:

- To preserve, protect and defend the independence, sovereignty and territorial integrity of Singapore.
- To safeguard the freedom, and advance the well-being, of Singaporeans, through representative and democratic government.
- To forge a nation of Singaporeans; to build a multiracial society, fair, just, and tolerant to all, whatever their race, language and religion; to infuse into Singaporeans a sense of national identity and to bind them together by patriotism and commitment to Singapore.
- To build a dynamic society which is disciplined and self-reliant, and in which rewards are in accord with each Singaporean's performance and contribution to society, and which also has compassion for the aged, the sick and handicapped, and the less fortunate.
- To achieve the optimum in economic development, and social and cultural fulfilment through harmonious and cooperative social relationships. Within the overriding interests of the good of society, to provide equal opportunities for all Singaporeans to strive to fulfill themselves and to achieve their maximum potential through education and training so that there will be a place and a role for every Singaporean, whatever his contribution.

23

The Mentoring and the Apprenticeship

A Lesson in the Rain

THE December monsoon rain beat down mercilessly and he was drenched but on an open-air, makeshift stage at Fullerton Square, Lee Kuan Yew was talking about fire.

Despite the downpour, he had been speaking for about an hour and now, as he wrapped up his speech, he told his audience: "I can go on for another hour but I won't. You've got the message, you've got to help me test out a new team. They are doing well. There is only one thing they are not learning as fast and that is how to enthuse you, how to put a bit of fire into you."

The way he said it, one could almost hear the sizzle in the word "fire".

And that was enough of a payoff for many in the lunchtime crowd who had chosen to stay where they were in front of the stage—in their wet shoes, in their soaked office clothes—when they could have left earlier, as some had done, after the first big, fat raindrops came pelting down. Those who had come prepared with umbrellas were not spared from getting wet either; such was the ferocity of the rain carried by the wind that blew in from the sea across the old esplanade.

The rain gave the whole proceedings a heightened sense of drama that Lee exploited to maximum effect. It also provided an opportunity for him to give an impromptu lesson on the art of moving people to his handpicked successors who were seated on the stage behind him. As bright as they were, the young men were technocrats untested before a crowd. They would have to learn how to hold their audiences under all kinds of unexpected circumstances.

Lee would tell them afterwards: "Politics is about human beings and their lives. It is an art, not a science. It is the art of the possible...

"The dialogue and the feedback, the explanation and the persuasion, the coaxing and the cajoling, and when necessary … the coercing, they are important aspects of good government.

"To be trusted by the people as the older leaders have been trusted, the younger leaders must learn to translate ... figures and hard-headed analyses of complex problems into warm, simple and human terms which the ordinary people can understand...

"With experience, a few can acquire that sensitive political touch which is essential for the rapport between the government and the people, so that a people and its leaders feel and throb as one...

"It is part inborn, part learning from experience."

⌘

THE lunchtime rally at Fullerton Square was a fixture and a highlight of every general election until after 1998, when redevelopment works at the Fullerton Building began. Fullerton Building became the Fullerton Hotel in 2001.

When Lee spoke at the 1980 rally that rainy afternoon, four days before the people went to cast their votes on December 23, he was speaking with some urgency. He would be 65 in 1988 and he wanted to put in place a successor team of PAP leaders by then. He told his audience that he and his old colleagues would see through that election and perhaps the next one. But a younger team would have to take over, to build on what they had achieved.

When he said that the new team had not learnt how to put the fire in the people, he added that he was confident they would learn to do so in eight years. "But," he told the crowd, "I tell you what you have to do. You have got to know this young team, they have got to know you, and you've got to jell and build on what we have built. Otherwise, all that Singapore has achieved will go down the drain."

That year, PAP had a clean sweep victory, its fourth since 1968. It would also be the last time it did so.

⌘

Early Tests in the Political Arena

SUCH was the urgency of Lee's renewal plans that he began to test Goh Chok Tong and Lim Chee Onn in the larger political arena by early 1979. This was barely three years after the two men had come onboard— Goh in the 1976 general election and Lim in the 1977 Bukit Merah by-election. Goh was 38 years old at the time and Lim, 35.

Lee put them in charge of the campaign to fight the by-elections in seven vacated wards, which he had called for after he had sacked three MPs and another three had resigned at the same time. The seventh ward, Anson, had been vacant after its MP, veteran trade unionist P Govindasamy, died.

Among the new PAP candidates was 38-year-old banker Tony Tan, who would become another key member of the second-generation team.

That Lee obviously had difficulties finding young talent with ministerial potential was reflected in the choice of three not-so-young candidates: Devan Nair, 56, secretary-general of the NTUC and a founding member of PAP; Howe Yoon Chong, 55, who had just retired as head of the civil service; and Teh Cheang Wan, 50, who was the former chief executive officer of HDB and chairman of JTC. They really belonged among the Old Guard.

As Howe said expansively at a press conference held to announce his candidacy, with his arms thrown around the shoulders of Goh Chok Tong on one side and Lim Chee Onn on the other: "These are my younger colleagues with very broad shoulders. I won't be standing in the way of these people. Any time they are ready, I am ready to move off. This is the beauty of staging an old horse."

In the midst of the hustings—polling day was February 10—Lee disclosed that Goh and Lim, together with Ong Teng Cheong, 43, and Ahmad Mattar, 39, another two men identified as part of the second echelon team, had been moved to take up key positions in PAP's central executive committee (CEC).

The posts for Goh Chok Tong, Ong Teng Cheong and Ahmad Mattar were new and created specially for them so that they could understudy the Old Guard who remained in the CEC—Toh Chin Chye, the chairman; Goh Keng Swee, first vice-chairman; Ong Pang Boon, first assistant secretary-general; and Chua Sian Chin, treasurer.

Goh Chok Tong was made second assistant secretary-general; Ong Teng Cheong, second vice-chairman; and Ahmad, second assistant treasurer. As first assistant treasurer, Lim Chee Onn replaced Jek Yeun Thong, who was away as Singapore's high commissioner in London.

On February 10, the five PAP candidates whose wards were contested won with a 74.53 per cent share of the votes. Teh, together with another candidate, Koh Lip Lin, a 43-year-old academic, enjoyed a walkover.

Goh said after the results were announced that the by-elections had all the characteristics of a general election since the five constituencies contested were representative of Singapore. "We can say the people of Singapore ... very convincingly, once again, have shown their faith in PAP ... Over the next 10 to 15 years we are confident that we will have the support of the people," he said.

He was on an upward trajectory. By April, when the two-year long task force exercise facilitated by Hwang Soo Jin was finally completed, Lee made Goh and Lim the first and second organising secretaries of PAP respectively, replacing Phua Bah Lee, a Nanyang University graduate and former civil servant who had joined the party in 1968. Phua would remain the MP for Tampines and senior parliamentary secretary in the Ministry of Defence until 1988 when he retired at 56 years old.

When the 1980 general election came round, Goh and Lim were put in charge of the campaign again. Together with the four other men—Ong Teng Cheong, Tony Tan, S Dhanabalan and Ahmad Mattar—identified as members of the core team who would take over from Lee and his peers, they also organised that year's party conference which Lee described as a watershed one.

At the conference held on December 7, Lee said: "This meeting ... is the last time that the original team presides over events and dispenses the solutions. By the second half of the 1980s, the original core group will not be here to settle the proceedings in the party as it has done all these years. And that is as it should be."

Lee pointed out that the process of self-renewal became a conscious effort in 1970 when five MPs stood down in mid-term by-elections to be replaced by five younger men. The process had not stopped and would be given impetus with 18 new candidates in the coming general election.

To those who had qualms about the pace of self-renewal—and there were some even in the CEC—Lee explained: "My colleagues and I can keep on solving problems until we are dead. One day, one by one, we shall cease to be able to solve Singapore's problems. This is for sure ... We have to bring together the best team possible in Singapore ... men who can meet new, startling and unexpected problems, think out the possible answers..."

The 1980 general election proved to be an easy fight for the ruling party as Lee had predicted. It was the most tranquil general election in his life, he had said at the Fullerton Square rally. PAP not only had a clean sweep of all 75 wards—37 were walkovers—but it also improved its share of votes to 77.7 per cent, from 74.09 in 1976 and 74.53 in the 1979 by-elections.

But Lee did not care to celebrate the victory. As soon as the election was over, in a meeting in the new year, he got all six men in the second-generation leadership team to fill in the top slots of the CEC.

Toh Chin Chye, 59, who was chairman of the party since it was formed in 1954 and first vice-chairman Goh Keng Swee, 62, gave up their posts but remained members in the party's top policy-forming body.

The new line-up in the CEC:

Chairman: Ong Teng Cheong
1st vice-chairman: Ong Pang Boon
2nd vice-chairman: Lim Chee Onn

Secretary-general: Lee Kuan Yew
1st assistant secretary-general: Tony Tan
2nd assistant secretary-general: Goh Chok Tong

Treasurer: Chua Sian Chin
1st assistant treasurer: S Dhanabalan
2nd assistant treasurer: Ahmad Mattar

Members: Goh Keng Swee, S Rajaratnam, E W Barker , Toh Chin Chye and Lee Khoon Choy

THE surprise in the new line-up was the sudden catapulting of Tony Tan from outside the CEC to the post of first assistant secretary-general, replacing Ong Pang Boon, who became first vice-chairman. Goh Chok Tong, whom political watchers had assumed would move up to take over that post, remained as second assistant secretary-general.

Lee did alert him that he was making Tony Tan first assistant secretary-general. "He asked me if I minded," Goh recalled years later. "I said I didn't. I am not the type to fight for positions."

Tony Tan was proving to be popular with the people, Goh said. Nonetheless, he believed he would still have been the more popular choice among the cadres. In organising three election campaigns, he had been exposed to most of the grassroots leaders. But he stood by Lee's decision.

Mentoring Lunches

BY now, Lee would have had a good gauge of Goh, Tony Tan and Lim Chee Onn. Ever since he made them organising secretaries, he had been having regular working lunches with Goh and Lim. He also lunched separately with Tony Tan who, as minister of state in the education ministry, was put under the wings of his deputy, Goh Keng Swee, who was then also the education minister.

When Lee approached Tan to stand on a PAP ticket in 1979, he offered him the post of a minister of state and suggested that he could either go to the education or finance ministry. He would probably acquit himself well in the finance ministry because of his banking background. He was the general manager of OCBC Bank when he joined PAP. In the education ministry, however, he would be working for a very demanding and impatient man, Goh Keng Swee. But, Lee told the young man, Goh Keng Swee was the brightest spark in the cabinet and an original thinker, and he would learn a lot from him.

Tan took up Lee's challenge. He opted for the more demanding job and found Goh Keng Swee to be an excellent mentor. In an interview in his MINDEF office in Bukit Gombak in 2003, the 64-year-old deputy prime minister and defence minister said: "What I learnt from Dr Goh was really to get down to the basics of any problem and attack it from all angles. And always to be practical. He wrote beautiful memos, very clear in their analyses of problems."

Both Lim Chee Onn and Goh Chok Tong described their lunches with Lee as mentoring sessions. Lim, who joined Keppel Corporation in 1983 and became its executive chairman in 2000, said: "Mr Lee passed on a lot of his experience, his way of thinking, his way of analysis and of course, his own interpretations and assessments of situations. Not just the related facts, but also the way you looked at things. To that extent, I was very privileged. He is one of a kind."

Goh believed that "most of the transmission of knowledge from Mr Lee and most of his assessment of us was done through the lunches. He would tell you stories and you had to draw lessons from them. His style was also to squeeze information out of you."

Some instructive lessons Goh came away with from those lunches were these: how to get people to serve; the need to build a successor team right away; the vulnerability of Singapore and its unique situation since it was born through an accident in history; and leadership principles such as never allowing oneself to be led by populist pressures, the need to take tough and painful measures when necessary, and the importance of mobilising people behind them.

Goh said the lunches, which would usually last for an hour and a half or two hours, were always serious affairs. "We didn't discuss light topics. It was always political ... what was happening in the region and how [these events] would affect us."

"Luckily," he said with a laugh, "Mr Lee had a good chef and he had very exacting demands."

Lee had three menus: a small cut of steak, roast chicken or *ikan kurau* (snapper). There would be consommé and fruit.

Over the years, there were many occasions when Goh got to observe how Lee taught others in the leadership ranks. "He's a good mentor and you learn how he teaches people," he said.

Lee himself said of those mentoring lunches: "No, you sit down, you talk about problems. You talk and you get to know their worldview, and they get to know how we look at things. And you see how they react. It's not mentoring in the sense that you're training them for a specific job because you cannot predict the kind of crisis, problems that they are going to meet.

"But you must try and find out what kind of a response you will get from the man when he's faced with a crisis. Is he likely to curl up and face the wall, is he likely to be alert and say, 'okay, I've got to fight, find a way out for the country'? That really is what you're trying to find out."

⁂

Anson Lessons: The Art of Politics

IN 1981, Goh Chok Tong and Lim Chee Onn were once again put in charge of a by-election campaign—this time in Anson, whose MP Devan Nair was going to be made the state president and had to give up his parliamentary seat.

Although the two men had organised the previous three campaigns, Lee had led the charge. This time, he was taking his hands off. Goh and Lim would have to fight the by-election entirely on their own. The PAP candidate was a new face, Pang Kim Hin, a 32-year-old manager. His opponent was J B Jeyaretnam, the secretary-general of the Workers' Party (WP) since 1971 and a veteran of many elections. The participation of

Harbans Singh, seen by many people as a political clown because of his bizarre theatrics during elections, made it into a three-corner fight.

Just 11 months earlier, in the 1980 general election, PAP's Nair had polled 84.1 per cent of the votes against an unknown from Harbans' United People's Front. It was hard to believe that the ground had shifted in the short period since then but during the campaign, the PAP team sensed that it had. Lim Chee Onn had doors slammed in his face when he went canvassing. On one of the evenings, when Goh Chok Tong was making his speech at a rally, someone from a nearby HDB high-rise threw down two packets of *char kway teow*, or fried noodles, into the crowd.

There was a confluence of factors that led to the shift in voter sentiment. First, the choice of the candidate proved to be a wrong one. The largely working-class voters in Anson were used to having a heavyweight MP who stood for unionised workers—first, P Govindasamy and then Devan Nair. They did not see the young and well-scrubbed Pang as someone who could relate to their problems, much less fight on their behalf.

And they had problems. Public utility charges and food prices had gone up. And so had bus fares. During the campaign, there were newspaper reports—which later turned out to be inaccurate—that there would be another hike in bus fares.

There was also anxiety about housing. More than 1,000 PSA workers who were housed in nine blocks of flats in Blair Plain had earlier been given eviction notices—some to vacate by 1982, others by 1983—as the blocks were to be torn down to make way for the expansion of the port's container wharf facilities. They wanted priority in resettlement but were denied it. They had to join a long queue of 100,000 applicants for HDB flats and were understandably unhappy about it. That Pang happened to be the nephew of Lim Kim San, then the chairman of PSA, stacked the odds higher against PAP.

Another 3,500 voters had applied to buy new HDB flats. The prices of HDB flats, meanwhile, had gone up by 35 per cent because of rising costs. What was worse—those in the central area or near Anson had shot up by nearly 100 per cent. And in anticipation of further increases in costs, Teh Cheang Wan, then-minister for national development, had warned that prices might by go up by another 15 per cent.

All these figures came up only later in the PAP's post-mortem of the by-election. In the heat of the campaign, although Goh could sense a shift on the ground away from PAP, he did not think the party would lose the by-election. It would not have 1980's 77.7 per cent of the votes but he reckoned it would still win with a 60 per cent vote or slightly less. Lim Chee Onn and the two veteran grassroots leaders who were helping them in the campaign, Ch'ng Jit Koon and Ong Ah Heng, shared his reading of the ground.

By late afternoon on polling day, October 31, Ong Ah Heng, the PAP's Anson branch secretary, got wind that the bookies in the coffeeshop in Block 105, Jalan Bukit Merah, had reversed the odds of a PAP win. They were now betting on a 70 per cent chance that PAP might lose.

Ong, a grassroots leader since the mid-1960s who would become an MP in 1997, was not one to dismiss bookies' odds. These illegal gamblers played to win. They had an effective network on the ground that could sometimes pick up signals more clearly than the political parties that were too busy fighting the elections. But there was nothing he could do at this late hour. He remained hopeful but was prepared for the worst.

As it turned out, PAP lost by 653 votes. Its share of the votes was a dismal 47 per cent. Jeyaretnam got 52 per cent and became the first man since 1968 to beat PAP at the polls. Harbans Singh made history of a different kind as the candidate with less than 1 per cent of the votes.

When the result was announced just before 11 pm at the counting centre in Gan Eng Seng Secondary School that was then in Anson Road, there was near pandemonium in the crowd that had gathered there. The whole stretch of Anson Road from Palmer Road to Telok Ayer Market was jam-packed with vehicles, many of whose drivers tooted their horns in celebration.

Jeyaretnam's supporters could not stop cheering and it took a while before he could give his victory speech. On the dais where the election agent had announced the result, he declaimed with theatrical flourish: "There is a new sun breaking out tomorrow morning. Let us welcome the dawn of a bright, prosperous, happy Singapore ... I am sure the Anson voters want me to regard myself not only as their MP but the MP for the silent majority."

Nineteen years later, in his cluttered cubicle in a rented office in Sim Lim Tower in Jalan Besar, Jeyaretnam, still feisty at 77 years old, looked back on that night as "a momentous time for Singapore and the people". He believed that by 1981, people were desperate to escape from what they felt to be PAP's complete dominance not only in parliament but also over their lives.

"It's quite true to say that in almost every Singaporean breast, there was the longing that there should be some channel or outlet for them. This is true even of people who would have voted PAP. That, of course, was shown by the reaction produced after the by-election. There was, as it were, a sense of relief, something that was sort of lifted from their shoulders," he said.

Working the ground for eight days in Anson, a largely working-class ward, Jeyaretnam said he sensed that the longing among the voters was even more acute.

He brushed aside the local factors that PAP had cited for its loss. Of the PAP's campaign, he said: "I don't know if it would have been different if Lee (Kuan Yew) had come, but Goh Chok Tong certainly did not get any good reception in Anson."

He also believed that he would still have won the by-election even if PAP had not fielded a novice. "I think people were clamouring for some voice in parliament. And of course, they won't just vote for anybody, just because it's opposition. I'm sorry that it looks like trumpet-blowing, but I think they saw in me someone who would voice their opinions in parliament."

At Gan Eng Seng Secondary School, Pang Kim Hin emerged from the counting room before the result was announced and tried to mount the dais to make a speech. Technically, no candidate could make a speech until after the returning officer had announced the result. Still, despite Ong Ah Heng pulling his hand and trying to dissuade him from doing so, he got up on the dais.

But he could not make that speech. His voice was drowned out by the loud jeers from WP's contingent of supporters. He lost what little composure he had left and stomped off. PAP said later it would field him in the next election but it did not eventually because he had so obviously failed his crucial first test.

There is a lesson here for an aspiring politician—one should never lose one's cool on the battlefield.

That night, when Lee Kuan Yew got Goh Chok Tong to call him towards midnight, it was not to find out the result, which he had already known. Lee was at a dinner function at the Shangri-La Hotel with Tony Tan that evening; the latter remembered Lee was calm when an aide came to deliver the bad news. Goh said of the telephone call: "He really wanted to find out if I had melted."

The crowd had largely dispersed by the time Goh was summoned to call Lee. He walked about a kilometre from the school compound to the PAP branch office to make the call.

He recounted: "The first question he asked me was, 'What happened?' I said we lost. I gave some reasons why we lost. He was calm; I was calm."

It was a brief exchange but long enough for Lee to establish that Goh was holding up well. He noted too that Goh had stayed back at the counting centre when most of the supporters had already left. His press secretary, James Fu, who was at the centre, reported to him later that Goh had remained collected throughout that night.

Another lesson from Pang's unfortunate experience is that you do not alienate the grassroots leaders when you rope in your friends to help you in an election campaign. Your friends may be highly qualified professionals, as Pang's were, but they cannot get to know the local terrain as well as the grassroots leaders can in the short period of the hustings. You may end up with two or more factions in your own camp pulling in different directions. Pang's friends did him no favours either when they descended on the ward every evening in what must have been seen by the residents as a convoy of fancy cars.

At Gan Eng Seng, in the sudden frenzy that ensued after the announcement of the result, PAP's Fong Sip Chee showed himself to be the veteran trooper that he was by quickly calming down the group of PAP supporters who felt threatened by the unruly opposition crowd. He got them to move to a corner of the school field where he then arranged for them to sit in a circle on the grass behind a police cordon.

Goh Chok Tong remembered Fong's quick reflexes that night. He had always felt indebted to the veteran who had helped him fight his first election in Marine Parade in 1976. When he was plonked into the newly created ward, he was put under the charge of Yeoh Ghim Seng, the MP in neighbouring Joo Chiat. The latter planned to fight in his own constituency as well as Goh's with only one set of activists—his—and he told the newcomer that the setting up of a branch office in Marine Parade could wait until after the election.

So Goh found himself without any branch office and supporters to speak of. He recalled that Goh Keng Swee called him one day to check how he was doing. When he said he did not have a branch office, the older Goh simply said: "Don't worry, just put up a table and a chair there, and then go and fight the election."

"It was really a guerilla concept," said Goh, laughing at the memory.

Luckily for him, Fong Sip Chee extended him a much-needed helping hand. Fighting in Chai Chee, Fong was also tasked with coordinating the campaigns for the constituencies in the east. When he found out about Goh's situation, he dug into his own war chest to provide him with some funds and diverted a few of his supporters who were Marine Parade residents to help run Goh's campaign.

Fong was not fighting against a lightweight. He was up against J B Jeyaretnam, the fiery leader of the WP. The PAP leaders had to take him seriously and field a strong candidate against him. Fong was the man. He was moved from his Stamford ward at the last minute to fight in Chai Chee. He certainly needed all his resources, yet he was generous enough to help the younger man out.

In 1976, Goh could speak only English at the rallies and he marvelled at how the veteran could speak three languages—English, Chinese and Malay—and work the crowds. Toh Chin Chye, who had brought Fong into PAP in 1963, had described him as "a street-fighter, a man who could stand on a platform and talk".

Fong was later openly resentful of some of the fast-trackers Lee moved into positions above his but he maintained a good relationship with Goh. He felt he was being penalised for not having gone to the university but Lee has said in his memoirs that that was not the case. He was parliamentary secretary and then senior parliamentary secretary for most of his years in government. He did make minister of state in 1981 but for only a term. In 1988, he quit politics altogether.

He died of lung cancer in 1992 when he was only 54. He left behind two sons. Arthur, the elder son, who worked in a bank, joined PAP as an activist in 1993 and became an MP for the West Coast GRC in 2001. Fong's anecdotal history of the party, *The PAP Story: The Pioneering Years*, which was published in 1979, still remains a valuable resource book.

⋰⋱⋰⋱

LOOKING back on the 1981 lesson more than two decades later, Goh acknowledged that he was too mathematical and logical in his approach to fighting the by-election. Yes, there were local grievances and the ground had shifted. But the previous candidate had scored 84.1 per cent, had he not? Goh could not imagine the vote going down to less than 50 per cent in just 11 months.

But much like stock market prices, one cannot predict the votes of the people by hard logic and mathematical models alone. And time frames may not count for much. "That's the real lesson of politics," said Goh. "Don't assume the last votes will not change too drastically. The ground can turn, depending on the issues and how the candidates campaign."

As Lee Hsien Loong had learnt since his first foray into politics in the 1984 general election: "Nine days is a very long time during an election campaign. You start with a certain set of issues you want to make election issues, but you never know how the mood will develop within the nine days ... As the rallies go, the mood changes, and you sense it on the ground. And then somewhere which you can't always predict, some constituencies or some issues will get hot. You will never have one which just goes peacefully, and then you coast along to the end. Somewhere along the way, there will be an issue which catches the imagination. The battle is joined and you are fully committed in it."

During the campaign in Anson, Goh did not think the situation warranted Lee Kuan Yew's involvement. When the latter called him to check, he reported that he sensed a shifting of the ground and that the percentage might go down to 60. But he was confident that the party would not lose. Lee left it at that.

On hindsight, Goh thought perhaps he should have alerted Lee earlier. His mistake, he said, was in the final judgement. It was not as if he did not know that the situation on the ground was bad. It was just that he did not have the seasoned politician's instincts to know how bad it actually was.

After the loss, some people told him he might get the chop given Lee's well-known intolerance of less than satisfactory performances. But at a meeting with PAP MPs the following month during which he gave a detailed analysis of PAP's loss, Lee said: "It is painful to suffer the jolt of PAP's first by-election defeat in 15 years since 1966. I have seen the by-election committee after the defeat. They have been through a minor trauma. They will be none the worse for it. Indeed, the experience will temper them. They will fight harder and better the next time."

The Anson defeat was an unfortunate misadventure that might not be without its blessings, he said. It put more pressure on the Old Guard for self-renewal, both at the top and the lower ranks.

In his post-mortem, he provided the figures of the number of PSA workers who were given eviction notices, the number of other residents who wanted new HDB flats, and how high the prices of these flats had gone up.

"We got cheap housing for several years until Malaysian construction boomed. Now, we are strapped for workers," he said. He suggested that the state build a core of Singaporean construction workers in five to seven years. Meanwhile, the HDB would have to seek out workers from beyond Malaysia and the region.

Housing took up a major part of Lee's post-mortem speech. The issue was not just one of housing but of security as well, he pointed out. The SAF was a citizen army and the people would not fight to defend the country if they owned nothing of it. Between HDB prices and CPF savings, a sound formula would have to be worked out so that the majority of Singaporeans could own an HDB flat and be able to service their monthly mortgage instalments with their CPF money.

"No Singaporean will lose out on his HDB home because he was born later or got married later," he promised.

Lee said the PAP government had subsidised only health, education and housing in the 23 years of its rule. They were investments, not consumption. On the other hand, subsidies on consumption were wrong and would only lead to more consumption and more subsidies. He cited how they had ruined the British and had been the cause of troubles in the American economy.

A new generation of Singaporeans had grown up who did not know hardship, he said, and if they were not lucky, they might discover at great cost that an opposition could cause much confusion by "raising false expectations of unattainable benefits from greater welfare spending, as in Britain and in so many third world countries".

On a more philosophical note, he said he had come to the conclusion that "each generation must learn its own lessons. What we, the elders, can do is to save our young Singaporeans from unnecessary, self-inflicted wounds."

The final part of his speech was really a lesson in the art of politics. Losing Anson, he said, was part of the price of learning. "There will be sharper and more acerbic debates with one opposition member in parliament. It is necessary experience for the new PAP ministers and MPs … Some may develop the cut and thrust of the fencing foil. Some will learn to wound with the rapier."

It was here that he spoke about how politics was an art and not a science, and how the younger leaders would have to learn how to win the people's trust, how to move them and make them feel as one.

His first lesson in politics "was that the speeches I made in parliament did not count as much as the speeches I made on constituency tours".

"The speeches made in parliament were of more interest to the press, the gallery and some of the intelligentsia. But when I went down and explained to people in the streets, in the kampungs and when I solved their constituency problems—roads, drains, schools, community centres, veterinary stations, clinics, jobs and housing—that was what settled the issues and enabled us to win in 1963, and again in 1968, in 1972, 1976, and again in 1980."

He ended his speech by underlining the need for a fighting spirit and the will to win. He said: " ... When we lost Hong Lim in April 1961 and Anson in July 1961, we marched back from the counting centre to our HQ in South Bridge Road with our heads high and banners fluttering.

"We made defiant speeches. Barisan thought we were done for. In the face of defeat, we were defiant. We had the will to win. By our example, we inspired our party workers to fight back. We fought back resolutely and intelligently. We went back to Anson and won in September 1963.

"We went back to Hong Lim in 1963, and again we lost. We swore to continue the fight in Hong Lim. We went back to Hong Lim in a by-election in May 1965 and we won.

"Those without this indomitable fighting spirit had better go and sell stocks and shares. This task is not for the faint-hearted. It is for people with deep and abiding convictions."

<hr>

Goh's Application

GOH Chok Tong in his first 10 years in politics was like a sponge absorbing lessons from a wide range of people besides Lee Kuan Yew. He learnt mostly by observing and interacting with them.

S Rajaratnam took a keen interest in the younger leaders and watched them fairly closely. Goh had no doubt that he would also have given his own assessment of the men to Lee. When he was a young minister and giving speeches at events, he would see Rajaratnam in the audience observing him with a smiling face. Trained as an economist, it was natural that he would pepper his speeches with figures. It was Rajaratnam who advised him against doing so. "Don't do that. People cannot remember the figures and find them boring," he told Goh.

On television, Rajaratnam advised him he would have to assume his audience had the mental age of a 16-year-old. People watched TV not to be educated but to relax. "You give them facts and figures, they will not listen to you," said the veteran politician.

Rajaratnam was, in effect, giving him pointers on the art of telling stories, Goh said.

Lim Kim San was good in assessing potential candidates. Goh would observe him and test his own assessment of a candidate against his. "But this thing you can't teach, you can't pass it on," he said. Still, from watching him closely, Goh learnt, up to a point, how to assess a person by asking the right questions and watching his responses.

From Goh Keng Swee, he learnt that one had to be bold in one's ideas and to carry them out even if all one had was a table and a chair.

Veteran grassroots leaders like Ch'ng Jit Koon and Ho Kah Leong were the ones who could marshal resources and organise rallies and large-scale community events. They worked the ground and had a finger on the pulse of the people. Goh found he could learn much from them too.

During breaks in parliamentary sessions, he found out that while the English-educated ministers and MPs milled around upstairs in Parliament House, the Chinese-educated like Ong Pang Boon and Jek Yeun Thong would congregate in a room downstairs. Ong was still a popular figure with the masses. From time to time, Goh would go downstairs and mingle with them. Perhaps because he did so, the Chinese-educated Old Guard leaders who were bitter at being displaced did not show him any animosity. His soft skills were apparent even then.

When Goh attended his first parliament sitting in 1977, after the 1976 GE, Lee Kuan Yew set a poser in his speech: "This is psephology ... Take two similar constituencies, both HDB estates. One, Marine Parade and the other, Buona Vista ... Both are new constituencies.

"Marine Parade has no one-room flats. Buona Vista ... has 1,300 one-room flats ... The member for Buona Vista (Ang Kok Peng) won 82.75 per cent of the votes. The member for Marine Parade (Goh Chok Tong), with the most five-room flats, with the most four-room flats, with no one-room flats, got 78.62 per cent."

Why did Ang get 82.75 per cent and Goh only 78.62? He wanted the members to figure it out.

Goh did figure it out. The races might have come together after independence, but people still tended to vote along racial lines 20 years later. Although both he and Ang faced relatively unknown Malay opponents, he had a larger pool of Malay voters in his constituency and most of them had obviously voted for the Malay candidate, one Monsor Rahman of the United Front.

So he would have to learn to win the trust of the Malay ground. He sought out veteran grassroots leader Ya'acob bin Mohamed, MP for Kampong Ubi and minister of state in the PMO, and learnt from him how he could reach out to the Malay community.

Goh's application, his total commitment and his performance in three successive "hard" ministries—trade and industry, defence and health— must have impressed Lee. By September 1984, Goh had replaced Tony Tan as first assistant secretary-general in the CEC. Tan was made vice-chairman, replacing Lim Chee Onn who quit the post in August 1983.

Lim, who was appointed secretary-general of the NTUC in 1981, began a renewal programme by moving young scholarship holders to key positions in the labour body. But perhaps in his eagerness to inject fresh blood and ideas into the union body, he failed to pay enough attention to the elected, incumbent leaders. They felt they were being shoved aside.

The plunge in morale among these old-timers was a problem Lee could not ignore. He moved Lim out of the NTUC in April 1983 and had Ong Teng Cheong take over his place.

In the following year, Goh Chok Tong would learn another lesson in the elections when, for the first time, PAP votes fell sharply across the board.

There were lessons too to be learnt from the performance of the opposition parties. After 1984, they stood a real chance of becoming a force to be reckoned with. But, as Chiam See Tong ruefully admitted years later, they did not take advantage of the momentum built up by then. Instead, they were "a disparate group, each going on their own way".

"We didn't really understand what was going on. But PAP understood it. Lee Kuan Yew took the results very seriously, and their whole machinery started cranking again," he said.

Jeyaretnam maintained that it was Chiam's which was a disparate group. "With all due respect to Chiam, why didn't he get his act together?" he said.

Still, unlike the leaders in PAP, both Chiam and Jeyaretnam failed to groom a potential successor. Both had messy squabbles with their own party leaders, and had to leave their parties eventually.

Jeyaretnam's "new dawn" did not come about.

24

The Titanium in the Wood

Coffee at Tony's

AFTER PAP's setback in the 1984 general election, some among the second-generation leaders were not sure if the leadership renewal should be followed through as had been planned.

In the plan, two among them would take over the two deputy prime minister positions vacated by Goh Keng Swee, who tendered his resignation to Lee Kuan Yew in the middle of the year, and S Rajaratnam who suffered a heart attack in the United States and underwent a bypass operation in London the previous year. The man named first deputy prime minister should, barring unforeseen circumstances, succeed Lee when the time came for the latter to step down.

If some of the others had their doubts, Tony Tan certainly was clear that the renewal should not be held back. As he recounted 20 years later: "We knew we had a setback. Our feedback from the newspapers was that things were very bad and very uncertain. But my own feeling was that if you hesitated now, and people saw that you were uncertain as to what to do, they would lose confidence in you. So we should press ahead ... I felt that very strongly."

He acted quickly. On the evening of December 30, less than a week after the results were announced, he rounded up the key second-generation leaders and got them to go over to his Bukit Timah house. There, over coffee and orange juice, they would pick from among themselves the two men who would succeed Goh and Rajaratnam

The group, comprising Tan, Ong Teng Cheong, S Dhanabalan, Ch'ng Jit Koon, Lee Hsien Loong and four men from the 1980 cohort—Yeo Ning Hong, S Jayakumar, Lee Yock Suan and Tay Eng Soon—arrived fairly quickly at a unanimous decision. Goh Chok Tong would be first deputy prime minister and Ong Teng Cheong, the second deputy.

Because he had a community event at Marine Parade, Goh Chok Tong arrived late at Tan's house, at about 9.30 pm, by which time the decision had already been taken. After Tan had offered him a slice of chocolate cake, he asked: "So okay, what have you decided?"

Tan, smiling, replied: "You."

Goh was not surprised. Neither did he hesitate in his acceptance of the group's decision. "Well, this is a tough job," he said to them. "Since you have asked me to do the job, I will try and do it to the best of my ability. I hope you chaps will support me."

Looking back on that moment, Goh remembered that his one thought was: *Somebody had to do the job; it was critical for self-renewal.* "That someone didn't have to be me. It could be someone else. But if it had to be me, then I could not say no," he said.

As soon as Goh had said yes to the group's decision, Tan telephoned Ahmad Mattar to ask him to come over to his house. He had not been able to reach Ahmad earlier. As the latter remembered it, he had gone out with his wife that evening. When he received Tan's call, it was almost midnight. Briefed on the group's decision after he arrived at Tan's house, he said he was all for it.

There were a few previous meetings where Lim Chee Onn and Bernard Chen, another potential second-generation leader, were also involved. Ahmad did not attend those because a leg fracture sustained a month before the election had put him in hospital for six weeks, and afterwards, he had to hobble on crutches for another month or so. Now with Ahmad in, Tan felt he had a full quorum.

Tan said he included Ch'ng Jit Koon in the meeting because the group could test their judgement with the veteran grassroots leader. Ch'ng, a Nanyang University graduate, joined PAP in 1968 and proved to be one of its most effective mobilisers on the ground. For many years, he managed Lee Kuan Yew's constituency work in Tanjong Pagar, besides his own in Tiong Bahru. Lee Hsien Loong was invited to the meeting as an observer because he was, according to Tony Tan, the best man in the 1984 cohort.

Like the others, Ch'ng believed that to complement Goh, the second deputy should be someone who was conversant in Chinese and could connect more readily with the Chinese-speaking population base. He felt Ong Teng Cheong was the right choice. Although Ong obtained his architecture degree from the University of Adelaide in Australia and a master's degree in civic design from the University of Liverpool in England, he was essentially Chinese-educated. He had his secondary school education in Chinese High, at the time the premier Chinese-language school in Singapore.

The meeting in Tony Tan's house was a historic moment. But as with many of such moments in the story of PAP after the 1970s, it was business-as-usual, with little or no fuss, and certainly no drama. It demonstrated, as Jayakumar was to tell the party organ, *Petir*, in a 1987 interview, "a watershed in the group's ability to consult and establish a consensus".

It is significant that Lee Kuan Yew refrained from choosing his own successor. Four years earlier, after the 1980 general election, he had told the second echelon leaders that they had to choose their own man to succeed him. He hoped to step aside as prime minister in 1988 when he turned 65. He had sized up the top contenders for the job—Goh Chok Tong, Ong Teng Cheong, Tony Tan, Lim Chee Onn and S Dhanabalan—and given them his blunt assessment of their respective strengths and weaknesses.

In his interviews for this book, Lee explained why he would not pick his own successor: "I'm going to give my opinion, but you choose. I'm not choosing because if I choose, you may not support the man and then there'd be big trouble. You choose … and the leader you have chosen, you have to support him. That was my logic and I think the logic worked."

In the second volume of his memoirs, *From Third World to First,* he says: "I had seen how Deng Xiaoping had failed with his appointees, Hu Yaobang and Zhao Ziyang. I also remembered how Anthony Eden, chosen by Winston Churchill, failed."

If he were to appoint his own successor, his first choice, he said, would have been Tony Tan. He was impressed with both Tan's quickness of mind and decisiveness.

Goh Chok Tong might be quicker but he tended to try to please everybody, allowing, for instance, journalists to badger him and drag on a meeting unnecessarily, Lee observed. While he could be effective in one-on-one and small group discussions, he was ill at ease when addressing a large audience. Like many of his peers who grew up speaking Hokkien at home and then learnt English at school, he often lapsed into using the same tonal accents of the dialect when he spoke in English that could make him sound awkward. Lee ranked him second in his assessment.

Ong Teng Cheong was third. Lee thought he was equable, patient, fair and decisive. But he was more at ease with Mandarin than with English. Mandarin may be important in the domestic arena, but English is the country's working currency and the language of international science and commerce. The prime minister of Singapore had to be adept in it.

Lee judged Lim Chee Onn to be taciturn and someone who did not know how to look people in the eye.

He ruled out S Dhanabalan because the hard reality was that Singapore's ethnic Chinese majority population was not ready for an ethnic Indian prime minister.

Now, four years after Lee had given them his assessment, the core group of second-generation leaders went to him with their unanimous choice of Goh and Ong for the new deputy minister positions. Lee accepted the group's decision and worked with them on the new cabinet positions.

On 1 January 1985, Goh—flanked by his team—held a press conference at the Istana to announce the new cabinet line-up. The positions of the key players:

Goh Chok Tong would be first deputy prime minister and at the same time, retain his previous defence portfolio.

Ong Teng Cheong would be second deputy prime minister while remaining head of the labour movement, the NTUC.

Tony Tan would keep his finance portfolio and swap the trade and industry job for those of education and health. He would, in effect, have three portfolios.

S Dhanabalan would remain the minister for foreign affairs and double up as the minister for community development.

Yeo Ning Hong, who was the minister for communications, would become the minister for an enlarged Ministry of Communications and Information, which absorbed the information portfolio of the former Ministry of Culture, and also remain second minister for defence (policy). The culture portfolio was absorbed by the new Ministry of Community Development.

S Rajaratnam, who contested in the election, was made the senior minister in the PMO, a specially created post. In deference to him, the younger ministers agreed that he would be second on the protocol list.

Lim Chee Onn would remain in the backbench where he had gone after his fallout from NTUC in 1983.

Using the analogy of soccer, Singapore's most popular spectator sport, Goh said he would be the centre forward and striker, and Lee, as prime minister, the goalkeeper.

He said: "We have discussed this with the prime minister. He's very happy that we are going to play the leadership role. The exercise of self-renewal is irreversible. He has planned for this and is delighted that we are prepared to take the challenge to play a more dominant role in the cabinet in running the country's affairs ... The prime minister will take a back seat but he will not play the role of the back seat driver. He will play the role of goalkeeper."

But what if the views of the new generation leaders differed from Lee's? How would the differences be resolved? "Unless the issues are so fundamental that they involve national security and the survival of the country, we would not expect the prime minister to overrule us," Goh answered, and added unequivocally: "We will run this place and we must be left alone to run the country ... Our views must prevail."

At the same press conference, Ong Teng Cheong said: "The seven of us (Goh, Ong, Tan, Dhanabalan, Ahmad Mattar, S Jayakumar and Yeo Ning Hong) have been working closely for a number of years ... and know one another very well. We meet and discuss many times in a week.

"We know one another's thinking and stand, and what is best for Singapore. We have differences of views but we are all moving in the right direction. The self-renewal started many years ago and we have come to the final phase. This is the best time to shift the centre of gravity."

Tony Tan added: "We have had many discussions and I am extremely happy that Goh Chok Tong is ready to act as the leader man, the striker. His choice, without any reservations, has the full support of all of us as well as the ministers of state."

⚜

Knock on Wood

LEE Kuan Yew might have accepted the second-generation leaders' choice of Goh Chok Tong as their leader in 1984 but he unsettled both them and the public four years later, at the National Day rally in August, when he made public his 1980 assessment of the five key men.

His blunt statement on how he thought Goh tried to please too many people when he should not and that his first choice as successor was Tony Tan although he had known by 1984 that the latter was not interested in the job, shook the people.

Goh, who was "puzzled and stunned" by the speech, remembered the awkwardness at the reception after the event. "How would the people come and greet me? It was very awkward. They looked at me … they didn't know whether to smile or to sympathise with me," he said.

His good friend Ahmad Mattar was furious, he said. He told Ahmad in jest: "If the prime minister does this to me again next year, I'll walk out." "I'll walk out with you," Ahmad said to him.

Goh's wife, equally puzzled, asked: "Why did he say that?"

Lee caused yet another stir among the people a few days later—at a session with students from the National University of Singapore and the Nanyang Technological Institute, now Nanyang Technological University—when he described Goh as "wooden" and said that he might have to see a psychiatrist about it .

In pointing out how Goh could not convey through television and mass meetings what he could in individual face-to-face or small group discussions, he said: "I have suggested to him [to seek] perhaps a bit of psychological adjustment, maybe [see] a psychiatrist … something holds him back. He is … before a mass audience … he gets wooden—which he is not. When you speak to him one-to-one, he has strong feelings. Get him on television, it's difficult [to see that]. He has improved, I will say, about 20 per cent. He needs to improve by more than 100 per cent."

Someone differently constituted from Goh could have been thrown on the mat by so harsh a public judgement and not get up after the count of 10 but not Goh. Looking back, he said simply: "It did not hurt … I knew Mr Lee well. He's not a man to slam you for nothing. He was never personal. So I did not feel he wanted to insult me … He had his purpose in saying what he said. I think he was disappointed with me for my inability to mobilise the ground. So he wanted to get me to do something about it."

He added: "I knew myself. I was a block of wood. So? It was the truth. But I was prepared to take on the job. If I could not do the job, then so be it. That was my strength. I was not chasing after the job. If I were, if my ambition was to be prime minister, then I'd be furious that my chances had diminished."

This did not prevent him from speculating that Lee could still have wanted Tan to be the successor although Tan and his peers had plumped for him. Lee could have made his less than favourable public assessment of Goh to see if the PAP cadres and MPs would reject him as a result.

If they did, then Tan, however reluctant he was, would have to take his place. Tan was well liked by the people, Goh said, but he believed he was more popular among the cadres than Tan since he had worked closely with them for many years.

As it turned out, it was Tony Tan and Lee Hsien Loong who led the cadres and the people to rally round Goh. At a PAP rally at the Singapore Conference Hall on August 21, Lee Hsien Loong made it clear that all the cabinet ministers and all the members of the party's central executive committee (CEC), except Lee Kuan Yew, worked for Goh Chok Tong.

"We acknowledged him as our leader and in fact, we—that means the younger ministers—discussed it among ourselves and have decided that he'll be the next prime minister," he said to loud applause from the party cadres.

"He brought many of us into politics, including me. If comrade Goh had not invited me to stand, I would not be in politics because I cannot volunteer," he added.

At a community event in Sembawang on the same day, Tony Tan told reporters that the second-generation leaders had met after the 1984 general election and decided unanimously that Goh should lead them and take over from Lee eventually. "I see no reason at all why that decision should be changed, and the task for all of us is to support Goh Chok Tong in his very difficult job," he stressed.

Goh himself did not remain silent. At a National Day dinner at his Marine Parade ward a week after Lee's rally speech, he said to his constituents: "I told the prime minister many times ... I will not change my style. It is part of my temperament and personality, and I cannot change my personality or my temperament.

"But habits, if they are not so good habits and if they can be improved upon, certainly, I should change those habits. But style is part of my temperament. It cannot be changed."

On Lee's point about his desire to please people, he said: "I would not use the word 'please' to describe my attitude. I would use the word 'accommodate'. In other words, I listen, I talk, I try to persuade and try to bring as many people on board as possible...

"I regard this style of mine as a strength, not a weakness. Karate chops have to be executed when necessary. But I like to use them only sparingly."

At the National Day rally speech, Lee had said that getting people to perform was not a matter of smiling and kissing babies and patting people on the back all the time. "There are times when a very good, firm karate chop is necessary. And deliver it cleanly. Don't have two chops where one would do."

Ong Keng Yong—who was Goh's press secretary from 1998 to 2002 when he left for Jakarta to head the Asean Secretariat, the central administrative organ for the group of Southeast Asian countries—observed that Goh would not reject any suggestion or idea outright, whether in the cabinet, in community work or interacting with his staff.

"He would listen to the pros and cons, work out a balance and match it with his own opinion. In this disarming way, he would bring people around to a particular idea," Ong said.

"He might be patient but no issue was left to stew for too long. If something had to be left on the burner for a slow boil, it would have been a deliberate decision ... His style was [that] he would get into the deep end of the swimming pool with you and knock around a particular idea. Once you got out of the pool, you actually wanted to deliver results as quickly as possible. Because he had indulged you, he had listened to you, given you some ideas, polished some rough edges and then asked for action to be taken. He didn't need to give you a deadline. You knew you had failed him if he had to remind you of the task."

⋘⋙

WHEN Lee spoke to the students, he did elaborate on Goh's qualities. He had no doubts about the latter's integrity and dedication, he said. Goh had shown that he could not be bought when he was head of the Neptune Orient Lines. He had to do business with very wealthy people, like shipping magnate Y K Pao, but he was not seduced by their way of life.

Since 1980, Goh had found 30 of the 61 candidates that PAP fielded in 1981 and 1984, and would field in the 1988 election. Most importantly, he was not afraid to pick able men, men who could be his contenders. Lee cited, in particular, his son Lee Hsien Loong and the Cambridge-trained biochemist Yeo Ning Hong.

Goh had first-class interpersonal skills but he was no softie. He was not afraid to make tough decisions and push them through in parliament after he had worked the ground, selling them to the people. In the case of the CPF cut and wage restraint during the 1985 recession, for instance, he and his peers spent three months talking to all the unions.

"They pulled it off. The workers accepted not only a 15 percentage point cut in the employers' contribution but also two years of wage restraint, which is a major triumph, not attempted anywhere else in the world," Lee told the students.

But reading the newspaper reports on the event the following day, most people were drawn only to the sensational bit—that Goh was wooden and needed to see a psychiatrist.

For the many Singaporeans who wondered what Lee was up to in assessing his successor Goh in so public and blunt a fashion, he cleared the air a month later, at the PAP's lunchtime rally at Fullerton Square for the 1988 general election. He told the crowd that his recent candid assessment of Goh was "not a bad gambit".

Since he "put up that balloon", Goh had become more natural on television and in front of mass audiences, he said. It was his duty to tell Singaporeans his honest assessment of Goh. At the same time, he wanted to decide, from the way Goh reacted, whether he could be his own man.

"I said: 'Speak up! Be yourself. If you are angry, say so!' The result? He's no longer inhibited. He can talk about his inability to react naturally with crowds and in the process, he has come through."

He urged the people to give Goh and his team "a ringing endorsement".

In his interviews for this book, Lee elaborated on the reasons he made public his assessment of Goh. He said: "I knew it would cause some discomfort. But this was a very critical question ... it was choosing the right man for the job. I laid down my cards. They (the second-generation leaders) chose Goh Chok Tong. Well, he had got to make the effort.

"And because I said all those things, he felt uncomfortable. But I said to him: 'Look, you may not be a natural speaker but you've got to start learning, because you can't be a leader when you can't communicate.'

"I told him when I was doing my campaigning in 1960 and 1961, every lunchtime I was eating and learning Hokkien from scratch. And by the end of the campaign, I was able to make some speeches in Hokkien. So he was willing to do it. He knew he had to make the effort. And he made the effort. As the years progressed, he improved."

The majority of the ethnic Chinese population in Singapore are descendants of immigrants who had come from the southern Chinese province of Fujian, where Hokkien is the principal dialect. In the 1960s, most of the people were uneducated, hence Lee's need to master Hokkien. After Goh Keng Swee introduced national service in 1967, he found he had to form separate Hokkien-speaking platoons because many of the

18-year-olds could not understand the English and Malay instructions of their officers. It would take another two decades before the need for such platoons was made redundant, thanks to universal education.

Panjang from the *Longkang*

THAT Goh Chok Tong made the effort was clearly evident in the annual National Day rally speeches which he had been giving since he became prime minister in 1990. Usually held at the Kallang Theatre in those years, the event was broadcast live on national television. In the first couple of years, Singaporeans who loved him would sit on the edge of their chairs and will that he would not stumble. In subsequent years though, they could afford to sit back and just listen to him, and even laugh with him.

He did not have to consult a psychiatrist. What he did was to find himself a good speech trainer who also taught him how to be less inhibited when speaking in public.

Ong Keng Yong explained how thoroughly Goh prepared for his annual speeches. Goh would write the draft himself because he believed he would remember better his own words and he wanted to speak with conviction. His staff would help him gather the necessary material.

Each time he finished a section, he would practise it in front of Ong and his principal private secretary. They would tell him if a particular joke was not funny or if he mispronounced certain words. He spent whole weekends writing and polishing the draft of the speech and rehearsing it.

By the time Ong became his press secretary in 1998, Goh was so practised in delivering his speeches that his audience could not tell how much effort he still put into their preparation. When Ong suggested to him that he might no longer need to labour so hard over his draft, Goh said: "No, you must do it properly. You must always find the right word to put in the right place."

Over the years, even as he polished up his articulation, eliminating as much as possible the rough Hokkien tonal edges, he found he could also use Hokkien to his advantage in a joke or a Singlish phrase, which would often have the crowd at the Kallang Theatre breaking out into laughter and applause. Certainly, he was no Lee Kuan Yew and he would never shake off his awkwardness and Hokkien tonal accents entirely. But he connected with the people all right.

In picking up Lee's gauntlet, Goh had shown he was not made of wood. As Ong Keng Yong put it, he had the resilience of a titanium rod in a golf club—deceptively light-weight yet able to resist being broken by hard knocks of any kind.

⤜⧫⤐

"EVERY man is led by one of three things: by an appetite … and I class ambitions among the appetites; or by an idea; or by an inspiration," a revolutionary leader says in D H Lawrence's most political novel, *The Plumed Serpent*. All his life, Goh Chok Tong had been led primarily by an idea—the idea of duty.

Since he was a student in Raffles Institution (RI), the leading secondary school whose history goes back to Stamford Raffles, Goh had always had responsibility thrust upon him. It might be because his height of 1.88m marked him out—his neighbourhood friends called him Panjang ("tall" or "long" in Malay)—but he was obviously more mature than boys of his age.

He was the eldest of five children. When he was nine, he was summoned from school to the bedside of his father who was dying from tuberculosis. His father's last words to him were: "Look after your mother, look after your brother and sisters, study hard." The loss of his father at that early age and the heavy responsibility placed on him made him mature earlier than others of his age.

In any case, the young Goh was not one to say no when called upon to perform one duty or another. He was the class monitor, school prefect, swimming team captain, scout patrol leader, editor of the school magazine and even the students' representative on the tuckshop committee. As chairman of the school's historical society, he had invited then-chief minister David Marshall and opposition leader Lee Kuan Yew to speak to the students.

He said: "I have always had this sense of responsibility. I have never turned down any job that I am asked to do … It's this sense of responsibility, not so much as outstanding leadership skills, which somehow people felt. You could be trusted to do the job … they asked you to do the job."

It would be this sense of responsibility and duty that led him into politics and to eventually become the prime minister of Singapore.

⤜⧫⤐

GOH grew up in his grandmother's house in Pasir Panjang, near the sea, together with his four uncles and three aunts. At any one time, there were at least three families of boarders. His grandmother had divided up the rooms in the house into smaller ones and built more in the enclosed courtyard to take in boarders to support the extended family. His grandfather, a small-time trader in Chinatown, had died early.

Goh has a brother and three sisters. Together with his mother, they lived, squeezed into one of the rooms. Later, when he moved into a room of his own, it was just long enough to fit in his tall frame. The house had only one bathroom and one toilet shared by some 20 people.

Very few Singapore homes had a flush toilet at the time. People generally used a black bucket, over which they squatted. The bucket system was organised islandwide and there was an army of night soil carriers who visited homes every morning to replace the buckets, two at a time, which they balanced on a yoke between their shoulders. These men would come in a truck custom-built to have two tiers of compartments on either side to hold the buckets. The collected waste would be transported to the two night soil treatment centres, one in Park Road and the other in Albert Street, both in Chinatown. There, the waste would be converted into a sludge fertiliser.

The last of the night soil carriers were phased out only as late as 1979. A public campaign had to be carried out in the 1980s to teach people the habit of flushing every time they went into a public toilet because many had not yet been accustomed to doing so.

When the street lamps came up on the main road, Goh's grandmother did not have the money to run the electrical wires into her house that was about 30 metres away from the road. There was no electricity for a long time. Kerosene lamps were lit come nightfall.

Goh's father came to Singapore with his parents from Yongchun, near Quanzhou in the Chinese province of Fujian. His father and grandfather traded in sundry goods out of a small Chinatown shop. Both of them died early. After his father's death, Goh's mother became a primary school teacher to help support the family.

In 1963, when the PAP government built an HDB estate in Queenstown, one of the island's earliest ones, she bought a three-room flat there and moved in with her family. Goh was by then a final year student at the-then University of Singapore.

The eldest uncle, who worked in a biscuit factory, was the principal breadwinner in the extended family. Over time, he would have six children. The aunts moved out one by one after they got married.

Goh was close to the fourth and youngest uncle who put himself through school and was influenced by the left-wing movement of the time. This uncle introduced Russian literature—Gorky, Turgenev, Tolstoy—to the young Goh. The hardcover books were English translations, beautifully bound and in glossy paper, perhaps subsidised by the Russian government, Goh thought on looking back. He was also the one who took the boy to the election rallies of PAP, then a newly formed opposition party. Sadly, this uncle died when he was only 44.

At the back of the house ran a large monsoon drain, or *longkang*, which would be filled with rushing water from the sea when the tide came up. It was here that Goh learnt how to swim. He would become the swimming captain at RI.

Goh went to RI where he received a government bursary. He was also a bursary student at the university, where he did English, geography and economics in his first year. He did well enough to qualify for an honours year in any of the three subjects. His geography professor encouraged him to take the subject but he chose economics and graduated with first class honours in 1964.

He had hoped to go on a doctorate course. But the government bursary required that he served five years in the civil service. His first stint was at the PMO's Economic Planning Unit, at a salary of $830. When Shell had an opening, a job that offered $1,100, he applied for it. The Anglo-Dutch oil company had rigorous tests for new recruits, which Lee Kuan Yew would later adapt to select his party candidates. Goh did well in his tests and Shell snapped him up, giving him a loan to buy out his bond.

But Goh Keng Swee, who was the finance minister, recognised the young man's potential and snatched him back. Chok Tong had married his school sweetheart after he clinched the Shell job and was on honeymoon in his in-laws' house in Kuala Lumpur when Shell cabled him to return to Singapore urgently. The older Goh had wanted him back, he was told by the people at Shell. But, they added, he could choose not to return to the civil service since he had already signed the contract and the bond had been bought out. There was no question though about the choice he had to make. And so it was back to the Economic Planning Unit.

In 1966 his immediate boss, Joe Pillay—the top civil servant who helped Hon Sui Sen manage the conversion of the British bases to productive enterprises—sent him on a fellowship to Williams College in Massachusetts in the United States where he topped the master's degree class. Upon his return the following year, he was sought out by Lee Kuan Yew, who was then casting around for a new principal private secretary. "I'm looking for a general factotum, an errand boy," he told Goh. "When can you start?"

Pillay would have none of it. He got then-finance minister Lim Kim San to convince Lee that the young man was more useful where he was.

Soon after, Goh Keng Swee wanted someone to join the World Bank to understand how it worked, in case Singapore needed to apply loans from it. He got the younger Goh a three-year stint as a project officer at the world body based in Washington DC.

Chok Tong found that the salary would not be enough to support the family especially since his wife had just delivered a pair of twins and, in moving to Washington, she would have to give up her work as a lawyer as well. After some checking, he found that his World Bank job was equivalent to that of a first secretary in a foreign mission who, on top of his salary, was entitled to housing and other allowances. He asked if he could be given the allowances too.

When the senior Goh, known for his fiscal prudence, said no, Chok Tong turned down the job. The former was understandably furious because he had gone out of the way to get him the job that normally went to PhD holders only.

Back at the Economic Planning Unit, Chok Tong told Pillay: "Why don't you second me to NOL instead for some private sector exposure?" NOL is Neptune Orient Lines which Goh Keng Swee had started a year earlier.

And so he joined the national shipping line as its planning and projects manager, and rose quickly to become its financial director and then managing director. He was 32 years old then. He was buying container ships that cost between $15 million and $20 million. He had a chauffeur-driven Mercedes 200 and a company house. He was courted by shipping tycoons like Y K Pao.

It could be heady for a young man, especially one who, as a poor student, had studied by the light of a kerosene lamp. But Goh did not lose himself. Because NOL was not making money yet, he insisted on flying economy class, even on long-haul flights, to set an example to his staff. Before long, he was starting to make money for NOL. And that was when

Hon Sui Sen, then the finance minister, approached him to join PAP.

Duty called. He had benefited from the PAP government and had seen what it had done for the people. He could not say no.

~❧~

DUTY makes demands of one. Sometimes, in the line of duty, one must overcome certain qualms and take actions that may affect people's lives. But an effective leader of a country cannot flinch from doing what he believes is right for his people, even when in doing so he may alarm them to a certain degree initially. Truth will out and people will renew their respect for him if what he has done proves to be in their interest in the end.

The closing years of the 1980s would make such demands on Goh Chok Tong. He had to deal with a Marxist group. He had to also tackle an opponent in the 1988 general election who was ushered into the ring by probably well-intentioned American State Department officers who wanted Singapore to be their model of democracy for the rest of Asia, especially an awakened China which had rolled up its bamboo blinds.

Goh would be tested and this time, not by Lee.

25

Puppets and a Dangerous Game

BY the 1980s, Singapore had become a bustling metropolis. It had a "boom town" feel about it as everywhere one looked, there was construction work going on. The skyline was cluttered with so many building cranes that the cranes came to be dubbed the national bird. There was full employment, the people had a home to go back to after work and few went hungry. The days of political strife and social unrest were long over. A new generation had grown up knowing only peace, stability and relative affluence. Who would have thought that in this transformed society, a militant ideology that had been defeated in the 1960s would rear its ugly head again?

As it happened, Singaporeans were generally surprised, some even incredulous, when they were told in May 1987 by the government that it had arrested 16 Marxist conspirators who were plotting against it from under the cover of Catholic church-based organisations and student bodies. Except for four of them, the 16 men and women were English-educated graduates and professionals. In their profiles published in the newspapers, they came across as idealistic do-gooders who had found their cause among the less unfortunate, including domestic maids from the Philippines and Indonesia.

But as government statements subsequently revealed, these 16 men and women were being manipulated by a former student activist and committed Marxist, Tan Wah Piow, who had fled to Britain in 1976 to escape national service. Growing up in a pro-communist family—his two elder brothers were associated with the Malayan Communist Party (MCP) in the 1960s—Tan was drawn early to left-wing politics. He was a student agitator who operated under the banner of a Christian group and then sought to politicise the University of Singapore Students' Union when he got himself elected as its president in 1974. He was then an architecture student at the university.

In the same year, Tan was involved in an industrial dispute in Jurong that led eventually to rioting by some workers at a trade union office. In

1975, after a trial that lasted more than 40 days, he was found guilty for unlawful assembly and rioting and sentenced to a year's jail.

Released after eight months in prison, he was called up for national service, which is compulsory for all male citizens when they turn 18 or, in Tan's time, when they had finished their tertiary education or had stopped their studies. He went into hiding and subsequently found his way to Britain with a forged renewed passport endorsement.

His leftist contacts there got him a place at Bradford University, which secured him a student visa. He did not cease his Marxist activities and according to government statements, plotted to subvert Singapore through the group of people who were detained. In 1987, when he was 35 years old, he was a second-year law student at Balliol College, Oxford University.

His co-conspirator in Singapore was a 40-year-old lay church worker Vincent Cheng who was identified by the government as the leader of the Marxist group. The men's association went back to the days of the Jurong industrial dispute when they were both in the same student Christian body.

Cheng, who has a master's degree in theology, saw Tan as a mentor. He was also very much influenced by liberation theology, a popular militant movement at that time which argued for the Catholic Church's involvement in the overthrowing of oppressive state regimes. It had grown out of the churches in South American countries and spread to countries like the Philippines whose population was largely Catholic.

According to government statements, Cheng had made several visits to the Philippines where he established contacts with clergymen linked to the communist party in the country. He studied the ways the Communist Party of the Philippines had captured control of certain church social action agencies and set up front organisations under the Catholic banner to advance its cause.

Back in Singapore, Cheng had some members in his group infiltrate the Workers' Party (WP) in the early 1980s. While keeping a low profile, they helped to print and distribute the party's pamphlets in the 1984 general election. They took control of the party's publication, *The Hammer*, to disseminate anti-government propaganda and stir up dissatisfaction.

When asked about it in an interview at his Sim Lim Tower office, J B Jeyaretnam, who was at the time secretary-general of the WP, said it was "the biggest hoax that PAP put out in 1987, that we were being infiltrated by Marxists". He was aware of a group helping out in the party but they were not in the frontline, he said.

Jeyaretnam claimed he knew only one of them, a lawyer named Teo Soh Lung. In 1986, Teo was a key witness in a parliamentary select committee hearing on the proposed Legal Profession (Amendment) Bill. Lee Kuan Yew had asked for changes to the Legal Profession Act to tighten disciplinary procedures and to disqualify errant lawyers from standing for election, after Francis Seow, a former solicitor-general, was elected to be the president of the governing council of the Law Society in January of that year.

Lee knew well Seow's less than illustrious career as a lawyer. The latter had left the Legal Service, where he had worked for 15 years, after a scandal in 1971. He started his own firm but was suspended from practice twice—for a year in 1973 for improper conduct in relation to a chit-fund company's pyramid-selling scam, and for six months in 1984 after he was convicted and fined $1,000 in the High Court in 1982 for making a false declaration when he reapplied for a practising certificate in 1980. (Lawyers had to apply for the certificate every year.) He had a judgement against him for more than $100,000 that he did not disclose. He was also heavily in debt and had been so since his time in the Legal Service.

In September, S Jayakumar, then home affairs minister and second law minister, said before a debate on the proposed bill in parliament that the issue at the heart of the new legislation was "integrity and responsibility in the highest quarters of the legal profession". After the debate by several PAP MPs and the only two opposition MPs, J B Jeyaretnam and Chiam See Tong, both of whom spoke out against it, he sent it to a select committee.

Meanwhile, Teo Soh Lung and another lawyer in the Marxist group, Tang Fong Har, helped organise an extraordinary meeting where more than 400 lawyers, including the entire council of the Law Society, voted a motion to reject the bill.

Both Teo and Tang, together with Seow and several other witnesses, appeared at the select committee hearing at the Parliament House Annexe in October before a panel chaired by the speaker of parliament, Yeoh Ghim Seng. They faced relentless questioning by Lee, law minister E W Barker and Jayakumar. The proceedings, held over two days, were televised. At the end of the hearing, all were agreed that the Law Society should keep out of politics.

According to government statements, Teo Soh Lung and Tang Fong Har had worked to turn the society into a political pressure group. Earlier in the year, at their instigation, Seow had issued a public statement that criticised the proposed Newspaper and Printing Presses (Amendment) Bill. The bill was meant to restrict the circulation of offshore publications if they were deemed by the government to be interfering in domestic politics. As the society's past president Harry Elias testified at the hearing, the statement was an unprecedented action taken by the body which had previously been concerned only with its own professional matters.

After having been passed by parliament in late October, the Legal Profession (Amendment) Act was put into force in early November. It ended Seow's 10-month long presidency of the 1,335-strong Law Society.

⁕

BESIDES taking over control of *The Hammer,* Vincent Cheng's group also took over Catholic church publications. It used them to question the usefulness of national service, attack the alleged exploitation of workers by the multinationals and portray the social system as "unjust" and "repressive".

Goh Chok Tong said he played an active role in the arrest of the 16 after Internal Security Department (ISD) reports alerted the top leadership to the group's activities but Lee Kuan Yew made the final decision. And it was Lee who moved in to intervene when it looked like the Catholic Church and the government could be heading towards a collision course.

There were ripples in the 105,000-strong Catholic community following the arrest of the group, 10 of whom were active church workers, both paid staff and volunteers. A fair number of Catholics could not bring themselves to see the church workers as subversives.

Lee arranged for Archbishop Gregory Yong, the 62-year-old head of the archdiocese of Singapore at the time, and a delegation of five priests, a nun and three lay leaders to visit the Istana where they were shown documents by the home affairs ministry before he met them to brief them on the reasons for the arrests. At a press conference after the meeting, the archbishop told reporters that he accepted the government's position because Vincent Cheng himself had admitted that he was using the Church as a cover.

Three days later, the archbishop met with his 80 priests to order them not to mix politics and religion in their sermons. He also suspended four priests who had earlier resigned from their positions in various church organisations, including Edgar D'Souza, the Church's spokesman who also edited the *Catholic News*. He had used it to agitate Catholics against the arrest of Cheng and company.

Cheng was detained for two years. Four detainees were released in June, even as six more, including Tang Fong Har, were arrested. All of them, except for Cheng, were released after they had given statements about their activities to the ISD and appeared in interviews on television.

Of the Marxist group, Goh said: "Some were conscious of what they were doing. Many [of the others] had their own ideals for Singapore but they were not fully aware that they were being manipulated by other people."

He confirmed that ISD investigations found "there were connections between Tan Wah Piow and a few others, and the MCP who had then relocated their broadcasting station from Malaysia to southern China".

In a speech which he gave at a PAP Youth Wing seminar in July 1987, Jayakumar had suggested that Tan was not the puppet master behind the Marxist plot but a puppet "in a larger, more sinister and dangerous game". There were many unanswered questions surrounding Tan's escape from Singapore and his 10-year exile in Britain. He seemed well provided for. "Who gave him the thousands of pounds sterling needed to set up his typesetting firm in London?" Jayakumar asked.

Tan denied he was a communist and expressed the hope to return to Singapore when the political climate was more conducive. "Jeyaretnam's Anson victory broke the hegemony of PAP ... Lee Kuan Yew sensed a problem for his second echelon in the trend amongst my generation not to take things as they were before," he told a Malaysian newspaper.

"What I want is to humanise capitalism. In Singapore, we can introduce a great deal of political reform by strengthening the structures of democracy."

⚜

IF it was Lee who had ordered the first arrest, it was Goh who ordered the re-arrest of eight members of the group when in April 1988, they issued a joint statement which alleged that the government had fabricated the

Marxist plot and had tortured the detainees to compel them to admit to the lies that made up that plot. Lee was away in Italy then, on a stopover after his visit to the United States where President Ronald Reagan had welcomed him warmly. Also arrested was a lawyer, Patrick Seong, who had instigated the group to come out with the statement.

Goh said of the re-arrest: "I decided on it because having released those people, when they issued the statement, it was like they were throwing a bomb in your face. If we didn't re-arrest them, it would be very difficult to handle them and subsequently, people like them, because it would have shown that our case was weak. So we had to re-arrest them."

With the re-arrest, the government announced that it would hold a commission of inquiry into the matter. But the inquiry would prove unnecessary. Soon after their arrest, they and other former detainees gave sworn statutory declarations in which they reaffirmed that the statements given to the ISD and in the television interviews were indeed true.

Investigation reports subsequently released by the government revealed that the joint statement was not just an innocent attempt by the eight to clear their names. It was a political ploy to discredit the government in an election year. The plan was to build up a campaign of smears about the government's alleged illegal use of force and improper use of the Internal Security Act (ISA) to detain the group. The offshore press, which included the *Far Eastern Economic Review*, *Asiaweek* and the *Asian Wall Street Journal*, were made use of in the campaign, as were western human rights groups like Asia Watch.

The government suggested that those who had signed the joint statement were not the prime movers behind the campaign. It said: "The arrest and re-arrest of the Marxist conspirators raise a larger political issue, one which Singaporeans must determine for ourselves.

"It is for Singaporeans to decide how Singapore should be governed, and whether powers like detention without trial for subversion, secret society activities and drug trafficking, and measures like the death penalty are necessary for the safety and security of the Republic.

"Overseas interest groups, the foreign press and foreign powers have no right to interfere ... These are internal issues and the next election will resolve them in a decisive manner."

Another Foreign Hand

FRANCIS Seow did have an illustrious beginning in his career as a lawyer. After having been called to the Bar, he was made deputy public prosecutor under the British colonial government in 1956. In 1963, Lee Kuan Yew got him to help chief justice Wee Chong Jin carry out a commission of inquiry into the boycott of the secondary four examinations by the Singapore Chinese Middle School Students' Union (SCMSSU).

The union had charged that the PAP government was going to scrub out Chinese language and culture, and staged the boycott to protest against it. This was in the midst of PAP's campaign to have Singapore join Malaya in a merger and against a backdrop of unrelenting communist agitation.

Seow acquitted himself well, showing during the 79-day inquiry that the Chinese school students had been manipulated by the communists, just as the undergraduates and staff of Nanyang University had.

Before he was made solicitor-general in 1967, he was a star public prosecutor, taking on high-profile cases that packed the courtrooms and got maximum exposure in the press. But in 1971, after a police raid on his woman friend's apartment, he used his influence and friendship with the then-director of the Corrupt Practices Investigations Bureau, Yoong Siew Wah, to have the four officers who had conducted the raid sacked. The attorney-general Tan Boon Teik intervened to reinstate the four officers. Seow was allowed to resign rather than have his actions investigated because of his track record in the Legal Service. Yoong was also asked to quit.

Seow dropped out of public attention until 1986 when he appeared in the televised proceedings of the select committee hearing on the proposed amendments to the Legal Profession Act. Questioned by Lee on his fitness to head the Law Society, he put on an insouciant show, addressing the former as "my dear prime minister" repeatedly until he was told to stop doing so. Lee, on his part, allowed his impatience with the impertinent man to show.

Seow was one of those slick types who seemed to have been made for television. Although he was 59 years old, he had retained a smooth and fair face, was stylishly dressed and was articulate. That he dared to stand up to the stern Lee won him fans. "Overnight, a TV star had been born," he gloats in a self-regarding memoir published in the United States in 1994.

His bandit-hero stature grew in 1988 when he was arrested under the

ISA. He had acted as counsel for one of the Marxist detainees, Teo Soh Lung, the previous year. In 1988, after the eight in the group were arrested again together with Patrick Seong, he was counsel for both Teo and Seong. In May, he was suddenly detained.

The arrest shook many people. They wondered if the PAP government had gone overboard just to shut out a potential political opponent. But the government revealed soon enough that two senior American State Department officers, Joseph Snyder, the former director of the Indonesia, Malaysia, Brunei and Singapore affairs, and David Lambertson, deputy assistant secretary of state for East Asia and Pacific affairs, and their subordinate on the ground, E Mason Hendrickson, had instigated Seow and several lawyers to take part in the coming election against PAP.

Hendrickson, who was the first secretary (political) at the embassy, was asked to leave the country in 48 hours. The American government complied and retaliated by booting out Singapore's first secretary (political) in Washington DC, Robert Chua Hian Kong.

It became clear that the joint statement issued by the ex-detainees had a link to the attempted American interference in Singapore's internal affairs. As Goh Chok Tong told his Marine Parade grassroots leaders at a dialogue: "The joint statement was meant to confuse the ground and sour the mood of the people against the government. At the same time, the US official (Hendrickson) worked on the lawyers to stand together with Francis Seow during the election."

In interviews for this book, Goh said the PAP government's assessment of the episode was that Snyder, Lambertson and Hendrickson were not against Singapore specifically. He said: "They did not want Singapore to be a model for China in the way we ran our country. They wanted us to be a successful country more in the image of America so that China would follow that model."

The American officers' fears were not unfounded. China was beginning to open up and since Deng Xiaoping's visit to Singapore in 1978, a constant stream of Chinese officials had been coming to this city-state in the Nanyang ("south seas" in Mandarin) to study its methods of governance and its very successful public housing programme, among other things.

In a press conference, Goh cited another reason for the interference by the American officers whom he thought did not have the backing of the Reagan administration. The strategic interest of the United States could be served by having both a friendly government and friendly opposition in Singapore, he pointed out.

In parliament in June, Goh touched on how Hendrickson's meddling could lead to the destruction of Singapore's system, one built over a period of 30 years. Hendrickson had chosen to back a man whose personal character and professional conduct were contrary to what Singaporeans expected their leaders to be, he said. "He was undermining a basic traditional strength of our society—that only honourable men and women should be in parliament. It is this lack of understanding of our society and our philosophy of government which upsets us ...

"I am prepared to believe that Hendrickson probably meant Singapore no harm and was acting out of ignorance. Indeed, he may even have thought that instigating and contriving an effective opposition led by Francis Seow was good for Singapore ... But he had no idea that he would have done immense harm to Singapore had his scheme succeeded."

Hendrickson and his State Department minders call to mind the earnest but politically naive US officer in Graham Greene's *The Quiet American* (1955), the novel that anticipated the American war in Vietnam. In the book, while the French Army was grappling with Vietminh in Indochina, the US officer planned some boy-scout actions which, if they were not eventually aborted, would have proven disastrous to all parties.

Asked by the BBC in a telephone interview if Singapore's international reputation had been damaged by what it called "heavy-handed tactics by the government against its opponents", Lee Hsien Loong, then the trade and industry minister, said that, on the contrary, the nation's standing would be damaged if it allowed itself to be manipulated and subverted.

"If Singapore can show that it can be firm with a good strategic ally like the US and put its house in order without rupturing long-term links, then Singaporeans will learn ... those who subvert will learn that this is the way Singapore is and outsiders, please lay off..."

This was not the first time that foreign groups had used Singaporeans as proxies to influence domestic politics in Singapore, the government pointed out. In 1957 and 1958, the CIA funnelled $700,000 (a big sum at the time) to Chew Swee Kee, the education minister in Lim Yew Hock's government, through Taiwan.

According to the PAP government, in 1971, millions were channelled through Donald Stephens, the former chief minister of Sabah who had retired in Australia, to prop up the *Singapore Herald*, a newspaper that had set itself up as an alternative to the mainstream *Straits Times*. It tried to mimic the press in the US and Britain, publishing articles which challenged the government and glamourising the more permissive and disruptive lifestyle which had been brought about by the countercultural waves of the 1960s.

Despite its western veneer, Singapore was still very much an Asian society. It has opened up a lot since then but in the 1970s, the PAP leadership believed strongly it was certainly not ready to have the kind of anti-establishment anomie and decadence that dissipated the energies of the young in the west.

⚜

The 1988 General Election

GIVEN the good relations Singapore had always enjoyed with the United States, the so-called "Hendrickson Affair" blew over quickly enough.

When Francis Seow was arrested, there were charges in the opposition camp that it was to prevent him from taking part in the election. But although he was detained for a year, he was released in July, in time for the September election, and he secured a WP ticket to stand in the Eunos Group Representation Constituency (GRC).

It was in the 1988 general election that the PAP government first introduced the GRC system. The House passed it after a 13-member parliamentary select committee, which included opposition MP Chiam See Tong, had held a three-day hearing on it. The GRC clustered together three single-seat wards—it would later be expanded to up to six—and at least one of its candidates had to be from a minority race, whether Malay, Indian or Eurasian.

Since the building of new HDB estates in the late 1960s—it allowed the PAP government to break up the racial enclaves encouraged by the British and reshuffle the population—it was inevitable that the ethnic Chinese, who form the majority in the population, would also form the majority in all the wards.

Lee had noted earlier in the year that the younger people were now voting for individuals, not their parties, and the danger of minority race candidates not being voted into parliament was very real. That the people still voted along racial lines was clear in the last few general elections. As seen in Chapter 23, Goh Chok Tong and Ang Kok Peng of Buona Vista faced relatively unknown Malay opponents in the 1976 elections. But Goh had a larger pool of Malay voters in his constituency, hence his 78.62 per cent votes against Ang's 82.75 per cent.

The opposition insisted that it was an election ploy by PAP. In any case, 10 three-member GRCs and 40 single-seat wards were contested.

Seow chose to contest in Eunos as it was the largest GRC, with 75,723 voters. The second biggest was Aljunied, with 65,351 voters. The other GRCs had numbers ranging from more than 40,000 to more than 60,000. His teammates were Lee Siew Choh, the old warhorse from Barisan Sosialis, and a 37-year-old part-time comedian, Mohd Khalit B Md Baboo.

PAP moved Tay Eng Soon from Tanglin where he was originally slated to contest to head its team in Eunos. Tay had joined PAP in the 1980 general election and was the minister of state in the education ministry. The other two candidates were Zulkifli Mohammed, a grassroots leader and political secretary in the community development ministry, and Chew Heng Ching, the general manager of a publishing house.

Seow's rallies drew large crowds, which caused traffic jams along those roads that led to the rally venues. He made good political theatre, quick with his wit and what the television folks call "sound-bites". But as smooth as he was, he was often speaking over the heads of many in the audience. He was obviously someone who had lived apart from the masses all his life.

The ISA and the arrest of the Marxist group did not turn up as hot election issues, as PAP had anticipated. Instead, what dominated the hustings were a proposal made by Lee to allow for an elected president who would safeguard the nation's reserves and the integrity of its civil service, and the Town Councils Act.

Under the Act, all constituencies would have their own town councils to take care of their municipal needs by early 1991. The HDB and other central government agencies, which had been looking after these needs, would devolve the responsibilities to the individual town councils. As chairman of the town councils, an MP in a single-member ward would work with a yearly budget of about $3 million while the three MPs in a GRC would have an annual budget of $9 million. The councils would be formed in phases over the two and a half years after the election.

PAP believed that the change would make for a more stable political system because voters would have to look at election candidates very carefully before voting for those who would run their estates. It would also give the people a bigger say in how they wanted their precincts run.

Seow said in his rallies that Lee had proposed the change for an elected president because he wanted the post to remain in power. Making capital of Lee's assessment of Goh Chok Tong, he said the latter was "second-rate" and would be "a political eunuch in Lee's court" when Lee became the elected president.

(The Presidential Election Act was finally passed in parliament in 1991, after two readings of the bill and an exhaustive study by a select committee. It took effect in November 1992. Lee did not stand for the election that was held on 28 August 1993. Instead, Ong Teng Cheong contested for the post against a former accountant-general turned banker Chua Kim Yeow. He was elected and assumed office on 1 September 1993.)

On its part, PAP charged that Seow had been threatened with bankruptcy five times and had debts amounting to $1.3 million. He also faced tax evasion charges. How could he be trusted to run a town council that had an annual budget of some $10 million?

The fight in Eunos was PAP's most intense among all the fights in the wards and GRCs. PAP wanted to make sure Francis Seow did not get voted in. It succeeded but by the thinnest of margins—1,279 votes. The close shave vexed PAP particularly, because it felt that there was a certain moral blindness among the voters. Here was someone whose flawed character was so patently obvious and yet the people could still be so easily seduced.

That close shave in Eunos aside, PAP had a decisive victory despite facing the broadest challenge since 1972 in terms of the number of seats contested (81 in all). It lost only one seat, to Potong Pasir incumbent Chiam See Tong.

It did not succeed though in recapturing the ground it had lost in the 1984 general election; its share of the total votes in 1988 was 63.2 per cent, down 1.6 per cent from the 1984 results. But the leadership's biggest fear had not come to pass. It arrested the almost 13 per cent swing to the opposition in the previous election.

At a 3.40 am press conference on September 5 after the results were announced, Lee said that with PAP's solid majority, the transition from the Old Guard to the New was now complete. The future was up to them. It was indeed. Goh confirmed at the same press conference that he would be ready to take over from Lee within two years.

The last of the Old Guard had all stepped down before the election. They included Toh Chin Chye, S Rajaratnam, E W Barker, Ong Pang Boon and Jek Yeun Thong. Learning from the poor exit management practices of the past, Goh made sure he gave the credit that was due to them and nine others who had made way for younger leaders.

⚬⚬❧⚬⚬

ALTHOUGH he failed at the polls, Francis Seow could still get into parliament as a Non-Constituency MP (NCMP). Constitution changes made in 1984 allow for up to three non-constituency seats to be offered to the top losers of the opposition parties, if fewer than three opposition candidates win. The NCMPs can speak, debate motions and ask questions in parliament, although they cannot vote on critical matters.

In the 1984 general election, a WP candidate, P D Nair, qualified for the one NCMP seat available after the two other seats were won by J B Jeyaretnam and Chiam See Tong. The WP had rejected the seat at the time, saying the scheme undermined the growth of a genuine opposition.

But Seow would not allow the WP to shackle him. He said both he and Lee Siew Choh, who qualified to become NCMPs, would take up the seats. The WP acquiesced, its righteous objections to the scheme in 1984 conveniently forgotten.

Seow did not get his way, however. By the time the new parliament convened in early 1989, he was disqualified for an NCMP seat as he was found guilty on his tax evasion charges. Seow did not appear in court to face the charges though. He had gone to New York to attend a Human Rights Watch event and according to him, to undergo treatment by an American heart specialist at the same time. He would not return to Singapore.

American human rights groups have a soft spot for those they consider political dissidents whether they were genuine or false. They took good care of Seow. He obtained a fellowship at Yale Law School in 1989 and another fellowship at Harvard Law School in 1990. From the comfort of his new home in Massachusetts, he would write a memoir and two books on Singapore.

Would Seow have made a difference if he had been voted in? Certainly, there would be more political theatre in parliament where he could imagine himself cutting Lee Kuan Yew down to size before a cheering populace.

Not for him though the mundane chores of managing a town council or attending the weekly meet-the-people sessions which someone like Chiam See Tong had been doing conscientiously on the ground-floor void deck of an HDB block of flats since he took Potong Pasir. No, Seow would not have lasted long as an opposition MP but he would have wreaked enough havoc for PAP.

Lee Siew Choh was an NCMP for one term. He was by then in his early 70s and although he could still make eloquent speeches, the fire of his early days had burned out long ago.

Just Another Day in Singapore

IN June 1990, Goh Chok Tong told parliament that he would take over from Lee in November. Lee would be asked to remain in cabinet as senior minister. There would be some cabinet changes but Goh told the House, "It will be a cabinet that reflects continuity rather than change".

He spoke about new regional cooperation and his plans for a growth triangle in which Singapore would work with Johor across the causeway and the Indonesian Riau islands of Batam and Bintan. It could grow faster than the rest of ASEAN and could link with other points of growth. Singapore would also have to go international and a new breed of Singaporeans had to be prepared to work abroad.

Singapore was a middle-class society and there were new middle-class aspirations. These would have to be met. The underclass would not be forgotten either. It would be a gentler society but the government would remain tough-minded. He made it clear that it would not govern by popular polls and would not flinch from making critical decisions on issues that would be for the long-term national good. There would certainly not be a welfare state.

The end of the 1980s saw the collapse of the Berlin Wall and the break-up of the Soviet Union. Closer to home, the triumph of people power in the Philippines saw Corazon Aquino rise to become president. The world had turned. People expected a freer society.

"There will be greater freedom for Singaporeans to make their own choices and to express themselves," Goh promised, but warned, "this freedom is not extended to actions which rock the boat".

On November 27, dressed in a dark grey suit over a blue shirt and a tie, he attended a five-minute ceremony at the Istana where then-president Wee Kim Wee formally appointed him prime minister. Goh handed to the president a folder that contained the details of the new cabinet line-up.

There were no surprises. Goh had made known all new appointments in three press conferences since early October. Lee Kuan Yew would be senior minister in the PMO, second to Goh in the protocol list. Goh would have two deputy prime ministers, Ong Teng Cheong and Lee Hsien Loong. Goh would retain his defence portfolio, assisted by second minister for defence and minister for communications Yeo Ning Hong and senior minister of state for defence Lee Boon Yang. A new ministry of information and the arts would be set up. Acting minister George Yeo, who would also be senior minister of state for foreign affairs, would head it.

Goh was sworn in the next evening at City Hall in a fuss-free ceremony that was televised live. The last time the same ritual took place was 31 years ago and thousands had thronged the city centre to witness Lee Kuan Yew take office as prime minister. But this time, people stayed home to watch the historic event.

Cherian George, an academic who at the time was a reporter in *The Straits Times*, captured memorably the business-as-usual transition in an essay that he included in his book, *The Air-Conditioned Nation*. Police stopped the traffic on St Andrew's Road when the time approached for the new prime minister and his cabinet to make their appearance on the City Hall steps.

George went up to a motorcycle rider who had been stopped at the head of the queue of vehicles. He asked the man if he knew what was going on. The motorcycle rider nodded. When asked how he felt about being stopped for the event, he said simply: "It's okay. I'm not in a hurry."

He was literally the man in the street. His answer perhaps rang more eloquently than the many opinion editorial pieces in the newspapers about the smooth transfer of power. It had been carefully planned for over many years. It was nothing less than remarkable that Lee Kuan Yew had voluntarily given up his premiership to a younger man—and yet, it was for the motorcycle rider and many other Singaporeans just another day in Singapore.

As Goh Chok Tong told the president after the Istana ceremony, "We start another chapter. Life goes on."

26

The New Divide—1991

Goh? Wait

WHEN Lee Kuan Yew handed over the premiership to Goh Chok Tong in November 1990, he did not, however, relinquish all power. He stayed on as secretary-general of PAP, a post that he had held since 1954 when PAP was founded. As party chief, he had the power to replace Goh as prime minister if he should find it necessary to do so.

Goh was sanguine about it. He said: "When I became prime minister, he was not sure whether I would succeed or not. Nobody could be sure. I could not be sure myself. So he said to me: 'Better for me to hold on to the secretary-general post for one or two years.' "

On his part, Lee said: "When I stepped down in 1990, there was no guarantee that he would succeed completely. I had slowly left out all the old guards. Rajaratnam, Barker, all gone. I was the only one left.

"In 1988, I said: 'You ready to take over?' He said, no, he wanted two more years. I said: 'Okay, take your time, get accustomed to it.' But already I was passing him the major decisions. Any paper that came up, I said: 'Look, this is my view but you decide.'

"There was no guarantee he was going to succeed. So I said: 'You take over but I will remain the secretary-general.' In other words, if anything went wrong, there was a chance to pull it back."

Goh could understand Lee's caution. In his long political career, Lee had seen many bright young stars fail him. His lieutenants and allies had betrayed him. And he knew well that power could get to a man's head and lead him to do foolish things.

Lee would eventually give up the top party position to Goh in 1992. As senior minister in the new cabinet, he saw his main role as helping Goh politically, especially in the crafting and presentation of policies to the electorate.

He told the *International Herald Tribune* in September 1988: "He doesn't need help to succeed administratively. He can administer as well as I can. But to do it with political savvy so that at the end of the day, the vote comes out right—that's different." He made it clear that he had no overriding power over Goh. "Once he's got the buttons, they are his. He has to press them."

In fact, by 1988, Lee had already entrusted the government to Goh and his team, as he would reveal at a National University of Singapore forum in July 1990. The style of government had changed even earlier, after the 1984 general election, although that change was gradual. It only became more marked after the 1988 general election.

Lee said at the forum he expected more changes in the style and pace of government under Goh but he emphasised: "There will be continuity in major policies because the underlying factors have not changed. Our basic strengths and weaknesses have not altered."

Singapore's small size, its geographical position among large neighbouring countries such as Malaysia and Indonesia, and its demographic make-up of different races were "fundamental constants which Singaporeans ignore at their peril".

Goh would bide his time for the secretary-general post. After all, he had waited two years for the prime minister's seat. In his patience, he showed that indeed he "was not chasing after the job". It also pointed to a political side to the man, a side often overlooked by those who were disarmed by his geniality. He had, after all, graduated from a political apprenticeship under the most demanding of tutors. Others had not acquitted themselves as well.

One does not need to look farther than Malaysia to see how an ambitious politician, shrewd as he was, was felled by his own impatience. Anwar Ibrahim owed his meteoric rise in the dominant UMNO party to prime minister Mahathir Mohamad. He then quickly manoeuvred his way through the thickets of the political jungle that was UMNO to become deputy prime minister in December 1993.

Soon he was chafing at the bit, encouraging his supporters at home to press for a more rapid succession in the prime minister's office. Abroad, he courted the western media and projected himself as a moderate Muslim intellectual and Southeast Asia's best hope for liberal democracy. He became a poster boy in the regional news magazines.

But he was up against an even shrewder political player, someone whom Lee had once called a *tok guru silat* ("master pugilist" in Malay). Mahathir took his time, carefully preparing the ground before he bloodlessly removed his challenger from both the government and the UMNO supreme council in September 1998. Afterwards he threw him in jail, using the ISA. The former deputy was released only in 2004 by the new government of Abdullah Ahmad Badawi.

⚜

GOH Chok Tong's first make-or-break task as prime minister was the National Day rally speech. It is the annual state-of-the-nation address, televised live, which over the years Lee had set a formidable benchmark with his impossibly articulate and impassioned speeches that could go on for at least three hours.

When he finally went on the stage at the Kallang Theatre on 11 August 1991, Goh let the audience know he was not going to even approximate Lee's style. Pointing to the two contraptions before him, he said: "They are auto cues to assist me in my Malay and Mandarin." It had the audience laughing and on his side right away.

He delivered his speech in a conversational manner, making effective use of personal anecdotes to drive home his points. In a departure from Lee's rally speeches, he did not brandish statistics and charts. He appeared relaxed and confident. He had come through.

"After I finished my speech, I could hear the collective sigh of relief. The audience clapped!" Goh was to recall 13 years later in his final National Day message as prime minister. "And I saw senior minister Lee beaming away. He looked immensely relieved. He wanted the younger team to succeed. Had I failed, I would have jeopardised the process of self-renewal."

⚜

Upgrade of the Less Able

IN his speech, Goh said he sensed a loosening of the bond that had held Singapore together. He did not quite say it, but implied in his speech was his sense that there was a growing social divide between the able and the less able.

Under Singapore's meritocratic system, there had been schemes put in place in the past 10 years to allow the more able to flourish, such as independent schools and programmes for gifted children. These schemes which had served the country well would stay, Goh said.

The less able, however, saw these as "elitist" programmes. They had begun clamouring for them to be dismantled and the funds for them to be spread evenly among all schools. As PAP saw it, in trying to pull back those who had run ahead of them, they could end up dragging everyone down to the mean. Human nature being what it is, the mean would keep being lowered until it reaches the bottom of the heap. In the end, it would lead not to equal prosperity for all but equal poverty and misery instead, as had been demonstrated in the failed communist countries.

At the same time, the able appeared to be more self-centred, Goh observed. They felt no obligation to the system that had helped make them successful, and so did not see the need to help the less able and to contribute to society as was the way in the past.

He would make it one of his goals to reinforce the bond between the people. There had to be a sense of family, of a common purpose and a shared destiny. For a start, he would want to balance those schemes that focused on the more able with new programmes for the average Singaporeans. He would concentrate on three basic areas: education, health care and housing.

On education, there would be Edusave, a scheme that he had announced earlier in the year. It would allow annual cash grants to be given to primary and secondary school students to pay for enrichment programmes or to buy additional resources. It would later be fine-tuned to reward students who performed well or who made good progress in their academic and non-academic work. Grants would be given to schools too to allow them to give bursaries and scholarships to such deserving students.

More autonomy would be given to schools following the example set by the independent schools. At the post-secondary level, there would be two more polytechnics, making it a total of four, to cater to some 40 per cent of students. A new revamped body for technical education would absorb those students who could be trained to perform high-level skilled jobs that the new industries demanded. The two existing universities would expand their intakes. For working adults who had missed out on tertiary education but who wished to better themselves, Goh proposed the setting up of a distance learning Open University.

"All these programmes would be for the benefit of the bulk of Singaporeans," Goh said as he pointed out that spending on education would be raised from 3.5 per cent of Singapore's gross domestic product to 4 per cent.

In an assurance to Singaporeans concerned about rising health costs, the new prime minister promised to make essential health care affordable to one and all. The government would continue to provide large subsidies so that the average lower middle-income earner who needed to be hospitalised could afford a B2 class bed and the average lower-income worker a C class one.

Medisave, which docks a compulsory sum in the CPF account of every working individual—a scheme which, as the health minister, Goh introduced in the 1980s—would help to cover costs on top of the subsidies. For the very poor who were chronically ill, the government would top up their Medisave accounts.

A new medical endowment fund, Medifund, would be initiated with money built up from the annual surpluses. It would be a safety net of last resort for needy Singaporeans whose Medisave savings and Medishield insurance coverage, if they had any at all, could not adequately cover their medical bills.

In housing, 90 per cent of Singaporeans were home owners, and this less than 30 years after the PAP government launched its public housing programme. Of the bottom 10 per cent who lived in rental flats, Goh said he would like to see at least half of them becoming home owners as well by providing them with the necessary leg-up.

He touched on the proposed nationwide Housing and Development Board (HDB) upgrading programme, which national development minister S Dhanabalan first announced in 1989. The government would subsidise the programme to the tune of between $10 billion and $15 billion over the course of the next 20 years. The first demonstration phase would begin in six estates in 1993.

Residents who lived in older HDB estates could vote to have their flats retrofitted and enjoy a new utility room, or a balcony, or additional bedroom space, depending on the size of their flat. The estate's environment would be spruced up. HDB blocks would be given a fancier facade. Open car parks next to the blocks would be transformed into landscaped gardens and multi-storeyed car parks built near by. There would be plazas, children's playgrounds, barbeque pits and covered walkways. In short, the upgraded HDB estates would not be very different from private condominiums.

Depending on the type of flat and upgrading package they voted for, the residents would have to fork out between 7 per cent and 42 per cent of the upgrading costs, using either cash or their CPF savings and paying in instalments.

Although it was Goh who would implement the programme, the idea was Lee's. As seen earlier, by the 1980s, Lee had seen a new divide emerging between those who had succeeded in the meritocratic system and those who had not. "In percentage terms, the society was already stratified, not now by wealth but by ability … ability which was translated into professional qualifications, which were translated into income," he said.

As the forces of globalisation and technologial change made income disparity wider, stratification could become more marked. So Lee came up with the idea of upgrading the older estates, which was, in effect, giving the HDB dwellers·a capital grant. An upgraded flat would have a market premium of up to 20 per cent over a similar one that had not been given the makeover.

He said: "I pay for your water, light, electricity three months of the year … so we take some of the burden off you at the lower end. I give you another $50,000 worth of assets in your house … I upgrade the whole flat. You pay $5,000; I pay $50,000. You can sell it … or keep it and your children will have it. So there is some equity. In the market, you're not entitled to this … but as a government, we say, the successful owe this to you, the unsuccessful. We carry you … which I think is a way you build cohesion in a society…"

Some seed money for Edusave, Medifund and the housing upgrading programme would come from the reserves but these schemes would not draw on—and drain—the reserves. To sustain them, the PAP government had to make sure it continued to perform well, generating enough surpluses so that some of the money could be channelled into the schemes. For Medifund, even the capital sum built up from the surpluses would not be touched. Only its interest income could be disbursed.

This was a signature PAP policy. Wealth could be redistributed but there would be no direct cash handouts and no dipping into the reserves. Since they came into power as democratic socialists, Lee and his leaders had seen how socialist welfare programmes had hobbled the Western European economies. A socialist ideal counted for nothing if it did not work for the larger good.

The situation had not improved 30 years later in the 1990s. In

Germany, for instance, an "entitlement culture" ran through the society where even the well-off took from the state what they were entitled to rather than what they needed. Fed up with the high labour costs, German firms voted with their feet. They were making foreign investments at a pace unrivalled in the country's history. They scaled down their operations at home, shuttering up factories where necessary. In 2005, 5.2 million or 12.6 per cent of the population was unemployed, the highest in 70 years. But unemployment benefits were so generous that there was no urgency among the jobless to seek work. German president Horst Koehler warned: "Our total debt is 7.1 billion euros ... that's 330 per cent of our gross domestic product. Do we finally see what a burden this is for our children and grandchildren?"

<hr />

An Early Election

EDUSAVE, Medifund and the HDB upgrading programme were the three most concrete initiatives in Goh's election manifesto when he called for the polls, more than two years ahead of schedule, soon after he gave his National Day rally speech. Nomination day would be August 21 and election day August 31. Singaporeans would cast their votes in 21 single-seat wards and 15 four-member Group Representation Consitutencies (GRCs).

The manifesto, which emphasised a more consultative and participatory style of government, was based on the book, *The Next Lap*, which Goh had issued earlier in the year. It was a blueprint to achieve for Singapore a developed country's standard of living by 1999.

In keeping with the new participatory style, the manifesto was "built on the ideas of many Singaporeans", said Goh in the preface of the 160-page book. More than 1,000 names were listed in the back of the book. These were civil servants and private sector leaders who had sat on various committees to share ideas for Singapore's long-term development in all areas, including sports and the arts.

Goh explained to the electorate why he called for an early election. He had inherited the position of prime minister but he would not know to what extent he could pursue his style of consultative government and carry out his more liberal programmes unless he had the mandate of the people.

He cited the examples of James Callaghan, who took over as Britain's prime minister after Harold Wilson resigned in mid-term in 1976, and Gerald Ford, who became the American president after Richard Nixon was forced to quit in 1974. The two leaders could not carry out fundamental changes under their watch because they lacked political clout. They had not led their parties to election and won. In the end, both lost at the polls.

Goh said that in calling for an early election, he was doing what Lee Kuan Yew did in 1968 after the British announced they were withdrawing their forces from Singapore. Lee called for an election immediately after the announcement. Fifty-one of the 58 seats were returned unopposed, following a boycott by the Barisan Sosialis. PAP won all the seven seats contested with an average of 86.72 per cent of the votes. That gave Lee the strength, after the British withdrawal, to carry out massive and initially painful programmes which eventually transformed Singapore.

To the electorate, Goh said: "Without your endorsement, I will not be able to move quickly and decisively on (my) programmes ... Every vote that you withhold from me, or worse, you give to the opposition, will weaken my political position. Every vote that you give me will increase my political weight in the country, in the cabinet and in parliament.

"Not everyone supports these programmes, especially the old who think that I am being too liberal and too accommodating, and too free-spending," he warned, suggesting that his *Next Lap* initiatives and consultative style might be reversed should the electorate not give him a clear mandate.

But what would make for a clear mandate?

It was an English don, Michael Leifer, who first suggested that a drop to below 60 per cent of the votes for PAP would mean a vote of no confidence for Goh. In the 1988 election, PAP had won 63.2 per cent of the valid votes.

Speaking on BBC, Leifer, a close Singapore watcher who taught international relations at the London School of Economics, said there would be a groundswell within PAP for Lee Hsien Loong to replace Goh if there was such a drop. He saw "a latent challenge" in the younger man, and said: "Certainly, Lee Hsien Loong is a very ambitious young man."

Goh did not want to be pinned down on a figure, saying it was up to the electorate to decide what would constitute a clear mandate. But he conceded that he was looking at an improvement over the 1988 result.

In his National Day dinner speech at his Tanjong Pagar ward two days after nominations closed with 40 of the 81 seats to be contested, Lee Kuan Yew pronounced: "Goh Chok Tong is really the one fighting in every one of the 40 constituencies. If he increases the percentage of votes over the last elections, it will be a signal to investors that the younger generation is firmly behind him."

Deputy prime minister Lee Hsien Loong, however, said the issue of the mandate was not a clear cut numerical one. "We are not looking for a number but a clear signal across the board for good support," he said.

Speaking at a PAP Youth Wing event, he said a fair analysis of the results could be made if only a count was done of those seats which were contested in the 1988 general election. "Otherwise, you are not comparing apples with apples. You are comparing apples with oranges."

The opposition was challenging PAP for 40 seats, much smaller than the 70-seat fight in 1988. Also, it had to be assumed that the uncontested GRCs were PAP strongholds. He said he was no statistician but the point was made. If all 70 seats and the GRC strongholds were contested, it would arguably have made for a higher percentage of votes than whatever it was that PAP was going to have in the election.

Earlier, responding to Leifer's suggestion that he might take over from Goh should the percentage fall below 60, he insisted that PAP was fighting as a cohesive team and there was "no internal leadership contest". He stressed: "We have settled the succession. Mr Goh is our leader; we are his team; and we want your support. If you vote against Mr Goh, it is a vote against us."

❦

THAT the nominations closed with 40 seats to be contested out of 81 did not come about by random chance.

The fight for 20 seats in single-seat wards and 20 in five GRCs was a deviously clever tactic worked out by Chiam See Tong's Singapore Democratic Party (SDP). Knowing that Singaporeans wanted some opposition at the same time that they wished to have PAP remain in power, the tactic was to allow the ruling party to secure a majority on nomination day. Voters could then take their chances with the opposition if they chose to. They could have their cake and eat it after all.

SDP got the Workers' Party (WP) and the other smaller parties to work together in the "by-election effect strategy". Only the Malay party, PKMS (Pertubuhan Kebangsaan Melayu Singapura or Singapore Malay National Organisation) refused to be part of it.

And so for the first time since 1968, Singaporeans knew for sure that PAP would form the government even before they cast their votes. As Chiam said in a press conference, the outcome was "simply beautiful". In limiting the fight, the general election had been turned into a by-election.

Goh's response was: "You can call it a by-election ... the fact remains that I am the issue ... I called this election and I remain the issue in the constituencies to be contested."

To fight the SDP's by-election tactic, he announced that he would hold by-elections within the next 12 to 18 months. He gave two reasons for them: to continue to inject new blood into PAP and to allow J B Jeyaretnam to contest a seat.

Jeyaretnam had charged that the election had been called early to prevent him from taking part in it. MP for Anson, he was disqualified from parliament in 1986 and barred from contesting elections for five years after he was convicted of false declaration and fraudulent transfer of party funds. His disqualification would end only in November, making him ineligible for the August poll.

As in the 1988 general election, PAP concentrated its firepower in the Eunos GRC. It moved the seasoned Malay MP Sidek Saniff to Tay Eng Soon's team because this time round, in the place of Francis Seow in the WP camp was businessman Jufrie Mahmood, a firebrand who was expected to stoop to communal politics.

In a constituency where 23 per cent of the voters were ethnic Malays, Jufrie did play the communal card, bringing up real or imagined grievances in the Malay community, never mind that 16 Malay grassroots bodies had pledged their backing for Goh in an unprecedented public show of support. He accused Malay MPs in PAP, including Sidek, as having sold out their community and of not representing Malay interests. The other WP heavyweight in Eunos was again Lee Siew Choh, who let Jufrie hog the limelight and gamely put in a stout supporting role.

In what was later seen as a miscalculated move, PAP decided not to hold rallies, preferring to have dialogues with groups of residents instead on top of door-to-door visits. PAP rallies had always drawn a smaller turnout than those organised by the opposition but that did not make rallies any less useful. High visibility of the candidates mattered, even if they were ministers, or especially if they were ministers. A mass event in an open space is also where the candidates can best make an emotional connection with the people.

In the heat of the battle, during which he made himself the central issue of the election and distracted as he was by Jufrie's communal politics, Goh omitted to spend time elaborating on his proposed programmes: Edusave, Medifund and the HDB upgrading exercise. If he had done so—spelling out the details of these programmes that would benefit the majority of the population—he might have won more votes. Admittedly, these schemes would take several years before the people could feel their full impact. The demonstration phase of the upgrading programme, for instance, would finish only in 1995 when the result would be clear for all to see.

In the end, PAP lost four seats and saw its percentage dip from 63.17 to 61. The four seats lost were all single-ward seats. Chiam kept Potong Pasir. The other three wards that went to the opposition were all newly created in the last election in 1988. Chiam's two SDP colleagues, Ling How Doong and Cheo Chai Chen, took Bukit Gombak and Nee Soon Central by razor-thin margins, 654 and 168 votes respectively. Low Thia Khiang of the WP performed better in Hougang, securing 10,621 votes against the PAP incumbent Tang Guan Seng's 9,487.

PAP must have been relieved that Jufrie Mahmood and his teammates failed to capture Eunos and that its 52.4 per cent share of the votes was higher than 1988's 50.9. But it was little comfort.

At the pre-dawn press conference after the results were announced, a visibly disappointed Goh said: "No matter how popular my style is to the people, there is such a thing called the bottom line. This style has cost me four seats this time. Will it cost me another four in future? So I've got to review my style."

He said of the overall result: "Well, it's not a slap in the face but certainly it's not a pat on my back ... So I've got to understand what that means."

The Silent Majority Struck Back

GOH Chok Tong's disappointment over the election result drew a spontaneous outpouring of letters from the people that quashed doubts about his popularity. They all said, more or less, that the result was not a rejection of him and his consultative style. Why, some of them suggested, if he had not been the prime minister, PAP would have lost more votes and seats. Even the opposition was moved to assure him that he was not on the wrong track in his Next Lap.

As a letter published in *The Straits Times* said: "Even in his disappointment, Mr Goh must still know that the people accept him. Where else in the world does a population have to console its political leader when he has won 77 out of 81 seats? And where else in the world do vanquished parties have apologetic words for victorious prime ministers?"

Low Thia Khiang, the WP candidate who took Hougang, said: "Mr Goh has won a clear majority of 61 per cent and should not be disappointed. He should press ahead with the programmes outlined in *The Next Lap...*"

After studying the results, PAP saw that a large segment of the electorate did not care or understand the significance that Goh was the central issue of the election. This segment, made up largely of the Chinese-educated and more conservative HDB dwellers, formed the silent majority who, except for a hardcore 20 per cent, had always voted for PAP in the past. But this time round, many had voted against it.

Their main grievance, as first cited by Ong Teng Cheong at a Chinese Press Club talk in September, was that they felt the PAP government had taken them for granted. It was too eager to please the English-educated as was shown in its relaxation of film censorship guidelines. The English-educated were a vocal group and had pushed for more liberalisation in areas like film censorship.

The terms "cosmopolitans" and "heartlanders" had not been in currency then but one can say that the 1991 election was a case of the heartlanders striking out at what they perceived as PAP's bias towards the cosmopolitans. It was Harvard Business School professor Rosebeth Moss Kanter who first made the distinction between "cosmopolitans" and "locals" in her popular 1995 book, *World Class*. They refer to the two new classes of people in any society that has been changed or is being changed by the new global economy.

The cosmopolitans have an international outlook, make good money and are highly mobile because they have the education and the skills. The locals or heartlanders, on the other hand, are inward-looking and still bound by traditions. Their skills are not marketable beyond their society. They resent the cosmopolitans whom the society's leaders seem to pamper although these are the very ones who are most likely to up their stakes and flee at the first sign of trouble.

The divide between the cosmopolitans and the heartlanders would be a nagging problem that simply would not go away. Goh Chok Tong would use the two terms in his 1999 National Day rally speech when he spoke about the importance of maintaining cohesion between these two categories of Singaporeans.

In Singapore in 1991, the heartlanders were made up of the largely Chinese-educated and the bottom 20 to 30 per cent of the education ladder. Lee Kuan Yew identified this latter group as an emerging class that could express its unhappiness through the ballot box. Speaking to Singaporean journalists while on a visit to Kazakhstan in September that year, he said the government would have to try to improve the earning capabilities of the people in this bottom segment and enable them to upgrade themselves.

He also pointed out that the Chinese-educated were telling the government that it was not attending to their concerns such as their fear of the dilution of the Chinese language, culture and identity. They saw the government as paying more attention to the English-educated and the Malay community.

Lee admitted: "We came to the conclusion that the English-speaking were becoming the majority but in fact they were not. And indeed, the silent majority decided to remind us that this was not so."

He believed that the Chinese-educated would continue to be the majority for the next 10 to 15 years. The English-educated liberals might have chafed at the government restraints and clamoured for more relaxation but as Lee saw it, they were never good mobilisers. Some of them might have voted against the party but their number could not have been very significant.

The ground feeling of the Chinese-educated came through most clearly in the three wards that went to the opposition, he said. The voters in Bukit Gombak, Nee Soon Central and Hougang had switched their votes not because they were not doing well economically. After all, they were children of the Chinese-educated who had moved into the four- and five-room and executive flats in the new estates. They were not the old or unsuccessful who were left behind in the older wards.

"I think it was a sense of being squeezed out of the mainstream, that they were no longer getting the kind of attention that as a majority community they should have. I think that caused the switch," Lee said.

It was significant that two of the opposition winners in the three wards were the Chinese-language Nanyang University graduates—Low Thia Khiang and Cheo Chai Chen.

Dialect and clan loyalties were still strong, he discovered. He did not elaborate on this observation but post-mortem reports in the media made several pertinent points. Low Thia Khiang won the largely Teochew constituency of Hougang by making rally speeches in that dialect. Cheo Chai Chen was a local boy made good. The 40-year-old businessman, who lived just outside the ward, had spent 30 years in the area. His grandfather was the foreman of the former rubber estate that belonged to Lim Nee Soon, the tycoon who gave the area its name.

The decision by the Yishun Town Council not to provide incense burners to residents during the Hungry Ghost Festival, when other town councils did, was seen as the "most burning" issue in Nee Soon Central.

That the festival fell smack during election time made the issue more immediate to the residents. In order to avoid a fine of up to $1,000 for damaging the grass turf, they had to buy their own incense burners. They saw the English-speaking town council officers, who had spent money building a big park, as dismissive of their religious faith.

GOH Chok Tong, who said that he felt better about the election result after a detailed analysis of the four seats lost, made the distinction between the Chinese-educated intellectuals and the lower-income, Chinese-speaking Singaporeans. The small group of intellectuals might be disturbed by what they saw as the erosion of the Chinese language and culture but the main concerns of the larger lower-income group were simply bread-and-butter issues.

He said: "They are a big group of Singaporeans who really only care about daily life—lower taxes, lower levies, cheap hospital charges, cheap education services. They want a firm government. All they are interested in is stability, progress and prosperity. That's a signal for us. So we've got to reach out (to them)."

He had in fact said he was going to focus his policies on the lower

80 per cent of the population during the hustings, he pointed out. "That is coming but they haven't seen it yet, so they felt neglected. Had they given me more time—three, four or five years—they will see that some policies will be percolating down to them."

But would he be given time? In the week after the election, the financial markets were hit by rumours that he would resign as prime minister. Goh was quick to deny the rumours through the wire news agencies such as Reuters, Associated Press and Agence-France Presse. He said in no uncertain terms that he planned to stick around long enough to achieve the goal of making Singapore a First World country.

"Which means by 1999, my job will be done ... then somebody else can take over," he said.

The 1991 general election was a sobering lesson for Goh. But he would prove to be a fast learner.

27

A Double Whammy and Then a Triumph

Two Heavy-hitters Leave the Field

BARELY a week after the 1991 general election, Goh Chok Tong made a surprise announcement. Two PAP heavy-hitters, Tony Tan and S Dhanabalan, were quitting politics to return to the private sector. The two men were still relatively young. Tan, 51, would leave on 31 December 1991 and Dhanabalan, 54, the following year.

If the people were surprised, Lee Kuan Yew was certainly less than happy with their resignation. It was "a serious crisis" for the PAP government, he still maintained years later. "They had voted for him (Goh). If I had appointed him and they resigned, I could understand that. But they chose him and then they resigned. I said: 'You are irresponsible. You must at least see him through one term.' "

He could understand though why not every minister would want to stay on for the long haul. "It's an onerous job, you see. The pay is not attractive. The work hours are horrendous. The burden is on you all the time. Whether you go to bed or wake up in the morning, it's still there over you—this problem you have to solve."

Goh, on the other hand, was not too exercised over the resignations. He did not see the episode as a crisis, although the two men's departure would weaken the cabinet temporarily. In his view, it would have been a crisis if Tan and Dhanabalan had strong views against him, had challenged him and had threatened to quit if he did not come to a compromise with them. But they did not resign because they had differences with him.

Looking at it from the bright side, he suggested that more individuals might be attracted to join the government when they saw that ministers did not have to serve life terms, as it were. "I hope that if I can allow them to go back and resume their private careers successfully, it will be a signal to other younger men and women outside to join me. And that when they join us in the cabinet, they can serve for 10, 15 years, and then they can go back to a good position in the private sector," he said.

Tan had wanted to quit as early as 1988, after the general election that year. Dhanabalan had made his decision before the general election. But Goh had persuaded them to stay on long enough to contest in his crucial 1991 election.

The two men were among the strongest of his peers. They set education and national development in a new direction to meet the demands of the times. In education, Tan had set up independent schools that were less centrally organised, allowing individual principals greater flexibility to run their schools more efficiently. At the tertiary level, he converted the Nanyang Technological Institute, which had offered diploma courses only, into a second university and also set up a third polytechnic.

Dhanabalan saw that Housing and Development Board (HDB) estates did not have to be just cookie-cutter, functional blocks. He encouraged more variations in the design of new estates so that each would have its own distinctive features. Architects in the private sector could tender for a new design-and-build scheme. He launched the HDB upgrading programme and devised the concept plan for a Singapore that could accommodate comfortably a population of four million, a figure that the government had projected for the near future.

The two heavyweight ministers, as Goh called them, did not give any specific reasons for their resignations at the time. Tan said he would return to OCBC (Overseas Chinese Banking Corporation) to become its chairman and CEO. He was its general manager when he was called into politics in 1979. Dhanabalan, who had worked in DBS Bank previously, had not made any plans.

Why indeed did they quit? The question to ask in Tan's case is not so much why he quit but why, in the first place, did he not want the job of prime minister when Lee Kuan Yew had made it quite clear that he was his first choice as successor? It was he, after all, who initiated that milestone meeting in his house where Goh was picked by the younger leaders to be Lee's successor. But he had ruled himself out before he started the meeting, according to Dhanabalan.

In his interview for this book, Tan said he had a family tradition to fulfill. His grandfather was the head of the old Overseas Chinese Banking Corporation. His uncle was its chairman for many years. He himself was general manager of the bank. His father, who died when he was still a student, would have wanted to see him become the chairman of the bank.

· In the colonial days, no Chinese man could expect to head a British bank. The Overseas Chinese Banking Corporation was the biggest local bank then and to be its chairman was to be the number one man in the local business community. It was a notion which Tan's father held until he died, although by the time Tan joined the bank as its head, it was no longer the biggest local bank.

In 1992, when Tan became chairman and CEO of OCBC Bank, it ranked third among the "Four Big Singapore Banks", behind DBS Bank and United Overseas Bank. The smallest among the four was Overseas Union Bank. Though it ranked third, its assets, which included insurance, property and a sizeable land bank, gave OCBC the highest international credit ratings among the four, which were all listed on the stock exchange.

If Tan had longed to fulfil his father's wishes, the bank, on its part, had also wanted him badly as chairman and CEO. Teo Cheng Guan, who took over from Yong Pung How as chairman in 1989 after the latter was appointed chief justice, felt he was too old for the job. He was hitting 70 and had come out of retirement to head the bank. Tan said Teo had told him more than once: "I'm just sitting here, waiting for you to take over. When are you coming back?" Tan was also the first choice of Lee Seng Wee, who represented the largest single shareholding interest in the bank and was also chairman of the executive committee, the bank's highest policy-making body.

Tan joined OCBC but remained an MP in the new Sembawang Group Representation Constituency (GRC) and kept his post as deputy chairman in the PAP's central executive committee (CEC). In 1993, he was made the chairman. At the same time, he continued to play a role in the education ministry as chairman of a new university grants committee which was set up to recommend the allocation of funds and resources for the various university programmes.

S Dhanabalan left in September 1992. His reason for quitting, as he put it some 12 years later, was one of conviction. "My philosophy is one where I need to have complete conviction about some key policies and if I have differences, it doesn't mean that I'm against the group. I still want to make sure the group succeeds, but I have to try and live with myself if I have some disagreements on some things," he said. He had different views on some government policies and although "they were not so sharp that I wanted to leave immediately ... I could see for myself it could pose problems in the future for the group and me".

Goh did not wish to go into the specifics, but in his interviews for this book, he revealed for the first time that Dhanabalan was not comfortable with the way the PAP government had dealt with the Marxist group in 1987. He said: "At that time, given the information, he was not fully comfortable with the action which we took ... His makeup is that of a very strong Christian so he felt uncomfortable and thought there could be more of such episodes in future. So he thought since he was uncomfortable, he'd better leave the cabinet. I respected him for his view."

⋘⋙

Then a Double Whammy

IN their resignation letters, both Tony Tan and S Dhanabalan assured Goh Chok Tong that they would return to the government should there be a pressing need for their services. Little did they know how soon he would need the services of at least one of them.

On 16 November 1992, the Singapore stock market was hit by heavy selling, following rumours that some senior government leaders were ill. The Straits Times Industrial Index took a dive. After trading closed, Goh released a statement which confirmed the worst of fears—both his deputies, Lee Hsien Loong and Ong Teng Cheong, had cancer.

Ong, then 56 years old, suffered from a low-grade malignant lymphoma. The 40-year-old Lee, too, had lymphoma but his was deemed intermediate-grade. (Lymphoma encompasses a variety of cancers specific to the lymphatic system which is an important network of glands, nodes and vessels that makes up the body's main line of defence against infections.)

While Ong did not need treatment immediately because low-grade lymphoma was something that was slow growing, Lee had begun chemotherapy at the Singapore General Hospital the day before the statement was released.

Ong was found to have lymphoma in August after his doctors had established that a swelling on his neck was due to enlarged lymph nodes and ordered a biopsy. In Lee's case, three small polyps were discovered in his rectum during a routine medical examination in October. Tests showed intermediate-grade lymphoma but thankfully, it was confined to the rectum and did not spread to the other organs.

Apart from their own doctors in Singapore, both deputy prime ministers were examined by two top specialists over in the United States—Saul Rosenberg of the Stanford University Medical Center, who was popularly known as the "Father of Lymphoma", and Fernando F Cabanillas of the University of Texas' M D Anderson Cancer Center.

The two specialists agreed with Ong's doctor in Singapore, Tan Yew Oo, that no treatment was necessary at that time, in view of the slow growing nature of his cancer. They also supported the recommendation made by Lee's doctors at the Singapore General Hospital—senior physician Ong Yong Yau, senior colorectal surgeon Goh Hak Su and medical oncologist Ang Peng Tiam—that he should undergo a course of chemotherapy.

Said Rosenberg: "We believe, at this point, that there is only a limited amount of disease and that therefore, a standard course of chemotherapy would offer a good chance at long-term cure." Cabanillas was confident that Lee had a 90 per cent chance of being cured.

The chemotherapy course was divided into six cycles, each lasting three weeks, or 18 weeks in all. If he had a full remission after the treatment and if the cancer did not recur in the next five years, the chances of its returning would be very slim, the doctors said.

Nothing tests a man's strength of character more than a life-threatening illness. One is subjected to all kinds of indignities in the hospital treatment rooms; then there is always the pain, and often treatment brings with it very uncomfortable side effects. The two deputy prime ministers bore their illness with a stoic dignity. Undergoing chemotherapy, especially, was no walk in the park but Lee added to it a dose of humour. When his hair fell out because of the therapy, he did not hide his bald head from public view.

The two men set the tone with which they would manage their illness when they met the media on the day after the release of the press statement. At the Singapore General Hospital, Lee readily unbuttoned his batik shirt to show reporters a tube that was inserted into a vein in his chest. A portable pump that he carried with him would feed both chemotherapy and anti-nausea drugs into his body through the tube at regular intervals. This managed the drug level, ensuring that it would not become toxic.

"I don't think you would enjoy it," he said wryly.

Asked about his ministerial duties, he replied that the problem was one of getting more people to share the workload. But, for the longer term, he said: "It is not just a matter of finding a group of candidates to run the country for the next 20 or 30 years. People fall ill. Anything untoward can happen to one's successors too. A person is answerable for his own life. The people of Singapore cannot possibly count on one man's life to decide their own fate. Therefore, we must look for more successors."

He said it was important that he had the emotional support of his family. Friends and well wishers provided moral support. "We will fight to live. If it works and if the odds are with me, that's fine. If not, well, you've done your best. And that's your stand," he said matter-of-factly.

Ong Teng Cheong said he wanted to live "every minute of my life" and press on with his work at the NTUC where he was secretary-general. Cancer apparently had not affected his generally optimistic outlook. He said: "I am already 56 ... going to be 57 soon. If I were 30 years old, it might be different."

Rosenberg had told him that the median span of life for patients with a similar illness was between 10 and 11 years. Some might live longer, some shorter. "I'll just have to wait and see," he said.

While Ong could carry on with his work, Lee was advised by his doctors to do light duty while he underwent treatment. He had to stay away from crowds because there was a period during each cycle of the chemotherapy when the white blood cell count was likely to drop which would lower his resistance to infections.

Goh Chok Tong persuaded S Dhanabalan, who had left the National Development Ministry barely three months ago and had not gone on to another job yet, to take over Lee's trade and industry portfolio while the latter underwent treatment. He also relieved Lee of his work as chairman of the ministerial committee on health policies. Dhanabalan made it clear that he would still want to return to the private sector after Lee had finished his treatment and been given a clean bill of health by his doctors.

Tony Tan, however, was not recalled. He had gone over to OCBC for just about a year and it would be unsettling for the bank to lose him so soon, Goh said.

⋘⋙

By-election Effect Turned on its Head

GOH Chok Tong had promised in the 1991 general election to hold by-elections in 12 to 18 months. He kept his promise. In early December

1992, despite the fact that both his deputies were ill, he called for a by-election in his own Marine Parade GRC. Nomination day would be on December 9 and election on December 19.

All four PAP MPs in the GRC—Lim Chee Onn, Othman Haron Eusofe and Matthias Yao, as well as Goh—resigned their seats on December 1. The attorney-general had advised Goh that he did not have to resign as prime minister to contest the by-election. But Goh said he would resign as prime minister if he were not re-elected. Yao, the parliamentary secretary in the defence ministry, who was also contesting the by-election, would retain his office but like Goh, he would resign if the team lost.

Goh later revealed that Othman, who was the assistant secretary-general of the NTUC, would also be part of his by-election team. Othman was MP for Geylang Serai from 1980 to 1988 and was re-elected as MP for Marine Parade GRC in 1988 and 1991.

Lim Chee Onn, who had long expressed a desire to leave politics altogether, was replaced by newcomer Teo Chee Hean. The 38-year-old Teo was clearly ministerial material, and one of the reasons for the by-election was to induct him into parliament, Goh pointed out. Teo had been awarded both the president's scholarship and the SAF scholarship, was a first class honours student, and had two master's degrees in computing science and public administration. In his 20 years in the SAF, he had held various command and staff appointments. In 1991, he was appointed the chief of navy and was promoted to the rank of rear-admiral before he resigned to contest in the election.

Teo, like his modest father, OCBC's Teo Cheng Guan, was not one given to talking about himself. He would only say that when he left school, he wanted to do something that had a wider purpose than just contributing to a company's bottomline. He said: "I'd always felt that three professions were inherently satisfying: a doctor because you healed people; a teacher because you taught people, you helped them develop themselves; and a civil engineer because you built physical things—bridges, dams, buildings—which made people's lives better.

"Well, as it turned out, I didn't become any of them. But I found the navy very interesting because it allowed me to do things which served a larger purpose."

The Marine Parade GRC was formed in 1988 when the Marine Parade, Joo Chiat and Geylang Serai constituencies were combined. In

1991, the GRC absorbed MacPherson as well. The Marine Parade ward, where Goh had been the MP since he began his political career in 1976, was made up exclusively of HDB flats, 56 blocks to be exact, all built on reclaimed land. Five of them were rental blocks but on the whole, the estate could be described as middle-class. MacPherson was a much older estate, whose residents were mainly blue-collar workers, while Geylang Serai had a mix of HDB blocks and private dwellings.

When Goh called for the by-election, it was Lee Kuan Yew who cast the first vote of confidence in him. He handed over to him the PAP secretary-general post, one that he had held since the founding of the party in 1954. Lee would make two appearances at the PAP rallies towards the end of the nine-day campaign. At the first one in Marine Drive, he told the crowd that with the two deputy prime ministers ill, he could have played it safe and remained the secretary-general of PAP.

"I decided that Singapore will do better at this critical junction if I publicly showed confidence in Goh Chok Tong. And I stepped down and handed over control of the party to him. It is to consolidate the government and Singapore's future," he said.

Goh would fight the contest as both prime minister and leader of PAP. He told a press conference: "The issue is clear. The stakes are very high. The issue is whether the Goh Chok Tong government continues and the stakes are what follows after the 19th—whether we have certainty of government or whether we enter into a period of uncertainty ... If I lose, there may be a PAP government but there will be no Goh Chok Tong government. So my views, my policies, my philosophy, my values, may or may not be continued by somebody else."

In putting his head on the chopping block, as it were, he made political leadership the central issue of the election. It was no longer a local election but, as he declared, a "by-election with an unintended general election effect". A decisive victory would mean that the people had given him the endorsement that he thought they had not given him in the 1991 general election. His position as the prime minister would be consolidated.

It did not matter that the voters were the 74,000 residents in the GRC and not the whole population of Singapore. Since a freak election result would mean losing Goh Chok Tong, and perhaps even PAP, the stakes had been raised to the national level. "The whole of Singapore is watching Marine Parade," Goh said on another occasion. "The future of Singapore depends on voters here."

It was a new Goh here, as fighter and masterful political strategist. He had kept his promise to hold by-elections. And in choosing to hold just one by-election in his own ward, he had turned the opposition's successful 1991 by-election tactic on its head.

Without a doubt, he was also taking a risk even if it was a carefully calculated one. PAP had won 73.8 per cent of the total votes in the GRC in 1988 and 77.2 per cent in 1991. There was only one opponent in the GRC in both elections, the Singapore Justice Party (SJP), which posed no threat. The by-election would see a four-corner fight, with Chiam See Tong's Singapore Democratic Party (SDP) and the National Solidarity Party (NSP) joining in the fray, besides the SJP.

No bookie would bet that Goh would lose the fight. But how wide would his winning margin be? Two close political observers, Bilveer Singh of the National University of Singapore and Derek da Cunha of the Institute of Southeast Asian Studies, expected PAP's share of the votes to fall to between 65 and 70 per cent, given the tougher competition from SDP.

After his block visits and rallies, Chiam was confident that SDP would win 40 per cent of the votes. If it did, PAP's share of the votes would fall below 60 per cent. Goh would no longer be able to stay on long as the prime minister, much less claim to have the people's endorsement.

The nine days of campaigning was intense and bruising for S Puhaindran, the PAP's Marine Parade branch secretary since 1976. He said: "It took a lot out of me. The pressure was just so great." Then 55 years old and an inspector of primary schools at the Ministry of Education, he took three weeks' leave of absence to help organise the campaign. What heartened him was that when he held the first meeting to call for campaign volunteers, some 300 residents showed up. In previous elections, the typical number was 30 to 40 people.

Even so, he worked day and night on the campaign. And while he was all jangling nerves, Goh, on the other hand, "was very cool, very relaxed, shaking the hands of the residents warmly, and inviting them to tea," Puhaindran recounted.

The failure of the Workers' Party (WP) to field a team was an indictment of its leader J B Jeyaretnam. It was he, after all, who had accused Goh for calling for an early election the previous year just to lock him out of it since he was barred in 1986 from contesting elections for five years. But now that he could take part in it, he had chosen not to.

Many observers believed that he opted out because he had failed to persuade SDP to join forces with him and fight the by-election under the WP banner. SDP's response to his call was that if WP wished to join forces, it should do so under the SDP banner. This obviously Jeyaretnam would not agree to; he would not play second fiddle to Chiam. He knew he could not afford to go it alone. WP would most likely lose out not only to PAP but also to SDP. And it would be the end of his party if it could not garner enough votes to get back its election deposit.

Chee Soon Juan, who would become very much a thorn in PAP's side the way Jeyaretnam had been in the 1980s, first made his appearance at this by-election. The 30-year-old PhD holder, who taught neuropsychology at the National University of Singapore, was SDP's prized catch. But while he cast himself as a champion for political freedom and human rights, it was clear that he was a man who had once been wounded and it was the wound that drove him into politics where he could work out his rage.

He betrayed this hurt in his emotional rally speeches when he recounted how the university had rejected him as a student and he had to pursue his studies in the United States. Wasn't it such an irony, he asked, that the university which had rejected him as a student had now employed him as a lecturer? The bitterness of that rejection had obviously stayed with him.

The other SDP candidates were Low Yong Nguan, a former PAP MP; Mohamed Shariff Yahya, a clerk; and Ashleigh Seow, who was the general manager of Bukit Gombak and Nee Soon Town Councils. The last was also the son of Francis Seow although he appeared the more sober of the two. He had contested in the two previous general elections.

❧

IN the end, Goh and his team romped home with a 72.9 per cent lead. SDP managed to garner 24.5 per cent of the votes while both NSP and SJP lost their deposits with only 1.4 per cent and 1.1 per cent of the votes, respectively.

The result was the endorsement Goh had sought. At the midnight press conference held after the announcement of the vote count, he attributed the victory to the sound judgment of the voters and the bonding between them and the PAP candidates. He made the call to all Singaporeans, especially the young, to join the party or to support it to meet the new challenges ahead. "There are going to be some big problems ahead of us in the years to come and I want to consolidate this unity," he said.

His emphatic win came as a relief for those who had feared that he would have to give up his open, consultative style of government as he had said after the previous year's setback. Goh's hand had been strengthened and his style would prevail after all.

For Goh, the success was a personal milestone in his political career. Puhaindran, who had worked closely with the man since he first set up the Marine Parade ward, observed: "He was not fully confident as a politician before that. But after the 1992 by-election, you could see that he had become a very confident leader."

⚜

Ong as Elected President

THE following year saw another election. It was the first of its kind—the people would elect the president.

Lee Kuan Yew had the idea of an elected president as far back as the early 1980s. Typically of him, he was thinking far down the road and working out all the what-ifs. The PAP government had built up formidable reserves but a profligate government could clean out the savings in a very short time. "In one five-year spending spree, Singapore can be rendered prostrate and bankrupt," he had warned at the 1984 National Day rally.

The idea, as it evolved, was for an elected president who had the power to safeguard the reserves and integrity of key public service appointments. He could be the guardian of a key in a "two-key safeguard mechanism". The prime minister and his cabinet would hold the other key.

Since independence, the president of Singapore was appointed by the government and acted on its advice. His role was a largely ceremonial one although as the mass turnout for the wakes of Singapore's first two presidents, Yusof Ishak and Benjamin Sheares, had shown, the presidential office added to the people's sense of nationhood. The elected president would continue with the ceremonial role but he would also serve as a check on the government.

The scheme was debated and painstakingly drafted and redrafted through the 1980s. It was made an issue by the opposition parties in the 1988 general election when they charged that Lee was creating the office for himself, as we saw in Chapter 25. By the time the Constitution of the

who joined PAP in 1980, third-generation ministers who had come on board in the 1984 general election and after staffed the cabinet.

Four ministers were shouldering double portfolios. Besides Mah Bow Tan, there were Richard Hu (finance and national development), S Jayakumar (law and home affairs) and Yeo Cheow Tong (health and community development).

In a later reshuffle, Yeo took over the trade and industry portfolio while Lee Boon Yang, another third-generation leader, took on defence on top of his labour ministry duties. As deputy prime minister, Lee Hsien Loong oversaw both the trade and industry, and finance ministries.

It was not exactly a happy situation for Goh and he saw the need now to persuade Tony Tan to return to the cabinet. He would be made deputy prime minister and defence minister. This time, unlike the first occasion when he was approached to join PAP, it took Tan a good six months to make the decision. In the short time that he was in OCBC Bank, he had expanded its operations significantly and helped turn in record profits. He had relished the challenges and had expected to stay in his office in OCBC Building on Chulia Street until his retirement.

In the end, however, he felt he had to honour the word he had given Goh in his resignation letter, that he would return should there be a pressing need for his services.

Tan returned to the cabinet on 1 August 1995 and would prove invaluable to Goh, not only in the defence ministry but also in the area of higher education where he was put in charge in 1997.

28

Goh Between the Lees

Torn between Two Leaders?

GOH Chok Tong's 1992 by-election triumph consolidated his position as prime minister. Or, did it?

Catherine Lim, a Singaporean author of short stories and novels, did not think so, at least not in 1994. She penned two critical commentary pieces, published in *The Straits Times*, which suggested that Goh was not really in charge.

In the first commentary which the paper carried in September, she asserted that there was a "Great Affective Divide" between the PAP government and the populace. This was because PAP had continued to be stern, impersonal and pre-emptive in its actions. It concentrated, as it had done in the past, on only the material well-being of the country. The citizens' more emotional, non-material concerns were not attended to, resulting in their estrangement from the government, she said.

In her second piece, which was published in November, Lim argued that the PAP government had been torn between Goh's promised consultative style and Lee Kuan Yew's authoritarian approach, and that the latter had prevailed. But Singapore society had changed. The authoritarian style grated on the people especially when the younger leaders who did not have Lee's stature and record of leadership took to imitating his style.

Goh did not respond to the first piece but he did after the second one was published. In a letter to *The Straits Times*, his press secretary challenged her to enter politics and take responsibility for her views.

At a PAP event, Goh made clear that Lim had "gone beyond the pale" to imply that he had allowed himself to be overwhelmed by Lee. "When my authority is being commented on or undermined by wrong observations, I have to correct them, or the view will prevail that I am indeed not in charge of Singapore," he said.

In the Asian context especially, it was important that the authority of the prime minister be upheld and not be undermined by "writers on the fringes", he said. If left unchecked, snide comments would, over time, erode the people's respect for the office.

The challenge to Lim to enter politics led to a debate in the letter pages of *The Straits Times*. Why should those who wished to comment on public affairs join a political party or form one? Could they not speak up as concerned citizens? Or was it, as some cynics described it, a "sign-up-or-shut-up" policy?

In parliament in January 1995, Goh clarified his government's stand. It welcomed debate on its policies, he said. And no, those who wished to air their views did not have to join a political party, but the government reserved the right to respond—"robustly", if need be—to views that it considered wrong and that might undermine the country's interests. "I can assure all these intellectuals that they need not fear retribution. They must expect a rebuttal where we disagree with them. A rebuttal is not retribution," he said.

Goh's use of the term "intellectuals" was useful in putting the debate in context. While the episode might seem like a big affair among the small, westernised elite who followed it, most Singaporeans who lived in the heartland did not pay it much attention.

The concerns of these Singaporeans were more material, bread-and-butter issues, as PAP had found out at some cost in the 1991 general election. They had felt neglected and resented the government's seeming bias towards the more vocal educated elite. So while Goh had promised to open up the society, there were limits to how much, and how fast, he could do so.

The more liberal pundits might argue that bread-and-butter issues and the political concerns of the educated elite were not mutually exclusive. Journalist-turned-academic Russell Heng, for one, asserted that the two were indeed intimately related. In an article in *The Straits Times*, he posed the challenging question: "If not enough attention was focused on the hardship of less affluent Singaporeans ... is it because there has been too little or too much political openness?"

Heng's idealistic assumption was that if there were more political openness, the educated elite's first impulse would be to speak up on behalf of the less fortunate. But this group's clamour had really been in their own areas of concern—less censorship in the arts and entertainment, HDB homes for singles, gay rights and the right to criticise government policies without having to worry about the consequences.

The government's liberalisation of theatre in the mid-1990s, for instance, was followed by a plethora of English-language plays that centred on gay issues. If there were productions that examined the larger issues of the society at large, they were staged mainly by the vernacular groups.

In its liberalisation of the arts scene, PAP showed it could not disregard the educated elite even as it attended to the bread-and-butter issues. The opening up of society was a delicate balancing act and was best approached in a cautious, evolutionary way, as opposed to a radical shift. As Goh's then-press secretary Chan Heng Wing said: "We have all seen what has happened in Eastern Europe, Russia and the former states of the Soviet Union. They went for glasnost or the 'Big Bang', as against gradualism in China and Vietnam."

When Catherine Lim later sent Goh an apology, the prime minister took the opportunity to say in his reply to her, which was published in the papers: "I have to set out the out-of-bounds markers clearly so that everyone knows the limits of openness and consultation."

An out-of-bounds marker, or OB marker, is a golfing term which would become part of the political vocabulary in Singapore. The OB markers delineated the line where commentators on government policies should not cross. Venture beyond the markers and you risk a "robust" response from the government, or worse, a penalty.

Time and again, critics and non-government organisations would press the government to define the OB markers. As one cynic put it, the OB markers acted like an invisible electric fence that ranchers could use to keep in their cattle or sheep. Once a bull or a sheep hits against the fence, it will get a jolt of electricity. The critics did not want the jolts whose wattage the government determined. Also, since the OB markers were not defined, the government could move them arbitrarily to suit its needs, they charged.

But Lee Hsien Loong, in his interviews for this book, said: "The whole point is wherever you draw the line, they (the critics and NGOs) will be on the other side, pretending that they are on this side."

Also, OB markers could not remain fixed. "As our society matures and grows more stable, and the population becomes better educated and more discerning, the limits of debate—the OB markers—will widen," he said in a 2000 speech. He made a distinction, however, between debates on policies and attacks on the government and its fitness to rule. The

PAP government could not, obviously, accept the latter as constructive feedback.

"The government will continue to set the tone for public debate," he said. "The government cannot promise that its responses will always be meek and mild. But we do promise to take criticisms seriously and to give them carefully considered responses."

Lee's Knuckle-dusters

LEE Kuan Yew had kept silent during the Catherine Lim episode. But after the issue was debated in parliament in January, he finally gave a piece of his mind the following month. He told the afternoon daily, *The New Paper*, that he was glad that Goh had reacted to Lim's commentaries.

He said: "Everybody now knows that if you take on the prime minister, he will have to take you on ... If he didn't, then more people will throw darts ... put a little poison on the tip and throw them at him."

He dismissed Catherine Lim's views as "the popular theory the Western press writes about". He said: "They see conspiracies in shadows. She's wrong."

In a reference made to the Catherine Lim commentaries in the book, *Lee Kuan Yew: The Man And His Ideas* by Han Fook Kwang, Sumiko Tan and Warren Fernandez, published in 1998, Lee is quoted as saying: "Supposing Catherine Lim was writing about me and not the prime minister ... She would not dare, right? Because my posture, my response has been such that nobody doubts that if you take me on, I will put on knuckle-dusters and catch you in a cul-de-sac ... There is no other way you can govern in a Chinese society."

"Robust" as his response was to Lim's pieces, Goh did not take out his knuckle-dusters. That he had chosen not to use them was, in itself, an eloquent rebuttal to her charge that he had ceded control to Lee. In fact, the episode made her a star of sorts when previously she was known only in Singapore's small literary circle and among those students who studied her short stories as examination texts. Dressed in her trademark cheongsams, she would appear regularly in the papers and on television.

Interviewed for this book in 2004, the writer, vivid and vivacious at 62, conceded that there had been a "loosening up" since that time. "Nobody but nobody will call him a seat-warmer now," she said, referring to Goh who, in his initial years, was seen by his critics to be warming the seat for Lee's son, Lee Hsien Loong.

But the loosening up was part of a larger trend, she said. The pragmatic PAP government had seen the benefits of opening up. The world had changed, and "they have no choice but to do it," she said, adding: "Only, they are doing it very incrementally, on their own terms."

She maintained that Lee's presence had remained dominant. "It is one thing to be still formally part of decision making and another thing to have so much influence that even a recollection of Lee Kuan Yew, a reminder of Lee Kuan Yew's displeasure, would already make people shrink. Absolutely, and this is what is happening, as long as he's around."

Yet, she said: "Lee Kuan Yew is sui generis. There is nobody like him, and his uniqueness is imprinted on our model so that it has permeated, disappearing, of course, with the younger generation, but it is still there."

The best test of his concern for Singapore was that he handed over power when he was still politically young. "Lee Kuan Yew knew that a younger man would be more in tune with the younger generation. And then again, you had the best of both worlds. He would be senior minister, some kind of wise counsellor. And I thought: great, this is a mark of greatness, true leadership."

National University of Singapore sociologist Chua Beng Huat, known for his outspoken views, had never hidden his conviction that Lee should have stepped down altogether when he passed over the baton to Goh. He related how, at academic talk-shops overseas, he found he could not make the other participants accept that Goh was the one in charge of the country and not Lee. "Most people absolutely refused to buy that line," he said.

"The thing was, one really didn't know what Lee Kuan Yew had done in the last 14 years. Everybody looked at his past. So even if he had come out and said, 'I didn't do anything at all', nobody would have believed him ... Did his presence stifle the next generation? We would never know. We would never know, for example, what else Goh's generation would have done if he weren't there," he said.

There were yet others who clung to their beliefs that Lee Kuan Yew was still the man running the show during all the years that Goh was the prime minister. Old opposition warhorse J B Jeyaretnam was one of them. He said: "Goh Chok Tong tried to give the appearance that he was his own man. He wasn't."

Lee still occupied the same room in the Istana which he did when he was the prime minister and Goh "was told to go and put up his office somewhere further down the corridor", or at least that was what he was reliably told, he said.

"Can you imagine a UK prime minister who's been defeated still saying, 'Well, I'll stay on at 10 Downing Street; you go and occupy another place'?" he asked.

⁂

The Banyan and the Tembusu

AUGUSTINE Tan, a PAP MP from 1970 to 1991, probably spoke for many Singaporeans when he said, in response to a question during an interview for this book: "When Chok Tong took over, I must confess, in retrospect, that I had misgivings because of course, consciously or unconsciously, I was comparing him with Lee Kuan Yew. But it turned out my misgivings were wrong and he had actually proven himself to be a very good prime minister.

"I was also nervous or apprehensive that the power configuration might not be the best for Singapore. I was apprehensive of potential conflicts because Lee Kuan Yew was still around. His son would be there and Chok Tong would be in the middle. But thank God, it had worked out well."

Tommy Koh, Singapore's best-known diplomat, shared Tan's view that the power configuration had worked out well. At a press conference at the end of a civil society conference organised by the Institute of Policy Studies in 1998, he likened the period under Lee to a banyan tree. The tree, revered in Asian culture, is deep-rooted and strong and has a large canopy that casts a big shadow. It was a metaphor borrowed from the seminal civic society speech that George Yeo made in 1991 when he was acting minister for information and the arts.

Yeo, who was the only candidate in the 1988 general election to have been installed as a minister almost immediately, made the case for a strong civic society which involved as many people as possible. In involving them, it would help them form an emotional attachment to the country. Otherwise, Singapore could just be a hotel with revolving doors, especially for those with portable skills. But because the first phase of nation building was a centralised one, the government did not pay attention to the building of that civic layer between state and family.

"The problem now is that under a banyan tree, very little else can grow," he said. "When state institutions are too pervasive, civic institutions cannot thrive. Therefore, it is necessary to prune the banyan tree so that other plants can also grow."

Tommy Koh took the tree metaphor further and suggested that the era under Goh was like the tembusu tree. It is as tall and firm a tree as the banyan but with only a small canopy, it allows more plants below to grow around it. "As advances in information technology make knowledge the driving force of the world economy, civil society will expand and become more powerful as the role of the state shrinks," he said.

Over lunch at the canteen in the Ministry of Foreign Affairs building six years later, Koh said the point he wanted to make in that 1998 speech was "that there had been a gradual transition from the banyan tree to the tembusu tree and that the transition had actually gone quite smoothly".

Credit should go to Lee for making that transition possible, he said. He recounted how when Goh asked him to chair the censorship review committee in 1992—he was then also the chairman of the newly formed National Arts Council—he went to see Lee about it. "Do I have your support for this?" he asked. "I'm going to propose liberalisation."

Lee replied: "Oh yes, this is very important for the prime minister. The times have changed. We have a new electorate. It's important for the prime minister to be seen to be his own man. Yes, it's very important. You should do this."

Goh himself had used the tree metaphor as early as 1985 when he spoke in an interview with *The Asian Wall Street Journal* about how Lee was making way for the second-echelon leaders. "The prime minister's such a giant. Fortunately for us, he is aware that his presence will prevent others from coming up. So the prime minister has consciously started pruning branches. Otherwise, we'll never get through."

It is not surprising that Goh had used a tree metaphor. As he said at a National Day rally in 1999, he—and Lee before him—were possibly the only prime ministers in the world who monitored the work of a National Parks Board gardening committee whose job was to plan, implement and track projects to beautify the island. Singapore is a 'garden city' because the meticulous manicure of its trees and shrubs and flowers had the attention of the prime minister, no less.

In his office in 2004, when asked how he managed what Augustine

Tan had called the power configuration, Goh said it was principally Lee Kuan Yew who made sure that it worked. As senior minister in the PMO, Lee observed protocol strictly, whether publicly or in private, he pointed out. If there was a function where both he and Lee had been invited, Lee would make sure he showed up before him, no matter how informal the function. Likewise, in private, when the two men had something to discuss, Lee would insist on going up to his third-floor office in the Istana Annex which was a floor above Lee's own.

The Istana, which is Malay for "palace", was built in the nineteenth century by British Indian convict labour to house the governor. Hidden behind a thick cover of mature trees off Orchard Road and nestled deep inside the sprawling 100-acre grounds, it is a statuesque building, with its classical European columns and deep tropical verandahs. It is where the president receives and entertains state guests.

One could not, however, describe the unadorned offices of Goh and Lee in the annex as grand. Their rooms were functional, the furniture simple and spare.

Yes, Lee kept his old office but Jeyaretnam had heard incorrectly about Goh being told to set up his office "somewhere further down the corridor". As Goh related it, Lee had insisted on giving up his office to him when he became the prime minister but it was he himself who suggested that Lee stayed put. All he had to do was to convert the disused floor above Lee's into his office.

This gesture of deference was very much in keeping with Goh's personality. He said: "(Lee) was the one who risked his life to build this place. He had stepped aside willingly. You inherited his place. How could you not respect him now just because you had become the prime minister? It's in my nature. I'm just as respectful of people like Lim Kim San and Goh Keng Swee."

Lee might not have to give up his room for Goh but he gave him room to grow as the leader of the country. In Goh's initial years as prime minister, he deliberately kept himself out of the front sections of the papers. He made few speeches on domestic matters, choosing instead to comment on international issues, away from the country, and for audiences outside it.

As a statesman whose track record that even his harshest critics could not disregard, Lee was helping to project Singapore on the world stage in a new era of globalisation. Said Goh: "I did not have the reach yet so it was very useful for Singapore."

In order that Goh could build up his links with the other ASEAN leaders, Lee did not visit any ASEAN country for some time. It would take him 10 years to go across the causeway to Malaysia.

Lee made his first major speech as senior minister in parliament only in January 1994 when he felt compelled to argue for the case that ministers' salaries be raised and pegged to top professionals'.

It was when he was confident that Goh could hold his own that he began to voice his views on issues that exercised him. Lee being Lee, he could not speak less than vigorously. In some instances, as in a Singapore Airlines management union dispute in 2004, he seemed to just charge in and intervene.

But Goh maintained that Lee cleared every of his moves with him. In the Singapore Airlines case, for example, it was "old business". Lee had intervened in a similar dispute when he was the prime minister and Goh felt he was the best man to deal with it.

In the cabinet, Lee's role was largely that of a tutorial master, Goh said. As prime minister, Goh would begin his weekly cabinet meetings with what he called a "pre-cab" session, when the ministers and the ministers-of-state would exchange their views freely on the issues of the day. Lee would not be present at these sessions.

The senior minister would join the team only after the pre-cab session for the cabinet meeting proper, during which decisions on policy issues were taken. Goh directed the meeting and only occasionally would Lee give his views on certain issues. The cabinet would hear them out and discuss them. Goh was still the one who made the final calls. As prime minister, the buck stopped with him.

When the meeting was over, Lee would share with the ministers whatever matters he thought were useful and where he could, he would bring his own experiences and wide reading to bear. "They were story-telling sessions," Goh said. "He had a lot of historical experience, he had more time to read and he would share his wisdom and insights. That was the principal value of having him among us in cabinet meetings. If we had kept him upstairs, we would have lost out on a lot ... the younger ones, especially, would have lost out on a lot."

In persuading potential office-holders to come on board early when they had indicated that they preferred to sign up at a later time, Goh found that it helped to tell them: "You'd better come in when Mr Lee is still around. You sit in Cabinet, you listen to him and you'll learn a lot." It worked invariably.

⸎

IN his office below Goh's, Lee said it did not make sense for him to undermine his successor. "To undermine him after working so hard for the succession would have been to defeat myself," he said. "It worked because it was not planned but at each stage, we adjusted … or I adjusted. I said: 'You are the boss; you decide.' "

He recounted how he managed the transition of power: "First, I was the pilot and he was the co-pilot. Then, between '88 and '90, even when I was the pilot, I was leaving the controls to him. He was at the back but actually piloting the plane. I was the master control. I could take over at any time. After that, he was in front and I was at the back. And after two, three years, when he had found his feet, I just left him alone. But from time to time, I just said: 'Oh, watch that meter.' The relationship stabilised and he was comfortable with me, and he knew I was helping him to succeed."

Lee's contribution to Goh's government was, of course, more than just that of a tutorial master and co-pilot. Cherian George, a *Straits Times* journalist whose often thoughtful and trenchant coverage of the political scene in the 1990s made him a known name before he left to pursue an academic career, says in his book, *Singapore: The Air-Conditioned Nation* (2000): "Lee Kuan Yew remained Singapore's long-range strategist. Ironically, the cabinet's oldest member was frequently its most visionary and boldest thinker ... He remained Singapore's most influential leader. People knew the government really meant business when he invested his moral authority behind a policy."

George cites as an example of Lee's several critical initiatives, the massive reform of the financial sector after 1997, although the work was carried out by Lee Hsien Loong. The senior minister's hand was also apparent in firm positions taken in the problematic dealing with the Malaysian government, he notes.

If there were Singaporeans who wished Lee had stepped down altogether, there were certainly many others, including expatriates who worked here, who were grateful that he was still around. He received letters regularly from expatriates who had enjoyed their stints in Singapore and wished to thank him personally.

A typical example was Mrs P Cattheral, an Englishwoman, who wrote him a letter in 1998 as she prepared to leave the country where she had spent 12 years. She came first as a dependant with her husband and later set up her own business. She said in her letter to Lee: "During my husband's frequent extended absences on business, I have been able to live here, even to go out alone in the evenings, feeling completely safe and comfortable, a basic human right which is unfortunately not now available to women in many countries...

"Singaporeans are most fortunate to have had as visionary a leader as you, Mr Lee, and also to have had a government that has enabled the implementation of your vision. The success of Singapore sets an example for the rest of the world."

A German radio journalist Carsten Peters, who had visited the country more than 10 times, felt compelled to write to Lee in 2004: "Looking at the present situation in my home country, I sometimes wish we would, and could, learn something from your model ... Our ex-chancellor, Helmut Kohl, was right when he called you 'a great statesman'."

❧

Three-in-one: A Winning Combination

GOH Chok Tong said he had never felt uncomfortable with Lee Hsien Loong as his deputy. "I appointed him," he said. It was a choice between Lee and Ong Teng Cheong. Goh canvassed views from his team before he made his decision. After all, as his potential successor, Lee had to have the support of the team. In the end, he chose Lee because he wanted a deputy who was younger than he was, not older. Ong was five years older than he was while Lee was a good 11 years younger. "It would not reflect well on our self-renewal drive if I picked someone older than I. That might mean I was protecting my position. As it turned out, he (Lee) was a very good deputy," Goh said.

After he had recovered from his cancer, Lee worked tirelessly as the second-in-command. He took on a variety of challenging tasks, especially economic ones. Because he was the more articulate of the two, Lee would also often be the one who spoke on behalf of the government. When it came to election broadcasts on television, it was Lee who spoke for PAP.

Goh pointed out that in cabinet, Lee the son had disagreed with some of the views of Lee the father. "Loong had different experiences. They looked at things differently ... At home, he might listen to his father's advice but in the end, he made his own decisions. I took comfort in passing over to him," he said.

In his office in the main Istana building in 2005, a year after he had become the prime minister, Lee Hsien Loong said the power configuration had proved to be an effective one. Lee Kuan Yew provided advice and the benefit of his years of experience; and Goh, as the prime minister, set the direction of the country and held a strong team together to work in that direction. "He set the tone, the pitch and the political presentation."

"And me, working with Mr Goh, knowing what he wanted to do and putting the pieces together to achieve the political objective which he as prime minister had decided on. So together we settled on the right directions, designed policies which worked, and then made sure that Singaporeans accepted and supported them," he said.

Certainly, the three men had very different temperaments. So when they approached a problem, they would bring to the table three different perspectives but the younger Lee said "our perspectives complemented one another's".

"Once we had agreed on a direction to take, (Lee Kuan Yew) would often start with the political objective: what was it that you wanted to achieve? Mr Goh would look at it from the point of how to present it to the public, how it would go down. I would look at the details: what was the best way to do it, what were the problems that needed to be solved and what changes needed to be made?"

Lee Hsien Loong said: "Mr Lee, as the senior minister, was supposed to be in semi-retirement but not actually in retirement at all. And all of us were working on different aspects. You could not have done it with just one person. It was not a matter of abilities but the scope, the amount of work."

His view of the power configuration was: "There was a job to be done and I think we had a team which could do it better than any single one of us could ... I think if any one of us had been missing from that team, something would have been lost."

On his working relationship with Goh, Lee pointed out that he had known Goh for a long time even before he entered politics. When he was director of the joint operations and plans directorate and chief of staff of the general staff in the army, he reported to Goh, who was the-then defence minister. "So there was already a good degree of understanding of each person's temperaments and mindsets, and how to adapt and work with one another," he said. "We didn't always agree completely on issues. With big decisions, we had to debate them: which way to go, whether to go quickly, slowly, whether to negotiate harder or what concessions to offer. These are things reasonable people disagree over. So we had thorough discussions. Usually, we would discuss it with a group of ministers and reach a consensus."

But was Goh in any way constrained by Lee Senior's presence, as some critics had charged. Could bar-top dancing, for example, which Goh allowed in August 2003, have been introduced much earlier if Lee Hsien Loong were the prime minister?

"I don't know ... Maybe ... I'm not sure!" Lee said, and laughed. "No, in the end, the prime minister sets the tone because he appoints the ministers and he has to carry the responsibility. The ministers can make all kinds of recommendations but if the prime minister doesn't agree with the thrust or doesn't agree with the way the proposals are presented, it cannot be done. Because, he has to stand up and defend the policies. And if he doesn't believe in them, it will show straightaway."

The PAP government had to cut CPF contribution rates and make changes to the system during the recession of 2002 following the 9/11 attacks in the United States. Lee said: "If the prime minister didn't agree that we had to reform the CPF, then when he was asked a difficult question in an election rally or an interview, everyone could see immediately that he was not his own man."

⚜

THAT Goh was his own man was abundantly clear as he grew in stature as both the country's leader and a statesman who could work well on the global stage to further the interests of Singapore. Yet, he would be the first to stress that his achievements were as much the result of the collective effort of his capable team which included the two Lees, his other deputy Tony Tan, and his ministers such as Wong Kan Seng, George Yeo and Lim Boon Heng.

As home affairs minister since 1994, Wong had ensured the country's stability in a turbulent time. In dealing with crimes, he balanced toughness with an enlightened approach. Wong was also very much in charge of party affairs as second assistant secretary-general in PAP's CEC and as vice-chairman of the People's Association (PA), which oversaw the running of the islandwide grassroots network. He organised the party's successful campaigns in the 1991, 1997, 2001 and 2006 general elections.

George Yeo was Goh's point man in his government's liberalisation programme in the arts. Put in charge of the newly created Ministry of Information and the Arts in 1991, he opened up the space for artists and forged a lively arts scene. He also helped make Singapore a media hub by courting the international media companies and getting them to set up their Asian bases in Singapore. These included Hallmark, MTV and HBO.

In the late 1980s, the government had problems with various regional publications and at one time or another, restricted for a time their circulation in the country. Yeo repaired the troubled relationships with the media conglomerates that owned these publications. Many of these publications, such as *The Asian Wall Street Journal*, *The Financial Times*, *Newsweek* and *Time*, are now printed in Singapore.

Lim Boon Heng had joined the NTUC in the early 1980s and risen up the ranks. Ong Teng Cheong was a hugely popular leader of the labour movement and was a difficult act to follow but Lim proved to be a capable, if not as popular, a leader after he became the NTUC's secretary-general in 1993. He introduced seamless membership so that workers could continue to be members as they switched from one firm to another. The numerous incentives offered by the NTUC cooperatives had also helped to retain and enlarge the membership base, which grew from 230,000 in August 1993 to 460,000 in April 2005.

To make the Singapore labour market a more nimble and competitive one, Lim oversaw a major wage-restructuring programme. A worker's wage was no longer a fixed sum. There was a fixed component and a flexible one that was tied to his own performance and his employer's. The flexible component of the workers' wages allowed companies to make quick adjustments to shorter business cycles.

Globalisation brought with it the new phenomenon of structural unemployment, which Lim had to tackle together with the Ministry of Manpower. A number of those unemployed could not take up jobs that were available because they did not have the skills for them. They had to be re-trained.

Goh's team was a cohesive one, perhaps because working together at the top, he, Lee Kuan Yew and Lee Hsien Loong had already set that very tone.

29

A Goal Fulfilled

Upgrading and the 1997 Polls

KIM Keat Court, a grouping of three blocks in Lorong 7, Toa Payoh, has the features of a new Housing and Development Board (HDB) estate. It has a road leading into it, framed at the entrance by a polished granite arch. There is a two-storey covered car park at the back, which borders Lorong 8. The grounds within are paved and landscaped with trees and shrubs. Walkways link the blocks to one another, as well as to pavilions, and a large, open community hall. The blocks are painted a vivid canary yellow against a pastel green background. The lifts have tiled lobbies.

The year is 2005 and Kim Keat Court can easily pass off as a development that is not more than 10 years old. But Blocks 1, 2 and 3 are almost 40 years old. They were among the first HDB blocks to be built in Toa Payoh, back in 1968. The flats in all the three blocks are three-room units. In each unit, there are two bedrooms, a living/dining room, a kitchen and a toilet-cum-bathroom.

In 1992, the three-block cluster was picked by the PAP government to undergo an extensive makeover as part of a demonstration phase of its 15-year upgrading programme to rejuvenate the older HDB estates. Five other precincts were also chosen: Marine Parade, Lorong Lew Lian, Ang Mo Kio, Clementi and Telok Blangah.

First announced in 1989, the $15 billion to $20 billion upgrading programme formed part of PAP's campaign in the 1991 general election. But at the time, voters had no idea what the programme meant as there was nothing concrete to look at.

But in 1995, when the upgrading work was completed, the results were there for everyone to see. And were the results impressive! To borrow a *Straits Times* headline, the upgraded HDB blocks had gone "from featureless to fabulous".

As in the other five precincts, the three blocks in Lorong 7 had taken on a whole new look and were given a name, Kim Keat Court. The lifts, which previously did not stop on every floor, now did. Each flat, which had a floor area of 66 sq m, had an extra 6-sq-m room added to it. Adjoining the kitchen, it could be used by its owners as a small bedroom, a study or utility room. Thinner polyvinyl pipes had replaced the bulky cast-iron pipes that used to take up much space in the toilets.

The external environment had also been transformed, as has been described above.

Upgrading work in Kim Keat Court had begun in 1992, after more than 90 per cent of its 572 home owners had voted for it. Those in Blocks 2 and 3 had each paid $4,500 for the upgrading exercise, or 10 per cent of the cost. Residents in Block 1 had opted to pay $3,000 more each for a larger (7.2 sq m) additional room. The government picked up the rest of the $27.5 million tab.

The demonstration phase of the upgrading programme was completed in the midst of a boom in the Singapore property market. Between 1989 and 1993, the government had introduced a series of policy changes that boosted demand for resale HDB flats. Against the backdrop of a strong economy, this demand drove up prices in not just the public property sector but the private one as well. HDB dwellers who could afford it were upgrading into condominiums and landed property.

The upgraded flats in the six precincts saw their value in the resale market shoot up by at least 20 to 30 per cent more than similar flats that had not been upgraded. The average prices of three-room and five-room flats transacted in 1996 were $182,000 and $468,000 respectively, according to National Development Ministry figures. One upgraded three-room flat in Marine Parade actually fetched $340,000 while one five-room unit went for a breath-stopping $668,000.

In Kim Keat Court, the selling price of the flats doubled, said Ho Tat Kin, then the chairman of the Toa Payoh Town Council. The residents had, as Lee Kuan Yew said, been given a capital grant. Those who chose to keep their flats now enjoyed a better quality of life, with their home environment made more pleasant.

Across Lorong 8 in Toa Payoh, the HDB blocks in the opposition-held ward of Potong Pasir looked decidedly drab in comparison. Flat-owners there could not hope to see the value of their flats go up by very much. Ho, who was also an MP in the Toa Payoh Group Representation Constituency (GRC), said: "If you look across the road from your flat on the Potong Pasir side, won't you be envious (of the Kim Keat Court residents)?"

Indeed, HDB residents liked what they saw. "When is our turn?" became the most asked question in the various housing estates.

⁓⊱❦⊰⁓

THE HDB upgrading programme was the centrepiece of PAP's campaign in the January 1997 general election. Although the programme was a national one, precincts that voted for PAP would get to be upgraded first besides enjoying other benefits.

It proved to be the "single, most important factor" in the party's 65 per cent victory, as Goh Chok Tong disclosed at a party convention a year after the election. The result was its best showing since the 1980 general election and it reversed a slide that began in the 1984 general election. PAP also regained two of the four seats it had lost in the 1991 general election. Cheo Chai Chen and Ling How Doong of the Singapore Democratic Party (SDP) lost their seats after only one term.

By linking priority of upgrading to electoral support, PAP effectively checkmated the opposition's by-election strategy. The ruling party had obviously thought hard about how it could counter the clever strategy after the 1991 general election. By 1992, it had found the answer.

In April that year, at a press conference after a community visit, Goh served notice that how Singaporeans voted in future elections would determine how quickly their estates were refurbished under the HDB upgrading programme.

Two months later, in a speech to party activists, he said: "We cannot deny voters in opposition wards the benefits of national programmes like Edusave, Medifund and the HDB upgrading programme ... But it is perfectly legitimate to serve constituencies which voted for the programme first as against those which did not. Can you imagine how silly I would have sounded had I said that where two constituencies had equal claims on the HDB upgrading programme, the ward which voted against the government programme would be served first?"

The upgrading programme was a key plank in PAP's strategy to fight the election at the constituency level. After the 1991 general election, the PAP government had devolved the management of housing estates to the town councils, which were headed by the MPs of the respective constituencies. The individual town councils took over the management of municipal matters which had previously been carried out by central government agencies like the HDB and Public Utilities Board.

How efficient a town council managed its ward could thus be a quantifiable measure of the effectiveness of its MP. Residents who voted in an ineffectual MP would have to live with the consequences for five years before they could kick him out in the next election.

For the 1997 general election, PAP MPs drew up plans for the building of a range of facilities in their respective wards as well as improvements to the housing estates, including upgrading. The MPs made clear that they would carry out these plans only if they were voted in. The general election was also a local election, as Goh said.

Although PAP did not articulate it, it obviously believed that those who voted for the opposition for the sake of opposition ought to feel some pain. They should not be allowed to be "free riders", a problem which the National Trades Union Congress (NTUC) had faced.

The national union body had suffered a decline in membership, largely because workers who refused to join a union still got to enjoy the benefits that the union had won through collective bargaining. The problem was solved and its membership base built up after the NTUC tied tangible benefits to membership. Union members had discounts at the NTUC-run supermarket chain, FairPrice, and its numerous recreational centres.

PAP also maintained that it needed to carve up the constituencies into smaller precincts of about 5,000 voters each so that it would know exactly which precincts showed it the strongest support. The votes of the different precincts were counted at different centres. The Cheng San GRC, for instance, had 25 counting centres. (This decentralisation of the wards was first carried out in the 1993 presidential election when Ong Teng Cheong beat Chua Kim Yeow for the job at the Istana.)

Voters were assured that their votes would still be secret. PAP might know how 5,000 voters in a precinct voted but it would never know how any individual among the 5,000 voted.

In the din of protests that followed at the opposition rallies, Low Thia Khiang of the Workers' Party (WP) raised a shrewd political point: "The real purpose of this is not to decide which precinct will get upgraded first. PAP wants to use this method to redraw the electoral boundaries accurately next time so that they can ensure that opposition votes will always remain in the minority."

At the time, PAP did not wish to engage Low on it. But asked about it some years later, Wong Kan Seng, who had organised PAP's campaign, said: "Mr Low Thia Khiang was making a political point and as the opposition, he was entitled to politicise this and hold different views.

"The rationale for having smaller polling districts of about 5,000 electors each was for the purpose of knowing which precinct supported PAP's electoral programmes, including upgrading.

"There are many reasons why the opposition remains weak and a minority, for example, poor leadership, lack of a political platform which appeals to all voters, inability to attract quality candidates and ineffectiveness even as MPs in parliament and in the constituency. Ling How Doong and Cheo Chai Chen failed to take charge of their town councils in Bukit Gombak and Nee Soon Central, for example. It is certainly not because of small electoral precincts."

⊱⋅☼⋅⊰

PAP'S strategy of tying the local vote to upgrading and other benefits did not go down well in certain quarters.

More than a week before the polls, the US State Department took a shot at it, pronouncing: "We believe that voters everywhere should be able to vote without fear of repercussions from the government as a result of their responsibilities as citizens."

The meddling infuriated the usually even-tempered Goh, who responded: "This is a local election and what we offer the people as a programme is no more different from what any candidate anywhere else would offer their electorate."

George Yeo could not resist taking a swipe at the US: "I am quite surprised that the Americans should raise an issue about how we run democratic politics in Singapore when their pork-barrel politics is something of a long tradition."

After the election, in response to a critical piece written by The Roundtable, a political discussion group, which was published in *The Straits Times*, PAP took the opportunity to point out that the Americans had developed what they called pork-barrel politics into a fine art. To keep themselves in the favour of their home folks, American politicians had always lobbied for slices of federal "pork" for their constituencies—money for infrastructure projects, military bases and defence contracts.

The party contended that the HDB upgrading programme was not pork-barrel politics. It was offered to all Singaporeans who lived in HDB estates and did not benefit a small group at the expense of the general population. It said: "The advantage of faster upgrading is available to all those who vote for it. Upgrading depends on growth and surpluses. Surpluses require a good and sound government pursuing long-term policies that can generate growth and wealth for all.

"Good government can endure only if people vote for it. So voters who help to elect a good government are making a contribution to Singapore. Those who vote against good government, and yet hope to benefit from it, are free-riding on those who vote for good government.

"We must give people an incentive to support good government with their votes ... This is both necessary and right."

As Goh had said before the polls, Singapore was in a peculiar situation where opposition parties did not provide voters with an alternative set of policies but campaigned only on the need to check the PAP government. In other democracies, voters had a choice between at least two alternative sets of programmes presented by rival political parties and candidates.

To give the voters a real choice, an opposition party should seek to field a full slate of candidates and draw up its alternative set of policies which might also include upgrading. Should the voters choose the opposition party over PAP, it could then form the government and implement its alternative programmes.

<hr/>

No Sedan Chair for Chinese Advocate

PAP had an unexpected threat in the 1997 general election. From the left field sprang Tang Liang Hong, a pugnacious 61-year-old lawyer who was, until then, a relatively unknown figure outside the Chinese cultural scene. He joined forces with J B Jeyaretnam of the WP to contest in the five-member Cheng San GRC against a PAP team led by the soft-spoken education minister Lee Yock Suan.

Tang had tried to enter parliament as a nominated MP in 1992 but PAP rejected his application because of his uncompromising views on the Chinese language. He did not hide his conviction that the standard of Chinese had declined because the largely English-educated PAP leaders did not pay it enough attention.

Since the early 1990s, he had been a speaker at public forums and seminars where issues on the Chinese language and culture were discussed. He was a strident speaker, given to emotional outbursts. At one forum, he charged that the English-educated and Christians dominated the government. The Chinese-educated had ended up carrying the sedan chair instead of sitting in it, he said. Remarks such as these had made many members of the Chinese intelligentsia uncomfortable even if they shared his view that the standard of Chinese had declined.

The PAP MPs who represented the ethnic Chinese ground judged that Tang was treading dangerous ground. He could express his intemperate views as a private individual without causing much harm but if he were allowed into parliament, those views could make for divisive politics. They voted against his application to become a nominated MP.

Tang had always believed in the supremacy of Chinese culture. Growing up in his immigrant grandfather's laundry shop in Chinatown, he was exposed to Chinese folk culture early and he developed a passion for all things Chinese. Because he linked his identity with his ethnicity, he had perhaps felt it a personal slight that the once great Middle Kingdom had fallen behind in the last few hundred years and had allowed the "fair-skinned devils", or westerners, to bully it at will.

In the 1950s, when the Chinese High School was a hotbed for leftist rebels, the young Tang was in his element, agitating for all kinds of causes. He helped collect funds for the building of Nanyang University, or Nantah. But for all his passion, he left Nantah after a year there. He was realistic enough to see that he could not have much of a future with a degree from a Chinese-language university. Instead, he went to the-then University of Singapore to read law. His heart, though, remained with Nantah. When the government closed it in 1980, it was another personal slight.

To be fair to the man, Tang had no quarrels with the other races in Singapore. He learnt Indian dance when he was a student and he could read and speak Malay fluently. His anger was directed at those English-educated Chinese Singaporeans whom he saw as shallow and deracinated. He had once said: "English-educated Chinese who do not have a good grasp of their culture and do not feel embarrassed about it are likely to lack respect for their own kind and confidence in themselves."

But it was not as though PAP was not alive to the danger of people being uprooted and displaced. Lee Kuan Yew himself had warned about it way back at the National Day rally in 1978: "… I say a person who gets deculturalised—and I nearly was, so I know the danger—he loses his self-confidence. You get a sense of deprivation. For optimum performance, a man must know himself, know the world. He must know where he stands."

In the 1997 hustings, however, Lee sounded the alarm against someone like Tang Liang Hong. At a lunchtime rally held at UOB Plaza, he said that even if China became the world's greatest power and Chinese one of the world's leading languages, Singapore could not afford to be more Chinese and less multiracial. Singapore remained a fragile nation-state within Southeast Asia, with deep fault lines along race, language and religion. If Tang's views prevailed, the Chinese-educated would become more assertive and demand a more dominant role for Chinese language and culture. The multiracial balance would be upset, he warned.

Goh Chok Tong said in interviews for this book, that "if he (Tang) had come into parliament and if he had argued the way he had done for the Chinese language and culture, it would have caused alarm among the Malays and Indians, and even the Chinese, because not all Chinese think like him."

PAP pulled out all the stops to make sure Tang did not get into parliament. Goh, his two deputies and Lee all weighed in. It was a winner-take-all fight, Goh declared. In the end, PAP won by a narrow margin of 54.8 per cent in Cheng San.

During the hustings, Tang filed a police report against PAP and threatened to sue its top leaders. PAP counter-sued. Tang fled the country, having made all the necessary preparations to do so.

The Cocktail-circuit Freedom Fighter

WHEN he first entered the political arena as an SDP candidate in the 1992 Marine Parade by-election, the 30-year-old Chee Soon Juan was touted as a rising star. He was articulate and armed with a PhD. But by the time he fought in the 1997 general election as leader of the SDP, he had become inconsequential in the domestic political arena.

Chee was a lecturer at the National University of Singapore when he contested in the by-election. In the following year, he was sacked from the university for misusing research funds. It concerned a small sum of $226 so public sympathy was with him. But he squandered the sympathy through a series of ill-judged actions over the next few years.

He went on a hunger strike to protest against his expulsion. Pragmatic

Singaporeans were unconcerned and more so after the media revealed that he was feeding himself glucose water. He was no Gandhi, certainly.

That he had secretly taped conversations with his former department head S Vasoo, a PAP MP, and then denied it when he was caught out, cast doubts on his character.

Eight months after he joined SDP, he had party chief Chiam See Tong sacked for breaching party rules. He swiftly installed himself as the secretary-general of the party. Chiam successfully sued the party CEC and was reinstated as an ordinary member.

In 1995, Chee lost much public goodwill when he went to Williams College in Massachusetts, US, to be a party-pooper at a ceremony to honour Goh Chok Tong. The university where Goh had earned his master's degree in 1967 had chosen to give its illustrious alumnus an honorary degree. But a group of students and academics were opposed to it on the grounds that Goh was running a police state that had the temerity in 1994 to cane an American delinquent for acts of vandalism.

The American media's feeding frenzy on the Michael Fay case had rallied Singaporeans behind their country's stand. Now, proud that their prime minister was being honoured by an august American institution, they saw Chee as being disloyal to Singapore when he accepted the anti-Goh group's invitation to take part in a protest against the award ceremony.

The PAP government's strategy in tackling Chee was to simply give him enough rope to hang himself. When he charged that the cost of living in Singapore was too high and that health care was not subsidised, the government formed a cost review committee and a select committee on health care, and invited Chee and his team mates to present their evidence to be scrutinised.

Chee and gang floundered in both the hearings but instead of admitting to the mistakes, he kept trying to weasel his way out of them. After the health care select committee hearing, the team was accused of perjury, prevarication, misconduct and wilfully giving false information, and fined for contempt of parliament.

In the lead-up to the 1997 general election, after a protracted public debate with PAP's Matthias Yao, Chee was cornered into contesting against Yao in MacPherson which was carved out of the Marine Parade GRC specifically for the one-on-one fight. Yao, the incumbent, easily beat him with a 65.1 per cent margin.

Chee cried when the result was announced but his defeat could not have hurt him much. For he had perhaps by now found his true calling—as a cocktail-circuit democracy fighter outside of Singapore. Well-funded NGOs in the United States, Europe and Australia whose aim was to promote what they believed to be universal civilisation were happy to have him on their roster of talking heads.

Domestic politics was no longer a real concern of his, even if he had started out with a chip on his shoulders. It was only necessary so long as it got him on one junket after another.

Goh Chok Tong's judgment of Chee was that he used the network of these organisations for his purpose. "He wants to go on study courses; he wants to be invited to give speeches," he observed.

Likewise, the NGOs were using him for their cause. It was clear, however, that these NGOs were not targeting Singapore specifically. So PAP did not see Chee as a dangerous subversive.

Also, Goh said: "He has big character flaws. He's always trying to elude you when you pin him down. But people can see him shifting positions all the time. So he's no threat."

In the 1997 general election, the SDP was also roundly trounced, with Ling How Doong and Cheo Chai Chen losing their Bukit Gombak and Nee Soon Central seats respectively. They had won their seats narrowly in the 1991 general election but as Wong Kan Seng said, they had not managed their town councils properly when they were MPs. Veteran PAP grassroots leaders, Ang Mong Seng and Ong Ah Heng, snatched back the wards with more than 60 per cent margins.

However inept the two SDP leaders were, the triumph of Ang and Ong was instructive. Singapore might have become a First World country but there was still a sizeable Third World segment in the population who could be reached only through grassroots politics. The folks in this segment certainly could relate to someone like Ong Ah Heng, popularly known as the *kopitiam* ("coffeeshop" in Hokkien) MP.

Chiam See Tong, who joined the Singapore People's Party (SPP) to contest the election after he was unceremoniously turfed out of his own party, kept his Potong Pasir seat. His margin plunged though, from 1991's 69.6 per cent to 55.2 per cent. Behind the swing could be those residents in Lorong 8, Toa Payoh, who wanted their flats to be upgraded like Kim Keat Court's.

On the other hand, Low Thia Khiang's 58 per cent win at Hougang put paid to the cynical view that Singapore voters could be "bought" with upgrading programmes and other benefits. Low had proven to be an effective MP both in parliament and on the ground. That his voters had chosen him over material incentives and a weaker opponent—PAP had fielded a first-timer—reflected a certain maturity among the electorate.

❧❦❧

PAP's Big Win amid the 2001 Gloom

AS if he had not discredited himself enough, Chee Soon Juan made yet another costly mistake in the 2001 general election. This time, he was contesting in the Jurong GRC. While on a campaign trail in Jurong East one Sunday morning, he caught sight of Goh Chok Tong and his team at a food centre. As he made his way towards Goh, his running mates and supporters thought he was going to shake the prime minister's hand, like a gentleman politician. Instead, he suddenly shouted at Goh at the top of his voice: "Mr Goh! Mr Goh! Come here, Mr Goh! I want to talk with you. Come here! Where is our money, Mr Goh? You can run but you can't hide."

He was referring to the $17 billion he had alleged that Goh and Lee Kuan Yew had lent to the besieged Indonesian president Suharto during the Asian financial crisis in the late 1990s. (The allegation turned out to be baseless after all and he had to make a public apology to both men.)

The fallout from his unduly emotional heckling was irreparable, especially when television replayed the clip repeatedly. If the voters had not already judged him as a poor politician, they did now. In the end, the PAP team led by Lim Boon Heng beat Chee's by an overwhelming 79.8 per cent margin, the biggest win among all the GRCs.

Goh had originally planned to call for the election in early 2002 but moved it to 3 November 2001 after the 9/11 terrorist attack on the World Trade Center and the Pentagon in the United States. Dark clouds had gathered as global confidence was shaken by the shocking event.

Singapore was going into a deep recession. There would be a loss of some 25,000 jobs by the end of the year and another 15,000 in the following year, Goh told reporters. To save jobs, there would be wage cuts in all sectors. In addition, the government also issued New Singapore Shares and announced an off-Budget package of $11.3 billion to help affected Singaporeans cope with the downturn.

On the ground, morale was low and the mood grim. People were anxious about their jobs, their future and their children's future. Goh said he wanted the election out of the way so that the country could focus on creating jobs and building up its home security defence.

"The government couldn't have asked for a better made-to-order electorate with a laser-like focus on the big issues," said Han Fook Kwang, then the political editor of *The Straits Times*. "When the world is on such a knife edge, when there is so much uncertainty about the future and so much danger of the region undergoing another catastrophic upheaval, minds will begin to concentrate on the important and the urgent. I believe the Singapore electorate is in such a state," he wrote in a commentary.

Han was proven right. PAP romped home with a 75.3 per cent win, its biggest since 1980's 77.7 per cent.

Chiam See Tong clung to his Potong Pasir seat by a whisker—751 votes. He had formed an alliance of four parties but the other candidates made no headway.

Low Thia Khiang retained his seat in Hougang for the third time although his share of votes dipped from 58 to 55 per cent.

Low had replaced J B Jeyaretnam as leader of the WP. The latter had been found guilty of defaming the organisers of the 1995 Tamil Language Week in an article in the WP's organ, *The Hammer*. He had to pay them more than half a million dollars in damages and costs. Because he could not rustle up the sum, he lost his non-constituency MP seat and was barred from contesting in the election.

PAP's slate of candidates in 2001 was radically different from those in the previous elections. There was no SAF scholar. Only two of the 25 new faces were from the public sector. There were seven women candidates, three of them single. One of the singles, lawyer Indranee Rajah, was the first Indian woman candidate since 1965. There was also a *tudung*-wearing Malay woman candidate, Halimah Yacob, a trained lawyer who was a popular senior officer in NTUC.

PAP also included a few candidates known to hold some different views from the party—Raymond Lim, a founder of the political discussion group, The Roundtable; Tharman Shanmugaratnam, whose name came into public attention in 1992 when, as a director of the economics department of the Monetary Authority of Singapore, he was charged with breaching the Official Secrets Act; and Vivian Balakrishnan, who had spoken up against PAP policies as an active student leader at the university.

Shanmugaratnam was a rebel in his school days and at the London School of Economics, he was in a study group with Tan Wah Piow. He was questioned by the Internal Security Department (ISD) when he returned in 1982. During the Marxist conspiracy episode in 1987, he was again questioned by the ISD "day and night for one week".

This slate had popular appeal, especially among the post-1965 voters who formed one-third of the electorate.

❧

DURING the hustings, Goh had announced that the general election would be his last as prime minister. He would be handing over the reins to his successor some time before 2007, he said.

If Goh could look back on his years as the PAP's secretary-general with some satisfaction, it was because he had fulfilled a key goal that he had set out for himself. He said: "The question I asked myself was, how was it that PAP, which I regarded as the most competent party with the right policies, was losing ground over the years after 1981. '81, '84, '88, we were losing ground. Why? So we had got to solve the problem. We could not govern if we could not solve the problem. In time to come, we might be out.

"There was no doubt in my mind that PAP was the white knight for Singapore … to be able to deliver the goods and a better life for the people. But why were we losing support? That worried me and intrigued me. My goal therefore, when I took over, was to reverse this trend."

And reverse the trend he did, in only three general elections.

30

Finally, Lee Hsien Loong as Prime Minister

The Long Stint as Deputy

FOURTEEN years is a long time to be a deputy prime minister. "Yes, I was one of the most senior deputy prime ministers in the world," said a laughing Lee Hsien Loong in his Istana office on a clear September morning in 2005. Slightly more than a year ago, he finally took office as prime minister, at age 52.

Did he think the 14 years were... "Wasted?" he asked. Not wasted, but could it perhaps have been shorter? "It could have been," he said, "but I mean, what's the loss?"

When he entered politics in 1984, many Singaporeans assumed he would succeed his father, Lee Kuan Yew. But the father believed the son should succeed on his own merit and not simply inherit his office.

Still, when Goh Chok Tong was made prime minister in November 1990 and he appointed Lee Hsien Loong as his deputy, many people saw Goh as a seat warmer for the younger Lee. They figured that Goh would occupy the prime minister's office for a couple of years before the younger Lee took over.

Two months before he became premier, in an interview with Hong Kong journalists, Goh made clear there was no arrangement for his appointment to be merely a transitional one.

A journalist had noted that in Taiwan, after President Chiang Kai-shek died in 1975, his successor, the former vice-president Yen Chia-kan, ruled for three years only before Chiang Ching-kuo, a son of Chiang Kai-shek, took over. Would such a scenario happen in Singapore, he asked.

"But I am not a seat warmer," Goh replied. "Being a seat warmer means there is an arrangement by all concerned that you come into this job and you stay for a certain period until somebody is ready to take over. There is no such arrangement," he maintained.

In 1996, six years after he had been in the premier's seat, at a dialogue with grassroots leaders at the Kallang Theatre, Goh said to loud applause:

"When I first took over, I remember people touting me as a seat warmer. I think I can qualify as the longest seat warmer in history. In the coming election, if you signal that you want me to continue, I shall leave the seat so warm that my successor will have to find a new chair."

It was not a statement of bravado. For several years, Goh had endured taunts from critics, both abroad and at home, that he was just a seat warmer. But now six years into the job, there was no question that he was fully in charge. It was a statement from someone who was confident in his position and comfortable under his own skin.

Yet, a year later, during the 1997 general election, he began thinking about the succession, Goh revealed. His obvious choice as successor was Lee Hsien Loong, whom he believed to be the best man for the job. Lee had just cleared the critical five-year period during which he did not suffer a relapse of his cancer. His doctors had told him that he could be considered cured if the lymphoma did not recur in the five years after his remission.

Goh was only 56 years old then but he had to take into account that Lee was already 45. If his peers endorsed him as well, Lee should take over the job when he was still in his early 50s so that he would have at least 10 to 15 years at the helm, as Goh saw it. He himself became prime minister when he was 49.

In planning for the succession, Goh set himself two targets: the changeover had to take place at a time when the economy was in good shape and PAP had to recover the ground it had lost since 1991. With Lee's age in mind, it was quite clear to him that he should not serve another two full terms as prime minister. If he should wait till 2007, Lee would be 55.

"There would not be too many years left. And of course, also by then, he might become a little stale with the public. Twenty years as deputy prime minister before you take over, what new ideas would you have? That was my thinking," he said.

The 2001 general election would be his last as prime minister, he decided, and he should hand over the reins perhaps two or three years after the event. He prepared the public for the changeover by announcing during the hustings that the general election would be his last as premier.

PAP did recover its ground in the 2001 general election with a handsome 75.3 per cent win, 10 per cent more than 1997's showing and 14 per cent more than 1991's. But the country had gone into a recession, following a year of stagnant growth and then the fallout of 9/11. The succession had to wait. Goh got Lee to work out a series of tough measures, including radical changes to the CPF, to fight the recession. The measures worked. There were signs of recovery.

Then the outbreak of a new, deadly virus called SARS (Severe Acute Respiratory Syndrome) in the first half of 2003 set back the recovery.

Unlike the case in China, Hong Kong and Taiwan, which were also badly affected by SARS, the government and the people in Singapore responded to the outbreak in a manner so exemplary it won the respect of the World Health Organisation (WHO) and many countries. To combat the epidemic, the PAP government had to take what, in more tranquil times, would be called draconian measures which included compulsory home quarantine for those who came into contact with suspected SARS victims. But the readiness in which the people responded to the measures showed the deep reservoir of trust the party had built up among the populace over the years.

The SARS crisis tested Singaporeans like no other in the past 20 years or more. They passed the test, emerging the stronger for it after the WHO declared in June that the worst was over.

But economic recovery required more time. At the National Day rally in August, even as he spoke about succession and made clear that his choice of successor was Lee Hsien Loong, Goh said: "But I am not stepping down yet. My immediate priority is to get Singapore out of the economic gloom."

The gloom lifted towards the end of 2003 when it became clear that the economy had turned around. By then, Goh felt the time was right for him to pass the baton. Of course, he could not simply appoint his own successor. Lee Kuan Yew did not appoint him; his peers picked him. Likewise, the choice of his successor had to be supported by the ministers. In May 2004, at a lunch arranged by Wong Kan Seng, the ministers gave their unanimous support of Lee as the next prime minister.

Goh instituted an additional process. It would not just be the ministers but all MPs as well who would decide on a new leader each time a prime minister stepped down. Accordingly, he summoned the MPs to a meeting at Parliament House where he asked if any of them wished to propose candidates other than Lee. No one did.

A final decision still had to be taken by the party's 18-member central executive committee (CEC). The CEC's decision was also unanimous—

Lee would be the next prime minister. Wong Kan Seng, the party's second assistant secretary-general, made the public announcement.

Goh and Lee then spent the next few months preparing for the changeover. "It was not that difficult," Lee said. "The main thing was the message and in this case I had two—the swearing-in followed by the National Day rally a week later. That set the tone for the new leadership."

They also had to settle on a new cabinet line-up. Said Lee: "Originally, Mr Goh was going to do the reshuffle but it took longer than we expected. So finally we decided, better for me to take the responsibility. So we had about May until August, about three months, to work this out. It was very long. In other countries, the prime minister resigns and tomorrow you find someone new."

The date for the changeover—August 12—was announced to the public in the middle of July.

Two days before the historic event, in a brief ceremony at the Istana in the morning, Goh tendered his resignation as prime minister to president S R Nathan and Lee presented himself to accept the president's call to form a new government. Goh's resignation, on behalf of himself and his government, would take effect on the evening of August 12, immediately before the new prime minister was sworn in.

On the same day, Lee unveiled his new cabinet line-up. Balanced between the new and the old, the line-up was seen by political observers as a transitional one. Lee Kuan Yew himself told *The Straits Times:* "This is a smooth transition rather than a drastic change of players. The incoming prime minister has redeployed some of his players and also reinforced the team with several backbench MPs. I believe there could be further deployments, especially after the next general election."

Lee Hsien Loong kept his finance portfolio. Both Lee Kuan Yew, 81, and Goh Chok Tong, 63, stayed in the new cabinet, as minister mentor and senior minister respectively. Minister mentor was a post specially created for the older Lee. Tony Tan, 64, remained as deputy prime minister although he would step down in September the following year and be replaced by Wong Kan Seng, 58. Contrary to widespread speculation, the prime minister-designate did not appoint a third-generation leader as the other deputy. Instead, he picked S Jayakumar, 65, a second-generation leader, for the job.

The ministers who were redeployed were George Yeo, 50; Yaacob Ibrahim, 49; and Lim Hng Kiang, 50. Yeo crossed over from trade and industry to foreign affairs; Yaacob moved to an expanded Ministry of Environment and Water Resources; and Lim took over trade and industry.

The three acting ministers who had come in during the 2001 general election—Ng Eng Hen, 45, at the manpower ministry; Khaw Boon Wan at health; and Tharman Shanmugaratnam, 47, at education—were confirmed as full ministers.

Two junior ministers from the 2001 batch were also promoted. Raymond Lim, 45, was made the acting second finance minister and senior minister of state for foreign affairs. Vivian Balakrishnan, 43, became the acting minister at the Ministry of Community Development, Youth and Sports (MCYS) and senior minister of state for trade and industry. "Youth" was added to the Ministry of Community Development and Sports to signal "the government's commitment to engage young Singaporeans in shaping the future", said Lee in a statement.

For the first time in three years, there were two women political office-holders in the front bench. Lim Hwee Hua, 45, was made the minister of state for finance and transport. Yu-Foo Yee Shoon, 54, took the job of minister of state for MCYS. First-term MP Amy Khor, 46, replaced Yu-Foo as the mayor of Southwest Community Development Council.

Veteran Lee Yock Suan, 58, was the only minister who retired.

⚬౷ஓ౷⚬

The Inauguration and the Rally

IN a departure from the two previous inauguration ceremonies, which were held inside the City Hall where only a limited number of members of the establishment were present, Lee Hsien Loong's was held on an open lawn in the Istana. Among the 1,400 guests were community leaders, leading businessmen, teachers, nurses, artists and even taxi-drivers and hawkers. The ceremony was televised live on state television.

After the president had sworn him in at 8 pm, Lee, dressed in a formal suit, gave two brief speeches in Malay and Mandarin before he spoke in English. In the speech, he underlined the diversity that made up the fabric of the nation. As the country progressed, no one would be left behind, he stressed. "We will look after the less educated and the elderly who have helped build Singapore. And we must also have a place in our hearts and our lives for the disabled, who are our brothers and sisters."

The political transition was not just a change of prime ministers, he pointed out. "It is a generational change for Singapore, a shift to the post-independence generation in a post-Cold War world."

The majority of Singaporeans were now those who were born after 1965. They grew up in a different Singapore from their parents'. They could expect an open and inclusive country where the government would continue to expand the space for individuals.

Lee said: "Our people should feel free to express diverse views, pursue unconventional ideas or simply be different. We should have the confidence to engage in robust debate so as to understand our problems, conceive fresh solutions and open up new spaces. We should recognise many paths of success and many ways to be Singaporean."

Lee's speech embraced all Singaporeans, strong or weak. He could have taken heed of Goh's advice to show his compassionate side which, although not often seen by the public, was evident to those who had worked with him in the cabinet and others who knew him well.

In his final National Day rally in the previous year, Goh had said some Singaporeans were uncomfortable with Lee. They had got used to his gentler style and would like Lee to be more approachable. The latter's public persona was that of a no-nonsense, uncompromising and tough minister. Goh had said: "But it is not fair to expect him to be like me, just as it was not fair to expect me to be like the senior minister ... I found my way to communicate with you, the people. Likewise, I believe Hsien Loong will find his own way to establish rapport with you. He is not me and he is not his father."

If Lee did not convince enough Singaporeans in his swearing-in speech that he was not his father and that he was not as uncompromising and tough as he was perceived, he certainly went some way to do so in his first National Day rally speech more than a week later.

For slightly more than three hours, as he ranged over a number of issues, he had the audience's rapt attention. He was articulate, even in Malay and Mandarin, and he made effective use of down-to-earth anecdotes to illustrate his points. He spoke with passion, yet showed compassion, and surprised many with his sense of humour. His jokes, because they were taken from life on the ground, had the audience laughing in recognition.

After the rally, Goh gave the performance the thumbs-up, saying it was "masterful". In an interview in 2005, he said: "Of course he's very good with words and I think he's able to balance the depth of his ideas with the need for a certain light touch in putting across the ideas."

Sociologist Kwok Kian Woon said he doubted if there was any other person in the cabinet who could have performed as well and projected the kind of effectiveness that Lee did. It was not just ability, he said. It showed "the will to be flexible, to make the necessary adjustments, in an intelligent response to the signs of the times".

"The presentation of self, the ability to command attention, the execution … he certainly had it but it must have also taken a lot of preparation. There were many issues and he handled them very well. People would recognise the ability and the effort," he said.

Kwok, the head of sociology at the Nanyang Technological University, said Lee's speech reminded him of those made by former Malaysian Prime Minister Mahathir Mohamad that he had watched over television. Mahathir's speeches could tug at the people's heartstrings so effectively that he practically had them eating out of his hand. "Ordinary people would go up and surround him," he said. Lee showed he had that same kind of charisma on the podium.

"There must be those whose hearts went out to him. These are people who feel he shouldn't be punished just because he's Lee Kuan Yew's son," Kwok said.

⁓⁓⁓

IN his speech, as with the one at his inauguration, Lee Hsien Loong first paid tribute to his predecessor. "… Chok Tong won the support of voters and the respect and affection of Singaporeans, and brought us all closer together as one people, and for that, I think we all thank Chok Tong."

He asked for a mindset change because the world had turned and so had Singapore. He said: "We are so capable, we are so efficient, we are so comfortable that we stick with what we have tried and tested, and found working, and we are reluctant to take risks and try new things. And that is a weakness. It's a weakness which we have to overcome.

"The key to overcoming this is a mindset change. We have to see opportunities rather than challenges in new situations, we have to be less conventional, we must be prepared to venture and you've got to do this as individuals, we've got to do this as a government, and I think we have to do it as a society."

To put the money where his mouth was, the new prime minister showed he was willing to risk losing some political capital by bringing up the controversial issue of the setting up of casinos in Singapore. He said: "Some people told me, 'Don't raise it. It's your first rally speech ... very dangerous', but I'm going to do it anyway."

Since the idea was first floated earlier in the year, many Singaporeans had expressed strong reservations about it. Religious groups had objected to it strongly. In his speech, Lee gave the reasons why the idea could no longer be summarily thrown out of the window as it had been many times whenever it came up.

The situation had changed. Circling the international waters around Singapore were cruise ships where people went to gamble; there were 13 casinos in the nearby Indonesian island of Batam; and almost every tour group that came to Singapore would go to Genting Highland in Malaysia whose main attraction was a casino. Macau, long a casino centre, had opened up with new operators who offered more games and more shows. The new wave of newly rich Indian and Chinese tourists had money to spend and if gambling was one of the activities that they sought, should Singapore say no?

Lee said: "We will consider all views before deciding. Finally, if we decide against it, then I think we will have had a valuable debate in our society ... and sent a strong signal that we are prepared to discuss all sorts of things and reopen long settled issues.

"But if we decide to proceed, then the final solution which we implement will have to address the valid concerns which Singaporeans have raised. So, it's not black and white ... Increasingly, the world is going to be like that."

Given that the world was what it was, Lee spoke on the five priorities that his government would tackle: external relations, economic restructuring, older Singaporeans, the post-independence generation and education.

Before he finished his speech, he also spoke about the problem of babies, or more specifically, the lack of. Singaporeans were cheered by the good news he delivered along the way—longer maternity leave, lower maid levy, the baby bonus which would be extended to the first and fourth child, a five-day working week for civil servants, the same medical benefits for both male and female civil servants and some 3,000 more teachers over the next six years.

The five-and-a-half-day working week was long a sacred cow

Lee himself had previously spoken up for it. He had maintained that productivity would be affected if it were cut down to a five-day week. But here he was, making the U-turn.

But what in the speech connected and touched the people most were Lee's human touches. Even in his big-picture presentations, people were not just statistics charted on graphs, something that Lee's father used to do at his National Day rallies, although that was a different era.

On grooming the new generation, for example, he said, "Guide them, but don't constrain them."

When Lee spoke about adding new teachers to primary and secondary schools and the junior colleges, he said it was for the schools to decide how to use them, not the Ministry of Education. There was a lot that the schools could do.

"But there is one thing which we shouldn't do," he said, "and that is that when we add more teachers, we'd better not add more homework or increase the syllabus because that just defeats the whole purpose … We've got to teach less to our students so that they will learn more."

To parents who fretted over their children's schoolwork, he advised: "Let them grow up in their own time … I think we have to let go a little."

The big dip in procreation was a national problem, he pointed out, but added that it was also "an intensely personal business". Again, in raising the subject, he was taking a risk. Lee Kuan Yew raised it in his 18th National Day rally which created a storm of controversy. Goh waited for his 10th National Day rally to talk about it.

The new prime minister did not hesitate to touch on the topic in his first rally speech. But his approach was that it was "a matter of values, not of incentives".

A hard-headed type would say he got "touchy-feely" here but he was speaking as a father of four children: "We want people to have babies because they want them and they love them … It's fulfilling to bring up a child. You can have the most successful career, you can be the richest man on earth or the most powerful man or woman on earth but if you don't have a family and don't have children, I think you're missing something.

"It starts off with missing changing nappies when you have a child but then you miss watching a child learning to walk, learning to talk, going to school, getting sick, depending on you, walking with you, playing with you …

"So, these are not things you can translate into dollars and cents, or careers and promotions. It's fulfilling. It's sad if you don't have it ... So, have two, three."

But he was quick to stress: "We are not going to micromanage your lives ... What we can do is we'll make it easier for families to marry and to have children. You make the decisions."

Lee finished his speech by saying, "We are building something unique and precious here ... I think this will always be work-in-progress because we will never be satisfied. We always want to move on, do better. But I think ours should be a future of opportunity and promise."

⋙⋘

The Firm Statesman

IN July, a month before he became prime minister, Lee Hsien Loong made a three-day visit to Taiwan.

An upset Beijing issued a statement immediately, saying that Lee had made the visit despite several representations made by China. The visit "damaged China's core interest and the political foundation for China-Singapore relations, and hurt the feelings of 1.3 billion Chinese people", it said. Chinese Foreign Ministry spokesman Kong Quan said the ministry hoped Singapore would "face up to the gravity of the issue and take concrete actions to win the confidence of the people of China".

Relations were strained as China suspended several scheduled important exchanges between the two countries. Over the Internet, Chinese citizens posted fairly vehement attacks on Singapore and invariably mocked its small size for good measure.

Lee stood firm and kept a dignified silence. It was only at the National Day rally when he was speaking on external relations that he made his considered response to the issue. He devoted 20 minutes of his speech to it. First, he explained why he had to make the trip to Taiwan. The cross-straits tension was the most dangerous problem in the region and as prime minister, he might have to make some difficult judgment calls should tensions become worse.

Also, if other countries were to take Singapore's views and assessments of the tension seriously, they had to see Singapore as informed, impartial and balanced. Though it was small and unable to influence events, Singapore could provide vital input to help the key players avoid mistakes and misjudgements.

Hence, his need to talk to the leaders in both the Democratic Progressive Party (DPP) and Kuomintang (KMT) parties in Taiwan face-to-face so that he could make an objective assessment with conviction and knowledge. He could not just do it remotely from his office in Singapore.

Which was precisely the problem of the Taiwanese government leaders and civil servants, he said. Unlike the businessmen, they were not allowed to visit China. So they were making policies on China based on reports but not on firsthand knowledge of how China had changed.

Lee also found the Taiwanese media a parochial lot, chasing after sensational news and speculation. They covered only domestic news, with very little or no reporting of the situation in North Korea, the war in Iraq, the war against terrorism and the US elections.

The DPP and KMT were also so bogged down by domestic politics that they did not have the time to reflect about Taiwan's future, about how to manage relations with China and how best to reconcile the aspirations of the Taiwanese people with the realities of their international position.

Lee then stated unequivocally: "Singapore's one-China policy will not change. A move by Taiwan towards independence is neither in Singapore's interest nor in the region's interest. If Taiwan goes for independence, Singapore will not recognise it. In fact, no Asian country is going to recognise it. Nor will the European countries. China will fight. Win or lose, Taiwan will be devastated...

"The problem is that it's not going to be just Taiwan which is going to be damaged. It will be a grave setback for the whole region. Our hope for China to emerge peacefully and for the region to prosper through investments and trade, and tourism will be shattered."

Unfortunately, Lee said, he met only very few Taiwanese who recognised the reality of the situation.

A Hong Kong Chinese-language weekly, *The Observer Star*, said Lee's "firmness and unequivocal tone in that speech demonstrated spirit and vision. It was a diplomatic masterstroke, the political wisdom of which is likely to earn the respect of senior diplomats in Beijing".

Wang Gungwu, the head of the East Asian Institute in the National University of Singapore and a highly regarded authority on Chinese history and the Chinese diaspora, said Lee's reply was "certainly well crafted". He had reservations, though, on why Lee chose to visit Taiwan at the time. "He underestimated (Taiwanese President) Chen Shui-bian's willingness to exploit his visit for his own advantage. It was just before the legislative elections and media coverage of the visit was maximised," said Wang.

The Observer Star noted that although Chen might have seen the visit as a major diplomatic coup, Lee's message against Taiwanese independence was a heavy blow to Chen and his pro-independence cause. It expected China's strained relations with Singapore to thaw soon. It said: "Mr Lee, in effect, used his own unique way to tell Beijing that while his Taiwan visit might have damaged China's interests, he rendered help to China by expressing a serious warning to Mr Chen which will provide an unseen and unique contribution to stabilising the situation in the Taiwan straits."

Relations between the two countries did return to normal by 2005. A not insignificant point to note is that despite China's displeasure over the Taiwan visit, it took care to "give face" to Lee when he was installed as prime minister. Its ambassador in Singapore, Zhang Yun, was present at Lee's inauguration ceremony at the Istana.

When Lee made his first official visit to China in October 2005, he received a formal welcome from his counterpart Wen Jiabao and had back-to-back meetings with Wen, President Hu Jintao, National People's Congress chairman Wu Bangguo and Jia Qinglin, chairman of the Chinese People's Political Consultative Conference, the country's top political advisory body. They were China's top four leaders and it was rare for a visiting head of state to meet all of them in consecutive meetings.

❧

His Early Years

WHEN Lee Kuan Yew became prime minister in 1959, he chose not to live in Sri Temasek, his official residence on the Istana grounds. He did not want his three children to grow up in grand surroundings, fussed over by butlers and orderlies. "It would have given them an unrealistic view of the world and their place in it," Lee said in the second volume of his memoirs.

Lee Hsien Loong and his two younger siblings, Wei Ling (1955) and Hsien Yang (1957), grew up in their parents' unassuming Oxley Road home. Hsien Loong, like Hsien Yang after him, went to Catholic High School, then a top Chinese-medium school. He did his two-year post-secondary education at the National Junior College where English was the main medium.

His childhood was crammed with studies—he was tutored in Jawi

(Malay written in the Arabic script) and Russian, among other subjects. He played the clarinet in the school band. He was also the drum major and editor of the school magazine. But he found time to play too with friends he made at school.

There were certainly constraints such as the presence of security officers everywhere he went but it was as normal a childhood as it could be, he said in 1984 when he first contested on a PAP ticket. Given that he was Lee's son and that he had a formidable intelligence, probably not many school mates dared to go near him. He could have been a lonely child in school but he made an effort to make friends, many of whom still remain close to him to this day.

As one of the top performers nationwide, Lee won both the President's and the Singapore Armed Forces' scholarships. He studied mathematics at Trinity College in Cambridge, graduating with first class honours in 1974, having completed the course in two years instead of three and spent the third year earning a postgraduate diploma in computer science, again with distinction.

Back in Singapore, Lee served in the army, holding various staff and command posts. He was trained in field artillery at Fort Sill, Oklahoma, and in 1978, spent a year at the US Army Command and General Staff College at Fort Leavenworth in Kansas. The following year, he took a master's degree in public administration at Harvard University.

In the army, his buddy was a Hokkien *peng*, a dialect-speaking staff sergeant, Lim Hock Lee, who dropped out of primary school and joined the army when he was 18. Both men shared a passion for the military and came up with ways to improve the army. Their friendship endured even as Lee rose up the ranks to become brigadier-general and after he joined politics. When Lee's first wife, Wong Ming Yang, died in 1982, Lee asked Lim to be one of the pall-bearers. Lim told *The Straits Times* in 2004: "I was surprised that he gave me the honour. I have no education; I have nothing. I was touched by his honest, sincere, forthright way with me all these years."

Lee met his wife-to-be in Cambridge in 1973 while she was studying to be a doctor at Girton College, the same college where his mother had studied. She was from Kuala Lumpur, Malaysia, and was the daughter of an insurance firm manager and a teacher in a Chinese school. They kept up their courtship after he returned to Singapore the following year while she worked in a hospital in Cambridge. Their marriage in May 1978 was a low-key affair. They had a simple ceremony at the Registry of Marriages and a small reception for 100 at Sri Temasek in the evening. Four short years later, Lee's wife died of a heart attack after giving birth to a son, Yipeng. She also left behind a 19-month-old daughter, Xiuqi.

Lee was stricken but when duty called, when Goh Chok Tong approached him to join PAP and take part in the 1984 general election, he said yes.

He had formed the conviction that he wanted to play a role in shaping Singapore from a young age. He had followed his father to election rallies when he was a child. He had witnessed the tumult of the 1960s. In Cambridge, when his tutor tried to persuade him to pursue a career in mathematics as he had done exceptionally well, he wrote him a letter to explain why he could not do so. "... Singapore is where I belong and where I want to be," he said in the letter.

Lee remarried in December 1985, to Ho Ching who was at the time the deputy director of both the Defence Science Organisation and the Materials Management Organisation in the defence ministry. The couple had met at work and begun their courtship in 1984. Ho Ching would bear Lee two sons and would also look after her two stepchildren as her own.

Both husband and wife must have agreed that Ho Ching would not have to switch to the slow lane in her career path. She eventually became executive director and CEO of Temasek Holdings, an umbrella government investment firm whose linked companies include a wide range of blue-chip stalwarts, industrial giants and technology outfits. Even lifestyle operations like the Singapore Zoo, Night Safari and the Jurong Bird Park all come under a company linked to Temasek.

⁂

The Reformer Who Listens

IN politics, Lee showed early that he was a reformer who could see ahead of the curve. After the 1984 general election, which saw PAP's share of votes take a dive almost across the board, it was he who crafted the post-mortem report that set a new direction in PAP's style. The report is impressive in its lucidity. The simple style and the economy with words reflected the author's command of the language.

In 1985, when the country went into a recession, the Economic Committee (EC) that he chaired took the bold step of slaughtering a sacred cow. It recommended that the CPF contribution rates be cut from 50 per cent to 35 per cent, to cut down on wage costs. The EC and its eight sub-committees were made up of more than 1,000 participants who included leaders in both the private and public sectors, business organisation representatives, unionists, bankers, lawyers and academics.

Earlier in the year, Lee had made one of his first speeches in parliament and, among other things, he had defended the CPF policy which Toh Chin Chye, a backbencher by then, had criticised.

"CPF, is that an overhead? Is that something which the government takes away from the workers or is it something which is part of the salary which belongs to the workers, something which the workers use to spend for Medisave, for a house, for old age?" he had asked. His own answer was that it was not an overhead but a component of a worker's salary.

Yet as the recession deepened, Lee revealed, "... [A]s we operated the Economic Committee, I got educated and people persuaded me we had to do something about the CPF. It was an overhead; it was cost. Yes, it is wages but it cannot be helped."

Lee's about-turn on the CPF showed his willingness to listen to others and to adopt what was right even if it meant changing what had worked well previously.

On one wall in Lee's Istana office is a dominant calligraphic work which reads: *Ju an si wei, jie she yi jian.* ("Watch for danger in times of peace. Be thrifty in times of plenty.")

It was one of the more than 200 statements that Prime Minister Wei Zheng (580–643) wrote to Emperor Tang Tai Zong (598–649) during the 17 years he served him. The emperor brought about a new era that laid the foundation for prosperity, development and progress for which the Tang dynasty became known. During the 23 years of his reign, known as Zhenguan, the people enjoyed unrivalled peace, stability and prosperity.

Tang Tai Zong was acknowledged as a wise ruler who was receptive to advice from his close courtiers, especially Wei Zheng. On his part, the prime minister had never been afraid to speak up against some of the emperor's ideas or initiatives if he believed they would eventually hurt him and the country. To this day, Wei Zheng is celebrated in China as that rare, righteous government official who dared to speak his mind.

In Lee Hsien Loong's office, the calligraphic work speaks of more than just alertness and thrift. It says too about how he views his responsibility and the kind of leader he wants to be.

31

Youthful and "Not Square" at 50

Young and Old at Anniversary Rally

THE Singapore Indoor Stadium was filled with some 7,000 people and they were making a huge racket.

Young cheerleaders on the stage shouted out the chorus of a British pop group's anthem, "We Will Rock You", and the crowd hollered in response as they kept time with the drum beats with the inflated plastic clappers in their hands. At the end of each round of chorus, they cheered loudly. The cheerleaders added to the din by blowing on their whistles.

This was call-and-response, a common routine in stadium rock concerts except that the event was not a rock concert. It was a PAP mass rally. The crowd was made up of party members, all dressed in white.

Different sections of the stadium held members of the five different districts as well as representatives of the National Trades Union Congress (NTUC) and the Young PAP (formerly known as the Youth Wing). Each section had its own bright colour for the party clappers. There were splashes of blue, pink, red, yellow, dark green, brown and light green, beating in unison against a sea of white.

It was 5 December 2004. The mass rally was the culmination of a series of celebrations to mark the party's 50th anniversary.

The crowd had arrived in chartered buses as early as 1 pm. A percussion group kept them entertained after they had been seated. At 3 pm, the cheerleaders, all members of the Young PAP (YP), went on stage to work them into a carnival mood. The party members had come prepared to have a good time so it was not difficult to get them to participate in the call-and-response routine and to clap along. These were volunteers who took party activities seriously, whether at the branches or during the elections. But this was a day to let their hair down even if they had turned up in their white-on-white uniforms.

When Lee Kuan Yew, Goh Chok Tong and Lee Hsien Loong arrived, after the past and present MPs had streamed in, the crowd broke into a long, sustained round of cheering and clapping that could rival that of an audience at a Rolling Stones concert.

A month earlier, at the 28th ordinary conference of the party, Lee Hsien Loong, freshly made prime minister, had taken over the secretary-general position from Goh Chok Tong. Tony Tan had stepped down as chairman. He was replaced by the labour leader, Lim Boon Heng.

When Lee went up on the stage to speak, it was his first speech as the new leader of the party. Eighty PAP members from all walks of life had taken up their places on raised platforms on the stage behind him and they remained seated throughout his speech. It was a gesture of inclusion which was Lee's key theme as prime minister and the secretary-general of the 50-year-old party.

His speech was rousing, which fitted in with the mood in the stadium. The audience would beat their clappers and cheer each time he made a rallying statement such as: "We may be a small island but we can be a great nation. A nation at peace with our neighbours, prospering with Asia, forming a Singapore community which stretches beyond our shores."

Lee did not mind the least the interruptions to his speech. He was beaming and in good cheer.

In outlining his vision for a better Singapore, he called on the people to seize the opportunities around them, ride on the growth of the region and take the country to a new level of prosperity. "We are at the centre of a region which is undergoing historic transformation," he said. China was changing day by day. Southeast Asia was not doing badly either. "Singapore has to move forward with them because we have the resources, we have the organisation, we have the skills to prosper with our neighbours."

The new secretary-general also spoke about self-renewal, a staple of party conferences. "Our self-renewal continues, and we have to search for new candidates and potential office holders ... I can tell you we've invited a lot of people to tea. We've drunk a lot of tea and we've got some promising names." He called for more, younger Singaporeans to join PAP and help shape the future Singapore. At the same time, he paid tribute to the Old Guard who had kept the party strong and connected to the ground. In particular, he cited a 74-year-old stalwart, Choo Siu Heng, who had served PAP for almost five decades.

Choo joined the party in 1956. In the following year, seen as a pro-communist by the British colonial government, he was thrown into Changi Prison together with some other activists. In 1958, he was among some

100 detainees who were put on a boat to China. He was only 28. He spent four years working on a farm in Guangdong province. It was only after PAP had won the 1959 general election and with the help of Ong Pang Boon, who had secured a seat on the Internal Security Council and could make recommendations on his behalf, that he was able to return to Singapore in 1962.

He did not abandon party work upon his return. Instead, he plunged into it with greater vigour at the Ulu Pandan branch and was still the branch's vice-chairman when Lee cited him in his speech, 41 years later.

In an interview, Choo said he was disenchanted by the widespread hypocrisy he had witnessed in communist China. Senior army officers wore silk under their uniforms and lived well while the foot soldiers went around in rags.

He was grateful he could return to Singapore and was happy to serve PAP as a cadre while he ran his own small business. Like other Singaporeans, he had benefited from the system. He had come from a poor family in Johor. He had met and married his wife when he was exiled to China. Now, they lived in a comfortable, five-room HDB flat in Holland Drive. Their two daughters were teachers and their two sons, businessmen.

⁓⁂⁓

THE indoor stadium rally also featured speeches by new chairman Lim Boon Heng and Halimah Yacob, the NTUC's assistant secretary-general and an MP for Jurong GRC. In between the speeches, there was a three-part video presentation of PAP's 50-year journey.

Lim, who had been the leader of the labour movement for 11 years, said: "Our future lies in continuing to stay close to the ground ... As we bring into our fold the increasing number of professionals and executives, let us not forget the workers and the unions. The unions have been our mass base and today they still are." In the crowd were more than 1,000 unionists and they led in cheering Lim's remarks.

Halimah spoke about the close relationship between PAP and NTUC, and explained why it was important that each new generation understood that this should remain so.

The rally ended with the PAP members taking the party pledge and breaking into thunderous applause.

Penny Low, 37, the youngest of the three single women MPs elected in the 2001 general election, said the event showed how PAP could move with the times, "invigorated by a new vibrancy while keeping its core values".

The "new vibrancy" was not contrived. It reflected the youthfulness of the event's organisers. Instead of having veteran hands organise it, the PAP leadership had entrusted the task to a committee of YP members led by a 29-year-old public relations consultant, Linda Lim.

Lim, whose father was a police coast guard, had suffered from a benign brain tumour when she was doing her final year as an English literature major at the National University of Singapore. After recovering from the illness, she felt she wanted to do something positive in her life besides having a career in an international public relations firm. In late 2000, she and her younger sister volunteered to draft appeal letters at the weekly meet-the-people sessions of Nee Soon East MP, Ho Peng Kee. She got more involved during the 2001 general election when she took no-pay leave to help out in Ho's campaigning.

The branch's YP chairman, Ong Seh Hong, who became an MP in the Aljunied GRC after the election, had noticed her organising potential and people skills and roped her into the YP's Executive Committee, where she became its assistant secretary and public affairs coordinator.

Lim was modest about her abilities. She said she was often noticed by others because "I was always a big kid". In St Nicholas Convent, she had been class monitor, then prefect and finally head prefect. She had also been the leader of the school band and in junior college, had been the band major.

The 50th anniversary rally was the first time she coordinated such a big event. She said she consulted with YP chairman Vivian Balakrishnan and Yaacob Ibrahim who oversaw the event's organisation.

Since she joined the party, Lim said she could see that there was a greater need for the party to be relevant to the young. "Its greatest challenge must be to make sure it doesn't lose the strong bonds which it had built up with the people over the years," she said.

After Ong Seh Hong became an MP, she began to help out at his weekly meet-the-people sessions in Kembangan. If there was one obstacle the party faced among its young volunteers, it was to get them to see the importance of ground-level work, she said. "This is the bread-and-butter work but sometimes, there is hesitation among the younger volunteers to go down to the ground," she pointed out. "But we should all be little engines, operating in every corner of Singapore."

Another challenge was to get people to join the party without expectations of any tangible rewards because there were none.

Young, cosmopolitan Singaporeans tended to view association with PAP as "uncool" and so there were YP members who preferred not to be open about their links with the party. But not Linda Lim who had a little party flag on her desk in the office where she worked. She said: "People don't laugh at the fact that you're a PAP member if you admit to it and talk matter-of-factly about it. If you speak sensibly and conduct yourself properly, you find your opinions are listened to."

The YP held a joint celebration of its 18th birthday and the party's 50th at Singapore's trendiest disco, Zouk, in September. It drew more than 1,500 YP members and their friends. The new YP chairman, Vivian Balakrishnan, dressed in a white linen shirt and a pair of white trousers, got the crowd down to the dance floor to party soon after it began at 7 pm.

Lee Hsien Loong, who arrived at 9 pm and spoke from the disc jockey's console, confessed it was strange to address his comrades in Zouk. But, he said, although PAP was a serious party, "we're not a 'square' party. We have some serious people but we know how to enjoy ourselves too."

He joined the others on the dance floor. Also merrily dancing away were Lim Swee Say, the former YP chairman; Lim Hwee Hua, chairman of the PAP's Women's Wing; and first-term MPs Irene Ng, Indranee Rajah, Penny Low, Chong Weng Chiew and Ong Seh Hong.

⊷⊷⊷

But One Candle Stayed Lit

OTHER events held to commemorate the 50th anniversary of PAP included a gala dinner at Suntec City in October and a ceremony to mark the party's inauguration at the Victoria Concert Hall on November 21.

The dinner was an informal affair which was attended by some 1,500 party cadres and a group of mainly business and civic leaders whom the party leaders addressed as "friends of PAP". They often donated to the party's charity funds or gave of their time. Seated at the two head tables and hosted by Lee Kuan Yew and Goh Chok Tong were Old Guard leaders Toh Chin Chye, Lim Kim San, Ong Pang Boon and Othman Wok.

Goh Chok Tong, then still the secretary-general, addressed the diners. He described PAP as "a quiet national movement of people who believe in Singapore and are willing to contribute to make Singapore succeed. Without PAP, the history of Singapore would be totally different. I do not see another group of men and women who can do a better job of looking after Singapore than PAP."

The old generation systematically identified and prepared the next generation to take over. It stepped aside when the successor generation was ready. "This is the way to defy the march of time, retain the party's youthfulness and continue to appeal to the electorate," he said. "However," he stressed, "while we pass on power as individuals, we must retain it as a political party. PAP is a positive force."

He reminded his audience of the party's low-key profile as represented by its modest headquarters, a three-storey building in the heart of a housing estate in New Upper Changi Road manned by a staff of only nine.

As was related to him by Lim Swee Say, a Chinese Communist Party (CCP) official made an observation after he had visited the headquarters: "The achievement of the party is everywhere but the party itself is nowhere to be seen." Goh said: "And may we stay this way forever ... hardly visible but invincible; no party bureaucracy but lots of dedicated activists and volunteers."

After the speech, members of the party's central executive committee (CEC) went on stage where a cake with five candles on it, all lit up, was wheeled out. Joining Goh to blow out the candles were party chairman Tony Tan, first assistant secretary-general Lee Hsien Loong and second assistant secretary-general Wong Kan Seng.

A huff and a puff, and four candles went out. Lee Kuan Yew, who was standing behind the four men, stepped forward and blew off the remaining lit candle to loud applause and much laughter. Even when it came to blowing off candles, Lee's presence was still required.

A pictorial book which recorded the 50 years of PAP was launched at the event.

Afterwards, the leaders went around to the different tables to greet and shake the hands of past and present party cadres, and the business and civic leaders. Old comrades who had not seen one another for a long time used the occasion to catch up, moving freely among the tables. The atmosphere was akin to an old school mates reunion, with much hand-pumping, back slapping and hearty laughter.

Back at the Vic, 50 Years Later

THE ceremony to mark the party's inauguration at the Victoria Concert Hall on 21 November 2004 was a dignified one, befitting the occasion. It was exactly 50 years ago, on this same date and at this same venue— though it was then called Victoria Memorial Hall—that the People's Action Party was formed.

About 1,500 activists, mainly trade union members and Chinese middle school students, had sat on wooden armchairs as a perspiring Lee Kuan Yew, then only 31 years old, introduced the other 13 convenors on the stage and unfurled the new party's platform. Lee had made an impassioned speech calling for the creation of a democratic state as the crowd shouted *merdeka* ("independence" in Malay). Nine of the convenors were elected into the pro-tem CEC, with Toh Chin Chye as chairman and Lee as secretary. The event had lasted four hours but no one left the hall early.

Toh was present again at the 50th anniversary ceremony as were some Old Guard stalwarts who had been at the original inauguration such as Ong Pang Boon, Joe Conceicao, Chor Yeok Eng and Chan Chee Seng.

The hall packed in a crowd of 1,000 selected cadres and office-holders. Hosted by first-term MP Amy Khor, who had recently been made mayor of the Southwest District, the event began at 5 pm.

Lee, now 81, began his address by saying it was a privilege given to a very few to be present at the founding of a political party and also at its 50th anniversary. "I could not have imagined that 50 years after Sunday, 21 November 1954, I would be in this same hall, on the same date and also a Sunday, to celebrate the tumultuous journey of PAP."

But instead of looking back on past achievements, the elder statesman spoke about self-renewal: "At every general election, we must induct younger men and women of ability, integrity and commitment for PAP to remain vigorous, sensitive to changes and never complacent.

"We have established a unique political culture of clean and honest politics in Singapore. Our institutions are unsullied and uncorrupted, even though we have remained in power for 45 years. This is because we have had men and women of integrity in parliament and in charge of government...

"The key to PAP's longevity is self-renewal continually, inducting younger men and women of ability and integrity, and with high energy levels. It does not matter what their political views and philosophies are, as long as they are pro-Singapore. Arguments on alternative policies and different futures can be intra-party (within the party) rather than inter-party (between parties)."

PAP had begun as an anti-colonial, nationalist, democratic-socialist party. But after finding that socialism did not work and noting how it had failed in Britain, the party became anti-doctrinaire and pursued pragmatic policies, moving towards the free market and free competition. The pragmatic approach had allowed it to keep up with a world that was changing at a faster pace as the forces of technology and globalisation affected every society.

Lee told his audience: "PAP must from time to time re-examine all its assumptions and policies. However successful they may have been in the past, they may not be relevant for the future. They may have to be modified, changed or abandoned."

What must remain constant though, he stressed, was integrity and the party's commitment to a just, fair and caring society. "We have to enable the less successful to have a decent life commensurate with our overall standards, and give a fair and equal chance for their children to compete on par and to excel in their generation ... This task is never done," he said.

After his speech, with the other pioneer party members on the stage, Lee unveiled a commemorative plaque to mark the occasion. The evening ended with three cheers of "Majulah PAP, Majulah Singapore!"

⚜

Refreshing the Party

AT the December 2002 ordinary party conference, Goh Chok Tong noted that there would be a major demographic shift by 2007. Those who were born after 1965 would come to comprise 60 per cent of the population. They had "no direct knowledge of the poverty, pain and struggle of our initial years".

It was imperative, therefore, that PAP re-brand itself to reach out to the post-65ers, even as it retained the support of the older people. There was no need for a complete makeover since the party's fundamentals had remained relevant. But there was a need to "refresh" the party. The task fell to Teo Chee Hean. He would head a committee that would make recommendations to drive the party forward and present its report before the 2003 party convention.

In its study of the party objectives, attributes and style, the committee would have dialogues with party members in the five districts as well as those in the YP and the Women's Wing.

The five districts corresponded to the five Community Development Councils (CDCs), each headed by a mayor, which were formed in the late 1990s as a way for the government to devolve its municipal duties. The CDCs could be seen as district governments, providing social services and administering the districts under their charge.

In an interview in June 2003, before the committee's report was finalised, Teo said he approached his task guided by certain principles. The party stood for certain fundamental values which should not be changed. Its social objective was to do the most good for the most number of people. The objective would remain but the ways to achieve it could be updated. He said: "We have to look at the number of new challenges that are taking place. I think the main ones that the party will look at are its organisation, the ageing population and the new electorate who are younger and better educated, and have higher and different expectations."

At the party convention in November, Teo said his committee recommended that the party's core values and objectives be reaffirmed since members endorsed them strongly. It was the presentation of these values that had to be changed so that they could be easily communicated to the young.

The YP demonstrated how this could be done by encapsulating the party's core values and attributes in a diagram of three concentric circles. Appropriately, the launch pad for this diagram was the computer mouse pad, copies of which were distributed to all the cadres at the convention.

In the centre of the three rings is the PAP logo and the words "Fair and Just Society". The party's core values are captured in the second ring: "Honest, Multiracial, Self-reliant and Meritocratic". On the outer ring are the PAP attributes: "Reliable (Can Trust), Pragmatic (Can Work), United (Can Stick Together), Far-sighted (Can See Ahead), Decisive (Can Do), Compassionate (Can Feel), Resilient (Can Last)".

Teo recommended a more ground-up approach in party activities rather than top-down which was the style of the past. Members would put in more energy and enthusiasm in party activities and programmes if these were driven by their interests and were seen as more relevant to them, he said. The approach would also draw more ideas from existing members and draw in new members too.

The committee proposed several ways to achieve this such as elections to the Headquarters' Executive Committee, a PAP policy forum and new initiatives in the YP and Women's Wing.

The Headquarters' Executive Committee ran the daily operations of the party. Headed by Wong Kan Seng, the first assistant secretary-general, it met bi-monthly with its 12 sub-committees and five district chairmen.

On the YP, the "refreshing PAP" committee recommended that there be more activities organised at the district level. This would provide a critical mass of members to support more diverse activities. The YP district chairman and vice-chairman would no longer be appointees. They had to be elected from among the YP branch chairmen. Once elected, they would automatically become members of the YP executive committee which met once a month.

The first election was held at the party headquarters in March 2004. According to Linda Lim, its assistant-secretary, the committee's calendar in 2004 included the party in Zouk, the 50th anniversary rally and a two-day school camp.

Lim Hwee Hua, chair of the Women's Wing, said it would focus on two key areas: political activities at the branches such as meet-the-people sessions and house visits, and policy dialogues and activities with professional women outside of the party and grassroots organisations.

In a speech she made at the 2002 party convention, she asked for a mindset change among its members. "Many anecdotes have been cited on how women who are able and willing to help out, say at meet-the-people sessions, are prevented from doing so by the current mindsets of male activists," she said.

She clarified that remark in an interview later. The men did not set out to be discriminatory, she said, it was just that they had been helping out at the branches for a much longer time. "But," she said, "they do need to be aware that circumstances have changed and that actually it is the party's loss if they do not open the doors to women because women can serve."

To make sure the women activists could play a bigger role at the branches, Lim organised training sessions for them that covered the range of skills needed in meet-the-people sessions and house visits. The Women's Wing also intensified its efforts to match these activists with the branches where their skills would be properly tapped.

Veronica Tee, the chairman of the Women's Wing in Sembawang branch, helped conduct interviews with the residents who went to the meet-the-people sessions. She pointed out that in some instances, residents felt more comfortable opening up to a woman than to a man. There were, for example, battered wives and some men who had family problems. "We are better listeners; we are good with eye contact and in our body language," said Tee, who was in her mid-50s. She had been a party activist since 1997.

Women professionals were a fast growing constituency but PAP had previously not engaged them. These women usually had no time for grassroots work but Lim Hwee Hua felt it was still useful to tap their views even if they did not become party members. She organised dialogues with members of professional women bodies and collaborated with them on specific projects and workshops which covered such issues as work-life balance, preventive health care and juvenile delinquency.

In another initiative, the Women's Wing and YP came together to form a new arm called Young PAP Women (YPW) which aimed to reach out to women aged between 17 and 40. It was launched in April 2005.

At a press conference a month before the launch, YP chairman Vivian Balakrishnan said: "There currently isn't any political group that taps exclusively on the energy, talents and ideas of young women, speaks directly to them or is their platform to contribute to nation-building. YPW will be this conduit for PAP to reach out to young women and be their voice."

Previously, a woman aged below 40 who joined the party automatically became a member of YP and the Women's Wing. Now, she would also become a member of the YPW. The multiple memberships would offer her an unprecedented range of diverse activities. There would be the inevitable overlap but as Lim Hwee Hua said, "The overlap will not bother us. To us, it's the more the merrier. We want to maximise our outreach."

The idea of the YPW came from feedback from YP women activists. Lim put up a paper on it and after more positive feedback from young women members, cleared it with the party's CEC.

Through YPW, the party hoped to increase young women's participation in the political process. It would also be a platform where promising candidates could be trained to become political leaders. Linda Lim was made its chairman.

A new third pillar in PAP, besides the YP and the Women's Wing, was the policy forum. It was what committee member Raymond Lim called "the party's internal communication vehicle", where rank-and-file members could be involved in its policy-making process. It comprised 188 members, with two representatives from each of the 84 branches and 10 each from the YP and Women's Wing.

Lee Hsien Loong disclosed that the setting up of the policy forum was discussed very carefully in the party's top decision-making body. The CEC considered this: What was it that members wanted when they joined the party? The answer was that they were not seeking tangible compensation or even personal recognition "but the chance to have contact with the MPs, to have access, and therefore, have their views heard and, at the same time, to be able to make a contribution". The policy forum would allow members the access to MPs and ministers. "And that access, I think, is an honourable and good foundation for the people to want to join the party," Lee said.

In an interview in 2005, Ellen Lee Geck Hoon, the first chair of the Policy Forum Council, said it had conducted several dialogues with the party leaders who included Lee Hsien Loong before he became prime minister, Khaw Boon Wan, Ng Eng Hen and Vivian Balakrishnan. These dialogues saw encouraging attendances of more than 200 each time, she said. Even those who were not members of the policy forum were keen to take part in the sessions, and they were invited to them.

Soon after it was set up, the policy forum conducted a survey among party members on the issues that concerned them most. Five representatives from each of the 84 branches were asked to participate in the survey. Ellen Lee, 48, was heartened by the 100 per cent response.

At the PAP conference in November 2004, she presented the findings of the survey. They showed there was clear concern over affordable health care, greater flexibility in education and structural unemployment.

⚜

PAP at 50 was certainly very different from what it was in its early formative years. Its shape and style had changed. With Lee Hsien Loong at the helm and a new generation of Singaporeans, it will but continue to evolve.

The diagram distributed to PAP members that
summarises the party's objectives and attributes.

32

Transforming Singapore,
but First the General Election

Most Contested Election Since 1988

LEE Hsien Loong played a less hasty hand than his predecessor when it came to calling his first general election as prime minister. Goh Chok Tong called his nine months after he became prime minister and two years ahead of schedule. Lee waited 20 months after he had assumed office to have the polls on 6 May, 2006.

The economy was on an upswing. Gross domestic product growth was 8.7 per cent in 2004 and 6.6 per cent in 2005, up from a dismal 2.9 per cent in 2003, and looked set to rise above 7 per cent in 2006. According to Lee in one of his election speeches, the PAP government created 113,000 jobs in 2005, and unemployment was down to 2.6 per cent.

Lee had also rolled out two major policies to help the less well-off Singaporeans. There was the ComCare scheme, which provided funds for projects put up by community and grassroots leaders to reach out to the needy. The $200-million scheme, launched in 2005, would eventually be topped up to $500 million. There was also the Opportunity Fund, which schools could tap to help poor students to participate in extra-curricular activities. Between $50 million and $100 million had been allocated for it.

Two hot political potatoes were also thoroughly tackled in the year preceding the election. First, the PAP government's proposal to build two integrated resorts with casinos in them was extensively debated, with views canvassed from all quarters. That took almost a year before the government decided to go ahead with them.

Then there was the scandal surrounding the high-profile charity outfit, the National Kidney Foundation (NKF). Its CEO, T T Durai, a poster-boy for successful fund-raising, had taken out a defamation suit against *The Straits Times* over an article it had published on him and the NKF, but as it turned out, the court case brought to light his extravagant pay and perks and issues concerning transparency and accountability.

The charity reached out not only to the better off but also across the board to all Singaporeans, through popular programmes such as the specially produced television extravaganzas telecast annually. When Durai's excesses were made public, the people were outraged and they bayed for blood. Many also directed their anger at the government for its oversight of Durai's wrongdoings, even though the NKF was not a government body.

The government acted swiftly. It put in a new board to replace Durai and his directors, and sent in its agencies to conduct a full-scale probe into the charity's practices. After six months of investigation, evidence of wrongdoing was found. In April 2006, just a week before nomination day on April 27, Durai, three of his directors and an employee were charged in court for offences including intention to deceive the NKF and falsifying accounts. The new NKF board also filed a civil suit to recover some $12 million from Durai, three former board members and a business associate. The courts scheduled the civil case and the criminal trial to be heard back-to-back in January 2007.

According to some political pundits, the NKF scandal might have cost the PAP votes if the election had been held a year earlier. But since Durai and his henchmen were going to be dealt with in court after all, it was no longer an issue among the voters in the May 2006 election, as informal polls showed.

The 2006 election turned out to be the most contested one since 1988. For the first time in 18 years, the party was not returned to power on nomination day. The opposition fought in 47 out of the 84 seats, taking on seven group representation constituencies (GRCs) and all nine single-seat wards. One million two hundred thousand Singaporeans got to vote in the election. Forty per cent of them were post-65ers, born after Independence.

PAP fought the election on the theme, Staying Together, Moving Ahead. Lee cited three reasons for calling the polls: to secure a mandate, to decide on a future direction where no one would be left behind and to endorse a team to lead Singapore over the next 15 to 20 years. The party fielded 24 new candidates, including four Malays and two Eurasians. Ten of them contested, while the rest enjoyed walkovers.

Lee clearly wanted PAP to win all seats. He assigned Goh Chok Tong to help the candidates in Potong Pasir and Hougang—Sitoh Yih Pin, 42, and Eric Low, 57—to wrest back the two wards held by Chiam See Tong of the Singapore Democratic Alliance (SDA) and Low Thia Khiang of the Workers' Party (WP). In addition to the weight of former prime minister Goh, the party also dangled two juicy upgrading plans before the voters—to the tune of $80 million in Potong Pasir and $100 million in Hougang.

The two incumbents had seen their winning margins shaved in 2001. Chiam, 71, especially, had seen his share of the votes falling since his peak of 69.6 per cent in 1991. In 2001, his share of the votes was 52.4 per cent; he had beaten Sitoh by a mere 751 votes. He led a team of 20 in his SDA, which was a coalition of four parties. There were eight new faces, among them three graduates and four post-65ers. The team boasted at least six professionals.

Low, 49, had replaced J B Jeyaretnam as secretary-general of the WP in 2001. He led a team of 20 candidates, 15 of them contesting for the first time. Eleven were born after Independence. There were 15 graduates among them and 10 professionals. The team was clean-cut and well scrubbed, and would not be out of place in a PAP line-up.

Both WP and SDA fought in three GRCs and four single-seat wards each. Of the two teams, the WP was the more impressive at the hustings, where it showed itself to be better organised and disciplined. Besides Low, it also had a popular candidate in Sylvia Lim, 40, who had joined the party after the 2001 general election and was elected to the post of party chairman in 2003.

Lim's father was a police inspector who studied to become a lawyer. She took the opposite route; she studied to be a lawyer, obtaining an honours degree from the National University of Singapore and a Master's from the University of London, then joined the police force as an inspector. However, she quit the force after three years because of what she saw as gender bias in promotions. She practised as a lawyer for four years before becoming a law lecturer in Temasek Polytechnic. Lim led what the media billed as WP's A-team in Aljunied GRC, against the PAP team led by foreign minister George Yeo.

The WP also fielded a team comprising some of its youngest candidates—average age 33—in Ang Mo Kio GRC to take on the prime minister. Low said he wanted to give voters, especially those in the former Cheng San GRC, part of which was absorbed into Ang Mo Kio, a chance to vote. The WP had strong support in the Cheng San GRC in the 1997 general election. Also, Low wanted Lee to have a contest. He might or might not have been ironic when he declared: "I'm sure we don't want a "walkover" prime minister. It will be bad for Singapore and internationally. I believe it will even affect the legitimacy of the government." His tactic of course was to tie Lee down in Ang Mo Kio, so that the latter could not range quite so freely over the other constituencies to rally support for his candidates in those constituencies

The contest would be Lee's third. When he first joined politics in 1984, he stood in the single-seat Teck Ghee and trounced the United People's Front (UPF) candidate with an 80.4 per cent win. In 1988, he won 79.1 per cent of the votes against an independent candidate. Since the Ang Mo Kio GRC was formed in 1991, with Teck Ghee as one of its wards, Lee had not faced any challenger.

In its 52-page manifesto, WP stated openly that its long-term goal was to be an alternative government. Among its many proposals were the scrapping of the ethnic quotas in Housing and Development Board (HDB) estates, the GRC, the elected presidency, and grassroots organisations such as the residents committees and the citizens consultative committees.

In contrast to WP and SDA, the Singapore Democratic Party (SDP) looked decidedly like a spent force even before campaigning began. Its leader Chee Soon Juan had been declared a bankrupt earlier in the year when he could not pay the damages that the High Court awarded to Goh Chok Tong and Lee Kuan Yew for defaming them during the 2001 general election. He had accused the two senior leaders of misleading parliament over an alleged $17-billion loan to former Indonesian president Suharto. Besides his bankruptcy, Chee's two prior convictions in 2002 also effectively barred him from standing for the 2006 election. His sister, Chee Siok Chin, led a team in the six-member Sembawang GRC to fight health minister Khaw Boon Wan on the NKF issue, while old warhorse Ling How Doong, 70, contested the single seat in Bukit Panjang.

That SDP was disunited was clear from the start. Before the hustings, Lee Kuan Yew and Lee Hsien Loong had served letters of demand on the party's 12 central executive committee (CEC) members for alleging in articles printed in the party newsletter that both leaders knew about the problems in NKF and deliberately covered them up. The CEC members claimed they had no sight of the articles before they were printed. Three of them broke ranks with Chee and apologised to the Lees before nomination day. In the end, all of the others, including Ling and the four candidates who were standing in Sembawang, decided to apologise and pay damages to the Lees. Only Chee's sister did not do so. The sixth candidate in the Sembawang team was not a CEC member.

Ling disclosed to the media that he had tried to oust Chee in 2003. On another occasion during the hustings, he said: "Chee has been focusing a lot on foreign issues but the voters tend to look at bread-and-butter issues ... Human rights issues are important but we should look at these human rights issues here, not the cases based overseas." At that time, Chee chaired the Alliance for Reform and Democracy in Asia and was a member of the Directors for Democratic Leaders in Asia Pacific. Both were NGOs. Another member of the CEC, Abdul Rasheed Abdul Kuthus, said: "Chee is not concerned about local politics. He's more into the 'big picture' ideal of democracy."

The disarray was embarrassing during the party's press conferences and rallies. Key players either did not show up, or they showed up late and appeared distracted.

⚜

Battle in Aljunied

THE hottest battle was fought in Aljunied GRC, where WP fielded its A-team led by Sylvia Lim. The heat was turned up by the so-called "James Gomez saga". Gomez, 41—a researcher who founded the political discussion group, The Think Tank, in 1999—was a member of the WP team in Aljunied. Besides Lim, the others were Tan Wui-Hua, 39, a financial controller; Mohamad Rahizan Yaacob, 49, a businessman; and Goh Meng Seng, 35, also a businessman.

The PAP team comprised George Yeo, 51; minister of state Zainul Abidin Rasheed, 58; minister of state Lim Hwee Hua, 47; deputy general manager of Fairprice and chairman of the Aljunied Town Council Cynthia Phua, 48; and Consumers' Association of Singapore chairman Yeo Guat Kwang, 45.

Gomez was in the WP team that tried to contest in Aljunied GRC in 2001, but the team was disqualified because the candidates' papers were not in order. This time round, it looked like he might have blundered again when on the eve of nomination day he turned up at the Elections Department (ELD) to collect his minority certificate and was told he had not made any application. A GRC team must have a minority candidate who has to submit a duly filled minority certificate on nomination day.

In Gomez's case, he did not need a minority certificate because Aljunied GRC was designated as one meant for a Malay candidate.

At the ELD, however, Gomez insisted that he had filled in the form and returned it on the spot at the department. That same afternoon, an official telephoned him to say that its security cameras showed that he had indeed filled the form at the counter. However, he did not hand it in, and instead slipped it into an envelope which he then put in his bag and left the office.

Two days later, the ELD made public a video clip of the incident as well as the transcript and audio clip of the telephone call. PAP leaders came out in full force to press WP for the "full story" of what had actually happened and asked Gomez to "come clean". At a rally that night, Gomez admitted to his mistake and read out an apology to the ELD. PAP was "making a mountain out of a molehill", said Low.

But PAP did not let up its pressure on Gomez and WP. Wong Kan Seng who, as deputy prime minister was in charge of the ELD, maintained that Gomez's apology and Low's statement had "carefully avoided dealing with what really happened". The issue was not a simple one of whether Gomez had forgotten if he had handed in his form, he said. What were Gomez's real intentions for going to the ELD in the first place if he did not need a minority certificate?

Voters interviewed by *The Straits Times* said Gomez had made a mistake and as he had apologised, it was time to move on. But PAP was not moving on. Instead, it was turning the episode into a major election issue. Did it have something else on Gomez that it had not yet disclosed? As it turned out, it did.

Four days before polling day, Ang Mo Kio GRC candidate Inderjit Singh disclosed at a press conference that he had met Gomez on nomination day at Pei Chun Public School. In the course of their conversation, he asked Gomez about his supposedly botched minority certificate application. Gomez replied that it was just another *wayang* ("theatre" in Malay) to play along with the media, since they had speculated that he was going to stand in Ang Mo Kio GRC. Singh's testimony was corroborated by a retired civil servant who was one of the assenters for the PAP candidates contesting in Ang Mo Kio GRC.

It was a fairly serious indictment on Gomez. The episode was not an honest mistake after all, even though, if Gomez was to be believed, it was a prank to fool the media. And what kind of politician would disclose something like this to a member of a rival party, not knowing that it could so easily be used against him? Gomez had turned out to be the WP's weak link that the PAP could break and use to cast doubts on the party.

At a rally the same evening, party chairman Sylvia Lim dismissed Inderjit Singh's disclosure as an example of why one just could not talk too much to the PAP.

On the same day after Singh had held his press conference, Wong issued an 11-page statement declaring that Gomez had stage-managed the whole episode—not to play with the media but to set up the ELD. "He was playing an even more elaborate *wayang* to claim that the PAP government and the ELD had no integrity," Wong charged.

What if there had been no security cameras? Wong asserted in the statement: "Mr Gomez would have accused the PAP of depriving him of his right to stand in a constituency of his choice. He would have questioned the integrity of the whole election process in Singapore. Other Workers' Party candidates would have taken up the theme. The government and the ELD would have been brought into disrepute."

In his first rally speech that evening, minister mentor Lee Kuan Yew called Gomez a liar and a liability, and asked Low to drop him as a candidate. "They are left with four candidates, the election goes on, the election is not cancelled," he said.

But WP closed ranks. Lim said the party remained focused on the elections and was proceeding with the campaign with a clear conscience. Gomez refused to comment on his being called a liar by both Lee and Wong.

Public sentiment, or at least that of the educated middle class, appeared to be forgiving of Gomez. So he had been exposed as the weak link in WP but his stunt to fool the media was not a crime. There was no need for PAP to keep on hammering the issue. Some voters saw it as the party playing its signature hardball politics the way it did against Francis Seow in 1988 and Tang Liang Hong in 1997.

The following day, at a lunchtime rally at UOB Plaza in the city's business centre, Lee Hsien Loong said he had received feedback that the party's onslaught against Gomez might backfire against the party. "But," he said, "it was not an honest administrative mistake. Gomez was dishonest. He planned this dastardly trick to discredit the Elections Department and the Government, and that's why we can't just move on."

However, the next day, with just two days to go before polling day, Lee said it was time to refocus the general election on Singaporeans' future. He led his ministers in a coordinated bid to set aside the James Gomez affair. There would be a proper resolution after the election, he said.

In a last-minute effort to win over the Aljunied voters, just a day before the polls, George Yeo and his team sent out a letter to every one of the 43,500 homes in the GRC. Written in English and Chinese, it listed not only what the PAP team had done in the last five years but detailed as well its future plans for the area. The plans—which would benefit the elderly, the young working adults, the unemployed and the housewives—included lifts that stopped on every floor and ramps for the elderly; health clubs, wireless hot spots and hub activities for the young; and a one-stop centre in each of the divisions to help those who had lost their jobs and housewives who were looking for part-time work.

Zainul Abidin Rasheed thought there was a need to reach out to the Malays as well. He got his wife and daughter to help translate the letter and had his supporters distribute the copies in his Eunos ward, where Malays formed about 24 per cent of the voters. "We went out to drop the letters at the flats till the eleventh hour, well, till just before midnight, which was the cut-off time," said Zainul. "That showed what our activists could do, and their commitment. It was, for me, one of the important highlights of the election."

At the 11 Aljunied counting centres on the night of the polls, the way the votes were stacking up in the first hour or so made for a lot of anxiety for PAP MPs, who were allowed to watch the counting process together with their rivals. Cynthia Phua, MP of the Paya Lebar ward in the GRC who covered four centres, recalled some months after the event: "I was really anxious. My heart was beating so fast." She kept in touch on the phone with the other MPs and with George Yeo, who calmed her. She was so overwhelmed by the tension at the counting centres that she burst into tears when she arrived later at Serangoon Stadium, where the result would be announced, and saw her nine-year-old son rushing up to her.

Yeo went to two centres, and as he spoke to the other MPs who were in the other centres, it was clear to him after more than an hour of counting that PAP was ahead, if only just. And when it was finally announced that his team had polled 56.1 per cent of the valid votes, the PAP camp at the stadium heaved a collective sigh of relief and burst into smiles. It was a small margin of victory but not exactly a close shave either. Interviewed in his office the following year, Yeo said the James Gomez issue was a matter of concern that "had to be laid bare for the people to see". He added: "But I think in hindsight it was overplayed and people got fed up."

Wong Kan Seng, when interviewed a year later, said he did not think the PAP's handling of the Gomez issue affected the voting. "The issue was really a question of the integrity of the system and the questioning of that integrity," he said. It was also about the values that WP tried to espouse of its candidates—character, capability and credibility. Gomez had shown himself to lack these values, and in protecting him, WP had done itself no favour.

Over a glass of wine at the Shangri-La Hotel's lobby lounge some six months after the polls, WP's Sylvia Lim said: "Although it's very hard to be sure how the effect went, my own guess is that we lost votes overall because of that incident." The yuppie and educated segment might think differently, but the PAP's drumming of the issue did cast doubt among the heartland voters on Gomez, and by extension, on the WP as well, she believed.

⸎

Lee's Strong Mandate

PAP won the May 2006 general election with 66.6 per cent of the valid votes, up from the 65 per cent in 1997, 61 per cent in 1991 and 63.2 per cent in 1988. Its 75.3 per cent win in 2001 was widely seen as a one-off outcome with the threat of terrorism following 9/11 and the recession. The people had given Lee a strong mandate.

Lee's wish to win all seats was not realised though. Low Thia Khiang and Chiam See Tong not only kept their Hougang and Potong Pasir seats but fared better than previously as well. Low secured his highest margin of victory—62.7 per cent—in his ward since he first contested there in 1991. Chiam, whom Goh Chok Tong had described as lacking in energy and stamina because of his age, scored 55.8 per cent of the votes, more than the 52.4 per cent in 2001 and 55.2 per cent in 1997. Many voters in the two wards had clearly rejected the multi-million-dollar upgrading carrots that the PAP had dangled before them. Goh, popular though he was, just could not sway them.

The biggest loser was the SDP, which was no surprise. Chee Siok Chin's team in Sembawang GRC managed to get only 23.3 per cent of the votes, while Ling How Doong in Bukit Panjang got 22.8 per cent.

In Ang Mo Kio GRC, Lee's team scored 66.1 per cent against the young WP team, which he had dubbed "the suicide squad". As he pointed out in the traditional post-election press conference, many first-time voters in the newer estates like Anchorvale and Fernvale had supported his team. With 40 per cent of the electorate born after Independence, it was obvious that the young, first-time voters had not abandoned PAP, which the party had seen as one of its challenges.

As for the party's loss in Hougang and Potong Pasir, Lee said he respected the choice of the voters. PAP had tried very hard to win the two wards back, but the verdict showed that Low and Chiam were "credible people" with "standing on the ground".

He also pointed out that voters wanted a credible opposition that was of higher quality, which augured well for the future. WP, which averaged 37 per cent of the votes, did best because it had better quality candidates compared to those in the past and to other opposition parties. SDP fared poorly because "voters reject the sort of politics which SDP and Chee Soon Juan represent—more interested in impressing foreign supporters than in serving Singaporean voters".

With the election over, Lee urged all Singaporeans "to come together again as one people". He said: "Whichever party you voted for, let's close ranks." His speech at the post-election conference was healing, after the tumult of the hustings. He was calm, he was inclusive in his words, and he displayed grace, which was not a virtue that the PAP had been known for.

The WP's Aljunied team, having scored highest among the losers, qualified for a non-constituency MP seat. The party nominated Sylvia Lim for it. As for James Gomez, he returned to Stockholm where he worked in a research firm.

Transforming Singapore

WITH the election over, Lee Hsien Loong could concentrate on building on his vision to transform Singapore into a top-league global city. He also needed to address the potential problems that would come out of an ageing population and a widening income gap brought about by globalisation.

To tackle the latter two challenges, he announced a slew of measures to help the elderly needy and the lower-income citizens in his National Day rally address in August 2007. These measures included a higher return on Central Provident Fund (CPF) savings, bigger housing grants, more Workfare bonus to reach out to more people, and a way to unlock the value of a two- or three-room HDB flat so that the elderly could still live in their homes and have money to see them through their retirement years.

Workfare bonus, which was first given out to 330,000 people in May 2006, is essentially an income top-up scheme that rewards those at the bottom who stay employed. It would become a permanent feature that forms the fourth pillar of the social safety net, besides the CPF, the 3Ms of medical care—Medisave, Medishield and Medifund—and public housing.

The transformation of the island would take some time, but work had already begun and signs of changes were already apparent even before the election. After the gloom and doom of the early 2000s, Lee ushered in a period of prosperity and optimism, and he was making best use of the boom and positive mood to achieve his goals.

The boom did not come as a matter of course; it was thanks to the work done from 2001 to 2003 by the Economic Review Committee which Lee chaired when he was deputy prime minister. Under his direction, the economy was diversified so that pharmaceuticals and transport now play a big part in the manufacturing sector when previously there was an over-reliance on electronics. Services and the construction sector have also become key drivers of growth. These and other measures have made Singapore more resilient to external shocks.

PM Lee also had other plans. He wanted the city, previously known for its many prohibitions, to become a city of many possibilities. One obvious sign is alfresco dining, and not just in those areas where upscale restaurants cluster but also in the HDB heartlands. At the neighbourhood coffee shops, tables and chairs spill out onto the pavements and side alleys and are often crowded and lively with the chatter of the people. In the evenings, there is vivid, bustling street life. In the 1950s and 1960s, people went out into the streets to escape from their crammed quarters in the slums and squatter colonies. Now, people are out in the streets because there is a buzz and they want to be a part of it.

Singapore has a large network of 14 reservoirs, 32 rivers and more than 7,000 km of canals and drainage channels. These used to be out of bounds. That will change. Early in 2007, a plan to draw people to the water was unveiled by the Public Utilities Board. Over the next 10 to 15 years, the island's reservoirs, rivers and canals will be transformed into vibrant recreational centres—bare concrete canals will be turned into landscaped channels and some reservoirs will become sports havens. Speaking at the opening of an exhibition of some of the projects in the plan, Lee said Singapore would become "a city of water and gardens". He said: "In the past, we used to protect our water resources by keeping people away from them. Now, we bring people closer to the water so that they will enjoy it and cherish it more."

For a preview of things to come, the 2007 National Day Parade was staged on a floating platform in the calm waters of Marina Bay. It was a bold undertaking, markedly different from previous parades which were held either at the Padang or the National Stadium. It signalled the beginning of a new era.

Marina Bay would be the centrepiece of Singapore's redevelopment. By 9 August 2015, Singapore's 50th birthday, a whole new downtown would have risen in the area, as Lee had first disclosed in his 2005 National Day rally speech. There would be a new business and financial centre where banking houses stood next to residential spaces and hotels, and one of the two planned multi-billion-dollar Integrated Resorts would open its doors there. A barrage would dam up the mouth of the bay and convert it into a fresh water lake. And when the stunning Gardens By The Bay is completed, there would be not one, not two, but three gardens, all linked by walkways, bridges and promenades.

The heartlands, where most Singaporeans live, were not forgotten and would also be made anew. In his National Day rally address in 2007, after he had dealt with the issues of a widening income gap and an ageing population, Lee wowed his audience by unveiling plans to turn the north-eastern suburb of Punggol into the next showcase HDB town. Calling it Punggol 21-plus, it was a bolder and jazzier version of Punggol 21, which had been launched by Goh Chok Tong as a vision for the future back in 1996.

In the blueprint for Punggol 21-plus, the Punggol and Serangoon rivers would be dammed up to create a fresh water lake. A waterway would be cut diagonally through the estate to link the rivers. Blocks of flats would line the waterway, giving residents the kind of view that homebuyers paid a premium for in private developments. The estate would have water sports facilities for kayaking and canoeing, gardens and parks with jogging and cycling tracks, and outdoor dining. Viewed on the high-resolution screen where Lee presented it, the plan looked breathtaking.

Lee also talked about the older estates, which he said would not be overlooked. In those areas where a big piece of land could be cleared up, the whole site could be made over and turned into a new estate. Describing the plan for the old Dawson estate in Queenstown as an example, he said that pockets of empty land in the area would be replaced by new blocks of flats designed by award-winning architects. These blocks would be integrated with a new park, which is to be built on top of the covered Alexandra Canal that snaked through the estate. Old landmarks, such as a wet market and a plaza, would be preserved to give residents a sense of place and belonging.

In time to come, all older estates would be made over, with residents having a say in the renewal plans of their neighbourhoods. Lee said: "No other city in the world can do this. Public housing that's attractive, that's affordable, that's appealing, that gives a quality home for every citizen and gives you an asset which will appreciate in value and also help to provide for your old age ... We will remake the whole city. It will take us 20, 30 years but eventually, the whole country will be transformed. And this is what Singaporeans call home."

More than 50 years since it was formed and now under its third generation leadership, the PAP has more than fulfilled its 1954 objectives of "establishing an economic order which will give to all citizens the right to work and the full economic returns for their labour and work; and to ensure a decent living and social security to those who through sickness, infirmity or old age can no longer work".

PART THREE

BY

Sonny Yap, Richard Lim and Leong Weng Kam

33

From White Men to Men in White

THE Kingdom and the Beauty, the Chinese classic film about the ill-fated love between a Ming Dynasty emperor and a country maiden, was entering its 31st record-breaking day. A live broadcast of the lying-in-state of Sultan Ibrahim in Johor Bahru was keeping listeners tuned to Radio Singapore. Three men robbed a Kallang Road tailor of six rolls of cloth worth $300.

On the sporting front, the big debate raged on: Should Choo Seng Quee continue to be the national coach for the Malayan team? Or should he make way for Frank Soo, the former Stoke City player and the first Chinese to don England colours? The ebullient Choo had angered the football authorities once again with his trenchant comments in the press.

The market place was shaken by jitters and rumours. Companies planned to move from Singapore to Kuala Lumpur. Property prices slumped. *The Straits Times* on 6 June 1959 reported that "first grade" rubber fell below the dollar level on a "watchful" market while the index for industrials remained at 89.10, little changed from 88.99 on the previous day. As the correspondent summed up, the market was at a "standstill" as it awaited the formation of the new government.

If the whole of Singapore was holding its collective breath, it was because of a momentous event which had unfolded in City Hall the day before. Businessmen, civil servants and the English-educated were apprehensive, fearing that the communists might have slipped into power. But the Chinese-speaking and illiterate masses were jubilant. Neglected by the British colonialists, discriminated in education and employment, victimised by corrupt officials and incensed by the privileges showered on the elite, they saw in the new socialist government hope for a better life.

5 June 1959 was the day that changed the course of the island forever. At 4 pm, a 36-year-old Cambridge-educated lawyer was sworn in as the prime minister of a new government which pledged to strive for a more just and equal society. Just six days earlier, his five-year-old People's

Action Party (PAP) had polled 54 per cent of the votes cast and won 43 out of 51 seats to end 140 years of colonial rule.

The 40-minute ceremony was devoid of pomp and protocol. Lee Kuan Yew and his eight ministers were all garbed in white open-neck shirts and trousers. Queen Elizabeth II's portrait was removed. Sir William Goode, the former governor who became Yang Di Pertuan Negara (Head of State) to preside over the event, had to shed his ceremonial plumage for a lounge suit. He had to make his way to City Hall as the new government refused to hold the swearing-in at the then-Government House, now known as Istana, where he resided.

The message was unmistakable: the governor's "summoning" days were over. Power had shifted to the duly elected representatives of the people for the first time in Singapore's history. Power had shifted from the white men to the men in white.

Former journalist, politician and diplomat Lee Khoon Choy was a parliamentary secretary in the 1959 government. He recalled that many PAP members, including himself, were unable to enter the chamber. "Only the ministers who were to be sworn in together with the PM could go in. It was a very low-key affair. We even forgot to take pictures."

Not a single photograph of the historic event existed as it was closed to the press and public. There was no TV then. When Singapore artist Lai Kui Fang was commissioned to re-enact the swearing-in 31 years later, he had to spend six months interviewing people who attended the ceremony and poring over photographs of the pioneering politicians in newspaper archives.

His wall-sized oil painting measuring 2.1 m by 3 m shows Lee Kuan Yew being flanked by Sir William Goode, aide-de-camp Captain J L Carruthers and assistant cabinet secretary Wong Chooi Sen. The ministers portrayed were Ong Pang Boon (home affairs), K M Byrne (labour and law), Ahmad Ibrahim (health), Toh Chin Chye (deputy prime minister), Ong Eng Guan (national development), Goh Keng Swee (finance), S Rajaratnam (culture) and Yong Nyuk Lin (education).

Imagine the mood of the people on that hot, humid day. While the English-educated were gripped by fear of the unknown, the masses were brimming with optimism. Then, as now, the euphoria of the common folks was reflected in a punting frenzy. When Lee was spotted driving his Mercedes Benz SS 6566, people betted so heavily on the number that bookmakers were forced to ban it.

Tang Chong Kuan was a 17-year-old student of Chung Cheng High School when he read about the swearing-in in the Chinese daily, *Min Pao*. The founding chairman of an event management and design company remembered how elated the Chinese school students were then. "Lee was like a god to us. He had helped us as our legal adviser and identified with us even though he was not Chinese-educated."

He described the change from colonial rule to PAP government as "*fan tian fu di*" or "heaven and earth turned upside down". Under the British, he said, the Chinese-educated were suppressed as they could not find jobs in the government. But after the PAP took over and created the People's Association and the Works Brigade, the public sector was thrown open to them.

Foong Choon Hon was the Mandarin broadcaster who covered the PAP victory rally for Radio Singapore two days earlier. Recollecting the 50,000-strong crowd at the Padang, he said: "The atmosphere was electrifying. People were overjoyed that some good men and women were finally going to govern the country. I remember Rajaratnam telling me what Lee said: 'Look at the crowd. If we do well, everybody will be happy. If not, we will be in trouble.' "

The reaction of the press and readers ranged from cautious welcome to nervous trepidation. In its editorial on 5 June 1959, *Sin Chew Jit Poh* called on the new government to strike a balance between minority and majority interests in policy-making. The Chinese daily was concerned that with PAP dominance in the chamber, the government might disregard alternative views and turn authoritarian.

Nanyang Siang Pau's June 6 editorial acknowledged the calibre of the PAP leadership and predicted that the new government would perform well. But the Chinese newspaper noted that it would have to work with many constraints as self-governing Singapore had yet to gain full sovereignty. As it stood, foreign affairs and defence were to remain in British hands.

The same issue carried a profile of Lee as a leader with "a heart for workers". Journalist Mok Lee Kwang related how Lee once confided in him about a dilemma he faced as a lawyer: An injured construction worker sought compensation from his employer who hired Lee as his lawyer. But "Lee couldn't bear to see the poor worker uncompensated for his injuries. So he suggested that the matter be settled out of court, resulting in the contractor having to pay a sum of money to the worker."

As for *The Straits Times* report on the same day, it chose to weigh in on the cabinet line-up, commenting on the way the ministerial functions were being consolidated and the emphasis placed on the creation of the powerful ministry of national development. Noting the PAP's position that teamwork mattered more than personalities, it concluded that "success will obviously call for much more than the collective endeavour and abilities of the leadership. Much will depend on the performance of the civil service, and on the response of the people as a whole."

Earlier, on June 3, the British-run daily had published a profile headlined "Lee Kuan Yew: He's the most puzzling politician I've met." Pondering why a Cambridge-educated politician was taking such a virulently anti-British stand, Vernon Bartlett asked: "Is he basically anti-European or merely anti-colonial?" Describing Lee's thinking as quite similar to his, the British columnist said that he found it "difficult to believe that, with the great responsibility that now is his, he will do things which will irretrievably damage Singapore in Western eyes".

Lee's response came in an interview with British Independent TV News. Watched by 25 million people in Britain, and as reported in *The Straits Times* on June 6, he made it very clear that he was anti-colonial but not anti-white, that the PAP government would not permit foreign capital to intervene in domestic affairs, and that he was a firm believer in the freedom of the press.

The letters in the same issue reflected the widely divergent views of *Straits Times* (ST) readers who often wrote under pseudonyms in those days. M H B wanted Goh Keng Swee to clarify his statement that the English-educated were about to lose their privileges. Pointing out that English was the language of international trade, he contended that "the law of supply and demand, and not Dr Goh, will dictate the value of the English-educated". M G G Pillai believed that if the anti-PAP parties had put up a united front, they could have reduced the PAP's majority of 35 in the new chamber to about seven.

D C sought to give a positive spin to the PAP victory, noting that Lee "was essentially an individualist" and a "fervent believer in the British way of life, excelling in tennis and golf". He wrote: "I cannot for a moment believe that Mr Lee will be prepared to sacrifice all these in favour of the communist subversion of the state." Merdeka felt that people voted PAP into power because they wanted to see an end to corruption, hawker persecution and privileges for the few.

To the foreign press, the PAP government was viewed alarmingly as a pro-communist takeover. The *Times of Indonesia* warned that the left-wing government would owe its loyalty to China. Britain's *Sunday Times* said that PAP "is known to be dangerously infiltrated with disguised communists". Labelling Lee "an angry young man", the *New York Herald Tribune* editorialised that "anti-communist countries like Malaya and SEATO will need all their vigilance to contain the threat within the island that Raffles built".

⊶⊱⋇⊰⊷

TRY visualising what Singapore was like in 1959. Tap the memory bank of ageing baby-boomers and the elderly, and you will be fed with heart-wrenching and gut-churning stories of abject poverty, urban squalor, spiralling unemployment, social unrest, industrial strife and rising crime and corruption.

It was a Singapore where cows grazed along the roadside depositing dung at regular intervals, where goat-herders delivered recycled bottles of unpasteurised milk at doorsteps, where pig-swill collectors presented a squawking chicken to every household as a gesture of appreciation during Chinese New Year.

It was a Singapore where *attap* ("palm leaf") and scrap material were used to construct squatter huts, where wood was cut from trees to make fire, kerosene pumped into lamps to shed flickering light and rainwater collected in oil drums. Former PAP legislative assemblyman Ong Chang Sam remembered how his constituents in Chua Chu Kang used to draw and carry well water daily, and how he had to lobby very hard to obtain a standpipe for 20 families.

It was a Singapore where most people lived on very little. To 17-year-old Tang Chong Kuan, a typical meal consisted of plain white broken rice seasoned with dark soya sauce or lard and salted vegetables. Clothes usually meant just a pair of shorts with no shirt. Home was a Chinatown cubicle with no electricity. "We used an oil lamp at night but I usually studied under a street lamp as it was brighter," he recalled.

The spectre of joblessness haunted the PAP government from day one. With a soaring rate of 10 per cent, how was it going to create enough jobs for a population of 1.58 million and one which was growing by 4 per cent or 63,000 a year? Teenagers who failed to attend or dropped out of school were swelling the ranks of the jobless by 32,000 to 34,000 a year. Able-bodied men gratefully thanked the deities when they found jobs as labourers, fitters, welders, lathe operators, boiler-makers, carpenters, bricklayers and electricians. Some 50,000 people were reported to be plying the roads as hawkers, trishaw riders and taxi drivers. In those days, securing a job as a teacher or a clerk epitomised career success.

When the PAP government set up the People's Association in 1960, Tang was one of 6,000 people who applied to be organising secretaries. To this day, he still remembered how his mother rushed to his workplace with the PA letter of appointment. "She shouted: 'Son, you got a civil servant job!' I never saw my mother so happy. That was the first time she took a taxi in her life."

Tang spoke sadly of how his mother toiled as a rubber cutter in a factory for $3 a day. Ong Chang Sam, who laboured as a quarryman and a shop assistant before he joined politics, said that people were happy if they could find a job which paid $50 to $60 a month. A government survey in 1959 found that about 58 per cent of workers earned between $36 and $45 per week while about 34 per cent earned less than $35 per week.

The Singapore that Lee and company inherited also had the dubious distinction of harbouring the most overcrowded slums in the world. When Lim Kim San visited a ghetto on Upper Nankin Street, he was stunned to meet residents who shared their trousers and took turns to sleep on wooden planks. The sorry spectacle strengthened the resolve of the then-Housing and Development Board chairman to expedite the public housing programme.

Visiting Queenstown as a Progressive Party's candidate in the 1955 elections, war heroine Elizabeth Choy was shocked by the sight of "so many people living in such horrible conditions". Describing the slums as "some of the worst in the world", she said that those who "lived in luxury and plenty should go and see how the poor lived". She admitted that she was rejected by the constituents because they saw her as a representative of a rich men's party.

In 1959, it was estimated that a quarter of a million people were living in slums with another third of a million in squatter areas. A typical Chinatown structure would have a frontage serving as a shop and a back portion as workers' quarters. Often built up to four storeys, it would be sub-divided into small cubicles. Tang's family of six occupied a second-level cubicle in a shophouse on Upper Hokkien Street; they shared a common kitchen and bathroom with seven other families on the same floor.

This proliferation of ramshackle dwellings was prone to fire as they were made of flimsy and flammable material. Between 1955 and 1959, at least one major fire broke out each year in either the squatter settlements or the congested slums. Floods caused by poor drainage following a torrential downpour led to more anguish and misery.

Not surprisingly, the first welfare activity of the budding PAP was to help victims in such disasters. Party founding member Samad Ismail remembered Lee wading into a Bedok flood and meeting Lim Chin Siong for the first time. Recalled Choy: "It was during one of those devastating floods when the water was above one's waist and washing away the squatters' huts that I first met Lee. He was there with some friends who were ready to help the flood victims. I could already see his determination written all over his young face."

Of course, Singapore in 1959 was not an unmitigated portrait of Dickensian poverty. There was a British upper crust of colonial officials supported by a small English-educated middle class of civil servants, professionals and businessmen who were mainly Eurasians, Straits-born Chinese and Indians.

For glimpses into their lives and lifestyles, just scan *The Straits Times* the day after the historic swearing-in. As conjured up by the advertisements, their notion of a good life was to live in a landed property in Katong, Thomson and Holland Road, and drive an Austin Healy, Ford Prefect or Morris Minor. They would like to listen to the news on a National radio, savour Nescafe coffee with Huntley and Palmers biscuits, and peel Sunkist California oranges. The health-conscious could ingest Ridto syrup to "get rid of worms" and Waterbury's compound to "stop tired blood and build zip". The fashion-conscious could aspire to wear Carl Zeiss sunglasses, put on Yardley lipstick, and shop for sapphire and silver blue mink from Ali Joo furriers.

Pleasure-seekers unperturbed by the advent of the new socialist government could go dancing at the Great World Air-Conditioned Cabaret on Kim Seng Road, or wine and dine at the air-conditioned Singapore Hotel on Geylang Road to the music of Lionel Ventura and his Modernaires and the songs of Miss Margi Poon. For a puff or two, their choice could be du Maurier, Rothmans or Player's.

There was no Singapore Girl then. For the well-heeled, one great way to fly would be to travel by Malayan Airways to Bangkok every Saturday.

Single: $201; return: $362. The plane would leave at 7.45 am, stopping over in Kuala Lumpur and Penang before arriving in Bangkok at 2.30 in the afternoon!

These two faces of Singapore present a society sharply divided between the well-off who lived in bungalows, terrace houses and apartments, and the rest huddled in squatter colonies, Chinatown cubicles and rural farms; between the upper and middle classes who spoke mainly English, and the toiling masses who bantered in a babel of Chinese dialects, Malay and Tamil.

The ever-widening income gap generated social discontent which provided fertile ground for communist exploitation. Official statistics for 1959 cited 40 strikes and lockouts resulting in the loss of 26,587 man-days. Altogether there were 504 industrial disputes involving the port, bus companies, sawmills, canning plants and factories. Former journalist Foong Choon Hon remarked that the industrial climate was so bad that even cake shops went on strike!

As if all these problems were not enough on their plate, Lee and his young, inexperienced ministers had to grapple with a crime rate and vice trade which placed Singapore in the top ranks of Asia's sin cities. To the Western mind, Singapore became synonymous with seediness and sleaze. Many parts of the island were virtually controlled by triad societies which ran extortion rackets, gambling dens and prostitution rings with impunity.

To top it all, the new leaders were saddled with an administration whose standards were sliding fast. Older Singaporeans would remember the 1950s as a time when bribes and kickbacks were part of the way of life. People had to grease palms to obtain licences, permits, immigration papers, public housing and coveted places in schools. Retired architect Lee Kip Lin had no qualms about describing the Lim Yew Hock administration as "being corrupt from head to toe".

Indeed it was the failures in governance that compelled PAP to go all out for victory in the 1959 general election. Mrs Lee Kuan Yew recalled her husband's gnawing concern that if Lim Yew Hock were to continue for another term, the standards of administration would fall so rapidly that by the next elections, "the damage would have been beyond repair".

You name it, Singapore had it then—riots, strikes, pickets, protests, demonstrations, squalor, poverty, joblessness, corruption, vice, crime, fires, floods, diseases. "It was a journalist's paradise," reminisced former

ST news editor Felix Abisheganaden who reported on many of the social and political dramas of the day. "It was a Marxist recipe for revolution," reflected former finance minister Goh Keng Swee many years later.

When Lee raised his right hand before Sir William to promise to "serve the state faithfully", he had no illusion about the monumental tasks ahead. He and his British-trained associates had joined forces with the Chinese-educated communists to win mass support and capture power. After witnessing what had happened to the David Marshall and Lim Yew Hock governments, he knew that his troubles with the communists were just beginning.

As he recollected in an oral history interview: "Having watched what happened to them and how their ground support turned sour on them, how people were manipulated and turned against them, how they were made to appear as destroyers of Chinese culture and civilisation and stooges of the imperialists and representatives or the protectors of the bourgeoisie and the capitalists, I knew I was in for a rough ride. And it'll need all my skills, all knowledge of their tactics and really a cool head to handle them."

For new finance minister Goh, the greater preoccupation was with the ever-swelling legions of the jobless. He often spoke about how he met jobless people who turned up in his Kreta Ayer ward to seek help. When he failed to see them again, he presumed that they had died of starvation. His personal encounters and social research convinced him that "the more important and lasting problem is how to provide a livelihood for our rapidly growing population. There is a limit to the extent to which we can live by taking in each other's washing."

⚬◦✳◦⚬

WHEN Lee moved to his spartan City Hall office overlooking the Padang and ploughed through *The Straits Times* on his full first day as PM on 6 June 1959, he would have discerned the dark clouds on the horizon. Amid the coverage on the installation of the new government were gloomy news reports which painted a regional backdrop of political instability and uncertainty.

Malaya's ambassador to the United States, Nik Kamil, told a New York audience that communist subversion was still the greatest menace facing the federation. Calling the communists terrorists, he warned that their objective was to establish a communist state in Malaya. Another news report noted that seven British demolition experts were making their rounds in the peninsula to destroy explosive dumps belonging to the terrorists.

In Indonesia under President Sukarno, rumours of an army coup surfaced once again. Army chief Nasution dismissed Suharto as commander of the Diponegoro division after he was found to be using his military office to demand money from Central Java businesses. No reader would have guessed that the Javanese officer would seize power from Sukarno eight years later.

Fearing that Indo-China would go red and have a domino effect on Southeast Asia, the Americans began stepping up their involvement in Vietnam. This was to lead to the 15-year Vietnam War which ended in American defeat in 1975 and the loss of an estimated 5 million lives.

In China, Mao Zedong resigned as head of state in favour of Liu Shao-chi but remained as chairman of the Chinese Communist Party. An uprising against Chinese rule in Tibet was crushed and the Dalai Lama fled to India. Communist leader Fidel Castro came to power in Cuba after overthrowing dictator Fulgencio Batista. Charles de Gaulle was proclaimed first President of the new Fifth Republic in France.

The year 1959 also saw the continuing polarisation of the world stemming from the Cold War, the term used to describe the titanic ideological struggle between the United States and its allies and the Soviet Union and its satellites. Tension rose as each superpower sought to gain influence over emerging nations in Asia, Africa, the Middle East and Latin America.

On a lighter note, 1959 witnessed the debut of the Barbie doll. "Breaking Up is Hard to Do" was the smash hit from Neil Sedaka and Howard Greenfield. *The Sound of Music*, based on the story of the Von Trapp family, premiered on stage in Broadway. The 3½-hour epic *Ben Hur* made Charlton Heston a household name. Readers lapped up Philip Roth's *Goodbye, Columbus* and Alan Sillitoe's *The Loneliness of the Long Distance Runner*. Singapore philanthropist Tan Kah Kee established the Overseas Chinese Museum in Xiamen. The Russians launched a rocket with two monkeys into space.

By the way, the year that saw the advent of a government that would pilot Singapore from Third World backwardness to First World ranking was also the year that unveiled a device that would change the world beyond recognition. American electrical engineer Jack Kilby invented a network of interconnected transistors and tiny electronic components fabricated on a thin piece of semiconductor material—the integrated circuit or the microchip.

⁂

MOVIE-GOERS were flocking to see *The Village* in cineplexes all over the island, making it the No 1 box office hit. The supernatural thriller, directed by M Night Shyamalan and starring Joaquin Phoenix, Sigourney Weaver and Adrien Brody, tells the spine-tingling tale of a community confronted by unknown creatures lurking in the surrounding woods.

Crime took on a high-tech edge with news of criminals stealing CashCards from cars and syndicate members using fake credit cards. Making the headlines on the same day were reports on fires causing more deaths in the year and the inquiry into the cave-in at Nicoll Highway that killed four workers at the Circle Line MRT station worksite.

It was also the day before the opening of the Olympic Games in Athens and naturally the big buzz revolved around the medal prospects of the 16 Singapore athletes. Once again, thoughts turned to Singapore's sole Olympic medallist Tan Howe Liang. A writer to *The Straits Times* forum page pleaded for a gymnasium to be named in honour of the ageing former weightlifter who won the silver in the Rome Olympics in 1960.

Such was the expectant mood in the country that even a slip by the ST index was given a positive twist. As reported in *The Straits Times*, the ST index slipped "a prosperous 8.01 pts" to 1888.18 points, which was interpreted to spell good fortune for the Chinese. In Cantonese, the number "8" sounded like the character for "prosperity".

This was a snapshot of Singapore captured by the English daily on the day that 52-year-old Lee Hsien Loong was sworn in as prime minister. The contrast between the two historic ceremonies could not have been more striking: On 5 June 1959, the elder Lee in cotton white was sworn in, in City Hall on a sultry afternoon at 4 pm. On 12 August 2004, the younger Lee, in suit and tie, recited his oath at the Istana lawn on a balmy evening at 8 pm.

While his father's swearing-in was attended by a small select audience and barred to the press, PM Lee's was witnessed by 1,400 guests from all walks of life and televised live. The telecast was watched by 1.3 million viewers in Singapore, and seen and heard on the Internet via webcasts, podcasts and vodcasts around the world. Not a single photograph was snapped of the first swearing-in. PM Lee's moment in history was preserved for posterity in a mind-boggling array of TV footage, audio clips, photographs and digital images.

When entrepreneur Tang Chong Kuan watched the August 12 ceremony on TV, his mind flashed back to the first swearing-in that he had read about as a Chinese school student in 1959. Then the PAP was rather tentative as it took steps in forming a government, he recalled. "But in 2004, after 45 years in running the country, the PAP had become so much more confident. It had grown from strength to strength."

The local press expressed full support for the new PM but struck a cautionary note. Outlining the challenges of a rapidly ageing society, *Lianhe Zaobao*, the Chinese morning daily which was formed in 1983 from the merger of *Sin Chew Jit Poh* and *Nanyang Siang Pau*, said that the top priority for the younger Lee "would be to win over the younger generation and at the same time retain the support of the old".

Coincidentally, three letters in the ST forum page dwelled on the issue of a greying population. Two readers supported the call for a state pension to be paid to those aged 80 and above, while the third urged people to start saving early for old age.

The ST editorial, however, took a different tack commenting on Lee's vision of making Singapore an inclusive society and his call to young people to come forward and serve without waiting to be invited to tea. It surmised that this could be problematic as "it simply is alien to Singaporeans' nature to advertise themselves as keepers of the national trust".

Lee Hsien Loong's premiership was welcomed by the regional media. *The Jakarta Post* noted that the PM had displayed "an adroitness in discussing bilateral and regional issues within the context of Asean" and that "he is a man that Indonesia should be able to get along with". Malaysia's *New Straits Times* said the change was an opportunity "to throw away the deadweight of historical baggage which has plagued bilateral relations".

⁂

"LET us shape our future together: PM Lee" This was the page one headline of *The Straits Times* of 13 August 2004. If a time-traveller from the Singapore of 1959 were to land on the island on that day and pick up the papers, he would be bewildered by the cornucopia of goodies and goods advertised by NTUC Fairprice, Cold Storage and Giant supermarkets and OG, Takashimaya and Isetan department stores.

The transistor radio, the gramophone record, the Rediffusion box, the black rotary dial telephone and typewriter with its smudgy carbon had given way to a bedazzling range of high-tech devices—plasma TV, high definition TV, DVD player, home theatre system, laptop, notebook, mobile phone, bluetooth, MP3 player, digital camera, personal digital assistant and blackberry.

He would surely be confounded by the enticing offers inviting him to recline on an Osim massage chair costing up to $7800, join The Pines Town Club, snap up a property in Port Dickson, Auckland or Shanghai, or sign up for a stock market and futures trading seminar.

Should he wander around Bukit Timah and Bukit Panjang, he would be puzzled over the disappearance of the animal and vegetable farms. Dairy Farm had become the name of a condominium estate. He would be astounded to learn that children visit the bird park and the zoo to see chickens, ducks, geese and pigs, or stay in farms in Australia to find out how eggs were hatched and cows milked.

Whatever happened to the squatter colonies, kampungs and zinc-roofed houses in the vicinity, he might wonder? Everywhere he turned, he would catch glimpses of towering public housing estates, shining condominiums and clusters of semi-detached houses and bungalows.

The malnourished, lice-infested, half-naked children who ran barefooted had been replaced by strapping, well-fed kids in stylish T-shirts and jeans listening to their iPod, hurriedly composing a text message on their mobile phone, logging on to Facebook, playing cyber-games or downloading e-mail in a wi-fi hotspot.

Gone were the buses which belched surrealistic black smoke and the *pa ong chia* ("pirate taxis" in Hokkien) which ferried passengers in hair-raising rides. In their place were Mass Rapid Transit trains and public buses which provided air-conditioned travel for commuters at the swipe of an EZ-link card. Mud tracks and lateritic lanes had turned into roads and expressways where the most expensive cars in the world whizzed under gantries which deducted tolls electronically.

No longer would he see the sweatshops and factories that churned out garments, soap, mosquito coils, cooking oil, biscuits, soft drinks and batteries, or the plants which canned pineapples and processed coconut and palm oil. Instead he would come across industries unimaginable in 1959—wafer fabrication, semi-conductor chips, disk drives, petrochemicals, pharmaceuticals, biotechnology, precision engineering, infocommunications and aerospace.

Incredible as it might seem to him, he would not find a trace of the industrial strife endemic in the 1950s. There was not a single strike in 2004. The frightening Hokkien cry "*ba gang*" had disappeared. The word on every unionist's lips was training and retraining. Union leaders were more likely to be seen teeing off at Orchid Country Club than manning a picket line.

As the time-traveller strolled along the banks of the Singapore River, he would be amazed to discover that the flowing sewer with its bobbing bumboats and coolies on the gangplanks had been transformed into a picturesque waterway. There was enough sparkle in the waters to tempt the inebriated to take an occasional dip.

The storytellers on the bridges by the river, who regaled labourers huddled around a burning incense stick with tales from ancient Chinese folklore, had vanished. Entertainment along the banks now came from feet-stomping discotheques and swanky bars converted from rundown warehouses.

One "time-traveller" who visited Singapore in 2004 was Chin Peng, the former secretary-general of the Malayan Communist Party. During his three-day trip, the man who waged a 12-year insurgency to set up a communist republic was quoted as saying that "the advocacy of violence no longer has any place in Singapore and Malaysia because people's living conditions have improved so much that it would no longer be possible to ask people to put their lives on the line". He acknowledged that "Lee had made great contributions to Singapore although he had also made mistakes".

Unlike the elder Lee who inherited an impoverished and strife-torn island in 1959, the younger Lee took over a prosperous and peaceful Singapore in 2004. It was a Singapore which embodied the 14-year achievements of his predecessor Goh Chok Tong, who took over from Lee in 1990 and built on his 32-year stewardship of Singapore.

The best testimonies came not from scholars, think tanks or foreigners but from ordinary Singaporeans who lived through the span of PAP rule. Singapore's Third-to-First World trajectory is mirrored in the rags-to-riches life stories of a generation of Singaporeans such as Tang Chong Kuan.

In 45 years, Tang had gone from being an $80-a-month clerk in a spare parts shop to become the owner of a design company with a staff strength of 70 and an annual turnover of about $7 million. From a Chinatown cubicle, he moved in to a 7,000-sq ft bungalow in tree-lined Siglap, and from taking bus rides, he now reclined in the comfort of a Mercedes S280.

His family circumstances were typical of many in 1959. The Tangs were so poor that he and his elder brother had to take turns to attend classes at Yeung Ching School as they could not afford to pay the monthly fees for both. It was only after his brother dropped out of school to be an apprentice in a machinery shop that he was able to continue with his primary school education. If not for the financial aid of his art teacher in Chung Cheng High, Yeo Hwee Bin, he would not have managed to complete his secondary school education. In a dramatic reversal of fortune, thanks to his thriving business in a prospering Singapore, he could afford to send his two sons to the United States for higher studies.

Drawing an analogy, Tang said that Singapore's progress could be tracked through the quality of the rice that was consumed. In the 1950s, most people ate broken rice grains from Pakistan. In the 1960s, they had rice from China. In the 1970s and 1980s, they enjoyed Thai rice and by the 1990s, it was royal Thai fragrant rice.

But if you need more than anecdotal proof of Singapore's success, let the statistics do the talking. When Lee and company took over the languid colonial outpost in 1959, its per capita GDP was $1,306. Loosely speaking, per capita GDP is the output per person, and GDP or Gross Domestic Product, the total output of all residents in the country. By the time Goh Chok Tong took over in 1990, per capita GDP had soared to $21,915 or up by about 16 times. It doubled to $44,282 by 2004 when Goh passed the premiership to Lee Hsien Loong. In 2007, it stood at $52,994.

The GDP for 1959 is not available. The record shows that the GDP measured at current market prices leapt from $2,149.6 million in 1960 to $66,778.1 million in 1990. By 2004, it had hit $184,508 million. In 2007, the figure was $243,168.8 million.

When finance minister Goh Keng Swee inspected the coffers in 1959, he discovered that the previous government had dipped into the reserves and spent $200 million. He duly reported that a deficit of $14 million would be incurred for the year. According to the Singapore annual report, the reserves had fallen from $322 million in 1953 to $87 million in 1958.

The scrimping and saving by a government reputed for its legendary thriftiness and frugality began to pay off. When Singapore's official foreign reserves were first published for the year 1963, the figure was $1,151.4 million. By 1990, the reserves had shot up to $48,478.7 million. By 2004, it had rocketed to $183,464.0 million, and by 2007 the amount was $234,545.6 million.

The Republic's reserves are now managed by the Government of Singapore Investment Corporation, which operates as a global fund manager. It made the headlines in January 2008 amid the credit crisis shaking the global financial system when it invested 11 billion Swiss francs (S$14.3 billion) in Swiss bank UBS and US$6.88 billion (S$9.82 billion) in American banking giant Citigroup.

In 1959, the government faced a 10 per cent unemployment rate. By 1990, it reported a record low of 1.7 per cent. But in 2004, the jobless rate went up to 3.4 per cent amid an economic downturn. In September 2007, Singapore was back to 1.7 per cent—and full employment.

Nowhere were the Republic's achievements more visible than in public housing. In 1959, only 9 per cent of the population lived in public housing. In 1990, 80 per cent owned their HDB flats. In 2004, the figure went up to 82 per cent. By 2007, the number of residential units built since 1960 was nearing a million.

In 1996, Singapore was accorded the status of an "advanced developing country" by the Organisation for Economic Co-operation and Development, the "rich man's club" based in Paris. In 1997, it was classified as an "advanced economy" by the International Monetary Fund.

Perhaps the best compliment of the year came in the ST issue which covered the swearing-in of PM Lee. Tucked inside was a news report in which London mayor Ken Livingstone announced that the Singapore-style road pricing system to cut congestion in the city centre had been so successful that it would be extended to cover a bigger area. Following a study of the pioneering Singapore system, the British capital had introduced a £5 daily charge on vehicles entering the city centre. Who would have thought that the country, which once presided over a great empire and was known as the cradle of industrial revolution, would one day take a leaf from a former colony in traffic management?

Goh left an enduring legacy for PM Lee to build on—14 years of peace and prosperity, a culture of greater openness and public engagement, and a higher international profile for Singapore. His leadership was vividly demonstrated in the way he rallied the people through the Asian financial crisis in 1997, the aftermath of the September 11 attack on New York in 2001 and the SARS epidemic in 2003. His empathy for the less well off was reflected in wealth-sharing policies such as Edusave and Medifund.

But what PM Lee inherited did not come on a silver platter. He had helped to build up the country since he entered politics in 1984. As deputy prime minister and finance minister, he often had to push through unpopular and controversial policies. Goh had described Lee as "not only a most supportive and valuable deputy, but also a key minister handling many jobs at any one time".

As Singapore's third PM raised his right hand before President S R Nathan and recited the same oath that his father did 45 years ago, he was acutely aware that he faced a different set of challenges from those confronting his father and his predecessor who were appointed minister mentor and senior minister respectively in his cabinet.

In his inauguration speech, he articulated his vision of a government that will be open and inclusive in its approach towards Singaporeans, whether young or old, disabled or able-bodied, rich or poor. He urged Singaporeans to step forward to make a difference to themselves, their fellow citizens and their country.

How the worlds of 1959 and 2004 have changed in a cosmic wink of an eye. The elder Lee and his team faced the do-or-die challenges of combating communism and communalism; curbing corruption and crime; providing housing, schools and health care; creating jobs and developing Singapore's economy against all odds after it was ejected from Malaysia.

The younger Lee and his associates had to grapple with the challenges of growing the economy against global competition, transforming Singapore into a global cosmopolitan city without losing its Asian values, ensuring multi-racial harmony amid the threat of Islamic terrorism, and maintaining social cohesion in the face of widening income disparities.

❧

REMEMBER what the region and the world were like in 2004? As PM Lee thumbed through the ST issue of 13 August 2004 on his first day at work in the Istana, he would have scanned the headlines that summed up the tremendous challenges of an increasingly globalised, volatile and unpredictable world.

The headline "China's thirst for oil grows despite surge in world prices" continued to tell the earth-shaking rise of a new economic superpower growing at a blistering pace. Napoleon had been proven right when he said that "China is like a sleeping dragon, when she wakes up, the whole world will take notice". PM Lee faced a China that was exporting goods while his father faced a China that was exporting revolution.

A sense of foreboding was evoked by another headline in the same issue: "Taiwan can resist invasion for 2 weeks." The report on the tension between Taiwan and China as they staged their annual war games was quoting military sources in Taipei to allay fears that the city could be captured in six days according to a computer simulation.

The new PM would understand the situation well as he had first-hand experience of cross-straits sensitivities. A month before he assumed the premiership, he paid a private visit to Taiwan to update himself on developments in the island. The trip sparked off a diplomatic rift between Singapore and China. It took some time for bilateral relations to return to normal.

Yet another sign of the troubling times was a report about the deaths of three people from bird flu in Vietnam. Earlier in the year, the H5N1 type of bird flu virus had killed 16 people in the country and eight in Thailand, raising the spectre of a global pandemic. The ripple effect hit home on August 18 when the government banned the import of eggs and poultry from Malaysia following a bird flu outbreak in Kelantan.

The haze that wafted from the blazing forests in Sumatra was a seasonal hazard that threatened public health and tourism in the region. Kuala Lumpur appealed to Jakarta to cooperate as the smog reduced visibility in various parts of the peninsula. Singapore kept its fingers crossed that its sky would continue to be blue and the air free from toxic particles.

If PM Lee discerned any bright spot, it was regional stability. Southeast Asia was much more equable in 2004 than in 1959 when communist regimes and insurgencies threatened to knock down the non-communist countries like dominoes. The formation of ASEAN, APEC and other regional entities helped to anchor the region in peace and prosperity.

In particular, Singapore enjoyed smoother relations with Malaysia. Malaysia's prime minister Abdullah Badawi, who succeeded Mahathir

Mohamad the previous year, steered the UMNO-led Barisan National to its most successful victory in the country's history. Unlike Mahathir who was hostile towards Singapore, Abdullah chose to mend bilateral ties.

In Indonesia, retired general Susilo Bambang Yudhoyono was destined to be the country's first directly elected president. In Thailand, Prime Minister Thaksin Shinawatra was serving his second term in office. In the Philippines, Gloria Arroyo, who replaced Joseph Estrada as president in 2003, won the election in May 2004. All three leaders maintained strong ties with Singapore.

The most ominous news of the day continued to emanate from Iraq where American forces were leading a full-scale assault in the southern holy city of Najaf against the militia of radical Shi'ite cleric Moqtada al-Sadr. The war on terror waged by US president George W Bush, who was re-elected after beating John Kerry in November, was turning into an orgy of bloodletting triggered by suicide bombings.

Some things never changed. While the older Lee faced the threat of terrorism from communist insurgents, the younger Lee faced a similar threat but from Islamic jihadists. The danger was all too real. In 2001 and 2002, 31 men were detained for planning to bomb Yishun MRT station, water pipelines, embassies and US naval vessels docked in Singapore. They were linked to Jemaah Islamiah, a militant Islamic body which vowed to create an Islamic Southeast Asia.

Most tragically, the year that Lee Hsien Loong became PM saw an apocalyptic event in the region that would be seared in the memories of generations. On Boxing Day, the seas rose to swallow more than 200,000 people from Sumatra to Sri Lanka to Africa in the most deadly tsunami in 50 years. More than 5 million people lost their homes. Seventeen Singaporeans died in Thailand.

Singaporeans reacted to the catastrophe with an unprecedented outpouring of compassion and aid. They raised $150 million to help victims as Singapore non-government organisations swung into action. The government staged its greatest humanitarian relief operation in history when it mobilised SAF personnel, aircraft and helicopters to ferry food and medical supplies, tents and blankets, equipment and material to affected areas. It was Singapore's finest hour in one of the darkest moments in Southeast Asia's annals.

THREE years into Lee Hsien Loong's premiership, the accolades kept pouring on the little red dot. Top honours became so routine that Singaporeans barely stifled a yawn when they read about their island being ranked variously as the most competitive, freest and safest economy or the most globalised, best-run and least corrupt country in Asia or the world.

The Republic has been ranked consistently by the World Bank among the top 10 per cent of well-run countries. It scored in rule of law, regulatory quality, government effectiveness, control of corruption and political stability.

No wonder Singapore governance has been regarded as a model by scholars, think tanks and international agencies, and has spawned a cottage industry in case studies and books. Singapore's competitiveness became a classic case study in Harvard Business School and its public sector expertise, an export item. Politicians and policy-makers come from all over the world to find out what makes the island tick.

To be sure, the Singapore system is not without its imperfections and deficiencies. The World Bank report in 2007 gave the Republic lower scores for voice and accountability, which measures the degree of freedom of expression and association. The Hong Kong-based Political and Economic Risk Consultancy also warned that Singapore was increasingly vulnerable to corruption in other countries.

The island was taken to task for maid abuse and action against the opposition by the US-based Human Rights Watch. Its rankings fell near the bottom in press freedom indices compiled by the Washington-based Freedom House, which promotes democratic values, and the Paris-based Reporters Without Borders which campaigns for press freedom.

The constant refrain among local scholars was that the country's economic openness was not matched by political openness. Foreign critics maintained that the country was run with absolute control by a small elite which brooked no dissent and resorted to undemocratic measures to crush the opposition.

On 21 November 2004, PAP celebrated its 50th anniversary with a ceremony on the same day and at the same place where it was inaugurated—the Victoria Concert Hall. By 2009, PAP would have been running the country for 50 years. This makes it the only elected party in the world to have ruled a country uninterruptedly since assuming power. The only other elected party with unbroken rule is UMNO although it governs Malaysia as part of a coalition.

The Colorado Party of Paraguay could have held the record after ruling for 61 years if it was not thrown out in the country's 2008 elections amid a growing groundswell of anger over gross inequality of income, poverty and corruption.

Before that, Partido Revolucionario Institucional or the Institutional Revolutionary Party enjoyed that distinction. It ruled Mexico for more than 70 years until it was ignominiously ousted in the 2002 polls for being synonymous with corruption and electoral fraud.

In 2000, after half a century of total power, Taiwan's Kuomintang (KMT) or Nationalist Party fell to the Democratic Progressive Party (DPP). Despite the country's stellar economic achievements, the people were alienated by the rampant corruption in the party, its arrogance and unresponsiveness to popular grievances. What dealt the final blow was the split in the party which allowed the DPP to win the elections with only 39 per cent of the vote. In 2008, the KMT recaptured power.

In Japan, the 38-year rule of the powerful Liberal Democratic Party came to an end in 1993 with the puncturing of the country's miracle economy and exposure of corruption in government.

Similarly the Congress Party which led India to independence in 1947 strode the political landscape like a colossus until it collapsed in 1977 following widespread anger over emergency rule and unpopular measures, such as the mass clearance of slums and forced sterilisation of men. The party was to fall two more times in 1989 and 1996.

The earlier defeat was caused by the Bofors scandal which involved prime minister Rajiv Gandhi; he was accused of receiving kickbacks from a Swedish company manufacturing Bofors machine-guns. The loss in 1996 was attributed to fears of prime minister Narasimha Rao's economic liberalisation policy and bribery of parliamentarians. The party returned to government as part of a coalition in 2004.

Many ruling parties in Africa, which wrested freedom from the colonialists in the 1950s and 1960s, have either fallen or disappeared into oblivion. Think of Jomo Kenyatta's Kenya Africa National Union, Kwame Nkrumah's Convention Peoples Party of Ghana, Julius K Nyerere's Tanganyika African National Union of Tanzania, Kenneth Kaunda's United National Independence Party of Zambia and Milton Obote's Uganda Peoples' Congress.

The reasons ranged from tribal warfare, ethnic conflicts, corruption, malfeasance and economic mismanagement to extravagant spending on prestige projects, Marxist and socialist dogmas, army coups and dictatorships. Or to sum it up simply: non-governance or poor governance.

Even long-dominant parties in developed nations could not maintain their grip on power. Having ruled Sweden for nearly eight decades, the Social Democrat Party was regarded as one of the most successful political parties in the world. Yet in the 2006 general election, the oldest and largest party in the country lost power to a centre-right coalition. Its demise was attributed to its welfare policies which led to high unemployment, complacency, tiredness and loss of direction.

So how do you account for PAP's political success and longevity? How does it manage to avoid the pitfalls which have led to the decline of so many ruling parties the world over? Speak to scholars, politicians and community leaders and you will receive a wide spectrum of answers: leadership and leadership renewal, integrity, incorruptibility, meritocracy, multi-racialism, the ability to deliver the goods, social compact between the leaders and people, rule of law, national security, discipline and sacrifice, technocratic competence, infrastructure development, political control, social engineering and social equity.

We put the question to entrepreneur Tang Chong Kuan who has lived through nearly 50 years of PAP rule and this was his down-to-earth answer: "Singapore's success did not come from heaven, but from hard work, some luck and very importantly, a good government." In a nutshell—good governance.

What are the key factors in the PAP governance that have enabled the men in white to stay on top for so long? Will the party survive in the age of wrenching social changes and global economic uncertainties? Or is hubris just around the corner? Is the downfall of the party inevitable?

34

In Search of PM No 4

WHEN Lee Kuan Yew embarked on his island-wide constituency tours from November 1962 to September 1963, the man assigned to accompany him and plan his itinerary was a 29-year-old administrative officer from the land office by the name of Lee Wai Kok.

The junior civil servant was given the job as he was conversant in English, Chinese and Malay, and could thus help Lee attend to the grievances and requests raised by the residents in each ward. Before a tour, Lee Wai Kok would visit the constituency to work out the itinerary with village elders—where they would welcome the prime minister; which lanes he would trudge through; and where, on a wooden stage in an open space, he would address the residents.

On one occasion when he was showing the prime minister the itinerary for a certain rural constituency they were going to tour, he was asked to stop when they came to the spot where the wooden stage would be set up. Lee Kuan Yew asked him: "Where will the sun be when I get up on stage to talk? Will it be in my eyes?"

"I was befuddled," Lee Wai Kok said. The day before, he had personally checked the stage, the microphone and the sound system, but it had never occurred to him to check if the prime minister would be facing the sun at the hour when he would get up on stage.

"You don't use your brain!" the prime minister scolded him. Lee Wai Kok survived his boss' wrath and went on to work in the prime minister's office for 15 years. The anecdote, which he recounted in an interview for this book four decades later, captures the quintessential Lee Kuan Yew, a man who planned many steps ahead and left nothing to chance. This unflinching attention to details and getting even the smallest things right characterised his roll-up-your-sleeves leadership style.

"Unbelievably hands-on," was how former *Straits Times* news editor Felix Abisheganaden described Lee during his field visits in the early days. "He would stop at a site and ask why is the construction of this building so slow? Or he would say I saw garbage here last week, why is it still here?"

Ngiam Tong Dow still remembered his first "love-letter" from Lee. One day, as permanent secretary in the ministry of communications, he received a note which read: "Last night I went for a walk and found a lot of graffiti on the walls of the general post office. This is a disgrace. Please have it removed by noon." Ngiam said: "Lee really went down to the ground and looked at all these things. He was very meticulous; without the political will and discipline he imposed, we would not have a clean and green Singapore."

Of all his leadership attributes, it was Lee's never-give-up never-say-die spirit that changed the course of Singapore's history. There were moments in the 1960s when PAP was on the ropes and some of his despairing associates contemplated throwing in the towel and letting the leftists take over, but Lee clung on tenaciously.

As Francis Thomas, a former minister in the Labour Front government (1955-1959) wrote in *Memoirs of a Migrant*, many people thought that Lee would be devoured by the communist tiger during the monumental battle between PAP and the leftists. "It happened the other way round ... Lee has never been a man to let himself be devoured or still more to let the country he leads be devoured."

In the lexicon of historian Wang Gungwu, the phrase that jumped up was the will to power. "From my study of history, there is such a thing as will to power. It's an intangible thing but the human will has to be very strong otherwise you can't do it. If you don't have it, then you stay out of politics, you will have to work for somebody else. Not many people have it. Mao Zedong had it. Lee had it.

"Looking back, if not for that tremendous willpower, he couldn't have survived. I mean brain's not good enough by itself, oratory not good enough, cunning not good enough, money not good at all, no use at all, it's that will to power."

The professor expressed admiration for the way Lee swung the Chinese-educated to his side during those politically tumultuous days. "If he didn't have the capacity, he could have failed and missed the boat. But he managed to do that. Some call it genius. That's leadership."

In the reflections of Ngiam: "In the end, it's the leadership that counts. If Lee was not the leader, the leftists would have swarmed over Singapore easily. People have suffered under his hands but in the bottom of their hearts, they know that without him, there would be no Singapore."

Othman Wok lived through it all as a minister in Lee's cabinet during the struggle with the communists, the merger with Malaysia, the race riots and the trauma of separation. "Those were the toughest times," he asserted emphatically, "without Lee, we could have collapsed under all those pressures, particularly the problems with Malaysia."

Of course, as many of our interviewees were quick to qualify, Lee's leadership could not have prevailed without the unwavering support of his team. Goh Keng Swee was singled out for his instrumental role in the social and economic transformation of Singapore. Toh Chin Chye was cited for holding the party together in difficult times. S Rajaratnam was the indefatigable communicator of ideas. Ong Pang Boon helped to muster the support of the Chinese-speaking.

Former PAP MP P Selvadurai: "The combination of talent in the cabinet then was unbeatable. Goh Keng Swee had a tremendous mind. Rajaratnam got a mind of his own. Then there was Toh Chin Chye. All these fellows were working at their highest intellectual powers."

Former civil servant Goh Sin Tub: "It was a very happy coincidence in history that we had this band of brothers coming together at a very crucial moment."

Former permanent secretary Sim Kee Boon: "The thinkers, doers and speakers complemented each other very well. Lee was helped by Goh as a thinker of policies. Rajaratnam amplified what Lee said. He could find an ideological basis for Lee's ideas. It was a marvellous team."

Lee's leadership has been depicted as the "revolutionary" type thrown up by the political and social upheaval of the time—Japanese occupation, British colonialism and the fight for independence. A different kind of leadership emerged under Goh Chok Tong, one dictated by the imperatives of economic management and nation building.

While Lee subscribed to the Machiavellian maxim of being feared rather than being loved, Goh believed in gathering public feedback and softening the harsh ruling style of his predecessor. He came to be associated with the gentler and kinder face of government.

Goh's former press secretary Ong Keng Yong conjured up the imagery of *wuxia* ("sword-play" in Mandarin) to dramatise the differences between the two prime ministers. "Lee was this very fearsome warrior who charged at you, whereas Goh was this swordsman who didn't have to take out his sword, and he's got *qing qong* ("light touch")."

PAP leadership assumed a more consultative and collective style which continued under PM Lee Hsien Loong when he took over from Goh in 2004. The autocratic approach became less and less apparent as the new-generation leaders sought to involve a wider spectrum of society in governance and accommodate a wider range of opinions. Their buzzword was "inclusive".

It might sound like an oversimplification, but political commentator Catherine Lim had characterised the respective governing styles of Lee, Goh and the younger Lee as "hard power", "soft power" and "smart power". The last referred to a blend of the first two approaches.

As successive waves of new ministers and MPs with fresh ideas and different perspectives emerged, the PAP leaders took pains to reiterate that the core values should remain—integrity, meritocracy, multi-racialism, performance, rule of law and social equity.

Of all these values that now make up the much-envied and much-studied Singapore model of governance, integrity was upheld as the pivotal principle. Goh had declared time and again that if PAP ever turned corrupt, it deserved to be thrown out of power. For the men in white, being whiter than white continued to be their mantra.

Lee's integrity, as former diplomat Maurice Baker defined it, lay in his insistence on absolute honesty and his utter ruthlessness in cracking down on corruption. Referring to past ministers Lee had acted against without compunction, he said: "You may be a very good man, you may be a very good friend of Lee, but if you are corrupt, out you go."

P Ramasamy, a Malaysian academic who became second deputy chief minister of Penang in 2008, observed that Singapore was able to avoid the corruption which was so rampant in Malaysia, Indonesia and Sri Lanka because of the integrity of its leadership. "The top is clean. The elite is actually committed to getting rid of corruption, so you have a society that takes corruption very seriously."

If Singapore had become one of the most highly ranked countries in the world, it was because of the quality and character of its leadership, pronounced Ted Haner who headed the American rating organisation, Business Environment Risk Intelligence (BERI). "No corruption. No nepotism. No demonstrations of wealth out of the reach of successful working people. The citizens have confidence that there are plans and programmes that will give them jobs, hope for a better future, and security."

In the view of Henri Ghesquiere, a former International Monetary

Fund economist who wrote the book *Singapore's Success: Engineering Economic Growth*, the Republic succeeded because its leadership was assiduous, highly intelligent in a practical way, determined to achieve shared prosperity, and committed to act with integrity.

American academic Thomas Bellows had been tracking the ups and downs of the party since he visited the island in the 1960s and wrote the groundbreaking book, *The PAP of Singapore: Emergence of A Dominant Party System*. Attributing the country's success to brainpower, institutions and the ability to identify new problems and develop responses, he concluded that "what remained unchanged was the indisputable importance of a top meritocratic elite".

⁓⁓⁂⁓⁓

WHAT could be more pressurising for lawyer Christopher de Souza than a court trial or the bar examinations? Answer: the psychological interview for prospective PAP election candidates.

"It was like going under mental surgery," recalled the youthful Eurasian MP in an interview in 2007. "The questions were extremely probing ranging from my childhood to my marriage."

He was studying law at King's College London on a bond-free Shell scholarship when he received a job offer from then-chief justice Yong Pung How to be his law clerk. After clinching a first class honours degree and a master's in civil law at Oxford University, he returned to Singapore to take up the offer in 2002. Two years later, he became a deputy public prosecutor. The following year, he was invited to the customary tea session and later met cabinet ministers S Jayakumar and Teo Chee Hean who asked if he was keen on entering politics. He replied that he was enjoying his career in government and needed time to consider.

Despite his reservations, he found himself at a meeting with prime minister Lee Hsien Loong, senior minister Goh Chok Tong, minister mentor Lee Kuan Yew and almost the whole cabinet. "They asked me why I chose to return from England when I was not bonded by the Shell scholarship. My classmates had joined law firms in London and New York where the money was better and the exposure greater. My answer was I wanted to contribute back home. My sense of the interview was that they were assessing my loyalty to the country, what I could contribute and where I could contribute best."

The ministers told de Souza that if he were to go into politics, he could contribute more to Singapore. He met the PM again and sought the advice of ministers Lim Swee Say and George Yeo and his mentor, Yong Pung How. At the end of 2005, he went with his wife on a holiday to India where he thought long and hard about the offer. He decided to take the plunge. He quit the civil service and joined Lee and Lee.

As he reflected on the rigorous psychological interview, he said: "It was an extremely searching and very intrusive experience, but I understood the necessity for it and so I was not offended. It was looking for the base plate of morality."

Like de Souza, Jessica Tan Soon Neo found the questions for the psychological test very personal, admitting that "they took a lot out of me". She realised that the questions reflected the scale and magnitude of a PAP MP's role and the lack of privacy that went with it.

"I was concerned about my suitability so the test was useful for me. From the questions, you got a sense of what to expect of the role, what kind of values they were looking for," said the Microsoft Asia Pacific senior general manager in 2007. She remembered spending two afternoon sessions with the psychologists, each lasting about four to five hours. "The people who did the test were very professional. They made it fun. I didn't know what to expect. One minute you had an IQ test, the next it was something else."

Tan was first invited to tea by defence minister Teo Chee Hean in early 2004. Later she met then-deputy prime minister Lee Hsien Loong and two other ministers. Her third session was with Mah Bow Tan in early 2005. Then Teo popped the question. Her answer was no as she was worried about career implications. Urged by Teo to think about it, she talked to her employers and her husband, a civil servant. "He was apprehensive. As it was, I was spending so little time with my family," the mother of three said.

A week later, Tan told the minister that although she had not made up her mind, she was open to it. She went through the three formal rounds of interviews, as well as the psychological test. Afterwards she was exposed to grassroots work. "Both the exposure to the grassroots work, and the discussions with the various leaders convinced me to say yes. The selection process helped me to understand the party and align myself to it. It helped me make my decision."

Both de Souza and Tan were among the 24 new candidates fielded by the ruling party in the general election on 6 May 2006. Aged 30 and 40 then, they were returned as MPs for Holland-Bukit Timah GRC and East Coast GRC respectively.

The gruelling psychological assessment for potential PAP candidates comprised psychometric tests and in-depth clinical interviews. Since the 1980 general election, the assessment has been conducted by clinical psychologist Fred Long Foo Yee and psychiatrist Teo Seng Hock, then-medical director of Woodbridge Hospital. When the latter retired in the 1990s, Long conducted the tests on his own until the 2001 general election, when he roped in clinical psychologist Elizabeth Pang to help him.

Trained in Australia and Britain, Long was head of the government psychological service in Woodbridge Hospital and Institute of Mental Health from 1984 until his retirement in 2002. He was a member of the team which helped to provide psychological support in the aftermath of the MI 185 and SQ 006 air crashes of 1997 and 2000 respectively.

According to him, when Lee Kuan Yew was prime minister, he wanted the tests to assess a candidate's intellectual ability, emotional stability, integrity, sense of judgement, character and loyalty to a cause and to the group. He also wanted to know the person's motivation, aspirations, fortitude, leadership and organisational and communication skills. When Goh Chok Tong took over the premiership, he requested the inclusion of qualities such as emotional intelligence, creativity and community service.

The assessment comprised IQ tests, pen-and-paper personality quizzes numbering about 1,000 questions and two face-to-face clinical interviews. Candidates were probed about their family dynamics, childhood and early life events, educational history, national service experiences, psychosexual history, marriage and family life, personal habits, social activities and lifestyles, health issues, work record, finances, philosophy of life and political motivation.

Long stressed that the assessment did not directly determine the suitability of a candidate. "The purpose is to provide the requesting authorities with the kind of personal information needed for their decision-making. Candidates do not pass or fail the so-called 'test'." For each candidate, he would submit a detailed report to the PAP leaders.

What could his tests uncover? The psychologist was not at liberty to divulge individual details but he gave the example of a candidate who came armed with impressive university degrees. After he was put through the intelligence tests, it was found that his IQ level was just average. Long noted that most candidates performed well and were open about themselves although there were some who were not as candid as they claimed to be.

There were some candidates who had high "lies" scores which suggested attempts at "faking good" on the personality questionnaire. In an interview in 2004, Lee spoke about a candidate who did well in the psychological tests but his gut instincts told him otherwise. He believed the person "faked well" and said he was proven right later.

As Wong Kan Seng, a PAP selection panel member since 1988, acknowledged, the psychological test could not be the sole determinant. "No matter how thorough we can be, sometimes we may miss something in the person and that may not surface until much later. Ultimately you've got to see the person on the ground, how he relates to people and how he conducts himself."

From our interviews, we learnt that some shortlisted candidates were not fielded because of adverse grassroots feedback. One eminent member of the establishment today passed the initial rounds but was not approved by Lee. Some became MPs but served only one term before they were found wanting. High-flyers who failed to live up to expectations were grounded. The same fate awaited those who performed well but could not connect with the ground.

⁓⧉⁓

ASK founding party chairman Toh Chin Chye how PAP candidates were picked for the 1959 elections and his reply would be brutally frank: "Anybody who walked in. So long as from hearsay the chap was not pro-communist or communist, he could stand for us."

Those were the days when the party was desperately short of talent as it was shunned by the English-educated and the professional class. It was looked down as a poor men's party peddling a socialist agenda. Lee and associates were even suspected to be camouflaged communists.

Names were plucked randomly from party branches and trade unions. Candidates were asked to recommend candidates. Friends and relatives were rounded up. There were no tea parties, interviews or background checks. The party even had to drop a candidate at the eleventh hour when it discovered he was not a Singapore citizen.

Reporter Lee Khoon Choy was stopped in a car park and asked if he could stand for PAP. Bank clerk Chan Chee Seng resisted, saying that he lacked qualifications. Shop assistant Ong Chang Sam protested, lamenting that he was financially broke. Seamstress Ho Puay Choo pointed out that she could not speak English. But the party order was unyielding: sorry, you had to stand.

The result was an all-and-sundry slate which included teachers, journalists, trade unionists, barbers, tradesmen, farmers, shopkeepers and dressmakers. The party's prized catch were two doctors—Lee Siew Choh and Sheng Nam Chin—whose professional credentials, unfortunately, did not ensure party allegiance. They defected to Barisan Sosialis later.

What kept the British-educated leaders aloft on a wave of mass support was its partnership with populist politicians from the left who could deliver inflammatory speeches and exploit issues unashamedly. That was when politicking skills mattered more than policy-making acumen.

It was only after PAP had vanquished the leftists and gained complete dominance of parliament because of the Barisan boycott that Lee began to inject new blood with higher qualifications. Wong Lin Ken, Augustine Tan and Chiang Hai Ding were among the first doctorate-holders to be parachuted into the august chamber. They were soon joined by a stream of academics, lawyers, doctors and former senior civil servants. Orthopaedic surgeon Ong Leong Boon was hailed as a rising star while Singapore's first Rhodes scholar Tan Eng Liang was touted as a future prime minister.

In the meantime, Lee initiated the painful process of phasing out the party's grassroots politicians. An elitist, but a pragmatic one, he judged that the activists who had fought alongside him in the early difficult days were not up to the task of running the country. Most of them were Chinese-educated and did not have tertiary education. They were handicapped by Lee's policy of retaining English as the language of government.

His search for a second generation leadership took on added urgency when in 1974, one of his closest lieutenants and friends, Hon Sui Sen, then 60, told him that he was standing down. The then-finance minister told him that investors were confident with Lee and the ministers in charge. But they were looking beyond and behind the ministers to see who would replace them. Hon pointed out that chief executive officers (CEOs) of American corporations had to retire at 65. Several years before a CEO's retirement, he had to put before the board of directors one or more candidates for them to choose one as his successor.

Resolving to entrust Singapore in competent hands before he retired, Lee scoured the length and breadth of the island for men in their 30s or early 40s who had an excellent academic record and who had proven themselves in their careers.

Lee's belief in psychological tests for IQ and character was reinforced in 1987 by a meeting with Hans Jürgen Eysenck, the British psychologist famed for his controversial theories on the role of genetics in IQ differences. He told Lee that Mobil had a team of psychologists who assessed applicants before recruitment as well as executives before promotion.

In Lee's mind, that was the missing link, the Eureka moment. As he told our writers: "Ability with words and figures, reasoning and presentation skills could be determined but not character, temperament, values and motivation." He asked psychologists in the army and education ministry to administer tests on people being considered for important jobs and scholarships. He acknowledged that the assessment could not be foolproof as it was very difficult to gauge a person's character and motivation but it could help to reduce errors.

Later, to assess the potential of PAP candidates, he adopted the system devised by Shell which ranked individuals against four basic qualities: the ability to look at things from a high vantage point and at the same time zoom in on critical details, power of analysis, imagination and a sense of reality.

For many of the 18 new candidates fielded in the 1980 general election, Lee also put them through an exhaustive psychological test administered by Fred Long.

But as fate or luck would have it, even before the 1980 polls, the core group of the second echelon leadership was already taking shape—namely Goh Chok Tong, Ong Teng Cheong, Tony Tan, Lim Chee Onn, S Dhanabalan, S Jayakumar and Ahmad Mattar.

The most promising minister tipped to be Lee's successor was Lim Chee Onn. But he was dropped suddenly after being stripped of his post as the National Trades Union Congress secretary-general in 1983. The ostensible reason was that he had no rapport with rank-and-file unionists. There were, however, murmurs that his supporters were pushing too hard for him to be prime minister.

Against their will, however, the Old Guard leaders began to make their exits—some gracefully, some with parting shots dripping with sarcasm and bitterness. By 1984, except for Lee and two veteran grassroots MPs, Ch'ng Jit Koon and Ho Kah Leong, the central executive committee (CEC) consisted wholly of second-generation leaders.

Toh Chin Chye objected vehemently to Lee's leadership renewal plan and the pace with which it was being carried out. He believed that leaders could be groomed from the ground but Lee disagreed. As Lee put it in an interview: "You will get activists, yes. You will get enthusiasts, yes. You will get committed, dedicated workers, yes. But managers, thinkers, implementers?"

The former deputy prime minister also contended that he and his colleagues, being in their 50s then, were not that old yet. A frail 81-year-old Toh told us in 2002: "We gave our lives to building Singapore right from the beginning. We never thought of building a career. So when we were dropped, how were we going to seek a new livelihood all of a sudden?"

For many veteran PAP MPs, the memory of being dropped still rankled. Former Changi MP Robin Sim Boon Woo was particularly embittered as he had helped to rebuild the party after The Big Split of 1961. When contacted in 2003, he said angrily that he had nothing more to do with the party and slammed down the phone.

Betraying traces of rancour and melancholy, several others said that it was futile to talk about the past. A former minister of state recalled that when he was asked by Lee to step down, he was told that the then-PM would also be doing so. "Well, it had been more than 20 years since I retired but Lee has still not retired!" he lamented. One MP who served his ward for 24 years spoke poignantly of how he went in and out of then-PM Goh's office in one minute. He knew what was coming and did not want to sit through it.

In a party speech in 2002, PM Goh recounted his experience in breaking the bad news: "Not only were the MPs my comrades but, in the initial years, they were also all senior to me. They had put in years of dedicated service. Many had fought the communists and communalists. All had served selflessly. They had toiled to build a better Singapore. I was air-dropped into office and wet behind the ears.

"It was difficult to find the right words to tell those who had sacrificed many years of their lives for the party that they had to make way for younger people. I do not think I always got my words right. I could see the anguish and pain in some of their eyes."

꩜

WHERE in the world can you find a leadership succession system in which candidates are identified from a database, invited for tea, wooed assiduously by the most powerful men in the country, put through psychometric tests, reluctantly inducted into politics and meticulously groomed to be ministers?

In most democratic countries, people are driven by ambition, idealism and a sense of social injustice to go into politics. They usually start at the grassroots rising through the rank and file, earning their spurs in hard-won elections and building a power base before vying for a top position.

Witness the marathon, hard-slogging ascent of Barack Obama in the United States, Kevin Rudd in Australia, Lee Myung-bak in South Korea and Ma Ying-jeou in Taiwan in 2007-08. They cut their political teeth and honed their leadership skills in exhausting party and electoral combat. They had to harness immense resources and expend tremendous energy on the campaign trail and withstand unending criticisms from robust opponents and a rambunctious media. In contrast, as critics relished pointing out, some Singapore ministers had yet to fight in an election because of walkovers.

Just across the causeway, politicians in UMNO had to marshal ground support and fend off fierce opposition even within their own party to fight their way up. By the time they were fielded in the general election, they would have undergone a baptism of fire in branch elections. As PAP MP Charles Chong noted wryly: "Our Malaysian counterparts are hard-boiled politicians. That's why when they meet us, they say you fellows are not politicians, you're all technocrats. In a way it is true, many of our ministers and MPs are technocrats parachuted into the branches."

Public policy scholar Neo Boon Siong agreed that a leadership system in which people were persuaded to enter politics and nurtured to be ministers was unique. In countries where party politics was very strong, he said, the loyalists would have the first bite rather than outsiders.

By planning for leadership renewal, in the view of political science lecturer Ho Khai Leong, the party ensured political stability and continuity. Open contest would thus be avoided and factional struggle minimised, he said, as candidates were endorsed and supported by the CEC and the cadres.

Prominent intellectual Kishore Mahbubani commented that it was very unusual for PAP to keep on recruiting younger and younger people to avoid keeping the same people in office. The nearest equivalent of such a system he could think of was that of the Chinese Communist Party which sought to recruit and promote the best talents in the country. "In some ways, it's even more ruthless than the PAP as it has a very strict age limit."

But while pundits acknowledged the strengths and virtues of PAP-styled leadership rejuvenation, they could not help wondering if there might be possible pitfalls in a system in which intellectually brilliant technocrats and high-flying scholars were inducted as political leaders.

Look, they choroused, these parachuted politicians never had to fight tooth and nail to reach the top, they never experienced the trials and tribulations of political life, they never had to spend sleepless nights agonising over what a freewheeling media might dig out from their past, they never had to face boisterous street protests against their policies, they never had to confront a hostile opposition baying for their blood.

So if they had never suffered an electoral reverse or the dire consequences of a policy fiasco, how would they acquire the Hillary Clinton-like qualities of resilience and tenacity? Would they have the mettle and stamina to surmount a crisis or fight off a serious political challenge? As Ngiam Tong Dow put it: "Supposing the opposition throws up a Lee Kuan Yew, can the young PAP leaders face up to him?"

Ponder this poser raised by former researcher Russell Heng in an essay: "When a party offers its potential candidates an extremely high chance of winning, it is never going to know if these young men and women, whatever their many talents, have a stomach for a fight when the risk of losing is significantly higher. Let's call this an X-factor, that special something any politician should have. So long as the PAP deploys its immense power to maintain the status quo, it will never know how much of that precious X-factor its recruits really have."

Some scholars insisted that the ability to lead was innate rather than acquired. Given a better educated and increasingly cosmopolitan population with high expectations of accountability and transparency, they asked, would instant technocrats-turned-politicians be able to command the respect and standing to persuade, cajole and rally the people behind them in a time of crisis?

Ho Khai Leong expressed concern that ministers were looking and sounding more and more like CEOs. "They have little sense of the political contestation on the ground. Without grassroots experience, there is a kind of disconnect between them and the people. Whether they can win hearts and minds is questionable."

Retired diplomat Maurice Baker was especially perturbed that leaders accustomed to a privileged scholastic and career track might not have the ground feel and empathy. He recalled that at the height of the unemployment problem in 2003, he heard a minister referring to it as "only five per cent". He exclaimed indignantly: "Did he see issues only in economic terms? Did he not know what that figure meant in real terms—the number of families affected and the scale of human suffering?"

Others raised a big question mark over motivation: Would inducted politicians be driven by a strong sense of public service and self-sacrifice or were they attracted to politics only because of the million-dollar pay cheque? As Workers' Party (WP) chairman Sylvia Lim cautioned: "If I were in the PAP leadership, I would be quite careful in assessing the motivations of the people joining because you are now in an organisation which is like a blue-chip company. So people may want to buy your stocks because they derive benefits from it. My question would be: Are you really interested in the people or is it something else?"

If there was a weakness in the leadership system, pinpointed Neo Boon Siong, it was that the party needed to retire one-third of its MPs each term to make way for new candidates. He noted that in other countries people became politicians in their 50s, but in Singapore politicians in that age group were on the verge of retirement. After two terms, he said, MPs would have built up their grassroots experience and political acumen. "They are about to be more settled and more seasoned politicians who begin to have a sense of the ground. And then they are rooted out. Are the people well-served by this turnover, by being constantly a training ground for new MPs?"

Neo, who co-authored a book with Geraldine Chen on the civil service titled *Dynamic Governance: Embedding Culture, Capabilities and Change in Singapore*, argued that ministers could not be compared to executives. Enumerating the characteristics of successful corporate executives, he noted that they could "act, move fast, solve problems and mobilise resources and have energy and good thinking capability".

But these characteristics might not be the same ones that made a successful minister, he said. "As a minister you no longer have to do all those things. Basically you're thinking about a more complex set of issues, policies which have multiple internal conflicts and dilemmas which requires a maturity in thinking which is quite different from what you see in executives trying to prove themselves."

If you asked Kishore Mahbubani, he would say that the main shortcoming of the system was the selection of leaders from a relatively narrow band of Singaporeans. "Increasingly, they tend to come from the civil service or the army. I think it would be good to broaden the base and get different personality types, so that they are not all cut from the same cloth." He believed that some cabinet members should have solid private sector experience.

This was one view Lee Kuan Yew would readily agree with as he had often stressed the need to recruit people from outside the system to build a balanced and well-rounded team. His great concern was that having like-minded people in the cabinet would result in "intellectual in-breeding".

He recalled that he had a more diverse team in 1959 as his ministers came from different backgrounds. But present leaders went through the same school and university system, the same training and career progression, he said, "so they understood each other very well and had the same world view and same methodology of tackling problems. But that has disadvantages in that nobody puts the egg upside down and says, 'Look, perhaps it can be tackled this way.' "

Recounting the colourful career of his old guard colleague Lim Kim San who ran his father's petrol kiosk and later his father-in-law's pawn shops, and invented a sago milling machine before he became minister, Lee said: "He had a different kind of mind. You got to find people like him."

Well, what kind of a person would he have in mind? Lee mentioned Olivia Lum, the founder and CEO of Hyflux, the water treatment system company. The Perak-born orphan had a very rough life before she became a successful entrepreneur, he said. "We should get people like her to join because she'll bring a completely different background. She'll have a different kind of instinct for how things can get done."

Abandoned at birth in a hospital in Kampar, Lum was adopted by an illiterate Chinese woman who gambled heavily. From the age of nine, she became the breadwinner, weaving rattan bags, playing the clarinet in funeral processions and selling fruits, sandwiches, ice cream and jeans in and out of school every day. Arriving in Singapore by bus at age 16 with $10 and a results slip with seven As and one B, she knocked on the doors of more than 10 schools before she was admitted to Tiong Bahru Secondary. To pay her way, she gave tuition and worked as a waitress and store promoter. By sheer grit, she made it to the science faculty of the National University of Singapore, worked as a chemist with Glaxo and then struck out on her own.

"Supposing she had been through our system," said Lee, "she would not have turned out that way. Supposing she was born a Singaporean, she would have gone to our school, got a scholarship, gone off to Harvard, Yale, Princeton or Stanford, come back and be moulded in the process.

"I think there must be people like her outside the system. We have to go outside the system and find them. You just got to keep your eyes wide open and say: 'Oh yes, that's a different career path, different mindset, different experiences, bring him or her in.'"

TO the cacophony of criticisms levelled at the PAP leadership system, the robust rejoinder would be that it was much easier to train a technocrat to be a politician than the other way round and that the party's track record of achievements spoke for itself.

Its best testament would be the succession of strong and capable leaders from 1959 to 2008 who had steered Singapore to greater progress and prosperity. The Goh team had battled and overcome one serious challenge after another—from the Asian financial crisis in 1997 to the post-September 11 slump in 2001 to the severe acute respiratory syndrome (SARS) outbreak in 2003. In 2009, the Lee Hsien Loong team faced its biggest test as it grappled with Singapore's worst economic crisis since the Second World War.

American professor Larry Diamond specialised in the study of democracy all over the world. Like many Western scholars, he did not see eye to eye with the PAP model of governance. He took issue with the government for what he described as the lack of level playing field for opposition parties, the unfair nature of Singapore's electoral system, the media bias and the lack of a free climate for criticism. But he acknowledged that the recruitment of highly capable political and governmental talent was one positive factor behind the party's remarkable performance.

According to distinguished historian Wang Gungwu, what mattered most under this system was not politics but performance—the government was able to promise and deliver because it had the analytical skills to solve problems and the foresight and ability to plan over several electoral terms.

Lee's brilliance, he expounded, lay in creating an institution to enshrine the legitimacy of a group of leaders who were not political like he was in the 1950s and 1960s, and in ensuring that the party would win in every general election so that it could take the long-term view while implementing short-term policies.

The professor argued that the present leadership should not be compared to the first-generation leadership which was charismatic and political. "A technocratic leadership is not the normal political leadership. It is never really inspiring. It is efficient, it can be trusted to do certain things well. The criteria are performance, capability in getting things done, looking ahead, planning, system management." The current leaders were not selected, he said, for the purpose of being tested in the hurly-burly of street politics but for their performance skills which could be assessed.

Political science professor Jon Quah highlighted not just the party's crisis management skills but also its ability to anticipate crises and pre-empt them. No one really knew what problems the PAP government had to nip in the bud especially in the sensitive areas of foreign relations, race, religion and language. "The mark of a good leader is that you anticipate the future, you anticipate a crisis. You don't wait for a crisis to come. Once the crisis comes, it's too late. It is better to take safety precautions to prevent a fire rather than let the fire start and then call the fire engine," he said.

Chua Beng Huat had been a vocal critic of PAP but he was not worried that the technocrats-turned-politicians could not rise to the challenges. The sociologist said: "I actually think that crisis times will throw up crisis heroes. I actually think every time there is an economic crisis, the PAP would do better rather than worse—and it has always been the case."

What about concerns that parachuted politicians lacked an understanding of the ground? Five-term PAP backbencher Charles Chong, known for his strong rapport with his constituents, believed that elections would have a sobering effect on inducted newcomers. "Politicians face elections so they have to sell their policies and get them accepted by the electorate. So elections actually keep the technocrats humble in the sense that they have to go down to the ground knowing that everybody has got one vote each."

Scholar general-turned-minister George Yeo understood all too well the importance of keeping in touch with the people, having had to fend off a ferocious challenge from WP in Aljunied GRC in the 2006 elections. "Unless you really grew up with a silver spoon in your mouth, which very few Singaporeans did, I think you would know most of the political ground that you got to face."

He maintained that PAP leaders were acutely aware of the danger of being cut off from the people. "If you don't go to the hawker centre, the wet markets and you don't know what life is like in Asia, then you are in danger of being eliminated by the people you serve."

On whether the range of PAP leaders was too narrow, Teo Chee Hean reiterated that PAP was an inclusive, not exclusive, party and that it had roped in people from think tanks, religious and clan associations and social activist groups to serve as ministers and MPs. "The PAP had a very broad roof under which we're prepared to bring in people with quite a wide range of views on issues. What we agreed upon are core values. But other than that, we are actually not ideological. We are logical in how we approach problems. We see them, we analyse them, we try and find the best solutions for them," he said.

Political commentators had noted that the party not only co-opted some of the best and brightest but also made a conscious effort to reel in critics such as Vivian Balakrishnan and Raymond Lim. There was a time when the party would not consider having a *tudung*-wearing Malay Muslim and single women in their parliamentary ranks. Not anymore.

Grassroots politicians were not ignored altogether. It was a tribute to them that they, and not the scholars, were invariably fielded against tough opponents in single-seat wards. In the 1997 polls, Ong Ah Heng and Ang Mong Seng recaptured Nee Soon Central and Bukit Gombak from Singapore Democratic Party's Cheo Chai Chen and Ling How Doong.

As for the concern over the one-third turnover of PAP parliamentarians in every general election, PM Lee Hsien Loong did not think that it was too fast. According to his calculations, such a turnover would work out to an average of three terms per MP or about 15 years.

"So if you come in at around 37, in 15 years, you're already in your early 50s. It's a long time. There will be some who will stay only one term, some who will stay just two terms and then leave or retire for various reasons. So to make the three-term average, you must have some MPs who stay four, some five terms, and that is not easy. It is physically and emotionally a very demanding job to be an MP.

"In order to stay current with a new generation, we need this continuing induction of new faces, new ideas, and balance them with people who have that leadership and battle experience, so that we have a rounded team. I think one-third is an ambitious target, but so far we've been able to manage it."

⁂

CALL it the Republic's equivalent of the Holy Grail—the search for prime minister No 4. Prime minister No 3 had barely settled down in the Istana when he said that the party was looking for people in their 30s, young enough to be still young in 10, 15 years. As Lee Hsien Loong announced in a speech in 2007: "I want to be able to assemble the best possible group so that we can offer Singaporeans the best choice. Ten years from now, one of them at least will be ready to take over as PM."

Elaborating in an interview, he said that it was not possible for the leadership to be chosen by successively anointing the next person. "I choose you, you choose him, and then he chooses the next person, each one chooses a successor, and so make sure that his own retirement will be comfortable."

The leadership had to jell, he explained, and for the leadership to jell, the leader had to emerge naturally from the group who must choose him and support him. "Ultimately, it's really the PAP MPs who must have confidence in him, because constitutionally, the prime minister is the person who commands the confidence of the majority of the MPs in parliament."

For all the scintillating success of the system in bringing on board a constant stream of very able ministers, there seemed to be a never-ending anxiety, if not paranoia, over the perceived lack of talent in government. PAP leaders worried incessantly about the exodus of bright Singaporeans overseas and the reluctance of promising private sector people to take their chances in public life.

Not surprisingly, questions have been raised about the viability and relevance of the leadership selection system and whether the party could be blindsided in its quest for talent. If past performance was not necessarily indicative of future performance, as that fund manager's caveat went, how certain was the PAP that the leaders it drew would be the right ones?

People we interviewed believed that a different type of leadership would be needed to seal a new compact with an increasingly mixed and mobile population and to navigate Singapore through an age of profound social changes and global economic unpredictability.

Political science academic Kenneth Paul Tan contended that PAP would have to move from the transactional to the transformative type of leadership. By transactional leadership, he was referring to the party's ability to deliver the goods in exchange for the support of the people. That was fine in the earlier years when the only thing that mattered was economics, he said, but with Singaporeans becoming more globally exposed and media savvy, leadership would have to be "more inspirational, more to do with values, identity and other higher order things and envisioning Singapore as a place that is interesting, worth living in and more inclusive".

Just because the leadership formula had worked well so far, said Wang Gungwu, it should not mean that the same kind of leadership should be reproduced again and again. "The new leaders would have to be upfront, respond fast, take risks, put their money where their calculations are and say that's the future. Even if they don't anticipate everything correctly, they should be quick in recognising a mistake and rectifying it."

To take Lee at his word, perhaps it is time to turn over the egg and ask: Is the current system the only way to ferret out potential leaders? Has PAP really explored all options and exhausted all avenues in scouting for new leaders? Has it fully tapped the potential of women who make up half the population?

Is talent too narrowly defined by the PAP headhunters? Is the party so pre-occupied with the academically brilliant that it might have overlooked other potential sources of leadership, for example, the creative and the entrepreneurial? Isn't the blogging community worth trawling for talent? Wouldn't rebels, mavericks and non-conformists make the best change agents?

Is it that heretical to source for talent in the 150,000-strong Singapore diaspora? Must a leader be picked from those with four As? What about the non-scholarly street-smart types who have the X-factor to energise and lead people? Why not consider the advocates in non-government organisations whose public spiritedness and passion would more than compensate for their lack of technocratic credentials?

There are other leadership assumptions that could be turned on their head: Does it really take such a long tutelage to be a prime minister when many a great leader including Lee had slipped into their job from day one?

With ever-lengthening life-spans, is it necessary to retire outstanding ministers in their 50s? Why not co-opt matured non-government people at the height of their leadership and intellectual powers? Must ministers be affiliated to the ruling party?

If PAP has reached the limit or the end of its tether in the search for new leaders, why not think the unthinkable: free up the political system completely so that potential leaders who want to serve the nation without prompting or inducement and without having to wear white can surface.

Who knows, a bright new star might burst into the political firmament and capture the popular imagination with an electrifying agenda. It happened in 1959 when a 36-year-old lawyer in private practice emerged from the opposition to change the destiny of a nation.

35

Lee: "You Are Equal To Me"

DATE: 11 December 1950. Time: after 1 pm. As private secretary to the British governor of Singapore, Mike Gorrie was working in Government House, now known as the Istana, when he received a desperate call on the phone: "Please come and rescue us."

The plea came from one of two daughters of a British colonial official who had been shopping in Raffles Place when it all blew up. Curfew was imposed suddenly. People rushed off frantically. Taxis and buses stopped running. The girls were stranded—and frightened.

Gorrie, all of 26 years then with visions of being a knight in shining armour, jumped into an official car, took over the wheel from the Malay driver, raced through Orchard Road and into Battery Road to rescue the two damsels. On the return journey, he did what he was to describe in his oral history interview in 1991 as "an extremely stupid thing". From Battery Road, he sped past Connaught Drive and, despite the sight of a blazing car beside Raffles Hotel, headed towards Arab Street.

As a former pilgrimage officer who spoke Malay fluently, he thought he knew the Indian Muslim traders of Arab Street well enough and wanted to see for himself what was happening. "We were turning the corner when suddenly we saw this crowd and they saw us. They saw these *orang puteh* ("white people" in Malay) and they saw it was a big car, and they came with a great roar.

"The nearest man was actually running. As he was running, he was also wheeling a bicycle. He picked up his bicycle and he flung it to the car. It hit the car ... I put my foot on the accelerator and I whisked off, down into Rochor Road and back, and then I realised the full implication, because never before had anybody dreamt of attacking Europeans, I mean, it was unheard of and they were coming for us. We would have been slaughtered."

The Scottish colonial administrator, who later became a Singapore citizen and a much-respected human resource practitioner, was recalling his close shave during the Maria Hertogh riots which erupted on that fateful day. For three days, mobs of Malay and Indian Muslim rioters attacked Europeans and Eurasians, barricaded major roads, and set cars and houses on fire. In all, 18 people were killed and 173 injured.

The carnage was sparked off by a custody battle over the 13-year-old Maria between her adoptive Malay family and her Dutch-Eurasian parents. During the Japanese occupation of Java, Maria was handed over to Aminah binte Mohamed, an Indonesian woman who raised her as a Muslim named Nadra. After the war, the Hertoghs learnt that their daughter was in Malaya and launched a legal battle for her custody.

The tragic chain of events began when the colonial court in Singapore removed Maria from her adoptive Muslim family and placed her in a Catholic convent. When the judge dismissed Aminah's appeal and awarded custody to her biological mother, the massive crowds outside the court rioted. They saw it as no less than an all-out assault on their religion and way of life. It was the day that Gorrie received the call.

Date: 22 July 1964. Time: around 7.30 am. Ahmad Mattar was driving his brand new car—a white Ford Cortina with a striking turquoise stripe on each side—to the Singapore Polytechnic on Prince Edward Road where he was scheduled to give a lecture. As he turned into Guillemard Road in front of Singapore Badminton Hall, he stopped behind two cars. Thuggish youths began swarming all over the cars and peering through the windscreens. They allowed the first and the second car to go. "The moment they came to my car, they saw me, they said '*pak*'," as Ahmad recalled. *Pak* means "beat" in Hokkien.

In a flash, the 24-year-old physics graduate of Arab origin realised he was being confronted by Chinese rioters. "I opened the door of the car and ran for my life. It was fortunate that it happened early in the morning. The rioters had not warmed up yet. During the struggle I lost my glasses. They threw something sharp at me and I got cut. Bleeding, I ran to my grand uncle's place on Lorong 25 and called for the ambulance."

When he arrived at Singapore General Hospital, he saw many victims—the innocent as well as the rioters. He was shocked by the sight of a journalist whose leg was pierced by a spear. "Apparently he was trying to take a picture of the riot in Chinatown. They didn't want any evidence so they speared him. He died." The ambulance which later sent him home passed through Guillemard Road. Ahmad saw his three-week-old car burnt into a charred hulk.

The academic, who would later serve the nation as cabinet minister and minister-in-charge of Muslim affairs for 16 years, counted his blessings. He could have joined the casualty toll of 23 killed and 460 injured in the Chinese-Malay riots which broke out the day before during a procession celebrating Prophet Mohammed's birthday.

These near-death accounts by Gorrie and Ahmad evoked the racial and religious strife of the 1950s and 1960s when Singapore was a transient and disunited society, a simmering cauldron of emotions which was all too easily stoked up by demagogues, chauvinists, racists, extremists and fanatics.

The demographic jigsaw revealed the racial segregation, religious polarisation and linguistic fragmentation of the time. Singapore Malays used to be the dominant community until the mid-1830s when a flood of Chinese immigrants altered the racial composition permanently. By 1959, the Chinese numbered 1.19 million, the Malays 217,000 and the Indians 134,600. Eurasians and others, totalling about 37,500, made up the rest.

Although the Chinese formed the majority, they were far from being a monolithic community as they were divided and sub-divided by dialect groups—Hokkien, Hockchew, Hockchia, Teochew, Cantonese, Hainanese, Hakka, Henghua and Shanghainese. One distinct group was the Straits-born Chinese.

The Malays might appear homogencous but they also spanned a wide spectrum of ethnic groups—Rhio Malays, Johor Malays, Baweanese, Minangkabau, Achinese, Batak, Boyanese, Javanese, Sundanese, Bugis and Banjarese. What they had in common was their adherence to Islam.

Ditto with the Indians who comprised southern Indian and Sri Lankan Tamils, Malayalees, Sikhs, Bengalis, Chettiars, Sindhis, Telegus and Gujeratis. They spoke vernacular languages which were incomprehensible to one another. English-speaking Eurasians and Europeans accounted for the rest of the population.

Compounding the racial mosaic were myriad religious affiliations. Most Chinese subscribed to a mix of Taoism, Buddhism and Confucianism. Virtually all Malays were Muslims, while Indians were mainly Hindus with a fair number of Muslims. Together with some middle class Chinese and Indians, the Eurasians and Europeans were invariably Christians. Almost all the world's faiths converged on the island.

Delve deeper into Singapore's history and you will find it strewn with blood from ethnic clashes and religious violence. In 1851, secret societies attacked Chinese Christians in Punggol and Serangoon fearing that mass conversion would threaten clan and triad membership. By the time the riot was quelled, some 500 Chinese including many Catholic converts had been slaughtered.

Yet another horrifying episode was the Indian sepoy mutiny of 1915. When Indian Muslim sepoys or native soldiers serving under British command in Singapore heard rumours that they would have to fight Muslim Turks in the Middle East, they went on a rampage massacring more than 40 British officers and civilians. The mutineers roamed the streets killing Europeans on sight before they were put down.

After the Second World War, as Singapore approached enfranchisement and self-government, race, language and culture became a combustible cocktail as politicians of all hues and shades began championing the interests of their ethnic communities to win popular support.

Communal agitation was par for the course. In the 1960s, the PAP government was accused by both the Chinese and Malay communities of exterminating their language and culture. Fiery Chinese students backed by the Chinese intelligentsia staged sit-ins and demonstrations and clashed with the police. Malay extremists aided by UMNO and Utusan Melayu hoisted the banner of "religion, race and homeland".

The psyche of older Singaporeans has been indelibly scarred by memories of the 1964 racial bloodletting. How can they ever expunge the bone-chilling fear of being caught in a riot or a curfew or reading a leaflet that screamed: "The Chinese are planning to kill Malays. Before Malay blood flows in Singapore, it is best to flood the state with Chinese blood."?

❧❀❧

YEAR: 2007. Meet Chung Kwang Tong in his workplace and he would appear like any young executive on the go. Switching effortlessly from Mandarin to English as he handed you his business card, he was scrolling his laptop screen to check on his day's schedule.

But catch him at a religious festival and you would hardly recognise him under a black hat and garbed in a red ceremonial robe presiding over an elaborate ritual. Chanting prayers in Cantonese, he was invoking the deities and asking them for their blessings.

His office: The San Qing Gong temple on 21 Bedok North Avenue 4.

His designation: administrator of Taoist Federation of Singapore and secretary-general of Taoist Federation Youth Group (Singapore). His profession: Taoist priest.

When he was interviewed, the 22-year-old master had been a practising priest for four years. Educated in Red Swastika Primary, Pasir Ris Secondary and Nanyang Polytechnic where he obtained a diploma in multi-media and infocomm technology, he found his calling after he met a Hong Kong master and was initiated into the Quan Zhen Long-men (Dragon Gate) sect of Taoism.

Not surprisingly, his youthfulness would arouse much curiosity among the religious representatives at inter-faith dialogues. "They often ask me: 'How do you get ordained at such a young age? What do Taoists really believe in? Do they believe there's one God who created the universe? What do they pray about?' "

The strapping priest admitted that he had to dispel many myths and misconceptions about his religion: "For example, when they ask why we pray to the statue of Guan Gong, the god of war, we explain that we pray to remind ourselves of the warrior's values of courage and loyalty."

By the same token, Chung said that if he had any questions about the other religions, he would seek clarification. "If I don't understand any part of the Bible, I would ask about its meaning and interpretation. Through these dialogues, I got to know the five pillars of Islam, why Muslims pray five times a day and go on the haj to Mecca."

Did he experience any friction with the religious participants? "No, no, we all know the ground rules. Our main objective is to promote inter-faith harmony, to learn and trust each other. We are having a dialogue, not debating who's correct and who's wrong. No, nobody says that my god is the right god, and my way is the right way."

What he found most engrossing were the discussions on life, death and the afterlife. In seeking to understand each other's religion, they would discover that they shared some common views, he said. "The differences are mainly due to beliefs and traditions, but the teachings of all religions are more or less the same—to help mankind, to do good, to be kind to people and so on."

Indeed Chung's sentiments were shared by his religious counterparts who were often surprised to discover the commonalities among the various faiths. Alami Musa, who headed Majlis Ugama Islam Singapura (MUIS) or the Islamic Religious Council of Singapore, said: "For example, the idea of fasting is shared by many religions. The idea of goodness, the idea of seeking truth, these ideas are shared by many religions.

"If there are any differences, we will acknowledge them. Each side will articulate what they believe in. The other side will listen and ask questions to clarify and vice-versa. And that's how it goes. Each meeting ends with an appreciation of differences and that's very, very enriching."

If inter-faith dialogues had become a regular fixture which astonished foreign visitors, so did the multi-faith prayer services conducted in supposedly strictly secular Singapore—from the passing-out parades of Singapore Armed Forces officer cadets to the opening ceremonies of public works projects to the memorial services for the victims of catastrophes such as the SQ006 crash in 2000 and the Asian tsunami in 2004.

A typical service would see religious elders from the Inter-Religious Organisation of Singapore (IRO) reading from their scriptures, praying and giving their blessings together. They represented almost all of the world's major religions—Baha'i, Buddhism, Christianity, Hinduism, Jainism, Judaism, Islam, Sikhism, Taoism and Zoroastrianism. Founded in 1949, the IRO is reputed to be the oldest inter-faith organisation in the world.

Step into a mosque and you might be greeted by a plaque listing the 10 desired attributes of a good Muslim. They included holding strongly to Islamic principles while adapting to changing contexts; appreciating other civilisations and being confident in interacting and learning from other communities; and being a contributing member of a multi-religious society and a secular state.

Visit the National Council of Churches of Singapore website and you will come across exhortations to Christians not to denounce other religions and to recognise that there are many non-Christians who have high standards of conduct. In an apparent response to complaints about Christian insensitivity to Chinese traditions, the umbrella body of Protestant churches made it clear that Christians can attend wakes or funerals conducted under the rites of other religions.

Speak to a Sikh community leader and he would have you know that when the Sikhs pray at their seven *gurdwaras* or temples and in their homes daily, they would remind themselves that they are members of a multi-racial and multi-religious society and pray for the well-being of all.

Every July, religious leaders recite the declaration of religious harmony in churches, mosques and temples or disseminate the message through their activities. The declaration affirms five values: recognise the secular nature of the state, promote cohesion within society, respect each other's freedom of religion, grow common space while respecting diversity, and foster inter-religious communications to avoid conflict and disharmony in Singapore.

Every morning all over the island, students pledge themselves "as one united people, regardless of race, language or religion, to build a democratic society based on justice and equality so as to achieve happiness, prosperity and progress for our nation". Ironical as it may seem, all schools celebrate racial harmony day on July 21 which marks the anniversary of the 1964 racial slaughter.

Racial and religious harmony is one of five shared values displayed in plaques in government departments. They were conceived to embody the common values binding the diverse communities as a nation. The other values are: nation before community and society above self; family as the basic unit of society, community support and respect for the individual; and consensus, not conflict.

After the September 11 attack on New York and the arrests of Jemaah Islamiyah militants in Singapore in 2001, a new grassroots movement sprang up to foster goodwill and understanding among the races. The name: Inter-Racial and Religious Confidence Circles (IRCC). In July 2006, the Central Singapore Community Development Council went orange, the universal colour for racial harmony. More than 300,000 orange ribbons and collar pins were distributed as part of a month-long campaign to raise awareness of racial harmony.

Inter-faith dialogues, multi-religious prayer sessions, declarations of religious harmony, daily pledge, racial harmony day, shared values, confidence circles, orange ribbons—one could go on and on. The placidity and ordinariness of these activities in 2007 could not have been more diametrically different from the blood-splattered imagery of racial and religious violence in the 1950s and 1960s.

⁂

NO white-haired *ang moh* (Hokkien for "Caucasian") could possibly feel more at home in Singapore than Sharon Siddique. She could haggle with market vendors in fractured Hokkien or polished Malay. She was once mistaken for a Chinese albino by a taxi driver because she wore sunglasses and spoke Singlish.

The American-born scholar of multi-culturalism sank her roots in the island after marrying an Indian Singaporean diplomat. In 2007, amid a neon strip of bars, pubs and karaoke lounges on Duxton Hill, she and her partner ran a research consultancy which conducted political risk assessments of countries in the region.

Having lived in Singapore for 40 years and studied its social evolution, the Muslim Singaporean and sociologist took the pulse of multi-racialism in the country. Her verdict: the Republic's racial divide had become more pronounced because of the pervasive presence of Chinese nationals and Chinese-biased policies.

But taking an overview, she noted that there had been no racial violence on the island since 1969 when Singapore suffered from a spillover of the May 13 riots in Malaysia. "That's an incredible achievement!" she exclaimed. "That's a hugely positive track record. I mean, what other country in the world can say that? This is one of the most harmonious places in the entire world."

Siddique's encomium was echoed in almost all the interviews we conducted with academics, community leaders and past and present politicians for this book, and in many published accounts by scholars and think tanks. To appreciate Singapore as a model of communal peace, as they summed up, one had only to survey newspaper headlines depicting racial strife from Brixton to Paris to Bondi Beach, from Kosovo to Sri Lanka to Fiji, from American city ghettoes to European ethnic enclaves.

Many resource-rich African countries, which won independence at about the same time as Singapore, had been ripped apart by ethnic cleansing and tribal warfare. By favouring one race or one tribe over the others and suppressing the minorities instead of reconciling and balancing competing interests, they had spiralled downwards into savagery, mayhem and impoverishment.

Singaporeans need not look beyond the region to fathom the havoc wreaked by racial and religious strife. In 2007, Buddhist Thailand and Roman Catholic Philippines were still struggling to put down Muslim separatists in their southern regions. Buddhist Burmans in Myanmar were battling Christian minorities in the mountains and cracking down on Muslim Rohingyas.

Even Malaysia, which touted itself as a multi-racial model, had not been spared from a new surge in racial animosity over its *bumiputra* policy of favouring Muslim Malays as the "sons of the soil". Chinese discontent continued to simmer. The Indians, led by the Hindu Rights Action Force (HINDRAF), felt so marginalised they took to the streets in 2007 to protest against racial discrimination.

How did Singapore manage to avoid racial and religious conflict for nearly 40 years? The collective answer: by deciding from the outset not to opt for majoritarianism, or rule by the majority race, and by putting in place a series of policies that kept the peace among the races.

P Ramasamy, a Malaysian scholar who became a deputy chief minister in Penang in 2008, said he was struck "by the way Singapore protected its minorities rather than its majority". Unlike Sri Lanka, Fiji, Malaysia and other countries which took the majoritarian route, the PAP government chose to prevent dominance by the majority race. "If the government had decided to please or appease the Chinese majority in 1959, 1963 or 1965 by pandering to their wishes, Singapore would have turned out very differently today."

Or as American political science professor Larry Diamond put it: "The PAP did not engage in the degree of blatant ethnic chauvinist policies that drove the Tamils to open, secessionist rebellion in Sri Lanka. The more open, competitive politics of Sri Lanka, in the context of an extremely ill-suited electoral system, served to polarise politics, promote ethnic out-bidding, and frustrate the quest for compromise."

After scrutinising the PAP government's track record on race relations, New Zealand-based academic Raj Vasil concluded in his book *Asianising Singapore: The PAP's Management of Ethnicity*: "Looking around the world today and watching the viciousness and savagery of ethnic conflict, it is not unreasonable to say that today's Singapore stands as the most monumental achievement of its rulers and its people.

"It is to the credit of the PAP rulers that they have not allowed themselves to be overly influenced by the fact that more than three-quarters of Singapore's population has consisted of the Chinese. They chose, and throughout adhered to, the concept of cultural democracy as the founding principle of the Singapore state which allowed the distinctively different ethnic components of the island's population cultural autonomy and a role and status as persons and citizens of equal worth."

Ask Singapore's founding father how this model of governance came about and Lee Kuan Yew's reply was that he could not quite recollect, saying that it just evolved over the years. "We did not consciously formulate these principles. When a crisis confronted us, we reacted to overcome it. We made decisions for the long-term good of the people. Over time principles had been drawn from the policies and actions we took."

He remarked wryly that scholars could "abstract principles" and make it appear as if PAP had performed a "miraculous transformation" when in actual fact the leaders were "then learning on the job, struggling for survival and making sure the races did not collide". Noble notions did not cross their minds in the heat of the moment.

But while one could debate how multi-racialism arose, said law and multi-culturalism scholar Eugene Tan, there was no question that the government implemented, innovated and institutionalised the model. "PAP's greatest claim is really to operationalise multi-racialism successfully."

Among Singaporeans who lived through PAP rule, there was undisguised pride and relief that the country's multi-racialism had held for so long. Methodist bishop Robert Solomon noted that it had become a much-envied model in the world. China scholar Gwee Yee Hean was convinced that it had evolved to a stage where incidents involving the races no longer attracted racial undertones. Association of Malay Professionals chairman Imram Mohamed pronounced race relations "stronger than ever". Islamic Religious Council of Singapore (MUIS) president Alami Musa described Singapore as an "an oasis in a troubled world".

So how did carnage turn into an oasis?

⚬⚬⚬

GEOFFREY Abisheganaden's eyes lighted up when he recounted how he and eight people were holed up in a room in the Supreme Court for six months in 1966 poring over voluminous documents and listening to views from community leaders and interest groups.

They consulted the constitutions of former British colonies, sought advice from chief justices in the Commonwealth and figured out how to consolidate the scattered pieces of legislation. The result was the report of the Constitutional Commission on Minority Rights.

Looking frail in his Chancery Court apartment in 2007, the 87-year-old retired lawyer said with a sudden animated burst: "What was accepted was equal rights and freedom of worship for all races. Our commission decided that Malay, Mandarin, Tamil and English should be the official languages. If you ask me, the equality of races was Lee Kuan

Yew's greatest achievement!"

If there was a defining moment in the history of multi-racialism in Singapore, it was the setting up of this commission under then-chief justice Wee Chong Jin in December 1965 to safeguard minority rights and interests and to ensure parity of status for all races and languages.

Did the Chinese push for more rights in view of their overwhelming majority? "The idea of the equality of races was accepted with no heated argument," Abisheganaden replied with no hesitation. "The Chinese understood the sensitivities of living in the Malay archipelago and were simply too sensible to want to lord over the other races."

Describing his stint with the commission as his "most memorable recollection", he said: "It's a wonder of the world that four major races should have equal rights here. We all accept one another as equals. Look at what happened in Sri Lanka, Fiji and Africa where people are still at each other's throats because of ethnic jealousy."

Arumugam Ponnu Rajah, the then-deputy chairman of the commission, said that they took the position that "there was no such thing as special rights for the minorities and that everybody must be treated alike". He remembered dismissing as "absurd" a Sikh representation that no Sikh should be allowed to cut his hair under the constitution.

In a nutshell, the commission report declared that "no one citizen has, or ought to have, less or more rights than another citizen".

From where did this idea of multi-racialism spring forth, the idea that all races should be equal in law and political representation in a racially diverse country? Was it by chance or design that Singapore managed to evolve a multi-racial polity that allowed it to escape the ethnic strife plaguing other countries?

One could go back to the Malayan Forum days in London when the young Goh Keng Swee and other students were mulling over how to free Malaya from British shackles. Inspired by socialism, which decreed the equality of men, and incensed by the colonial policy of racial segregation, they were all seized by the notion of multi-racial solidarity.

Lee's nascent views could be gleaned from his first political speech to the forum in Malaya Hall on 28 January 1950 as a 27-year-old law graduate from Cambridge University. He argued for the development of a society which was not Malay or Chinese or Indian but Malayan based on racial harmony and cooperation. He was concerned that Malaya might end up like Palestine with one race pitted against another.

When the idealistic British-educated students returned to Singapore and continued brainstorming the formation of a new party in No 38 Oxley Road, they envisaged a multi-racial, socialist, non-communist Malaya which included Singapore. The multi-racial ideal was crystallised in the PAP party symbol, manifesto and constitution.

One could also trace the idea further back to 1946 when the Malayan Union was formed and granted equal citizenship rights to all regardless of race. But the union was strongly opposed by the Malays and was quickly replaced by the Federation of Malaya in 1948 which recognised the special rights of the Malays. Eventually Malaya chose to go the route of communal politics with UMNO being the party for Malays, MCA for Chinese and MIC for Indians.

Singapore counted itself lucky for not going into communal politics, according to former Progressive Party (PP) leader A P Rajah. "As far as PP was concerned, what was to be avoided at any cost was communal politics—Chinese forming Chinese parties, Malays forming Malay parties and Indians forming Indian parties. This we thought would be the worst thing that could happen to Singapore."

He recalled that MCA tried to break into Singapore politics after the formation of his party in 1947. "But strangely enough, it didn't catch on, you know, communal politics. That much I will say for the Singaporean. He saved himself. Whereas the people in Malaya took to communal politics like ducks take to water." In his view, if MCA had started earlier, it might have succeeded and Singapore politics could have been communal as in Malaya. "We eventually succeeded in keeping them out. If the Progressives had not been that keen on keeping Singapore non-communal, today the history of Singapore might be different."

Rajah pointed out that after the Progressives came the Labour Party and PAP, both of which were non-communal. "So, mainly, politics in Singapore was conducted from the time of its inception up till now on a non-communal basis. So, PAP were not originators of non-communal politics here. They say so but they were not. We were the originators of non-communal politics."

Originator or not, PAP adopted a multi-racial strategy right from the start to mobilise mass support. It was no coincidence that the trade unions, which helped the party to romp to victory in the 1959 general election, cut across all ethnic communities. And since many PAP activists were unionists, the experience of fighting for the workers of all races ingrained in them the importance of multi-racialism.

Othman Wok related how as secretary of the Singapore Printing Employees' Union, he learnt to mix with Chinese and Indian workers for the first time in his life. Former trade unionist Mahmud Awang said he left UMNO for PAP because he believed that it was better to work for all races than to work for only one race.

Even among the Chinese-educated, multi-racial convictions ran deep. Tay Boon Too said he joined PAP to help Eurasian minister K M Byrne in the 1959 polls because he believed in the party platform of equal treatment for all. Most notably, old guard leaders such as Ong Pang Boon, Jek Yeun Thong and Lee Khoon Choy had no truck with those who clamoured for a Chinese-dominant society and a higher status for Chinese language and culture. If they had been tempted to play the Chinese card and defected to the pro-Chinese Barisan Sosialis during The Big Split of 1961, the story of Singapore would have taken a dramatically different turn.

In one of his musings, former PAP MP Chan Chee Seng said he often wondered why the other parties seemed to be so ignorant of one important principle in Singapore politics that PAP understood so well—that a party seen as being associated with any one particular race would have no electoral future, whether it was UMNO, MCA, MIC, Partai Rakyat or Barisan.

⁂

THE first glimpse of PAP-style multi-racialism frightened the wits out of the English-educated middle class. When Ong Eng Guan became PAP mayor of the city council from 1957 to 1959, he gave higher priority to vernacular languages over English in speeches, official correspondence and counter service. At times, English was left out deliberately from notices, just to confound the colonial officials.

The onus was on civil servants to look for translators to help people and not the other way round. Simultaneous translations of official proceedings became standard practice. For the first time, people in singlets and shorts could saunter into the august City Hall and listen to council meetings in their native tongues.

When Lee and company assumed power in 1959, they began putting their own stamp on multi-racialism. It was less extreme than mayor Ong's but still nerve-wracking to the anglicised middle class. For a start, they embarked on a Malayanisation exercise, renaming English-named streets and buildings to reflect the multi-racial character of Singapore.

They also placed legislative assemblymen in government ministries to help liaise with the masses in their mother tongues. Ong Pang Boon remembered that as minister for home affairs, he made sure that all official forms were printed in the four languages. He said that while it made civil service work less efficient, it was politically the right thing to do.

A poster of a drawing depicting four hands, each reflecting a different skin tone and clasped to one another, came to symbolise the party's commitment to multi-racial solidarity. *Aneka ragam ra'ayat* ("people's variety concerts" in Malay) featuring dances and songs from the four language streams were staged on the steps of City Hall and the National Theatre.

The fusion of ethnic cultures to develop a pan-Malayan culture was promoted by the newly set up ministry of culture under S Rajaratnam. As he explained: "It is true that we are trying to create a Malayan culture deliberately in the shortest possible time by pressure cooking ... I do not believe that the creation of a Malayan culture is an impossible task or that we need hundreds of years to evolve one."

This cultural initiative was to lead to the curious D J Enright affair. Enright was a British academic with the University of Singapore who argued that it was futile to institute a "sarong culture complete with *pantun* competitions". A *pantun* is a traditional form of oral Malay verse.

Maintaining that culture should at best be left to itself and the people who lived it, he said: "Who can decide in advance which seeds will fall on barren ground and which will grow ... art does not begin in a test-tube, it does not take its origin in good sentiments and clean-shaven upstanding young thoughts ... it begins where all the ladders start, in the foul rag-and-bone shop of the heart."

The next morning, he was summoned by a minister and given a letter accusing him of overstepping his role as a university professor and meddling in Singapore's domestic affairs. Stating a position which is still in force against foreigners seen to be taking part in local politics, the letter read: "This is to inform you that should you again wander from the bounds of your work for which you were granted entry into the country, then your professional visit pass will be cancelled as in all such cases. You are being paid handsomely to do the job which you are presumably qualified to do, and not to enter into the field of local politics which you are unqualified to participate.

"You would do well to leave such matters to local citizens. It is their business to solve these problems as they think fit. They have to live and die in this country. You will be packing your bags and seeking green pastures elsewhere if your gratuitous advice on these matters should land us in a mess."

In line with the PAP's election manifesto which recognised the special position of the Malays, and pending merger with Malaya, the PAP government gave precedence to Malay and made it the national language. This explained why Singapore's national emblems reflected Malay identity and culture rather than the heritage of the dominant Chinese race in Singapore.

Toh Chin Chye was assigned by the cabinet to find a new anthem to replace "God Save the Queen". The former deputy prime minister with a love for classical music picked a tune by Indonesian composer, Zubir Said, which he felt "will appeal to all races, strike no discord, be easily understood and easily remembered". "Majulah Singapura" was composed in Malay and had never been translated.

Toh was also involved in the design for the national flag. After discussions with Malay legislative assemblymen, he revealed that a crescent moon would be added to the five stars to represent an emerging country. He said: "The proposal was accepted in deference to Malay sentiments as there were also five stars on the flag of the People's Republic of China. It helped to remove any apprehension that we were building a Chinese state." The crescent moon is often seen as a symbol of Muslim identity and brotherhood.

Then came Malaysia—and the trauma of the race riots and separation. After the merger in 1963, Lee and Goh realised that their notion of multi-racialism differed dramatically from that of Malaysian prime minister Tunku Abdul Rahman and his deputy, Tun Abdul Razak. UMNO wanted a Malay-dominant model of multi-racialism. PAP sought a Malaysian Malaysia which put all races on par.

The clash of diametrically opposing ideologies opened up a Pandora's box of raw emotions which was to lead to the race riots in July and September 1964 and the eventual separation of Singapore on 9 August 1965.

The bloodletting and Singapore's experience in Malaysia was to shape the PAP leaders' thinking on multi-racialism profoundly. When Lee visited Geylang in the aftermath of the riots, he resolved that racial enclaves should be broken up and minority groups integrated into mainstream society.

As community leaders looked back, they agreed that the Malaysian episode compelled a generation of Singaporeans to be alive to the peril of ethnic animosity. Sikh advisory board chairman Surjit Singh Wasan observed that it led to "strong government involvement and deliberate actions to ensure harmony among the communities". Tamils Representative Council president R Theyvendran said that "it taught PAP that there should be moderation in racial, religious and cultural matters".

Scholars took the same view. Norman Vasu said that the riots pushed to the forefront "the importance of managing inter-communal relationships". Eugene Tan believed that the Malaysian experience gave PAP the impetus to develop its own brand of multi-racialism. With PAP's failure to institute a Malaysian Malaysia, Sharon Siddique noted, the idea was transposed to the island as Singaporean Singapore.

If there was a silver lining in those dark days, it was the emergence of a grassroots movement which had since become the most tangible symbol of racial harmony today. Forged in the crucible of carnage, the goodwill committees had evolved into the present network of citizens' consultative committees, community centre management committees, residents committees, inter-racial and religious confidence circles and the community engagement programme.

Recovering from the shock of separation, Lee and his cabinet had to think through their approach to multi-racialism: How best can Singapore go forward in developing race relations? How do you re-assure the traumatised Malays that they have a place in Singapore? How do you temper the rising expectations of the jubilant Chinese who believe that their day in the sun has finally arrived?

The PAP government's philosophy could be discerned from Lee's remarks in his post-separation press conference. Voicing his disdain of the Malaysian model, he said: "We are going to build up a system in which nobody can come in and say "one voice". Nobody can say *satu bangsa, satu bahasa, satu ugama*—one race, one language, one religion."

In another speech, Lee declared that the government would make Singapore a model multi-racial society, one which did not belong to any race but to all races. "We are an equal society. You are equal to me. Nobody is more equal than others." He guaranteed that the constitution would be redrawn with entrenched clauses to protect the minorities and could not be cancelled by any government. The constitutional commission was formed and Geoffrey Abisheganaden invited to be a member.

Reflecting on the landmark event, Muslim community leader Wan Hussin Zoohri said that Lee could have gone with the majority sentiments and favoured the Chinese but chose to go multi-racial. Alami Musa agreed that Singapore could have been a Chinese-dominated country. "I am thankful that the founding members of PAP have chosen the multi-racialism path so I know I have equal rights with my fellow Chinese countrymen."

What the PAP government did then was very unusual, according to scholars. It could have followed the path taken by neighbouring countries and favour the dominant race and its language over the minorities, for instance, Thai over Chinese in Thailand, Malay over Chinese and Indians in Malaysia, Indonesian over Chinese in Indonesia, Burman over the ethnic groups in Myanmar, and Sinhalese over Tamil in Sri Lanka.

What if Singapore had made Chinese the national language?

⚬⚬⚬

THE Malays in Singapore were devastated by separation. Suddenly they found themselves transformed overnight from being the majority community in Malaysia to a minority community in independent Singapore. To re-assure them, the constitution continued to recognise their indigenous position while granting parity of status for all races. But unlike the Malaysian constitution, it did not provide for affirmative action.

Just to recap, Article 152 (1) states that it shall be the government's responsibility "to care for the interests of the racial and religious minorities in Singapore." Article 152 (2) says that "the government shall exercise its functions in such manner as to recognise the special position of the Malays, who are the indigenous people of Singapore, and accordingly it shall be the responsibility of the government to protect, safeguard, support, and promote their political, educational, religious, economic, social and cultural interests and the Malay language." Note that the key word used is interests, not rights.

If the Chinese were too sensible to want to lord over the Malays, the Malays were too realistic to demand special rights, according to Wan Hussin Zoohri. S Rajaratnam said that the Malays had no choice but to come to terms with PAP, knowing that UMNO would never be able to form the government in Singapore.

One potential racial minefield in those years was the challenge of breaking up the Malay bastions of Geylang Serai, Kampong Kembangan and Southern Islands, and resettling the residents in public housing estates where the racial mix would mirror that of the national population.

As several former Malay PAP MPs recollected, many Malays resisted moving from what they regarded as their heartlands. This situation was not helped by UMNO leaders who began to exploit the fears of the community. Othman Wok remembered meeting an *Utusan Melayu* editor from Kuala Lumpur who asked him: "Do you expect the Malays to live in flats? Your flats look like pigeonholes from afar. How can they keep their goats and chicken?" I said: 'This is urban society, they've got to change.' " Insisting that it was against Malay culture to be uprooted from their kampungs, the editor wrote an article discouraging the Malays from moving into flats.

But in what must be the height of irony, in 1965 an UMNO-funded housing cooperative society bought 82 two-room flats in three blocks in Geylang from the Housing and Development Board (HDB) and sold them to Malays with low instalments. Then-Malaysian minister of agriculture and cooperatives Mohamed Khir Johari was moved to describe the achievements of HDB as "the greatest social evolution in Singapore".

The government's aim was to achieve a multi-racial mix in public housing estates through balloting. But by 1980, it was observed that the races were beginning to regroup in certain areas because of the sale of resale flats on the open market. The solution was the ethnic quota policy announced in 1989.

For HDB neighbourhoods, the racial limits were capped as follows: Chinese 84 per cent; Malays 22 per cent; and Indians and others 10 per cent. For HDB blocks, limits were set three percentage points higher namely, Chinese 87 per cent, Malays 25 per cent, and Indians and others 13 per cent.

The quotas sparked off a controversy which lingered to this day. One fierce critic was Rajaratnam who said: "Where in our constitution does it say there must be 75 per cent Chinese, 15 per cent Malays and 7 per cent Indians? It's stupid and dangerous ... I think it was a wrong proposal. Once you are a Singaporean, there is no race."

Defending the policy in an interview in 2007, Lee reiterated that the racial quotas ensured that the minorities were absorbed into mainstream society. Referring to the arrest of Jemaah Islamiyah militants, he noted that the policy helped in the campaign against terrorism as this meant that jihadists could not operate in isolation anywhere on the island. He added that other countries were learning from Singapore's experience.

Integration, however, did not preclude giving more autonomy and space to the Malays. Their way of life and religion was preserved with the enactment of the Administration of Muslim Law Act, the formation of MUIS as a statutory board and the setting up of a fund to build mosques in new towns.

There were other concessions. PAP Malay MPs formed a caucus to make representations to the government on issues such as the non-enlistment of Malay youths for national service and the over-zealous pinyinisation of school and estate names. Later Mendaki, a self-help group, came into being to tackle educational under-performance in the community.

The constitutional commission led to the formation of the Presidential Council for Minority Rights in 1970 to ensure that laws passed would not discriminate against any racial or religious community. In 1988, the group representation constituency (GRC) scheme was introduced to ensure the election of Malay and Indian MPs.

But the most important concession given by the government was free education for Malays from primary school to university level. It was regarded as the best way to help the economically disadvantaged Malays catch up with the Chinese.

Othman Wok recalled how the Malay MPs were brainstorming ideas to alleviate the poverty of their community when some suggested giving financial assistance in trade and industry. "But when we put it to PM Lee, he said no, the key is education. He said if a Malay is well-educated, you give him a few cents he can make $500. If he's not educated, you give him $500, it becomes 50 cents! So we agree." In 1990, the automatic waiver of university fees for Malay students was scrapped and the subsidy diverted to Mendaki to administer.

Perhaps one early litmus test of the community's confidence in the PAP government came when Malaysian PM Tunku Abdul Rahman offered land in Johor to Singapore Malays who wished to leave. Former senior minister of state Ya'acob Mohamed, known for his stirring speeches sprinkled with Koranic injunctions, recounted how he gave a robust rebuff to the offer. At Lee's request, it was repeated thrice on national radio.

This was his response: "Even though Malays had been colonised by the Portuguese, Dutch and British, and then by Japan and back to British, the Malays have never moved from their homeland. Where the feet are firmly standing on the land, that's where the rest of the life will be spent. This is our land. Why should we migrate when other people tell us to do so?" He noted that only some Malays living in Lorong 3 in Geylang took up Tunku's offer.

When it came to the Chinese community, Lee and company faced a completely different challenge—how to temper their rising expectations and demands. Given their demographic dominance and after being suppressed by British, Japanese and Malay rule for so long, the culture champions felt that it was time to re-assert their identity.

As Raj Vasil put it, many Chinese viewed Singapore as a Chinese city-state where the Chinese majority were expected to control their own destiny and organise the polity and society in terms of their own aspirations, interests and priorities.

"PAP's difficult task was to deny the Chinese this natural, and to many, an entirely rightful, urge. PAP had to persuade the Chinese not to behave and act as a dominant majority and treat Malays and Indians not as subordinate minorities that enjoyed lesser status and rights similar to those accorded to Chinese minorities elsewhere in the region. It had to educate them to view Singapore not as a Chinese city-state but as a multi-racial society that belonged equally to all its component ethnic segments."

In his memoirs, Lee gave a vivid account of how the Chinese Chamber of Commerce wanted to boost the status of the Chinese language and culture after separation. Its call was backed by the Chinese teachers' unions, owners and editors of Chinese newspapers, and leaders of clan associations.

On how he scotched the move before it grew into a campaign, Lee wrote: "On October 1, I restated that all four major languages in Singapore were official and equal ... five days later, under the full glare of TV lights, I met the committees of all four chambers of commerce. I left the Chinese representatives in no doubt that I would not allow anyone to exploit the Chinese language as a political issue. That put an end to their attempts to elevate the status of the Chinese."

Fortunately this clamour was confined to the more extreme section of the intelligentsia. Having just experienced the racial turbulence of 1964 and witnessed Singapore's acrimonious problems with Malaysia, most

Chinese grasped the sensitivities of living in a Malay region and accepted parity of status with all races.

According to Rajaratnam, the Chinese saw the danger of Malay racialism and decided to make the necessary sacrifices to make independent Singapore work. If not for the Malaysian experience, they would have resisted, he said. "So this was one of the unexpected benefits of going into Malaysia and coming out."

In the view of historian Lee Guan Kin, many ethnic Chinese accepted equality of status with the other races as they had always regarded the Malayan peninsula, not China, as their home. She pointed out that quite a number of the pioneering generation of Nantah (Nanyang University) students were caught up in the fervent tide of Malayan nation building; they learnt Malay and subscribed to the multi-racial ideal.

China scholar Gwee Yee Hean's explanation was cultural, citing studies which showed that Chinese all over the world adapted very well to local customs and cultures. "This was why Singapore Chinese accepted the reality of living in the Malay heartlands of Southeast Asia and were prepared to concede to parity of status with the Malays."

⚬≈⚬≈⚬

TEARS flowed when news broke that the last Tamil medium school in Singapore would close down in 1982. For the closely-knit Muslim Tamils who traced their roots to Kadayanallur in India, the Umar Pulavar Tamil High School on Maxwell Road had been part of their history.

Many were newspaper vendors who saw the school as their last bastion of the Tamil language. Through blood, sweat and tears, they had raised funds to build the school in 1946 and made monthly contributions for its maintenance.

S Chandra Das still remembered how emotionally distraught the school management committee members were when he announced that the government was shutting down the school because of falling enrolment and the lack of job prospects for its students. The Indian community leader and former PAP MP had put it to them: "If your children continued studying Tamil up to secondary level, what jobs could they hold? Could they all get jobs as TV announcers and *Tamil Murasu* journalists or would they all end up as office boys?

"I said, no point keeping the school. But I told them the government has a bilingual programme. 'Your children can still study Tamil, but they don't have to study all those subjects in Tamil. So I persuaded them to accept the closure. Then they said: 'Okay, but we want to retain the name.' "

He negotiated with the ministry of education, and the Tamil Language Centre on Beatty Road was renamed Umar Pulavar Tamil Language Centre. The name was also retained in the Umar Pulavar Secondary School on Maxwell Road. On top of that, a government compensation amounting to several hundred thousand dollars was used to set up the Umar Pulavar Scholarship Trust Fund.

The pain and anguish was just as acutely felt by the Chinese and Malay communities when their vernacular schools were replaced by national stream schools which used English as the main language of instruction.

Lee Guan Kin lamented that the Chinese school system in the 1950s was at "its most fully developed, with teaching in the mother tongue being offered from kindergarten to tertiary level". But within three decades, Chinese-medium primary and secondary schools ceased to exist. In 1980, Nanyang University was forced to merge with University of Singapore to form National University of Singapore.

The years between the 1960s and 1980s were the most agonising for the Chinese intellectuals, the academic said, as they were overcome by "a sense of crisis when they saw the Chinese language falling in importance and losing its place with the people. They felt hurt, helpless and pessimistic, and were worried about the irrevocable damage to the entire Chinese educational system".

Similarly the Malays were saddened by the demise of Malay schools although their *madrasahs* or religious schools were spared. They had high hopes for the Malay language and wanted their children to study in a Malay university. Yaacob Mohamed spoke mournfully of how he had to switch his children from Malay to English primary schools after separation.

Wan Hussin Zoohri admitted that the Malay community was upset by the downgrading of Malay even though it was retained as the national language. Recalling those troubled days, he said: "I saw a total shift in policy. When we were going into Malaysia, there was a series of pro-Malay policies. When we're out, there came a series of non-Malay policies, sad but inevitable."

The passing of vernacular schools was emotionally wrenching for the ethnic communities which had built and endowed the schools with their own resources—no thanks to the colonialists. As Lee once said, the people could not understand why they could run these schools under the British but had to forego them under independent Singapore.

What happened, although it was not decreed let alone enshrined in the constitution, was that over the years English had assumed a status more equal than the other languages. It became the pre-eminent language of government, courts, university, business and industry, science and technology. As a neutral medium, it became the key component of Singapore's multi-racialism.

Lee had said that if he were to state the policy openly, it would have led to problems with the Chinese community. So he let parents make the language choice themselves. Increasingly they switched their children to English-medium schools when they realised their children would have better job prospects.

Enrolment in Chinese-medium schools dropped from 45.9 per cent in 1959 to 28.5 per cent in 1965, and from 11.2 per cent in 1978 to only 2 per cent in 1982. By 1977, 99 per cent of Malay parents had opted for the English stream. In 1983, just less than 1 per cent of those eligible had registered in Chinese-medium primary schools and none in Malay-medium and Tamil-medium primary schools. In 1987, English became the sole medium of instruction in all schools.

What the British could not do without causing riots, independent Singapore had done so, marvelled Raj Vasil. "For Singapore to have achieved this dramatic change without any bloodshed, and with the concurrence of its multi-lingual populace, is a measure of the remarkably successful political management by the PAP leadership and the maturity of the Singapore people."

On the ascendance of English, Gwee Yee Hean commented: "Lee solved the multi-racial problem with the use of a language that belonged to nobody." Sharon Siddique: "It was a brilliant stroke. By promoting English as the first language for everyone, it meant that no one had a community stake in English but everyone had an economic stake in English." Wan Hussin Zoohri: "It was right for Singapore to put English ahead as the survival of the country came first."

Reflecting on his momentous decision to go with English, Lee said that this was the right move as it helped Singapore plug into the global economy. "After 1965, we had to make a decision on the common language. If we made Chinese the common language, then Chinese culture would be the dominant culture and it would have led to a breakup in society.

"So the only language that could give everybody an equal chance was English so that everybody played on the same playing field. It's not your language, it's not my language, and this was a language that connected us to the world and enabled us to survive."

⊰⊱

THEN came the great about-turn in the 1980s. As a keen observer of the education scene, Maurice Baker said he could not help being struck by the constant change in the PAP government's language policies, particularly in the way Chinese was "emphasised, de-emphasised and re-emphasised".

"Initially the government allowed Chinese, Malay, Tamil and English schools to co-exist but when many Chinese students became disposed to communism, it decided to cut down on their influence by promoting English."

With the disappearance of the Chinese schools, Lee began to realise the cultural consequences, the former academic and diplomat said. "Having almost destroyed Chinese education, Lee then reversed the policy. He saw the danger to a society not rooted in the language. He saw what happened to the West Indies people who lost their culture and spoke broken English."

Political pundits pointed out that PAP leaders became very concerned with what they viewed as the onslaught of less desirable Western values and the spectre of deracination and de-culturalisation. They feared that Singapore might end up as a Westernised society which had lost its Asian cultural moorings.

The result: a renewed emphasis on mother tongues to provide Singaporeans with cultural ballast and keep a lifeline to their ancestral cultures and history. The ethnic communities were encouraged to re-establish their identities through language campaigns and cultural festivals. Self-help groups were set up to tackle educational and social problems within their communities.

In 1979, the Speak Mandarin campaign was launched. A year later, the government converted several Chinese secondary schools into special assistance plan schools to arrest falling standards in Chinese and preserve traditional Chinese ethos. There was even a short-lived experiment to introduce religious knowledge in schools with Confucian ethics as one option. The programme collapsed because it aroused ethnic suspicions and raised the danger of cross-proselytisation.

Scholars described this turnaround in policy as the re-ethnicisation of Singapore. Speak to Lee Guan Kin and she would say that the change started at the end of the 1970s when the political leadership believed that ethnic cultures were weakening and that Western culture was causing a rise in individualism and loss of family values.

"The melting pot idea couldn't work anymore. The government encouraged the different ethnic groups to seek their cultural roots. Confucianism and Asian values were promoted. Chinese intellectuals who were marginalised were given more space," said the academic who had written extensively on the plight of the Chinese intelligentsia.

In his book *Asianising Singapore: The PAP's Management of Ethnicity*, Raj Vasil cited a political reason for re-ethnicisation—the need to shore up the electoral support of the Chinese-speaking population because of declining votes from the Malays in the 1988 elections. Lee Guan Kin noted that it was when the dissatisfaction of the "silent majority" was reflected in the big swing to the opposition during the 1991 general election that the government paid more attention to the Chinese community.

Not unexpectedly, the move to re-Asianise Singaporeans ran into stiff opposition especially from its harshest critic, S Rajaratnam. In one speech, he said that Singaporeans must "remember that this exercise is like searching at night in a dark room for a black hen which may be running around in China, India or in the sands of Arabia.

"The search for roots has imperceptibly drifted into a search to strengthen Chinese, Indian, Malay and now, for the first time, a Eurasian identity. At this rate, there will be a long ethnic queue of Singapore citizens proclaiming Sikh identity, Jewish identity, Ceylon Tamil identity, Indian Tamil identity, Cantonese identity, Hokkien identity—and goodbye Singapore identity."

The collision of views was captured most memorably in the Singaporean Singapore versus return-to-roots debate with Rajaratnam calling for a common identity to subsume all ethnic identities and Lee contending that the different races should develop their ethnic identities as a cultural counterweight against undesirable Western values. Older Singaporeans might remember the extraordinary verbal spat on the Speak Mandarin campaign in 1990 between Rajaratnam and Ow Chin Hock, a PAP MP and staunch advocate of Chinese culture.

As Maurice Baker saw it: "Rajaratnam was working towards a Singaporean Singapore society in which people did not think of ethnic identities. But Lee wanted to emphasise ethnicity to maintain cultural roots. It is very difficult to pronounce whether this is good or bad. It depends on your attitude to culture."

On reflection, Wan Hussin Zoohri thought that Rajaratnam's view was too utopian. "The hard reality is that human beings are what they are. They are bound by their race and religion. Rajaratnam forgot that Muslims are very religious. I'm not sure the Chinese want to forget their long history. Rajaratnam was a thinker but in terms of human practice, Lee had better judgment."

Indian community leader R Theyvendran concurred. "The Rajaratnam model would not have worked in Singapore. History is in favour of Lee. You cannot just overlook the ethnicity of a people. It is better to recognise it, accept it—and then build "an all-inclusive society" from it."

⁂

THE iron hand in the velvet glove is a metaphor often used to characterise the PAP government. Certainly while it preferred the soft approach in managing race relations, it had no qualms about playing hardball with those who crossed the line—whether they were communalists or chauvinists, religious zealots or racist bloggers, Islamic militants or Christian sects deemed prejudicial to public order.

Action had been taken against those who identified with the agendas of their motherlands and sought to import them to Singapore—Chinese who championed Maoism; Malays who wanted to re-create an Islamic state; Sikhs who celebrated the assassination of Indian Prime Minister Indira Gandhi; and Tamils who supported the Tamil Tigers' war against the Sri Lankan government.

In 1987, the authorities had a showdown with the Catholic Church when it accused a group of "Marxist conspirators" of using church bodies as "cover" organisations for political agitation. Fifteen years earlier, Jehovah's Witnesses was banned because its members refused to do military service and swear allegiance to the state.

The crackdown against militant Islamic groups started in the 1960s. One was the *Angkatan Revolusi Tentera Islam Singapura* or the Revolutionary Islamic Army of Singapore accused of inciting communal clashes between Chinese and Malays. Another was the Singapore People's Liberation Organisation group charged with seeking to overthrow the government through violence.

With the rise of new media came a new challenge. In 2005, two Chinese bloggers were jailed for mocking Islam and insulting Malays; they became the first to be charged under the Sedition Act. In 2007, the Criminal Penal Code was amended to cover racial and religious slurs over the Internet and electronic media.

Over the decades, the government had assembled an arsenal of laws to keep the peace. The most significant was the Maintenance of Religious Harmony Act enacted in 1990 to keep religion out of politics. It was designed to stop religious leaders from mounting political campaigns and to curb overzealous proselytisation.

When it came to racial and religious harmony, it was clear that the PAP's approach was not to leave anything to chance. As one observer commented: "This is one area where the government does not leave it to market forces, to natural evolution, to self-correcting mechanisms; the government's hand will come whenever it sees anything amiss."

Or as Tamils Representative Council chief R Theyvendran put it: "This is a government which believes in nipping a problem in the bud. No problem is allowed to brew, fester and grow—and that's how it has kept the peace all these years."

⋰⋱⋰⋱

WHITHER multi-racialism? As Singaporeans and scholars peer into an uncertain future, they wonder and worry if the country's carefully woven multi-racial fabric can absorb the rapid influx of new immigrants and ever-swelling foreign workforce, as well as bear the full brunt of globalisation and cosmopolitanism, without snapping.

There is already a growing disquiet about heightened racial consciousness stemming from ethnic-based policies and rising religious fervour. The soul-searching debate on the question of national identity sees no end for at the heart of the Singapore model lies a conundrum—on one hand, it expects the various races to develop a common identity; on the other it encourages them to maintain their ethnic identities.

Apart from trying to reconcile these contradictions, a whole gamut of issues is staring Singaporeans in the face: How will a projected population of 6.5 million affect the racial balance? Shouldn't the current race categorisation be re-examined in view of the growing trend of inter-marriages and the rise of multiple identities? Does race matter when you don't know what your grandchildren will look like? Is there a danger of race conflicts in Malaysia spilling over the causeway?

Will Singapore be increasingly sinicised? Will Chinese Singaporeans develop a greater ethnic identification with China when it emerges as a global superpower? Can new immigrants from mono-cultural countries be socialised into the values of multi-racial living? Why should rich and mobile new citizens living in their own enclaves bother about local sensitivities? Will cosmopolitan values override multi-racial values?

Will religious revivalism prove to be a chink in Singapore's multi-racial armour? Might Christian evangelism pose a bigger problem than Islamic fundamentalism? Thinking the unthinkable, can Singaporeans rally together and keep their faith in one another in the event of a terrorist attack involving Islamic militants?

The questions keep piling up as the new-generation leaders wrestle with the colossal challenges of multi-racialism in an age of wrenching social changes and unprecedented economic volatility. Their predecessors had kept the racial peace for the last 40 years. Can they do the same for the next 40 years?

36

Wealth-sharing Singapore-style

PROMINENT Chinese tycoon Tan Lark Sye was incensed when an expanse of rolling land in Redhill owned by the Hokkien clan association was gazetted for acquisition by the PAP government in 1961.

The chairman of the Singapore Hokkien Huay Kuan, which looked after the welfare of immigrants from Fujian province in China, was incredulous that the compensation for some 20 hectares amounted to no more than $570,000 or 26 cents per sq foot. Tan, who was famously known as founder of the defunct Nanyang University, blasted the socialist-styled government for being "worse than the communists" in the way it took over what the clansmen regarded as ancestral property.

The government, which was barely three years old, retorted that if the rubber magnate were living in a communist country, he would have been branded an exploiter of the people and his property confiscated without even a cent of compensation.

In 1979, it was the turn of the Cantonese and Hakka clans to stagger from a big blow. Their century-old Chinese burial ground called Peck San Theng (or "jade mountain pavilion") was suddenly earmarked for acquisition. Sprawled over 10 hillocks and covering 121 hectares, it was the final resting place for about 170,000 mainly Chinese immigrants. Its owner was the Singapore Kwong Wai Siew Peck San Theng, an umbrella body for 16 Cantonese and Hakka clan associations. As clan adviser Leong Siew Kwai recalled in 2008: "We were shocked when we received the news because it meant the end of burial services for our members."

With its future hanging in the balance, Peck San Theng decided to switch from burial to cremation to maintain the tradition of ancestor worship and promote the Confucian value of *shen zhong zhui yuan*, meaning "to hold a proper funeral for deceased parents and pay regular respect to them".

In exchange for the cemetery, following negotiations with the authorities, the clan body was given a three-hectare piece of land on a

99-year lease and a cash compensation of $4.95 million or about 2 cents per sq ft. A 100,000-niche columbarium, a community hall and other amenities were built on the land.

Fast forward to 2008. The Redhill site acquired from the Hokkien Huay Kuan had turned into a housing estate bounded by Leng Kee Road, Jalan Tiong and Lengkok Bahru opposite Redhill MRT station. Redhill or *ang sua* in Hokkien, so-called after its red lateritic soil, had become a much-coveted residential area because of its redevelopment and proximity to the city.

What the Hokkien clan lost, a generation of Redhill residents gained— not just a home and a vibrant estate with every conceivable public amenity but undreamed-of asset appreciation. In the 1960s, a three-room flat was bought for about $6,000. In 2008, it exchanged hands at about $240,000. One five-room flat was resold for a staggering $620,000.

What happened to Peck San Theng cemetery? By 2008, it had been transformed into Bishan New Town housing more than 100,000 people. Any superstitions about living on a former graveyard were swiftly dispelled when the first HDB flats to be put on sale were snapped up like hotcakes. "I remember I waited for nearly six years before I got my new five-room executive apartment on Bishan Street 11 in 1986," said artist and art lecturer Wee Beng Chong.

Bishan had since acquired the social cachet of being the Tanglin of public housing—a self-contained town with an MRT station and bus interchange, shopping, business and entertainment facilities, government offices, big banks and premier schools. Raffles Institution stood cheek-by-jowl with Peck San Theng columbarium.

This unprecedented and breathtaking act of acquiring land at very low prices to build heavily subsidised public housing for the masses had often been acclaimed as the PAP government's greatest act of socialism.

When the party came into power in 1959, it discovered that the state did not own even half of Singapore's total land area. Up to the time when Singapore became independent in 1965, it owned no more than 10 per cent of the land in the central business district.

It began amending the Land Acquisition Ordinance of 1920, which covered only waste and arable land, to ensure that landowners could not profit from accidental fires and that land reclamation could be carried out without having to pay huge compensations to landowners who lost their sea frontages.

Further changes were made giving the government more and more power to acquire land. All these culminated in the Land Acquisition Act of 1966 which basically compelled all private landowners to give up whatever land or property they owned when the government required them for public purposes.

Former permanent secretary Ngiam Tong Dow recalled writing a policy paper in which he made the case for the price of acquired land to be pegged at the price of undeveloped land. "The argument is very simple. If the state were to put in the facilities to make your land more valuable, it would pay you for just the ownership of the land but not for the improvement of the land."

As then-law and national development minister E W Barker made clear, the amount of compensation was based on two principles. First, that no landowner should benefit from development which had taken place at public expense and, second, that the price paid for acquired land should not be higher than what the land would be worth had the government not carried out development in the area.

Was it any wonder that the draconian act had been called the Robin Hood law as it meant taking from the rich to give to the poor? Indeed it struck fear in the landowning class. Vast tracts of plantations and farmland were acquired. Even prime property on Orchard Road was not spared. No land was sacrosanct, not even sacred burial ground.

Retired businessman Pang Tai Heng remembered his sense of panic when 4,000 sq ft of his land in Geylang was acquired. He thought that Singapore was turning into a communist state but was relieved to learn later that the government would give some compensation and use the land for public benefit.

It was reported that Goodwood Hotel tycoon Khoo Teck Puat gave up 1.4 million sq ft of private land. Bukit Sembawang lost its rubber estates in Seletar and Yio Chu Kang. Overseas-Chinese Banking Corporation, Lee Rubber and Straits Trading were among the big companies whose land was also acquired.

By 1976, 10 years after the act came into effect, the percentage of state-owned land went up to 67 per cent, from less than 50 per cent in 1959. By 1985, the figure shot up to 76 per cent. By 2004, about 90 per cent of land was owned by the government and its statutory boards, according to the Singapore Land Authority.

No less than then-prime minister Lee Kuan Yew admitted in 1985 that the PAP government had been playing Robin Hood by using overriding power to acquire land cheaply for low-cost public housing. His declared aim: "a 100 per cent property-owning democracy".

Given his legal training in Cambridge, he knew that the act would breach a fundamental tenet in British constitutional law. But he believed that the sanctity of a society seeking to preserve itself should prevail over the sanctity of property—an Englishman's home may be his castle but not the Singaporean's.

Retired academic Lee Ting Hui described the law as a great socialist act which redistributed the country's resources between the haves and have-nots. "Without it, landowners could demand millions and millions of dollars from the government and there could be no cheap public housing for the people, especially the poor."

The leftists viewed the drastic legislation as Singapore's equivalent of land reform. Chan Sun Wing, a former PAP parliamentary secretary who later became a communist guerrilla, compared it to the situation in revolutionary China when the communists seized land from the landowning classes and gave it to the peasants. He said that PAP did not want to be like the Kuomingtang which was reviled for conniving with wealthy landowners to oppress the people when it ruled China.

But not everyone saw land acquisition as an act of socialism. Scholar Neo Boon Siong contended that the government was targeting the land not the ownership. "Land wasn't just acquired from the rich, it was also acquired from the poor. The objective was not to redistribute but to develop the country."

Lim Chin Joo was a former collector of land revenue. In 1972 and 1973, he was involved in evicting several hundred families of mainly Hakka smallholders from Pulau Tekong as the island was needed by the defence ministry. He remembered spending two months going from house to house to talk to the residents. "They were all unhappy as they were being uprooted from a place where they had lived for generations. I felt very sorry for them because they were poor, unlike landowners and corporations. They were paid about 30 to 40 cents per sq ft. It was an emotional experience for me as I felt as if I was removing one whole community."

His view was that heavily subsidised public housing was achieved at the expense of the people—rich and poor—whose land was acquired cheaply. His hope was that the successful Singaporeans of today would never forget the sacrifices made by previous generations for the public good.

Looking back on the acquisition of Peck San Theng cemetery, clan elder Leong Siew Kwai said they were glad that they gave up the land for the good of the country. "After all, Lee Kuan Yew had once said that while the needs of the dead must be looked after, those of the living were even more urgent."

Reflected former PAP-turned-Barisan Sosialis legislative assemblyman Low Por Tuck, who represented the clan group in negotiating with the authorities: "If not for the land acquisition act, how could 90 per cent of Singapore's population become property owners in such a small country?"

⚬⚬❧⚬⚬

TO the pioneering generation, land acquisition and public housing encapsulated the notion of social equity in action. Together with leadership and leadership renewal, incorruptibility, meritocracy and multi-racialism, they formed the PAP bedrock of governance.

Just what is social equity? By one definition, it means the more you have, the more you give to upkeep the larger public good; the less you have, the more you receive from the state to give you a lift-up. Some take it to mean full and unfettered participation in the political, economic and cultural life of the community. Others prefer to see it as a means to help the disadvantaged and discriminated and to redress past and present injustices.

Political science academic Ho Khai Leong equated social equity with "narrowing the gap between the rich and the poor". Governance scholar Neo Boon Siong saw it as "equalising opportunities for all citizens, irrespective of family background and income". To former top policy-maker Ngiam Tong Dow, it meant equal access to jobs, housing and education.

Put simply in the Singapore context, social equity can be described as sharing the fruits of progress and prosperity through economic growth, job creation, education, housing, health care and other public goods. Lee Kuan Yew used to say that it meant "doing the most good for the most people most of the time".

If you read Part One of this book, you would be able to trace the swirling notions of social equity in the PAP to the socialist ideals and mindsets of its founding members. As students in Britain ruled by Clement Attlee's Labour Party, they were much influenced by its socialist policies. A system in which the people owned and managed the means of production and distribution of goods was seen as the unquestionable solution to the capitalist exploitation of Malaya and Singapore.

Goh Keng Swee joined the Fabian Society which laid the ideological foundation for the Labour Party. Toh Chin Chye was enamoured of Britain's national health service which provided free services for all citizens. Lee campaigned assiduously for a Labour Party MP.

At about the same time, the Chinese-educated founding members of PAP were inspired by the rise of socialism in newly independent Asian and African countries and by the emergence of communism in China.

When Ong Eng Guan became mayor from 1957 to 1959, the people had a taste of PAP-style socialism and egalitarianism. His wildly populist oratory and radical changes in the city council won mass support for the party and paved the way for its victory in the 1959 general election. He held rousing meetings for peons and cleaners and increased the pay for subordinate staff and daily rated workers. He ended the exclusive recruitment of the English-educated by giving jobs to vernacular-school leavers. He sacked expatriates and civil servants who did not serve the public to his satisfaction.

The mayor's municipal achievements gave the public a sneak preview of what could be achieved by the PAP at the national level—public clinics and mobile dispensaries for the poor, electricity and gas supply for homes, crèches for working mothers, street lamps in remote areas, improved drains, new and renovated public lavatories, bus shelters, children's playgrounds and parks.

Ong was hailed as Robin Hood by former PAP MP Fong Sip Chee who said that the mayor "did tremendous good by arousing the people while Lee played elder statesman in the legislative assembly". Reminisced former politician Ong Chang Sam: "In the eyes of the people, he was a hero."

Given the fear and terror that the Ong mayorship struck among the English-educated upper and middle classes, imagine their nervous trepidation when the PAP finally swept into power in May 1959.

Here's a flavour of the leaders' fiery socialist rhetoric at the hustings: A speech on labour indicted the then-Lim Yew Hock government for helping employers more than workers and for being lax in acting against companies that breached the labour code. A speech on the economy alleged that $800 million of Singapore's capital was invested in overseas projects and foreign investments which did not benefit the people and accused the government of giving large grants to favoured businessmen.

As the men in white moved into City Hall, the uppermost question was: Would they implement a socialist agenda? Businessmen and investors were on tenterhooks. British companies were especially fearful of asset seizure and made plans to move to Malaya. Landowners lived in mortal fear that their properties would be expropriated.

If there were growing differences in the party between what was called the moderate camp led by Lee and the radical leftists led by Lim Chin Siong, they were not apparent at that time. Very few were aware of the divergence of views over social and economic policy.

Plough through the oral history interview with James Puthucheary and you will catch some glimpses of the ideological tussle between the former leftist economist and then-finance minister Goh Keng Swee over the proposal for a steel mill. As the then-head of the Industrial Promotion Board, the predecessor of the Economic Development Board (EDB), Puthucheary swore by state ownership.

But Goh and Albert Winsemius, the former United Nations Development Plan (UNDP) mission leader, overruled him. Puthucheary said: "I want it to be state-owned, they thought it should be private. I saw the steel industry as the nub of all industrialisation and I didn't want to give it to one or two or X number of private individuals. And I think with the wisdom of hindsight, Singapore did well to kick me out."

As he reflected on how Singapore had turned out under PAP, he said: "I've been very critical of Goh during the fight. I have very great regard for him. I mean I have not shared his great beliefs in private enterprise but I supposed he was right and I was wrong. Singapore had benefited from it."

CERTAINLY the Singapore of today would not have materialised if Puthucheary's views had prevailed over Goh's. Just imagine what the island would be like if socialist orthodoxy had won the day. Cuba? Burma?

Very early on in the government, Goh and Lee began to distance themselves from the doctrinaire socialism that they espoused during their election campaign to garner popular support. Even though it was ostensibly a labour government, they were determined not to be held ransom to dogma. It started to clamp down on industrial strife by clipping the wings of militant unions, introducing legislation to favour business and investments, and retaining the powers of preventive detention. Pragmatism overrode ideology.

Realising the limitations of an entrepôt economy and uncertain prospects of a common market with Malaya, Goh cottoned on to the idea of developing export industries and attracting investments from multi-national companies at a time when they were taboo to newly independent countries.

In 1960, Dutch industrialist Winsemius and his secretary I F Tang visited Singapore on a UNDP mission. Soon after, Singapore's economic masterplan was rolled out. Jurong industrial estate was born. So were EDB, DBS, JTC, NOL, PSA and all the acronyms which encapsulated The Singapore Story.

As Goh explained then: "The scope for realising socialism in Singapore is narrow. The entrepôt trade cannot be socialised. Such factories as we now have are hardly worth nationalising and they should remain in private ownership. PAP will save every cent it can before it thinks of putting up taxes. Private enterprise, both of local and overseas origin, will be encouraged and helped; capital loans will be available to private industry through EDB and there will be no restrictions on the transfer abroad of profits and capital." He could not have sounded more capitalistic.

To Lee and Goh, it was crystal clear that indulging in ideological jargon was a meaningless exercise when the life-and-death priority was to develop the economy to create jobs, jobs and more jobs at a time when unemployment was spiralling into double digit.

"Without economic growth, we die," Goh famously said. His oft-quoted dictum best summed up the PAP philosophy for Singapore. The primacy of economic growth continued to be upheld by his successors to this day.

Ngiam Tong Dow was privy to Goh's thinking as permanent secretary (finance) and EDB chairman. As he elaborated: "The government's philosophy is to bake the cake first, then worry about how to slice it. Grow the economy first, then talk about how to share the income. Most countries think of just distributing the income and end up sharing misery."

Full employment and rising income was thus seen as the best way to achieve social equity. Ngiam said: "In those early days, our focus was very clear—the creation of jobs. We just concentrated on creating jobs, any kind of jobs as long as they were legal, of course. There were no high-tech or low-tech jobs.

"Goh used to say to me: 'Look, Ngiam, I don't care how you do it. Every week I must open three factories.' So I said: 'What about joss paper?' He said: 'I don't mind.' So he opened factories for joss paper, peanut butter, things that you really consider low-tech today."

This explained why garment factories sprouted in those days as they could absorb a large number of workers readily. Pictures of rows of women treading on sewing machines were proudly displayed in official publications. There were factories which produced matchsticks, plastic tooth brushes, cotton wool, zip fasteners and yes, chewing gum.

Today job creation remained the unswerving focus of the new-generation leaders. What any man in the street wanted, as minister-cum-labour leader Lim Swee Say expounded passionately in 2008, was to earn a good living and live a good life. "Since the PAP came to power, decade after decade it has been able to create high employment for Singaporeans of all backgrounds."

Governance guru Neo Boon Siong had gone through a wide range of public policies in Singapore with a fine academic tooth comb. "But ultimately, the main social policy is to create jobs," he concluded. "If you're employed, you can feed your own family. And if the economy is moving, income will increase faster than inflation. Jobs are very important. You can be a university graduate but if there are no jobs, you can't go anywhere. That's why some of our foreign domestic maids who are graduates come here to work. They are educated but can't find jobs in their country."

Explaining why employment mattered in terms of social equity, the professor said: "Housing and health care are consumption, they provide a baseline so that you don't fall below. Education is linked to employment. The last two allow anyone regardless of his current state to move up socially. So that's dynamic. Employment is a very critical part."

⚓

AFTER technician Leong Yin and his wife, Choo Bat Eng, tied the nuptial knot, they bought a three-room HDB flat in Toa Payoh in 1969 for $7,800. To their delight, their main asset kept appreciating in value year after year.

In 2000, the block they were living in was among those picked by the Housing and Development Board (HDB) for the selective en bloc redevelopment scheme. Under this scheme, old flats were demolished to make way for new ones. The aim was to intensify land use while keeping residents within the neighbourhood.

When the new flats were ready, the couple and their four children were allotted a spanking new four-room unit on the 35th floor. Thanks to a $30,000 grant from the HDB, all they had to shell out was another $30,000. Suddenly, lo and behold, the Leongs found themselves living in a flat with a panoromic view worth a quarter of a million dollars in 2006.

The story of Singapore is really the story of how ordinary Singaporeans have benefited from subsidised public housing and enjoyed asset appreciation under five decades of PAP rule. Many had capitalised on rising HDB resale flat prices to upgrade to private property and build on their wealth.

If land acquisition formed one side of the socialist equation, then public housing represented the other. It was regarded as the most visible face of social equity. Ngiam saw public housing as "the most tangible manifestation of progress." Political science scholar Ho Khai Leong described it as "the policy of an enlightened leadership willing to share the prosperity of the country".

By subsidising home ownership, as the argument went, the government had buffered Singaporeans against rising housing costs and brought about a redistribution of wealth which benefited all races. It was noted that even in successful countries such as Japan, South Korea and Taiwan, affordable quality housing still proved elusive.

As the centrepiece in its 1959 party manifesto, public housing was the top priority of the PAP government from day one. Confronted by urban squalor depicted by the Western press as one of the worst in the world, it had to live up to its pledge of providing cheap mass housing.

HDB was thus formed in 1960. Within 10 years, under the no-nonsense stewardship of Lim Kim San, it broke the back of the housing problem by building 147,000 flats. In 1960, only nine per cent of the population lived in public housing. In 2007, 81 per cent resided in about 900,000 flats.

As he looked back on the progress of public housing, Liu Thai Ker, who was HDB chief architect and chief executive between 1979 and 1989, kept repeating how lucky Singaporeans were to enjoy hefty subsidies and the benefits of painstaking town planning that went into each HDB estate.

For some smaller flats, he noted, the government even had to subsidise construction cost. Convinced that the rent of a one-room flat in 2008 was the same as in 1960—about $40—he asked this writer to check with HDB. He was right. What this meant, he said, was that "the government is totally committed to making sure everybody has a place to live in."

But what really exemplified social equity and made it the social marvel of the world was universal home ownership. In 2008, about 95 per cent of the flats were owned by residents. This meant that almost every citizen had a tangible stake in the country and its future, a stake whose value corresponded with the growth in the economy. According to a survey in 2006, each HDB household was estimated to have an average housing equity worth about $154,000.

The sale of subsidised flats, however, did not mark the end of the government's social equity exercise. Public housing estates had been maintained continuously to keep them spick and span and upgraded periodically to enhance their value. "This is why our apartments such as those in Marine Parade which are 20 years old still look good. Take a bus across the causeway, and look at the condition of the public housing apartment blocks there. You will know the difference," S Dhanabalan pointed out.

According to the former national development minister, the government viewed the upgrading of older public housing estates as another way of redistributing wealth. As upgrading was highly subsidised, he said, what flat-owners paid was nowhere near the full cost. What's more, he added, Singaporeans were allowed to buy a second HDB flat. "That means they had two bites of the cherry which I really think is very, very generous. In the early days, most people could only afford a three-room flat. When their incomes went up and their family got bigger, they wanted a bigger apartment, so they had to be given another bite of the cherry."

Another social equity consideration came into play when HDB decided to prevent the emergence of segregated estates based on class and income level. Thus three-room and five-room flats were blended in an estate so that the residents would come from different educational and occupational backgrounds. Such a policy would also throw up leaders to head the various grassroots bodies to look after the neighbourhood.

The injection of condominiums into public housing estates such as Toa Payoh, Simei, Bishan and Ang Mo Kio was also seen as another initiative to counter social stratification. "So you don't have a situation where workers live in one area, and the professionals in another area. They all live together and intermingle," explained Dhanabalan.

He related an anecdote by a lecturer from India about a government housing estate in New Delhi where residents were housed based on the type of work they did. "Those doing menial jobs are concentrated in one area and take a particular bus. So if you queue up there for the bus, people know you are from that part of the public housing."

HDB had also built public housing in the central area where land value was much higher. This was to ensure that HDB flat-buyers enjoyed a wider range of location choices as well as to facilitate social integration in all residential areas including the prime districts.

One breathtaking example of HDB's new generation of public housing within walking distance of the central business district was the 50-storey Pinnacle@Duxton. Comprising seven blocks connected by sky bridges at the 26th and 50th storeys, it would pierce the sky as the island's tallest public housing project when completed in end-2009. What made the iconic project even more significant was its location on the spot where the first two HDB blocks in the Tanjong Pagar area were built. Blocks 1 and 2 on Cantonment Road were launched in 1963 by then-PM Lee Kuan Yew.

No account of the public housing success story would be complete without mentioning the Central Provident Fund (CPF) scheme which made universal home ownership for Singaporeans possible. Although home ownership was introduced in 1964, it did not take off until 1968 when people were allowed to use their CPF savings to finance their flats. Under the scheme, Singaporeans could buy their own flats without forking out any cash. By taking up subsidised mortgage loans offered by HDB, many found that their monthly instalment through CPF was less than the rent of a similar-sized private apartment.

In recent years, however, the social equity element in public housing had been clouded by controversy over the issue of subsidy. In the early days, subsidies for public housing were clear-cut but when the method of calculation changed from a cost-based to a market-based approach from the mid-1990s, house buyers began to question HDB's definition of subsidy. They noted that the prices of new HDB flats were based on the market prices of resale HDB flats and not the cost of construction. As land was acquired at a low pre-development price and as flat prices kept rising, they asked, where was the subsidy? The criticism was especially strident among those who bought and resold at a loss or found themselves with negative equity.

As early as in 1985, then-PM Lee had explained the need to switch to market-based pricing. He said that "each block has to be priced differently because they are differently priced. We know that when they are resold, whether in Tanjong Pagar or Whampoa, there's a tremendous difference in prices." Three years later, then-national development minister S Dhanabalan told parliament: "We must safeguard land for our children. The only way we can be fair to all in our present and future generations is to value HDB land at market rates ... As long as the HDB sells its flats at a price below what they can fetch in the market, the purchasers enjoy a subsidy."

Affordability had also become a bone of contention for many young and less well-off Singaporeans who feared that continuing price hikes would put new and resale flats out of their reach. They were also apprehensive that they would miss out on the asset gains reaped by an earlier generation.

HDB's response was that it benchmarked new flat prices to comparable resale flat prices in the vicinity and priced new flats below it so that buyers enjoyed a generous subsidy. In a letter to *The New Paper* in 2008, it noted that the subsidies were reflected by the average deficit of about $530 million incurred under HDB's home ownership activity over the past three years. It added that 70 per cent of new flat buyers were able to service their mortgage loans entirely by their CPF contributions without the need for cash payments.

⚬⚭⚬

SAM Tan Chin Siong could have gone to Chinese High after primary school. But he chose Tuan Mong High so that he could walk to school and use the school uniform and textbooks of a neighbour's son who had dropped out.

From primary and secondary school to Hwa Chong Junior College and on to the National University of Singapore, the middle of five children had to depend on the waiver of school fees, bursaries and a People's Association scholarship to see him through. His father was a taxi driver who died of stomach cancer when he was in secondary school. His mother worked as a coffee shop assistant to make ends meet. His sisters gave up their dreams of higher education because of poverty.

In 2008, Tan was the executive director of the Chinese Development Assistance Council (CDAC) and an MP for Tanjong Pagar GRC. He lived with his teacher wife and three children in a three-storey terrace house in Upper Serangoon. As he ruminated: "Before my father died, he said the only way out of poverty was through receiving a good education. There was no way I could have done better in life without the opportunities offered to me in the Singapore education system."

His is a familiar story mirroring the lives of legions of Singaporeans who assumed leading positions in government, economy, society, business and the professions. The cabinet minister who sold noodles in his boyhood, the permanent secretary whose father drove a taxi, the CEO whose mother washed clothes for a living ... such were the innumerable examples which embodied the Singapore Dream.

In Neo Boon Siong's view, social mobility was the biggest but most underplayed achievement of the PAP government. Housing and health care constituted consumption, employment provided a means of livelihood, but it was education which enabled a person to improve continuously and rise beyond his station in life.

"That's why, for many of us, we can move from very low income working class to middle income class in one generation," said the public policy professor who graduated from National University of Singapore and received his doctorate from Pittsburgh University in America. He lived with his wife and two children in a semi-detached house in Bukit Timah, a far cry from the Jalan Besar three-room flat that he grew up in with his younger brother. His father was a taxi driver who never went to school, his mother a housewife.

Former history lecturer Lee Ting Hui also related his life story to make the point that it was very difficult to over-estimate the importance of education. If not for bursaries, he said, he would not have had the chance to attend school and university. His three sisters did not go to school so that he and his younger brother could do so. To this day, he felt conscience-stricken and duty-bound to look after his sisters because of their sacrifice.

Singapore in 1959 was teeming with the illiterate and semi-literate masses. Many youngsters dropped out of school to work and support the family. Former senior parliamentary secretary Chan Chee Seng, who had only four years of formal schooling, recalled that many of his fellow legislative assemblymen did not complete their studies. "Most people of my generation were not educated. Many of us couldn't even write our names."

Education did not take top priority until the PAP government resolved its most pressing problems, according to Ngiam. "In the first phase of development, the most compelling problem was jobs. So Lee sent Goh Keng Swee to the ministry of finance and Hon Sui Sen to the economic development board to create jobs. After the first 10 years, we almost reached full employment.

"In 1965, it was defence. By around the end of the 1970s, our defence force was quite credible. From then on, we were spending a lot of money on education. That's worth it because education means increasing the knowledge of the people so that they can fish by themselves. That is the basis of Singapore's strength."

The progress of education can be gleaned from these statistics: primary school enrolment increased from 266,625 to 336,163 between 1959 and 1963 when one new school was built every three weeks; secondary school enrolment jumped from 48,723 to 84,425 during the same period. In 2006, the total enrolment stood at 530,423 including 30,726 in junior colleges and the centralised institutes.

Before Chan Kai Yau became director of education from 1975 to 1982, he was a mathematics teacher. He remembered that by about 1960, close to 5,000 teachers from English, Chinese, Malay and Tamil schools were under training. If they taught in the afternoon, they were trained in the morning and vice-versa. Schools had to run two sessions each day.

Having witnessed the transformation of Singapore from 1959 to 2008, he singled out education as the most important factor in social mobility. "You can't measure success in education within 5 or 10 yrs. It has to be 30, 40 yrs. Now you can see the tremendous difference in the well-being of the people."

Drawing from his personal experience, he noted that in the 1950s most people finished only primary school and ended up as blue-collar workers and odd job labourers. These days, when he met people of that generation at the wedding ceremonies he solemnised as a justice of peace, he would discover that at least half of their children were university graduates.

What struck him most were the spectacular strides in higher education. When he was studying in the University of Malaya—the only tertiary institution on the peninsula in the 1950s—he was one of about 500 to 600 students. In 2008, some 32,000 students were enrolled in the

National University of Singapore alone and it was just one of three public universities here not counting the five polytechnics and two polytechnic-level arts colleges.

Dhanabalan was struck by the makeover of the Institutes of Technical Education (ITEs) which provided new and exciting career pathways for the less academically inclined. "Just look at the resources being lavished on the ITEs to help young people boost their earning power. At one time they were considered dead-ends. Now you see the image change. There are good teachers, good facilities, great emphasis and promotion."

Indeed, to many interviewees, equality of access to education was considered the best form of social equity as it redistributed resources across all classes and provided the key to social and economic advancement.

As Neo Boon Siong summed it up: "Equal opportunity means equal access. We are all measured by the same yardstick so if you don't do well, you don't go to a good class. Your social status does not matter. You cannot pay your way to go to a better class. Regardless of parents' background or income, you and I have the same opportunity as everyone else."

Of course, education never failed to attract more than its fair share of critics. Not all scholars shared Neo's view. Sociologist Chua Beng Huat argued that meritocracy worked only if everybody started from the same base. "How can meritocracy work in society when some don't even have money to send their children to schools?"

When policies distinguished the elite from the non-elite, said Ho Khai Leong, "you end up giving so much resources to people who are better off. For example, these days those who get President's scholarships are the well-to-do. So how does meritocracy help the poor in this case?"

A growing sentiment among many was that as the income gap widened, an education system so heavily reliant on the tuition industry would favour those with access to paid assistance and expensive enrichment opportunities. If even affluent top students received tuition, they asked, how would it be possible for the promising poor to be on the same level playing field?

There is a whole gamut of public policies in which social equity weighs heavily in decision-making such as the adequacy of CPF savings for retirement, health care and the provision of public amenities. There is no space to dwell on these issues except to note that health care once saw an ideological battle between Toh Chin Chye, who championed a free national health service, and Lee who opposed welfarism.

THE poorest and least skilled have been the hardest hit. For many families, hardship has been a way of life for over a decade. They have to run faster just to stand still. The malign combination of wage stagnation, low wage decline and rising inequality is potentially poisonous for the social compact.

Lest you think these are the wild misinformed criticisms of an opposition politician, they are actually the carefully considered comments of Yeoh Lam Keong, economic and strategy director of the Government of Singapore Investment Corporation. His findings were published in an article in *Ethos*, the monthly publication of the Civil Service College, in October 2007.

Without pulling any punches, Yeoh documented a new and alarming wage phenomenon in which the bottom 30 per cent of working families had been experiencing stagnating real household incomes for eight to ten years. The median monthly starting pay for cleaners and labourers had also fallen by nearly a third, from S$860 to S$600, between 1996 and 2006.

"Our poorest decile, numbering some 90,000 to 100,000 households, still earn around S$160 per month per capita, the equivalent of around S$640 a month for a family of four. This compares to a measure of average basic expenditure needs of S$1,040 estimated by the department of statistics, and a guideline of around S$1,500 used by many public agencies to indicate the need for social assistance."

He concluded that these families might "have little left over for the enrichment opportunities that could gradually lift them out of poverty—such as tuition, training courses, computers or IT services—access to which marks the boundaries of true social inclusion."

What was it like to belong to the bottom 10 per cent of society? To see one such statistic in flesh and blood, sweat and tears, we met Siew Kong Chong and his family in June 2008. Siew, 45, and his wife, Jeanie Tan, 38, lived in a three-room flat in Yishun with their three children aged 14, 11 and 9. The couple had only primary school education.

When Siew lost his job as a Chinese restaurant cook which paid $2,500 a month, he was unable to find full-time work that paid just as well. He ended up as an odd-job helper earning about $1,000 a month. To supplement the family income, his wife worked as a part-time supermarket cashier bringing home about $700 a month.

The result: left on their own, their children did poorly in school. Tan stopped work to supervise them. Their debts mounted—the monthly repayment for the flat was $400, the outstanding loan $90,000. Fortunately, they had some help from CDAC to meet their day-to-day expenses.

A *Straits Times* article in 2007 highlighted the plight of two cleaners —one in Bukit Panjang who earned $400 a month and had not received a pay rise in two years, and the other in Holland Village who earned $440 a month, $60 less than what she received nine years ago in the same job.

During the 2008 budget debate, PAP MP and mayor Zainudin Nordin spoke indignantly of a school cleaner whose salary dropped each time the cleaning contract was awarded to a new vendor. "So far, she has had three different employers, three salary reductions, but she is still doing the same task—cleaning the same classrooms and toilets at the same school!"

They might not command as much attention as middle class preoccupations over private property trends and electronic road pricing, but these very low-income earners represented an emerging underclass who posed the greatest social equity challenge to the government: Why was their pay regressing after five decades of progress and prosperity under PAP rule? Why were they paid a pittance when Singapore basked in the glow of a First World GDP per capita—US$35,000 (S$53,000) in 2007, the second highest in Asia after Japan?

Income inequity is commonly measured by the Gini coefficient, an internationally recognised index which ranges between 0 and 1. If income distribution is perfectly equal, the Gini will be 0; the greater the inequality, the closer the coefficient approaches 1.

A Reuters report in 2008 observed that Singapore had an income inequality profile more in line with Third World countries: its Gini coefficient of 0.472 in 2006 put the island in the same league with the Philippines (0.461) and Guatemala (0.483), and worse than China (0.447). Other wealthy Asian nations such as Japan, Korea and Taiwan had more European-style Ginis of 0.249, 0.316 and 0.326.

Another report in *Today* newspaper noted that the Republic's Gini overtook that of the United States in 2006 and rose further in 2007 to 0.485. A *Bloomberg News* columnist commented that it reflected "a very high level of disparity for a society with an educated workforce". Scholar

Ho Khai Leong said: "It indicated the huge gap between the rich and poor. It is fair to say that Singapore is a very inequitable society."

When PAP assumed power in 1959, it strove to achieve a more just and equal society. By embarking on land acquisition, public housing, job creation and other programmes, it managed to narrow the social gap. In fact the island's Gini kept falling—from 0.477 to 0.432 between 1980 and 1990. Then it shot up. So what happened?

The social disparities and ever-widening income gap had been attributed to several causes: the flood of cheap foreign labour which had depressed the pay of local workers and dampened investment in local productivity; the growing trend of outsourcing which had forced pay down to boost bottom lines; and globalisation which awarded high pay to the government and business elite.

Yeoh Lam Keong put it down to many factors: a globally integrated labour force competing on a scale never before seen, offshore outsourcing, replacement of workers by IT systems, structural unemployment, the inability of the less skilled to adapt and upgrade, and one of the highest rates of unskilled and semi-skilled immigration in the world.

To date the government's approach had been to work with the labour movement to retrain workers and redesign their jobs to raise their pay. Its most innovative scheme was Workfare which provided an annual income supplement for low-wage workers aged 35 and older.

The other major initiatives to help the lower-income group cope with the shortfall in earnings and rising costs of living were the provision of utilities and rental rebates, CPF top-ups, growth dividends and other handouts from the annual budget. An array of schemes administered by grassroots bodies and non-government organisations comprised another safety net.

But would these measures suffice as the government faced the spectre of a rapidly ageing population with insufficient retirement savings, increasing health care needs and ballooning costs of living? Could more be done without eroding the government's anti-welfare philosophy?

Despite their socialist origins, PAP leaders had been against going down the welfare route taken by Western countries where, for example, single mothers received benefits and all citizens were entitled to free medical services. But at the same time, they shunned the unbridled winner-take-all capitalism practised by the Americans—by ensuring that the fruits of progress were shared with the people.

Given the soaring pay at the high end and the declining pay at the low-end, there was increasing public sentiment that the government should rethink its social philosophy. Was enough being done to protect lowly paid workers from trigger-happy retrenchment, abuse of outsourcing and contracting and foreign competition, and to prevent them from plunging into abject poverty?

Indeed critics often queried why the country's ever-swelling massive reserves were being kept for the proverbial rainy day when the poor and needy were already being hit by thunderstorms. Would it not be a terrible shame, they said, if the money being withheld from them today were to be squandered by a future profligate leader on grandiose projects?

If the government was so averse to the word welfarism, why not forget about it, suggested Ho Khai Leong. "Substitute it with say social equality, social justice or social harmony. These are universal values that we would want to adhere to. If a society has not achieved social justice, then it is the government's job to do so.

"And if you think that communitarianism is one core value you want to preserve, then you really have to create harmony—*he xie she hui*. If the problem of high Gini coefficient is not resolved, it would jeopardise this principle or ideology."

Well, what solutions had these commentators thrown up to tackle social inequity? Ideas bandied about included using the reserves to set up an endowment fund for the structurally unemployed and poor retirees, helping people to adopt healthy habits to minimise medical expenses, and plucking children from dysfunctional families and placing them in a conducive environment to study.

Yeoh Lam Keong proposed social risk pooling to address the inadequacy in financing for retirement, health care and education costs, unemployment insurance, an expanded Workfare programme, a well-integrated continuing education and training system, and a more discriminating immigration policy against unskilled labour.

Chua Beng Huat's suggestion: give the bottom 10 per cent a minimum income. If a family with parents and two children needs $1,500 a month to survive and if the family's income is just $800 a month, top it up to make it $1,500. With such a top-up, the government can do away with all the various welfare schemes, thus saving a lot of trouble and manpower.

By all means, help those at the bottom get up on their feet but beware of the give-me-more mentality. This was the view of those who worried about going down the slippery slope to welfarism and saw the annual budgetary giveaways as disguised welfarism. As Ngiam Tong Dow warned: "Once a subsidy is given, no government can ever take it back."

Neo Boon Siong was also firmly of the view that there was less benefit in sharing wealth as people would always want more and more. It was better to share opportunity. "Share wealth means you just wait for a part of it to be given to you. Share opportunity means you have to work hard as well."

In defence of the present model, Sam Tan said that it sought to strike a delicate balance between helping the poor and needy and making sure they did not lose the motivation and the need to work. "They know that once they put in some effort to help themselves, then the whole train of government assistance will arrive to help them, not just for themselves but also for the children."

He believed that the government should not compress the income gap artificially. "Let the able realise their full potential. This is based on the assumption that the more successful they are, the more wealth they generate for themselves as well as for the whole economy."

PM Lee Hsien Loong acknowledged that the government could do more to uplift the poor. "I cannot cause those at the peak to be pulled down. I also cannot make those at the bottom to reach the top. It is impossible. But I can make sure that Singaporeans are not left behind at zero base and that their lives improve as the economy grows."

He conceded that attitudes towards welfare might change as elected leaders had to respond to ground pressure. Right now, the government could defend its "you don't work, you don't get" Workfare policy with the electorate. But would people still support this line in 20 years? "From year to year, generation to generation, the norms shift. How successive leaders respond and the system evolves, it's impossible to say," he commented.

How the concept of social equity will evolve and be manifested in future policies in a globalised Singapore will depend on the outlook and values of future leaders. How will they view and interpret social equity? How much weight will they give to social equity in policy-making? Will they agonise over equity considerations as much as their pioneering predecessors?

They will have to decide whether they can hang on to the government's anti-welfare philosophy in the face of rapid demographic changes and wrenching social challenges. Can they hold the line on social spending when nearly a million Singaporeans or about 20 per cent of the population will be aged 65 and above by 2030?

Will future PAP leaders be driven by renewed socialist impulses to ameliorate the harsh effects of global capitalism? Will they still regard the narrowing of income gap as a legitimate political objective? Or will they just wring their hands and resign themselves to the consequences of globalisation?

What about the mood and attitude of the young Singaporeans who will eventually determine the ethos of the country? Brought up in affluence and immersed in unending self-development, untrammelled materialism and economic competitiveness, will they care about social equity?

Let us hope that the new-generation leaders and electorate will never accept that this is an unfair world. Because if they do, it will spell the end of idealism, volunteerism, public-spiritedness, civic-consciousness and the sense of duty and obligation. Without social equity, politics is just an exercise of power for the benefit of vested interests.

Think about it. If the PAP old guard leaders had accepted the inequities under the British colonial system and the 1955-1959 Lim Yew Hock government, the Singapore of today would not have come about. Remember it was widespread social unrest fuelled by abominable income inequalities which led to the emergence of a young charismatic political leader who pledged to make Singapore a more just and equal society.

While the elder Lee succeeded in achieving his vision by 1990, the younger Lee would find it much more daunting to level society during his tenure. Society has become less equal and more stratified as Singapore bears the full brunt of globalisation as manifested in the ever-widening income disparities, lack of job security and influx of better-educated immigrants.

PM Lee can no longer redistribute blue chips the way his father did. He cannot afford to scare away the foreign investors and the super-rich that the country is courting to grow the economy. How can his government keep the social compact from fracturing? What can it do to prevent the politics of envy from turning toxic? Can it ever bring down the Gini coefficient and once again make Singapore a more just and equal society? This is a new social equity story that is beginning to unfold.

37

Can PAP Survive LKY?

PAP has fallen. The longest ruling elected political party in the world has finally been voted out of power in the general election. As a thoroughly devastated prime minister concedes defeat, jubilant leaders of the united opposition front begin talks to form a coalition government.

The message from the ballot box is unmistakable: Singaporeans have lost their legendary trust and confidence in the party which has ruled the island since 1959 and once ushered in a golden era of peace, progress and prosperity.

For the past seven years, the republic has been bogged down in an economic quagmire which saw double-digit unemployment, hyperinflation, currency devaluation, the collapse of the property and stock markets and a massive withdrawal of foreign investments.

The government's abysmal failure to stage an economic turnaround time and again is compounded by its sheer impotence to defuse the social unrest spawned by mind-boggling income disparities. Protests in cyberspace have spilled onto street space. Its much-vaunted social compact with the people has vanished like the morning mist.

The outflow of young well-educated Singaporeans abroad threatens to turn into an exodus as the inflow of expatriates and foreign workers slows to a trickle. Overseas graduates prefer to join the Singapore diaspora rather than take their chances back home. Affluent citizens transfer their assets to safe havens. Permanent residents pull up stakes.

To the long-suffering electorate, the straw that finally broke the camel's back was the shocking corruption scandal involving the top political leadership. A series of exposes in the international financial media which went "viral" in the online world revealed that billions of dollars in state investments have been siphoned off to private Swiss bank accounts.

Unthinkable? Unimaginable? Impossible? Improbable? You might dismiss such an account as a figment of a feverish imagination or the wishful fantasy of hardcore anti-PAP dissidents. But this composite scenario is actually reconstructed from interviews with politicians past and present and pundits local and foreign.

In broad dramatic strokes, it captures the main factors frequently cited as possible causes for the fall of the PAP government: corruption, arrogance and abuse of power, loss of rapport with the people, social inequity, complacency, poor leadership, technocratic incompetence and a long, drawn-out economic recession.

Indisputably, corruption was singled out as the death knell for PAP rule. Political pundit Terence Chong struck a common refrain when he said that a major corruption scandal involving the top PAP ministers would bring down the government. Yes, they would try to hush it up, he said, but once the news hit the headlines, PAP would lose its moral authority to govern.

The younger PAP ministers were just as unambiguous about what would destroy their government. Yaacob Ibrahim: "If you become corrupt, that's the end." Vivian Balakrishnan: "If we do not remain true to our core values, we will lose power." Lui Tuck Yew: "For a government that prides itself on integrity, a scandal will bring it down."

Even the PAP supremos did not rule out such a scenario. As prime minister and senior minister, Goh Chok Tong had warned repeatedly that if PAP ever turned corrupt, it would be voted out of power. Lee Kuan Yew had declared that the moment PAP became less than honest, "we will be out—and we deserve to be out".

One source of gnawing concern was the increasingly intricate ties between business and government in view of the latter's trusteeship and stewardship of several hundred billion dollars of foreign reserves and people's money in state enterprises and overseas investments. Might this nexus open up a goldmine of temptations for the less-than-scrupulous?

An academic drew attention to how the old Kuomintang in Taiwan and the Liberal Democratic Party in Japan were so deeply embedded in big business that their politicians became embroiled in conflict-of-interest situations and were tainted by shady deals. "The more profound the inter-relationship between government and business, the more opportunities there are for corruption," cautioned Kenneth Paul Tan of the Lee Kuan Yew School of Public Policy.

Henri Ghesquiere, a former International Monetary Fund economist and author of *Singapore's Success: Engineering Economic Growth*, warned that PAP's downfall could be caused by "corruption related to state investments". He did not doubt the integrity of the current stewards of public funds but believed that trust in moral character and reliance on checks and balances should not preclude public accountability.

The next most commonly cited cause for the collapse of PAP rule was a protracted and severe economic downturn. The PAP government had an outstanding track record of overcoming economic crises since 1959 but they were seen as relatively short-lived. The view was that if the slump extended beyond an electoral term and brought extreme hardship and suffering to the people compounded by gross social inequalities, the ground would turn against the party.

Terence Chong belonged to the school of thought which believed that if an economic downturn were to go on for six or seven years, the mood of the nation would surely change. People would blame the government for not fulfilling its promises and vote for the opposition, said the scholar with the Institute of Southeast Asian Studies (ISEAS).

American professor Larry Diamond, who had lectured and researched on democracy issues in 25 countries for over 30 years, commented that "PAP's hegemony rests heavily on its successful performance. If there was a prolonged lapse in economic prosperity, that could generate a political crisis for the party."

As political analyst Yeo Lay Hwee wrote in the book *Electoral Politics in Southeast and East Asia*: "Since PAP legitimacy is so much tied to its ability to deliver economic results, a prolonged economic recession would affect it. This, coupled with a generational change, makes a scenario of PAP being voted out of power not unlikely."

Interestingly, the same sentiment was shared by some young PAP MPs who entered the political arena in the 2006 elections. Hri Kumar felt that PAP had become a victim of its own economic success. "No matter how good Singapore's system is, it can be affected by world events it has no control over. If people feel that their lives are not improving, they may well turn to an alternative."

Teo Ser Luck thought that a short downturn might not work against PAP as people would expect the party to see it through. Even if it went on for four or five years, he believed that the government would not fall although it might lose more single wards and perhaps a group representation constituency in the polls. "But if the economic slump goes beyond that," he said, "that's when people will get impatient and want to look for a change. And if that coincides with the rise of an opposition led by some good leaders, then it could be 1959 all over again when Lee Kuan

Yew emerged to capture power."

In Masagos Zulkifli's view, if the government could not handle issues and difficulties, people would start to think that somebody else should do the job. Grace Fu was very clear that "if we don't do our work properly, the government will be replaced quickly. We cannot take for granted that things will be handed down to us on a platter."

Yet another factor that could spell the end of PAP rule could be summed up as arrogance of power and loss of rapport with the people. At the 50th anniversary celebrations of the party in 2004, then-prime minister Goh Chok Tong sounded this alert: "If success gets into our heads and we begin to lose touch with the people, that will be our downfall."

In the words of minister Yaacob Ibrahim: "When we refuse to listen to people, when we refuse to understand the ground, that will cost us dearly. Policies will have to be thought through but at the end of the day, you have to understand the people, you have to be in touch. If you become arrogant, that's the end."

Complacency. To Kishore Mahbubani, dean of the Lee Kuan Yew School of Public Policy: "That's the first and most obvious threat because most PAP leaders have got used to the idea that they will win elections. It is very dangerous if they cannot conceive of the possibility of defeat."

He recalled that when PAP lost the Anson by-election to J B Jeyaretnam in 1981, he asked Goh Keng Swee what happened. "He said: 'Very simple, Kishore. We lost the elections because we did not even conceive of the possibility that we're going to lose. We were so confident we were going to win. We thought we've always won every election. We assumed we're going to win, so it came as a total shock to us.' "

As the champion of Asian values and chronicler of the Asian renaissance put it ominously: "If you cannot conceive of the possibility of failure, you're in trouble."

⋙⋘

OF all the scenarios that stirred the public imagination, perhaps the most-talked-about or much-whispered-about would be: What happens when Lee Kuan Yew finally leaves the political stage? Will the party see a return to the feuding and factionalism of the 1960s? Can PAP survive Lee?

When the Colorado Party of Paraguay was defeated in the 2008 polls after ruling the country for 61 years, the news was not picked up in

Singapore's mainstream media but in online chatter which duly declared that PAP had taken over as the longest ruling elected party in the world. Some netizens could not resist warning the party that it would eventually suffer the same fate.

By 2009, PAP would have governed Singapore for 50 years. Actually, UMNO's unbroken rule was longer by two years, but the Malay party did not run Malaysia by itself but as part of a race-based coalition government.

Survey the history of long ruling elected political parties around the world and the record would show that they had all fallen from power at one time or another—be it the Kuomintang in Taiwan, the Liberal Democratic Party in Japan, the Congress Party in India, the Social Democrats in Sweden and the Liberals in Canada.

Under a succession of names, the Institutional Revolutionary Party (Partido Revolucionario Institucional or PRI) once had the distinction of enjoying the longest uninterrupted rule by an elected party. It governed Mexico for more than 70 years until it was beaten in the 2002 elections. The honour then shifted to Paraguay's Colorado Party.

Many ruling parties in Asia and Africa, which wrested freedom from Western colonialists in the 1950s and 1960s, have sunk into oblivion. Even UMNO, which headed the Barisan National coalition, lost its aura of political invincibility when the alliance lost its two-third parliamentary majority in the 2008 elections and faced the possibility of being ousted by a new opposition grouping.

Seen against this backdrop, the irresistible question posed by pundits is: Can PAP defy the odds of history and prove to be the exception to the rule? If the rise and fall of political parties is inexorable, what makes its leaders think they can ward off the inevitable?

The lesson of history, Kishore Mahbubani expounded, was that no one party could maintain its dominance forever. "So at some point the political space that the PAP occupies in Singapore will be definitely reduced. We don't know when or how but it will happen."

The first 40 years of Singapore from 1965 to 2005 were extraordinary years, he said. "You name it, we have it—political stability, peace, prosperity ... Well, it cannot carry on. There will be political instability at some point in time. There will be political challenges. All this is inevitable, it's going to come.

"As a student of history, I always say change always comes when you least expect it. So it's only in Singapore that you have this very strange view of history where you can manage change and control outside forces. You can't. The idea that Singapore will always go on sailing smoothly is a bizarre idea. We should actually prepare ourselves for the opposite, that there will be discontinuities rather than continuities."

The influential intellectual could not figure out how the party would change. "You can never tell. You don't know how much of that glue and that cohesiveness is natural and how much of it is due to extraordinary leadership. So when Lee leaves the scene, the party will change. How it will change, I don't know."

In a variation on the same theme, political science scholar Kenneth Paul Tan said that if he were the government, he would assume that nothing was permanent. "If you have a perfect system, it will start to degenerate. So I would think the party must know this, what its future is going to be, how it would try to extend its future in a way that doesn't do damage to the country."

His worry was that the ruling party might be convinced that being in power was completely consistent with Singapore doing well, but sometimes they could go in two different directions. "When the main concern is staying in power, then a lot of good decisions will be sacrificed. So I think PAP needs to be very mindful of this possibility.

"If I were in PAP, I will prepare for the day when I have to leave. I will prepare to leave graciously so that I can be written into textbooks and history books in a favourable way. Many parties have collapsed and died, and whatever good they have done are buried with them."

In one of her open letters to the government circulated on the Internet, political commentator Catherine Lim predicted a decline in the quality of PAP leadership. She noted that the government assumed that excellence of leadership would go on and on because of its painstaking process of self-renewal.

"Here's where this idealised picture falls apart. It ignores the inevitability of change through time. Twenty, thirty years down the road, there is certain to be a change in quality in the leadership. And it will be a change in the direction of decline, simply because in a globalised world of rapid, overwhelming change that has greatest impact on the young, the original core PAP principles and values will steadily lose their influence and may even disappear altogether. Future PAP leaders will therefore be very different."

Or as former journalist-turned-academic Asad Latif described it: "There is no guarantee that this country will continue to succeed. This is because a certain paradox lies at the heart of its independence. Every year that passes without a crisis threatening the life of the nation attests to the successes which it has accumulated over the previous years. But every such year also dilutes the do-or-die resolve with which Singaporeans in 1965 decided to make those numbers a permanent date in their history."

For scholastic support, look no further than the classic text by Maurice Duverger titled *Political Parties: Their Organisation and Activity in the Modern State*. Having studied the evolution of political systems in various countries, the French jurist concluded that any dominant party would eventually wear itself out in office: "It loses its vigour, its arteries harden. It would thus be possible to show ... that every domination bears within itself the seeds of its own destruction."

Renowned for scanning beyond the horizon, PAP leaders are not oblivious to such dire prophecies. When PM Lee Hsien Loong was asked to envisage the future of his party in the next 20 to 30 years, one scenario he sketched was that of PAP losing its dominance vis-à-vis a charismatic opposition winning many seats in parliament. It would then be akin, he said, to the multi-party situation in Taiwan where "the social consensus is fractured and politics is in command—*zheng zhi gua shuai*".

So, in Lee Kuan Yew's absence, will challengers be emboldened to seek the overthrow of the government? Mahbubani was absolutely certain that PAP would face new political competition. "There are people who are thinking of challenging PAP but will not do so as long as Lee is politically active as they are all afraid of him. But once he goes, you will find lots of challengers coming out of the woodwork. This is inevitable. It's normal."

PM Lee agreed that contenders might emerge to challenge PAP. "If they find Lee is not active, not around, then I'm sure some people are waiting for that moment to come and try. That's why it's important for us to have a strong team and continue to bring in from the whole society the ablest and most committed to be part of the PAP team."

In 1961, PAP suffered two serious splits when former cabinet minister Ong Eng Guan broke away to form the United People's Party and a group of leftists defected to set up Barisan Sosialis. Will history repeat itself in the post-Lee period? Will infighting and power struggles return to PAP?

If you go by scholarly speculation, a split might occur if a prime minister wanted to adopt a hardline position but his fellow ministers did not agree, or the gulf between the liberals and conservatives was so wide it could not be bridged, or the differences over a controversial policy were so profound that dissenting ministers were forced to take their case to the public.

Stanford University professor Larry Diamond was of the view that if the party refused to open up, the more reform-minded members would eventually break away and start a serious opposition party. In similar vein, Ted Haner of Business Environment Risk Intelligence (BERI), an American research and forecasting agency, believed that if the party could no longer resolve issues by consensus, several members could defect and form a political alternative.

As Indian journalist and Singapore watcher Sunanda Datta-Ray saw it, the republic had been under de facto one-party rule for so long that it was very unlikely "for the extremely restrained nominal opposition to spring any surprise suddenly". "If there is dissent," he asserted, "it will have to emerge from within the PAP ranks, spearheaded by tried men who have the experience of handling the levers of power." Given the apolitical nature of PAP leadership, he said, "reform need not be the reason for such a rift. It is far more likely to be on personal grounds, although challengers may rationalise their ambitions by citing a programme."

As part of the pioneering batch of Chinese scholars who had researched extensively on Singapore in the early 1990s, Yang Mu had no doubt that there would definitely be changes in the post-Lee period. "Things will not remain the same—either the opposition will become stronger or there is a split in the party. Just look at what happened to UMNO which is now being challenged by a former UMNO leader," said the senior research fellow with the East Asian Institute, National University of Singapore.

Kenneth Paul Tan also foresaw a possible rupture in a post-Lee PAP but did not think that it would be like the break in the 1960s between the moderates and the mass mobilisers, or a straightforward split between conservative and liberal ministers. "If some leaders believe that the party is going the wrong way or feel disgruntled that some are considered more valuable than others or if they are being retired as ministers after only one term, their egos may be affected. That could possibly be a source of opposition energies."

The political analyst, however, qualified that a split could help to clarify the stand of the party, just as the split in 1961 distinguished the position of Lee and company from that of the leftists. Right now, by trying to be all things to all people, the PAP could lose its vision, he said. "So a split may help to strengthen the party by making its views clearer and forcing it to adopt a stronger position."

Surprisingly, some young PAP MPs did not dismiss questions of a split as rhetorical or heretical. Baey Yam Keng, who raised eyebrows in parliament by making a pitch for media freedom, championing the use of dialects and expressing sympathy for the gay cause, said he would not rule out the possibility of PAP politicians jockeying for power in the post-Lee era.

However, he thought they might not be doing so out of personal ambitions but because they held different views and convictions about what constituted the common good. Such a divergence might lead to a split and perhaps result in a dual party system for Singapore one day, he surmised.

Masagos Zulkifli pointed out that factionalism happened in all ruling parties in the world, saying "it will be inevitable in the PAP when the best and power-minded people are placed together". This meant that the prime minister of the day would have to be vigilant and ensure that no particular faction would do anything to undermine the interests of the nation, he said.

Younger Singaporeans might not know it but the idea of splitting the party was seriously contemplated by the leaders at one time. Goh Chok Tong once revealed that PAP considered dividing the party into two factions who agreed on the basics but disagreed on policies, timing and implementation. They would contest on the basis of personality and ability to articulate ideas. But in the end, the idea was given up as there were not enough talented people to go round, said the then-prime minister. Another novel idea of forming a group of PAP MPs not constrained by the party whip to challenge the frontbench was also floated and then shelved.

IN 1999, then-PM Goh said he would not rule out a split within the party but thought this was unlikely to happen in the next 10 years. This was because the younger ministers were interacting well and there were no personality or ideological clashes among them, he said in an interview published in a book to mark PAP's 45th anniversary.

Well, the years had whizzed by. What would the younger ministers expected to see Singapore through the immediate post-Lee period have to say? The responses of two of them interviewed in 2007 could be summed up as: yes there will be changes in PAP, yes there will be differences among them, but no the party will not break up.

Vivian Balakrishnan: "With or without Lee, the party must change because it has to keep bringing in newer members with their values, ways of thinking and ways of operating which are reflective of the younger generation."

On the big issues such as multi-racialism and meritocracy, he did not see much scope for disagreement. Perhaps the leaders might argue over how best to look after the interests of the average Singaporean in a globalised Asia, he said. "But whatever the differences, I do not see any split in the party as members know they can do much more in a united group than by falling apart and fighting for power."

Lim Swee Say contended that PAP after Lee would be a different PAP as the minister mentor with his global outlook, wisdom and experience was irreplaceable. Would it be less united? No, he stressed noting that the team under PM Lee was "already a manifestation of unity amid diversity". As he explained: "Each one of us thinks differently, talks differently, behaves differently and has different views. But our starting and ending point is not my idea against your idea but rather what we firmly believe to be for the good of Singapore.

"So we may attach different weightage in our discussion. Maybe some may attach weightage to making Singapore more competitive, some may attach greater weightage to keeping Singapore society inclusive. But at the end of the day, we always find a way to harmonise. PAP is a *da wo* ("we" in Mandarin) party."

Lui Tuck Yew was peeved by suggestions that it was Lee's presence that prevented ambitious people from showing their true colours and that he was the glue that held the party and country together. "That would be giving too little credit to the second and third generation leaders," he remonstrated. "From what I've seen in cabinet discussions, nobody jostles for power. It's not like in other countries where ministers try to outmanoeuvre one another."

The new-generation MPs did not envisage any party strife or leadership struggle either. If Lee were to retire from politics tomorrow, said Hri Kumar, "you would not see the cabinet disintegrating and ambitious ministers jockeying for power". Teo Ser Luck argued that they were already in a post-Lee government: "We share PAP values, and we will stick to them to keep the party intact to win elections and run the country."

As a five-term MP, Charles Chong had a close-up view of the to-ing and fro-ing in his party since 1988. He scoffed at any notion of a post-Lee scramble for power. He noted that top PAP leaders were not hardcore politicians like their UMNO counterparts who had the raging desire to take over the country. If they had their way, he mused, they would rather stay out of politics, be bankers, professionals or whatever, and lead quiet, private lives.

No dramatic surprises was PM Lee's response when asked what effect he thought his father's political exit might have on the party. After all, Lee was no longer involved in day-to-day policy-making, he said, and he had already built up a strong team. Wong Kan Seng pointed out that the ministers had been meeting to discuss policy issues and options in Lee's absence for years.

What about the thoughts of the man himself? Lee did not see a return to the power play of the 1960s when PAP was an amalgam of pro-communists and non-communists. "Now PAP comprises men and women committed to the good governance of Singapore. Any infighting will be over the principles of how to move forward."

Among local and foreign scholars, the overwhelming view was that PAP would survive Lee Kuan Yew—at least in the foreseeable future. They expressed confidence that the Lee Hsien Loong team would be able to rise to any political, economic and social challenges in the age of globalisation.

Neo Boon Siong was certain that Lee's absence would make no difference to the party. There might have been concerns if Lee had stepped down completely in 1990 when he handed the reins over to Goh Chok Tong. But Goh and his successor Lee Hsien Loong had demonstrated that they were their own men and were not taking instructions from Lee. It was to Lee's credit, the governance guru said, that Singapore could live with—or without—him.

In the view of Terence Chong, a split was not likely to happen in the next 10 to 15 years for two reasons. Firstly, differences between PAP leaders were always resolved internally. As ministers and MPs were picked through a cadre system—a "self-selection process"—they tended to be like-minded. Secondly, PAP occupied too much of the middle ground "so unless it veers suddenly to the left or to the right, it's very hard for a split to occur within the party".

If the political analyst had any reservations, it was that the new generation leaders seemed more comfortable dealing with economic problems and structural issues such as getting more foreign capital and talent than with primal, emotional issues relating to ethnicity and religion. "The first-generation leaders were more confident with such issues as they lived through it. After Lee is gone, would anyone command the same type of respect in handling religious and ethnic issues? I don't think so. Not for the moment."

While Asad Latif agreed that hypothetically a post-Lee PAP could split and lose power, he strongly believed that such a scenario could be pre-empted by two factors. The first was that the party drew power from a broad middle swathe of the population which meant that any ideological divergence by the opposition parties would not be significant.

The second was leadership renewal. He said: "A party that speaks, with almost mathematical precision, of first-, second- and third-generation leaders is planning for the future. Plans can fail, but there is a major difference between a party that seeks to remain in power and one that has accepted that the best it can expect is to share power with other parties in a future that is up for grabs."

Asad also made the point that unlike other ruling parties such as Congress in India, KMT in Taiwan or LDP in Japan, PAP did not have an autonomous political profile in national affairs which could lead to political intrigues, factional squabbles and personality clashes. Neither did it have a bureaucracy and apparatus that ran parallel to the administration.

"Of course, the PAP CEC is a powerful body, but its composition overwhelmingly reflects the composition of the cabinet. PAP does not constitute a power centre independent of the cabinet, which is where real executive power lies in Singapore. So long as executive power ensures that Singapore does well, PAP will do well," said the visiting research fellow with ISEAS.

For all his robust criticisms of PAP, Chua Beng Huat called it "an unsinkable boat". PAP after Lee did not hinge on the man but on the system and institutions that had been set in place, the NUS sociology professor said. The values and ethos had been well-internalised and he had faith that the ministers were capable of managing an increasingly complex society.

To Gillian Koh, the question about PAP's survival was a no-brainer. The party would most certainly survive for many years, the senior research fellow with the Institute of Policy Studies said noting that Lee's legacy would last at least a generation as he had recruited and mentored the present leaders. Her greater concern was whether the leaders had enough political savvy and ground feel.

The foreign scholars interviewed were just as sanguine about PAP's prospects. Henri Ghesquiere, who worked in the IMF for 27 years and studied the economies of more than 14 countries, predicted that the PAP government would continue to perform well over the next 10 to 15 years and strengthen its model of governance. His forecast: barring a steep world recession or unforeseen calamity, there would be an average sustainable growth rate of 5 per cent, continued further qualitative development and a broadening model with greater involvement of the citizenry.

Walter Lohman of Heritage Foundation, an American think tank, commented that the success of the PAP government was foremost a product of its commitment to open markets, and competent, efficient, transparent administration. "It is an approach to government that has been thoroughly institutionalised and will indeed survive Lee's departure from the scene.

"There is no credible alternative. The opposition is perennially hard pressed to make a case against PAP's remarkable success in governing. People are happy with their economic situation. More often than not, the opposition is reduced to running on the idea that there should be an opposition. While true, the principle is not concrete enough to turn out votes."

Ted Haner of BERI believed that PAP would not only survive but also continue to make Singapore the World Cup champion in country governance. He noted that the vast majority of Singaporeans felt that they were part of a successful socio-political system. His proviso: keep breeding the talent. Continue to develop these people into the champions of the present generation.

Referring to BERI's government proficiency measure which ranked Singapore consistently among the world's top nations, he said he was confident of the republic's future in the post-Lee era. His reason: "The 14 Goh Chok Tong years were the keys to stability and superior governance and Lee Hsien Loong added experience in senior positions, and the emergence of several competent leaders during this period gives the government depth to continue effectively."

Sunanda Datta-Ray was just as positive commenting that "PAP will not decline until and unless Singaporean expectations undergo radical change. If it declines, it will be because sated Singaporeans begin to look for more than the good things of life, that is, demand more than good administration."

Making the point that the PAP government fulfilled people's expectations by acting as an apolitical administration, the Indian scribe said he was not sure that most Chinese Singaporeans expected their ruling party to be "a political force" like Britain's Labour Party or India's Bharatiya Janata Party. "Politics implies a sense of mission, of ideology, if you like. PAP is not a political force like the other mass-based movements cited. This has a great deal to do with the pragmatism of Chinese culture."

The way Arun Shourie saw it, Singapore's survival without Lee would depend on whether the institutions set up outlast the founders and the legitimacy and authenticity of his successors. "If they are seen by the people as being equally beneficial to Singapore, equally selfless, that they are imposing discipline and moving against individuals not in their personal interest but in the interest of the country, then I think people will stand by these rulers, because governments are run not on police authority but on moral authority," said the Indian politician and pundit.

Having spent a year as an exchange student at the National University of Singapore (NUS) in 2001 and four and a half years as a post-doctoral fellow in the S Rajaratnam School of International Studies, Nanyang Technological University (NTU), from 2003 to 2007, Japanese scholar Hiro Katsumata had witnessed Singapore politics at close range. His prognosis: "I do not expect a regime change in the foreseeable future, at least for another decade or two." Why? "Because I am amazed by the extent to which people support the existing system centred on the PAP."

Of course, PAP will survive Lee Kuan Yew, pronounced Li Luqu, a professor from East China University of Political Science and Law in Shanghai and author of *Singapore's Road to Modernisation* which analysed the factors for the country's success. "When Lee is gone, there will definitely be changes, but not very much because PAP already has in place a system of leadership change and self-renewal. Besides, the party is corruption-free and able to attract good people. Without Lee, voices of dissent may be louder but PAP will still dominate and rule because there is no alternative to the party in sight."

Pose the same question to Lu Yuanli, the Chinese professor who set up the centre for Singapore studies in Shenzhen University in 2008, and his answer was unequivocal: "After ruling for nearly 50 years, the PAP government had not only given Singaporeans material success but also a system of government which would not disappear with Lee. Perhaps we should turn the question around: If Lee is still the prime minister, and all important decisions are still left to him to decide, would Singapore be able to achieve what it did today?"

FOR many Singaporeans grappling with the great unknown, however, the more pertinent and worrisome question is not whether PAP can survive Lee Kuan Yew but what comes after Lee Hsien Loong. Who will be the fourth prime minister of Singapore? Who will form the nucleus of the fourth generation leadership? What will be their world-view, values, convictions, reflexes and instincts?

Will the new leaders who take over in 15 to 20 years be able to sustain the country in peace, progress and prosperity? Or will they preside over what doomsayers predict as an inevitable decline? Will good leadership plus good luck continue to favour Singapore? Or will blackguards in white show their true colours?

As they contemplate the future of their children and grandchildren, they must wonder if the leaders of the next generation will espouse the same core values of whiter-than-white integrity, multi-racialism, meritocracy and social equity, and uphold the same moral sense of trusteeship over the massive accumulated assets belonging to the people of Singapore.

But leaders do not drop like manna from heaven. They will have to be voted in by the young of today who will form the bulk of the electorate tomorrow. Only they will know and decide what kind of leaders they want—not PAP, MM, SM, PM, the opposition or anyone else. As one of the best educated, best-travelled, most Internet-savvy and globally exposed populations in the world, will the new generation voters still accept PAP's leadership renewal system? Will they still buy into the party's vision and game plan? Or will their world view, or *weltanschauung*, as the Germans call it, be out of sync with that of the anointed PAP leaders?

Several scholars were quite sure that the new PAP leaders would not be able to forge the same social compact with the new generation that their predecessors did with the older one. They expressed doubts that the spirit of tripartism among government, employers and trade unions would even prevail. Reason: having gone through political upheavals and economic hard times together, the older generation and pioneering leaders had developed mutual trust and strong bonding. But the new generation accustomed to the good life with no memory of the republic's early struggles would have little or no emotional affinity for inducted technocratic leaders.

Never far from the Asian psyche is the notion that wealth is created by the first generation, spent by the second and lost by the third. So far, the PAP government has disproved the dictum but what guarantee does Singapore have that it will not be the fourth or fifth generation leaders who will finally do the plundering and the squandering.

Goh Chok Tong confessed that he spent sleepless nights agonising over the future leadership of the country. PM Lee expressed great concern over whether young Singaporeans would have the "sense of social cohesion, consensus and missionary zeal to keep the country going".

So which of the three scenarios sketched by PM Lee would materialise: an all-dominant PAP, a still dominant PAP but one which lost its élan, or a less dominant PAP vis-à-vis an emerging opposition? Or would a fourth scenario become reality—the fall of PAP?

There was one more scenario invoked by our interviewees. PAP leaders always assumed that if the opposition were to form the government, it would be a weak one which would ruin the country. The institutional safeguards they designed were supposed to prevent the emergence of a rogue government.

But what if the rogue government sprang from the bosom of the PAP itself? Was it inconceivable that a good PAP government might turn rotten mid-term or that a good prime minister could succumb to temptations along the way? How could the party be certain that it would always prove to be an exception to Lord Acton's dictum that power corrupts and absolute power corrupts absolutely?

Indeed the most nightmarish scenario cited by many interviewees would be a rogue PAP government in full control of all the levers of power and all the key institutions from the presidency, judiciary and civil service to the labour movement, grassroots associations, professional organisations and the mass media.

As Catherine Lim warned in a public forum in 2006, long after Lee had gone and his legacy diminished, "there could appear a self-serving and corrupt leader who, because he wears the trusted PAP mantle, will get away with it. This is a frightening but possible scenario".

Heaven forbid but if such a situation were to occur, would Singapore's highly ranked and much-envied system of governance be able to kick in with all its institutional locks and keys to check and oust a nefarious prime minister and his government?

Let's listen to what some PAP MPs said: yes, they would come into play. The elected president would veto the use of reserves and key public appointments and scrutinise the government's exercise of power in internal security and corruption cases. Honest ministers and MPs would act against a bad PM. Upright bureaucrats would rebel if forced to go against the civil service's best practices.

Perhaps they could take comfort in what George Yeo once said: "Nations with good institutions survive bad luck and bad leaders. In the nature of things, bad luck does not last forever. As for bad leaders, good institutions will eventually throw them out."

Commenting on such a scenario, Lee Kuan Yew said that the elected president and the parliamentary system would be a check against the excesses of any prime minister. "Singapore's prime minister remains in office only as long as he commands the confidence of the majority of MPs in parliament. If he turns bad, ministers and MPs will know that he will be a liability and not lead them to victory in the next elections. They can remove him by a vote of no confidence and/or the elected president can require the PM to seek a vote of confidence in the house."

He also maintained that it was not true that the prime minister could have all the important institutions under his control. Key appointments were subject to the agreement of the president and the council of presidential advisers, and top office-bearers could not be removed by the PM without the consent of the president.

What if all these institutional measures failed? The ultimate check, according to some MPs, would be an electorate which was one of the best educated, most media-savvy and globally attuned generations in the world. Having experienced and internalised the values of good governance, they would surely react with outrage and boot out a bad government through the ballot box.

Some foreign scholars ventured to say that internal political reaction would be matched by external countervailing forces. Henri Ghesquiere said that the thousands of multinational corporations in Singapore could act as a check against a PAP government going awry as their billion-dollar investments would be at stake.

Alarm bells would not only start ringing loudly among the Singapore public but also among the international investment community if the country's performance and governance rankings by global agencies fell drastically. Imagine the collective shivers if Transparency International were to rank Singapore as one of the most corrupt countries in Asia.

All these conjectures and concerns raise the perennial poser: Is it prudent to just depend on institutional checks and balances to keep Singapore safe and sound? It has been argued that no political scenario could be worse than a one-party system in which the ruling party collapsed one day out of internal rot and no other party could take over the reins of government. Depending on the army to run the country, as it has been suggested, was considered foolhardy going by the poor record of army-run regimes in the region.

Many people and pundits are coming around to the view that the best fallback would be a full, functioning bi-partisan system in which power could pass from one party to another, as in most developed democratic countries, without affecting political stability. Such a system was seen as a better safeguard and safety valve than depending on the invincibility and infallibility of the incumbent party and the citizens' blind trust in and complete reliance on the party. By a logical extension, a two-party's check-and-balance system would be expected to provide greater transparency and accountability than a one-party's self-checking system.

With a competitive political system, it was argued, people would have choices and learn to discuss options and issues and weigh costs and benefits. They would feel more engaged in the affairs of their nation and develop a sense of empowerment and belonging. They would gain political maturity from experiencing the consequences of their vote. Foreign investors would be less anxious when they realised that a political turnover would have no appreciable impact on their investments.

Among those who saw the merits of such a system was former top civil servant Ngiam Tong Dow. In an interview with *The Straits Times*, he said that Singapore would survive Lee provided he left the right legacy, which was to "open up politically and allow talent to be spread throughout our society so that an alternative leadership can emerge".

"It is the law of nature that all things must atrophy. Unless Lee allows serious political challenges to emerge from the alternative elite out there, the incumbent elite will just coast along. At the first sign of a grassroots revolt, they will probably collapse just like the incumbent Progressive Party to the left-wing PAP onslaught in the late 1950s."

Likewise, sociologist Chua Beng Huat believed that a two-party system would ultimately be better for Singapore as a nation as it constituted normal politics. One-party rule, he argued, was a historical aberration which should not be taken as the only logic. "The fact that we became a single-party state had to do with the mistake of Barisan Socialis. If Barisan had stuck to it, we would now have a two-party state. PAP would probably still be the dominant party but you would actually have a serious opposition party. The single-party dominance is a historical phenomenon. It shouldn't be taken as the only logic of politics."

Gillian Koh envisaged the political ideal as one which would ensure the survival of a country irrespective of which party was in power. Citing the example of Taiwan under the presidency of Democratic Progressive Party's Chen Shui-bian before he was replaced by Kuomintang's Ma Ying-jeou in 2008, the senior research fellow said: "The country can now survive in spite of who is in power. It's not going to collapse. So even if you have a president who has completely lost all confidence of the people, the country will survive. There is the business sector, there is the people sector, there is a bureaucracy that will keep it going."

Larry Diamond, a leading American scholar in the field of democracy studies, advanced the theory that what worked in economics should apply to politics as well. No matter how great the intellectual and administrative ability of a ruling elite, he said, rot and complacency would set in eventually without the discipline of competition.

"The PAP elite understand this on the economic side, which is why they pragmatically abandoned socialist inclinations and committed to market principles. Sooner or later they will need to realise that competition is just as important in governance as in economics, and that without the discipline of a true political marketplace, the storied governance miracle of Singapore will eventually begin to rot.

"The real challenge for PAP is a political one. How can they open up without risking their hold on power? I think they should have more confidence in their own high levels of governing competence, their ability to continue to deliver the goods of development. And I think they should

660 MEN IN WHITE—The Untold Story of Singapore's Ruling Political Party

have more confidence in their own citizens, who have the education and prudence to make sensible judgements about who should exercise power."

Even some PAP MPs supported the idea of a good opposition waiting in the wings to prevent a PAP-or-nothing situation. In countries with a robust two-party system, said veteran PAP MP Charles Chong, either party could keep the country going. "But here, if PAP collapses, Singapore will collapse too because really who is going to take over."

If the opposition had sufficient credibility to present itself as an alternative government, said Baey Yam Keng, it would be for the good of Singapore. "For us, it is good to have a challenge. It forces us to be on our toes and prove ourselves."

Lui Tuck Yew believed that the right opposing voices would strengthen Singapore. "At the end of the day, opposing voices that have the best interests of the people and country at heart must surely make for better policies and better programmes."

If you took a leaf from PAP history in the 1960s, as some older Singaporeans pointed out, it was the do-or-die competition from the communists and leftists which kept the party on a razor's edge and acutely sensitised to the people's needs. As Lee had admitted repeatedly, it was the standards set by his arch adversary Lim Chin Siong and comrades which compelled the English-educated leaders to match their dedication, tenacity, selflessness and integrity. As the oft-asked question goes: If there is no political competition, who will keep the PAP honest?

❧

IT is no surprise that Singapore's dominant-party system has been the object of scorn and derision among Western and Westernised liberals and human rights organisations and in the rapidly exploding online media. But what's amazing is that it has been attracting more than its fair share of advocates and admirers throughout the world— from Russia, Central Asia and Africa to the Middle East, India and China.

At a parlous time in Asia when multiple-party systems with their full suite of civil freedoms and constant turnover of governments were often embroiled in political scandals, social disorder and economic turbulence, the island was held up as an oasis of peace and progress.

The case for the Singapore way was that the 707-sq km-island was just too tiny, its multi-racial foundation too fragile and economic viability too tenuous to sustain a full-blown adversarial party system. Much time, energy and resources would be needlessly spent in partisan politicking and endless debates at the cost of long-range planning and development. Singapore's talent pool was considered too limited to produce a ruling A team and an alternative A team.

As its defenders argued, the present system would allow potential leaders with talent and character to be head-hunted and groomed through a thorough and painstaking process to ensure that they could eventually manage an increasingly complex economy and govern a socially and racially diverse country. They feared that a free-for-all multi-party system might open the floodgates for the incompetent, the opportunistic and the corrupt to enter the corridors of power.

A typical favourable view would go like this: true, the Singapore system did not fit the norms and niceties of the Westminster model but if it had enabled Singapore to go from Third World to First in a generation, who was it to question its moral and legal validity? Come on, were Singaporeans really deprived of their free choice to vote out the PAP if they really wished to?

Describing the republic as unique, Japanese scholar Hiro Katsumata who lived in Singapore for five years agreed that it was not a liberal democracy with no guarantee for freedom of speech. But making clear that it was not for him but for Singaporeans to determine their political system, he said that he was amazed by the people's support for PAP. "The legitimacy of PAP is founded on several elements such as economic performance, social safety and high-quality education and research. The so-called Singapore model is meant to bring about these elements and, indeed, in my view, it has been successful thus far."

Research fellow Asad Latif acknowledged that theoretically a multi-party system would be the best guarantee against a rogue PAP government. "However, what is there to say that it will not be a rogue multi-party system? Present institutional safeguards are perhaps not sufficient to prevent PAP from going bad, but what safeguards can there be to prevent the whole system from going bad?

"Certainly, competition is good in politics as it is in economics, but competition does not protect politics from cartels any more than deregulation prevented the conspiring cartels of Wall Street from bringing capitalism almost to its knees.

"I know of countries where parties are like pimps that take turns to pass the electorate from hand to hand in the raucous brothel of politics. The parties take turns at power, but the electorate is always sold. To say this is to suggest the limits of the competitive principle in politics, not to make a case against the opposition."

Comparing the two political systems that he had experienced, the Indian national-turned-Singaporean said that in the sub-continent, democracy was seen as an end—an expression of a fundamental contestation over the end goals of political and social life, while in Singapore it was deemed as no more than a means of good governance. "Here politics had moved from being a contest of ideas to being a form of negotiation over particular policies."

It seemed ironic that the Singapore system with limited freedoms had been warmly received by some politicians and pundits from the most populous and vibrant democracy in the world. One Indian enthusiast was Kamal Nath, dubbed the chief salesman for his country and author of *The Age of Entrepreneurship in the World's Biggest Democracy* which was made into a three-part television series.

Lauding Singapore as a highly developed free market economy admired across the world, he said he was struck by "its strong legal framework which is strictly enforced, defamation laws which keep public pronouncements responsible and honest, the almost corruption-free economic and social systems, low crime rates, stable prices and tremendous growth."

It was inappropriate to compare Singapore with Western models of liberal democracy, he argued, as any system had to be adapted to a country's characteristics and background. "Singapore has evolved its own model to suit its unique position as a small multi-racial and multi-religious country. Pragmatism, meritocracy, multi-racialism and an emphasis on community development have been important pillars of the governance structure of Singapore and they have done well to preserve this," said the commerce and industry minister in the Congress-led coalition government in an interview in 2008.

You could not find a more fervent advocate of democratic rights and press freedom than former Indian minister, newspaper editor and prolific author Arun Shourie. As editor of the Indian Express in the 1980s, he was the indefatigable crusader against corruption who brought down the chief minister of Maharashtra state and contributed to the fall of prime minister Rajiv Gandhi over the Bofors howitzer gun purchase scandal. He had won the International Editor of the Year and The Freedom to Publish awards.

When asked to comment on Singapore's democratic limitations in 2008, the former divestment minister in the Atal Bihari Vajpayee government from 2001 to 2003 said that it did not matter what the system was as long as it had integrity and could induct new talent and allow for change. He stressed that no particular system could guarantee good governance and that any model—bi-party, multiple-party or whatever—could be perverted.

What impressed him most about the Singapore system was leadership renewal. Referring to India's electoral system, he noted that it had many parties but it "was not throwing up people of requisite competence and integrity". Expressing his high regard for MM Lee, PM Lee, SM Goh and Foreign Minister George Yeo, he said: "If I meet your ministers and MPs, I know they are competent. That's what I admire—the absolute insistence on competence."

Yet another feature that resonated with him was Singapore's rule of law and firmness in enforcing it. Describing himself as a strong advocate of capital punishment, he noted how its enforcement had minimised the drug problem on the island. He related what some Indian nationals who lived in Singapore had told him: that they never had to worry about their children doing drugs and about their wives returning home safely after midnight.

Another political observer from India, Sunanda Datta-Ray, summed up the Singapore system as one characterised by "discipline, efficiency, orderliness of life, punctuality and a meticulous attention to detail." He attributed it to "Lee's vision and ability to translate dream into reality that shapes governance—and his extraordinary success in keeping the lid firmly on racial tensions".

"Singapore is a constant reminder that an economy can boom without any natural resources or exceptional human talents if people dedicate themselves to the cause of prosperity," said the former editor of *The Statesman* and author of a forthcoming book on Lee Kuan Yew and India. Singapore succeeded because it "does what others do but does it better and faster". Citing the example of the Central Provident Fund, he said that the scheme was left by the British in many of its colonies but it was Singapore that took it much further and turned it into a social marvel.

It sounded like the height of presumption but what lessons could a little red dot possibly offer to a sprawling continental-sized country, bourgeoning global power and ancient civilisation? If Chinese politicians, policy-makers and pundits were attracted to the Singapore model, it was because they saw a fascinating hybrid model which fused capitalistic and socialistic, Western and Asian elements imbued with a pragmatic problem-solving approach.

Drawing a political parallel between one-party rule in Singapore and China, they wanted to know how PAP was able to gain continuous support from the people to legitimise its rule since 1959, how it renewed its leadership ranks and remained incorruptible, and how it built up a track record of political stability, economic growth, industrial peace, social cohesion and racial harmony.

As they turned their attention from Singapore's social and economic accomplishments to its political management, they were especially interested in how PAP maintained its dominance and yet kept a low profile and not got in the way of government, how party and government were kept separate, the nuts and bolts of electoral politics, party organisation and grassroots mobilisation, government-labour relations and MPs' interaction with the people.

As Li Luqu from East China University of Political Science and Law in Shanghai explained: "China sees PAP's continuous rule in Singapore for 50 years under a parliamentary democracy system unusually interesting and worth studying. The Chinese leaders believe the one-party dominance and rule had helped economic development and growth for Singapore, and they want the same to happen in China.

"China knows that with economic growth and rising income levels of the people, change in the political system is inevitable. Their leaders believe the Singapore model, particularly the one-party dominance by PAP in an electoral system, is something to learn from."

Fellow scholar Yang Mu, based in the East Asian Institute at NUS, noted that pressures were piling on China's political system to be more democratic with elections, checks and balances and an independent judiciary. "As China emerges as a world leader, it cannot continue to rule under a Marxist or socialist system of government but to evolve into a system acceptable to the rest of the world. Singapore may be a good model for China."

This seemingly insatiable hunger to learn from Singapore was reflected in a proliferation of books, academic papers and articles in the media and party publications, and an upsurge of visits to the island by Chinese officials and scholars. Statistics showed that more than 4,000 articles on Singapore from academic journals were posted on the Internet between 1994 and 2006.

Chinese newspapers such as *Nanfang Doushibao* and *Yunnan Xinxibao* despatched journalists to Singapore to compile special reports. Two master's degree programmes were set up in NTU to cater to senior Chinese officials. Generous grants were given by Chinese research institutions and foundations for studies on topics related to politics in Singapore. A centre for Singapore studies was launched in Shenzhen University in 2008.

No less than the almighty Chinese Communist Party (CCP) had expressed keen interest in imbibing PAP's experience in running the party and the country. Between 2000 and 2008, *Xuexi Shibao*, the newspaper of the CCP central party school published 10 articles on Singapore's political system. Its January–February 2008 issue by the school's first year students who visited the island concluded that the Singapore system ensured PAP's continuous rule by the elite—by virtue of its corruption-free government and track record. By comparison, it cautioned, the Western form of democracy could result in opportunists gaining power and causing political instability, and in extreme social welfarism.

To the Chinese cadres and analysts, PAP was perceived as a party with the unswerving mission of serving the masses which recalled the familiar CCP's slogan "*wei ren min fu wu*" which meant "to serve the people". Cai Dingjian of the Political Science and Law University in Beijing was emphatic that Singapore's success did not lie with the way PAP ruled but with the way it served the people.

"If we only talk about PAP's authoritarian rule without discussing its electoral support and service to the people or talk about its strict discipline in governing the country without highlighting the high calibre of its civil service and rule of law, then it is a big misunderstanding of the Singapore experience. Service for the people is no lip service in Singapore, but something real in action," he wrote in an article for the China Youth newspaper or *Zhongguo Qingnian Bao Bingdian Zoukan*.

Some Chinese intellectuals believed that what was conspicuously missing in Western systems could be found in Singapore. "If we say freedom is the hallmark of Western societies, then what is worthy of praise in Singapore is harmony," expounded Chinese scholar Lu Yuanli who founded the centre for Singapore studies and authored a series of books on Singapore, the latest being the two-volume publication *Why Can Singapore Do It?*

Across the Taiwan Strait, the Singapore model also won kudos from Ma Ying-jeou just before he won the presidential elections in 2007. Conceding that Singapore was different from Taiwan as it did not emphasise democratisation, he told Singapore Chinese daily *Lianhe Zaobao*: "Nevertheless, it is professional, corruption-free and efficient, which is worth our learning. The Singapore government can reach consensus easily and there is no squabbling. When they have an idea, they work towards it."

In fact, Singapore had often been compared favourably with Taiwan by its leading current affairs magazine *Commonwealth* or *Tianxia*. As it commented in its 2006 report: "Viewing Singapore from every angle, we find it a model worth examining under a magnifying glass. Singapore is a rare example in today's world where democratic leadership in many countries is being challenged and political parties are embroiled in scandals."

It noted that although Singapore adopted a state-owned but privately run method of controlling most of the country's economic resources, its officials were not corrupt. If PAP was able to win the people's confidence in every election, it was because "it never fails to remind voters that it has always kept its promise of being an efficient and clean government".

Weighing the relative importance of freedom, democracy and rule of law in the political systems of the four predominantly Chinese territories, its chief editor Diane Ying wrote: "While there is freedom and rule of law in Hong Kong, it lacks democracy. There is democracy and rule of law in Singapore, but the republic is a little in want of freedom. After the lifting of martial law in Taiwan, there is freedom and democracy, but not rule of law. Mainland China is most unfortunate because it lacks all three."

The Magsaysay award-winning journalist contended that freedom did not mean bizarre politicking or allowing people to do as they pleased without regard for the law and that democracy without rule of law was mob politics in another form which would lead to gross abuse of privileges and political corruption. Her conclusion: without rule of law, freedom and democracy was just a mirage.

Perhaps what swayed many adherents to the Singapore model was the hard-to-fault argument that a long period of one-party rule would allow for development planning and progressive implementation that spanned several electoral terms. This would not have been possible, they said, if a ruling party was struggling to hang on to power all the time and forced to resort to short-term measures to woo voters.

Instead of just reacting to issues and solving problems on a piecemeal basis, they argued, a party with no real fear of being unseated could embark on comprehensive plans which would only bear fruit in the long run. It did not matter if the leaders would not be around to see to their completion. Overseas officials who visited various ministries in Singapore were often astounded to be shown blueprints of plans for the next 20 to 30 years.

Indian author and lawmaker Arun Shourie called it "imagining the future and engineering it into reality." Right from the outset, he said, the republic had a clear vision of its future. "It had systematically gone into manufacturing, then financial services, hardware, software, chips production, information technology, biotechnology and so on. The island is so small, it has nothing, no oil, no natural resources, but its leaders have made Singapore a world presence."

Extolling Singapore's ability to make long-term plans systematically, the 2008 report in Taiwan's *Commonwealth* magazine commented that while Taiwan was still bickering over water issues, Singapore was already managing its water resources comprehensively. It pointed out that Singapore had placed water as its top priority from its very first day of independence. Lamenting that Taiwan had lagged behind Singapore in per capita income and quality of life, it said: "There are many things we can learn from Singapore. They have long-term plans and yet they are able to be flexible and adapt to changes. They are also good at spotting trends and going with the flow."

According to governance scholar Neo Boon Siong, it was long-term planning by the PAP government which might account for the lack of a strong opposition. Knowing that the party would be inevitably returned to power, he said, the leaders developed "an internal discipline to think long-term and not take short cuts because they know that they cannot get away with it".

PAP leaders realised that they were unlike their counterparts in many countries who could peddle all sorts of plans to gain political mileage with little or no intent to carry them through. "But in Singapore, when they made promises, they knew they must keep them," he told *The Straits Times*.

No doubt about it, it was the long period of one-party rule which was behind Singapore's success, said American editor Nathan Gardels. Comparing Singapore with Japan and Sweden, he noted that it was not incidental that all three countries had very long periods of one-party rule. "This rule enabled these governments to pursue public policies—high investment in infrastructure and education and a secure safety net—over long periods of time to bring prosperity and social stability. In short, this kind of one-party rule has been validated largely because it works." Japan had been ruled almost continuously by the Liberal Democratic Party since 1955. Sweden was governed by the Social Democrats for nearly eight decades until it was defeated in the 2006 general election.

As he elaborated: "In Sweden, strong labour unions and an historic social consensus put government on an even keel with the private sector. In Japan, the powerful bureaucracy ensured the interests of the public at large over the private sector. In Singapore, the emphasis on a highly paid, super competent governing class has made the public interest on par with private interests. This matters, especially for small countries facing the gale of globalisation because it is up to the governing class to ensure that globalisation works for its small population. This, Singapore has done so far under PAP rule."

Taking another perspective, eminent historian Wang Gungwu said that what mattered in the Singapore model was not party politics but good governance. He commented that PAP had taken politics out from the streets and turned it into a performance for the public to evaluate in a general election.

This meant, he explained, that the party would be judged not by politicking skills but by performance indicators. "The weight of expectations is placed on this elite group to perform successfully again and again and again. What happened externally is beyond the control of the country's leaders. But internally, how you win is clear. The determining factors are very clear. The formula demands that each generation of politicians and the bureaucracy has got to reproduce itself in new ways to meet new challenges but ultimately, each time it must succeed to deliver."

As the chairman of the East Asia Institute observed, PAP had its own way of ensuring performance and was very tough on anyone who did not succeed. "The markers are very clear. If you join PAP, you know what you're up against. You have to deliver, or else you're out. If you don't deliver according to what you have promised to do, you're out."

TO frequent criticisms that the Singapore system was an undemocratic if not despotic regime which brooked no dissent and excluded the opposition, the response was that unlike the ruling communist parties, PAP had to renew its mandate in every general election. Under the one-man-one-vote system, people were free to vote for PAP or any of the opposition parties on the ticket.

In fact, about one-third of the voters opposed the ruling party consistently. A top PAP minister once said that when he walked down the street in his ward, out of 10 people he met, he was mindful that four and a half were against him. "If I am gruff or impolite, next time it may be five and a half," he said to explain why Singaporeans were not deterred from exercising their free choice.

Liberals would find it simply incredible but many Chinese scholars and politicians said that they were drawn to the island's model precisely because of "the competitive element in Singapore politics." A 2008 report in *Xuexi Shibao*, the newspaper of the CCP central party school, highlighted the fact that the Singapore system allowed other political parties to exist and contest in elections.

As Sun Jingfeng, a professor from Henan Normal University's school of political science and management and author of two books on PAP rule explained: "Although Singapore is ruled by one party for a long time, the political system is a competitive one with many parties vying for votes in each election. PAP faces pressure at every election when it campaigns for votes.

"In contrast, the Chinese system is non-competitive as there are no elections or contests. The ruling Chinese Communist Party co-operates, not competes, with the other eight political parties. There is no competition and therefore it lacks vitality and becomes complacent unlike PAP which has to be on guard all the time against challenges."

Time and again, Lee had sought to debunk the notion that Singapore was a one-party state. He pointed out that PAP was not synonymous with the government unlike the situation in China where there was no distinction between the CCP and the Chinese government. If the opposition could beat PAP, he said, it would take over a working system.

As he told a forum in 2004: "At the end of the day, if you're running the system properly, you must have a distinction between what is the party, what is the government so if you are voted out of office, the machinery is there for the next party to take over.

"So although we don't have much of an opposition, we keep the system going so that at any time the party is out, the government, parliament, the civil service will be there. The police, the armed forces will carry it through. It's not going to collapse."

In recent years, what had been exercising Lee's mind was not the fate of the party he founded with a few good men in 1954 but the continuation of good governance. On his 83rd birthday at the Raffles Forum in 2006, he expressed the wish that in 40 years "there will be a government that is equal to the job, as the PAP was".

His ambition was "not to preserve PAP but to preserve the system that produces the answers we must have as a society to survive." As he put it: "We have structured the system such that a competent group which gets in will find a machine that works. Don't tinker with it. Run the system properly on the basis of merit, not nepotism, and you will always find a way out of the problem."

Can the PAP model of governance be sustained by a non-PAP party? When this intriguing poser was put to Lee, he admitted that it was not easy to do so. "The PAP's first generation leaders took over 30 years to work out the system of governance before they handed it over to the next generation. The next generation had worked with the old guard generation from the 1970s to 1990.

"For a non-PAP party to uphold the same system of governance, it must have candidates who can match the integrity, capabilities and commitment of the PAP ministers and MPs. After two to three election terms, 12 to 15 years on the opposition benches in parliament, they will understand the system, and if they take over, there is a chance this system of governance can continue."

No one can foresee the future but wouldn't it go down in political annals as the supreme irony of ironies if the universally acclaimed Singapore system of governance conceived, improvised and honed to a fine art by the PAP should end up being run by a non-PAP party someday? Surreal as it may sound today, if and when such a scenario happens, it would be the best tribute to PAP—and represent its greatest legacy.

SOURCES

INTERVIEWS CONDUCTED
BETWEEN 2002 AND 2008

Abdul Ghani Hamid

Abdul Halim Kader

Abdul Majid bin Abdul Latiff

Abisheganaden, Felix

Abisheganaden, Geoffrey

Ahmad Mattar

Alami Musa

Anandan, Subhas

Ang Mong Seng

Ariff Suradi

Asad Latif

Baey Yam Keng

Baker, Maurice

Balakrishan, Vivian

Bellows, Thomas

Beng Kian Lam, Arthur

Bloodworth, Dennis

Bulat Hamid

Chan Chee Seng

Chan Chin Bock

Chan Kai Yau

Chan Sun Wing

Chandradas, Gopal

Chen Chi Yean

Chen Man Hin

Chen Say Jame

Chen Wing Sum, Michael

Cheong Yuen Chee, Eric

Chiam See Tong

Chin Harn Tong

Ch'ng Jit Koon

Chong, Charles

Chong Fun Liam

Chong, Terence

Choo Siu Heng

Choo Wye Foo

Chor Yeok Eng

Chow Chiok Hock

Choy Su-Moi, Elizabeth

Chua Beng Huat

Chua Boon Siong

Chung Kwang Tong

Das, S Chandra

Datta-Ray, Sunanda

De Silva, Gerry

De Souza, Christopher

Dhanabalan, Suppiah

Dhanam, Avadai (Mrs C V Devan Nair)

Lim Siew Ming, Arthur

Lim Swee Say

Lim, Sylvia

Lim Yew Kuan

Lin You Eng

Liu Bo

Liu Thai Kher

Lohman, Walter

Long Foo Yee, Fred

Low Choon Quee

Low Foo Yong

Low Por Tuck, Peter

Lu Yuanli

Lui Tuck Yew

Luo Yamei

Mahbubani, Kishore

Mahmud Awang

Masagos Zulkifli

Mofradi bin Haji Mohamed Noor

Mohamad Ismail Haji Pitchay

Mohamad Maidin Packer Mohamad

Mohamed Khir Johari

Nath, Kamal

Nathan, S R

Neo Boon Siong

Ng Boon Chong

Ng, Irene

Ng Kah Ting

Ng, Victor

Ngiam Tong Dow

Ong Ah Heng

Ong Chin Tee

Ong Chye Ann

Ong Hock Siang

Ong Keng Yong

Ong Kim Seng

Ong Pang Boon

Ooi Giok Ling

Othman Wok

Ow Chin Hock

Pang Cheng Lian

Pang Tai Heng

Phua, Cynthia

Pillay, J Y

Puhaindran, S

Puthucheary, Dominic

Quah, Jon

Quah Wee Ho

Ramasamy, P

Said Zahari

Samad Ismail

Selvadurai, Pathmanaban

Seng Han Thong

Seow Peck Leng

Shanmugam, K

Sheng Nam Chin

Shi Mei Chiao

Shourie, Arun

Siddique, Sharon

Sidek Saniff

Siew Kong Chong

Sim Boon Peng

Sim Kee Boon

Singh, Inderjit

Singh Wasan, Surjit

Sitoh Yih Pin

Solomon, Robert

Soon Loh Boon, Robert

ORAL HISTORY INTERVIEWS LODGED WITH
NATIONAL ARCHIVES OF SINGAPORE

Barker, Edmund William

Bloodworth, Dennis

Buang Omar Junid

Chan Kum Chee

Chang Yuen Thong

Chen Say Jame

Cheong Yuen Chee, Eric

Chio Cheng Thun

Chor Yeok Eng

Corridon, Richard Byrne

De Cruz, Gerald

Douglas-Hamilton, George Nigel
  (10th Earl of Selkirk)

Ede, John

Eu Chooi Yip

Fernandez, Michael

Fong Sip Chee

Goh Sin Ee

Gorrie, Mike

Guo Ren Huey

Ho Bee Swee

Ho Puay Choo

Kow Kee Seng

Kwa Geok Choo (Mrs Lee Kuan Yew)

Lee Gek Seng

Lee Khoon Choy

Lee Kuan Yew

Lee Yew Seng

Lim Hock Siew

Lim Kim San

Lingam, S V

Low Por Tuck, Peter

Low Tiow Lye

Marcus, Philip Carlyle

Marshall, David

Mohamed Khir Johari

Nair, Chengara Veetil Devan

Ng Kah Ting

Ong Chang Sam

Ong Teng Cheong

Othman Wok

Puthucheary, James

Rahmat Kenap

Rajah, Arumugam Ponnu

Rajah, T T

Rajaratnam, Sinnathamby

Sockalingam, S

Soon Loh Boon, Robert

Syed Esa Almenoar

Tan Chee Khoon

Tan Eng Joo

Tan Siew Sin

Tay Kum Sun

Teong Eng Siong

Toh Chin Chye

Woodhull, Sandrasegeram

Yaacob Mohamed

PRIVATE SOURCES

Goh Keng Swee • Lee Siew Choh's unpublished memoirs • Francis Thomas' unpublished memoirs • Maurice Baker's notes on Malayan Forum • S R Nathan's notes on the labour movement • Dennis Bloodworth's interviews with S Rajaratnam, James Puthucheary and Lord Selkirk

OTHER SOURCES

The Straits Times • *The Sunday Times* • *The Singapore Standard* • *The Singapore Free Press* • *Utusan Melayu* • *Nanyang Siang Pau* • *Sin Chew Jit Poh* • *Berita Harian* • *The Star* (Malaysia)

Legislative assembly and parliamentary records • PAP and Barisan Sosialis publications • PAP's analysis of 1984 general election • Internal Security Department, Ministry of Home Affairs, Singapore • National Archives of the United Kingdom, Public Record Office, London

Australia and the Formation of Malaysia (1961–66)—Australian Department of Foreign Affairs and Trade

Tianxia (Commonwealth Magazine), Taiwan 2006 & 2008 • *Xuexi Shibao*, China's CCP central party school newspaper • *Zhongguo Qingnianbao Bingdian Zoukan*, China Youth newspaper

BOOK SOURCES

The Singapore Story: Memoirs of Lee Kuan Yew. Times Editions, 1998.

From Third World To First: Memoirs of Lee Kuan Yew. Times Editions, 2000.

Lee Kuan Yew: The Man and His Ideas by Han Fook Kwang, Warren Fernandez and Sumiko Tan. Times Editions, 1998.

The PAP Story—The Pioneering Years by Fong Sip Chee. Times Periodicals, 1979.

The People's Action Party of Singapore: Emergence of a Dominant Party System by Thomas J Bellows. New Haven: Yale University, 1970.

Singapore People's Action Party by Pang Cheng Lian. Oxford University Press, 1971.

The Dynamics of One Party Dominance: The PAP at the Grassroots by Chan Heng Chee. Singapore University Press, 1976.

The Tiger And The Trojan Horse by Dennis Bloodworth. Times Books International, 1986.

Singapore: Struggle For Success by John Drysdale. Times Books International, 1984.

Singapore's Success: Engineering Economic Growth by Henri Ghesquiere. Thomson Learning, 2006.

The Economics of Modernisation by Goh Keng Swee. Federal, 1972, 1975.

Rajaratnam: The Prophetic and The Political edited by Chan Heng Chee and Obaid ul Haq. Graham Brash, 1987.

Socialism That Works by Devan Nair. Federal, 1976.

A History of Singapore 1819-1975 by C M Turnbull. Oxford University Press, 1977.

Singapore Politics Under The People's Action Party by Diane K Mauzy and R S Milne. Routledge, 2002

Leaders of Singapore by Melanie Chew. Resource Press, 1996.

A Sensation of Independence: David Marshall by Chan Heng Chee. Times Books International, 2001.

Lee's Lieutenants edited by Lam Peng Er and Kevin Tan. Allen and Unwin, 1999.

Governing Singapore by Raj Vasil. Eastern Universities Press, 1984.

Asianising Singapore: The PAP's Management of Ethnicity by Raj Vasil. Heinemann Asia, 1995.

Memoirs of a Migrant by Francis Thomas. University Education Press, 1972.

Looking Back: Monday Musings and Memories by Tunku Abdul Rahman Putra Al-Haj. Pustaka Antara, 1977

Reflections by Lim Yew Hock. Pustaka Antara, 1986.

Memoir on the Formation of Malaysia by Ghazali Shafie. Penerbit UKM, 1998.

That Fellow Kanda by Peter H L Lim. AUPE, 1996.

I Stomped The Hot Beat by Sit Yin Fong. Heinemann Asia, 1991.

Singapore: The Air-Conditioned Nation by Cherian George. Landmark, 2000.

To Catch A Tartar by Francis Seow. Yale University, 1994.

The Singapore Dilemma by Lily Zubaidah Rahim. Oxford University Press, 1998.

Dark Clouds At Dawn by Said Zahari. INSAN, 2001.

My Side of History by Chin Peng. Media Masters, Singapore, 2003.

Lim Chin Siong and his Times (Chinese) edited by The Other Side of Malaysian History Editorial Committee. INSAN and Wasasa Enterprise, 2000.

The Open United Front—The Communist Struggle in Singapore (1954–1966) by Lee Ting Hui. South Seas Society, 1996.

Life's Like A River—Lives of 16 Women from Singapore, Malaysia and Thailand (Chinese) edited by Qiu Yihong. Strategic Information Research Centre, Malaysia, 1984.

India Unbound by Gurcharan Das. Alfred A Knopf, 2000.

The Elephant Paradigm by Gurcharan Das. Penguin, 2002.

INDEX